# MACROECONOMICS

## PRINCIPLES AND APPLICATIONS

### SECOND EDITION

---

ROBERT E. HALL

DEPARTMENT OF ECONOMICS

STANFORD UNIVERSITY


MARC LIEBERMAN

DEPARTMENT OF ECONOMICS

NEW YORK UNIVERSITY

**South-Western College Publishing**
Thomson Learning™

Australia • Canada • Denmark • Japan • Mexico • New Zealand • Philippines
Puerto Rico • Singapore • South Africa • Spain • United Kingdom • United States

Developmental Editor: Dennis Hanseman
Sr. Marketing Manager: Lisa L. Lysne
Production Manager: Sharon L. Smith
Manufacturing Coordinator: Charlene Taylor
Internal Design: Hespenheide Design
Cover Design: Paul Neff Design
Photo Manager: Cary Benbow
Photo Research: Susan Van Etten
Production House: Pre-Press Company, Inc.
Printer: R.R. Donnelley & Sons, Willard Manufacturing Division

Printed in the United States of America
1  2  3  4  5  6  03  02  01  00

For more information contact South-Western College Publishing, 5101 Madison Road, Cincinnati, Ohio, 45227 or find us on the Internet at http://www.swcollege.com.

**For permission to use material from this text or product, contact us by**
• **telephone: 1-800-730-2214**
• **fax: 1-800-730-2215**
• **web: http://www.thomsonrights.com**

This book is printed on acid-free paper.

**Library of Congress Cataloging-in-Publication Data**

Hall, Robert Ernest
    Macroeconomics: principles and applications / Robert E. Hall, Marc Lieberman.—2nd ed.
      p. cm.
    Includes index.
    ISBN 0-324-07282-1 (alk. paper)
    1. Macroeconomics. I. Lieberman, Marc. II. Title.
    HB172.5 .H346 2001
    339—dc21                                                                          00-032942

# PREFACE—TO THE INSTRUCTOR

This book is about economic principles and how economists use them to understand the world. It was conceived, written, and for the second edition, substantially revised to help your students focus on those basic principles and applications

We decided to write this book because we thought that existing books often confused students about economics and what it is all about. In our view, the leading texts can be divided into three categories. In the first category are the encyclopedias—the heavy tomes with a section or a paragraph on every topic or subtopic you might possibly want to present to your students. The result is a book that covers too much—often superficially—with the central themes and ideas lost in the shuffle.

The second type of text we call the "scrapbook." In an effort to elevate student interest, these books insert multi-colored boxes, news clippings, interviews, cartoons, and whatever else they can find to jolt the reader on each page. While these special features are often entertaining, there is a tradeoff: these books sacrifice a logical, focused presentation of the material, and the central themes and ideas are lost.

Finally, the third type of text, perhaps in response to the first two, tries to do less in every area—a *lot* less. But instead of just omitting the extraneous or inessential details, these texts attempt to redefine introductory economics by throwing out key ideas, models and concepts. If these books could talk, they would say, "We don't trust our readers to think much or remember much, so we won't really bother." Students who use these books may think that economics is overly simplified and unrealistic. After the course, they may be unprepared to go on in the field, or to think about the economy on their own.

## A DISTINCTIVE APPROACH

Our approach is very different. We believe that the best way to teach Principles is to present economics as a coherent, unified subject. This does not happen automati-

cally. On the contrary, Principles students often miss the unity of what we call "the economic way of thinking." For example, they are likely to see the analysis of goods markets, labor markets and financial markets as entirely different phenomena, rather than as a repeated application of the same methodology with a new twist here and there. So the Principles course appears to be just "one thing after another," rather than the coherent presentation we aim for.

To help students appreciate the virtues of the economic approach, we have included some important features in this book. One is a consistent methodology. Most economists, when approaching a problem, begin by thinking about buyers and sellers, about goals and constraints. They move on to study equilibrium, then give their model a workout in a comparative statics exercise. To understand what economics is about, students need to understand this process, and see it in action in different contexts. To help them do so, we have identified and stressed four "Key Steps to Understanding the Economy" that economists use in analyzing problems. These are:

1. **Characterize the Markets.** Define the market or markets that best suit the problem being analyzed, and identify the decision makers (buyers and sellers) who interact in that market.
2. **Identify the Goals and Constraints.** Identify the goals that the decision makers are trying to achieve, and the constraints they face in achieving those goals.
3. **Find the Equilibrium.** Describe the conditions necessary for equilibrium in the market, and a method for finding that equilibrium.
4. **What Happens When Things Change?** Explore how events and government policies change the market equilibrium.

A full statement of each Key Step appears toward the end of Chapter 3. Thereafter, whenever the Key Step is used in future chapters, it is identified with a key symbol as shown in the margin. Through the use of Key Steps, students learn how to think like economists, and in a very natural way. And, they come to see economics as a unified whole, rather than a series of disconnected ideas.

Another way we stress the unity of economics is through a new capstone chapter developed for this edition:

> **Using All the Theory: The Stock Market and the Macroeconomy.** We also want to help students see macroeconomics as a unified subject, so we have included this capstone chapter. It brings together a variety of macro tools to study an issue that students find intriguing—the relationship between the stock market and the macroeconomy. More specifically, we look at the ways in which the economy affects the stock market as well as how the stock market affects the economy.

In this chapter, students come to see that much of what they read and hear in the media can be understood by using the tools that they've learned in their Principles course.

## CAREFUL FOCUS

Because we have avoided encyclopedic complexity, we have had to think hard about what topics are most important. As you will see:

**We avoid nonessential material.** When we believed a topic was not essential to a basic understanding of economics, we left it out. We also avoided interviews, news clippings, and boxed inserts with only distant connections to the core material. The features your students *will* find in our book are there to help them understand and apply economic theory itself, and to help them explore sources of information on their own using the Internet.

**We explain difficult concepts patiently.** Because we have omitted topics of minor importance, we can explain the topics we do cover more thoroughly and patiently. We lead students, step-by-step, through each aspect of the theory, through each graph, and through each numerical example. In developing this book, we asked other experienced teachers to tell us which aspects of economic theory were hardest for their students to learn, and we have paid special attention to the trouble spots.

**We use concrete examples.** Students learn best when they see how economics can explain the world around them. Whenever possible, we develop the theory using real-world examples. When we employ hypothetical examples, because they illustrate the theory more cleanly, we try to make them realistic. In addition, each chapter ends with a thorough, extended application focusing on an important real-world issue.

## FEATURES THAT REINFORCE

We have chosen features that reinforce the basic theory, rather than distract from it. Here is a list of the most important ones, and how we believe they help students focus on essentials.

**Dangerous Curves** inserts appear within many of the chapters These are designed to eliminate confusion that sometimes arises as students read the text—the kinds of mistakes we see year after year in their exams.

**Using the Theory** sections, which present extended applications, appear at the end of each chapter. While there are plenty of real-world examples and facts in the  body of each chapter, helping to illustrate each step along the way, we also felt it important to have one extended application that unifies the material in the chapter. In the Using the Theory sections, students see how the tools they have learned can explain something about the world—something that would be difficult to explain without those tools.

**Internet references** point students to resources that contain truly up-to-the-minute information. We prefer to integrate current events through Internet  references, rather than with news clippings in the text, for two reasons. First, we want to minimize distractions; and second, news clippings are usually stale by the time of publication.

## CONTENT INNOVATIONS

In addition to the special features just described, you will find some important differences from other texts in topical approach and arrangement. These, too, are designed to make the theory stand out more cleanly, and to make learning easier. These are not pedagogical experiments, nor are they innovation for the sake of innovation. The differences you will find in this text are the product of years of classroom experience.

## INNOVATIONS IN MACROECONOMICS

**Long-Run Macroeconomics** (Chapters 7 and 8): Out text presents long-run growth before short-run fluctuations. Chapter 7 develops the long-run, classical model at a level appropriate for introductory students, mostly using supply and demand. Chapter 8 then *uses* the classical model to explain the causes—and costs—of economic growth in both rich and poor countries.

We believe it is better to treat the long run before the short run, for two reasons. First, the long-run model makes full use of the tools of supply and demand, and thus allows a natural transition from the preliminary chapters (1, 2, and 3) into macroeconomics. Second, we believe that students can truly understand economic fluctuations only if they understand *how* and *why* the long-run model breaks down over shorter time periods. This, of course, requires an introduction to the long-run model first.

**Economics and Fluctuations** (Chapter 9): This unique chapter provides a bridge from the long-run to the short-run macro model, and paves the way for the short-run focus on *spending* as the driving force behind economic fluctuations.

**Aggregate Demand and Aggregate Supply** (Chapter 13): One of our pet peeves about other introductory texts is the too-early introduction of aggregate demand and aggregate supply curves, *before* teaching where these curves come from. Students then confuse the *AD* and *AS* curves with their microeconomic counterparts, requiring corrective action later. In this text, the *AD* and *AS* curves do not appear until Chapter 13, where they are fully explained. Our treatment of aggregate supply is based on a very simple mark-up model that our students have found easy to understand.

**Exchange Rates and Open-Economy Macroeconomics** (Chapter 16): Many students find international macroeconomics the most interesting topic in the course, especially the material on exchange rates and what causes them to change. Accordingly, you will find unusually full coverage of exchange rate determination in this chapter. This treatment is kept simple and straightforward, relying exclusively on supply and demand. And it forms the foundation for the discussion of open-economy macro policy that ends the chapter.

## ORGANIZATIONAL FLEXIBILITY

We have arranged the contents of each chapter, and the table of contents as a whole, according to our recommended order of presentation. But we have also built in flexibility. Once the core chapters (4 through 13) have been taught, the remaining chapters (14–16) can be taught in any order.

Finally, we have included only those chapters that we thought were both essential and teachable in a year-long course. But not everyone will agree about what is essential. While we—as authors—cringe at the thought of a chapter being omitted in the interest of time, we have allowed for that possibility. Nothing in Chapter 14 (monetary policy), Chapter 15 (fiscal policy), or Chapter 16 (international finance) is required to understand any of the other numbered chapters in the book. Skipping any of these should not cause continuity problems.

In many cases, a chapter can be assigned selectively. For example, an instructor who is anxious to get to the short-run macro model could freely select among the sections in Chapter 8 (Economic Growth and Rising Living Standards) and Chapter 9 (Economic Fluctuations).

## ABOUT THE SECOND EDITION

For the second edition of our text, we have undertaken a careful revision. First, there is a global change. To shine even more light on the unity of economics, we have replaced the first edition's *Eight Basic Principles* with the current edition's *Four Key Steps*. This shifts the emphasis from analytic *results* to analytic *methods*, but retains the "common thread" approach of the first edition.

Second, there are many specific changes. Indeed, every chapter of this text was reviewed and scrutinized for improvements. Most chapters were at least partially rewritten, and some are entirely new. The resulting changes from the first edition are too numerous to list here. However, we know that many instructors who invested time reading the first edition will want a list of specific changes, and we have posted that list on our Web site.

# TEACHING AND LEARNING AIDS

To help you to present the most interesting Principles courses possible, we have created an extensive set of supplementary items. Many of them can be downloaded from the Hall/Lieberman Web site. The list includes:

## FOR THE INSTRUCTOR:

- An *Instructor's Manual* that provides chapter outlines, teaching ideas, and suggested answers to end-of-chapter questions and problems.
- *The Macroeconomics Test Bank* containing over 2,000 multiple-choice questions. For this edition, the test questions have been arranged according to chapter headings and subheadings. This makes it easy to find the material needed to construct examinations.
- *ExamView Computerized Testing Software* contains all of the questions in the printed Test Banks. Exam-View is an easy-to-use test creation package compatible with both Microsoft Windows and Macintosh client software. You can select questions by previewing them on the screen, selecting them by number, or selecting them randomly. Questions, instructions, and answers can be edited, and new questions can easily be added. You can also administer quizzes online—over the Internet, through a local area network (LAN), or through a wide area network (WAN).
- *Full-Color Transparency Acetates* are available for almost all graphs and illustrations in the text.
- A *CNN Video* provides a variety of short clips on various aspects of economics.
- *PowerPoint Slides* of figures and tables are available.
- *Instructor's Resource CD-ROM* allows quick access to instructor ancillaries from your desktop. This easy-to-use CD allows you to review, edit, and copy exactly the material you need.

## FOR THE STUDENT:

- The *Mastery Study Guide* provides numerous exercises and self-tests for problem solving practice. It is a valuable tool for helping students strengthen their knowledge of economics.
- The *Student Study CD-ROM*, available packaged with the text, is a powerful study tool that pro-

vides access to useful technology tools and learning support.

- *Macroeconomics Alive! CD-ROM* is an interactive multimedia study aid that provides a high-tech, high-fun way to study economics. Through a combination of animated presentations, interactive graphing exercises, and simulations, the core principles of economics come to life in an upbeat and entertaining way. (ISBN: 0-538-86850-3)

  Ask your South-Western/Thomson Learning sales representative for more details, or visit the Economics Alive! Web site at *http://econalive. swcollege.com/*.

- *The Wall Street Journal Edition.* The Hall and Lieberman texts are available with a special 10-week *Wall Street Journal* subscription offer. Contact your South-Western/Thomson Learning sales representative for package pricing and ordering information.

- With *Infotrac® College Edition* students can receive anytime, anywhere, online access to a database of full-text articles from hundreds of scholarly and popular periodicals such as *Newsweek, Fortune, American Economist,* and the *Quarterly Journal of Economics.* It is a great way to expose students to online research using academically based and reliable sources. An Infotrac subscription card can be packaged with this text. Contact your South-Western/Thomson Learning sales representative for ordering information, or for more information on Infotrac, visit *http://www.swcollege.com/infotrac/infotrac. html.*

- *The New York Times Guide to Economics* by Sliger, Jennings, and Murphy is a collection of the best economics-related articles from *The New York Times.* It can be used in the classroom or informally as complementary reading. All articles are accompanied by exploratory exercises and probing questions developed by experts in the field. The guide is divided into six sections, allowing easy integration into any economics course. (ISBN: 0-324-04159-4)

## FOR INSTRUCTORS *AND* STUDENTS:

- The *Hall/Lieberman Web site (http://hall-lieb. swcollege.com)* contains a wealth of useful teaching and learning resources. Important features available at the Web site include:
  - Downloadable ancillary materials for instructors and students.

- *Online Quizzes* with feedback on correct answers. Completed quizzes can be e-mailed directly to the instructor
- Links to the Internet addresses referred to in the text.
- Links to relevant *EconNews Online, EconDebate Online,* and *EconData Online* articles and exercises for each text chapter.
- *Using the Theory Online* activities that ask students to use the Four Key Steps to analyze interesting questions. The answers can then be e-mailed to the instructor.
- An *Online Graphing Workshop* designed to help students master economic reasoning and graphical analysis. It includes a set of animated graphical tutorials—with audio explanations. Students are also asked to manipulate graphs (using a specially designed freehand graph-drawing tool) to describe specific scenarios, and then are presented with the correct graphical answer. Other scenarios are provided without answers, and students can submit their work to their instructor via e-mail.
- For additional course support, our South-Western *Economics Resource Center* Web site, accessible at *http://economics.swcollege.com,* contains a variety of content features and applications. They are added monthly and updated semiannually.

  These special online features include the following:
- *EconDebate Online* keeps students informed on today's most crucial economics policy issues. Each debate provides a primer on a single timely issue and includes links to background information and current, in-depth commentaries from experts around the world.
- *EconNews Online* provides summaries of the latest economics news stories. Each contains a three to five paragraph review of a news article and provides questions to spur further thought.
- *EconData Online* provides current and historical economic data with accompanying commentary, diagrams, analysis, and exercises.
- *EconLinks Online* gives students a navigation partner for further exploration of economics on the Web. Topic links provide a list of key economics Web sites, including "best bets."
- *WebTutor on WebCT* offers concept presentations, flashcards, Internet links, discussion questions, and tutorials. It also includes an internal e-mail system, chat and discussion areas, search capabilities, calendars, custom printing features, and instructor cus-

tomization options. For more information, visit the South-Western Electronic Learning site at *http://www.swcollege.com/elearning.html.*

## ACKNOWLEDGMENTS

Our greatest debt in this second edition is to the many reviewers who carefully read the draft manuscript and provided numerous suggestions for improvements. While we could not incorporate all their ideas, we did carefully evaluate each one of them. Among those whose suggestions we found particularly valuable are the following:

| | |
|---|---|
| Ljubisa Adamovich | Florida State University |
| Rashid Al-Hmoud | Texas Tech University |
| David Aschauer | Bates College |
| Richard Ballman | Augustana College |
| Chris Barnett | Gannon University |
| Sylvain Boko | Wake Forest University |
| Mark Buenafe | Arizona State University |
| Stephen Call | Metropolitan State University |
| Kevin Carey | American University |
| Steven Cobb | Xavier University |
| Dennis Debrecht | Carroll College |
| Selhattin Dibooglu | Southern Illinois University |
| John Duffy | University of Pittsburgh |
| James Falter | Mount Marty College |
| Sasan Fayazmanesh | California State University, Fresno |
| Satayjit Ghosh | University of Scranton |
| Rik Hafer | Southern Illinois University |
| Andrew Hildreth | University of California, Berkeley |
| Thomas Husted | American University |
| David Kaun | University of California, Santa Cruz |
| Philip King | San Francisco State University |
| Kate Krause | University of New Mexico |
| Viju Kulkarni | San Diego State University |
| Nazma Latif-Zaman | Providence College |
| Teresa Laughlin | Palomar College |
| Judith Mann | University of California, San Diego |
| Chris Niggle | University of Redlands |
| Farrokh Nourzad | Marquette University |
| William Rosen | Cornell University |
| Thomas Sadler | Pace University |
| Jonathan Sandy | University of San Diego |
| Ramazan Sari | Texas Tech University |

| | |
|---|---|
| Edward Scahill | University of Scranton |
| Mary Schranz | University of Wisconsin, Madison |
| Alden Shiers | California Polytechnic State University |
| Martha Stuffler | Irvine Valley College |
| Glen Whitman | California State University, Northridge |
| Robert Whaples | Wake Forest University |

A market survey was conducted in conjunction with the development of the second edition of this textbook. The results provided valuable information in preparing the revision. Many thanks go to the over 600 respondents, and in particular to the following instructors who participated in a more extensive market review:

| | |
|---|---|
| Erol Balkan | Hamilton College |
| Amanda Bayer | Swarthmore College |
| Cliff Bekar | Lewis and Clark College |
| Michael Ben-Gad | University of Houston |
| John Blair | Wright State University |
| Jack Chambless | Valencia Community College |
| Jai-Young Choi | Lamar University |
| James Cover | University of Alabama |
| Jerry Crawford | Arkansas State University |
| Audrey Davidson | University of Louisville |
| Al DeCook | Broward Community College |
| Amy Diduch | Mary Baldwin College |
| John Dodge | Indiana Weslyan University |
| Gary Ferrier | University of Arkansas |
| Fred Glahe | University of Colorado |
| Gary Greene | Manatee Junior College |
| Paul Grimes | Mississippi State University |
| Wayne Grove | Colgate University |
| Carl Gwin | Babson College |
| Steven Hackett | Humboldt State University |
| Bassam Harik | Western Michigan University |
| Emily Hoffman | Western Michigan University |
| Janet Koscianski | Shippensburg University |
| Shah Mehrabi | Montgomery College |
| Will Melick | Kenyon College |
| Diego Mendez-Carbajo | Florida International University |
| John Nader | Grand Valley State University |
| David O'Hara | Metro State University |
| Carl Parker | Ft. Hays Kansas State University |
| Min Qi | Kent State University |
| Richard Roehl | University of Michigan, Dearborn |

| | |
|---|---|
| George Samuels | Sam Houston State University |
| Edward Schumacher | East Carolina University |
| Eric Schutz | Rollins College |
| Barry Seldon | University of Texas at Dallas |
| Michael Smitka | Washington and Lee University |
| Martin Spechler | Indiana University–Purdue University Indianapolis |
| Brian Strow | Western Kentucky University |
| Edward Stuart | Northeastern Illinois University |
| James Sullivan | U.S. International University |
| Timothy Sullivan | Towson State University |
| Amy Quist Vander Laan | Hanover College |
| Craig Walker | Delta State University |
| Kathryn Wilson | Kent State University |
| William Wood | James Madison University |

We also wish to acknowledge the talented and dedicated group of instructors who helped put together a supplementary package that is second to none. Geoffrey Jehle of Vassar College co-wrote the *Mastery Study Guide* and supervised much of the other work on the supplements. Jane Himarios of the University of Texas, Arlington revised her *Instructor's Manual* and also helped in reorganizing the *Test Banks*. Arne Hallam of Iowa State University is responsible for the Animated Graphs feature. Adhip Chaudhuri of Georgetown University contributed the online *Try It!* and *Apply It!* features. Frederica Shockley and David Gallo of California State University, Chico wrote the *Using the Theory Online* exercises. Elizabeth Sawyer Kelly of the University of Wisconsin, Madison created the online quizzes. Philip Way of the University of Cincinnati helped strengthen and organize our Web site. And Theresa Curtis of Ohlinger Publishing Services coordinated the supplements.

The beautiful book you are holding would not exist except for the hard work of a talented team of professionals. Book production was overseen by Sharon Smith of South-Western College Publishing, and undertaken by The Pre-Press Company. At Pre-Press, all things are possible because of the dedicated work of Jennifer Carley and Kurt Jordan. Jennifer made the book happen, and Kurt made sure that the graphs were drawn clearly and accurately. A team of NYU students helped to locate and fix the few remaining errors. They included Jerry Revich, Mathew Venzon, Elizabeth Taylor, James Dec, Amarna Tolentino, David Feygenson and Brigitta Shtern.

The overall look of the book was planned by Joe Devine at South-Western and executed by Hespenheide

Design. Paul Neff designed the cover, and Cary Benbow ably managed the photo program, with a little help from Darren Wright. Charlene Taylor made all the pieces come together in her role as Manufacturing Coordinator.

Finally, we are especially grateful for the hard work of the dedicated and professional South-Western College Publishing marketing and sales team. Dennis Hanseman, our developmental editor for both editions, surpassed his own previous record for helpfulness and resourcefulness. His advice on content and writing proved invaluable, and he was relentless in his pursuit of excellence in this revision. Lisa Lysne has been a persuasive and passionate advocate for our text in her role as Senior Marketing Manager. Her creativity and sense of humor have made working with the marketing staff at South-Western both interesting and fun. And the South-Western sales representatives have been ex-tremely persuasive advocates for the book. We sincerely appreciate all their efforts!

## A REQUEST

Although we have worked hard on the first two editions of this book, we know there is always room for further improvement. For that, our fellow users are indispensable. We invite your comments and suggestions wholeheartedly. We especially welcome your suggestions for additional "Using the Theory" sections and "Dangerous Curves." You may send your comments to either of us care of South-Western College Publishing.

Bob Hall
Marc Lieberman

# ABOUT THE AUTHORS

**ROBERT E. HALL**

is a prominent applied economist. He is the Robert and Carole McNeil Professor of Economics at Stanford University and Senior Fellow at Stanford's Hoover Institution where he conducts research on inflation, unemployment, taxation, monetary policy, and the economics of high technology. He received his Ph.D. from MIT and has taught there as well as at the University of California, Berkeley. Hall is Director of the research program on Economic Fluctuations of the National Bureau of Economic Research, and Chairman of the Bureau's Committee on Business Cycle Dating, which maintains the semiofficial chronology of the U.S. business cycle. He has published numerous monographs and articles in scholarly journals, and co-authored a popular intermediate text. Hall has advised the Treasury Department and the Federal Reserve Board on national economic policy, and has testified on numerous occasions before congressional committees.

**MARC LIEBERMAN**

is Clinical Associate Professor of Economics at New York University. He received his Ph.D. from Princeton University. Lieberman has presented his extremely popular Principles of Economics course at Harvard, Vassar, the University of California, Santa Cruz, and the University of Hawaii, as well as at NYU, where he won the Economics Society Award for Excellence in Teaching. He is co-editor and contributor to *The Road to Capitalism: Economic Transformation in Eastern Europe and the Soviet Union.* Lieberman has consulted for the Bank of America and the Educational Testing Service. In his spare time, he is a professional screenwriter. He co-wrote the script for *Love Kills,* a thriller that aired on the USA Cable Network, and he periodically teaches screenwriting at NYU's School of Continuing and Professional Studies.

# BRIEF CONTENTS

# CONTENTS

## PART II

# MACROECONOMICS: BASIC CONCEPTS

## PART III

# LONG-RUN MACROECONOMICS

# PART IV

## SHORT-RUN MACROECONOMICS

# PART V

## MONEY, PRICES, AND THE MACROECONOMY

## PART VI

## MACROECONOMIC POLICY

# WHAT IS ECONOMICS?

*E*conomics. The word conjures up all sorts of images: manic stock traders on Wall Street, an economic summit meeting in a European capital, a somber television news anchor announcing good or bad news about the economy. . . . You probably hear about economics several times each day. What exactly *is* economics?

First, economics is a *social science,* so it seeks to explain something about *society.* In this sense, it has something in common with psychology, sociology, and political science. But economics is different from these other social sciences, because of *what* economists study and *how* they study it. Economists ask fundamentally different questions, and they answer them using tools that other social scientists find rather exotic.

## ECONOMICS, SCARCITY, AND CHOICE

A good definition of economics, which stresses the difference between economics and other social sciences, is the following:

> *Economics is the study of choice under conditions of scarcity.*

This definition may appear strange to you. Where are the familiar words we ordinarily associate with economics: "money," "stocks and bonds," "prices," "budgets," . . .? As you will soon see, economics deals with all of these things and more. But first, let's take a closer look at two important ideas in this definition: scarcity and choice.

### SCARCITY AND INDIVIDUAL CHOICE
Think for a moment about your own life—your daily activities, the possessions you enjoy, the surroundings in which you live. Is there anything you don't have right now that you'd *like* to have? Anything that you already have but that you would like *more* of? If your answer is "no," congratulations! Either you are well advanced on the path of Zen self-denial, or else you are a close relative of Bill Gates. The rest of us, however, feel the pinch of limits to our material standard of living. This simple truth is at the very core of economics. It can be restated this way: We all face the problem of **scarcity**.

**Economics** The study of choice under conditions of scarcity.

**Scarcity** A situation in which the amount of something available is insufficient to satisfy the desire for it.

At first glance, it may seem that you suffer from an infinite variety of scarcities. There are so many things you might like to have right now—a larger room or apartment, a new car, more clothes . . . the list is endless. But a little reflection suggests that your limited ability to satisfy these desires is based on two other, more basic limitations: scarce *time* and scarce *spending power*.

> *As individuals, we face a scarcity of time and spending power. Given more of either, we could each have more of the goods and services that we desire.*

The scarcity of spending power is no doubt familiar to you. We've all wished for higher incomes so that we could afford to buy more of the things we want. But the scarcity of time is equally important. So many of the activities we enjoy—seeing a movie, taking a vacation, making a phone call—require time as well as money. Just as we have limited spending power, we also have a limited number of hours in each day to satisfy our desires.

Because of the scarcities of time and spending power, each of us is forced to make *choices*. We must allocate our scarce *time* to different activities: work, play, education, sleep, shopping, and more. We must allocate our scarce *spending power* among different goods and services: housing, food, furniture, travel, and many others. And each time we choose to buy something or do something, we are also choosing *not* to buy or do something else.

Economists study the choices we make as individuals and how those choices shape our economy. For example, over the next decade, we may each—as individuals—decide to make more of our purchases over the Internet. Collectively, this decision will determine which firms and industries will expand and hire new workers (such as Internet consulting firms and manufacturers of Internet technology) and which firms will contract and lay off workers (such as traditional "brick and mortar" retailers).

Economists also study the more subtle and indirect effects of individual choice on our society. Will most Americans continue to live in houses, or—like Europeans—will most of us end up in apartments? Will we have an educated and well-informed citizenry? Will traffic congestion in our cities continue to worsen, or is there relief in sight? Will the Internet create faster economic growth and more rapidly rising living standards for years to come or just a short burst of economic activity that will soon subside? These questions hinge, in large part, on the separate decisions of millions of people. To answer them requires an understanding of how individuals make choices under conditions of scarcity.

## SCARCITY AND SOCIAL CHOICE

Now let's think about scarcity and choice from *society*'s point of view. What are the goals of our society? We want a high standard of living for our citizens, clean air, safe streets, good schools, and more. What is holding us back from accomplishing all of these goals in a way that would satisfy everyone? You already know the answer: scarcity.

In society's case, the problem is a scarcity of **resources**—the things we use to make goods and services that help us achieve our goals. Economists classify resources into three categories:

1. **Labor** is the time human beings spend producing goods and services.
2. **Capital** consists of the long-lasting tools people use to produce goods and services. This includes *physical capital,* such as buildings, machinery, and equipment, as well as *human capital*—the *skills and training* that workers possess.

**Resources**  The land, labor, and capital that are used to produce goods and services.

**Labor**  The time human beings spend producing goods and services.

**Capital**  Long-lasting tools used in producing goods and services.

**Human capital**  The skills and training of the labor force.

3. **Land** is the physical space on which production takes place, as well as the natural resources found under it or on it, such as oil, iron, coal, and lumber.

Anything *produced* in the economy comes, ultimately, from some combination of these resources. Think about the last lecture you attended at your college. You were consuming a service—a college lecture. What went into producing that service? Your instructor was supplying labor. Many types of capital were used as well. The physical capital included desks, chairs, a chalkboard or transparency projector, and the classroom building itself. It also included the computer your instructor may have used to compose lecture notes. In addition, there was human capital—your instructor's specialized knowledge and lecturing skills. Finally, there was land—the property on which your classroom building sits.

Besides the three resources, other things were used to produce your college lecture. Chalk, for example, is a tool used by your instructor, so you might think it should be considered capital, but it is not. Why not? Because it is not *long lasting*. Typically, economists consider a tool to be capital only if it lasts for a few years or longer. Chalk is used up as the lecture is produced, so it is considered a *raw material* rather than capital.

But a little reflection should convince you that a piece of chalk is itself produced from some combination of the three resources (labor, capital, and land). In fact, all of the raw materials needed to produce the lecture—the energy used to heat or cool your building, the computer paper used for your instructor's lecture notes, and so on—come, ultimately, from society's three resources. And the scarcity of these resources, in turn, causes the scarcity of all goods and services produced from them.

> As a society, our resources—land, labor, and capital—are insufficient to produce all the goods and services we might desire. In other words, society faces a scarcity of resources.

This stark fact about the world helps us understand the choices a society must make. Do we want a more educated citizenry? Of course. But that will require more labor—construction workers to build more classrooms and teachers to teach in them. It will require more natural resources—land for classrooms and lumber to build them. And it will require more capital—cement mixers, trucks, and more. These very same resources, however, could instead be used to produce *other* things that we find desirable—things such as new homes, hospitals, automobiles, or feature films. As a result, every society must have some method of *allocating* its scarce resources—choosing which of our many competing desires will be fulfilled and which will not be.

Many of the big questions of our time center on the different ways in which resources can be allocated. The cataclysmic changes that rocked Eastern Europe and the former Soviet Union during the early 1990s arose from a very simple fact: The method these countries used for decades to allocate resources was not working. Closer to home, the never-ending debates between Democrats and Republicans in the United States reflect subtle but important differences of opinion about how to allocate resources. Often, these are disputes about whether the private sector can handle the allocation of resources on its own or whether the government should be involved.

## SCARCITY AND ECONOMICS

The scarcity of resources—and the choices it forces us to make—is the source of all of the problems you will study in economics. Households have limited incomes for satisfying their desires, so they must choose carefully how they allocate their spending among different goods and services. Business firms want to make the highest possible profit, but they must pay for their resources, so they carefully choose *what* to produce, *how much* to produce, and *how* to produce it. Federal, state, and local government agencies work with limited budgets, so they must carefully choose which goals to pursue. Economists study these decisions made by households, firms, and governments to explain how our economic system operates, to forecast the future of our economy, and to suggest ways to make that future even better.

## THE WORLD OF ECONOMICS

The field of economics is surprisingly broad. It extends from the mundane—why does a pound of steak cost more than a pound of chicken?—to the personal and profound—how do couples decide how many children to have? With a field this broad, it is useful to have some way of classifying the different types of problems economists study and the different methods they use to analyze them.

### MICROECONOMICS AND MACROECONOMICS

**Microeconomics** The study of the behavior of individual households, firms, and governments; the choices they make; and their interaction in specific markets.

The field of economics is divided into two major parts: microeconomics and macroeconomics. **Microeconomics** comes from the Greek word *mikros*, meaning "small." It takes a close-up view of the economy, as if looking through a microscope. Microeconomics is concerned with the behavior of *individual* actors on the economic scene—households, business firms, and governments. It looks at the choices they make, and how they interact with each other when they come together to trade *specific* goods and services. What will happen to the cost of movie tickets over the next five years? How many jobs will open up in the fast-food industry? How would U.S. phone companies be affected by a tax on imported cell phones? These are all microeconomic questions because they analyze individual *parts* of an economy, rather than the *whole*.

**Macroeconomics** The study of the economy as a whole.

Macroeconomics—from the Greek word *makros*, meaning "large"—takes an *overall* view of the economy. Instead of focusing on the production of carrots or computers, macroeconomics lumps all goods and services together and looks at the economy's *total output*. Instead of focusing on employment in the fast-food industry or the manufacturing sector, it considers *total employment* in the economy. Instead of asking why credit card loans carry higher interest rates than home mortgage loans, it asks what makes interest rates *in general* rise or fall. In all of these cases, macroeconomics focuses on the big picture and ignores the fine details.

### POSITIVE AND NORMATIVE ECONOMICS

**Positive economics** The study of what *is*, of how the economy works.

The micro versus macro distinction is based on the level of detail we want to consider. Another useful distinction has to do with the *purpose* in analyzing a problem. **Positive economics** deals with what *is*—with *how* the economy works, plain and simple. If we lower income tax rates in the United States next year, will the economy grow faster? If so, by how much? And what effect will this have on total employment? These are all positive economic questions. We may disagree about the answers, but we can all agree that the correct answers to these questions do *exist*—we just have to find them.

**Normative economics** The study of what *should be;* it is used to make value judgments, identify problems, and prescribe solutions.

**Normative economics** concerns itself with what *should be*. It is used to make judgments about the economy, identify problems, and prescribe solutions. While positive economics is concerned with just the facts, normative economics requires us to make value judgments. When an economist advises that we cut government spending—an action that will benefit some citizens and harm others—the economist is engaging in normative analysis.

Positive and normative economics are intimately related in practice. For one thing, we cannot properly argue about what we should or should not do unless we know certain facts about the world. Every normative analysis is therefore based on an underlying positive analysis. But while a positive analysis can, at least in principle, be conducted without value judgments, a normative analysis is always based, at least in part, on the values of the person conducting it.

**Why Economists Disagree.**   The distinction between positive and normative economics can help us understand why economists sometimes disagree. Suppose you are watching a television interview in which two economists are asked whether the United States should eliminate all government-imposed barriers to trading with the rest of the world. The first economist says, "Yes, absolutely," but the other says, "No, definitely not." Why the sharp disagreement?

The difference of opinion may be *positive* in nature: The two economists may have different views about what would actually happen if trade barriers were eliminated. Differences like this sometimes arise because our knowledge of the economy is imperfect, or because certain facts are in dispute.

More likely, however, the disagreement will be *normative*. Economists, like everyone else, have different values. In this case, both economists might agree that opening up international trade would benefit *most* Americans, but harm *some* of them. Yet they may still disagree about the policy move because they have different values. The first economist might put more emphasis on benefits to the overall economy, while the second might put more emphasis on preventing harm to a particular group. Here, the two economists have come to the same *positive* conclusion, but their *different values* lead them to different *normative* conclusions.

In the media, economists are rarely given enough time to express the basis for their opinions, so the public hears only the disagreement. People may then conclude—wrongly—that economists cannot agree about how the economy works when the *real* disagreement is over which goals are most important for our society.

# WHY STUDY ECONOMICS?

Students take economics courses for all kinds of reasons.

## TO UNDERSTAND THE WORLD BETTER

Applying the tools of economics can help you understand global and cataclysmic events such as wars, famines, epidemics, and depressions. But it can also help you understand much of what happens to you locally and personally—the worsening traffic conditions in your city, the raise you can expect at your job this year, or the long line of people waiting to buy tickets for a popular concert. Economics has the power to help us understand these phenomena because they result, in large part, from the choices we make under conditions of scarcity.

Economics has its limitations, of course. But it is hard to find any aspect of life about which economics does not have *something* important to say. Economics cannot explain why so many Americans like to watch television, but it *can* explain how TV networks decide which programs to offer. Economics cannot protect you from a

**http://**

The Federal Reserve Bank of Minneapolis asked some Nobel Prize winners how they became interested in economics. Their stories can be found at http://woodrow.mpls.frb.fed.us/pubs/rgion/98-12/quotes.html.

robbery, but it *can* explain why some people choose to become thieves and why no society has chosen to eradicate crime completely. Economics will not improve your love life, resolve unconscious conflicts from your childhood, or help you overcome a fear of flying, but it *can* tell us how many skilled therapists, ministers, and counselors are available to help us solve these problems.

## TO GAIN SELF-CONFIDENCE

Those who have never studied economics often feel that mysterious, inexplicable forces are shaping their lives, buffeting them like the bumpers in a pinball machine, determining whether or not they'll be able to find a job, what their salary will be, whether they'll be able to afford a home, and in what kind of neighborhood. If you've been one of those people, all that is about to change. After you learn economics, you may be surprised to find that you no longer toss out the business page of your local newspaper because it appears to be written in a foreign language. You may no longer lunge for the remote and change the channel the instant you hear "And now for news about the economy. . . ." You may find yourself listening to economic reports with a critical ear, catching mistakes in logic, misleading statements, or out-and-out lies. When you master economics, you gain a sense of mastery over the world, and thus over your own life as well.

## TO ACHIEVE SOCIAL CHANGE

If you are interested in making the world a better place, economics is indispensable. There is no shortage of serious social problems worthy of our attention—unemployment, hunger, poverty, disease, child abuse, drug addiction, violent crime. Economics can help us understand the origins of these problems, explain why previous efforts to solve them have failed, and enable us to design new, more effective solutions.

## TO HELP PREPARE FOR OTHER CAREERS

Economics has long been the most popular college major for individuals intending to work in business. But in the last two decades it has also become popular among those planning careers in politics, international relations, law, medicine, engineering, psychology, and other professions. This is for good reason: Practitioners in each of these fields often find themselves confronting economic issues. For example, lawyers increasingly face judicial rulings based on the principles of economic efficiency. Doctors will need to understand how new laser technologies or changes in the structure of HMOs will affect their practices. Industrial psychologists need to understand the economic implications of workplace changes they may advocate, such as flexible scheduling or on-site child care.

## TO BECOME AN ECONOMIST

Only a tiny minority of this book's readers will decide to become economists. This is welcome news to the authors, and after you have studied labor markets in your *microeconomics* course, you will understand why. But if you do decide to become an economist—obtaining a master's degree or even a Ph.D.—you will find many possibilities for employment. Of 16,780 members of the American Economic Association who responded to a recent survey,[1] 65 percent were employed at colleges or universities. The rest were engaged in a variety of activities in both the private sector (21 percent) and government (14 percent). Economists are hired by banks to as-

---

[1]    *American Economic Review,* December 1993, p. 635.

sess the risk of investing abroad; by manufacturing companies, to help them determine new methods of producing, marketing, and pricing their products; by government agencies, to help design policies to fight crime, disease, poverty, and pollution; by international organizations, to help create aid programs for less developed countries; by the media to help the public interpret global, national, and local events; and even by nonprofit organizations, to provide advice on controlling costs and raising funds more effectively.

# THE METHODS OF ECONOMICS

One of the first things you will notice as you begin to study economics is the heavy reliance on *models*. Indeed, the discipline goes beyond any other social science in its insistence that every theory be represented by an explicit, carefully constructed *model*.

You've no doubt encountered many models in your life. As a child, you played with model trains, model planes, or model people—dolls. In a high school science course, you probably saw a model of an atom—one of those plastic and wire contraptions with red, blue, and green balls representing protons, neutrons, and electrons. You may have also seen architects' cardboard models of buildings. These are physical models, three-dimensional replicas that you can pick up and hold. Economic models, on the other hand, are built not with cardboard, plastic, or metal but with words, diagrams, and mathematical statements.

What, exactly, is a model?

> *A **model** is an abstract representation of reality.*

**Model** An abstract representation of reality.

The two key words in this definition are *abstract* and *representation*. A model is not supposed to be exactly like reality. Rather, it *represents* the real world by *abstracting*, or *taking from* the real world that which will help us understand it. In any model, many real-world details are left out.

## THE ART OF BUILDING ECONOMIC MODELS

When you build a model, how do you know which details to include and which to leave out? There is no simple answer to this question. The right amount of detail depends on your purpose in building the model in the first place. There is, however, one guiding principle:

> *A model should be as simple as possible to accomplish its purpose.*

This means that a model should contain only the *necessary* details.

To understand this a little better, think about a map. A map is a model—it represents a part of the earth's surface. But it leaves out many details of the real world. First, maps are two-dimensional, so they leave out the third dimension—height—of the real world. Second, maps always ignore small details, such as trees and houses and potholes. Third, a map is much smaller than the area it represents. But when you buy a map, how much detail do you want it to have?

Let's say you are in Boston, and you need a map (your *purpose*) to find the best way to drive from Logan Airport to the downtown convention center. In this case, you would want a very detailed city map, with every street, park, and plaza in Boston clearly illustrated and labeled. A highway map, which ignores these details, wouldn't do at all.

These maps are *models*. But each would be used for a different purpose.

**Simplifying assumption**  Any assumption that makes a model simpler without affecting any of its important conclusions.

**Critical assumption**  Any assumption that affects the conclusions of a model in an important way.

But now suppose your purpose is different: to select the best driving route from Boston to Cincinnati. Now you want a highway map. A map that shows every street between Boston and Cincinnati would have *too much* detail. All of that extraneous information would only obscure what you really need to see.

Although economic models are more abstract than road maps, the same principle applies in building them: The level of detail that would be just right for one purpose will usually be too much or too little for another. When you feel yourself objecting to a model in this text because something has been left out, keep in mind the purpose for which the model is built. In introductory economics, the purpose is entirely educational. The models are designed to help you understand some simple, but powerful, principles about how the economy operates. Keeping the models simple makes it easier to see these principles at work and remember them later.

Of course, economic models have other purposes besides education. They can help businesses make decisions about pricing and production, help households decide how and where to invest their savings, and help governments and international agencies formulate policies. Models built for these purposes will be much more detailed than the ones in this text, and you will learn about them if you take more advanced courses in economics. But even complex models are built around a very simple framework—the same framework you will be learning here.

## ASSUMPTIONS AND CONCLUSIONS

Every economic model begins with *assumptions* about the world. There are two types of assumptions in a model: simplifying assumptions and critical assumptions.

A **simplifying assumption** is just what it sounds like—a way of making a model simpler without affecting any of its important conclusions. The purpose of a simplifying assumption is to rid a model of extraneous detail so its essential features can stand out more clearly. A road map, for example, makes the simplifying assumption, "There are no trees," because trees on a map would only get in the way. Similarly, in an economic model, we might assume that there are only two goods that households can choose from or that there are only two nations in the world. We make such assumptions *not* because they are true, but because they make a model easier to follow and do not change any of the important insights we can get from it.

A **critical assumption**, by contrast, is an assumption that affects the conclusions of a model in important ways. When you use a road map, you make the critical assumption, "All of these roads are open." If that assumption is wrong, your conclusion—the best route to take—might be wrong as well.

In an economic model, there are always one or more critical assumptions. You don't have to look very hard to find them, because economists like to make these assumptions explicit right from the outset. For example, when we study the behavior of business firms, our model will assume that firms try to earn the highest possible profit for their owners. By stating this assumption up front, we can see immediately where the model's conclusions spring from.

## THE FOUR-STEP PROCESS

As you read this textbook, you will learn how economists use economic models to address a wide range of problems. In Chapter 2, for example, you will see how a simple economic model can give us important insights about society's production choices. And subsequent chapters will present still different models that help us understand the U.S. economy and the global economic environment in which it operates. As you read, it may seem to you that there are a lot of models to learn and remember . . . and, indeed, there are.

But there is an important insight about economics that—once mastered—will make your job easier than you might think. The insight is this: There is a remarkable similarity in the types of models that economists build, the assumptions that underlie those models, and what economists actually *do* with them. In fact, you will see that economists follow the same *four-step procedure* to analyze almost any economic problem. The first two Key Steps explain how economists *build* an economic model, and the second two Key Steps explain how they *use* the model.

What are these four steps that underlie the economic approach to almost any problem? Sorry for the suspense, but you'll have to wait a bit—until the end of Chapter 3—for the answer. By that time, you'll have learned a little more about economics, and the four-step procedure will make more sense to you.

## MATH, JARGON, AND OTHER CONCERNS . . .

Economists often express their ideas using mathematical concepts and a special vocabulary. Why? Because these tools enable economists to express themselves more precisely than with ordinary language. For example, someone who has never studied economics might say, "When used textbooks are available, students won't buy new textbooks." That statement might not bother you right now. But once you've finished your first economics course, you'll be saying it something like this: "When the price of used textbooks falls, the demand curve for new textbooks shifts leftward."

An on-line introduction to the use of graphs can be found at http://syllabus.syr.edu/cid/graph/book.html.

Does the second statement sound strange to you? It should. First, it uses a special term—a *demand curve*—that you haven't yet learned. Second, it uses a mathematical concept—a *shifting curve*—with which you might not be familiar. But while the first statement might mean a number of different things, the second statement—as you will see in Chapter 3—can mean only *one* thing. By being precise, we can steer clear of unnecessary confusion. If you are worried about the special vocabulary of economics, you can relax. All of the new terms will be defined and carefully explained as you encounter them. Indeed, this textbook does not assume you have any special knowledge of economics. It is truly meant for a "first course" in the field.

But what about the math? Here, too, you can relax. While professional economists often use sophisticated mathematics to solve problems, only a little math is needed to understand basic economic *principles*. And virtually all of this math comes from high school algebra and geometry.

Still, you may have forgotten some of your high school math. If so, a little brushing up might be in order. This is why we have included an appendix at the end of this chapter. It covers some of the most basic concepts—such as the equation for a straight line, the concept of a slope, and the calculation of percentage changes—that you will need in this course. You may want to glance at this appendix now, just so you'll know what's there. Then, from time to time, you'll be reminded about it when you're most likely to need it.

## HOW TO STUDY ECONOMICS

As you read this book or listen to your instructor, you may find yourself nodding along and thinking that everything makes perfect sense. Economics may even seem easy. Indeed, it *is* rather easy to follow economics, since it's based so heavily on simple logic. But *following* and *learning* are two different things. You will eventually discover (preferably *before* your first exam) that economics must be studied actively, not passively.

If you are reading these words lying back on a comfortable couch, a phone in one hand and a remote control in the other, you are going about it in the wrong way. Active studying means reading with a pencil in your hand and a blank sheet of paper in front of you. It means closing the book periodically and *reproducing* what you have learned. It means listing the steps in each logical argument, retracing the cause-and-effect steps in each model, and drawing the graphs that represent the model. It means *thinking* about the basic principles of economics and how they relate to what you are learning. It is hard work, but the payoff is a good understanding of economics and a better understanding of your own life and the world around you.

## S U M M A R Y

*Economics* is the study of choice under conditions of scarcity. As individuals, and as a society, we have unlimited desires for goods and services. Unfortunately, the *resources*—land, labor, and capital—needed to produce those goods and services are scarce. Therefore, we must choose which desires to satisfy and how to satisfy them. Economics provides the tools that explain those choices.

The field of economics is divided into two major areas. *Microeconomics* studies the behavior of individual households, firms, and governments as they interact in specific markets. *Macroeconomics,* by contrast, concerns itself with the behavior of the entire economy. It considers variables such as total output, total employment, and the overall price level.

Economics makes heavy use of *models*—abstract representations of reality. These models are built with words, diagrams, and mathematical statements that help us understand how the economy operates. All models are simplifications, but a good model will have *just enough detail for the purpose at hand.*

When analyzing almost any problem, economists follow a four-step procedure in building and using economic models. This four-step procedure will be introduced at the end of Chapter 3.

## K E Y   T E R M S

| | | | |
|---|---|---|---|
| economics | capital | macroeconomics | simplifying assumption |
| scarcity | human capital | positive economics | critical assumption |
| resources | land | normative economics | |
| labor | microeconomics | model | |

## R E V I E W   Q U E S T I O N S

1. Discuss (separately) how scarcity arises for households, businesses, and governments.

2. Would each of the following be classified as microeconomics or macroeconomics? Why?
   a. Research into why the growth rate of total production increased during the 1990s.
   b. A theory of how consumers decide what to buy.
   c. An analysis of Dell Computer's share of the personal computer market.
   d. Research on why interest rates were unusually high in the late 1970s and early 1980s.

3. Discuss whether each statement is an example of positive economics or normative economics or if it contains elements of both:
   a. An increase in the personal income tax will slow the growth rate of the economy.

   b. The goal of any country's economic policy should be to increase the well-being of its poorest, most vulnerable citizens.
   c. Excess regulation of small business is stifling the economy. Small business has been responsible for most of the growth in employment over the last 10 years, but regulations are putting a severe damper on the ability of small businesses to survive and prosper.
   d. The 1990s were a disastrous decade for the U.S. economy. Income inequality increased to its highest level since before World War II.

4. What determines the level of detail that an economist builds into a model?

5. What is the difference between a simplifying assumption and a critical assumption?

## P R O B L E M

1. Come up with a list of critical assumptions that could lie behind each of the following statements. Discuss whether each assumption would be classified as normative or positive.

   a. The United States is a democratic society.
   b. European movies are better than American movies.
   c. The bigger the city, the higher the quality of the newspaper.

## E X P E R I E N T I A L   E X E R C I S E

1. Go to the Bank of Sweden's Web page on the Nobel Prize in economic science at *http://www.ee.nobel.se/prize/memorial. html*. Review the descriptions of some recent awards and try to determine whether each of those awards was primarily for work in microeconomics or macroeconomics.

   http://

# APPENDIX

## GRAPHS AND OTHER USEFUL TOOLS

## TABLES AND GRAPHS

A brief glance at this text will tell you that graphs are important in economics. Graphs provide a convenient way to display data. Take the example of Len & Harry's, an up-and-coming manufacturer of high-end ice cream products, located in Texas. Suppose that you've just been hired to head Len & Harry's advertising department, and you want to learn as much as you can about how advertising can help the company's sales.

Table A.1 records the company's total advertising outlay per month in the left-hand column, and the company's ice cream sales during that same month are shown in the right-hand column. Notice that the data are organized so that advertising outlay increases as we move down the first column. Often, just looking at such a table can reveal useful patterns. In this case, it seems that higher advertising outlays are associated with higher monthly sales. This suggests that there may be some *causal relationship* between advertising and sales.

To explore this relationship further, we might decide to plot the data and draw a graph (see Figure A.1). First, we need to choose units for our two variables. We'll measure both advertising and sales in thousands of dollars. Different values of one variable are then measured along the horizontal axis, increasing as we move rightward from the origin. The corresponding values of the other variable are measured along the ver-

tical axis, increasing as we move upward, away from the origin.

Using the data in the table, let $X$ stand for advertising outlay per month, and let $Y$ stand for sales per month. Notice that each row of the table gives us a pair of numbers: The first is always the value of the variable we are calling $X$, and the second is the value of the variable we are calling $Y$. We often write such pairs in the form $(X, Y)$. For example, we would write the first three rows of the table as (2, 46), (3, 49), and (6, 58), respectively.

To plot the pair $(X, Y)$ on a graph, begin at the origin, where the axes meet. Count rightward $X$ units along the horizontal axis, then count upward $Y$ units parallel to the vertical axis, and then mark the spot. For example, to plot the pair (2, 46), we go rightward 2 units along the horizontal axis and then upward 46 units along the vertical axis, arriving at the point marked $A$ in Figure A.1. To plot the next pair, (3, 49), we go rightward from the origin 3 units and then upward 49 units, arriving at the point marked $B$. Carrying on in just this way, we can plot all remaining pairs in Table A.1 as the points $C, D, E,$ and $F$.

If we connect points $A$ through $F$, we see that they all lie along the same straight line. Now we are getting somewhere. The relationship we've discovered appears from the graph to be very regular, indeed.

Study the graph closely. You will notice that each time advertising increases (moves rightward) by $1,000,

| TABLE A.1 | | |
|---|---|---|
| **ADVERTISING AND SALES AT LEN & HARRY'S** | **Advertising ($1,000s per Month)** | **Sales ($1,000s per Month)** |
| | 2 | 46 |
| | 3 | 49 |
| | 6 | 58 |
| | 7 | 61 |
| | 11 | 73 |
| | 12 | 76 |

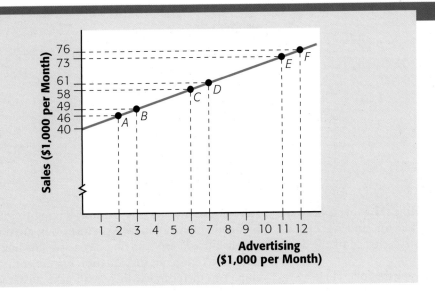

Y moves upward by $3,000. For example, when advertising rises from $2,000 to $3,000, sales rise from $46,000 to $49,000. By checking between any other two points on the graph, you will see that every time $X$ increases horizontally by one unit (here, a unit is $1,000), $Y$ increases vertically by three units (here, by $3,000). Thus, we conclude that that the *rate of change* in $Y$ is three units of $Y$ for every one-unit increase in $X$.

The *slope* of a graph tells us the rate at which the $Y$-variable changes for every one-unit change in the $X$-variable. The slope of a straight line between any two points $(X_1, Y_1)$ and $(X_2, Y_2)$ is defined as the change in $Y$—the vertical "rise"—divided by the change in $X$—the horizontal "run." This is why the slope is often described as "rise over run." Supposing we start at $(X_1, Y_1)$ and end at $(X_2, Y_2)$; then the change in the $X$-variable is $(X_2 - X_1)$. The corresponding change in the $Y$-variable is $(Y_2 - Y_1)$. We therefore compute the slope as follows:

$$\text{Slope of the line from } (X_1, Y_1) \text{ to } (X_2, Y_2) = \frac{\text{Rise along vertical axis}}{\text{Run along horizontal axis}}$$

$$= \frac{Y_2 - Y_1}{X_2 - X_2}$$

We sometimes use the capital Greek letter, $\Delta$ ("delta"), to denote a change in a variable. Here we would write $\Delta X = X_2 - X_1$ to denote the change in $X$, and $\Delta Y = Y_2 - Y_1$ to denote the corresponding change

in $Y$. We then could write that same formula for the slope more compactly as

$$\text{Slope of the line from } (X_1, Y_1) \text{ to } (X_2, Y_2) = \frac{\Delta Y}{\Delta X}.$$

## NONLINEAR GRAPHS

Although many of the relationships we encounter in economics have straight-line graphs, many do not. Still, graphs can help us understand the underlying relationships, and the concept of slope remains very useful.

As an example, look at the data in Table A.2, which records the price of a share of Len and Harry's stock at different points in time since the stock first appeared on the market. To understand how the price of this stock has behaved over time, we might again start by plotting a graph of the data in the table. It seems natural to measure time—in "weeks since launch"—on the $X$-axis and stock price—in "dollars per share"—on the $Y$-axis. As you can see in Figure A.2, Len and Harry's has had a rocky ride since it came on the market. In its first 10 weeks, the stock's price rose, so the slope of the underlying relationship was positive during that time. Over the next 10 weeks, the story changed: The stock's price decreased, so the slope of the relationship was negative then. Between weeks 20 and 30, things leveled off: There was no change in the stock's price, so the slope of the

| TABLE A.2 | | |
| --- | --- | --- |
| **PRICE OF LEN & HARRY'S STOCK SINCE LAUNCH** | **Weeks Since Launch** | **Stock Price** |
| | 3 | $20 |
| | 10 | 50 |
| | 18 | 35 |
| | 20 | 20 |
| | 25 | 20 |
| | 30 | 20 |
| | 40 | 75 |

graph was zero during that time. However, between weeks 30 and 40 things picked up, and once again the slope turned positive, since the price of the stock increased.

From this example, we can see the following:

- The slope is positive whenever an increase in X is associated with an increase in Y.
- The slope is negative whenever an increase in X is associated with a decrease in Y.
- The slope is equal to zero whenever an increase in X is associated with no change in Y.

## LINEAR EQUATIONS

Let's go back to the relationship between advertising and sales, as shown in Table A.1. What if you need to know how much sales the firm could expect if it spent $5,000 on advertising next month? What if it spent $8,000, or $9,000? Wouldn't it be nice to be able to an-

swer questions like this without having to pull out tables and graphs to do it? As it turns out, anytime the relationship you are studying has a straight-line graph, it is easy to figure out the equation for the entire relationship. You then can use the equation to answer any such question that might be put to you.

All straight lines have the same general form. If Y stands for the variable on the vertical axis and X for the variable on the horizontal axis, every straight line has an equation of the form

$$Y = a + bX,$$

where $a$ stands for some number and $b$ for another number. The number $a$ is called the vertical *intercept*, because it marks the point where the graph of this equation hits (intercepts) the vertical axis; this occurs when X takes the value zero. (If you plug $X = 0$ into the equation, you will see that, indeed, $Y = a$.) The number $b$ is the slope of the line, telling us how much Y will

| FIGURE A.2 | |
| --- | --- |

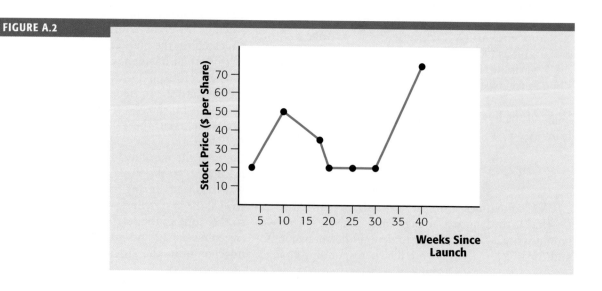

change every time $X$ changes by one unit. To confirm this, note that as $X$ increases from 0 to 1, $Y$ goes from $a$ to $a + b$. The number $b$ is therefore the change in $Y$ corresponding to a one-unit change in $X$—exactly what the slope of the graph should tell us.

More generally, if $X$ changes from some value $X_1$ to some other value $X_2$, $Y$ will change from

$$Y_1 = a + bX_1$$

to

$$Y_2 = a + bX_2.$$

If we subtract $Y_1$ from $Y_2$ to compute how much $Y$ has changed ($\Delta Y$), we find that

$$\begin{aligned} \Delta Y = Y_2 - Y_1 &= (a + bX_2) - (a + bX_1) \\ &= a + bX_2 - a - bX_1 \\ &= b(X_2 - X_1) \\ &= b\Delta X. \end{aligned}$$

Dividing both sides of the equation $\Delta Y = b\Delta X$ by $\Delta X$, we get

$$\frac{\Delta Y}{\Delta X} = b,$$

confirming that $b$ really does measure the slope.

If $b$ is a positive number, a one-unit increase in $X$ causes $Y$ to increase by $b$ units, so the graph of our line would slope upward, as illustrated by the red line in panel (a) of Figure A.3. If $b$ is a negative number, then a one-unit increase in $X$ will cause $Y$ to *decrease* by $b$ units, so

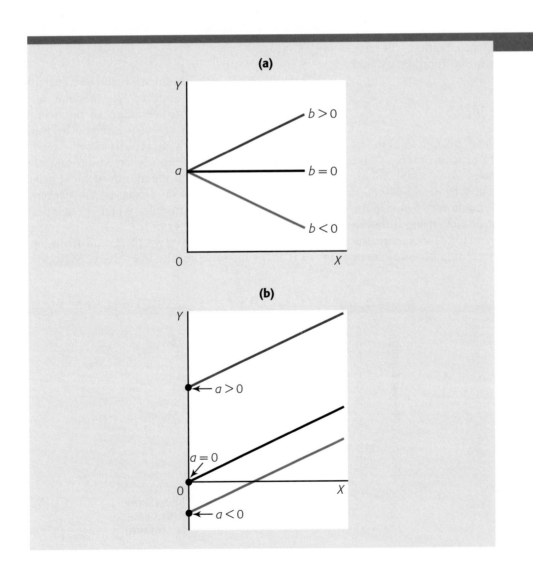

**FIGURE A.3**

the graph would slope downward, as the blue line does in panel (a). Of course, *b* could equal zero. If it does, a one-unit increase in *X* causes no change in *Y*, so the graph of the line is flat, like the black line in panel (a).

The value of *a* has no effect on the slope of the graph. Instead, different values of *a* determine the graph's position. When *a* is a positive number, the graph will intercept the vertical *Y*-axis above the origin, as the red line does in panel (b) of Figure A.3. When *a* is negative, however, the graph will intercept the *Y*-axis *below* the origin, like the blue line in panel (b). When *a* is zero, the graph intercepts the *Y*-axis right at the origin, as the black line does in panel (b).

Let's see if we can figure out the equation for the relationship depicted in Figure A.1. There, *X* denotes advertising and *Y* denotes sales. On the graph, it is easy to see that when advertising expenditure is zero, sales are $40,000. Therefore, our equation will have a *vertical* intercept of *a* = 40. Earlier, we calculated the slope of this graph to be 3. Therefore, the equation will have *b* = 3. Putting these two observations together, we find that the equation for the line in Figure A.1 is

$$Y = 40 + 3X.$$

*Now* if you need to know how much in sales to expect from a particular expenditure on advertising, you'd be able to come up with an answer: You'd simply multiply the amount spent on advertising by 3, add $40,000, and that would be your sales. To confirm this, plug in for *X* in this equation any amount of advertising from the left-hand column of Table A.1. You'll see that you get the corresponding amount of sales in the right-hand column.

## HOW LINES AND CURVES SHIFT

So far, we've focused on relationships where some variable *Y* depends on a single other variable, *X*. But in many of our theories, we recognize that some variable of interest to us is actually affected by more than just one other variable. When *Y* is affected by both *X* and some third variable, changes in that third variable will usually cause a *shift* in the graph of the relationship between *X* and *Y*. This is because whenever we draw the graph between *X* and *Y*, we are holding fixed every other variable that might possibly affect *Y*.

> A graph between two variables X and Y *is only a picture of their relationship when all other variables affecting Y are constant. Changes in any one or more of those other variables will shift the graph of X and Y.*

Think back to the relationship between advertising and sales. Earlier, we supposed sales depend only on advertising. But suppose we make an important discovery: Ice cream sales are *also* affected by how hot the weather is. What's more, all of the data in Table A.1 on which we previously based our analysis turns out to have been from the month of June, when the average temperature in Texas is 80 degrees. What's going to happen in July, when the average temperature rises to 100 degrees?

In Figure A.4 we've redrawn the graph from Figure A.1, this time labeling the line "June." Often, a

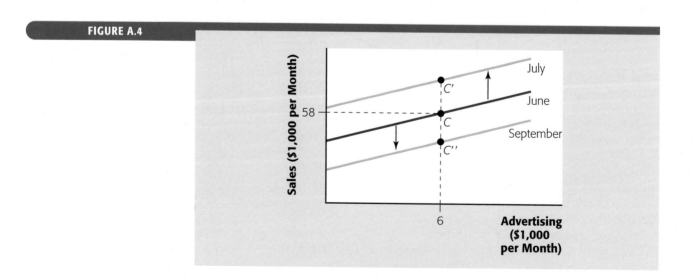

**FIGURE A.4**

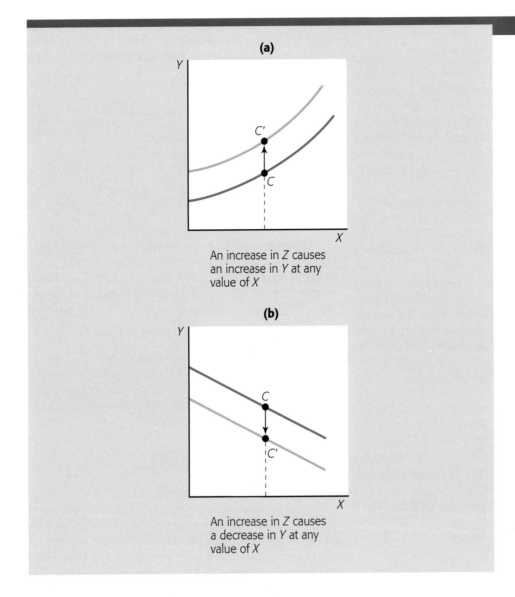

**(a)**

An increase in Z causes
an increase in Y at any
value of X

**(b)**

An increase in Z causes
a decrease in Y at any
value of X

good way to determine how a graph will shift is to perform a simple experiment like this: Put your pencil tip anywhere on the graph labeled June—let's say at point C. Now ask the following question: If I hold advertising constant at $6,000, do I expect to sell more or less ice cream as temperature rises in July? If you expect to sell more, then the amount of sales corresponding to $6,000 of advertising will be *above* point C, at a point such as C′. From this, we can tell that the graph will shift upward as temperature rises. In September, however, when temperatures fall, the amount of sales corresponding to $6,000 in advertising would be less than it is at point C. It would be

shown by a point such as C″. In that case, the graph would shift downward.

The same procedure works well whether the original graph slopes upward or downward and whether it is a straight line or a curved one. Figure A.5 sketches two examples. In panel (a), an increase in some third variable, Z, increases the value of Y for each value of X, so the graph of the relationship between X and Y shifts upward as Z increases. We often phrase it this way: "An increase in Z causes an increase in Y, *at any value of X.*" In panel (b), an increase in Z *decreases* the value of Y, at any value of X, so the graph of the relationship between X and Y shifts *downward* as Z increases.

## SOLVING EQUATIONS

When we first derived the equation for the relationship between advertising and sales, we wanted to know what level of sales to expect from different amounts of advertising. But what if we're asked a slightly different question? Suppose, this time, you are told that the sales committee has set an ambitious goal of $64,000 for next month's sales. The treasurer needs to know how much to budget for advertising, and you have to come up with the answer.

Since we know how advertising and sales are related, we ought to be able to answer this question. One way is just to look at the graph in Figure A.1. There, we could first locate sales of $64,000 on the vertical axis. Then, if we read over to the line and then down, we find the amount of advertising that would be necessary to generate that level of sales. Yet even with that carefully drawn diagram, it is not always easy to see just exactly how much advertising would be required. If we need to be precise, we'd better use the equation for the graph instead.

According to the equation, sales ($Y$) and advertising ($X$) are related as follows:

$$Y = 40 + 3X.$$

In the problem before us, we know the value for sales, and we need to solve for the corresponding amount of advertising. Substituting the sales target of $64,000 for $Y$, we need to find that value of $X$ for which

$$64 = 40 + 3X.$$

Here, $X$ is the unknown value for which we want to solve.

Whenever we solve one equation for one unknown, say, $X$, we need to *isolate* $X$ on one side of the equals sign and everything else on the other side of the equals sign. We do this by performing identical operations on both sides of the equals sign. Here, we can first subtract 40 from both sides, getting

$$24 = 3X.$$

We can then divide both sides by 3 and get

$$8 = X.$$

This is our answer. If we want to achieve sales of $64,000, we'll need to spend $8,000 on advertising.

By looking back over what we just did, we can come up with a useful formula that will help to solve similar equations. Starting with an equation of the form

$$Y = a + bX,$$

we first subtracted $a$ from both sides to get

$$Y - a = bX.$$

We then divided both sides by $b$ to get our answer:

$$\frac{(Y - a)}{b} = X.$$

This is a formula you can use to solve for $X$ whenever $X$ and $Y$ are linearly related and whenever $b$ is not equal to zero. Of course, not all relationships are linear, so this formula will not work in every situation. But no matter what the underlying relationship, the idea remains the same:

> To solve for X in any equation, rearrange the equation, following the rules of algebra, so that X appears on one side of the equals sign and everything else in the equation appears on the other side.

## PERCENTAGE CHANGES

It is often convenient to express changes in percentage terms, rather than absolute terms. While we are all quite used to thinking in percentages, a quick review of how to calculate them may be helpful. If some variable $X$ starts at one value and ends at another, the percentage change in $X$, denoted, $\%\Delta X$, is computed as follows:

$$\%\Delta X = \frac{\text{ending value of } X - \text{starting value of } X}{\text{starting value of } X} \times 100$$

Look at this formula for a moment. It says that, to calculate the *percentage* change in $X$, first compute the *change* in $X$ by subtracting the ending value from the starting value, and then divide by the "base," or starting value, of $X$. The resulting fraction is then multiplied by 100. The formula shows us that:

> Whenever a variable decreases, the percentage change in its value will be negative.
> Whenever a variable increases, the percentage change in its value will be positive.

| | | | | TABLE A.3 |
|---|---|---|---|---|
| **Variable** | **Beginning Value** | **Ending Value** | **Calculated Percentage Change** | **RULES OF THUMB FOR PERCENTAGE CHANGES** |
| $B$ | 100 | 103 | 3% | |
| $C$ | 20 | 21 | 5% | |
| $B \times C$ | 2,000 | 2,163 | 8.15% | |
| $B/C$ | 5 | 4.905 | 1.9% | |

Sometimes, we are interested in computing the percentage change in a product or a ratio. There are some useful rules of thumb that can simplify those computations. Specifically, we have:

*Product Rule:*   If $A = B \times C$,
               then $\%\Delta A = \%\Delta B + \%\Delta C$.

*Quotient Rule:*  If $A = \dfrac{B}{C}$,
               then $\%\Delta A - \%\Delta B = \%\Delta C$.

The product rule says that when $A$ is the product of $B$ and $C$, to find the percentage change in $A$, we simply *add* the percentage change in $B$ to the percentage change in $C$. The quotient rule says that when $A$ is the quotient $B/C$, to find the percentage change in $A$, simply *subtract* the percentage change in $C$ from the percentage change in $B$.

Strictly speaking, these rules are *approximations*. They are most accurate when the percentage changes in $B$ and $C$ are extremely small. Yet as long as those percentage changes remain "relatively small," the rules will provide "reasonably good" approximations. A few examples will help to convince you.

Suppose $B$ rises from 100 to 103, while $C$ rises from 20 to 21. To keep things straight, we've recorded the relevant data in Table A.3. The first two rows of the table record the beginning and ending values of $B$ and $C$, and the percentage change in each variable. The last two rows show the beginning and ending values for the product $B \times C$ and the quotient $B/C$, respectively, and the percentage change in each of these, calculated exactly.

Now look at what we have. Moving across the third row, we see that $B \times C$ rises from 2,000 to 2,163, a percentage increase of 8.15% when computed exactly. Notice that this is very close to what we would get if, instead, we just applied our product rule, adding the 3% change in $B$ to the 5% change in $C$ to get an estimate of 8% for the change in the product $B \times C$. Thus, our approximation is very close. Similarly, moving across the fourth row, we find that the quotient $B/C$ declines from 5 to 4.905, a percentage decrease of exactly 1.9%. Had we applied our quotient rule instead, we would have taken the 3% increase in $B$ and subtracted the 5% increase in $C$ to get $3\% - 5\% = -2\%$—again, very close to the exact result of 1.9%.

# 2

# SCARCITY, CHOICE, AND ECONOMIC SYSTEMS

W hat does it cost you to go to the movies? If you answered eight or nine dollars, because that is the price of a movie ticket, then you are leaving out a lot. Most of us are used to thinking of "cost" as the money we must pay for something. A Big Mac costs $2.50, a new Toyota Corolla costs $15,000, and the baby-sitter costs $8.00 an hour. Certainly, the money we pay for a good or service is a *part* of its cost. But economics takes a broader view of costs, recognizing monetary as well as nonmonetary components.

## THE CONCEPT OF OPPORTUNITY COST

The total cost of any choice we make—buying a car, producing a computer, or even reading a book—is everything we must *give up* when we take that action. This cost is called the *opportunity cost* of the action, because we give up the opportunity to have other desirable things.

**Opportunity cost** The value of the best alternative sacrificed when taking an action.

> The **opportunity cost** of any choice is all that we forego when we make that choice.

Opportunity cost is the most accurate and complete concept of cost—the one we should use when making our own decisions or analyzing the decisions of others.

## OPPORTUNITY COST FOR INDIVIDUALS

Virtually every action we take as individuals uses up scarce money, scarce time, or both. Hence, every action we choose requires us to sacrifice other enjoyable goods and activities for which we could have used our money and time. For example, it took a substantial amount of the authors' time to write this textbook. Suppose that the time devoted to writing the book could instead have been used by one of the authors to either (1) go to law school, (2) write a novel, or (3) start a profitable business.

Do all three of these alternatives combined make up the opportunity cost of writing this book? Not really. Choosing not to write the book would have released some time but not enough time to pursue all three activities. To measure opportunity cost, we look only at the alternatives that *would* have been chosen—the ones

**http://**

Is college worth the opportunity cost for you? Find out by trying Professor Jane Leuthold's COLLEGE CHOICE program at http://www.cba.uiuc.edu/college/econ/choice/choice.html.

that are actually given up. Suppose that for one of the authors the next best alternative to writing this book was to start a profitable business. Then the opportunity cost of co-authoring this book was the foregone opportunity to start the business. Since the other, less valuable alternatives would not have been chosen anyway, they are not part of the cost of writing the book.

To explore this notion of opportunity cost further, let's go back to the earlier question: What does it cost to see a movie? That depends on *who* is seeing the movie. Suppose some friends ask Jessica, a college student, to go with them to a movie located 10 minutes from campus. To see the movie, Jessica will use up scarce *funds* to buy the movie ticket and scarce *time* traveling to and from the movie and sitting through it. Suppose the *money* she uses for the movie ticket would otherwise have been spent on a long-distance phone call to a friend in Italy—Jessica's next best use of the money— and the *time* would otherwise have been devoted to studying for her economics exam—her next best use of time. For Jessica, then, the opportunity cost of the movie consists of two things given up: (1) a phone call to her friend *and* (2) a higher score on her economics exam. Seeing the movie will require Jessica to sacrifice *both* of these valuable alternatives, since the movie will cost Jessica both money and time.

Now consider Samantha, a highly paid consultant who lives in New York City a few miles from the movie theater, and who has a backlog of projects to work on. As in Jessica's case, seeing the movie will use scarce funds and scarce time. But for Samantha, both costs will be greater. First, the direct money costs: There is not only the price of the movie ticket, but also the round-trip cab fare, which could bring the direct money cost to $20. However, this is only a small part of Samantha's opportunity cost. Let's suppose that the time it takes Samantha to find out when and where the movie is playing, hail a cab, travel to the movie theater, wait in line, sit through the previews, watch the movie, and travel back home is three hours—not unrealistic for seeing a movie in Manhattan. Samantha's next best alternative for using her time would be to work on her consulting projects, for which she would earn $150 per hour. In this case, we can measure the entire opportunity cost of the movie in monetary terms: first, the direct money costs of the movie and cab fare ($20), and second, the foregone income associated with seeing the movie: ($150 × 3 hours = $450)—for a total of $470!

At such a high price, you might wonder why Samantha would ever decide to see a movie. Indeed, the same reasoning applies to almost everything Samantha does besides work: It is very expensive for Samantha to talk to a friend on the phone, eat dinner, or even sleep. Each of these activities requires her to sacrifice the direct money costs plus another $150 per hour of foregone income. Would Samantha ever choose to pursue any of these activities? The answer for Samantha is the same as for Jessica or anyone else: yes—*if* the activity is more highly valued than what is given up. It is not hard to imagine that, after putting in a long day at work, leisure activities would be very important to Samantha—worth the money cost *and* the foregone income required to enjoy them.

Once you understand the concept of opportunity cost and how it can differ among individuals, you can understand some behavior that might otherwise appear strange. For example, why do high-income

**DANGEROUS CURVES**

In some cases, the entire opportunity cost of a decision can be expressed as a single dollar figure. For example, Samantha's ticket, cab fare, and even the time spent at the movie are all easy to value in dollars (the value of the time is equal to the dollars Samantha could have earned at the next best alternative—working). But what if some part of opportunity cost *cannot* be easily measured in dollars? Then we simply express the opportunity cost as several different things, rather than a single number. For example, suppose that Samantha's next best alternative to the movie was not working, but attending a friend's birthday party instead. Then the opportunity cost of the movie would consist of both the *dollar* cost (ticket plus cab fare) *and* the missed birthday party.

people rarely shop at discount stores like Kmart and instead shop at full-service stores where the same items sell for much higher prices? It's not that high-income people *like* to pay more for their purchases. But discount stores are generally under-staffed and crowded with customers, so shopping there takes more time. While discount stores have lower *money* cost, they impose a higher *time* cost. For high-income people, discount stores are actually more costly than stores with higher price tags.

We can also understand why the most highly paid consultants, entrepreneurs, attorneys, and surgeons often lead such frenetic lives, doing several things at once and packing every spare minute with tasks. Since these people can earn several hundred dollars for an hour of work, every activity they undertake carries a correspondingly high opportunity cost. Brushing one's teeth can cost $10, and driving to work can cost hundreds! By combining activities—making phone calls while driving to work, thinking about and planning the day while in the shower, or reading the morning paper in the elevator—the opportunity cost of these routine activities can be reduced.

And what about the rest of us? As our wages rise, we all try to cram more activities into little bits of free time. Millions of Americans now carry cell phones and use them while waiting for an elevator or walking their dogs. Books on tape are becoming more popular and are especially favored by runners. (Why just exercise when you can also "read" a book?) And for some, vacations have become more exhausting than work, as more and more activities are crammed into shorter and shorter vacation periods.

## OPPORTUNITY COST AND SOCIETY

For an individual, opportunity cost arises from the scarcity of time or money. But for society as a whole, opportunity cost arises from a different source: the scarcity of society's *resources*. Our desire for goods is limitless, but we have limited resources to produce them. Therefore,

> *all production carries an opportunity cost: To produce more of one thing, society must shift resources away from producing something else.*

Let's discuss a goal on which we can all agree: better health for our citizens. What would be needed to achieve this goal? Perhaps more frequent medical checkups for more people and greater access to top-flight medicine when necessary. These, in turn, would require more and better-trained doctors, more hospital buildings and laboratories, and more high-tech medical equipment such as MRI scanners and surgical lasers. In order for us to produce these goods and services, we would have to pull resources—land, labor, and capital—out of producing other things that we also enjoy. The opportunity cost of improved health care, then, consists of all the other goods and services we would have to do without.

## PRODUCTION POSSIBILITIES FRONTIERS

Let's build a simple model to help us understand the opportunity cost we must pay for improved health care. To be even more specific, we'll measure production of health care by the *number of lives saved*. This variable is plotted along the horizontal axis in Figure 1. To measure the opportunity cost of health care, we'll make a simplifying assumption: that all goods *other* than life-saving health care can be lumped into a single category, and that we can measure how many units of these

**FIGURE 1**

**THE PRODUCTION POSSIBILITIES FRONTIER**

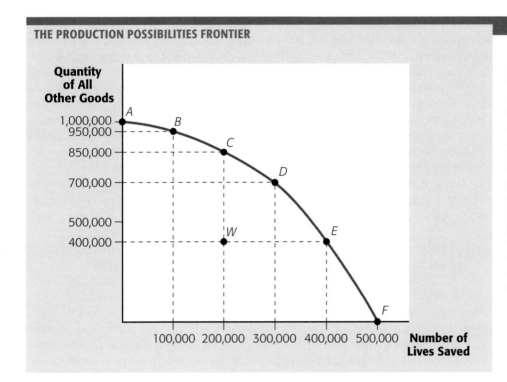

Points along a production possibilities frontier show combinations of two goods—here, lives saved and "other goods"—that can be produced using available resources and technology. At point *A*, all resources are used to produce other goods, and no lives are saved. At point *F*, 500,000 lives are saved, but no other goods are produced. The concave, bowed-out shape of the frontier reflects the law of increasing opportunity cost.

"other goods" we're producing. In Figure 1, the quantity of "other goods" is measured on the vertical axis.

Now look at the curve drawn in Figure 1. It is society's **production possibilities frontier (PPF)**, *giving the different combinations of goods that can be produced with the resources and technology currently available.* More specifically, this PPF tells us the *maximum quantity* of all other goods we can produce for each number of lives saved and the maximum number of lives saved for each different quantity of other goods. Positions outside the frontier are unattainable with the technology and resources at the economy's disposal. Society's choices are limited to points *on* or *inside* the PPF.

Let's take a closer look at the PPF in Figure 1. Point *A* represents one possible choice for our society: to devote all resources to the production of "other goods" and none to health care. In this case, we would have 1,000,000 units of other goods, but we would have to forego every opportunity to save lives. Point *F* represents the opposite extreme: all available resources devoted to life-saving health care. In that case, we'd save 500,000 lives, but we'd have no other goods.

If points *A* and *F* seem absurd to you, remember that they represent two *possible* choices for society but choices we would be unlikely to make. We want life-saving health care to be available to those who need it, but we also want housing, clothing, entertainment, cars, and so on. So a realistic choice would include a *mix* of health care and movies.

Suppose we desire such a mix, but the economy, for some reason, is currently operating at the undesirable point *A*—no health care, but maximum production of everything else. Then we need to shift some resources from other goods to health care. For example, we could move from point *A* to point *B*, where we'd be saving 100,000 lives. But as a consequence, we'd have to cut back on other goods, producing 50,000 fewer units. The opportunity cost of saving 100,000 lives, then, would be 50,000 units of all other goods.

**Production possibilities frontier (PPF)** A curve showing all combinations of two goods that can be produced with the resources and technology currently available.

**Increasing Opportunity Cost.**  Suppose we are at point *B*, and now we want to save even more lives. Once again, we shift enough resources into health care to save an additional 100,000 lives, moving from point *B* to point *C*. This time, however, there is an even *greater* cost: Production of other goods falls from 950,000 units to 850,000 units, or a sacrifice of 100,000 units. The opportunity cost of saving lives has risen. You can see that as we continue to save more lives—by increments of 100,000, moving from point *C* to point *D* to point *E* to point *F*—the opportunity cost of producing other goods keeps right on rising, until saving the last 100,000 lives costs us 400,000 units of other goods.

The behavior of opportunity cost described here—the more health care we produce, the greater the opportunity cost of producing still more—applies to a wide range of choices facing society. It can be generalized as the *law of increasing opportunity cost*.

**Law of increasing opportunity cost**
The more of something that is produced, the greater the opportunity cost of producing one more unit.

> *According to the **law of increasing opportunity cost**, the more of something we produce, the greater the opportunity cost of producing even more of it.*

The law of increasing opportunity cost causes the PPF to have a *concave* shape, becoming steeper as we move rightward and downward. To understand why, remember (from high school math) that the slope of a line or curve is just the change along the vertical axis divided by the change along the horizontal axis. Along the PPF, as we move rightward, the slope is the change in the quantity of other goods divided by the change in the number of lives saved. This is a negative number, because a positive change in lives saved means a negative change in other goods. The absolute value of this slope is the opportunity cost of saving another life. Now—as we've seen—this opportunity cost increases as we move rightward. Therefore, the absolute value of the PPF's slope must rise as well. The PPF gets steeper and steeper, giving us the concave shape we see in the Figure 1.[1]

Why should there be a law of increasing opportunity cost? Why must it be that the more of something we produce, the greater the opportunity cost of producing still more?

Because most resources—*by their very nature*—are better suited to some purposes than to others. If the economy were operating at point *A*, for example, we'd be using all of our resources to produce other goods, including resources that are much better suited for health care. A hospital might be used as a food cannery, a surgical laser might be used for light shows, and a skilled surgeon might be driving a cab or trying desperately to make us laugh with his stand-up routine.

As we begin to move rightward along the PPF, say from A to B, we shift resources out of other goods and into health care. But we would *first* shift those resources *best suited to health care*—and *least* suited for the production of other things. For example, the first group of workers we'd use to save lives would be those who already have training as doctors and nurses. A surgeon—who would probably not make the best comedian—could now go back to surgery, which he does very well. Similarly, the first buildings we would put to use in the health care industry would be those that were originally built as hospitals and medical offices, and weren't really doing so well as manufacturing plants, retail stores or movie studios. This is why, at first, the PPF is

---

[1]   You might be wondering if the law of increasing opportunity cost applies in both directions. That is, does the opportunity cost of producing "other goods" increase as we produce more of them? The answer is yes, as you'll see when you do Problem 2 at the end of this chapter.

very flat: We get a *large* increase in lives saved for only a *small* decrease in other goods.

As we continue moving rightward, however, we shift away from other goods those resources that are less and less suited to life-saving. As a result, the PPF becomes steeper. Finally, we arrive at point *F*, where all resources—no matter how well suited for other goods and services—are used to save lives. A factory building is converted into a hospital, your family car is used as an ambulance, and comedic actor Jim Carrey is in medical school, training to become a surgeon.

The principle of increasing opportunity cost applies to all of society's production choices, not just that between health care and other goods. If we look at society's choice between food and oil, we would find that some land is better suited to growing food and some land to drilling for oil. As we continue to produce more oil, we would find ourselves drilling on land that is less and less suited to producing oil, but better and better for producing food. The opportunity cost of producing additional oil will therefore increase. The same principle applies in choosing between civilian goods and military goods, between food and clothing, or between automobiles and public transportation: The more of something we produce, the greater the opportunity cost of producing still more.

## THE SEARCH FOR A FREE LUNCH

This chapter has argued that every decision to produce *more* of something requires us to pay an opportunity cost by producing less of something else. Nobel Prize–winning economist Milton Friedman summarized this idea in his famous remark, "There is no such thing as a free lunch." Friedman was saying that, even if a meal is provided free of charge to someone, society still uses up resources to provide it. Therefore, a "free lunch" is not *really* free: Society pays an opportunity cost by not producing other things with those resources. The same logic applies to other supposedly "free" goods and services. From society's point of view, there is no such thing as a free airline flight, a free computer, or free medical care. Providing any of these things requires us to sacrifice other things, as illustrated by a movement *along* society's PPF.

But what if an economy is not living up to its productive potential, but is instead operating *inside* its PPF? For example, in Figure 1, suppose we are currently operating at point *W*, where the health care system is saving 200,000 lives and we are producing 400,000 units of other goods. Then we can move from point *W* to point *E* and save 200,000 more lives with no sacrifice of other goods. Or, starting at point *W*, we could move to point *C* (more of other goods with no sacrifice in lives saved) or to a point like *D* (more of *both* health care *and* other goods).

As you can see, if we are operating inside the PPF, Friedman's dictum does not apply—there *can* be such a thing as a free lunch! But why would an economy ever be operating inside its PPF? There are two possibilities.

**Productive Inefficiency.** One reason an economy might be operating inside its PPF is that resources are being wasted. Suppose, for example, that many people who could be outstanding health care workers are instead producing other goods, and many who would be great at producing other things are instead stuck in the health care industry. Then switching people from one job to the other could enable us to have more of *both* health care *and* other goods. That is, because of the mismatch of workers and jobs, we would be *inside* the PPF at a point like *W*. Creating better job matches would then move us to a point *on* the PPF (such as point *E*).

Economists use the phrase *productive inefficiency* to describe the type of waste that puts us inside our PPF.

**Productive inefficiency** A situation in which more of at least one good can be produced without sacrificing the production of any other good.

> *A firm, industry, or an entire economy is **productively inefficient** if it could produce more of at least one good without pulling resources from the production of any other good.*

The phrase *productive efficiency* means the absence of any productive *in*efficiency. For example, if the computer industry is producing the maximum possible number of computers with the resources it is currently using, we would describe the computer industry as productively efficient. In that case, there would be no way to produce any more computers without pulling resources from the production of some other good. In order for an entire *economy* to be productively efficient, there must be no way to produce more of *any* good without pulling resources from the production of some other good.

Although no firm, industry, or economy is ever 100 percent productively efficient, cases of gross inefficiency are not as common as you might think. When you study microeconomics, you'll learn that business firms have strong incentives to identify and eliminate productive inefficiency, since any waste of resources increases their costs and decreases their profit. When one firm discovers a way to eliminate waste, others quickly follow.

For example, empty seats on an airline flight represent productive inefficiency. Since the plane is making the trip anyway, filling the empty seat would enable the airline to serve more people with the flight (produce more transportation services) without using any additional resources (other than the trivial resources of the airline meal). Therefore, more people could fly without sacrificing any other good or service. When American Airlines developed a computer model in the late 1980s to fill its empty seats by altering schedules and fares, the other airlines followed its example very rapidly. And when—in the late 1990s—a new firm called Priceline.com enabled airlines to auction off empty seats on the Internet, several airlines jumped at the chance, and others quickly followed. As a result of this—and similar efforts to eliminate waste in personnel, aircraft, and office space—many cases of productive inefficiency in the airline industry were eliminated.

The same sorts of efforts have eliminated some easy-to-identify cases of productive inefficiency in all types of industries: banking, telephone service, Internet service providers, book publishers, and so on. There are certainly instances of inefficiency that remain (an example appears at the end of this chapter). But on the whole, if you search the economy for a free lunch due to productive inefficiency, you won't find as many hearty meals as you might think.

**Recessions.** Another situation in which an economy operates inside its PPF is a *recession*—a slowdown in overall economic activity. During recessions, many resources are idle. For one thing, there is widespread *unemployment*—people *want* to work but are unable to find jobs. In addition, factories shut down, so we are not using all of our available capital or land either. An end to the recession would move the economy from a point *inside* its PPF to a point *on* its PPF—using idle resources to produce more goods and services without sacrificing anything.

This simple observation can help us understand, in part, why the United States and the Soviet Union had such different economic experiences during World War II. In the Soviet Union, the average standard of living deteriorated considerably as the war began, but when the United States entered the war, living standards improved slightly. Why?

Figure 2 helps to solve this puzzle. The PPF in Figure 2 is like the PPF in Figure 1. But this time, instead of pitting "health care" against "all other goods," we look at society's choice between *military* goods and *civilian* goods. When the United States

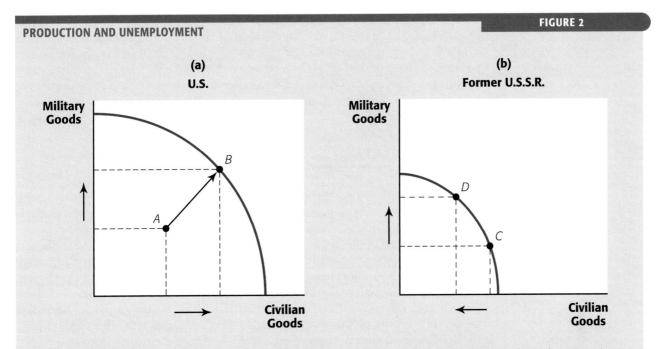

**FIGURE 2**

**PRODUCTION AND UNEMPLOYMENT**

At the onset of World War II, the U.S. economy was in a recession with high unemployment. This is shown by point *A* in panel (a), which is *inside* the production possibilities frontier. War production eliminated the unemployment as the United States moved onto its PPF at point *B* with more military goods *and* more civilian goods. The Soviet Union, by contrast, began the war with fully employed resources. It could increase military production only by sacrificing civilian goods and moving along its PPF from point *C* to point *D*.

entered the war in 1941, it was still suffering from the Great Depression—the most serious and long-lasting economic downturn in modern history, which began in 1929 and hit most of the developed world. For reasons you will learn when you study macroeconomics, joining the allied war effort helped end the Depression in the United States and moved our economy from a point like *A, inside* the PPF, to a point like *B, on* the frontier. Military production increased, but so did the production of civilian goods. Although there were shortages of some consumer goods, the overall result was a rise in the material well-being of the average U.S. citizen.

In the Soviet Union, things were very different. In the 1930s, the Soviet economy—which was internationally isolated—was able to escape entirely the effects of the depression that plagued the rest of the world. Thus, before the war, it was already operating on or near its PPF, at a point like *C*.[2] Entering the war—which meant an increase in military production—required a movement *along* its PPF, to a point like *D*. For the Soviet Union, the drop in civilian production—and the resulting drop in living standards—was the opportunity cost that had to be paid in order to fight the war.[3]

---

[2]    Because its economic system caused major productive inefficiencies, some would argue that the Soviet Union was never actually on or even near its PPF. In Figure 2, however, we take the Soviet economic system as a given. Being on the PPF means the economy is producing the maximum civilian output for any given quantity of military output *and* for the given Soviet economic system.

[3]    There is another explanation for the decline in living standards in the Soviet Union, and it, too, can be illustrated with PPFs. Unlike the United States, large parts of the Soviet Union were decimated during World War II, decreasing the land and capital available for production of any kind. Similarly, the Soviet loss of human life was staggering—about 20 times greater than the loss of American lives. These huge decreases in land, labor, and capital shifted the Soviet PPF significantly *inward*—with fewer resources, civilian production would have to be smaller for any given level of military production.

An economic downturn, such as the Great Depression of the 1930s, does seem to offer a clear-cut free lunch. But eliminating a recession is not *entirely* costfree. When you study macroeconomics, you will see that while a variety of government policies can help to cure or avoid recessions, these same policies risk creating other problems of their own. Of course, we may feel that it is worth paying the cost to end a recession, but there is, nevertheless, a cost. Once again, a truly free lunch is not so easy to find.

# ECONOMIC SYSTEMS

As you read these words—perhaps sitting at home or in the library—you are experiencing a very private moment. It is just you and this book; the rest of the world might as well not exist. Or so it seems. . . .

Actually, even in this supposedly private moment, you are connected to the rest of the world in ways you may not have thought about. In order for you to be reading this book, the authors had to write it. Someone (his name is Dennis Hanseman) had to edit it, to help make sure that all necessary material was covered and explained as clearly as possible. Someone else had to prepare the graphics. Others had to run the printing presses and the binding machines, and still others had to pack the book, ship it, unpack it, put it on a store shelf, and then sell it to you.

And there's more. People had to manufacture all kinds of goods: paper and ink, the boxes used for shipping, the computers used to keep track of inventory, and so on. It is no exaggeration to say that thousands of people were involved in putting this book in your hands.

And there is still more. The chair or couch on which you are sitting, the light shining on the page, the heat or the air conditioning in the room, the clothes you are wearing—all these things that you are using right now were *produced by somebody else*. So even now, as you sit alone reading this book, you are economically linked to others in hundreds—even thousands—of different ways.

Take a walk in your town or city, and you will see even more evidence of our economic interdependence: People are collecting garbage, helping schoolchildren cross the street, transporting furniture across town, constructing buildings, repairing roads, painting houses. Everyone is producing goods and services for *other people*.

Why is it that so much of what we consume is produced by other people? Why are we all so heavily dependent on each other for our material well-being? Why doesn't each of us—like Robinson Crusoe on his island—produce our own food, clothing, housing, and anything else we desire? And how did it come about that *you*—who did not produce any of these things yourself—are able to consume them?

These are all questions about our *economic system*—the way our economy is organized. Ordinarily, we take our economic system for granted, like the water that runs out of our faucets. But now it's time to take a closer look at the plumbing—to learn how our economy serves so many millions of people, enabling them to survive and prosper.

## SPECIALIZATION AND EXCHANGE

If we were forced to, most of us could become economically *self-sufficient*. We could stake out a plot of land, grow our own food, make our own clothing, and build our own homes. But in no society is there such extreme self-sufficiency. On the contrary, every economic system over the past 10,000 years has been characterized by two features: (1) **specialization,** in which each of us concentrates on a limited number of pro-

**Specialization** A method of production in which each person concentrates on a limited number of activities.

ductive activities, and (2) **exchange,** in which most of what we desire is obtained by trading with others, rather than producing for ourselves.

**Exchange** The act of trading with others to obtain what we desire.

> *Specialization and exchange enable us to enjoy greater production, and higher living standards, than would otherwise be possible. As a result, all economies exhibit high degrees of specialization and exchange.*

There are three reasons why specialization and exchange enable us to enjoy greater production. The first has to do with human capabilities: Each of us can learn only so much in a lifetime. By limiting ourselves to a narrow set of tasks—fixing plumbing, managing workers, writing music, or designing Web pages—we are each able to hone our skills and become experts at one or two things, instead of remaining amateurs at a lot of things. It is easy to see that an economy of experts will produce more than an economy of amateurs.

A second gain from specialization results from the time needed to switch from one activity to another. When people specialize, and thus spend more time doing one task, there is less unproductive "downtime" from switching activities.

Before considering the third gain from specialization, it is important to note that these first two gains—acquiring expertise and minimizing downtime—would occur even if all workers were identical. To see why, let's consider an extreme example. Suppose that three identical triplets—Sheri, Gerri, and Keri—decide to open up their own photocopy shop. They quickly discover that there are three primary tasks to be accomplished each day: making photocopies, dealing with customers, and servicing the machines.

Suppose first that the triplets decide *not* to specialize. Each time a customer walks in, *one* triplet will take the order, make the copies, collect the money, make the change, and give a receipt. In addition, each time a machine runs out of paper or ink, the triplet who is using the machine must remedy the problem. You can see that there will be a great deal of time spent going back and forth between the counter, the copy machines, and the supply room. Moreover, none of the triplets will become an expert at servicing the machines, dealing with customers, or making photocopies. As a result of the downtime between tasks and the lack of expertise, the triplets will not be able to make the maximum possible number of copies or handle the maximum possible number of customers each day.

Now, let's rearrange production to take advantage of specialization. We'll put Sheri at the counter, Gerri at the photocopy machine, and Keri keeping the machines in working order. Suddenly, all of that time spent going back and forth is now devoted to more productive tasks. Moreover, Sheri becomes an expert at working the cash register, since she does this all day long. Gerri becomes an expert at making copies, figuring out the quickest ways to select the proper settings, position originals, and turn pages. And Keri learns how to quickly diagnose and even anticipate problems with the machines. Each task is now performed by an expert. You can see that specialization increases the number of copies and customers that the triplets can handle each day, even though there is no difference in their basic abilities or talents.

Adam Smith first explained these gains from specialization in his book *An Inquiry into the Nature and Causes of the Wealth of Nations,* published in 1776. Smith explained how specialization within a pin factory dramatically increased the number of pins that could be produced there. In order to make a pin . . .

> *One man draws out the wire, another straightens it, a third cuts it, a fourth points it, a fifth grinds it at the top for receiving the head; to make the head requires three distinct operations; to put it on is a [separate] business, to*

Economics is a subject that has benefited from specialization and the division of labor. To get a feel for the many different subjects that economists investigate, take a look at the *Journal of Economic Literature*'s classification system at http://www.econlit.org/elcasbk.htm.

*whiten the pins is another; it is even a trade by itself to put them into the pa-per; and the important business of making a pin is, in this manner, divided into about eighteen distinct operations, which, in some manufactories, are all performed by distinct hands.*

Smith went on to observe that 10 men, each working separately, might make 200 pins in a day, but through specialization, they were able to make 48,000! What is true for a pin factory or a photocopy shop can be generalized to the entire econ-omy: Even when workers are identically suited to various tasks, total production will increase when workers specialize.

Of course, in the real world, workers are *not* identically suited to different kinds of work. Nor are all plots of land, all natural resources, or all types of capital equip-ment identically suited for different tasks. This observation brings us to the *third* source of gains from specialization.

### Further Gains to Specialization: Comparative Advantage.

Imagine a ship-wreck in which there are only two survivors—let's call them Maryanne and Gilli-gan—who wash up on opposite shores of a deserted island. Initially they are un-aware of each other, so each is forced to become completely self-sufficient.

On one side of the island, Maryanne finds that it takes her one hour to pick one quart of berries or to catch one fish, as shown in the first row of Table 1. On the other side of the island, Gilligan—who is less adept at both tasks—requires an hour and a half to pick a quart of berries and three hours to catch one fish, as listed in the second row of the table. Since both castaways would want some variety in their diets, we can assume that each would spend part of the day catching fish and part picking berries.

Suppose that, one day, Maryanne and Gilligan discover each other. After rejoic-ing at the prospect of human companionship, they decide to develop a system of production that will work to their mutual benefit. Let's rule out any gains from spe-cialization that might arise from minimizing downtime or from becoming an expert, as occurred in the photocopy shop example. Will it still pay for these two to spe-cialize? The answer is yes, as you will see after a small detour.

*Absolute Advantage: A Detour.* When Gilligan and Maryanne sit down to figure out who should do what, they might fall victim to a common mistake: basing their decision on *absolute advantage.* An individual has an **absolute advantage** in the production of some good when he or she can produce it using *fewer resources* than another individual can. On the island, the only resource being used is labor time, so the reasoning might go as follows: Maryanne can pick one quart of berries more quickly than Gilligan (see Table 1), so she has an *absolute advantage* in berry pick-ing. It seems logical, then, that Maryanne should be the one to pick the berries.

But wait! Maryanne can also catch fish more quickly than Gilligan, so she has an absolute advantage in fishing as well. If absolute advantage is the criterion for

**Absolute advantage** The ability to produce a good or service, using fewer resources than other pro-ducers use.

| TABLE 1 | | | |
|---|---|---|---|
| **LABOR REQUIREMENTS FOR BERRIES AND FISH** | | **1 Quart of Berries** | **1 Fish** |
| | Maryanne | 1  hour | 1 hour |
| | Gilligan | 1½ hours | 3 hours |

assigning work, then Maryanne should do *both* tasks. This, however, would leave Gilligan doing nothing, which is certainly *not* in the pair's best interests. What can we conclude from this example? That absolute advantage is an unreliable guide for allocating tasks to different workers.

*Comparative Advantage.* The correct principle to guide the division of labor on the island is comparative advantage:

> *A person has a **comparative advantage** in producing some good if he or she can produce it with a smaller* opportunity *cost than some other person can.*

**Comparative advantage** The ability to produce a good or service at a lower opportunity cost than other producers.

Notice the important difference between absolute advantage and comparative advantage: You have an *absolute* advantage in producing a good if you can produce it using fewer *resources* than someone else can. But you have a *comparative* advantage if you can produce it with a smaller *opportunity cost*. As you'll see, these are not necessarily the same thing.

Table 2 shows the opportunity cost for each of the two castaways to produce berries and fish. For Maryanne, catching one fish takes an hour, time that could instead be used to pick one quart of berries. Thus, for her, the opportunity cost of one fish is one quart of berries. Similarly, her opportunity cost of one quart of berries is one fish. These opportunity costs are listed in the first row of Table 2. For Gilligan, catching one fish takes three hours, time that he could instead use to pick two quarts of berries. The opportunity cost of one fish for Gilligan, then, is two quarts of berries, and the opportunity cost of one quart of berries is one-half of a fish. (Of course, no one catches half a fish unless they are fishing with a machete, but we can still use this number to represent a rate of opportunity cost.) Comparing the two numbers, we see that Maryanne has the lower opportunity cost for one fish, so she has a *comparative* advantage in catching fish. But when we turn our attention to berry picking, we see that it is Gilligan who has the lower opportunity cost—half a fish. Therefore, Gilligan—who has an *absolute* advantage in nothing—has a *comparative* advantage in berry picking.

Let's see what happens as the two decide to move toward specializing according to comparative advantage. What happens each time Gilligan decides to catch one fewer fish? Table 2 tells us that he frees up enough time to pick 2 quarts of berries. We can write the results for Gilligan's production this way:

Even castaways do better when they specialize and exchange with each other, instead of trying to be self-sufficient.

$$\text{Gilligan: Fish} \downarrow 1 \implies \text{Berries} \uparrow 2$$

Table 2 also tells us that each time Maryanne decides to catch one additional fish, she must sacrifice shift time away from berry picking, sacrificing 1 quart of berries:

$$\text{Maryanne: Fish} \uparrow 1 \implies \text{Berries} \downarrow 1$$

| | **Opportunity Cost of:** | |
| --- | --- | --- |
| | **1 Quart of Berries** | **1 Fish** |
| For Maryanne | 1 fish | 1 quart of berries |
| For Gilligan | ½ fish | 2 quarts of berries |

**TABLE 2**

**OPPORTUNITY COSTS**

Now, what happens to total production on the island each time the pair moves toward producing according to comparative advantage? As you can see, Maryanne makes up for the fish that Gilligan is no longer catching. But Gilligan *more than makes up* for the quart of berries that Maryanne isn't picking. In fact, each time the two move toward specialization, fish production remains unchanged, whereas berry production increases. The gains continue until Maryanne is spending all of her work time fishing, and Gilligan is spending all of his work time picking berries.

Since—by producing according to comparative advantage—total production on the island increases, total *consumption* can increase, too. Gilligan and Maryanne can figure out some way of trading fish for berries that makes each of them come out ahead. In the end, each of the castaways will enjoy a higher standard of living when they specialize and exchange with each other, compared to the level they'd enjoy under self-sufficiency.

What is true for our shipwrecked island dwellers is also true for the entire economy:

> *Total production of every good or service will be greatest when individuals specialize according to their comparative advantage. This is another reason why specialization and exchange lead to higher living standards than does self-sufficiency.*

When we turn from our fictional island to the real world, is production, in fact, consistent with the principle of comparative advantage? Indeed, it is. A journalist may be able to paint her house more quickly than a housepainter, giving her an *absolute* advantage in painting her home. Will she paint her own home? Except in unusual circumstances, no, because the journalist has a *comparative* advantage in writing news articles. Indeed, most journalists—like most college professors, attorneys, architects, and other professionals—hire house painters, leaving themselves more time to practice the professions in which they enjoy a comparative advantage.

Even comic book superheroes seem to behave consistently with comparative advantage. Superman can no doubt cook a meal, fix a car, chop wood, and do virtually *anything* faster than anyone else on the earth. Using our new vocabulary, we'd say that Superman has an absolute advantage in everything. But he has a clear comparative advantage in catching criminals and saving the known universe from destruction, which is exactly what he spends his time doing.

**Specialization in Perspective.**  The gains from specialization, whether they arise from developing expertise, minimizing downtime, or exploiting comparative advantage, can explain many features of our economy. For example, college students need to select a major and then, upon graduating, to decide on a specific career. Those who follow this path are rewarded with higher incomes than those who dally. This is an encouragement to specialize. Society is better off if you specialize, since you will help the economy produce more, and society rewards you for this contribution with a higher income.

The gains from specialization can also explain why most of us end up working for business firms that employ dozens, or even hundreds or thousands, of other employees. Why do these business firms exist? Why isn't each of us a *self-employed* expert, exchanging our production with other self-employed experts? Part of the answer is that organizing production into business firms pushes the gains from specialization still further. Within a firm, some people can specialize in working with their hands, others in managing people, others in marketing, and still others in keeping the books. Each firm is a kind of minisociety within which specialization occurs. The result is greater production and a higher standard of living than we would achieve if we were all self-employed.

Specialization has enabled societies everywhere to achieve standards of living unimaginable to our ancestors. But, if it goes too far, it can have a downside as well. In the old film *Modern Times,* Charlie Chaplin plays a poor soul standing at an assembly line, attaching part number 27 to part number 28 thousands of times a day. In the real world, specialization is rarely this extreme. Still, it has caused some jobs to be repetitive and boring. In some plants, workers are deliberately moved from one specialty to another to relieve boredom.

Of course, maximizing our material standard of living is not our only goal. In some instances, we might be better off *increasing* the variety of tasks we do each day, even if this means some sacrifice in production and income. For example, in many societies, one sex specializes in work outside the home and the other specializes in running the home and taking care of the children. Might families be better off if children had more access to *both* parents, even if this meant a somewhat lower family income? This is an important question. While specialization gives us material gains, there may be *opportunity costs* to be paid in the loss of other things we care about. The right amount of specialization can be found only by balancing the gains against these costs.

## RESOURCE ALLOCATION

It was only 10,000 years ago—a mere blink of an eye in human history—that the Neolithic revolution began and human society switched from hunting and gathering to farming and simple manufacturing. At the same time, human wants grew beyond mere food and shelter to the infinite variety of things that can be *made*. Ever since, all societies have been confronted with three important questions:

1. *Which* goods and services should be produced with society's resources?
2. *How* should they be produced?
3. *Who* should get them?

Together, these three questions constitute the problem of **resource allocation**. The way a society chooses to answer these questions—that is, the method it chooses to allocate its resources—will in part determine the character of its economic system.

Let's first consider the *which* question. Should we produce more health care or more movies, more goods for consumers or more capital goods for businesses? Where on its production possibilities frontier should the economy operate? As you will see, there are different methods societies can use to answer these questions.

The *how* question is more complicated. Most goods and services can be produced in a variety of different ways, each method using more of some resources and less of others. For example, there are many ways to dig a ditch. We could use *no capital at all* and have dozens of workers digging with their bare hands. We could use *a small amount of capital* by giving each worker a shovel and thereby use less labor, since each worker would now be more productive. Or we could use *even more capital*—a power trencher—and dig the ditch with just one or two workers. In every economic system, there must always be some mechanism that determines how goods and services will be produced from the infinite variety of ways available.

**Resource allocation** A method of determining which goods and services will be produced, how they will be produced, and who will get them.

Finally, the *who* question. Here is where economics interacts most strongly with politics. There are so many ways to divide ourselves into groups: men and women, rich and poor, workers and owners, families and single people, young and old . . . the list is endless. How should the products of our economy be distributed among these different groups and among individuals within each group?

Determining *who* gets the economy's output is always the most controversial aspect of resource allocation. Over the last half-century, our society has become more sensitized to the way goods and services are distributed, and we increasingly ask whether that distribution is fair. For example, men get a disproportionately larger share of our national output than women do, whites get more than African-Americans and Hispanics, and middle-aged workers get more than the very old and the very young. As a society, we want to know *why* we observe these patterns (a positive economic question) and what we should do about them (a normative economic question). Our society is also increasingly focusing on the distribution of particular goods and services. Should scarce donor organs be rationed to those who have been waiting the longest, so that everyone has the same chance of survival? Or should they be sold to the highest bidder, so that those able to pay the most will get them? Should productions of Shakespeare's plays be subsidized by the government to permit more people—especially more poor people—to see them? Or should the people who enjoy these plays pay the full cost of their production?

### The Three Methods of Resource Allocation.

**Traditional economy** An economy in which resources are allocated according to long-lived practices from the past.

Throughout history, there have been three primary mechanisms for allocating resources. In a **traditional economy,** resources are allocated according to the long-lived practices of the past. Tradition was the dominant method of resource allocation for most of human history and remains strong in many tribal societies and small villages in parts of Africa, South America, Asia, and the Pacific. Typically, traditional methods of production are handed down by the village elders, and traditional principles of fairness govern the distribution of goods and services.

Economies in which resources are allocated largely by tradition tend to be stable and predictable. But they have one serious drawback: They don't grow. With everyone locked into the traditional patterns of production, there is little room for innovation and technological change. Traditional economies are therefore likely to be stagnant economies.

**Command or centrally planned economy** An economic system in which resources are allocated according to explicit instructions from a central authority.

In a **command economy,** resources are allocated by explicit instructions from some higher authority. *Which* goods and services should we produce? The ones we're *ordered* to produce. *How* should we produce them? The way we're *told* to produce them. *Who* will get the goods and services? Whoever the authority *tells* us should get them.

In a command economy, a government body *plans* how resources will be allocated. That is why command economies are also called **centrally planned economies.** But command economies are disappearing fast. Until a few years ago, examples would have included the former Soviet Union, Poland, Rumania, Bulgaria, Albania, and many others. Beginning in the late 1980s, all of these nations have abandoned central planning. The only examples left are Cuba, China, and North Korea, and even these economies—though still dominated by central planning—are moving away from it.

**Market economy** An economic system in which resources are allocated through individual decision making.

The third method of allocating resources—and the one with which you are no doubt most familiar—is "the market." In a **market economy,** neither long-held traditions nor commands from above guide our economic behavior. Instead, people are largely free to do what they want with the resources at their disposal. In the end, re-sources are allocated as a result of individual decision making. *Which* goods and services are produced? Whichever ones producers *choose* to produce. How are they produced? However producers *choose* to produce them. *Who* gets these goods and services? Anyone who *chooses* to buy them.

There are, of course, limitations on freedom of choice in a market economy. Some restrictions are imposed by government to ensure an orderly, just, and pro-ductive society. We cannot kill, steal, or break contracts—even if that is our desire—without suffering serious consequences. And we must pay taxes to fund government services. But the most important limitations we face in a market economy arise from the overall scarcity of resources.

This last point is crucial: In a market system, individuals are not simply free to do what they want. Rather, they are constrained by the resources they control. And in this respect, we do not all start in the same place in the economic race. Some of us—like the Rockefellers and the Kennedys—have inherited great wealth; some—entrepreneur Bill Gates, the novelist Toni Morison, and the actress Julia Roberts—have inherited great intelligence, talent, or beauty; and some, such as the children of successful professionals, are born into a world of helpful personal contacts. Oth-ers, unfortunately, will inherit none of these advantages. In a market system, those who control more resources will have more choices available to them than those who control fewer resources. Still, in spite of the limitations imposed by govern-ment and the constraints imposed by limited resources, the market relies heavily on individual freedom of choice to allocate resources.

But wait . . . isn't there a problem here? People acting according to their own de-sires, without the firm hand of command or tradition to control them? This sounds like a recipe for chaos! How, in such a free-for-all, are resources actually *allocated*?

The answer is contained in two words: *markets* and *prices*.

**The Nature of Markets.** The market economy gets its name from something that virtually always happens when people are free to do what they want with the re-sources they possess. Inevitably, people decide to specialize in the production of one or a few things—often organizing themselves into business firms—and then sellers and buyers *come together to trade*. A **market** is a collection of buyers and sellers who have the potential to trade with one another.

**Market** A group of buyers and sell-ers with the potential to trade with each other.

In some cases, the market is *global*—that is, the market consists of buyers and sellers who are spread across the globe. The market for oil is an example of a global market, since buyers in any country can buy from sellers in any country. In other cases, the market is local. Markets for restaurant meals, haircuts, and taxi service are examples of local markets.

Markets play a major role in allocating resources by forcing individual decision makers to consider very carefully their decisions about buying and selling. They do so because of an important feature of every market: the *price* at which a good is bought and sold.

**The Importance of Prices.** A **price** is *the amount of money a buyer must pay to a seller for a good or service*. Price is not always the same as *cost*. In economics, as you've learned in this chapter, cost means *opportunity cost—all* that is sacrificed to buy the good. While the price of a good is a *part* of its opportunity cost, it is not the only cost. For example, the price does not include the value of the time sacrificed to buy something. Buying a new jacket will require you to spend time traveling to and

**Price** The amount of money that must be paid to a seller to obtain a good or service.

from the store, trying on different styles and sizes, and waiting in line at the cash register.

Still, in most cases, the price of a good is a significant part of its opportunity cost. For large purchases such as a home or automobile, the price will be *most* of the opportunity cost. And this is why prices are so important to the overall working of the economy: they confront individual decision makers with the costs of their choices.

Consider the example of purchasing a car. Because you must pay the price, you know that buying a new car will require you to cut back on purchases of other things. In this way, the opportunity cost to *society* of making another car is converted to an opportunity cost *for you*. If you value a new car more highly than the other things you must sacrifice for it, you will buy it. If not, you won't buy it.

Why is it so important that people face the opportunity costs of their actions? The following thought experiment can answer this question. Imagine that the government passed a new law: When anyone buys a new car, the government will reimburse that person for it immediately. The consequences would be easy to predict. First, on the day the law was passed, everyone would rush out to buy new cars. Why not, if cars are free? The entire stock of existing automobiles would be gone within days—maybe even hours. Many people who didn't value cars much at all, and who hardly ever used them, would find themselves owning several—one for each day of the week, or to match the different colors in their wardrobe. Others who weren't able to act in time—including some who desperately needed a new car for their work or to run their households—would be unable to find one at all.

Over time, automobile companies would step up their production to meet the surge in demand for cars, and then we would face another problem: the government's yearly "automobile budget," which would be hundreds of billions of dollars. Ultimately, we would all bear the cost of the increased car production, since the government would have to raise taxes. But we would pay as *taxpayers*, not as car owners. And our hefty tax bill would be supporting some rather frivolous uses for cars. Chances are, we would all be worse off because of this new policy. By eliminating a price for automobiles, and severing the connection between the opportunity cost of producing a car and the individual's decision to get one, we would have created quite a mess for ourselves.

> *When resources are allocated by the market, and people must pay for their purchases, they are forced to consider the opportunity cost to society of their individual actions. In this way, markets are able to create a sensible allocation of resources.*

**Resource Allocation in the United States.**  The United States has always been considered the leading example of a market economy. Each day, millions of distinct items are produced and sold in markets. Our grocery stores are always stocked with broccoli and tomato soup, and the drugstore always has Kleenex and aspirin—all due to the choices of individual producers and consumers. The goods that are traded, the way they are traded, and the price at which they trade are determined by the traders themselves. No direction from above is needed to keep markets working.

But even in the United States, there are numerous cases of resource allocation *outside* the market. For example, families are important institutions in the United States, and many economic decisions are made within them. Families tend to operate like traditional villages, not like market economies. After all, few families charge prices for goods and services provided inside the home.

Our economy also allocates some resources by command. Various levels of government collect, in total, about one-third of our incomes as taxes. We are *told* how much tax we must pay, and those who don't comply suffer serious penalties, including imprisonment. Government—rather than individual decision makers—spends the tax revenue. In this way, the government plays a major role in allocating resources—especially in determining which goods are produced and who gets them.

There are also other ways, aside from strict commands, that the government limits our market freedoms. Regulations designed to protect the environment, maintain safe workplaces, and ensure the safety of our food supply are just a few examples of government-imposed constraints on our individual choice.

What are we to make, then, of resource allocation in the United States? Markets are, indeed, constrained. But for each example we can find where resources are allocated by tradition or command, or where government restrictions seriously limit some market freedom, we can find hundreds of examples where individuals make choices according to their own desires. The things we buy, the jobs at which we work, the homes in which we live—in almost all cases, these result from market choices. The market, though not pure, is certainly the dominant method of resource allocation in the United States.

## RESOURCE OWNERSHIP

So far, we've been concerned with how resources are allocated. Another important feature of an economic system is how resources are *owned*. The owner of a resource—a parcel of land, a factory, or one's own labor time—determines how it can be used and receives income when others use it. And there have been three primary modes of resource ownership in human history.

Under *communal* ownership, resources are owned by everyone—or by no one, depending on your point of view. They are simply there for the taking; no person or organization imposes any restrictions on their use or charges any fees. It is hard to find economies with significant communal ownership of resources. Karl Marx believed that, in time, all economies would evolve toward communal ownership, and he named this predicted system **communism.** In fact, none of the economies that called themselves Marxist (such as the former Soviet Union) ever achieved Marx's vision of communism. This is not surprising: Communal ownership on a broad scale can work only when individuals have no conflicts over how resources are used. Therefore, communism requires the end of *scarcity*—an unlikely prospect in the foreseeable future.

**Communism** A type of economic system in which most resources are owned in common.

Nevertheless, there are examples of communal ownership on a smaller scale. Traditional villages maintain communal ownership of land and sometimes cattle. In some of the cooperative farms in Israel—called *kibbutzim*—land and capital are owned by all the members. Often there is a single television, a single kitchen, and a single children's playroom—all communally owned. Conflicts may result when individuals differ over how these resources should be used, but these conflicts are resolved by consensus, rather than by decree or by charging fees for their use.

Closer to home, most families operate on the principle of communal ownership. The house, television, telephone, and food in the refrigerator are treated as if owned jointly. More broadly, who "owns" our sidewalks, streets, and public beaches? No one does, really. In practice, all citizens are free to use them as much and as often as they would like. This is essentially communal ownership.

**Socialism**  A type of economic system in which most resources are owned by the state.

Under **socialism,** the *state* owns most of the resources. The prime example is the former Soviet Union, where the state owned all of the land and capital equipment in the country. In many ways, it also owned the labor of individual households, since it was virtually the only employer in the nation and unemployment was considered a crime.

State ownership also occurs in nonsocialist economies. In the United States, national parks, state highway systems, military bases, public colleges and universities, and government buildings are all state-owned resources. Over a third of the land in the country is owned by the federal government. The military, even under our current volunteer system, is an example in which the state owns the labor of soldiers—albeit for a limited period of time.

**Capitalism**  A type of economic system in which most resources are owned privately.

Finally, the third system. When most resources are owned *privately*—as in the United States—we have **capitalism.** Take the book you are reading right now. If you turn to the title page, you will see the imprint of South-Western College Publishing Company. This is a *private* company, owned by another company—Thomson Learning—that, in turn, is owned by *private* individuals. These individuals, in the end, own the facilities of South-Western: the buildings, the land under them, the office furniture and computer equipment, and even the reputation of the company. When these facilities are used to produce and sell a book, the private owners receive the income, mostly in the form of company profits. Similarly, the employees of South-Western are private individuals. They are *selling* a resource they own—their labor time—to South-Western, and they receive income—wages and salaries—in return.

The United States is one of the most capitalistic countries in the world. True, there are examples of state and communal ownership, as we've seen. But the dominant mode of resource ownership in the U.S. is *private* ownership. Resource owners keep *most* of the income from supplying their resources, and they have broad freedom in deciding how their resources are used.

## TYPES OF ECONOMIC SYSTEMS

We've used the phrase *economic system* a few times already in this book. But now it's time for a formal definition.

**Economic system**  A system of resource allocation and resource ownership.

> An **economic system** *is composed of two features: a mechanism for* allocating *resources and a mode of resource* ownership.

Let's leave aside the rare economies in which communal ownership is dominant and those in which resources are allocated primarily by tradition. That leaves us with four basic types of economic systems, indicated by the four quadrants in Figure 3. In the upper left quadrant, we have *market capitalism.* In this system, resources are *allocated* primarily by the market and *owned* primarily by private individuals. Today, most nations have market capitalist economies, including all of the countries of North America and Western Europe, and most of those in Asia, Latin America, and Africa.

In the lower right quadrant is *centrally planned socialism,* under which resources are mostly allocated by command and mostly owned by the state. This *was* the system in the former Soviet Union and the nations of Eastern Europe until the late 1980s. But in less than a decade, these countries' economies have gone through cataclysmic change, moving from the lower right quadrant to the upper left. That is, these nations have simultaneously changed both their method of resource allocation and their systems of resource ownership.

http://

The Center for International Comparisons at the University of Pennsylvania (http://pwt.econ.upenn.edu/) is a good source of information on the performance of economies around the world.

**FIGURE 3**

**TYPES OF ECONOMIC SYSTEMS**

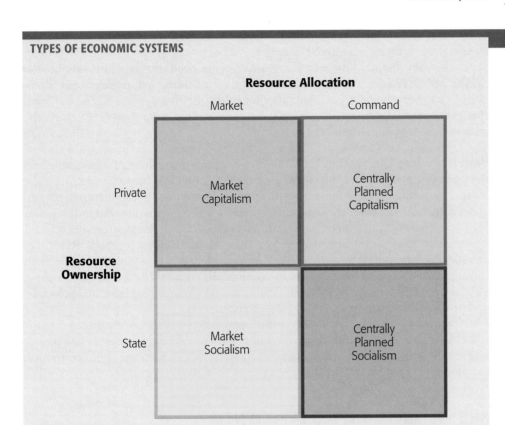

Although market capitalism and centrally planned socialism have been the two paramount economic systems in modern history, there have been others. The upper right quadrant represents a system of *centrally planned capitalism,* in which resources are owned by private individuals, yet allocated by command. In the recent past, countries such as Sweden and Japan—where the government has been more heavily involved in allocating resources than in the United States—have flirted with this type of system. Nations at war—like the United States during World War II— also move in this direction, as governments find it necessary to direct resources by command in order to ensure sufficient military production.

Finally, in the lower left quadrant is *market socialism,* in which resources are owned by the state yet allocated by the market mechanism. The possibility of market socialism has fascinated many social scientists, who believed it promised the best of both worlds: the freedom and efficiency of the market mechanism and the fairness and equity of socialism. There are, however, serious problems—many would say "unresolvable contradictions"—in trying to mix the two. The chief examples of market socialism in modern history were short-lived experiments—in Hungary and Yugoslavia in the 1950s and 1960s—in which the results were mixed at best.

**Economic Systems and This Book.**  In this book, you will learn how market capitalist economies operate. This means that the other three types of economic systems in Figure 3 will be, for the most part, ignored. Until 10 years ago, these statements would have been accompanied by an apology that would have gone something like this: "True, much of the world is characterized by alternative economic systems, but there is only so much time in one course . . ."

In the past decade, however, the world has changed dramatically: About 400 million people have come under the sway of the market as their nations have abandoned centrally planned socialism; another billion or so are being added as China changes course. The study of modern economies is now, more than ever before, the study of market capitalism.

**Understanding the Market.**  The market is simultaneously the most simple and the most complex way to allocate resources. For individual buyers and sellers, the market is simple. There are no traditions or commands to be memorized and obeyed. Instead, we enter the markets we *wish* to trade in, and we respond to prices there as we *wish* to, unconcerned about the overall process of resource allocation.

But from the economist's point of view, the market is quite complex. Resources are allocated indirectly, as a *by-product* of individual decision making, rather than through easily identified traditions or commands. As a result, it often takes some skillful economic detective work to determine just how individuals are behaving and how resources are being allocated as a consequence.

How can we make sense of all of this apparent chaos and complexity? That is what economics is all about. And you will begin your detective work in Chapter 3, where you will learn about the most widely used model in the field of economics: the model of supply and demand.

## ARE WE SAVING LIVES EFFICIENTLY?

In the chapter, you learned that if resources are being wasted, we will operate *inside* our PPF rather than on the PPF. In that case, by eliminating the productive inefficiency, we would free up resources. Some of the resources could be used to save more lives and some to produce more of other goods. In Figure 1, this would move us from a point like *W* to a point like *D*, where we end up saving more lives *and* having more of other goods.

But there could also be productive inefficiency in the saving of human lives. If that is the case—if it is possible to save more lives without devoting any additional resources to doing so—then we would, once again, be operating inside our PPF. And once again, we could have a free lunch—save more lives *and* have more of other goods—by eliminating the inefficiency.

Some economists have argued that we do, indeed, waste significant amounts of resources in our life-saving efforts. How have they come to such a conclusion?

The first thing to remember is that saving a life—no matter how it is done—requires the use of resources. For any life-saving action we might take—putting another hundred police on the streets, building another emergency surgery center, or running an advertising campaign to encourage healthy living—we need certain quantities of resources, and a certain number of lives would be saved. In a market economy, resources sell at a price. This allows us to use the dollar cost of a life-saving method to measure the value of the resources used up by that method.

Moreover, we can compare the "cost per year of life saved" of different methods. For example, in the United States we currently spend about $253 million on heart transplants each year and thereby add about 1,600 years to the lives of heart patients. Thus, the cost per year of life saved from heart transplants is $253,000,000/1,600 = $158,000 (rounded to the nearest thousand).

TABLE 3

THE COST OF SAVING LIVES

| Method | Cost per Life-Year Saved |
|---|---|
| Brief physician antismoking intervention: Single personal warning from physician to stop smoking | $150 |
| Sickle cell screening and treatment for African-American newborns | $236 |
| Intensive physician anti-smoking intervention: Physician identification of smokers among their patients; 3 physician counseling sessions; 2 further sessions with smoking-cessation specialists; and materials—nicotine patch or nicotine gum | $2,587 |
| Mammograms: Once every 3 years, for ages 50–64 | $2,700 |
| Mammograms: Annually, for ages 50–64 | $108,401 |
| Exercise electrocardiograms as screening test: For 40-year-old males | $124,374 |
| Heart transplants | $157,821 |
| Mammograms: Annually, for age 40–49 | $186,635 |
| Exercise electrocardiograms as screening test: For 40-year-old females | $335,217 |
| Heart Transplants | $157,821 |
| Seat belts on school buses | $2,760,197 |
| Anti-terrorist screening at airports | $8,000,000 |
| Asbestos ban in automatic transmissions | $66,402,402 |

*Sources:* Electrocardiograms: Charles E. Phelps, *Health Economics*, 2nd ed. (Reading, MA: Addison-Wesley, 1997). Regular exercise: L. Goldman, A. M. Garber, S. A. Grover, & M. A. Hlatky (1996). Task Force 6. Cost-effectiveness of assessment and management of risk factors (Bethesda Conference). *JACC*, 27(5), 1020–1030. Anti-smoking intensive intervention: *Journal of the American Medical Association*, Dec. 3, 1997. Anti-smoking brief intervention: Malcolm Law and Jin Ling Tang, "An Analysis of the Effectiveness of Interventions Intended to Help People Stop Smoking," *Archives of Internal Medicine*, 1995; 155: pp. 1933–1941, and authors calculations to convert "per life saved" to "per year of life saved." Annual mammograms: Kent Jeffreys, "Progressive Environmentalism: Principles for Regulatory Reform (Policy Report No. 194), National Center for Policy Analysis, June 1995. Benzene emission controls: Tammy O. Tengs et al., "Five Hundred Life-Saving Interventions and their Cost-Effectiveness," *Risk Analysis*, 1994. All other figures: Tammy O. Tengs, "Dying Too Soon: How Cost-Effectiveness Analysis Can Save Lives," School of Social Ecology, University of California, Irvine, NCPA Policy Report No. 204, May 1997. Anti-terrorist screening at airports: Robert W. Hahn, "The Cost of Anti-terrorist Rhetoric," *The Cato Review of Business and Government*, Dec. 17, 1996, and authors' calculations to convert "per life saved" to "per year of life saved."

Table 3 lists several of the methods we currently use to save lives in the United States. Some of these methods reflect legal or regulatory decisions (such as the ban on asbestos) and others reflect standard medical practices (such as annual mammograms for women over 50). Other methods are used only sporadically (such as seat belts in school buses). You can see that the cost per life saved ranges widely—from $150 per year of life saved for a physician warning a patient to quit smoking, to over $66,000,000 per year of life saved from the ban on asbestos in automatic transmissions.

The table indicates that some life-saving methods are highly efficient. For example, our society probably exhausts the potential to save lives from brief physician anti-smoking intervention. Most doctors *do* warn their smoking patients to quit.

But the table also indicates some serious productive *in*efficiencies in life saving. For example, screening and treating African-American newborns for sickle cell anemia is one of the least costly ways of saving a year of life in the United States—only

$236 per year of life saved. Nevertheless, 20 percent of African-American newborns do *not* get this screening at all. Similarly, intensive intervention to discourage smoking is far from universal in the U.S. health care system, even though it has the relatively low cost of $2,587 per year of life saved.

To get an idea of what this kind of productive inefficiency means, let's do some thought experiments. First, let's imagine that we shift resources from heart transplants to *intensive* antismoking efforts. Then for each year of life we decided *not* to save with heart transplants, we would free up $157,821 in medical resources. If we applied those resources toward intensive antismoking efforts, at a cost of $2,587 per year of life saved, we could then save an additional $157,821/$2,587 = 61 life years. In other words, we could increase the number of life-years saved without any increase in resources flowing to the health care sector, and therefore, without any sacrifice in other goods and services. A free lunch!

But why pick on heart transplants? Our ban on asbestos in automobile transmissions—which requires the purchase of more costly materials with greater quantities of scarce resources—costs us about $66 million for each life-year saved. Suppose these funds were spent instead to buy the resources needed to provide women aged 40 to 49 with annual mammograms (currently *not* part of most physicians' recommendations). Then for each life-year lost to asbestos, we'd save $66 million/186,635 = 354 life years from earlier detection of breast cancer.

The most surprising entry in the table may be the cost of the new antiterrorist screening procedures at airports, introduced in the late 1990s. The number relies on many critical assumptions. One is that, without current screening procedures, the number of fatalities from terrorist incidents on airlines would equal the rate we've had in the recent past—an average of 37 fatalities per year. If the rate would have *increased* without the new procedures, then the new procedures are actually saving more lives than assumed by economic studies, and the cost per life-year saved would be lower. On the other hand, the dollar figure assumes that current policies will be 100 percent effective in preventing fatal terrorist incidents. If this assumption is incorrect, the cost per life-year saved would be higher.

The largest component of the cost of antiterrorist screening is the increase in time it takes for the airlines to process luggage and passengers. This means a greater opportunity cost of time for passengers, who—on average—must arrive at the airport half an hour earlier. Suppose we value time at $44 per hour. (This is not unreasonable, since higher-income people—especially business travelers—take more flights than lower-income people.) Then, each half-hour delay carries an opportunity cost for passengers of $22. Multiplying that cost by 400 million annual passenger trips gives us a total opportunity cost of time of $22 × 400 million = $8.8 billion per year. This is by far the largest cost of the new antiterrorist screening procedures. Together with about $200 million of annual direct costs for equipment and personnel we get a total of about $9 billion per year, which implies an expenditure of $8 million per life-year saved.

What would happen if we applied this $9 billion to other life-saving methods? You can answer that question on your own, using Table 3. You will see that there are, indeed, more efficient ways of spending our money.

Or are there?

It may be that these studies have left out a lot. For example, *why* do we spend so much on fighting airline terrorism when very few have died from it? The answer might be that the public exaggerates the risk. And if they do, then there are benefits from responding to this risk that go beyond the actual number of life-years saved.

For example, it may be that the new, enhanced safety procedures have convinced tens of thousands—maybe even hundreds of thousands—of travelers to fly rather than use other, slower forms of transportation. These travelers *save* time with the new screening procedures. Further, many travelers—who would otherwise experience serious anxiety while flying—no doubt benefit from increased peace of mind after seeing how carefully the airlines are trying to prevent terrorist attacks. How much is increased peace of mind worth to travelers? It's hard to say, but it should not be ignored

One could make similar arguments about many environmental regulations, such as the ban on asbestos in auto transmissions. While their cost per life-year saved is exorbitant, they may have substantial—if intangible—benefits besides saving lives. (Can you imagine what some of these benefits might be?)

What can we conclude from all this? That life saving in the United States is no doubt plagued with productive inefficiencies. But the extent of the inefficiency is harder to measure than it appears at first glance.

## S U M M A R Y

One of the most fundamental concepts in economics is *opportunity cost*. The opportunity cost of any choice is what we give up when we make that choice. At the individual level, opportunity cost arises from the scarcity of time or money; for society as a whole, it arises from the scarcity of resources—land, labor, and capital. To produce and enjoy more of one thing, we must shift resources away from producing something else. The correct measure of cost is not just the money price we pay, but the opportunity cost: everything we give up when we make a choice. The *law of increasing opportunity cost* tells us that the more of something we produce, the greater the opportunity cost of producing still more.

In a world of scarce resources, each society must have an economic system—its way of organizing economic activity.

All *economic systems* feature *specialization*, where each person and firm concentrates on a limited number of productive activities—and *exchange*, through which we obtain most of what we desire by trading with others. Specialization and exchange enable us to enjoy higher living standards than would be possible under self-sufficiency.

Every economic system determines how resources are owned and how they are allocated. In a market capitalist economy, resources are owned primarily by private individuals and allocated primarily through markets. Prices play an important role in markets by forcing decision makers to take account of society's opportunity cost when they make choices.

## K E Y   T E R M S

opportunity cost
production possibilities frontier (PPF)
law of increasing opportunity cost
productive inefficiency

specialization
exchange
absolute advantage
comparative advantage
resource allocation
traditional economy

command economy
centrally planned economy
market economy
market
price
communism

socialism
capitalism
economic system

## R E V I E W   Q U E S T I O N S

1. "Warren Buffett is one of the world's wealthiest men, worth billions of dollars. For someone like Buffet, the principle of opportunity cost simply doesn't apply." True or false? Explain.

2. What are some reasons why a country might be operating inside its production possibilities frontier (PPF)?

3. Why is a PPF concave—that is, bowed out from the origin? Be sure to give an *economic* explanation.

4. What are three distinct reasons why specialization leads to a higher standard of living?

5. What is the difference between comparative advantage and absolute advantage? Which is more important from an economic viewpoint?

6. List the three questions any resource allocation mechanism must answer. Briefly describe the three primary methods of resource allocation that have evolved to answer these questions.

7. What are the three primary ways in which resources are *owned*? Briefly describe each of them.

8. Why can't the United States economy be described as a *pure market capitalist economy*?

9. True or false?: "Resource allocation and resource ownership are essentially the same thing. Once you know who owns the resources in an economy, you also know by what mechanism those resources will be allocated." Explain your answer.

# P R O B L E M S   A N D   E X E R C I S E S

1. Suppose that you are considering what to do with an upcoming weekend. Here are your options, from least to most preferred: (1) Study for upcoming midterms; (2) fly to Colorado for a quick ski trip; (3) go into seclusion in your dorm room and try to improve your score on a computer game. What is the opportunity cost of a decision to play the computer game all weekend?

2. Redraw Figure 1, but this time identify a different set of points along the frontier. Starting at point F (500,000 lives saved, zero production of other goods), have each point you select show equal increments in the quantity of other goods produced. For example, point H should correspond to 200,000 units of other goods, point J to 400,000 units, point K to 600,000 units, and so on. Now observe what happens to the opportunity cost of "200,000 more units of other goods" as you move leftward and upward along this PPF. Does the law of increasing opportunity cost apply to the production of "all other goods"? Explain briefly.

3. How would a technological innovation in life saving—say, the discovery of a cure for cancer—affect the PPF in Figure 1? How would a technological innovation in the production of *other* goods—say, the invention of a new kind of robot that speeds up assembly-line manufacturing—affect the PPF?

4. You and a friend have decided to work jointly on a course project. Frankly, your friend is a less than ideal partner. His skills as a researcher are such that he can review and outline only two articles a day. Moreover, his hunt-and-peck style limits him to only 10 pages of typing a day. On the other hand, in a day you can produce six outlines or type 20 pages.
   a. Who has an absolute advantage in outlining, you or your friend? What about typing?
   b. Who has a comparative advantage in outlining? In typing?
   c. According to the principle of comparative advantage, who should specialize in which task?

5. Suppose that one day, Gilligan (the castaway) eats a magical island plant that turns him into an expert at everything. In particular, it now takes him just half an hour to pick a quart of berries, and 15 minutes to catch a fish.
   a. Redo Tables 1 and 2 in the chapter.
   b. Who—Gilligan or Maryanne—has a comparative advantage in picking berries? In fishing? When the castaways discover each other, which of the two should specialize in which task?
   c. Can *both* castaways benefit from Gilligan's new abilities? How?

# C H A L L E N G E   Q U E S T I O N

1. Suppose that an economy's PPF is a straight line, rather than a bowed out, concave curve. What would this say about the nature of opportunity cost as production is shifted from one good to the other?

# EXPERIENTIAL EXERCISES

1. The transitional economies of Eastern Europe are often in the news as they shift from central planning to more of a market orientation. Take a look at the World Bank's Transition Newsletter at *http://www. worldbank.org/html/prddr/trans/WEB/trans.htm*. Choose one of these economies and try to determine how smoothly its transition is proceeding. What problems is that nation encountering? Do the problems seem to relate mostly to resource allocation, to resource ownership, or both?

2. The ability to measure the true cost of a choice is a skill that will pay you great dividends. Using Infotrac or a recent issue of the *Wall Street Journal*, try to find an article that discusses a decision some firm has made. Then review this chapter's section on "The Concept of Opportunity Cost." Finally, make a list of the kinds of cost involved in the firm's decision. Identify each item in your list as an explicit cost or an implicit cost.

# 3

# SUPPLY AND DEMAND

Father Guido Sarducci, a character on the early *Saturday Night Live* shows, once observed that the average person remembers only about five minutes worth of material from college. He therefore proposed the "Five Minute University," where you'd learn only the five minutes of material you'd actually remember, and dispense with the rest. The economics course would last only 10 seconds, just enough time for students to learn to recite three words: "supply and demand."

Of course, there is much more to economics than these three words. Still, Sarducci's observation had some truth. Many people *do* regard the phrase "supply and demand" as synonymous with economics. But surprisingly few people actually understand what the phrase means. In a debate about health care, poverty, recent events in the stock market, or the high price of housing, you might hear someone say, "Well, it's just a matter of supply and demand," as a way of dismissing the issue entirely. Others use the phrase with an exaggerated reverence, as if supply and demand were an inviolable physical law, like gravity, about which nothing can be done. So what does this oft-repeated phrase really mean?

First, supply and demand is just an economic model—nothing more and nothing less. It's a model designed to explain *how prices are determined in a market system*. Why has this model taken on such an exalted role in the field of economics? Because prices themselves play such an exalted role in the economy. In a market system, once the price of something has been determined, only those willing to pay that price will get it. Thus, prices determine which households will get which goods and services and which firms will get which resources. If you want to know why the cell phone industry is expanding while the video rental industry is shrinking, or why homelessness is a more pervasive problem in the United States than hunger, you need to understand how prices are determined. In this chapter, you will learn how the model of supply and demand works and how to use it. You will also learn about the strengths and limitations of the model. It will take more time than Guido Sarducci's 10-second economics course, but in the end you will know much more than just three little words.

# MARKETS

Put any compound in front of a chemist, ask him what it is and what it can be used for, and he will immediately think of the basic elements—carbon, hydrogen, oxygen, and so on. These elements are the basic building blocks of the materials we see in our world, and they help chemists make sense of what would otherwise appear rather chaotic.

Similarly, ask an economist almost any question about the economy, and he will immediately think about *markets*. As you learned in the last Chapter, the word *market* has a special meaning in economics.

> *A market is a group of buyers and sellers with the potential to trade.*

Economists think of the economy as a collection of markets. In each one, the buyers and sellers will be different, depending on what is being traded. There is a market for oranges, another for automobiles, another for real estate, and still others for corporate stocks, French francs, and anything else that is bought and sold.

And this is where the choices begin. A market, as you'll soon see, is an important part of a supply and demand model, like a wing is an important part of a model airplane. And just as we can choose to make a wing out of balsa wood or plastic or metal—depending on our purpose—so, too, we have many choices when we define a market.

## DEFINING THE GOOD OR SERVICE

Suppose we're interested in analyzing the computer industry in the United States. Should we define our market very broadly ("the market for computers"), very narrowly ("laptops under four pounds") or something in between ("portable personal computers")? Our choice will depend on the specific question we are trying to answer.

For example, if our goal is to predict how many households will be connected to the Internet by the year 2005, it would be best to combine all computers into one broad category, treating them all as if they were a single good. Economists call this process **aggregation**—combining a group of distinct things into a single whole. It would not do us much good to *disaggregate* computers into different types—desktops, laptops, handheld, faster than 450 Mhz, etc.—because such distinctions have little to do with Internet access and would only get in the way.

**Aggregation** The process of combining distinct things into a single whole.

But suppose instead we are asking a different question: Why do laptops always cost more than desktops with similar computing power? Then we should use a slightly narrower definition of the product, aggregating all *laptops* together into one good, and all desktops together into another, and then looking at the markets for *each* of these more narrowly defined goods.

How broadly or narrowly we define a good or service is one of the choices that distinguishes *macro*economics from *micro*economics. In macroeconomics, goods and services are aggregated to the highest levels. Macro models even lump all consumer goods—dishwashers, cell phones, blue jeans, and so forth—into the single category "consumption goods" and view them as if they are traded in a single, broadly defined market, "the market for consumption goods." Similarly, instead of recognizing different markets for shovels, bulldozers, computers, and factory buildings, macro models analyze the market for "capital goods." Defining goods in this very broad way allows macroeconomists to take an overall view of the economy without getting bogged down in the details.

In microeconomics, by contrast, we are interested in more disaggregated goods. Instead of asking how much we'll spend on *consumer goods*, a microeconomist might ask how much we'll spend on *health care* or *video games*. Although micro-economics always involves some aggregation—combining different brands of lap-top computers into one category, for example—in microeconomics, the process stops before it reaches the highest level of generality.

## BUYERS AND SELLERS

A market is composed of the buyers and sellers that trade in it. But who, exactly, *are* these buyers and sellers?

When you think of a seller, your first image might be of a business. Indeed, in many markets, you'd be right: The sellers *are* business firms. Examples are markets for restaurant meals, airline travel, clothing, banking services, and video rentals. But businesses aren't the only sellers in the economy. In many markets, *households* are important sellers. For example, households are the primary sellers in labor mar-kets, such as the markets for Web page designers, for accountants, and for factory workers. Households are also important sellers in markets for used cars, residential homes, and rare artworks. Governments, too, are sometimes important sellers. For example, state governments are major sellers in the market for education through state universities (such as the University of California, the University of Minnesota, and St. Louis Community College).

What about the other side of the market? When you think of *buyers*, your first thought may be "people" like yourself, or "households." Indeed, many goods and services are bought primarily by households: college education, movies, housing, clothing, and so on. But here, too, the stereotype doesn't always fit. In labor mar-kets, businesses and government agencies are the primary buyers. Businesses and government are also important buyers of personal computers, automobiles, and air-line transportation.

As you can see, the buyers in a market can be households, business firms, or government agencies. And the same is true of sellers. Sometimes, it's important to recognize that all three groups are on both sides of a market. But not always. Once again, it depends on our purpose.

When the purpose is largely educational, greater simplification is permitted. For example, to understand *how* the price of paperback books is determined, we would in most cases assume that households are the only buyers. True, business firms and government libraries also buy paperback books. But including these buyers would only complicate our model, without changing any of our conclusions about price. On the other hand, if we wanted to precisely forecast the revenues of booksellers from paperback books, it would be dangerous to ignore orders from businesses and government libraries.

## THE GEOGRAPHY OF THE MARKET

While a market itself is not an actual location, the participants in a market *do* live within some geographic area. When we speak of the geography of a market, we mean the geographic area within which the buyers and sellers are located.

It might appear that our choice of geography follows logically from the particu-lar good or service we are analyzing. For example, think about crude oil. It is rou-tinely transported across international waters and is freely traded among buyers and sellers in many different countries. So the market for oil should be a market of *global* buyers and sellers, right?

Not necessarily. Suppose we want to explain why oil is cheaper in the United States than in France? Then we'd need to define a *pair* of markets for oil and see how the price is determined in each one. In one market, global oil producers sell to buyers in France, and in another, the same producers sell to buyers in the United States. In each of these markets, global sellers trade with *national* buyers.

On the other hand, if we want to explain and forecast *world oil prices*, we'd gain little by distinguishing between French and American buyers. In this case, both sellers and buyers would be global.

> *In defining a market, we must choose the geographic area within which buyers and sellers are located. The buyers can be spread around the globe, or they can be a national, regional, or local group. The same is true of sellers. The geographic definition we choose depends on the specific question we are trying to answer.*

## COMPETITION IN MARKETS

A final issue in defining a market is how individual buyers and sellers view the price of the product. In many cases, individual buyers or sellers have an important influence over the market price. For example, in the market for cornflakes, Kellogg's—an individual *seller*—simply sets its price every few months. It can raise the price and sell fewer boxes of cereal, or lower the price and sell more. In the market for windshield wiper motors, Ford Motor Company—an individual *buyer*—can influence the price by negotiating special deals, or merely changing the number of motors it buys. The market for breakfast cereals and the market for windshield wiper motors are examples of *imperfectly competitive* markets.

> *In **imperfectly competitive markets**, individual buyers or sellers have some influence over the price of the product.*

**Imperfectly competitive market** A market in which a single buyer or seller has the power to influence the price of the product.

But now think about the national market for wheat. Can an individual seller have any impact on the market price? Not really. On any given day, there is a going price for wheat—say, $5.80 per bushel. If a farmer tries to charge more than that—say, $5.85 per bushel—he won't sell any wheat at all! His customers will instead go to one of his many competitors and buy the identical product from them. Each wheat farmer must take the price of wheat as a "given."

The same is true of wheat *buyers*: If one tries to negotiate a lower price with a producer, he'd be laughed off the farm. "Why should I sell my wheat to you for $5.75 per bushel, when there are others who will pay me $5.80?" Accordingly, each buyer must take the market price as a given.

The market for wheat is an example of a *perfectly competitive market*.

> *In **perfectly competitive markets** (or just **competitive markets**), each buyer and seller takes the market price as a given.*

**Perfectly competitive market** A market in which no buyer or seller has the power to influence the price.

What makes some markets imperfectly competitive and others perfectly competitive? You'll learn the complete answer when you are well into your study of *microeconomics*. One hint is that in perfectly competitive markets, there are many small buyers and sellers, and the product is standardized, like wheat. Imperfectly competitive markets, by contrast, have either a few large buyers or sellers, or else the product differs in important ways among different sellers.

http://
The Inomics search engine is devoted solely to economics (http://www.inomics.com/query/show?what=welcome). Use it to investigate topics related to supply and demand.

In the real world, perfectly competitive markets are rare. However, many markets come *close enough* that we can choose to view them as perfectly competitive. Think of the market for fast-food hotdogs in a big city. On the one hand, every hotdog stand is slightly different from every other. And each might be able to raise its price a bit above its competitors without losing all of its customers. For example, if his competitors are charging $1.50 for a hotdog, the individual vendor might be able to charge $1.60 or $1.70. In these ways, the market for sidewalk hot dogs resembles *imperfect* competition.

But because there are so many other hotdog vendors in a big city, and because they are not *that* different from one another, no vendor can deviate too much from the going price of $1.50. A vendor that charges $1.80 or $1.90, for example, might soon find himself without a business. So in some ways, the market is close to perfect competition.

How, then, do we decide whether to consider a market—such as the market for big-city hotdogs—as perfectly or imperfectly competitive? You won't be surprised to hear that it depends on the question we want to answer. If we want to explain why there are occasional price wars among hotdog vendors, or why some of them routinely charge higher prices than others, viewing the market as perfectly competitive would not work. To answer *these* questions, an individual seller's influence over his or her own price is important.

But if we want to know why hotdogs are cheaper than most other types of fast foods, the simplest approach is to view the market for hotdogs as perfectly competitive. True, each hotdog vendor does have *some* influence over the price. But that influence is so small, and the prices of different sellers are so similar, that our assumption of perfect competition works pretty well.

## SUPPLY, DEMAND, AND MARKET DEFINITION

The supply and demand model—which explains how prices are determined in a market system—is a very versatile model. It can be applied to very broadly defined goods (the market for food) or very narrowly defined goods (the market for Granny Smith apples). Households, business firms, or government agencies can appear in any combination on the buying side or the selling side. The buyers and sellers can reside within a small geographic area or be dispersed around the world.

But there is only one restriction that is always implicit in any supply and demand analysis: We must always assume that the market is perfectly competitive.

> *The supply and demand model is designed to explain how prices are determined in perfectly competitive markets.*

Does this mean we can only use the model when sellers and buyers have *no influence at all* over their price? Not really. As you've seen, perfect competition is a matter of degree, rather than an all-or-nothing characteristic. While there are very few markets in which sellers and buyers take the price as completely given, there are many markets in which a *narrow range* of prices is treated as a given (as in the market for hotdogs). In these markets, supply and demand often provides a good approximation to what is going on. This is why it has proven to be the most versatile and widely used model in the economist's tool kit. Neither laptop computers nor orange juice is traded in a perfectly competitive market. But ask an economist to tell you why the cost of laptops decreases every year, or why the price of orange juice rises after a freeze in Florida, and he or she will invariably reach for supply and demand to find the answer.

Supply and demand are like two blades of a scissors: The demand blade tells us how much of something buyers want to buy, and the supply blade tells us how much sellers want to sell. To analyze a market, we need both blades—and they must both be sharp. In this and the next section, we will be sharpening those blades, learning separately about supply and demand. Then, when we have a thorough understanding of each one, we'll put them together—and put them to use. Let's start with demand.

# DEMAND

When you come to a market as a buyer, what is your goal? In the most general terms, it's to make yourself as well off as possible. Then why don't you try to buy up everything you can in every possible market? After all, you'd be better off if you had more clothes, more airline travel, a bigger home or apartment, a faster Internet connection. . . . If your goal is to make yourself as well off as possible, you should try to grab up all these things. Right?

Not really. Because in addition to having a goal, you also face *constraints*. First, everything you want to buy has a *price*. Second, you have a limited income with which to buy things. As a result of these two constraints—prices and your limited income—whenever you decide to buy something, you must give up something else that you *could have bought* instead. That is, every purchase carries an opportunity cost. (Even if you have more income each year than you spend, you still pay an opportunity cost when you buy something because you will *save* less that year.)

Both the goals and the constraints of buyers like you play a role in determining the demand side of a market. That is why we do *not* define the quantity of a product demanded as how much a buyer would *like* to have if he could snap his fingers and just have it. Rather, it's how much he would actually *choose* to buy given the constraints that he faces.

> An **individual's quantity demanded** of any good is the total amount that individual would choose to buy at a particular price.

**Individual's quantity demanded** The total amount of a good an individual would choose to purchase at a given price.

When we turn our attention to demand in the market as a whole, we define a similar concept.

> The **market quantity demanded** of any good is the total amount that all buyers in the market would decide to buy at a particular price.

**Market quantity demanded** The total amount of a good that all buyers in the market would choose to purchase at a given price.

Notice two very important things about this definition. First, it refers to buyers' *choices*, not to the amount that buyers will *actually* buy. Will buyers, in fact, be *able* to buy what they decide to buy? Or will they be frustrated in their attempts because sellers are not supplying enough? This is a very important question but one that can't be answered until buyers and sellers—demand *and* supply—come together in the market. That will happen a little later in this chapter.

Second, notice that the influence of price is stressed in the definition of quantity demanded. This is for a good reason. The supply and demand model, you recall, is designed to explain how *prices* are determined in perfectly competitive markets. It seems natural, then, to begin our exploration of demand with the influence of prices.

## THE LAW OF DEMAND

How does a change in price affect quantity demanded? You probably know the answer to this already: When something is more expensive, people buy less of it.

This common observation applies to walnuts, air travel, magazines, education, and virtually everything else that people buy. For all of these goods and services, price and quantity are *negatively related*—that is, when price rises, quantity demanded falls; when price falls, quantity demanded rises. This negative relationship is observed so regularly in markets that economists call it the *law of demand*.

**Law of demand** As the price of a good increases, the quantity demanded decreases.

> The **law of demand** states that when the price of a good rises and everything else remains the same, the quantity of the good demanded will fall.

Read that definition again, and notice the very important words "everything else remains the same." The law of demand tells us what would happen *if* all the other influences on buyers' choices remained unchanged, and only one influence—the price of the good—changed.

This is an example of a common practice in economics. In the real world, many variables change *simultaneously*. But to understand the economy, we must understand the effect of each variable *separately*. Imagine that you were trying to discover which headache remedy works best for you. You wouldn't gain much information if you took an Advil, a Tylenol, and an aspirin tablet all at the same time. Instead, you should take just *one* of these pills the next time you get a headache and observe its effects. To understand the economy, we go through the same process—conducting mental experiments in which only one thing changes at a time. The law of demand tells us what happens when we change *just* the price of the good, and assume that all other influences on buyers' choices remain constant.

## THE DEMAND SCHEDULE AND THE DEMAND CURVE

To make our discussion more concrete, let's look at a specific market: the market for real maple syrup in Wichita, Kansas. In this market, the buyers are all residents of Wichita, whereas the sellers (to be considered later) are maple syrup producers in the United States or Canada.

**Demand schedule** A list showing the quantities of a good that consumers would choose to purchase at different prices, with all other variables held constant.

Table 1 shows a hypothetical **demand schedule** for maple syrup in this market. This is *a list of different quantities demanded at different prices, with all other variables that affect the demand decision assumed constant.* For example, the demand schedule tells us that when the price of maple syrup is $2.00 per bottle, the quantity demanded will be 6,000 bottles per month. Notice that the demand schedule obeys the law of demand: As the price of maple syrup increases, the quantity demanded falls.

Now look at Figure 1. It shows a diagram that will appear again and again in your study of economics. In the figure, each price-and-quantity combination in Table 1 is represented by a point. For example, point *A* represents the price $4.00 and quantity 4,000, while point *B* represents the pair $2.00 and 6,000. When we

| TABLE 1 | | |
|---|---|---|
| **DEMAND SCHEDULE FOR MAPLE SYRUP IN WICHITA** | **Price (per Bottle)** | **Quantity Demanded (Bottles per Month)** |
| | $1.00 | 7,500 |
| | 2.00 | 6,000 |
| | 3.00 | 5,000 |
| | 4.00 | 4,000 |
| | 5.00 | 3,500 |

## THE DEMAND CURVE

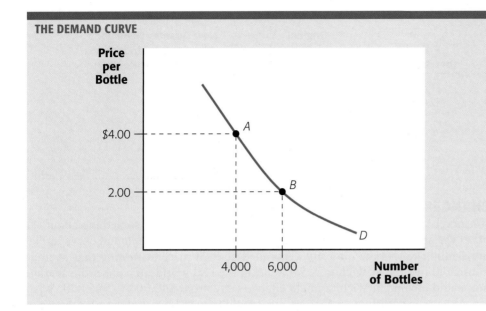

FIGURE 1

The downward-sloping demand curve, *D*, shows the quantity of maple syrup that would be purchased at each price, holding constant all other variables affecting demand. At $4.00 per bottle, 4,000 bottles of syrup are demanded (point *A*). At $2.00 per bottle, 6,000 bottles are demanded (point *B*).

connect all of these points with a line, we obtain the famous *demand curve*, labeled with a *D* in the figure.

> *The **market demand curve** (or just **demand curve**) shows the relationship be-tween the price of a good and the quantity demanded, holding constant all other variables that affect demand. Each point on the curve shows the total quantity that buyers would choose to buy at a specific price.*

**Market demand curve** The graphical depiction of a demand schedule; a curve showing the quantity of a good or service demanded at various prices, with all other variables held constant.

The demand curve for maple syrup in Figure 1—like virtually all demand curves we might observe—follows the law of demand: A rise in the price of the good causes a decrease in the quantity demanded. Graphically, the law of demand tells us that demand curves slope downward.

## CHANGES IN QUANTITY DEMANDED

Markets are affected by a variety of different events. Some events will cause us to *move along* the demand curve for a good. Other events will cause the entire demand curve to *shift*. It is crucial to distinguish between these two very different effects on demand, and economists have adopted a language convention that helps us keep track of the distinction.

Let's go back to Figure 1. There, you can see that if the price of maple syrup rises from $2.00 to $4.00 per bottle, the number of bottles demanded falls from 6,000 to 4,000. This is a movement *along* the demand curve, from point *B* to point *A*, and we call it a *decrease in quantity demanded*. More generally,

> *a change in a good's price causes us to move along the demand curve. We call this a **change in quantity demanded**. A rise in price causes a leftward move-ment along the demand curve—a decrease in quantity demanded. A fall in price causes a rightward movement along the demand curve—an increase in quantity demanded.*

**Change in quantity demanded** A movement along a demand curve in response to a change in price.

| TABLE 2 | | | |
|---|---|---|---|
| **INCREASE IN DEMAND FOR MAPLE SYRUP IN WICHITA** | **Price (per Bottle)** | **Original Quantity Demanded (Bottles per Month)** | **New Quantity Demanded After Increase in Income (Bottles per Month)** |
| | $1.00 | 7,500 | 9,500 |
| | 2.00 | 6,000 | 8,000 |
| | 3.00 | 5,000 | 7,000 |
| | 4.00 | 4,000 | 6,000 |
| | 5.00 | 3,500 | 5,500 |

## CHANGES IN DEMAND

Whenever we draw a demand curve, we are always assuming something about the other variables that affect buyers' choices. For example, the demand curve in Figure 1 might tell us the quantity demanded at each price, *assuming* that average household income in Wichita is $40,000. In the real world, of course, the average household income in Wichita might change—say, from $40,000 to $45,000. What would happen? With more income, we would expect households to buy more of *most* things, including maple syrup. This is illustrated in Table 2. At the original income level, households would choose to buy 6,000 bottles of maple syrup if the price is $2.00 per bottle. But after income rises, they would choose to buy 8,000 bottles at that same price. The same holds for any other price for maple syrup: after income rises, households will choose to buy more than before. In other words, *the entire relationship between price and quantity demanded has changed.*

Figure 2 plots the new demand curve from the quantities in the third column of Table 2. The new demand curve lies to the *right* of the old curve. For example, at a price of $2.00, the old demand curve told us that the quantity demanded was 6,000 bottles (point *B*). But after the increase in income, buyers would want to buy 8,000 bottles at that price (point *C*). Notice that the rise in household income has *shifted the demand curve to the right.* We call this an *increase in demand,* because the word *demand* means the entire relationship between price and quantity demanded.

More generally,

**Change in demand**  A shift of a demand curve in response to a change in some variable other than price.

> *a change in any determinant of demand—except for the good's price—causes the demand curve to shift. We call this a **change in demand**. If buyers choose to purchase more at any price, the demand curve shifts rightward—an increase in demand. If buyers choose to purchase less at any price, the demand curve shifts leftward—a decrease in demand.*

Language is important when speaking about demand. If you say, "People demand more maple syrup," you might mean that we are moving along the demand curve, like the move from point *A* to point *B* in Figure 1. Or you might mean that the entire demand curve has shifted, like the shift from $D_1$ to $D_2$ in Figure 2.

To avoid confusion (and mistakes on exams!), always use the special language that distinguishes between these two cases. When we *move along* the demand curve, we call it a *change in quantity demanded*. A change in quantity demanded is always caused by a change in the good's price. But when the entire demand curve shifts, we call it a *change in demand*. A change in demand is always caused by a change in something *other* than the good's price.

Now let's look at the different variables that can cause demand to change and shift the demand curve.

**Income and Wealth.** Your **income** is what you earn over a period of time—say, $3,000 per month or $36,000 per year. Your **wealth**—if you are fortunate enough to have some—is

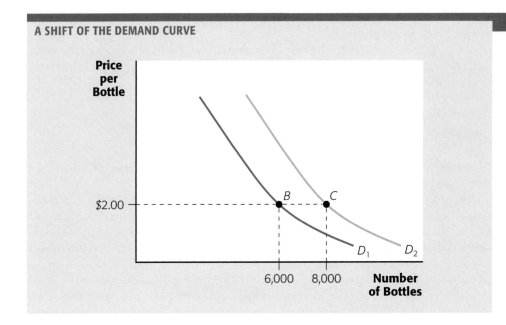

**FIGURE 2**

**A SHIFT OF THE DEMAND CURVE**

A change in any influence on demand besides the price of the good causes the entire demand curve to shift. An increase in income, for example, causes the demand for maple syrup, a normal good, to shift from $D_1$ to $D_2$. At each price, more bottles are demanded after the shift.

the total value of everything you own (cash, bank accounts, stocks, bonds, real estate, valuable artwork, or any other valuable property) minus everything you owe (home mortgage, credit card debt, auto loan, student loans, and so on).

You've already seen (in Table 2 and Figure 2) how an increase in income would increase the demand for maple syrup. And while income and wealth are different things, they have similar effects on demand. If someone's wealth increases—say, through inheritance or an increase in the value of their stocks or bonds—they tend to respond just as if their income had increased, even if their income remains unchanged.

A rise in either income or wealth increases the demand for most goods. We call these **normal goods**. Housing, airline travel, health club memberships and maple syrup are all examples of normal goods.

> *The demand for most goods (normal goods) is positively related to income or wealth. A rise in either income or wealth will increase demand for these goods, and shift the demand curve to the right.*

But not all goods' demand curves behave this way. For some goods—called **inferior goods**—a rise in income or wealth will *decrease* demand. Ground chuck is one example. It's a cheap source of protein, but not most people's idea of a fine dining experience. Higher income or wealth would enable consumers of ground chuck to afford more steaks, decreasing their demand for ground chuck. For similar reasons, Greyhound bus tickets, low-rent housing units, and single-ply paper towels are probably inferior goods. For all of these goods, an increase in consumers' income or wealth would decrease demand, shifting the demand curve to the left.

**Prices of Related Goods.** A **substitute** is a good that can be used in place of another good and that fulfills more or less the same purpose. For example, many people use maple syrup to sweeten their pancakes, but they could use a number of other

**Income** The amount that a person or firm earns over a particular period.

**Wealth** The total value of everything a person or firm owns, at a point in time, minus the total value of everything owed.

**Normal good** A good that people demand more of as their income rises.

**Inferior good** A good that people demand less of as their income rises.

**Substitute** A good that can be used in place of some other good and that fulfills more or less the same purpose.

things instead: honey, sugar, fruit, or jam. Each of these can be considered a substitute for maple syrup.

When the price of a substitute rises, people will choose to buy *more* of the good itself. For example, when the price of jam rises, some jam users will switch to maple syrup, and the demand for maple syrup will increase. In general,

> *when the price of a substitute rises, the demand for a good will increase, shifting the demand curve to the right.*

Of course, if the price of a substitute falls, we have the opposite result: Demand for the original good decreases, shifting its demand curve to the left.

There are countless examples in which a change in a substitute's price affects demand for a good. A rise in the price of postage stamps would increase the demand for electronic mail. A drop in the rental price of videos would decrease the demand for movies at theaters. In each of these cases, we assume that the price of the substitute is the only price that is changing.

**Complement** A good that is used *together with* some other good.

A **complement** is the opposite of a substitute: It's used *together with* the good we are interested in. Pancake mix is a complement to maple syrup, since these two goods are used frequently in combination. If the price of pancake mix rises, some consumers will switch to other breakfasts—bacon and eggs, for example—that *don't* include maple syrup. The demand for maple syrup will decrease.

> *A rise in the price of a complement decreases the demand for a good, shifting the demand curve to the left.*

This is why we expect a higher price for automobiles to decrease the demand for gasoline and a lower price for movie tickets to increase the demand for movie theater popcorn.

**Population.**  As the population increases in an area, the number of buyers will ordinarily increase as well, and the demand for a good will increase. The growth of the U.S. population over the last 50 years has been an important reason (but not the only reason) for rightward shifts in the demand curves for food, rental apartments, telephones, and many other goods and services.

**Expectations.**  Expectations of future events—especially future changes in a good's price—can affect demand. For example, if buyers expect the price of maple syrup to rise next month, they may choose to purchase more *now* to stock up before the price hike. The demand curve would shift to the right. If people expect the price to drop, they may postpone buying, hoping to take advantage of the lower price later. This would shift the demand curve leftward.

Expectations are particularly important in the markets for financial assets such as stocks and bonds and in the market for real estate. People want to buy more stocks, bonds, and real estate when they think their prices will rise in the near future. This shifts the demand curves for these items to the right.

**Tastes.**  Suppose we know the number of buyers in Wichita, their expectations about the future price of maple syrup, the prices of all related goods, and the average levels of income and wealth. Do we have all the information we need to draw the demand curve for maple syrup in Wichita? Not really. Because we do not yet know how consumers there *feel* about maple syrup. How many of them eat breakfast? Of these, how many eat pancakes or waffles? How often? How many of them *like* maple syrup, and how much do they like it? And what about all of the other goods and services competing for Wichita consumers' dollars: How do buyers feel about *them*?

The questions could go on and on, pinpointing various characteristics about buyers

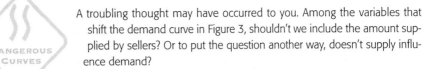

A troubling thought may have occurred to you. Among the variables that shift the demand curve in Figure 3, shouldn't we include the amount supplied by sellers? Or to put the question another way, doesn't supply influence demand?

The answer is no—at least, not directly. The demand curve tells us how much buyers *would choose* to buy at different prices. It provides answers to a series of hypothetical questions: How much maple syrup *would* consumers choose to buy if the price were $3.00 per bottle? If the price were $3.50 per bottle? and so on. Sellers' decisions have no effect on the demand curve, since they do not affect the answers to these hypothetical questions.

that influence their attitudes toward maple syrup. The approach of economics is to lump all of these characteristics of buyers together and call them, simply, *tastes*. Economists do not try to explain where these tastes come from or what makes them change. These tasks are left to other social scientists—psychologists, sociologists, and anthropologists. Instead, economists concern themselves with the *consequences* of a change in tastes, whatever the reason for its occurrence.

When tastes change *toward* a good (people favor it more), demand increases, and the demand curve shifts to the right. When tastes change *away* from a good, demand decreases, and the demand curve shifts to the left. An example of this is the change in tastes away from cigarettes over the past several decades. The cause may have been an aging population, a greater concerns about health among people of *all* ages, or successful antismoking advertising. But regardless of the cause, the effect has been to decrease the demand for cigarettes, shifting the demand curve to the left.

Figure 3 summarizes the important variables that affect the demand side of the market, and how their effects are represented with a demand curve. Notice the important distinction between movements *along* the demand curve and *shifts* of the entire curve.

## SUPPLY

Now we switch our focus from the buying side to the selling side of the market. When we discussed demand, we noted that each buyer comes to a market with a goal—to make himself as well off as possible. But the buyer also faces a constraint: He must pay for purchases out of a limited income.

A seller, too, comes to a market with a goal—to make as much profit as possible. And if the seller is a business firm (which we'll assume for most of this chapter), it faces an important constraint: Producing output (goods and services) requires the use of inputs. The quantities of those inputs needed are determined by the firm's *production technology*.

*A firm's **production technology** (or just **technology**) is the set of methods it can use to turn inputs (resources and raw materials) into outputs (goods or services).*

**Technology** The set of methods a firm can use to turn inputs into outputs

Continuing with our example, there are many different ways for a maple syrup farm to produce its output (maple syrup) from its inputs (land, maple trees, labor,

**FIGURE 3**

**CHANGES IN DEMAND AND IN QUANTITY DEMANDED**

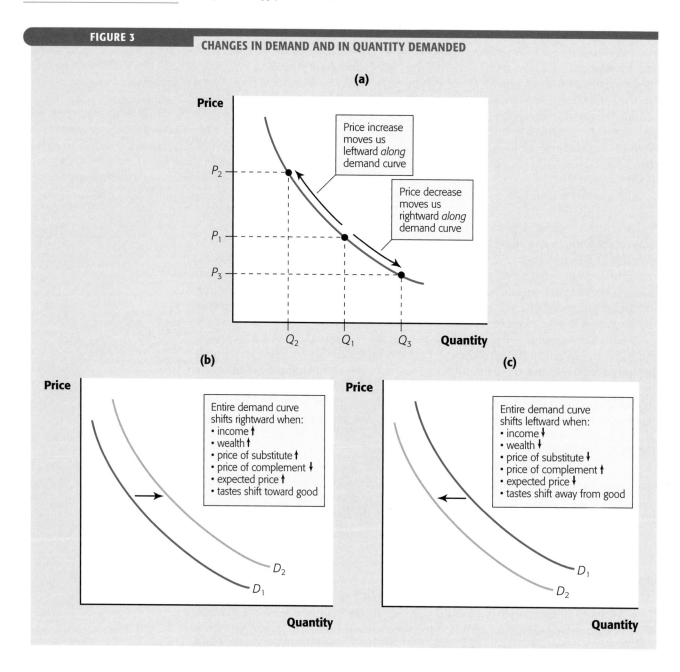

capital, fuel, transportation, glass bottles, etc.). The sap can be collected with buckets, bags, plastic tubing, or some combination of these. Syrup evaporators can be fueled with wood, oil, or natural gas, and they can include accessories such as preheaters, reverse osmosis, steam hoods, automatic draw-offs, and more. The syrup can be packaged in glass bottles or plastic bottles or metal tins, and it can be shipped across the country by train, truck, or aircraft. As you can see, there are hundreds if not thousands of different ways to combine inputs to produce a given quantity of maple syrup. Each of these production methods is a part of the known technology of this industry.

A firm's production technology tells us not only what the firm *can* do, it also tells us what it *cannot* do. For example, a firm cannot produce a thousand gallons of maple syrup per year with only 10 trees, no matter how much labor or equipment it uses, and it cannot produce *any* maple syrup at all using iron ore instead of maple trees.

The known technology in an industry is an important constraint on the firm. Another constraint is that it must *pay a price* for its inputs. Together, the technology of production and the prices of its inputs determine how much it will *cost* the firm to produce different quantities of output.

Finally, every competitive firm faces one more constraint: the market price. The firm is not free to set any price it wants for its output. Rather, it must accept the market price as a given.

In sum,

> *when a competitive firm comes to a market as a seller, it wants to make the highest possible profit. The firm can choose the level of output it wants to produce, but it faces three constraints: (1) its production technology, (2) the prices it must pay for its inputs, and (3) the market price of its output.*

Together, the firm's goal of earning the highest possible profit, and the constraints that it faces, determine the quantity that it will supply in the market.

More specifically,

> *a firm's **quantity supplied** of any good is the amount it would choose to produce and sell at a particular price.*

**Firm's quantity supplied** The total amount of a good or service that an individual firm would choose to produce and sell at a given price.

And when we turn to the market as a whole:

> *The **market quantity supplied** of any good is the amount that all firms in the market would like to produce and sell at a particular price, given the prices they must pay for their inputs, and given any other influences on their selling decisions.*

**Market quantity supplied** The total amount of a good or service that all producers in a market would choose to produce and sell at a given price.

Notice that quantity supplied—like quantity demanded—tells us about sellers' *choices*. The amount that will *actually* be sold will be discussed later, when we put demand and supply together.

## THE LAW OF SUPPLY

How does a change in price affect quantity supplied? When a seller can get a higher price for a good, producing and selling it become more profitable. Producers will devote more resources toward its production—perhaps even pulling resources out of other types of production—and increase the quantity of the good they would like to sell. For example, a rise in the price of laptop computers will encourage computer makers to shift resources out of the production of other things (such as desktop computers) and toward the production of laptops.

In general, price and quantity supplied are *positively related:* When the price of a good rises, the quantity supplied will rise as well. This relationship between price and quantity supplied is called the law of supply, the counterpart to the law of demand we discussed earlier.

> *The **law of supply** states that when the price of a good rises, and everything else remains the same, the quantity of the good supplied will rise.*

**Law of supply** As the price of a good increases, the quantity supplied increases.

Once again, notice the very important words "everything else remains the same." Although many other variables influence the quantity of a good supplied, the law of supply tells us what would happen if all of them remained unchanged as the price of the good changed.

## THE SUPPLY SCHEDULE AND THE SUPPLY CURVE

Let's continue with our example of the market for maple syrup in Wichita. Who are the suppliers in this market? Since maple syrup is easy to transport, any producer on the continent can sell in Wichita. In practice, these producers are located mostly in the forests of Vermont, upstate New York, and Canada. The market quantity supplied is the amount of maple syrup all of these producers together would offer for sale in Wichita at each price for maple syrup.

**Supply schedule**  A list showing the quantities of a good or service that firms would choose to produce and sell at different prices, with all other variables held constant.

Table 3 shows the **supply schedule** for maple syrup in Wichita—a *list of different quantities supplied at different prices, with all other variables held constant.* As you can see, the supply schedule obeys the law of supply: As the price of maple syrup in Wichita rises, the quantity supplied rises along with it. But how can this be? After all, maple trees must be about 40 years old before they can be tapped for syrup, so any rise in quantity supplied now or in the near future cannot come from an increase in planting. What, then, causes quantity supplied to rise as price rises?

Many things. First, with higher prices, firms will find it profitable to tap existing trees more intensively. Second, evaporating and bottling can be done more carefully, so that less maple syrup is spilled and more is available for shipping. Finally, the product can be diverted from other areas and shipped to Wichita instead. For example, if the price of maple syrup rises in Wichita but not in Kansas City, producers would shift deliveries away from Kansas City and toward Wichita.

Now look at Figure 4, which shows a very important curve—the counterpart to the demand curve we drew earlier. In Figure 4, each point represents a price-quantity pair taken from Table 3. For example, point *F* in the figure corresponds to a price of $2.00 per bottle and a quantity of 4,000 bottles per month, while point *G* represents the price-quantity pair $4.00 and 6,000 bottles. Connecting all of these points with a solid line gives us the *supply curve* for maple syrup, labeled with an *S* in the figure.

**Supply curve**  A graphical depiction of a supply schedule; a curve showing the quantity of a good or service supplied at various prices, with all other variables held constant.

> *The **supply curve** shows the relationship between the price of a good and the quantity supplied, holding constant the values of all other variables that affect supply. Each point on the curve shows the quantity that sellers would choose to sell at a specific price.*

Notice that the supply curve in Figure 4—like all supply curves for goods and services—is *upward sloping.* This is the graphical representation of the law of supply.

| TABLE 3 | | |
|---|---|---|
| **SUPPLY SCHEDULE FOR MAPLE SYRUP IN WICHITA** | **Price (per Bottle)** | **Quantity Supplied (Bottles per Month)** |
| | $1.00 | 2,500 |
| | 2.00 | 4,000 |
| | 3.00 | 5,000 |
| | 4.00 | 6,000 |
| | 5.00 | 6,500 |

**FIGURE 4**

**THE SUPPLY CURVE**

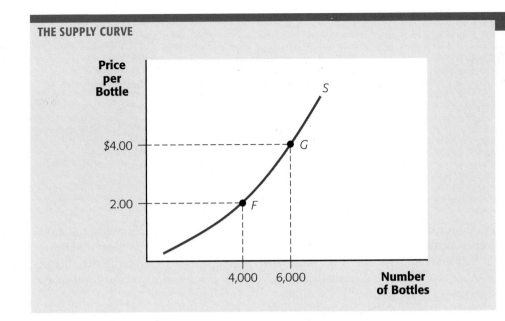

The upward-sloping supply curve, *S*, shows the quantity of a good that firms wish to produce and sell at each price, assuming constant all other variables affecting supply. At $2.00 per bottle, quantity supplied is 4,000 bottles (point *F*). At $4.00 per bottle, quantity supplied is 6,000 bottles (point *G*).

*The law of supply tells us that supply curves slope upward.*

## CHANGES IN QUANTITY SUPPLIED

Sellers' choices about how much to sell are affected by many different variables. One of these variables—the price of the good—causes sellers to *move along* a given supply curve. The other variables cause the entire supply curve to *shift*. Economists use the same language convention for supply that we discussed earlier for demand. Look once again at Figure 4. Notice that when the price of maple syrup rises from $2.00 to $4.00, the number of bottles supplied rises from 4,000 to 6,000. This is a movement *along* the supply curve, from point *F* to point *G*, and we call it an *increase in quantity supplied*.

More generally,

*a change in a good's price causes us to move* along *the supply curve. We call this a change in quantity supplied. A rise in price causes a rightward movement along the supply curve—an increase in quantity supplied. A fall in price causes a leftward movement along the supply curve—a decrease in quantity supplied.*

**Change in quantity supplied** A movement along a supply curve in response to a change in price.

## CHANGES IN SUPPLY

Both the supply schedule in Table 3 and the supply curve in Figure 4 assume given values for all other variables that might affect supply. For example, the supply curve in Figure 4 might tell us the quantity supplied at each price, *assuming* that maple syrup workers are paid $10 per hour. But what would happen if these workers' wages fell to $7 per hour? Then, at any given price for maple syrup, firms would find it more profitable to produce and sell maple syrup, and they would no doubt choose to sell more. This is illustrated in Table 4. For example, at the original wage of $10, maple syrup producers would choose to sell 6,000 bottles when the price is

**TABLE 4**

**INCREASE IN SUPPLY OF
MAPLE SYRUP IN WICHITA**

| Price (per Bottle) | Quantity Supplied (Bottles/Month) | Quantity Supplied After Increase in Supply |
|---|---|---|
| $1.00 | 2,500 | 4,500 |
| 2.00 | 4,000 | 6,000 |
| 3.00 | 5,000 | 7,000 |
| 4.00 | 6,000 | 8,000 |
| 5.00 | 6,500 | 8,500 |

$4.00. But if they could pay the lower wage of $7, they would choose to sell 8,000 bottles at that same price of $4.00 per bottle. The same holds for any other price for maple syrup: After the wage falls, sellers would choose to sell more than before. In other words, *the entire relationship between price and quantity supplied has changed.*

Figure 5 plots the new supply curve from the quantities in the third column of Table 4. The new supply curve lies to the *right* of the old curve. For example, at a price of $4.00, the old supply curve told us that quantity supplied was 6,000 bottles (point G). But after the decrease in the wage, sellers would choose to supply 8,000 bottles at $4.00 each (point J). The decrease in maple syrup workers' wages has *shifted the supply curve to the right.* We call this an *increase in supply.*

**Change in supply** A shift of a supply curve in response to some variable other than price.

> *A change in any influence on supply—except for the good's price—causes the supply curve to shift. We call this a* **change in supply.** *When sellers choose to sell more at any price, the supply curve shifts rightward—an* increase *in supply. When sellers choose to sell less at any price, the supply curve shifts leftward—a* decrease *in supply.*

**FIGURE 5**

A change in any nonprice determinant of supply causes the entire supply curve to shift. A decrease in labor costs, for example, causes the supply of maple syrup to shift from $S_1$ to $S_2$. At each price, more bottles are supplied after the shift.

**A SHIFT OF THE SUPPLY CURVE**

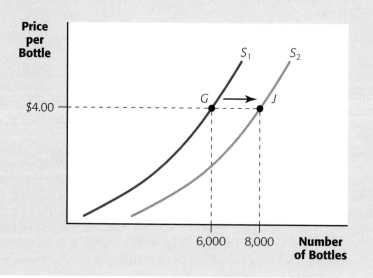

Now let's take a look at the different variables that can cause a change in supply and shift the supply curve.

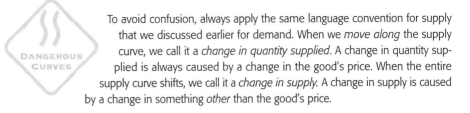

To avoid confusion, always apply the same language convention for supply that we discussed earlier for demand. When we *move along* the supply curve, we call it a *change in quantity supplied*. A change in quantity supplied is always caused by a change in the good's price. When the entire supply curve shifts, we call it a *change in supply*. A change in supply is caused by a change in something *other* than the good's price.

**Prices of Inputs.** Producers of maple syrup use a variety of inputs: land, maple trees, evaporators, sap pans, labor, glass bottles, bottling machinery, transportation, and more. A higher price for any of these means a higher cost of producing and selling maple syrup, making it less profitable. As a result, we would expect producers to shift some resources out of maple syrup production, causing a decrease in supply.

In general,

> *a rise in the price of an input causes a decrease in supply, shifting the supply curve to the left. A fall in the price of an input causes an increase in supply, shifting the supply curve to the right.*

Figure 5 has already illustrated one example of this: The supply curve shifted rightward when the wage rate paid to maple syrup workers fell. Now we can see that maple syrup workers are just *one* type of input among many for syrup producers. If the price of bottles, transportation, or any other input were to decrease, it would also shift the supply curve for maple syrup rightward, just as in Figure 5.

**Profitability of Alternate Goods.** Many firms can switch their production rather easily among several different goods or services, all of which require more or less the same inputs. For example, a dermatology practice can rather easily switch its specialty from acne treatments for the young to wrinkle treatments for the elderly. An automobile producer can—without too much adjustment—switch to producing light trucks. And a maple syrup producer could dry its maple syrup and produce maple *sugar* instead. Or it could even cut down its maple trees and sell maple wood as lumber. These other goods that firms *could* produce are called **alternate goods.**

**Alternate goods** Other goods that a firm could produce, using some of the same types of inputs as the good in question.

> *When an alternate good becomes more profitable to produce—because its price rises, or the cost of producing it falls—the supply curve for the good in question will shift leftward.*

In our example, if the price of maple *sugar* rises, and nothing else changes, maple sugar will become more profitable. Producers will devote more of their output to maple sugar, *decreasing* the supply of maple syrup.

**Technology.** A *technological advance* in production occurs whenever a firm can produce a given level of output in a new and cheaper way than before. For example, the discovery of a surgical procedure called Lasik—in which a laser is used to reshape the interior of the cornea rather than the outer surface—has enabled eye surgeons to correct their patients' vision with fewer follow-up visits and smaller quantities of medication. Similarly, in the late 1990s, several firms—including Ebay, Amazon.com, and Priceline.com—developed new software that enabled people and firms to trade used goods more cheaply over the Internet (compared to

The list of variables that shift the supply curve in Figure 6 does not include the amount that buyers want to buy. Is this a mistake? Doesn't demand affect supply?

The answer is no—at least, not directly. The supply curve tells us how much sellers *would choose* to sell at alternative prices. It provides answers to a series of hypothetical questions, such as How much maple syrup would firms choose to sell if the price were $4.00 per bottle? If the price were $3.50 per bottle? and so on. Buyers' decisions don't affect the answers to these questions, so they cannot shift the supply curve.

the previous method of running and searching through classified ads). These examples are technological advances because they enable firms to produce the same output (eye surgeries, used goods sales) more cheaply than before.

In maple syrup production, a technological advance might be a new, more efficient tap that draws more maple syrup from each tree, or a new bottling method that reduces spillage. Advances like this would reduce the cost of producing maple syrup, and producers would want to make and sell more of it at any price.

In general,

> *cost-saving technological advances increase the supply of a good, shifting the supply curve to the right.*

**Productive Capacity.** A market's productive capacity is determined by the number of producers in the market, and the plant and equipment possessed by each firm. Whenever productive capacity increases, the supply curve shifts rightward, since sellers would choose to sell a greater total quantity at each price. Similarly, a decrease in productive capacity will shift the supply curve leftward. For example, if a sudden blight destroyed maple trees in Vermont, the total productive capacity of maple syrup suppliers would shrink, decreasing the supply of maple syrup to any market. On the other hand, if—over time—more firms moved into the market and started their own maple syrup farms, supply would increase.

Changes in weather can cause sudden changes in productive capacity in many agricultural markets. Good weather increases the productive capacity of all farms in a region, shifting supply curves for their crops to the right. Bad weather destroys crops and decreases productive capacity, shifting supply curves to the left. Natural disasters such as fires, hurricanes, and earthquakes can destroy the productive capacity of *all* industries in a region, thereby causing sudden, dramatic leftward shifts in supply curves.

> *An increase in sellers' productive capacity—caused by, say, good weather or an increase in the number of firms—shifts the supply curve rightward. A decrease in sellers' productive capacity shifts the supply curve leftward.*

**Expectations of Future Prices.** Imagine that you are the president of Sticky's Maple Syrup, Inc., and your research staff has just determined that the price of maple syrup will soon rise dramatically. What would you do? You should *postpone* producing—or at least selling—your output until later, when the price will be higher and profits will be greater. Applying this logic more generally,

> *A rise in the expected price of a good will decrease supply, shifting the supply curve leftward.*

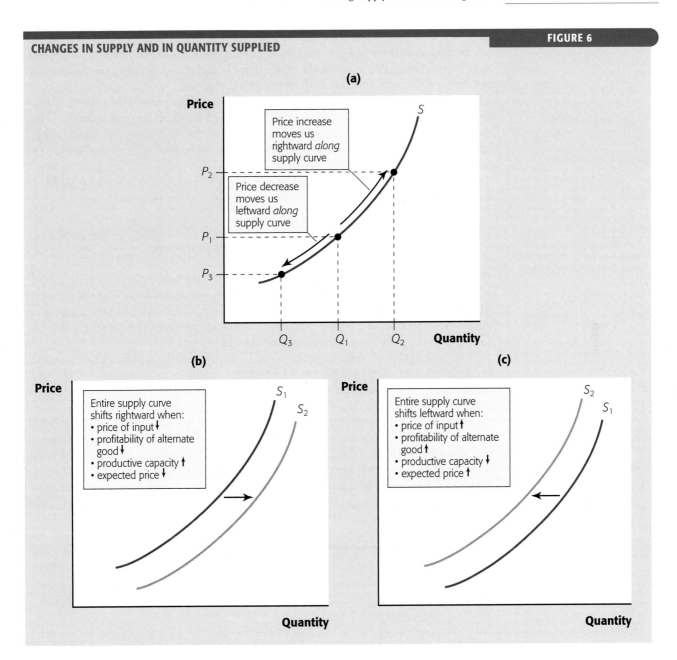

**CHANGES IN SUPPLY AND IN QUANTITY SUPPLIED**

**FIGURE 6**

**(a)**

Price increase
moves us
rightward *along*
supply curve

Price decrease
moves us
leftward *along*
supply curve

**(b)**

Entire supply curve
shifts rightward when:
• price of input ↓
• profitability of alternate
  good ↓
• productive capacity ↑
• expected price ↓

**(c)**

Entire supply curve
shifts leftward when:
• price of input ↑
• profitability of alternate
  good ↑
• productive capacity ↓
• expected price ↑

Figure 6 summarizes the different variables that change the supply of a good and shift the supply curve.

## PUTTING SUPPLY AND DEMAND TOGETHER

What happens when buyers and sellers, each having the desire and the ability to trade, come together in a market? The two sides of the market certainly have different agendas. Buyers would like to pay the lowest possible price, while sellers would like to charge the highest possible price. Is there chaos when they meet, with buyers and sellers endlessly chasing after each other or endlessly bargaining for advantage, so that trade never takes place? A casual look at the real world suggests not. In most markets, most of the time, there is order and stability in the encounters between buyers and sellers. In most cases, prices do not fluctuate wildly from moment to moment, but seem to hover around a stable value. This stability may be short lived—lasting only a day, an hour, or even a minute in some markets—but still, for this short time, the market seems to be at rest. Whenever we study a market, therefore, we look for this state of rest—a price and quantity at which the market will settle, at least for a while.

Economists use the word *equilibrium* when referring to a state of rest. More formally,

**Equilibrium** A state of rest; a situation that, once achieved, will not change unless some external factor, previously held constant, changes.

> *an **equilibrium** is a situation that, once achieved, will not change unless there is a change in something we have been assuming constant.*

What will be the price of maple syrup in Wichita? And how much will people actually buy each month? We can rephrase these questions as follows: What is the *equilibrium* price of maple syrup in Wichita, and what is the *equilibrium* quantity of maple syrup that will be bought and sold? These are precisely the questions that the supply-and-demand model is designed to answer.

Look at Figure 7, which combines the supply and demand curves for maple syrup in Wichita. We'll use Figure 7 to find the equilibrium in this market through the process of elimination. Let's first ask what would happen if the price of maple syrup in Wichita were $1.00 per bottle. At this price, we see that buyers would choose to buy 7,500 bottles each week, while sellers would offer to sell only 2,500 per week. There is an **excess demand** of 5,000 bottles. What will happen? Buyers will compete with each other to get more maple syrup than is available, offering to pay a higher price rather than do without. The price will then rise. You can see that $1.00 per bottle is *not* the equilibrium price, since—if the price *were* $1.00— it would automatically tend to rise.

**Excess demand** At a given price, the excess of quantity demanded over quantity supplied.

---

**FIGURE 7**

The intersection of the supply and demand curves at point *E* determines the market price of maple syrup ($3.00 per bottle) and the number of bottles exchanged (5,000). At a lower price, such as $1.00 per bottle, buyers would like to purchase more bottles (7,500) than producers are willing to supply (2,500). The resulting excess demand of 5,000 bottles causes the price to rise.

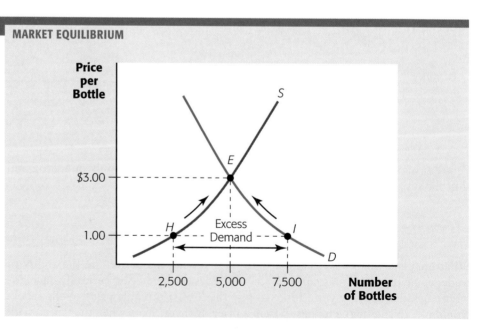

MARKET EQUILIBRIUM

Before we consider other possible prices, let's look more closely at the changes we would see in this market as the price rose. First, there would be a decrease in quantity demanded—a movement along the demand curve leftward from point *I*. At the same time, we would see an increase in quantity supplied—a movement along the supply curve rightward from point *H*. As these movements continued, the excess demand for maple syrup would shrink and, finally—at a price of $3.00—disappear entirely. At this price, there would be no reason for any further price change, since quantity supplied and quantity demanded would both equal 5,000 bottles per month. There would be no disappointed buyers to offer higher prices. In sum, if the price happens to be below $3.00, it will rise to $3.00 and then stay put.

Now let's see what would happen if, for some reason, the price of maple syrup were $5.00 per bottle. Figure 8 shows us that, at this price, quantity supplied would be 6,500 bottles per month, while quantity demanded would be only 3,500 bottles—an **excess supply** of 3,000 bottles. Sellers would compete with each other to sell more maple syrup than buyers wanted to buy, and the price would fall. Thus, $5.00 cannot be the equilibrium price.

**Excess supply**  At a given price, the excess of quantity supplied over quantity demanded.

Moreover, the decrease in price would move us along both the supply curve (leftward) and the demand curve (rightward). As these movements continued, the excess supply of maple syrup would shrink until it disappeared, once again, at a price of $3.00 per bottle. Our conclusion: If the price happens to be above $3.00, it will fall to $3.00 and then stop changing.

You can see that any price higher or lower than $3.00 is *not* the equilibrium price. If the price is higher than $3.00, it will tend to drop, and if it is lower, it will tend to rise. You can also see—in Figures 7 and 8—that if the price were exactly $3.00, there would be neither an excess supply nor an excess demand. Sellers would choose to sell 5,000 bottles per week, and this is exactly the quantity buyers would choose to buy. There would be no reason for the price to change. Thus, $3.00 must be our sought-after equilibrium price and 5,000 our equilibrium quantity.

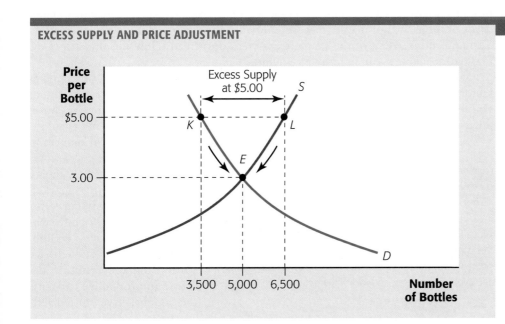

**EXCESS SUPPLY AND PRICE ADJUSTMENT**

**FIGURE 8**

At any price above $3.00 per bottle, the market for maple syrup in Wichita will be out of equilibrium. The excess supply of 3,000 bottles at a price of $5.00 causes the market price to fall. As the price falls, quantity supplied decreases and quantity demanded increases. At point *E*, the market is back in equilibrium.

No doubt, you have noticed that $3.00 happens to be the price at which the supply and demand curves cross. This leads us to an easy, graphical technique for locating our equilibrium:

> To find the equilibrium price and quantity in a competitive market, draw the supply and demand curves. The equilibrium is the point where the two curves intersect.

The intersection of the supply and demand curves helps us to understand the concept of equilibrium even more clearly. At the intersection, the market is operating on *both* the demand and the supply curves. When the price is $3.00, buyers and sellers can *actually* buy and sell the quantities they would *choose* to buy and sell at $3.00. There are no dissatisfied buyers unable to find the goods they want to purchase, nor are there unhappy sellers, unable to find buyers for the products they have brought to the market. This is why $3.00 is the equilibrium price. In this state of rest, there is a balance between the quantity supplied and the quantity demanded.

But that point of rest will not necessarily be a lasting one, as you are about to see.

## WHAT HAPPENS WHEN THINGS CHANGE?

Remember that in order to draw the supply and demand curves in the first place, we had to assume particular values for all the other variables—besides price—that affect demand and supply. If any one of these variables changes, then either the supply curve or the demand curve will shift, and our equilibrium will change as well. Economists are very interested in how and why an equilibrium changes in a market. Let's look at some examples.

### AN ICE STORM HITS THE NORTHEAST: A DECREASE IN SUPPLY

In January 1998, New England and Quebec were struck by a severe ice storm. Hundreds of thousands of maple trees were downed, and many more were damaged. In Vermont alone, 10% of the maple trees were destroyed. How did this affect the market for maple syrup in faraway Wichita?

Maple trees are part of the productive capacity of a maple syrup firm, just as factory buildings are part of the productive capacity of a toy manufacturer. And as you learned in this chapter (see Figure 6), a decrease in productive capacity causes a leftward shift of the supply curve in any market in which maple syrup is sold—including the local market in Wichita.

Figure 9 shows how the ice storm affected this market. Initially, the supply curve for maple syrup in Wichita was $S_1$, with the market in equilibrium at Point $E$. After the ice storm, and the resulting decrease in productive capacity, the supply curve shifted left-

**DANGEROUS CURVES**

It's tempting to use *upward* and *rightward* interchangeably when describing an increase in demand or supply and to use *downward* and *leftward* when describing a decrease in demand or supply. But be careful! While this interchangeable language works for the demand curve, it does *not* work for the supply curve. To prove this to yourself, look at Figure 6. There you can see that a rightward shift of the supply curve (an increase in supply) is also a *downward* shift of the curve. In later chapters, it will sometimes make sense to describe shifts as upward or downward. For now, it's best to avoid these terms, and stick with *rightward* and *leftward*.

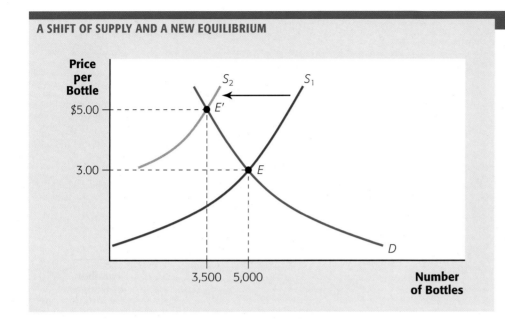

**FIGURE 9**

### A SHIFT OF SUPPLY AND A NEW EQUILIBRIUM

An ice storm causes supply to decrease from $S_1$ to $S_2$. At the old equilibrium price of $3.00, there is now an excess demand. As a result, the price increases until excess demand is eliminated at point $E'$. In the new equilibrium, quantity demanded again equals quantity supplied. The price is higher, and fewer bottles are produced and sold.

ward—say, to $S_2$. The result: a rise in the equilibrium price of maple syrup (from $3.00 to $5.00 in Figure 9) and a fall in the equilibrium quantity (from 5,000 to 3,500 bottles).

In this case, it was an ice storm that shifted the supply curve leftward. But suppose, instead, that the wages of maple syrup workers had increased or that evaporators became more expensive or that some maple syrup producers went out of business and sold their farms to housing developers. Any of these changes would have caused the supply curve for maple syrup to shift leftward, increased the equilibrium price and decreased the equilibrium quantity.

More generally,

> *any change that shifts the supply curve leftward in a market will increase the equilibrium price and decrease the equilibrium quantity in that market.*

### INTERNET ENTREPRENEURS GET RICH: AN INCREASE IN DEMAND

Since shifts in supply and demand work the same way in *any* market, let's leave Maple syrup for now and look at a different market: housing in San Francisco. In this market, something remarkable has happened recently: The average price of a single-family home[1] increased from $250,450 in mid-1995 to $373,750 in mid-1999. In just three and one-half year, the price almost doubled! What explains this dramatic rise in in San Francisco housing prices? Supply and demand can give us the answer.

First, let's define the market itself. The sellers are households and real estate companies who own homes in San Francisco. Figure 10 shows their supply curve for

In the late 1990s, an increase in wealth drove up housing prices in San Francisco.

---

[1]  The housing price data is for already-existing, detached homes only. It does not include the price of condominiums or apartments or of newly constructed homes.

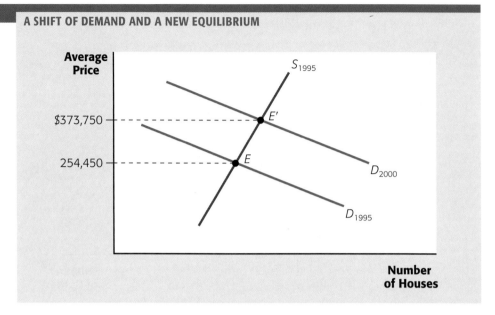

**FIGURE 10**

An increase in household incomes increased demand from $D_{1995}$ to $D_{2000}$. At the old price of $254,450, there was an excess demand. As a result, prices rose until excess demand was eliminated at point E'. In the new equilibrium, quantity demanded again equals quantity supplied. The price is higher, and more houses are sold.

**A SHIFT OF DEMAND AND A NEW EQUILIBRIUM**

housing in 1995, labeled $S_{1995}$. Notice that this curve sloped upward: A rise in housing prices—with no other change—increases the number of homes offered for sale.[2]

The demand side of the market consists of households who have the potential to *buy* homes in San Francisco. This includes anyone who works in San Francisco itself or within commuting distance of the city, as well as those who can consider moving to the city (getting jobs or retiring there). The market demand curve in 1995 is represented by the curve $D_{1995}$. Notice that this demand curve slopes downward: With a higher price (and no other change), buyers would want to buy fewer houses in San Francisco. Point E shows the equilibrium in 1995, the intersection between the demand curve and the supply curve, with an average price of $254,450.

Now, what happened from 1995 to 1999 that so significantly affected this market? The answer is: the Internet. More specifically, the 1990s was an era in which, by starting up successful companies in a new industry, people could become extremely wealthy in a very short period of time. For example, Pierre Omidyar founded the Internet trading community Ebay in 1995, when his girlfriend wanted to trade Pez dispensers online. The auction idea was a big hit, and by 1999 the 31-year-old Omidyar's wealth was estimated at $7.8 billion.

This story is not unique. About 200 people with ordinary incomes but extraordinary ideas for new Internet-related companies became *billionaires* in the 1990s. And hundreds of thousands more saw their stocks and stock options rise dramatically in value—doubling, tripling, or quadrupling their wealth within just a few years or less. Disproportionately, the newly rich lived and worked in the Silicon Val-

---

[2]   The supply curve for housing should slope upward even if we ignore new building activity in the city. To understand why, imagine that you own a home in your current town or city, and that housing prices are rising there. Is there a critical price beyond which you would decide to move elsewhere and cash in on the value of your home? For most people, the answer is yes. After all, even when you own a home, the opportunity cost of continuing to live in an area is the money you *could* have if you sold it and lived elsewhere. As the price of housing rises higher and higher, each additional person who decides to sell his or her home adds to the supply of housing, as shown by the supply curve.

ley area of Northern California—an area within commuting distance of San Francisco. Thus, they were part of the buying side in the housing market there.

As you've learned (see Figure 3), an increase in buyers' wealth causes the demand curve for a normal good—such as housing—to shift rightward. In this case, greater wealth leads people to choose bigger homes and sometimes multiple homes—an increase in the demand for housing. In Figure 10, this is shown as the rightward shift from $D_{1995}$ to $D_{1999}$, with the equilibrium moving from point $E$ to point $E'$. And this explains why the price rose from \$254,450 to \$373,750.

More generally,

> *any change that shifts the demand curve rightward in a market will increase both the equilibrium price and the equilibrium quantity in that market.*

Notice that the supply curve has not shifted in Figure 10; it remains at $S_{1995}$. There *has* been an increase in the quantity of housing supplied (a movement *along* the supply curve), but no change in the *supply* of housing (no shift of the entire curve). Why hasn't the supply curve shifted in Figure 10? Largely because we are dealing with a five-year period—a period too short for significant new construction to change the stock of available housing in a city. While the quantity of housing supplied has increased, it has done so largely because higher prices cause a more intensive use of the *existing* housing stock. This is represented as a movement along the supply curve.

## THE MARKET FOR DAY CARE: CHANGES IN BOTH SUPPLY AND DEMAND

So far, we've considered the consequences of a change in a single variable only. But what happens to the market equilibrium when two or more variables change simultaneously? Figure 11 illustrates how we would analyze such a situation, using the market for day care services.

**FIGURE 11**

**SIMULTANEOUS SHIFTS OF SUPPLY AND DEMAND**

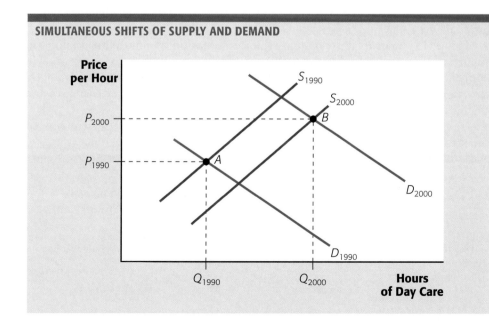

As more young mothers sought day care, the demand curve shifted right from $D_{1990}$ to $D_{2000}$. Simultaneously, more firms entered the market, increasing supply from $S_{1990}$ to $S_{2000}$. As a result, equilibrium moved from point $A$ to point $B$. Over the decade, both the quantity of day care services and the price of day care increased.

The story begins in the 1990s, when a variety of factors combined to increase total employment in the United States. Favorable economic conditions drew more and more workers in the labor force, and an increasingly competitive business climate led individuals to work ever-longer hours. By the end of the 1990s, the average American worker spent more time on the job than his or her counterparts in any other developed country. At the same time, legislative reform took thousands of individuals off the welfare reform and into jobs. The implications of these changes were wide-ranging and profound, but here we are interested in just one of them: the use of for-profit day care services.

As more and more women worked outside the home and worked longer hours, they sought care for their preschool children. Many of these women did not have access to the traditional providers of day care—relatives (especially grandparents), friends, or neighbors. So they began to seek day care services in the commercial sector. In terms of our supply and demand model, these changes led a rightward shift of the demand curve for day care services. In Figure 11, the demand curve shifted rightward, from $D_{1990}$ to $D_{2000}$.

At the same time, many business firms saw an opportunity in these developments. They realized that the labor market trends just described would continue, and perhaps even become stronger. Aiming to earn a profit, these firms set about obtaining office space, hiring teachers, and marketing themselves as high-quality providers of day care services. Large corporations, governments, and nonprofit agencies also got into the act by offering day care services themselves. The effect was to shift the supply curve of day care services to the right from $S_{1990}$ to $S_{2000}$.

As you can see in Figure 11, the original market equilibrium—in 1990—was determined where the original demand and supply curves intersected at point $A$. Over the course of the decade, both curves shifted rightward. Therefore, you should not be surprised that the quantity of day care services increased over the decade. But what about the price? In fact, the demand curve shifted farther during the decade than the supply curve did. As a result, the equilibrium in 2000—shown at point $B$—featured a larger quantity *and* a higher price. What if it were the other way around so that supply increased by more than demand did? In that case, the total quantity exchanged would still have increased, but the price would have fallen.

Figure 11 illustrates just *one* possible combination of simultaneous shifts in supply and demand. But there are others. Table 5 summarizes what we *know* will happen to the equilibrium price ($P$) and quantity ($Q$), and what remains uncertain, in each case. For example, to find what happens when demand increases and

| TABLE 5 | | | |
|---|---|---|---|
| **EFFECT OF SUPPLY AND DEMAND SHIFTS ON EQUILIBRIUM PRICE ($P$) AND QUANTITY ($Q$)** | **Increase in Demand (Rightward Shift)** | **No Change in Demand** | **Decrease in Demand (Leftward Shift)** |
| Increase in Supply (Rightward Shift) | $P? Q\uparrow$ | $P\downarrow Q\uparrow$ | $P\downarrow Q?$ |
| No Change in Supply | $P\uparrow Q\uparrow$ | No change in $P$ or $Q$ | $P\downarrow Q\downarrow$ |
| Decrease in Supply (Leftward Shift) | $P\uparrow Q?$ | $P\uparrow Q\downarrow$ | $P? Q\downarrow$ |

supply decreases, look at the bottom, leftmost cell: The equilibrium price rises, while the equilibrium quantity might rise, fall, or remain the same.

Remember the advice in Chapter 1—to study economics actively rather than passively. This would be a good time to put down the book, pick up a pencil and paper, and see whether you can *work* with supply and demand curves, rather than just follow along as you read. Try to draw diagrams that illustrate each of the possibilities in Table 5.

# THE FOUR-STEP PROCEDURE

In this chapter, we built a model—a supply and demand model—and then used it to analyze price changes in several markets. You may not have noticed it, but we took four distinct Key Steps as the chapter proceeded. Economists take these same four steps to answer almost *any* question about the economy. Why? Because they are so effective in cutting through the chaos and confusion of the economy and helping us see how things really work.

In this book, we'll focus on this *four-step procedure,* which forms the core of economists' unique methodology. And we'll start right now by listing and discussing all four steps.

> **Key Step 1—Characterize the Market:** *Decide which market or markets best suit the problem being analyzed, and identify the decision markers (buyers and sellers) who interact in that market,*

 Characterize the Market

In economics, we make sense of the very complex, real-world economy by viewing it as a collection of *markets.* Each of these markets involves a group of *decision makers*—buyers and sellers—who have the potential to trade with each other. At the very beginning of any economic analysis, we must decide which market or markets to look at and how these markets should be *defined.*

To define a market, we must define (a) the thing being traded (such as maple syrup); (b) the decision makers in the market (such as maple syrup producers in New England and Canada on the selling side and households in Wichita on the buying side); and (c) the nature of competition in the market (such as the perfectly competitive markets we've looked at in this chapter). Keep in mind that whenever we draw market supply and demand curves we are treating the market as perfectly competitive, in which each individual buyer and seller treats the price as a given.

> **Key Step 2—Identify the Goals and Constraints:** *Identify the goals that the decision makers are trying to achieve, and the constraints they face in achieving those goals.*

 Identify Goals and Constraints

In every market, we assume that each decision maker is trying to achieve a specific goal. Typically, the goal will involve *maximizing some quantity.* Business firms, for example, are usually assumed to maximize profit. Households maximize utility— their well-being or satisfaction. In some cases, however, we might want to recognize that firms or households are actually groups of individuals with different agendas. While a firm's owners might want the firm to maximize profits, the managers might want to consider their own power, prestige, and job security. These goals may conflict, and the behavior of the firm will depend on how the conflict is resolved.

While economists often have spirited disagreements about *what* is being maximized, there is virtually unanimous agreement that, in any economic model, everyone is maximizing *something*. Even the behavior of groups—like the decision makers in a firm or officials of the federal government—is assumed to arise from the behavior of different maximizing individuals, each pursuing his or her own agenda.

In addition to having goals, decision makers also face constraints. Firms are constrained by their production technology, the prices they must pay for their inputs, and the price they can get for their output. Households are constrained by the prices they must pay for their purchases and by their limited incomes. Government agencies are constrained by the prices of the things they buy and by limited budgets. And even entire nations, as a whole, are constrained in their choices by the resources at their disposal.

Find the Equilibrium

> **Key Step 3—Find the Equilibrium:** *Describe the conditions necessary for equilibrium in the market, and a method for determining that equilibrium.*

Once we've defined a market and the goals and constraints of the decision makers there, we can usually find the point at which the market will come to rest—the *equilibrium*. In the perfectly competitive markets we analyzed in this chapter, in which each decision maker takes the price as a given, the equilibrium price is the one at which quantity demanded and quantity supplied are equal. This equilibrium is easy to find on a graph once you've drawn the supply and demand curves. It's simply the point of intersection between the two curves.

But remember: Not all markets are perfectly competitive—or even close to it. When we analyze *imperfectly* competitive markets, we'll have to find the market equilibrium in a different way, as you'll learn when you study microeconomics.

What Happens When Things Change?

> **Key Step 4—What Happens When Things Change:** *Explore how events or government policies change the market equilibrium.*

Almost every economic analysis ends with an exploration of how an event or policy change affects one or more markets. For example, in this chapter, we explored how an ice storm affected the market for maple syrup, how sudden increases in wealth affected the price of homes in San Francisco, and how both supply and demand changes affected the market for day care services.

Do economists really follow this same procedure to analyze almost *any* economic problem? Indeed they do. They use it to answer important *microeconomic* questions. Why does government intervention in a market to lower the price of a good (such as apartment rents) often backfire and sometimes harm the very people it was designed to help? Why do some people earn salaries that are hundreds of times higher than others? Why are economists virtually always skeptical of anyone who says they can "beat" the stock market, even if they have done so in the past? Later in this text, when we turn our attention to these questions, the four-step procedure will play a central role.

Economists also use the procedure to address important *macroeconomic* questions. What causes recessions, and what can we do to prevent them? Why has the United States experienced such low inflation in recent years, and how long can we expect our recent good fortune to continue? How will the Internet and other new technologies affect the growth rate of the U.S. economy?

In this book, we'll be taking these four Key Steps again and again, every time we want to understand an aspect of the economy. But from now on, you'll recognize the steps as we develop new models, because we'll be calling them to your attention as we use them.

Some of the chapters that follow will concentrate on just one or a few of the steps, while in others, we'll use the entire four-step procedure. To help you keep track, you'll often see icons in the margins of this book that remind you of which of the four steps is being studied. Whenever you see one of these icons, think about how the corresponding step is being used. If you do this, you will soon find yourself thinking like an economist.

You have already seen one of the payoffs to this approach: It can explain how prices are determined in perfectly competitive markets, or in markets that come close to perfect competition. But the four-step procedure takes us even further. It helps us understand how *all* types of markets operate, whether they are perfectly competitive or not. It helps us predict important changes in the economy and prepare for them. And it helps us design government policies to accomplish our social goals and avoid policies that are likely to backfire.

## ANTICIPATING A PRICE CHANGE

In the late 1980s, many East Coast colleges purchased expensive equipment that would enable them to switch rapidly from oil to natural gas as a source of heat. The idea was to protect the colleges from a sudden rise in oil prices, like the one they had suffered in the 1970s.

Finally, an event occurred that gave the colleges a change to put their new equipment to use: In the fall of 1990, Iraq invaded Kuwait. As oil prices skyrocketed, the colleges switched from burning oil to burning natural gas. The college administrators expected big savings on their energy bills. But they were in for a shock. When they received the bills from their local utilities, they found that the price of natural gas—like the price of oil—had risen sharply. As a result, they did not save much at all. Many of these administrators were angry at the utility companies and accused them of price gouging. Iraq's invasion of Kuwait, they reasoned, had not affected natural gas supplies at all, so there was no reason for the price of natural gas to rise.

Were the college administrators right? Was this just an example of price gouging by the utility companies who were taking advantage of an international crisis to increase their profits? A simple supply and demand analysis will give us the answer. More specifically, it will enable us to answer two questions: (1) Why did Iraq's invasion of Kuwait cause the price of oil to rise, and (2) Why did the price of natural gas rise as well?

Figure 12 shows supply-and-demand curves in one of the markets relevant to our analysis: the market for crude oil. In this market, oil producers—including those in Iraq and Kuwait—sell to American buyers. Before the invasion, the market was in equilibrium at $E$ with price $P_1$ and total output $Q_1$.

Then came the event that changed the equilibrium: Iraq's invasion and continued occupation of Kuwait—one of the largest oil producers in the world.

Before the Iraqi invasion of Kuwait, the oil market was in equilibrium at point *E*. The invasion and the resulting embargo on Iraqi oil decreased supply to $S_2$. Price increased to $P_2$, and the quantity exchanged fell to $Q_2$.

**THE MARKET FOR OIL**

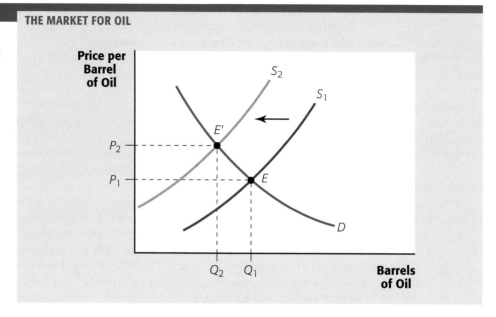

Immediately after the invasion, the United States led a worldwide embargo on oil from both Iraq and Kuwait. As far as the oil market was concerned, it was as if these nations' oil fields no longer existed—a significant decrease in the oil industry's productive capacity. If you look back at Figure 6, you will see that a decrease in productive capacity shifts the supply curve to the left, and this is just what happened. The new equilibrium at *E'* occurred at a lower quantity and a higher price. This change in the oil market's equilibrium was well understood by most people—including the college administrators—and no one was surprised when oil prices rose.

But what has all this got to do with natural gas prices? Everything, as the next part of our analysis will show.

Figure 13 shows the next market relevant to our analysis: the market for natural gas. In this market, world producers (which did not include Iraq or Kuwait) sell natural gas to American buyers. In this market, the initial equilibrium—before the invasion and before the rise in oil prices—was at point *F*. How did the invasion affect the equilibrium?

Oil is a *substitute* for natural gas. A rise in the price of a substitute, we know, will increase the demand for a good. (Look back at Figure 3 if you need a reminder.) In this case, the increase in the price of oil caused the demand curve for natural gas to shift rightward. In Figure 13, the price of natural gas rose from $P_3$ to $P_4$.

The administrators were right that the invasion of Kuwait did not affect the supply of natural gas. What they missed, however, was the invasion's effect on the *demand* for natural gas. With a fuller understanding of supply and demand, they could have predicted—*before* investing in their expensive switching equipment—that any rise in oil prices would cause a rise in natural gas prices. Armed with this knowledge, they would have anticipated a much smaller savings in energy costs from switching to natural gas and might have decided that there were better uses for their scarce funds.

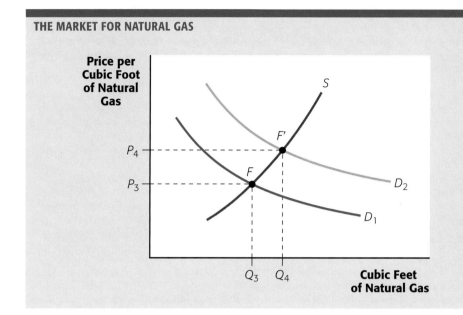

**FIGURE 13**

**THE MARKET FOR NATURAL GAS**

Oil is a substitute for natural gas. A rise in the price of oil increases the demand for natural gas. Here, demand for natural gas increases from $D_1$ to $D_2$ and the price rises from $P_3$ to $P_4$.

## S U M M A R Y

In a market economy, prices are determined through the interaction of buyers and sellers in *markets*. *Perfectly competitive* markets have many buyers and sellers, and none of them individually can affect the market price. If at least one buyer or seller has the power to influence the price of a product, the market is *imperfectly competitive*.

The model of *supply and demand* explains how prices are determined in perfectly competitive markets. The *quantity demanded* of any good is the total amount buyers would choose to purchase at a given price. The *law of demand* states that quantity demanded is negatively related to price; it tells us

that the *demand curve* slopes downward. The demand curve is drawn for given levels of income, wealth, tastes, and prices of substitute and complementary goods. If any of those factors changes, the demand curve will shift.

The *quantity supplied* of a good is the total amount sellers would choose to produce and sell at a given price. According to the *law of supply*, supply curves slope upward. The supply curve will shift if there is a change in the price of an input, the price of an alternate good, productive capacity, or expectations of future prices.

## K E Y   T E R M S

aggregation
imperfectly competitive
    market
perfectly competitive market
individual's quantity
    demanded
market quantity demanded
law of demand
demand schedule

market demand curve
change in quantity
    demanded
change in demand
income
wealth
normal good
inferior good
substitute

complement
technology
firm's quantity supplied
market quantity supplied
law of supply
supply schedule
supply curve
change in quantity supplied
change in supply

alternate goods
equilibrium
excess demand
excess supply

## REVIEW QUESTIONS

1. How does the way each of the following terms is used in economics differ from the way it is used in everyday language?
   a. market
   b. demand
   c. normal good
   d. inferior good
   e. supply

2. What is the difference between *demand* and *quantity demanded*?

3. List and briefly explain the factors that can shift a demand curve and the factors that can shift a supply curve.

4. What is the difference between substitutes and complements? Which of the following pairs of goods are substitutes, which are complements, and which are neither?
   a. Coke and Pepsi
   b. Computer hardware and computer software
   c. Beef and chicken
   d. Salt and sugar
   e. Ice cream and frozen yogurt

5. Rank each of the following markets according to how close you think it comes to perfect competition:
   a. Wheat
   b. Personal computer hardware
   c. Gold
   d. Airline tickets from New York to Kalamazoo, Michigan

6. Is each of the following goods more likely to be *normal* or *inferior*?
   a. Lexus automobiles
   b. Secondhand clothes
   c. Imported beer
   d. Baby-sitting services
   e. Recapped tires
   f. Futons
   g. Home haircutting tools
   h. Restaurant meals

7. What does the term *equilibrium* mean in economics?

8. Explain why the price in a free market will not remain above or below equilibrium for long, unless there is outside interference.

9. Determine whether each of the following will cause a change in demand or a change in supply, and in which direction:
   a. Input prices increase.
   b. Income in an area declines.
   c. The price of an alternate good increases.
   d. Tastes shift away from a good.

10. In the Using the Theory section at the end of this chapter, three of the Key Steps in the four-step procedure are mentioned explicitly, and one step is implicit.
   a. Identify the three Key Steps explicitly used in the analysis, and briefly describe *where* each is used.
   b. For the "missing step," write a sentence or two to be inserted in the analysis that would describe how the step is used.

## PROBLEMS AND EXERCISES

1. In the late 1990s, beef—which had fallen out of favor in the 1970s and 1980s—became popular again. On a supply and demand diagram, illustrate the effect of such a change on equilibrium price and quantity in the market for beef.

2. Discuss, and illustrate with a graph, how each of the following events will affect the market for coffee:

   a. A blight on coffee plants kills off much of the Brazilian crop.
   b. The price of tea declines.
   c. Coffee workers organize themselves into a union and gain higher wages.
   d. Coffee is shown to cause cancer in laboratory rats.
   e. Coffee prices are expected to rise rapidly in the near future.

3. The following table gives hypothetical data for the quantity of gasoline demanded and supplied in Los Angeles per month.

| Price per Gallon | Quantity Demanded Millions of Gallons | Quantity Supplied Millions of Gallons |
|---|---|---|
| $1.20 | 170 | 80 |
| $1.30 | 156 | 105 |
| $1.40 | 140 | 140 |
| $1.50 | 123 | 175 |
| $1.60 | 100 | 210 |
| $1.70 | 95 | 238 |

    a. Graph the demand and supply curves.
    b. Find the equilibrium price and quantity.
    c. Illustrate on your graph how a rise in the price of automobiles would affect the gasoline market.

4. How would each of the following affect the market for blue jeans in the United States? Illustrate each answer with a supply and demand diagram.
    a. The price of denim cloth increases.
    b. An influx of immigrants arrives in the United States. (Explicitly state any assumptions you are making.)
    c. An economic slowdown in the United States causes household incomes to decrease.

5. Indicate which curve shifted—and in which direction— for each of the following.
    a. The price of furniture rises as the quantity bought and sold falls.
    b. Apartment vacancy rates increase while average monthly rent on apartments declines.
    c. The price of personal computers continues to decline as sales skyrocket.

6. Draw supply and demand diagrams from two different markets, and label the markets A and B. Then use your diagrams to illustrate the impact of the following events. In each case, determine what happens to price and quantity in each market.
    a. A and B are substitutes, and producers expect the price of good A to rise in the future.
    b. A and B satisfy the same kinds of desires, and there is a shift in tastes away from A and toward B.
    c. A is a normal good, while B is an inferior good. Incomes in the community increase.
    d. A and B are complementary goods. There is a technological advance in the production of good B.

## C H A L L E N G E    Q U E S T I O N S

1. Suppose that demand is given by the equation $Q_D = 500 - 50P$, where $Q_D$ is quantity demanded, and $P$ is the price of the good. Supply is described by the equation $Q_S = 50 + 25P$, where $Q_S$ is quantity supplied. What is the equilibrium price and quantity?

2. A Wall Street analyst observes the following equilibrium price-quantity combinations in the market for restaurant meals in a city over a four-year period:

| Year | P | Q |
|---|---|---|
| (Thousands of Meals per Month) | | |
| 1 | $12 | 20 |
| 2 | $15 | 30 |
| 3 | $17 | 40 |
| 4 | $20 | 50 |

She concludes that the market defies the law of demand. Is she correct? Why or why not?

3. While crime rates have fallen across the country over the past few years, they have fallen especially rapidly in Manhattan. At the same time, there are some neighborhoods in the New York Metropolitan Area in which the crime rate has remained constant. Using supply and demand diagrams for rental housing, explain how a falling crime rate in Manhattan could make the residents in *other* neighborhoods *worse off*. (Hint: As people from around the country move to Manhattan, what happens to rents there? If someone cannot afford to pay higher rent in Manhattan, what might they do?)

## EXPERIENTIAL EXERCISES

1.  Visit the *Dismal Scientist* Web page at *http://www.dismal.com,* and find an article that you think involves supply and demand considerations. Once you understand the argument, try to present it, using a graph. What is the market being considered, and who are the suppliers and who are the demanders in this market (Key Step #1)? What are the goals of the decision makers on each side of the market, and what are their constraints (Key Step #2)? Is this a market in which the equilibrium is changing (Key Steps #3 and #4)? Explain.

http://

2.  You now have a basic understanding of supply and demand. Find a relevant current article using Infotrac or the *Wall Street Journal* and interpret it, using a supply and demand diagram. Explain at least one situation in which a curve shifts. What caused the shift, and how did it affect price and quantity?

# WHAT MACROECONOMICS TRIES TO EXPLAIN

You have no doubt seen photographs of the earth taken from satellites thousands of miles away. Viewed from that great distance, the world's vast oceans look like puddles, its continents like mounds of dirt, and its mountain ranges like wrinkles on a bedspread. In contrast to our customary view from the earth's surface—of a car, a tree, a building—this is a view of the big picture.

What, you may be wondering, could this possibly have to do with economics? Actually, quite a bit: These two different ways of viewing the earth— from up close or from thousands of miles away—are analogous to two different ways of viewing the economy. When we look through the *microeconomic* lens—from up close—we see the behavior of *individual decision makers* and *individual markets*. When we look through the *macroeconomic* lens—from a distance—these smaller features fade away, and we see only the broad outlines of the economy.

Which view is better? That depends on what we're trying to do. If we want to know why rents are so high in big cities, why computers are getting better and cheaper each year, or why the earnings of anesthesiologists are falling, we need the close-up view of microeconomics. But to answer questions about the *overall* economy—what determines the amount of unemployment, how fast the average standard of living will rise over the next decade, or how fast prices will rise—we need the more comprehensive view of *macroeconomics*.

## MACROECONOMIC GOALS

While there is some disagreement among economists about *how* to make the macroeconomy perform well, there is widespread agreement about the goals we are trying to achieve:

> *Economists—and society at large—agree on three important macroeconomic goals: rapid economic growth, full employment, and stable prices.*

Why is there such universal agreement on these three goals? Because achieving them gives us the opportunity to make *all* of our citizens better off. Let's take a closer look at each of these goals and see why they are so important.

## RAPID ECONOMIC GROWTH

Imagine that you were a typical American worker living at the beginning of the twentieth century. You would work about 60 hours every week, and your yearly salary—about $450—would buy a bit less than $8,000 would buy today. You could expect to die at the age of 47. If you fell seriously ill before then, your doctor wouldn't be able to help much: There were no X-ray machines or blood tests, and little effective medicine for the few diseases that could be diagnosed. You would probably never hear the sounds produced by the best musicians of the day, or see the performances of the best actors, dancers, or singers. And the most exotic travel you'd enjoy would likely be a trip to a nearby state.

Today, the typical worker has it considerably better. He or she works about 35 hours per week, and is paid about $31,000 per year, not to mention fringe benefits such as health insurance, retirement benefits, and paid vacation. Thanks to advances in medicine, nutrition, and hygiene, the average man can expect to live to age 73, and the average woman to age 80. And more of a worker's free time today is really free: There are machines to do laundry and dishes, cars to get to and from work, telephones for quick communication, and—increasingly—personal computers to keep track of finances, appointments, and correspondence. Finally, during their lifetimes, most Americans will have traveled—for enjoyment—to many locations in the United States and abroad.

What is responsible for these dramatic changes in economic well-being? The answer is three words: *rapid economic growth*. In the United States—as in most developed economies—our output of goods and services has risen faster than the population. As a result, the average person can consume much more today—more food, clothing, housing, medical care, entertainment, and travel—than in the year 1900.

Economists monitor economic growth by keeping track of *real gross domestic product (real GDP)*—the total quantity of goods and services produced in a country over a year. When real GDP rises faster than the population, output per person rises, and so does the average standard of living.

Figure 1 shows real GDP in the United States from 1920 to 1999, measured in dollars of output at 1996 prices. As you can see, real GDP has increased dramatically over the greater part of the century. Part of the reason for the rise is an increase in population: More workers can produce more output. But real GDP has actually increased *faster* than the population: During this period, while the U.S. population did not quite triple, the quantity of goods and services produced each year has increased more than tenfold. Hence, the remarkable rise in the average American's living standard.

But when we look more closely at the data, we discover something important: Although output has grown, the *rate* of growth has varied over long periods of time. From 1959 to 1973, output per person grew, on average, by 4.1 percent per year. But from 1973 to 1991, average annual growth slowed to 2.7 percent. Then, from 1991 to 1999, growth picked up again, averaging 3.6 percent per year. These may seem like slight differences. But over long periods of time, such small differences in growth rates can cause huge differences in living standards. For example, suppose that for the entire period from 1973 to 1999, output per person had grown at its previous pace of 4.1 percent per year, instead of its actual rate. Then we'd have produced more output in *each* of those 26 years. By 1999, our real annual GDP would have been $11,578 billion instead of $8,861 billion. That increase in GDP would have been enough to give every man, woman, and child in the country an additional $10,000 in goods and services from that year's production alone.

**FIGURE 1**

**U.S. REAL GROSS DOMESTIC PRODUCT, 1920–1999**

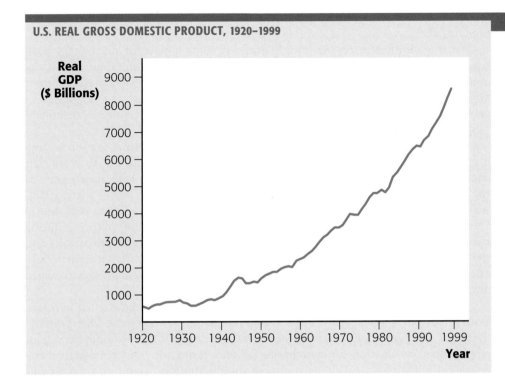

Real GDP has increased dramatically over the past 80 years. In the figure, real GDP is measured in dollars of output valued at 1996 prices. (The measurement of real GDP will be discussed in more detail in the next two chapters.)

Economists and government officials are very concerned when economic growth slows down. Growth increases the size of the economic pie, so it becomes possible—at least in principle—for every citizen to have a larger slice. This is why economists agree that growth is a good thing.

But in practice, growth does *not* benefit everyone. Living standards will always rise more rapidly for some groups than for others, and some may even find their slice of the pie shrinking. For example, since the late 1980s, economic growth has improved the living standards of the highly skilled, while less-skilled workers have actually become worse off. Partly, this is due to improvements in technology that have lowered the earnings of workers whose roles can be taken by computers and machines. But very few economists would advocate a halt to growth as a solution to the problems of unskilled workers. Some believe that, in the long run, everyone will indeed benefit from growth. Others see a role for the government in taxing successful people and providing benefits to those left behind by growth. But in either case, economic growth—by increasing the size of the overall pie—is seen as an important part of the solution.

## HIGH EMPLOYMENT

Economic growth is one of our most important goals, but not the only one. Suppose our real GDP were growing at, say, a 3 percent annual rate, but 10 percent of the workforce was unable to find work. Although the economy would be growing at a healthy pace, we would not be achieving our full economic potential—our average standard of living would not be as high as it *could be*. There would be millions of people who wanted jobs, who *could* be producing output we could all use, but who would not be producing anything. This is one reason why consistently *high employment*—or consistently *low unemployment*—is an important macroeconomic goal.

But there is another reason, too. In addition to its impact on our average standard of living, unemployment also affects the distribution of economic well-being among our citizens. People who cannot find jobs suffer. Their incomes, and their ability to buy goods and services, decrease. And even though many of the jobless receive unemployment benefits and other assistance from the government, the unemployed typically have lower living standards than the employed.

One measure economists use to keep track of employment is the *unemployment rate*, which is the percentage of the workforce that would like to work, but cannot find jobs. Figure 2 shows the average unemployment rate during each of the past 80 years. Notice that the unemployment rate is never zero—there are always *some* people looking for work, even when the economy is doing well. But in some years, unemployment is unusually high. The worst example occurred during the Great Depression of the 1930s, when millions of workers lost their jobs and the unemployment rate reached 25 percent. One in four potential workers could not find a job. More recently, in 1982 and 1983, the unemployment rate averaged almost 10 percent.

The nation's commitment to high employment has twice been written into law. With the memory of the Great Depression still fresh, Congress passed the *Employment Act of 1946,* which required the federal government to "promote maximum employment, production, and purchasing power." It did not, however, dictate a target rate of unemployment the government should aim for. A numerical target was added in 1978, when Congress passed the *Full Employment and Balanced Growth Act,* which called for an unemployment rate of 4 percent.

A glance at Figure 2 shows how seldom we have hit this target over the last few decades. In fact, we did not hit it at all through the 1970s and 1980s. But in the 1990s, we came closer and closer and finally—in January 2000—we reached the target again for the first time since the 1960s. In future chapters, you will learn why

**FIGURE 2**

The unemployment rate fluctuates over time. During the Great Depression of the 1930s, unemployment was extremely high, reaching 25 percent in 1933. In the early 1980s, the rate averaged 10 percent.

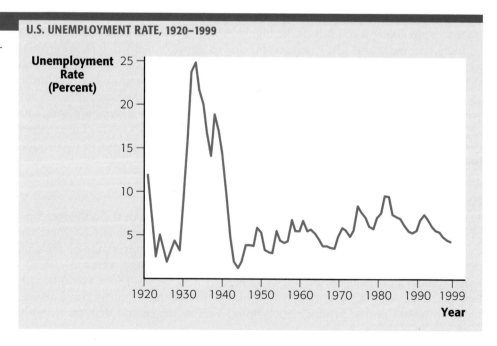

U.S. UNEMPLOYMENT RATE, 1920–1999

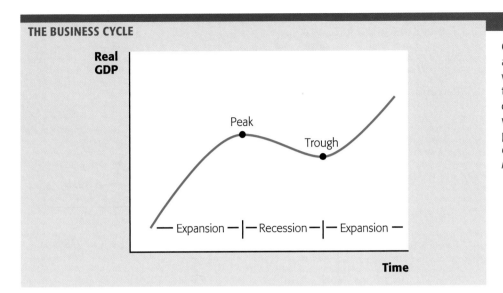

**THE BUSINESS CYCLE**

**FIGURE 3**

Over time, real GDP fluctuates around an overall upward trend. Such fluctuations are called *business cycles*. When output rises, we are in the expansion phase of the cycle; when output falls, we are in a *recession*.

the unemployment rate has often been higher than its target, why we were able to hit the target in January 2000, and—more generally—what the government can and cannot do to achieve its goal of low unemployment.

**Employment and the Business Cycle.** When firms produce more output, they hire more workers; when they produce less output, they tend to lay off workers. We would thus expect real GDP and employment to be closely related, and indeed they are. In recent years, each 1 percent drop in output has been associated with the loss of about half a million jobs. Consistently high employment, then, requires a high, stable level of output. Unfortunately, output has *not* been very stable. If you look back at Figure 1, you will see that while real GDP has climbed upward over time, it has been a bumpy ride. The periodic fluctuations in GDP—the bumps in the figure—are called **business cycles.**

Figure 3 shows a close-up view of a hypothetical business cycle. When output rises, we are in the **expansion** phase, which continues until we reach a **peak.** Then, as output falls, we enter a **recession**—a period of declining output. When output hits bottom, we are in the **trough** of the recession.

Of course, real-world business cycles never look quite like the smooth, symmetrical cycle in Figure 3, but rather like the jagged, irregular cycles of Figure 1. Recessions can be severe or mild, and they can last several years or less than a single year. When a recession is particularly severe and long lasting, it is called a **depression.** In the twentieth century, the United States experienced just one decline in output serious enough to be considered a depression—the worldwide *Great Depression* of the 1930s. From 1929 to 1933, the first four years of the Great Depression, U.S. output dropped by more than 25 percent.

But even during more normal times, the economy has gone through many recessions. Since 1959, we have suffered through two severe recessions (in 1974–75 and 1981–82) and several less severe ones, such as the recession of 1990 to 1991. Later in this book, you will learn about some of the causes of recessions, why we have not been able to eliminate them entirely, and what we *may* be able to do to make them milder in the future.

**Business cycles** Fluctuations in real GDP around its long-term growth trend.

**Expansion** A period of increasing real GDP.

**Peak** The point at which real GDP reaches its highest level during an expansion.

**Recession** A period of declining or abnormally low real GDP.

**Trough** The point at which real GPD reaches its lowest level during a recession.

**Depression** An unusually severe recession.

**FIGURE 4**

In most years, the inflation rate has been positive. The overall price level increased during those years.

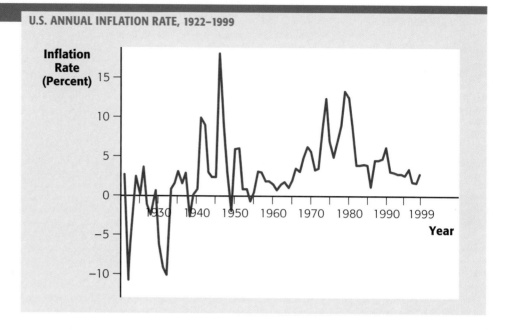

**U.S. ANNUAL INFLATION RATE, 1922–1999**

## STABLE PRICES

Figure 4 shows the annual inflation rate—the percentage increase in the average level of prices—from 1922 to 1999.[1] With very few exceptions, the inflation rate has been positive—on average, prices have risen in each of those years. But notice the wide variations in inflation. In 1979 and 1980, we had double-digit inflation—prices rose by more than 12 percent in both years. During that time, polls showed that people were more concerned about inflation than any other national problem—more than unemployment, crime, poverty, pollution, or anything else. During the 1990s, the inflation rate averaged less than 3 percent per year, and it has stayed low through early 2000. As a result, we hardly seem to notice it at all. Pollsters no longer include "rising prices" as a category when asking about the most important problems facing the country.

Other countries have not been so lucky. In the 1980s, several Latin American nations experienced inflation rates of thousands of percent per year. In the early 1990s, some of the newly emerging nations of Central Europe and the former Soviet Union suffered annual inflation rates in the triple digits. An extreme case was the new nation of Serbia, where prices rose by 1,880 percent in the single month of August 1993. If prices had continued to rise at that rate all year, the annual inflation rate would have been 363,000,000,000,000,000 percent.

Why are stable prices—a low inflation rate—an important macroeconomic goal? Because inflation is *costly* to society. With annual inflation rates in the thousands of percent, the costs are easy to see: The value of the currency—its purchasing power—declines so rapidly that people are no longer willing to hold it. This breakdown of the monetary system forces people to waste valuable time and resources bartering with each other—for example, trading plumbing services for dentistry services. With so much time spent trying to find trading partners, there is little time left for producing goods and services. As a result, the average standard of living falls.

---

[1]    The figure is based on the Consumer Price Index, the most popular measure of the price level, as well as historical estimates of what this index *would* have been in the early part of the twentieth century, before the index existed. We'll discuss the Consumer Price Index and other measures of inflation in more detail in later chapters.

With more modest inflation, like the double-digit rates the United States experienced in the late 1970s, the costs to society are less obvious and less severe. But they are still significant. And when it comes time to bring down even a modest inflation rate, painful corrective actions by government are required. These actions cause output to decline and unemployment to rise. For example, in order to bring the inflation rate down from the high levels of the early 1980s (see Figure 4), government policy purposely caused a severe recession in 1981–82, reducing output (Figure 1) and increasing unemployment (Figure 2).

The previous paragraph raises a number of questions. How, precisely, does a modest inflation harm society? Why would a recession reduce inflation? And how does the government create a recession? If you're a bit confused, don't worry. You are just beginning your study of macroeconomics, and we have a lot of ground to cover.

# THE MACROECONOMIC APPROACH

If you have already studied *microeconomics*, you will notice much that is familiar in *macroeconomics*. The *four-step procedure* plays an important role in both branches of the field. But the macroeconomic approach is different from the microeconomic approach in significant ways. Most importantly, in *microeconomics*, we typically apply our 4 Key Steps to *one market at a time*—the market for soybeans, for neurosurgeons, or for car washes. In *macroeconomics*, by contrast, we want to understand how the entire economy behaves. Thus, we will be applying the key steps to *all markets simultaneously*. This includes not only markets for goods and services, but also markets for labor and for financial assets like bonds and foreign currency.

How can we possibly hope to deal with all of these markets at the same time? One way would be to build a gigantic model that included every individual market in the economy. The model would have tens of thousands of supply and demand curves, which could be used to determine tens of thousands of prices and quantities. With today's fast, powerful computers, we could, in principle, build this kind of model.

But it would not be easy. We would need to gather data on every good and service in the economy, every type of labor, every type of financial asset, and so on. As you might guess, this would be a formidable task, requiring thousands of workers just to gather the data alone. And in the end, the model would not prove very useful. We would not learn much about the economy from it: With so many individual trees, we could not see the forest. Moreover, the model's predictions would be highly suspect: With so much information and so many moving parts, high standards of accuracy are difficult to maintain. Even the government of the former Soviet Union, which directed production throughout the economy until the 1990s, was unable to keep track of all the markets under its control. In a market economy, where production decisions are made by individual firms, the task would be even harder.

What, then, is a macroeconomist to do? The answer is a word that you will become very familiar with in the chapters to come: **aggregation**—the process of combining different things into a single category and treating them as a whole. Let's take a closer look at how aggregation is used in macroeconomics.

**Aggregation** The process of combining different things into a single category.

## AGGREGATION IN MACROECONOMICS

Aggregation is a basic tool of reasoning, one that you often use without being aware of it. If you say, "I applied for five jobs last month," you are aggregating five very different workplaces into the single category, *jobs*. Whenever you say, "I'm going out with my friends," you are combining several different people into

DANGEROUS
CURVES

In many English words, the prefix *macro* means "large" and *micro* means "small." As a result, you might think that in microeconomics, we study economic units in which small sums of money are involved, while in macroeconomics we study units involving greater sums. But this is not correct: The annual output of General Motors is considerably greater than the total annual output of many small countries, such as Estonia or Guatemala. Yet when we study the behavior of General Motors, we are practicing *microeconomics,* and when we study the causes of unemployment in Estonia, we are practicing *macroeconomics.* Why? Microeconomics is concerned with the behavior and interaction of *individual* firms and markets, even if they are very large; macroeconomics is concerned with the behavior of *entire economies,* even if they are very small.

a single category: people you consider *friends.*

Aggregation plays a key role in both micro- and macroeconomics. Microeconomists will speak of the market for automobiles, lumping Toyotas, Fords, BMWs, and other types of cars into a single category. But in macroeconomics, we take aggregation to the extreme. Because we want to consider the entire economy at once, and yet keep our model

as simple as possible, we must aggregate all markets into the broadest possible categories. For example, we lump together all the millions of different goods and services—computers, coffee tables, egg rolls, newspapers—into the single category, *output.* Similarly, we combine the thousands of different types of workers in the economy—doctors, construction workers, plumbers, college professors—into the category, *labor.* By aggregating in this way, we can create workable and reasonably accurate models that teach us a great deal about how the overall economy operates.

## MACROECONOMIC CONTROVERSIES

Macroeconomics is full of disputes and disagreements. Indeed, modern macroeconomics—which began with the publication of *The General Theory of Employment, Interest, and Money,* by British economist John Maynard Keynes in 1936—originated in controversy. Keynes was taking on the conventional wisdom of his time—*classical economics*—which held that the macroeconomy worked very well on its own, and the best policy for the government to follow was *laissez faire*—"leave it alone." As he was working on *The General Theory,* Keynes wrote to his friend, the playwright George Bernard Shaw, "I believe myself to be writing a book on economic theory which will largely revolutionize—not, I suppose, at once but in the course of the next ten years—the way the world thinks about economic problems." Keynes's prediction was on the money. After the publication of his book, economists argued about its merits, but 10 years later, the majority of the profession had been won over; they had become Keynesians. This new school of thought held that the economy does *not* do well on its own (one needed only to look at the Great Depression for evidence) and requires continual guidance from an activist and well-intentioned government.

From the late 1940s until the early 1960s, events seemed to prove the Keynesians correct. Then, beginning in the 1960s, several distinguished economists began to challenge Keynesian ideas. Their counterrevolutionary views—which in many ways mirrored those of the classical economists—were strengthened by events in the 1970s, when the economy's behavior began to contradict the most important Keynesian ideas. While some of the early disagreements have been resolved, others have arisen to take their place.

Some of today's controversies are purely *positive* in nature. For example, in a later chapter you will learn about the Federal Reserve System—the central bank in the United States—which can influence many important macroeconomic aggregates, such as output, employment, and the inflation rate. As this is being written (early 2000), most economists believe that the Federal Reserve (or "Fed") is doing an excellent job of managing these aggregates. They point out that the Fed has successfully engineered high employment and rapid economic growth for almost a decade, without overheating the economy and risking future inflation. A few economists, however, think that the Fed has made a mistake. They believe that it has indeed been overheating the economy, which will lead to higher inflation in the future. (Are you confused about the connections between rapid economic growth, overheating the economy, and future inflation? Don't worry: All of this will be explained in later chapters.)

To some extent, this is a *positive* disagreement: The two sides have different views about how the economy is performing now, and what that performance implies about the future. That is, it's in part a disagreement about *how the economy works*.

But for some, the controversy is also *normative*. We might find two economists who agree about the extent to which the Fed's current policies are risking future inflation. But they might disagree strongly about the wisdom of the gamble because of differences in *values*. One economist may place more weight on high employment and rapid growth, and may be willing to risk future inflation to achieve them. The other might put more weight on avoiding future inflation, even if it means lower employment and slower growth now.

Economists, like all other human beings, hold different values, and often hold them strongly. Not surprisingly, disagreements among economists are often emotionally charged. But there is also more agreement than meets the eye. Macroeconomists agree on many basic principles, and we will stress these as we go. And even when there are strong disagreements, there is surprising consensus on the approach that should be taken to resolve them.

## AS YOU STUDY MACROECONOMICS . . .

Macroeconomics is a fascinating and wide-ranging subject. You will find that each piece of the macroeconomic puzzle connects to all of the other pieces in many different ways. Each time one of your questions is answered, 10 more will spring up in your mind, each demanding immediate attention. This presents a problem for a textbook writer, and for your instructor as well: What is the best order to present the principles of macroeconomics? We could follow the line of questions that occur to the curious reader, but this would be an organizational disaster. For example, learning about unemployment raises questions about international trade, but it also raises questions about government spending, government regulations, economic growth, wages, banking, and much, much more. And each of these topics raises questions about still others. Organizing the material in this way would make you feel like a ball in a pinball machine, bouncing from bumper to bumper. Still, the pinball approach—bouncing from topic to topic—is the one taken by the media when reporting on the economy. If you have ever tried to learn economics from a newspaper, you know how frustrating this approach can be.

In our study of macroeconomics, we will follow a different approach: presenting material as it is *needed* for what follows. In this way, what you learn in one chapter will form the foundation for the material in the next, and your understanding of macroeconomics will deepen as you go.

But be forewarned: This approach requires considerable patience on your part. Many of the questions that will pop into your head will have to be postponed until the proper foundations for answering them have been established. It might help, though, to give you a *brief* indication of what is to come.

In the next two chapters, we will discuss three of the most important aggregates in macroeconomics: output, employment, and the price level. You will see why each

Two excellent print sources for news on the U.S. and world economies are *The Wall Street Journal* and *The Economist,* a British Magazine.

of these is important to our economic well-being, how we keep track of them with government statistics, and how to interpret these statistics with a critical eye.

Then, in the remainder of the book, we study how the macroeconomy operates, starting with its behavior in the long run. Here, you will learn what makes an economy grow over long periods of time, and which government policies are likely to help or hinder that growth.

Then, we turn our attention to the short run. You will learn why the economy behaves differently in the short run than in the long run, why we have business cycles, and how these cycles may be affected by government policies. Then we'll expand our analysis to include the banking system and the money supply, and the special challenges they pose for government policy makers.

Finally, we'll turn our attention to the special problems of a global economy. You'll learn how trade with other nations constrains and expands our macro policy options at home and how economic events abroad influence our own economy. You will also learn why the United States has run persistent trade deficits with the rest of the world and what that means for our citizens.

This sounds like quite a lot of ground to cover, and indeed, it is. But it's not as daunting as it might sound. Remember that the study of macroeconomics—like the macroeconomy itself—is not a series of separate units, but an integrated whole. As you go from chapter to chapter, each principle you learn is a stepping-stone to the next one. Little by little, your knowledge and understanding will accumulate and deepen. Most students are genuinely surprised at how well they understand the macroeconomy after a single introductory course, and find the reward well worth the effort.

## S U M M A R Y

Macroeconomics is the study of the economy as a whole. It deals with issues such as economic growth, unemployment, inflation, and government policies that might influence the overall level of economic activity.

Economists generally agree about the importance of three main macroeconomic goals. The first of these is rapid economic growth. If output—real gross domestic product— grows faster than population, the average person can enjoy an improved standard of living.

High employment is another important goal. In the United States and other market economies, the main source of households' incomes is labor earnings. When unemployment is high, many people are without jobs and must cut back their purchases of goods and services.

The third macroeconomic goal is stable prices. This goal is important because inflation imposes costs on society. Keeping the rate of inflation low helps to reduce these costs.

Because an economy like that of the United States is so large and complex, the models we use to analyze the economy must be highly aggregated. For example, we will lump together millions of different goods to create an aggregate called "output" and combine all their prices into a single "price index."

## K E Y   T E R M S

| business cycles | peak | trough | aggregation |
| expansion | recession | depression | |

## R E V I E W   Q U E S T I O N S

1. Discuss the similarities and differences between macroeconomics and microeconomics.

2. What is the basic tool macroeconomists use to deal with the complexity and variety of economic markets and institutions? Give some examples of how they use this tool.

3. List the nation's macroeconomic goals and explain why each is important.

4. Consider an economy whose real GDP is growing at 4 percent per year. What else would you need to know in order to say whether the average standard of living is improving or deteriorating?

## CHALLENGE QUESTION

Speculate about some factors that might help explain the post-1973 growth slowdown. What changes in the economy or in society as a whole may have contributed to this phenomenon? Why might growth have speeded up again in the late 1990s?

## EXPERIENTIAL EXERCISES

1. Which of the three macroeconomic goals mentioned in this chapter do you think is the most important today? Use *The Wall Street Journal* or Infotrac to support your conclusions. Do this by finding several recent articles that mention rapid growth, high employment, and stable prices. Then point to the emphasis each goal receives in these articles.

2. The Index of Leading Economic Indicators is an economic statistic that is sometimes used to predict how the economy will behave over the next several months. You can find it at *http://www.conference-board.org/products/frames.cfm?main=lei1.cfm*. Read up on the Index and see if you can explain how some of the individual components are related to overall economic performance.

http://

# 5 PRODUCTION, INCOME, AND EMPLOYMENT

On the first Friday of every month, at 8:00 A.M., dozens of journalists mill about in a room in the Department of Labor. They are waiting for the arrival of the press officer from the government's Bureau of Labor Statistics. When she enters the room, carrying a stack of papers, the buzz of conversation stops. The papers—which she passes out to the waiting journalists—contain the monthly report on the experience of the American workforce. They summarize everything the government knows about hiring and firing at businesses across the country; about the number of people working, the hours they worked, and the incomes they earned; and about the number of people *not* working and what they did instead. All of this information is broken down by industry, state, city, race, sex, and age. But one number looms large in the journalists' minds as they scan the report and compose their stories: the percentage of the labor force that could not find jobs, or the nation's *unemployment rate*.

Once every three months, a similar scene takes place at the Department of Commerce, as reporters wait for the release of the quarterly report on the nation's output of goods and services and the incomes we have earned from producing it. Once again, the report includes tremendous detail. Output is broken down by industry and by the sector that purchased it (ordinary households, businesses, government agencies, and foreigners), and income is broken down into the different types of earners—wage earners, property owners, and owners of small businesses. And once again, the reporters' eyes will focus on a single number, a number that will dominate their stories and create headlines in newspapers across the country: the nation's *gross domestic product*.

The government knows that its reports on employment and production will have a major impact on the American political scene, and on financial markets in the United States and around the world. So it takes great pains to ensure fair and equal access to the information. For example, the Bureau of Labor Statistics allows journalists to look at the employment report at 8:00 A.M. on the day of the release (the first Friday of every month). But all who see the report must stay inside a room—appropriately called the lockup room—and cannot contact the outside world until the official release time of 8:30 A.M. At precisely 8:29 A.M., the reporters are permitted to hook up their laptop modems, and then a countdown begins, ending at precisely 8:30 A.M. At that moment—and not a second before—the reporters are permitted to transmit their stories. At the same instant, the Bureau posts its report on an Internet Web site. (The URL is *http://stats.bls.gov/blshome.html.*)

The reactions to the government's reports come almost immediately. Within seconds, wire-service headlines appear on computer screens across the country—"Unemployment Rate Up Two-Tenths of a Percent" or "Nation's Production Steady." Within minutes, financial traders, regarding these news flashes as clues about the economy's future, make snap decisions to buy or sell, and prices move in the stock and bond markets. This creates further headlines—"Stock Market Plunges on Unemployment Data" or "Bonds Rally on Output Report." Within the hour, politicians and pundits will respond with sound bites, attacking or defending the administration's economic policies.

Why is so much attention given to the government's reports on production and employment, and—in particular—to those two numbers: gross domestic product and the unemployment rate? Because they describe aspects of the economy that dramatically affect each of us individually and our society as a whole. In this chapter, we will take our first look at production and employment in the economy. The purpose here is not to explain what causes these variables to rise or fall—that will come a few chapters later, when we begin to study macroeconomic models. Here, we will focus on the reality behind the numbers: what the statistics tell us about the economy, how the government obtains them, and how they are sometimes misused.

# PRODUCTION AND GROSS DOMESTIC PRODUCT

You have probably heard the phrase *gross domestic product*—or its more familiar abbreviation, GDP—many times. It is one of those economic terms that is frequently used by the media and by politicians. In the first part of this chapter, we take a close look at GDP, starting with a careful definition.

## GDP: A DEFINITION

The U.S. government has been measuring the nation's total production since the 1930s. You might think that this is an easy number to calculate, at least in theory: Simply add up the output of every firm in the country during the year. Unfortunately, measuring total production is not so straightforward, and there are many conceptual traps and pitfalls. This is why economists have come up with a very precise definition of GDP.

> *The nation's **gross domestic product** (GDP) is the total value of all final goods and services produced for the marketplace during a given year, within the nation's borders.*

**Gross Domestic Product (GDP)** The total value of all final goods and services produced for the marketplace during a given year, within the nation's borders.

Quite a mouthful. Is everything in this definition really necessary? Absolutely. To see why, let's break the definition down into pieces and look more closely at each one.

### The total value . . .

An old expression tells us that "you can't add apples and oranges." But that is just what government statisticians must do when they measure our total output. In a typical day, American firms produce millions of *loaves* of bread, thousands of *pounds* of peanut butter, hundreds of *hours* of television programming, and so on. These are *different* products, and each is measured in its own type of units. Yet, somehow, we must combine all of them into a single number. But how?

The approach of GDP is to add up the *dollar value* of every good or service— the number of dollars each product is *sold* for. As a result, GDP is measured in

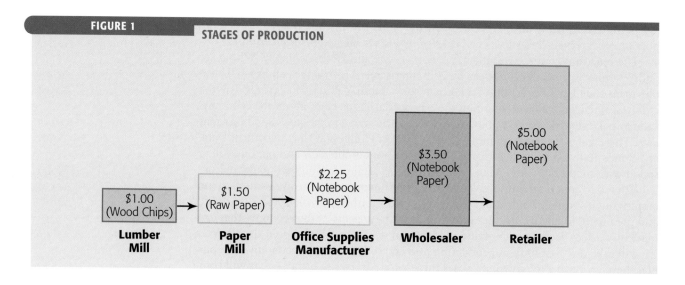

**FIGURE 1**

**STAGES OF PRODUCTION**

$1.00 (Wood Chips) — **Lumber Mill**

$1.50 (Raw Paper) — **Paper Mill**

$2.25 (Notebook Paper) — **Office Supplies Manufacturer**

$3.50 (Notebook Paper) — **Wholesaler**

$5.00 (Notebook Paper) — **Retailer**

dollar units. For example, in 1999, the GDP of the United States was about $9,248,000,000,000—give or take a few billion dollars. (That's about $9.2 trillion.)

Using dollar values has two important advantages. First, it gives us a common unit of measurement for very different things, thus allowing us to add up "apples and oranges." Second, it ensures that more valuable goods (like a hundred computer chips) will count more in our GDP than less valuable ones (a hundred tortilla chips).

*. . . of all final . . .*

When measuring production, we do not count *every* good or service produced in the economy, but only those that are sold to their *final users*. An example will illustrate why.

Figure 1 shows a simplified version of the stages of production needed to produce a ream (500 sheets) of notebook paper: A lumber company cuts down trees and produces wood chips, which it sells to a paper mill for $1.00. The mill cooks, bleaches, and refines the wood chips, turning them into paper rolls, which it sells to an office supplies manufacturer for $1.50. This manufacturer cuts the paper, prints lines and margins on it, and sells its to a wholesaler for $2.25. The wholesaler sells it to a retail store for $3.50, and then, finally, it is sold to a consumer—perhaps you—for $5.00.

Should we add the value of *all* this production, and include $1.00 + $1.50 + $2.25 + $3.50 + $5.00 = $13.25 in GDP each time a ream of notebook paper is produced? No, this would clearly be a mistake, since all of this production ends up creating a good worth only $5 in the end. In fact, the $5 you pay for this good already *includes* the value of all the other production in the process.

In our example, the goods sold by the lumber company, paper mill, office supplies manufacturer, and wholesaler are all **intermediate goods**—goods used up in the process of producing something else. But the retailer (say, your local stationery store) sells a **final good**—a product sold to its *final user* (you). If we separately added in the production of intermediate goods when calculating GDP, we would be counting them more than once, since they are already included in the value of the final good.

**Intermediate goods**  Goods used up in producing final goods.

**Final good**  A good sold to its final user.

> *To avoid overcounting intermediate products when measuring GDP, we add up the value of final goods and services only. The value of all intermediate products is automatically included in the value of the final products they are used to create.*

### . . . goods and services . . .

We all know a good when we see one: We can look at it, feel it, weigh it, and, in some cases, eat it, strum it, or swing a bat at it. Not so with a service: When you get a medical checkup, a haircut, or a car wash, the *effects* of the service may linger, but the service itself is used up the moment it is produced. Nonetheless, final services are as much a part of our GDP as are final goods. The services we are talking about include Internet access and the U.S. Navy, which you many not think of as services when you first hear the word.

> **DANGEROUS CURVES**
>
> You've learned that GDP excludes the value of many things that are bought and sold—such as land, financial assets, and used goods—because they are not *currently produced goods and services.* But all of this buying and selling *can* contribute to GDP indirectly. How? If a dealer or broker is involved in the transaction, then that dealer or broker is producing a current service: bringing buyer and seller together. The value of this service is part of current GDP.
>
> For example, suppose you bought a secondhand book at your college bookstore for $25. Suppose, too, that the store had bought the book from another student for $15. Then the purchase of the used book will contribute $10 to this year's GDP. Why? Because $10 is the value of the bookstore's services; it's the premium you pay to buy the book in the store, rather than going through the trouble to find the original seller yourself. The remainder of your purchase—$15—represents the value of the used book itself, and is *not* counted in GDP. The book was already counted when it was newly produced—in this or a previous year.

Services have become an increasingly important part of our total output in recent decades. The service sector has grown from 31 percent of total output in 1950 to more than half of total output in 1999.

### . . . produced . . .

In order to contribute to GDP, something must be *produced.* This may sound obvious, but it is easy to forget. Every day, Americans buy billions of dollars worth of things that are *not* produced, or at least not produced this year, and so are not counted in this year's GDP. For example, people may buy land, or they may buy financial assets such as stocks or bonds. While these things cost money, they are not counted in GDP because they are not "goods and services *produced.*" Land (and the natural resources on it or under it) is not produced at all. Stocks and bonds represent a claim to ownership or to receive future payments, but they are not themselves goods or services.

In addition, people and businesses buy billions of dollars in *used* goods during the year, such as secondhand cars, previously occupied homes, used furniture, or an old photo of Elvis talking to an extraterrestrial. These goods were all produced, but not in the current period. We include only *currently produced* output when figuring this year's GDP.

### . . . for the marketplace . . .

GDP does not include *all* final goods and services produced in the economy. Rather, it includes only the ones produced for the marketplace—that is, with the intention of being *sold.* Because of this restriction, we exclude many important goods and services from our measure. For example, when you clean your own home, you have produced a final service—housecleaning—but it is *not* counted in GDP because you are doing it for yourself, not for the marketplace. If you *hire* a housecleaner to clean your home, however, this final service *is* included in GDP; it has become a market transaction.

The same is true for many services produced in the economy. Taking care of your children, washing your car, mowing your lawn, walking your dog—none of these services are included in GDP if you do them for yourself, but all *are* included if you pay someone else to do them for you.

### . . . during a given year . . .

This part of the definition of GDP tells us that GDP is an example of a **flow variable**—a measure of a *process* that takes place over a *period* of time:

**Flow variable** A measure of a process that takes place over a period of time.

> *Gross domestic product is a flow variable: It measures a process—production—over a period of time.*

The value of a flow depends on the length of the period over which we choose to measure it. For example, if you are asked, "What is your *income*?" (another flow variable), your answer will be different depending on whether the question refers to your hourly, weekly, monthly, or yearly income. The same is true of GDP: We can measure it per day, per month, or per year. (For example, in 1999, the United States produced $25 billion worth of output on a typical day, $786 billion in a typical month, and $9,248 billion for the year as a whole. By tradition, the basic period for reporting GDP is a year.)

Not all macroeconomic variables are flow variables; some are **stock variables**—measures of things that *exist* at a *moment* in time. The U.S. population, the number of homes in the nation, the current value of your wealth—all these are stock variables because they are values measured at a particular instant. In this case, we never need to add the phrase *per week* or *per month*, since there is no *period* attached to the variable. (For example, it makes no sense to ask, "What is your wealth per month?" Instead, we would ask, "What is your wealth *right now*?")

**Stock Variable** A measure of an amount that exists at a moment in time.

### . . . *within the nation's borders.*

GDP measures output produced *within U.S. borders*—regardless of whether it was produced by Americans. This means we *include* output produced by foreign-owned resources and foreign citizens located in the United States, and we *exclude* output produced by Americans located in other countries. For example, when the rock star Sting, a resident of Britain, gives a concert tour in the United States, the value of his services is counted in U.S. GDP, but not in British GDP. Similarly, the services of an American nurse working in an Ethiopian hospital are part of Ethiopian GDP and not U.S. GDP.

## THE EXPENDITURE APPROACH TO GDP

The Commerce Department's Bureau of Economic Analysis (BEA)—the agency responsible for gathering, reporting, and analyzing movements in the nation's output—calculates GDP in several different ways. The most important of these is the *expenditure approach*. Because this method of measuring GDP tells us so much about the structure of our economy, we'll spend the next several pages on it.

In the expenditure approach, we divide output into four categories according to which group in the economy purchases it. The four categories are:

1. *Consumption goods and services (C),* purchased by households
2. *Private investment goods and services (I),* purchased by businesses
3. *Government goods and services (G),* purchased by government agencies
4. *Net exports (NX),* purchased by foreigners.[1]

This is an exhaustive list: Every purchaser of U.S. output belongs to one of these four sectors. Thus, when we add up the purchases of the four sectors, we must get GDP:

**Expenditure approach** Measuring GDP by adding the value of goods and services purchased by each type of final user.

> *In the **expenditure approach** to measuring GDP, we add up the value of the goods and services purchased by each type of final user:*
>
> $$\text{GDP} = C + I + G + NX.$$

---

[1] The meaning and measurement of the term *net exports* will become clear in a few pages.

As you can see in Table 1, applying the expenditure approach to GDP in 1999 gives us $GDP = C + I + G + NX$ = $6,255 + $1,621 + $1,629 + (−$257) = $9,248 billion.

Now let's take a closer look at each of the four components of GDP.

GDP is measured and reported each *quarter.* But be careful: Quarterly GDP is almost always reported at an *annual rate.* For example, in the first quarter of 1999, we produced $1,983. billion in final goods and services; but the GDP was reported at the *annual* rate of 4 × $1,983 billion = $7,933 billion. This is what we *would have* produced in 1999 if production had continued at the first quarter's rate for the entire year.

**Consumption Spending.** Consumption (C) is both the largest component of GDP—making up about three-quarters of total production in recent years—and the easiest to understand:

> *Consumption is the part of GDP purchased by households as final users.*

**Consumption (C)** The part of GDP purchased by households as final users.

Almost everything that households buy during the year—restaurant meals, gasoline, new clothes, doctors' visits, movies, electricity, and more—is included as part of consumption spending when we calculate GDP.

But notice the word *almost.* Two categories of things that households buy during the year are *not* part of consumption because they are not part of GDP at all. The two categories, referred to in an earlier Dangerous Curves warning, are *used* goods (such as secondhand textbooks or cars) and assets such as stocks, bonds, or real estate.

There are also some quirky exceptions to the definition of consumption. For example, two things are included even though households do not actually buy them: (1) the total value of all food products that farm families produce and consume themselves (meat, dairy products, fruit, and vegetables) and (2) the total value of the shelter provided by homes that are owned by the families living in them. The government estimates (and adds to GDP) what farm families *would* pay if they had to buy all of their farm products in the marketplace like everyone else. It also estimates the rent that homeowners *would* pay for their homes if they were renting from someone

**TABLE 1**

**GDP IN 1999: THE EXPENDITURE APPROACH (BILLIONS OF DOLLARS)**

| Consumption Purchases | | Private-Investment Purchases | | Government Purchases | | Net Exports | |
|---|---|---|---|---|---|---|---|
| Services | $3,656 | Plant and Equipment | $1,166 | Government Consumption | $1,333 | Exports | $ 996 |
| Nondurable Goods | $1,841 | New-Home Construction | $ 411 | Government Investment | $ 296 | Imports | $1,253 |
| Durable Goods | $ 758 | Changes in Business Inventories | $ 44 | | | | |
| Consumption = | $6,255 | Private Investment = | $1,621 | Government Purchases = | $1,629 | Net Exports = | −$257 |

$GDP = C + I + G + NX$
   $= $6,255 + $1,621 + $1,629 + (−$257)$
   $= $9,248$

*Source:* Economic Report of the President, 2000 (average of 1999 second and third quarter annual rates).

else. Another exception is that the construction of new homes—even when house-holds buy them—is not counted as consumption, but rather as private investment.

### Private Investment.

What do oil-drilling rigs, cash registers, office telephones, and the house you grew up in all have in common? They are all examples of *capital goods*—goods that will provide useful services in future years. When we sum the value of all of the capital goods in the country, we get our **capital stock.** As the name suggests, this is a *stock* variable—a value that exists at a moment in time.

Understanding the concept of capital stock helps us understand and define the concept of investment. A rough definition of **private investment** is *capital formation*—the *increase* in the nation's capital stock during the year. Investment, like the other components of GDP, is a *flow* variable—a process (capital formation) that takes place over a period of time.

More specifically,

> *Private investment has three components: (1) business purchases of plant and equipment; (2) new home construction; and (3) changes in business firms' inventory stocks (stocks of unsold goods).*

Each of these components requires some explanation.

*Business Purchases of Plant and Equipment.* This category might seem confusing at first glance. Why aren't plant and equipment considered intermediate goods? After all, business firms buy these things in order to produce other things. Doesn't the value of their final goods include the value of their plant and equipment as well?

Actually, no, and if you go back to the definition of intermediate goods, you will see why. Intermediate goods are *used up* in producing the current year's GDP. But a firm's plant and equipment are intended to last for many years; only a small part of them is used up to make the current year's output. Thus, we regard newly produced plant and equipment as final goods, and the firms that buy them as the final users of those goods.

For example, suppose our paper mill—the firm that turns wood chips into raw paper—buys a new factory building that is expected to last for 50 years. Then only a small fraction of that factory building—one-fiftieth—is used up in any one year's production of raw paper, and only a small part of the factory building's value will be reflected in the value of the firm's current output. But since the factory is produced during the year, we must include its value *somewhere* in our measure of total production. In calculating GDP, we therefore count the factory building as an investment good.

Plant and equipment purchases are always the largest component of private investment. In 1999, businesses purchased and installed $1,166 billion worth of plant and equipment, which was about 70 percent of total private investment spending that year. (See Table 1.)

*New Home Construction.* As you can see in Table 1, new home construction made up a significant part of total private investment in 1999. But it may strike you as odd that this category is part of investment spending at all, since most new homes are purchased by households and could reasonably be considered consumption spending instead. Why do we treat new home construction as investment spending in GDP?

Largely because residential housing is an important part of the nation's *capital stock.* Just as an oil-drilling rig will continue to provide oil-drilling services for many years, so, too, a home will continue to provide shelter services into the future. If we want our measure of private investment spending to roughly correspond to

**Capital stock** The total value of all goods that will provide useful services in future years.

**Private investment (***I***)** The sum of business plant and equipment purchases, new home construction, and inventory changes.

the increase in the nation's capital stock, we must include this important category of capital formation in investment spending.

*Changes in Inventories.*  Inventories are goods that have been produced, but not yet sold. They include goods on store shelves, goods making their way through the production process in factories, and raw materials waiting to be used. We count the *change* in firms' inventories as part of investment in measuring GDP. Why? When goods are produced but not sold during the year, they end up in some firm's inventory stocks. If we did *not* count changes in inventories, we would be missing this important part of current production. Remember that GDP is designed to measure total *production,* not just the part of production that is sold during the year.

To understand this more clearly, suppose that in some year, the automobile industry produced $100 billion worth of automobiles, and that $80 billion worth was sold to consumers. Then the other $20 billion remained unsold and was added to the auto company's inventories. If we counted consumption spending alone ($80 billion), we would underestimate automobile production in GDP. To ensure a proper measure, we must include not only the $80 billion in cars sold (consumption), but also the $20 billion *change* in inventories (private investment). In the end, the contribution to GDP is $80 billion (consumption) + $20 billion (private investment) = $100 billion, which is, indeed, the total value of automobile production during the year.

What if inventory stocks *decline* during the year, so that the change in inventories is negative? Our rule still holds: We include the change in inventories in our measure of GDP—but in this case, we must add a *negative* number. For example, if the automobile industry produced $100 billion worth of cars, but consumers bought $120 billion, then $20 billion worth of cars must have come from inventory stocks—cars that were produced (and counted) in previous years, but that remained unsold until this year. In this case, the consumption spending of $120 billion will *overestimate* automobile production during the year, and subtracting $20 billion corrects for this overcount. In the end, GDP would rise by $120 billion (consumption) − $20 billion (private investment) = $100 billion.

Inventory changes are included in investment spending, rather than some other component of GDP, because unsold goods are part of the nation's capital stock. They will provide services in the future, when they are finally sold and used. An increase in inventories represents capital formation: a decrease in inventories—negative investment—is a decrease in the nation's capital.

Inventory changes are generally the smallest component of private investment, but the most highly volatile in percentage terms. In 1999, for example, inventories increased by about $44 billion; one year earlier, they increased by $71.2 billion— almost twice as much, and in some years, inventories *decrease.* Part of the reason for this volatility is that, while some inventory investment is intended, much of it is *unintended.* During recessions, for example, businesses are often unable to sell all of the goods they have produced and had planned to sell. The unsold output will be added to inventory stocks—an unintended increase in inventories. During rapid expansions, the opposite may happen: Businesses find themselves selling more than they produced—an unintended decrease in inventories.

### Private Investment and the Capital Stock: Some Important Provisos.  A few pages ago, it was pointed out that private investment corresponds only *roughly* to the increase in the nation's capital stock. Why this cautious language? Because changes in the nation's capital stock are somewhat more complicated than we are able to capture with private investment alone.

Unsold goods, like those pictured in this warehouse, are considered inventories. The *change* in these inventories—positive or negative—is included as investment when calculating GDP.

First, an important part of the nation's capital stock is owned and operated not by businesses, but by government—federal, state, and local. Courthouses, police cars, fire stations, weather satellites, military aircraft, highways, and bridges are all examples of government capital. In any given year, some of the nation's capital formation consists of an increase in government capital, which is not included in our measure of private investment. Thus, private investment spending alone tends to *underestimate* the increase in the nation's capital stock. A better measure of capital formation would include both private and government investment:

> *Total investment during the year is the sum of private investment and government investment.*

In 1999, for example, the BEA estimated that $296 billion of government spending was devoted to capital formation, so that total investment in that year was

**Total Investment = Private Investment + Government Investment**
**= $1,621 billion + $296 billion = $1,917 billion.**

Second, in any given year, some of the nation's existing capital stock will wear out, or *depreciate*. Total investment spending, because it ignores depreciation, *overestimates* the increase in the nation's capital stock. We can fix this, however, by subtracting depreciation from total investment, to obtain *net investment spending*. This is the amount by which private and government investment actually causes the capital stock to increase:

**Net investment** Total investment minus depreciation.

**Net Investment = Total Investment − Depreciation.**

For example, the government estimates that in 1999, $1,141 billion of private and government capital depreciated, so that net investment for the year was

**Net Investment = $1,917 billion − $1,141 billion = $776 billion.**

Net investment comes close to being a true measure of the increase in the capital stock during the year. But in the minds of many economists, we are still not completely there, because we are still ignoring two kinds of capital formation. One is the purchase of *consumer durables*—goods such as furniture, automobiles, washing machines, and personal computers for home use. All of these goods can be considered capital goods, since they will continue to provide services for many years. In 1999, households purchased $758 billion in durables. If we deduct from this an estimate of depreciation on the existing stock of durables (say, $100 billion), we would get the increase in the stock of durables: $758 billion − $100 billion = $658 billion. Some economists would argue that *if* we included this $658 billion or so as part of investment, we would have an even better measure of the increase in the capital stock

Finally, our typical measures of capital formation ignore *human capital*—the skills and training of the labor force. Think about a surgeon's skills in performing a heart bypass operation, or a police detective's ability to find clues and solve a murder, or a Web-page designer's mastery of HTML and Java. These types of knowledge will continue to provide valuable services well into the future, just like plant and equipment or new housing. To measure the increase in the capital stock most broadly, then, we *should* include the additional skills and training acquired by the workforce during the year. But human capital growth—like growth in consumer durables—is *not* included in the official measure of investment by the BEA.

### Government Purchases.

In 1999, the government bought $1,629 billion worth of goods and services that were part of GDP—about a sixth of the total. This component of GDP is called **government purchases,** although in recent years the Department of Commerce has begun to use the phrase *gov-*

> Be *extremely* careful when using the term *investment* in your economics course. In economics, investment refers to capital formation, such as the building of a new factory, home, or hospital, or the production and installation of new capital equipment, or the accumulation of inventories by business firms. In everyday language, however, *investment* has a very different meaning: a place to put your wealth. Thus, in ordinary English, you invest whenever you buy stocks or bonds or certificates of deposit or when you lend money to a friend who is starting up a business. But in the language of economics, you have not invested, but merely changed the form in which you are holding your wealth (say, from checking account balances to stocks or bonds). To avoid confusion, remember that investment takes place only when there is new production of capital goods—that is, only when there is *capital formation.*

*ernment consumption and investment purchases.* Government *investment,* as discussed earlier, refers to capital goods purchased by government agencies. The rest of government purchases is considered government *consumption*—spending on goods and services that are used up during the year. This includes the salaries of government workers and military personnel, and raw materials such as computer paper for government offices, gasoline for government vehicles, and the electricity used in government buildings.

**Government purchases (G)** Spending by federal, state, and local governments on goods and services.

There are a few things to keep in mind about government purchases in GDP. First, we include purchases by state and local governments as well as the federal government. In macroeconomics, it makes little difference whether the purchases are made by a local government agency like the parks department of Kalamazoo, Michigan, or a huge federal agency such as the U.S. Department of Defense.

Second, government purchases include *goods*—like fighter jets, police cars, school buildings, and spy satellites—and *services*—such as those performed by police, legislators, and military personnel. The government is considered to be a purchaser even if it actually produces the goods or services itself. For example, if you are taking your economics course at a public college or university—like Western Illinois University or the City University of New York—then your professor is selling teaching services to a state or city government. His or her salary enters into GDP as part of government purchases.

Finally, it's important to distinguish between government *purchases*—which are counted in GDP—and government *spending* as measured by local, state, and federal budgets and reported in the media. What's the difference? In addition to their purchases of goods and services, government agencies also disburse money for **transfer payments.** These funds are *given* to people or organizations—*not* to buy goods or services from them, but rather to fulfill some social obligation or goal. For example, Social Security payments by the federal government, unemployment insurance and welfare payments by state governments, and money disbursed to homeless shelters and soup kitchens by city governments are all examples of transfer payments. The important thing to remember about transfer payments is this:

**Transfer payment** Any payment that is not compensation for supplying goods or services.

> *Transfer payments represent money redistributed from one group of citizens (taxpayers) to another (the poor, the unemployed, the elderly). While transfers are included in government budgets as spending, they are* not *purchases of currently produced goods and services, and so are not included in the government purchases or in GDP.*

The main source of information on U.S. GDP is the Bureau of Economic Analysis. Their Web page can be found at http://www.bea.doc.gov/.

**Net exports (NX)** Total exports minus total imports.

**Net Exports.** There is one more category of buyer for output produced in the United States: *the foreign sector*. In 1999, for example, purchasers *outside* the nation bought approximately $996 billion of U.S. goods and services—about 11 percent of our GDP. These exports are part of U.S. production of goods and services and so are included in GDP.

However, once we recognize dealings with the rest of the world, we must correct an inaccuracy in our measure of GDP the way we've reported it so far. Americans buy many goods and services every year that were produced *outside* the United States (Chinese shoes, Japanese cars, Mexican beer, Costa Rican coffee). When we add up the final purchases of households, businesses, and government agencies, we *overcount* U.S. production because we include goods and services produced abroad, which are *not* part of U.S. output. To correct for this overcount, we deduct all *imports* into the United States during the year, leaving us with just output produced in the United States. In 1999, these imports amounted to $1,253 billion—an amount equal to about 13.5 percent of our GDP.

Let's recap: To obtain an accurate measure of GDP, we must add the part of U.S. production that is purchased by foreigners—total exports. But to correct for including the goods produced abroad, we must subtract Americans' purchases of goods produced outside of the United States—total imports. In practice, we take both of these steps together by adding **net exports** (*NX*), which are total exports minus total imports.

> *To properly account for output sold to, and bought from, foreigners, we must include net exports—the difference between exports and imports—as part of expenditure in GDP.*

In 1999, when total exports were $996 billion and total imports were $1,253 billion, net exports—as you can see in Table 1—were $996 − $1,253 = −$257 billion. The negative number indicates that the imports we're subtracting from GDP are greater than the exports we're adding.

## OTHER APPROACHES TO GDP

In addition to the expenditure approach, in which we calculate GDP as *C* + *I* + *G* + *NX*, there are other ways of measuring GDP. You may be wondering: Why bother? Why not just use one method—whichever is best—and stick to it? Is the Bureau of Economic Analysis just trying to make life difficult for introductory economics students?

Actually, there are two good reasons for measuring GDP in different ways. The first is practical. Each method of measuring GDP is subject to measurement errors. By calculating total output in several different ways, and then trying to resolve the differences, the BEA gets a more accurate measure than would be possible with one method alone. The second reason is that the different ways of measuring total output give us different insights into the structure of our economy. Let's take a look at two more ways of measuring—and thinking about—GDP.

**The Value-Added Approach.** In the expenditure approach, we record goods and services only when they are sold to their final users—at the end of the production process. But we can also measure GDP by adding up each *firm's* contribution to the product *as it is produced*.

**TABLE 2**

**VALUE ADDED AT
DIFFERENT STAGES
OF PRODUCTION**

| Firm | Cost of Intermediate Goods | Revenue | Value Added |
|------|---------------------------|---------|-------------|
| Lumber Company | $ 0 | $1.00 | $1.00 |
| Paper Mill | $1.00 | $1.50 | $0.50 |
| Office Supplies Manufacturer | $1.50 | $2.25 | $0.75 |
| Wholesaler | $2.25 | $3.50 | $1.25 |
| Retailer | $3.50 | $5.00 | $1.50 |
| | | | Total: $5.00 |

A firm's contribution to a product is called its *value added*. More formally,

> *A firm's **value added** is the revenue it receives for its output, minus the cost of all the intermediate goods that it buys.*

**Value added** The revenue a firm receives minus the cost of the intermediate goods it buys.

Look back at Figure 1, which traces the production of a ream of notebook paper. The paper mill, for example, buys $1.00 worth of wood chips (an intermediate good) from the lumber company and turns it into raw paper, which it sells for $1.50. The value added by the paper mill is $1.50 − $1.00 = $0.50. Similarly, the office-supplies maker buys $1.50 worth of paper (an intermediate good) from the paper mill and sells it for $2.25, so its value added is $2.25 − $1.50 = $0.75. If we total the value added by each firm, we should get the final value of the notebook paper, as in Table 2.[2] The total value added is $1.00 + $0.50 + $0.75 + $1.25 + $1.50 = $5.00, which is equal to the final sales price of the ream of paper. For any good or service, it will always be the case that the sum of the values added by all firms equals the final sales price. This leads to our second method of measuring GDP:

> *In the **value-added approach**, GDP is the sum of the values added by all firms in the economy.*

**Value-added approach** Measuring GDP by summing the value added by all firms in the economy.

**The Factor Payments Approach.** If a bakery sells $200,000 worth of bread during the year and buys $25,000 in intermediate goods (flour, eggs, yeast), then its value added—its revenue minus the cost of its intermediate goods—is $200,000 − $25,000 = $175,000. This is also the sum that will be *left over* from its revenue after the bakery pays for its intermediate goods.

Where does this $175,000 go? In addition to its intermediate goods, the bakery must pay for the *resources* it used during the year—the land, labor, and capital that enabled it to add value to its intermediate goods.

Payments to owners of resources are called **factor payments**, because resources are also called the factors of production. Owners of capital (the owners of the firm's buildings or machinery, or those who lend funds to the firm so that *it* can buy buildings and machinery) receive *interest payments;* owners of land and natural resources receive *rent;* and those who provide labor to the firm receive *wages and salaries*. Finally, there is one additional resource used by the firm: *entrepreneurship*. In every capitalist economy, the entrepreneurs are those who visualize society's needs,

**Factor payments** Payments to the owners of resources that are used in production.

---

2   To keep our example simple, we assume that the lumber company simply cuts down trees and slices up lumber, using just land, labor, and capital. We thus assume it uses no intermediate goods.

mobilize and coordinate the other resources so that production can take place, and gamble that the enterprise will succeed. The people who provide this entrepreneurship (often the owners of the firms) receive a fourth type of factor payment—*profit*.

Now let's go back to our bakery, which received $200,000 in revenue during the year. We've seen that $25,000 of this went to pay for intermediate goods, leaving $175,000 in value added earned by the factors of production. Let's suppose that $110,000 went to pay the wages of the bakery's employees, $10,000 was paid out as interest on loans, and $15,000 was paid in rent for the land under the bakery. That leaves $175,000 − $110,000 − $10,000 − $15,000 = $40,000. This last sum—since it doesn't go to anyone else—stays with the owner of the bakery. It, too, is a factor payment—profit—for the entrepreneurship she provides. Thus, when all of the factor payments—including profit—are added together, the total will be $110,000 + $10,000 + $15,000 + $40,000 = $175,000—precisely equal to the value added at the bakery. More generally,

> *In any year, the value added by a firm is equal to the total factor payments made by that firm.*

Earlier, we learned that GDP equals the sum of all firms' value added; now we've learned that each firm's value added is equal to its factor payments. Thus, GDP must equal the total factor payments made by all firms in the economy. This gives us our *third* method of measuring GDP:

**Factor payments approach** Measuring GDP by summing the factor payments made by all firms in the economy.

> *In the **factor payments approach**, GDP can be measured by summing all of the factor payments made by all firms in the economy. Equivalently, it can be measured by adding up all of the income—wages and salaries, rent, interest, and profit—earned by all households in the economy.*[3]

The factor payments approach to GDP gives us one of our most important insights into the macroeconomy:

> *GDP—the total output of the economy—is equal to the total income earned in the economy.*

This simple idea—output equals income—follows directly from the factor payments approach to GDP. It explains why macroeconomists use the terms "output" and "income" interchangeably: They are one and the same. If output rises, income rises by the same amount; if output falls, income falls by an equal amount.

## MEASURING GDP: A SUMMARY

You've now learned three different ways to calculate GDP:

> *Expenditure Approach:* GDP = C + I + G + NX
>
> *Value-Added Approach:* GDP = Sum of value added by all firms
>
> *Factor Payments Approach:* GDP = Sum of factor payments made by all firms
> = Wages and salaries + interest + rent + profit
> = Total household income

---

[3]  Actually, this is just an approximation. Before a firm pays its factors of production, it first deducts a small amount for depreciation of its plant and equipment, and another small amount for the sales taxes it must pay to the government. Thus, GDP and total factor payments are slightly different. We ignore this difference in the text.

We will use these three approaches to GDP again and again as we study what makes the economy tick. Make sure you understand why each one of them should, in theory, give us the same number for GDP.

## REAL VERSUS NOMINAL GDP

Since GDP is measured in dollars, we have a serious problem when we want to track the change in output over time. The problem is that the value of the dollar—its purchasing power—is itself changing. As prices have risen over the past 100 years, the value of the dollar has steadily fallen. Trying to keep track of GDP using dollars in different years is like trying to keep track of a child's height using a ruler whose length changes each year. If we find that the child is three rulers tall in one year and four rulers tall in the next, we cannot know whether the child is really growing taller—or, if so, by how much—until we adjust for the effects of a changing ruler. The same is true for GDP and for any other economic variable measured in dollars: We usually need to adjust our measurements to reflect changes in the value of the dollar.

> *When a variable is measured over time with no adjustment for the dollar's changing value, it is called a **nominal variable**. When a variable is adjusted for the dollar's changing value, it is called a **real variable**.*

**Nominal variable** A variable measured without adjustment for the dollar's changing value.

**Real variable** A variable adjusted for changes in the dollar's value.

Most government statistics are reported in both nominal and real terms, but economists focus almost exclusively on real variables. This is because changes in nominal variables don't really tell us much. For example, from 1990 to 1991, nominal GDP increased from $5,743.8 billion to $5,916.7 billion. But production actually decreased over that period—the increase in nominal GDP was due entirely to a rise in prices.

> *The distinction between nominal and real values is crucial in macroeconomics. The public, the media, and sometimes even government officials have been confused by a failure to make this distinction. Whenever we want to track significant changes in key macroeconomic variables—such as the average wage rate, wealth, income, or GDP or any of its components—we always use real variables.*

> *Since our economic well-being depends, in part, on the goods and services we can buy, it is important to translate nominal values—which are measured in current dollars—to real values—which are measured in purchasing power.*

In the next chapter, you'll learn how economists translate nominal variables into real variables.

## HOW GDP IS USED

We've come a long way since 1931. In that year—as the United States plummeted into the worst depression in its history—Congress summoned economists from government agencies, from academia, and from the private sector to testify about the state of the economy. They were asked the most basic questions: How much output was the nation producing, and how much had production fallen since 1929? How much income were Americans earning, how much were they spending on goods and services, and how much were they saving? How much profit were businesses earning, and what were they doing with their profits? Had the economy continued to deteriorate in the previous year, or had it finally hit bottom? To the surprise of the members of Congress, no one could answer any of these questions,

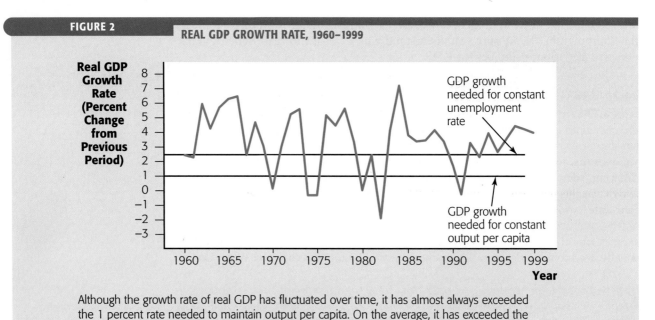

**FIGURE 2**

**REAL GDP GROWTH RATE, 1960–1999**

Real GDP Growth Rate (Percent Change from Previous Period)

GDP growth needed for constant unemployment rate

GDP growth needed for constant output per capita

Although the growth rate of real GDP has fluctuated over time, it has almost always exceeded the 1 percent rate needed to maintain output per capita. On the average, it has exceeded the 2.5 percent rate needed to prevent a rise in unemployment.

because *no one was keeping track of our national income and output!* The last measurement—which was rather incomplete—had been made in 1929.

Thus began the U.S. system of national income accounts—a system whose value was instantly recognized around the world and was rapidly copied by other countries. Today, the government's reports on GDP are used to steer the economy over both the short run and the long run. In the short run, sudden changes in real GDP can alert us to the onset of a recession or a too-rapid expansion that can overheat the economy. Many (but not all) economists believe that, if alerted in time, the government can design policies to help keep the economy on a more balanced course.

GDP is also used to measure the long-run growth rate of the economy's output. Indeed, we typically define the average *standard of living* as *output per capita*—real GDP divided by the population. In order for output per capita to rise, real GDP must grow faster than the population. Since the U.S. population tends to grow by about 1 percent per year, a real GDP growth rate of 1 percent per year is needed just to *maintain* our output per capita; higher growth rates are needed to increase it.

Look at Figure 2, which shows the annual percentage change in real GDP from 1960 to 1999. The lower horizontal line indicates the 1 percent growth needed to just maintain output per capita. You can see that, on average, real GDP has grown by more than this, so that output per capita has steadily increased over time.

Long-run growth in GDP is also important for another reason: to ensure that the economy generates enough additional jobs for a growing population. In order to prevent the unemployment rate from rising, real GDP must increase even faster than the population. In practice, a growth rate of about 2.5 percent per year—the upper horizontal line in the figure—seems to generate the required number of new jobs each year. You can see that real GDP growth has, on average, been sufficient for this purpose as well.

To sum up: We use GDP to guide the economy in two ways. In the short run, to alert us to recessions and give us a chance to stabilize the economy. In the long run, to tell us whether our economy is growing fast enough to raise output per capita and our standard of living, and fast enough to generate sufficient jobs for a growing population. You can see that GDP is an extremely useful measure. But it is not without its problems.

## PROBLEMS WITH GDP

Our GDP statistics are plagued by some important inaccuracies. One problem is *quality changes*. Suppose a new ballpoint pen comes out that lasts four times as long as previous versions. What *should* happen to GDP? Ideally, each new pen should count the same as four old pens, since one new pen offers the same *writing services* as four old ones. But the analysts at the Bureau of Economic Analysis (BEA) would most likely treat this new pen the same as an old pen and record an increase in GDP only if the total number of pens increased. Why? Because the BEA has a limited budget. While it does include the impact of quality changes for many goods and services (such as automobiles and computers), the BEA simply does not have the resources to estimate quality changes for millions of different goods and services. These include many consumer goods (such as razor blades that shave closer and last longer), medical services (increased surgery success rates and shorter recovery periods), and retail services (faster checkout times due to optical scanners). By ignoring these quality improvements, GDP probably understates true growth from year to year.

A second problem arises from the *underground economy,* which contains hidden economic activity, either because it is illegal (drugs, prostitution, most gambling) or because those engaged in it are avoiding taxes. These activities cannot be measured accurately, so the BEA must estimate them. Many economists believe that the BEA's estimates are too low. As a result, GDP may understate total output. However, since the *relative* importance of the underground economy does not change rapidly, the BEA's estimates of *changes* in GDP from year to year should not be seriously affected.

Finally, except for food grown and consumed by farmers and for housing services, GDP does not include **nonmarket production**—goods and services that are produced, but not sold in the marketplace. All of the housecleaning, typing, sewing, lawn mowing, and child rearing that people do themselves, rather than hiring someone else, are excluded from GDP. Whenever a nonmarket transaction (say, cleaning your apartment) becomes a market transaction (hiring a housecleaner to do it for you), GDP will rise, even though total production (cleaning one apartment) has remained the same. This can exaggerate the growth in GDP over long periods of time. Over the last half-century, much production has, indeed, shifted away from the home and to the market. Parenting, which was not counted in past years' GDP, has become day care, which *does* count, currently contributing several billion dollars annually to GDP. Similarly, home-cooked food has been replaced by takeout, talking to a friend has been replaced by therapy, and the neighbor who watches your house while you're away has been replaced by a store-bought alarm system or an increase in police protection. In all of these cases, real GDP increases, even though production has not.

What do these problems tell us about the value of GDP? That for certain purposes—especially interpreting *long-run* changes in GDP—we must exercise extreme caution. For example, suppose that, over the next 20 years, the growth rate of GDP slows down. Would this mean that something is going wrong with the economy? Would it suggest a need to change course? Not necessarily. It *could* be that the underground economy or unrecorded quality changes are becoming more important. Similarly, if GDP growth accelerates, it could mean that our living standards are rising more rapidly. But it might instead mean that economic activity is shifting out of the home and into the market even more rapidly than in the past.

**Nonmarket production** Goods and services that are produced, but not sold in a market.

When it comes to *short-term* changes in the economy, however, we can have much more confidence in using GDP. Look back at our discussion of problems with GDP in this section. The distortions we've discussed tend to remain roughly constant over the short run. If GDP suddenly drops, it is extremely unlikely that the underground economy has suddenly become more important, or that there has been a sudden shift from market to nonmarket activities, or that we are suddenly missing more quality changes than usual. Rather, we can be reasonably certain that output and economic activity are slowing down.

> *Short-term changes in real GDP are fairly accurate reflections of the state of the economy. A significant short-term drop in real GDP virtually always indicates a decrease in production, rather than a measurement problem.*

This is why policy makers, businesspeople, and the media pay such close attention to GDP as a guide to the economy from quarter to quarter.

# EMPLOYMENT AND UNEMPLOYMENT

When you think of unemployment, you may have an image in your mind that goes something like this: As the economy slides into recession, an anxious employee is called into an office and handed a pink slip by a grim-faced manager. "Sorry," the manager says, "I wish there were some other way. . . ." Perhaps, in your mind, the worker spends the next few months checking the classified ads, pounding the pavement, and sending out resumes in a desperate search for work. And perhaps, after months of trying, the laid-off worker gives up, spending days at the neighborhood bar, drinking away the shame and frustration, and sinking lower and lower into despair and inertia.

For some people, joblessness begins and ends very much like this—a human tragedy, and a needless one. On one side, we have people who want to work and support themselves by producing something; on the other side is the rest of society, which could certainly use more goods and services. Yet somehow, the system isn't working, and the jobless cannot find work. The result is often hardship for the unemployed and their families, and a loss to society in general.

But this is just one face of unemployment, and there are others. Some instances of unemployment, for example, have little to do with macroeconomic conditions. And frequently, unemployment causes a lot less suffering than in our grim story.

## TYPES OF UNEMPLOYMENT

Economists have found it useful to classify unemployment into four different categories, each arising from a different cause and each having different consequences.

**Frictional Unemployment.**  **Frictional unemployment** is short-term joblessness experienced by people who are between jobs or who are entering the labor market for the first time or after an absence. For example, imagine that you have a job, but that you think you'd be happier at some other firm. Since you can't search for a new job while working full time, you may decide to quit your job and begin looking elsewhere. In an ideal frictionless world, every potential employer would immediately know that you were available, and you would immediately know which job you'd prefer most, so you would become re-employed the instant you quit; you would not be unemployed between jobs. Of course, in the real world, it takes time to find a

**http://**

Employment-related information for the United States can be found at the Bureau of Labor Statistics' Web site: http://stats. bls.gov.

**Frictional unemployment**  Joblessness experienced by people who are between jobs or who are just entering or re-entering the labor market.

job—time to prepare your resume, to decide where to send it, to wait for responses, and then to investigate job offers so you can make a wise choice. It also takes time for employers to consider your skills and qualifications and to decide whether you are right for their firms. During all that time, you will be unemployed: willing and able to work, but not working.

There are other examples of this type of unemployment. A parent reenters the labor force after several years spent raising the children. A 22-year-old searches for a job after graduating from college. In both of these cases, it may take some time to find a job, and during that time, the job seeker is *frictionally* unemployed.

Because frictional unemployment is, by definition, short term, it causes little hardship to those affected by it. In most cases, people have enough savings to support themselves through a short spell of joblessness, or else they can borrow on their credit card or from friends or family to tide them over. Moreover, this kind of unemployment has important benefits: By spending time searching rather than jumping at the first opening that comes their way, people find jobs for which they are better suited and in which they will ultimately be more productive. As a result, workers earn higher incomes, firms have more productive employees, and society has more goods and services.

### Seasonal Unemployment.
**Seasonal unemployment** is joblessness related to changes in weather, tourist patterns, or other seasonal factors. For example, most ski instructors lose their jobs every April or May, and many construction workers are laid off each winter.

**Seasonal unemployment** Joblessness related to changes in weather, tourist patterns, or other seasonal factors.

Seasonal unemployment, like frictional unemployment, is rather benign: It is short term, and, because it is entirely predictable, workers are often compensated in advance for the unemployment they experience in the off-season. Construction workers, for example, are paid higher-than-average hourly wages, in part to compensate them for their high probability of joblessness in the winter.

Seasonal unemployment complicates the interpretation of unemployment data. Seasonal factors push the unemployment rate up in certain months of the year and pull it down in others, even when overall conditions in the economy remain unchanged. For example, each June, unemployment rises as millions of high school and college students—who do not want to work during the school year—begin looking for summer jobs. If the government reported the actual rise in unemployment in June, it would *seem* as if labor market conditions were deteriorating, when in fact, the rise is just a predictable and temporary seasonal change. To prevent any misunderstandings, the government usually reports the *seasonally adjusted* rate of unemployment, a rate that reflects only those changes beyond normal for the month. For example, if the unemployment rate in June is typically one percentage point higher than during the rest of the year, then the seasonally adjusted rate for June will be the actual rate minus one percentage point.

### Structural Unemployment.
Sometimes, there are jobs available and workers who would be delighted to have them, but job seekers and employers are *mismatched* in some way. For example, in the early 2000s, there have been plenty of job openings in high-tech industries, such as computer hardware and software design, satellite technology, and communications. Many of the unemployed, however, do not have the skills and training to work in these industries—there is a mismatch between the skills they have and those that are needed. The mismatch can also be geographic, as when construction jobs go begging in Northern California, Oregon, and Washington, but unemployed construction workers live in other states.

Unemployment that results from these kinds of mismatches is called **structural unemployment,** because it arises from *structural change* in the economy: when old,

**Structural unemployment** Joblessness arising from mismatches between workers' skills and employers' requirements or between workers' locations and employers' locations.

dying industries are replaced with new ones that require different skills and are located in different areas of the country. Structural unemployment is generally a stubborn, *long-term* problem, often lasting several years or more. Why? Because it can take considerable time for the structurally unemployed to find jobs—time to relocate to another part of the country or time to acquire new skills. To make matters worse, the structurally unemployed could benefit from financial assistance for job training or relocation, but—because they don't have jobs—they are unable to get loans.

Structural unemployment is a much bigger problem in other countries, especially in Europe, than it is in the United States. In November 1999, when the U.S. unemployment rate was 4.1 percent, the rate in Germany was 9.1 percent, in France 10.5 percent, and in Spain 15.4 percent. All three of those European countries have large groups of lower-skilled workers who are not qualified for the jobs that are available. Even Canada suffers from much more structural unemployment than does the United States—its unemployment rate at the end of 1999 was 6.9 percent, much of it concentrated in the maritime provinces. And within the United States, some areas have higher structural unemployment than others. For example, in early 2000 when the national unemployment rate was 4 percent, the rates in New York City and Los Angeles were closer to 6 percent.

The types of unemployment we've considered so far—frictional, structural, and seasonal—arise from *microeconomic* causes; that is, they are attributable to changes in specific industries and specific labor markets, rather than to conditions in the overall economy. This kind of unemployment cannot be eliminated, as people will always spend some time searching for new jobs, there will always be seasonal industries in the economy, and structural changes will, from time to time, require workers to move to new locations or gain new job skills. Some amount of microeconomic unemployment is a sign of a dynamic economy. It allows workers to sort themselves into the best possible jobs, enables us to enjoy seasonal goods and services like winter skiing and summers at the beach, and permits the economy to go through structural changes when needed.

Nevertheless, many economists feel that the levels of microeconomic unemployment in the United States are too high and that we can continue to enjoy the benefits of a fast-changing and flexible economy with a lower unemployment rate. To achieve this goal, they advocate government programs to help match the unemployed with employers and to help the jobless relocate and learn new skills. Note, however, that these are *microeconomic* policies—government intervention in particular labor markets or to help particular kinds of workers. Since frictional, seasonal, and structural unemployment have microeconomic causes, they need *microeconomic* cures.

Our fourth and last type of unemployment, however, has an entirely *macroeconomic* cause.

**Cyclical Unemployment.**  When the economy goes into a recession and total output falls, the unemployment rate rises. Many previously employed workers lose their jobs and have difficulty finding new ones. At the same time, there are fewer openings, so new entrants to the labor force must spend more than the usual "frictional" time searching before they are hired. This type of unemployment—because it is caused by the business cycle—is called **cyclical unemployment.**

**Cyclical unemployment** Joblessness arising from changes in production over the business cycle.

Look at Figure 3, which shows the unemployment rate in the United States for each quarter since 1960, and notice the rises that occurred during periods of recession (shaded). For example, in the recessions of the early 1980s, the unemployment rate rose from about 6 percent to almost 10 percent; in the more recent recession of 1990–1991, it rose from 5.3 percent to more than 7 percent. These were rises in cyclical unemployment.

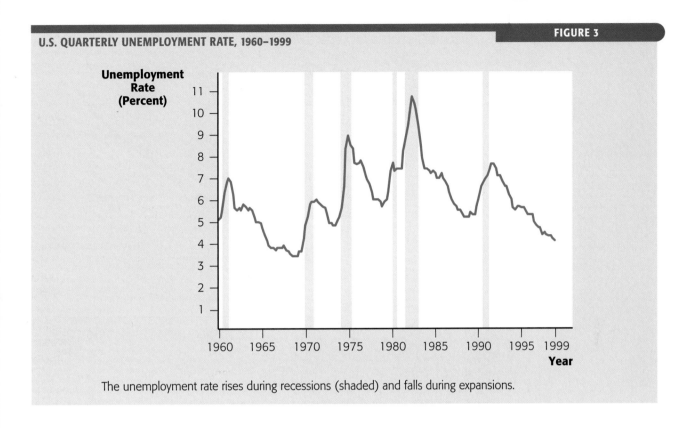

**FIGURE 3**

**U.S. QUARTERLY UNEMPLOYMENT RATE, 1960–1999**

The unemployment rate rises during recessions (shaded) and falls during expansions.

Since it arises from conditions in the overall economy, cyclical unemployment is a problem for *macroeconomic* policy. This is why macroeconomists focus almost exclusively on cyclical unemployment, rather than the other types of joblessness. Reflecting this emphasis, macroeconomists say we have reached **full employment** when we come out of a recession and *cyclical unemployment is reduced to zero,* even though substantial amounts of frictional, seasonal, and structural unemployment may remain:

> *In macroeconomics, full employment is achieved when cyclical unemployment has been reduced to zero. But the overall unemployment rate at full employment is greater than zero because there are still positive levels of frictional, seasonal, and structural unemployment.*

How do we tell how much of our unemployment is cyclical? Many economists believe that today, normal amounts of frictional, seasonal, and structural unemployment account for an unemployment rate of between 4 and 4.5 percent in the United States. Therefore, any unemployment beyond this is considered cyclical unemployment. For example, if the actual unemployment rate were 6 percent, we would identify 1.5 to 2.0 percent of the labor force as cyclically unemployed.

**Full employment** A situation in which there is no cyclical unemployment.

## THE COSTS OF UNEMPLOYMENT

Why are we so concerned about achieving a low rate of unemployment? What are the *costs* of unemployment to our society? We can identify two different types of costs: economic costs—those that can be readily measured in dollar terms—and noneconomic costs—those that are difficult or impossible to measure in dollars, but still affect us in important ways.

FIGURE 4

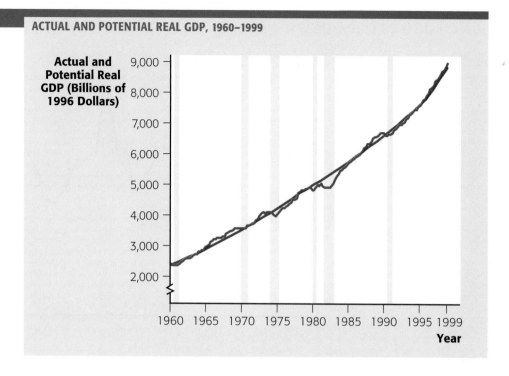

**ACTUAL AND POTENTIAL REAL GDP, 1960–1999**

**Economic Costs.**  The chief economic cost of unemployment is the *opportunity cost* of lost output—the goods and services the jobless *would* produce if they were working, but do not produce because they cannot find work. This cost must be borne by our society, although the burden may fall more on one group than another. If, for example, the unemployed were simply left to fend for themselves, then *they* would bear most of the cost. If they turned to crime in order to survive, then crime victims would share the burden. In fact, the unemployed are often given government assistance, so that the costs are spread among citizens in general. But there is no escaping this central fact:

> When there is cyclical unemployment, the nation produces *less output, and so some group or groups within society must* consume *less output.*

One way of viewing the economic cost of cyclical unemployment is illustrated in Figure 4. The blue line shows real GDP over time, while the red line shows the path of our **potential output**—the output we *could* have produced if the economy were operating at full employment.

**Potential output**  The level of output the economy could produce if operating at full employment.

Notice that actual output is sometimes *above* potential output. At these times, unemployment is *below* the full-employment rate. For example, during the expansion in the late 1960s, cyclical unemployment was eliminated, and the sum of frictional, seasonal, and structural unemployment dropped below 4.5 percent, its normal level for those years. At other times, real GDP is *below* potential output, most often during and immediately following a recession. At these times, unemployment rises above the full-employment rate. In the 1982–83 recession, the unemployment rate remained above 9.5 percent for more than a year

In the figure, you can see that we have spent more of the last 35 years operating *below* our potential than above it. That is, the cyclical ups and downs of the economy have, on balance, led to lower living standards than we would have had if the economy had always operated just at potential output.

**Broader Costs.** There are also costs of unemployment that go beyond lost output. Unemployment—especially when it lasts for many months or years—can have serious psychological and physical effects. Some studies have found that increases in unemployment cause noticeable rises in the number of heart attack deaths, suicides, and admissions to state prisons and psychiatric hospitals. The jobless are more likely to suffer a variety of health problems, including high blood pressure, heart disorders, troubled sleep, and back pain. There may be other problems—such as domestic violence, depression, and alcoholism—that are more difficult to document. And, tragically, most of those who lose their jobs also lose their health insurance, increasing the likelihood that these problems will have serious consequences.

Unemployment also causes setbacks in achieving important social goals. For example, most of us want a fair and just society where all people have an equal chance to better themselves. But our citizens do not bear the burden of unemployment equally. In a recession, we do not all suffer a reduction in our work hours; instead, some people are laid off entirely, while others continue to work roughly the same hours.

Moreover, the burden of unemployment is not shared equally among different groups in the population, but tends to fall most heavily on minorities, especially minority youth. As a rough rule of thumb, the unemployment rate for blacks is twice that for whites; and the rate for *teenage* blacks is triple the rate for blacks overall. Table 3 shows that the unemployment rates for January 2000 are consistent with this general experience. Notice the extremely high unemployment rate for black teenagers: 23.8 percent. Two years earlier—when the overall unemployment rate was 4.7 percent—the rate for black teenagers was even higher: 36.0 percent. This contributes to a vicious cycle of poverty and discrimination: When minority youths are deprived of that all-important first job, they remain at a disadvantage in the labor market for years to come.

## HOW UNEMPLOYMENT IS MEASURED

In January 2000, about 140 million Americans did not have jobs. Were all of these people unemployed? Absolutely not. The unemployed are those *willing and able* to work, but who do not have jobs. Most of the 140 million nonworking Americans were either *unable* or *unwilling* to work. For example, the very old, the very young, and the very ill were unable to work, as were those serving prison terms. Others were able to work, but preferred not to, including millions of college students, homemakers, and retired people.

**TABLE 3**

**UNEMPLOYMENT RATES FOR VARIOUS GROUPS, JANUARY 2000**

| Group | Unemployment Rate |
| --- | --- |
| Whites | 3.4% |
| Hispanics | 5.6% |
| Blacks | 8.2% |
| White Teenagers | 9.1% |
| Black Teenagers | 23.8% |

*Source: The Employment Situation: January 2000:* Bureau of Labor Statistics News Release, February 4, 2000.

**FIGURE 5**

BLS interviewers ask a series of questions to determine whether an individual is employed, unemployed, or not in the labor force.

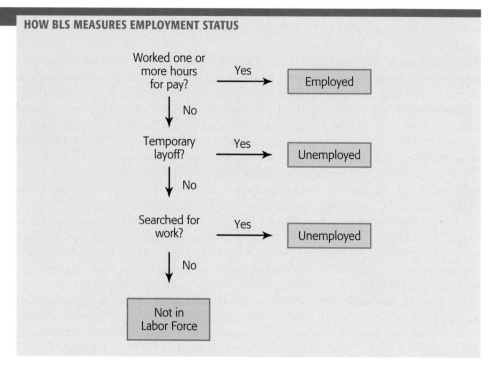

**HOW BLS MEASURES EMPLOYMENT STATUS**

But how, in practice, can we determine who is willing and able? This is a thorny problem, and there is no perfect solution to it. In the United States, we determine whether a person is willing and able to work by his or her *behavior*. More specifically, to be counted as unemployed, you must have recently *searched* for work. But how can we tell who has, and who has not, recently searched for work?

**The Census Bureau's Household Survey.** Every month, thousands of interviewers from the United States Census Bureau—acting on behalf of the U.S. Bureau of Labor Statistics (BLS)—conduct a survey of 60,000 households across America. This sample of households is carefully selected to give information about the entire population. Household members who are under 16, in the military, or currently residing in an institution like a prison or hospital are excluded. The interviewer will then ask questions to determine what the remaining household members did during the *previous week*.

Figure 5 shows roughly how this works. First, the interviewer asks whether the household member has worked one or more hours for pay or profit. If the answer is yes, the person is considered employed; if no, another question is asked: Has she been *temporarily* laid off from a job from which she is waiting to be recalled? A yes means the person is unemployed; a no leads to one more question: Did the person actively *search* for work during the previous four weeks. If yes, the person is unemployed; if no, she is not in the labor force.

Figure 6 illustrates how the BLS, extrapolating from its 60,000-household sample, classified the U.S. population in January 2000. First, note that about 64 million people were ruled out from consideration because they were under 16 years of age, living in institutions, or in the military. The remaining 208.8 million people made up the civilian, noninstitutional population, and of these, 135.2 million were employed, and 5.7 million were unemployed. Adding the employed and unemployed together gives us the **labor force,** equal to 135.2 million + 5.7 million = 140.9 million.

**Labor force** Those people who have a job or who are looking for one.

**FIGURE 6**

**EMPLOYMENT STATUS OF THE U.S. POPULATION–JANUARY, 2000**

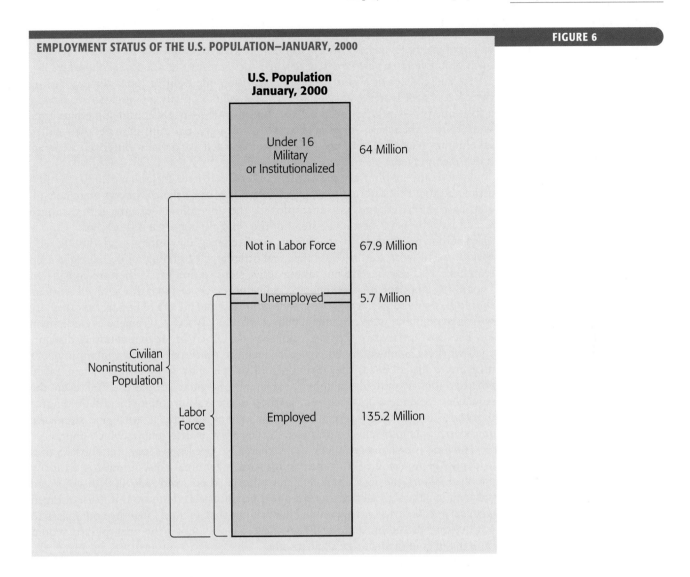

Finally, we come to the official **unemployment rate**, which is defined as the percentage of the labor force that is unemployed:

$$\text{Unemployment rate} = \frac{\text{Unemployed}}{\text{Labor Force}} = \frac{\text{Unemployed}}{(\text{Unemployed} + \text{Employed})}$$

Using the numbers in Figure 6, the unemployment rate in January 2000 was 5.7/(5.7 + 135.2) = 0.040 or 4.0 percent. This was the number released to journalists at 8:00 A.M. on the first Friday of February 2000, and the number that made headlines in your local newspaper the next day.

**Unemployment rate** The fraction of the labor force that is without a job.

## PROBLEMS IN MEASURING UNEMPLOYMENT

The Bureau of the Census earns very high marks from economists for both its sample size—60,000 households—and the characteristics of its sample, which very closely match the characteristics of the U.S. population. Still, the official unemployment rate suffers from some important measurement problems.

Many economists believe that our official measure seriously underestimates the extent of unemployment in our society. There are two reasons for this belief: the treatment of *involuntary part-time workers* and the treatment of *discouraged workers*.

As you can see in Figure 5, anyone working one hour or more for pay during the survey week is treated as employed. This includes many people who would like a full-time job—and may even be searching for one—but who did some part-time work during the week. Some economists have suggested that these people—called **involuntary part-time workers**—should be regarded as partially employed and partially unemployed.

**Involuntary part-time workers** Individuals who would like a full-time job, but who are working only part time.

How many involuntary part-time workers are there? In January 2000, the BLS estimated that there were about 3.5 million.[4] If each of these workers were considered half-employed and half-unemployed, the unemployment rate in that month would have been 5.3 percent, instead of the officially reported 4.0 percent.

Another problem is the treatment of **discouraged workers**—individuals who would like to work but, because they feel little hope of finding a job, have given up searching. Because they are not taking active steps to find work, they are considered "not in the labor force" (see Figure 5). Some observers feel that discouraged workers should be counted as unemployed. After all, these people are telling us that they are willing and able to work, but they are not working. It seems wrong to exclude them just because they are not actively seeking work. Others argue that counting discouraged workers as unemployed would reduce the objectivity of our unemployment measure. Talk is cheap, they believe, and people may *say* anything when asked whether they would like a job; the real test is what people *do*. Yet even the staunchest defenders of the current method of measuring employment would agree that *some* discouraged workers are, in fact, willing and able to work and should be considered unemployed. The problem, in their view, is determining which ones.

**Discouraged workers** Individuals who would like a job, but have given up searching for one.

How many discouraged workers are there? No one knows for sure. The BLS tries to count them periodically, but defining who is genuinely discouraged is a thorny problem. Using the BLS's rather strict criteria, there were 339,000 discouraged workers in January 2000. But with a looser, unofficial definition of "discouraged worker"—people who are not working but say they want a job—the count rises to 4.8 million. Including some or all of these people among the unemployed would raise the unemployment rate significantly.

There are also reasons to believe that the unemployment rate overstates the amount of joblessness as we usually think of it. Remember that a person is counted as unemployed if he or she did not work in the past week, but took some active steps to look for work in the past month. Some of those counted as unemployed did work earlier in the month, even though they were not at work in the survey week. Others whose principal activities are outside the labor market—going to school, keeping house, or being retired—are counted as unemployed because they checked the help wanted ads in the past month or talked to friends about what jobs might be available.

Still, the unemployment rate—as currently measured—tells us something important: the number of people who are *searching* for jobs, but have not yet found them. It is not exactly the same as the percentage of the labor force that is jobless even though willing and able to work. But if we could obtain a perfect measure of the latter, the unemployment rate—as currently measured—would be highly correlated with it.

Moreover, the unemployment rate tells us something unique about conditions in the macroeconomy. When the unemployment rate is relatively low—so that few peo-

---

[4]    This and other information about unemployment in January 2000 comes from *The Employment Situation: January 2000*, Bureau of Labor Statistics News Release, February 4, 2000.

ple are actively seeking work—a firm that wants to hire more workers may be forced to lure them from other firms, by offering a higher wage rate. This puts upward pressure on wages and can lead to future inflation. A high unemployment rate, by contrast, tells us that firms can more easily expand by hiring those who are actively seeking work, without having to lure new workers from another firm and without having to offer higher wages. This suggests little inflationary danger. Later in the book, we will discuss the connection between unemployment and inflation more fully.

## SOCIETY'S CHOICE OF GDP

*Using the*
**THEORY**

The title of this section might seem absurd: How can we say that society *chooses* its level of GDP? Wouldn't the citizens of any nation want their GDP to be as large as possible—and certainly larger than it currently is? The answer is yes. After all, GDP is certainly important to our economic well-being. Few of us would want to live at the levels of output per capita that prevailed 100, 50, or even 25 years ago. Increased output of medical care, restaurant meals, entertainment, transportation services, and education have all contributed to a higher standard of living and an overall improvement in our economic well-being.

But there is more to economic well-being than *just* GDP. Suppose that, over the next 10 years, real GDP per capita were to double. Further, suppose that our measure is entirely accurate (not plagued by the measurement problems discussed in the previous section). Would the average person be better off in 10 years? Maybe. But maybe not. We cannot say, because our GDP statistic ignores so many *other* things that are important to our economic well-being besides the quantity of goods and services at our disposal, and these things may be changing at the same time that GDP is changing.

What are these other things that affect our economic well-being? They include the leisure time we have to spend with family and friends; the cleanliness of our environment; the safety of our workplaces, homes, and streets; the fairness of our society; and more. None of these are included in GDP, which is, after all, just a measure of our output of goods and services.

But what does this have to do with society's choice of GDP? Remember that economics is the study of choice under conditions of scarcity, and just as individuals are constrained by a scarcity of time or income or wealth, society as a whole is constrained by the resources at its disposal. In many cases, we must choose between using our resources to have more of the output that is included in GDP or more of *other* things we care about that are *not* part of GDP.

For example, look at Figure 7, which shows the familiar production possibility frontier, or PPF, from Chapter 2, but with a new twist. In Chapter 2, we looked at the trade-off between two categories of *goods*—medical care versus everything else. Here, we explore the trade-off between real GDP on the horizontal axis and some other thing that we care about—something *not* in GDP—on the vertical axis. In this example, we've put *leisure time* on the vertical axis.

Why is there a trade-off between real GDP and leisure? Because with a given state of technology for producing output, a given population, and given quantities of other resources, the more labor time we devote to production, the more goods and services we will have. But more labor time means less leisure time: Either more people must become employed, or the employed must work longer hours. In either case, the total amount of leisure time enjoyed by the population will decrease.

Let's first identify the two extremes of the PPF in the figure. The maximum leisure time achievable would occur at point *A*—zero output. Here, people would

The production possibilities frontier shows that, for a given population and state of technology, a society must choose between the level of real GDP and the time available for leisure. At point *A*, people devote all their time to leisure, so GDP is zero. Point *D*, by contrast, represents the maximum GDP attainable if everyone works the maximum hours, year-round. *B* and *C* represent intermediate possibilities.

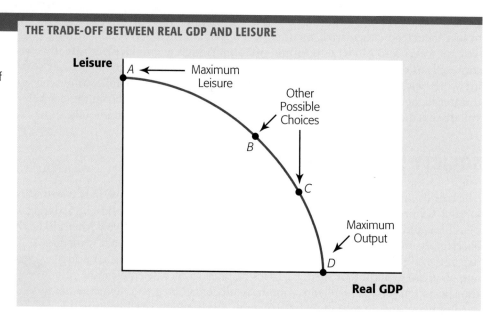

**THE TRADE-OFF BETWEEN REAL GDP AND LEISURE**

have to survive by eating fruit and nuts that fell to the ground, since even climbing trees or hunting animals would involve work. On the other hand, the maximum GDP achievable would require the lowest possible level of leisure—every able-bodied person working 16 hours per day, 365 days per year. This is indicated by point *D* in the figure. The curve that connects points *A* and *D* is the PPF that shows the maximum combinations of output and leisure achievable. (Why does the curve bow out from the origin? Review the material on PPFs in Chapter 2 if you need to.)

The PPF in Figure 7 makes it clear that society faces a trade-off and that, in any year, we choose our level of GDP subject to the constraints of this trade-off. We could draw a similar PPF illustrating the trade-off between a high GDP on the one hand and a clean environment or workplace safety on the other.

How does society choose its location on this kind of PPF?

In a market economy, the choice is made partly by individual households and firms. Suppose that most workers' tastes began to shift toward having more leisure and that they were willing to sacrifice income in order to have it. For example, workers might prefer a 20 percent cut in work hours, with a 20 percent cut in total compensation. Suppose, too, that there were no loss of efficiency from having people work shorter hours. Then any firm that refused to match these new worker preferences—cutting pay and work hours by 20 percent—would have to pay above-average wages in order to attract workers. With higher labor costs, the firm would have to charge a higher price for its output. Such a firm would not be able to compete with other firms that were offering the more desired, shorter work-week. As more and more firms moved toward a shorter workweek, society as a whole would move from a point like *C* in Figure 7 to a point like *B*—more leisure and a lower GDP.

Thus, at least to some extent, we can expect market pressures to adjust work hours to worker preferences for leisure on the one hand and income on the other. The result of these individual decisions will determine, in large measure, where we will be on the PPF in Figure 7.

Interestingly, the United States is farther down and to the right on this PPF (a point like *C*) than most European countries (which are at points like *B*). For example, the average workweek in manufacturing is more than 40 hours in the United States, but around 30 hours in Germany. In addition, the typical U.S. worker takes two weeks of vacation each year, while the typical German worker takes five weeks. To a great extent, these differences in labor hours reflect differences in worker tastes. For example, when Germany introduced Thursday night shopping in 1989, retail workers—who didn't want to work the additional two hours even for additional pay—went on strike. As a result of his greater taste for leisure, the typical German—and the typical French person, Italian, and Spaniard—enjoys more leisure each year than the typical American does. But Europeans pay a cost: a lower GDP, and therefore fewer goods and services per person than they would otherwise have.

Our location on the PPF is also determined by society as a whole, as a matter of public policy. We vote for our representatives, who make rules and regulations under which our firms must operate. If, for example, the majority prefers a higher GDP and less leisure, it can vote for representatives who promise to change work rules. In Germany, for example, it is *illegal* for workers to take another job during their five weeks of annual vacation.[5]

There are also other dimensions to our choice of GDP. For example, with economic growth, a nation can enjoy a greater GDP in the future *and* more of other things—say, workplace safety or leisure. But economic growth comes at a cost as well. We'll examine that cost—and society's choices concerning the rate of economic growth—a few chapters from now.

---

[5]    Daniel Benjamin and Tony Horwitz, "German View: You Americans Work Too Hard—And For What?" *The Wall Street Journal,* July 14, 1994, p. B1

## S U M M A R Y

This chapter discusses how some key macroeconomic aggregates are measured and reported. One important economic aggregate is *gross domestic product*—the total value of all final goods and services produced for the marketplace during a given year, within a nation's borders. GDP is a measure of an economy's total production. It is a flow variable that measures sales, to final users, of newly produced output.

In the *expenditure approach,* GDP is calculated as the sum of spending by households, businesses, governments, and foreigners on domestically produced goods and services. The *value-added approach* computes GDP by adding up each firm's contributions to total product as it is being produced. Value added at each stage of production is the revenue a firm receives minus the cost of the intermediate inputs it uses. Finally, the *factor payments approach* sums the payments to all resource owners. The three approaches reflect three different ways of viewing GDP.

Since nominal GDP is measured in current dollars, it changes when either production or prices change. *Real GDP* is nominal GDP adjusted for price changes; it rises only when production rises.

Real GDP is useful in the short run for giving warnings about impending recessions, and in the long run for indicating how fast the economy is growing. Unfortunately, it is plagued by important inaccuracies. It does not fully reflect quality changes or production in the underground economy, and it does not include many types of nonmarket production.

When real GDP grows, employment tends to rise and unemployment tends to fall. In the United States, a person is considered unemployed if he or she does not have a job but is actively seeking one. Economists have found it useful to classify unemployment into four different categories. *Frictional unemployment* is short-term unemployment experienced by people between jobs or by those who are just entering the job market. *Seasonal unemployment* is related to changes in the weather, tourist patterns, or other predictable seasonal changes. *Structural unemployment* results from mismatches—in skills or location—between jobs and workers. Finally, *cyclical unemployment* occurs because of the business cycle. Unemployment, particularly the structural and cyclical forms, involves costs. From a social perspective, unemployment means lost production. From the individual viewpoint, unemployment often involves financial, psychological, and physical harm.

## KEY TERMS

gross domestic product
  (GDP)
intermediate goods
final good
flow variable
stock variable
expenditure approach
consumption

capital stock
private investment
net investment
government purchases
transfer payment
net exports
value added
value-added approach

factor payments
factor payments approach
nominal variable
real variable
nonmarket production
frictional unemployment
seasonal unemployment
structural unemployment

cyclical unemployment
full employment
potential output
labor force
unemployment rate
involuntary part-time
  workers
discouraged workers

## REVIEW QUESTIONS

1. What is the difference between final goods and intermediate goods? Why is it that only the value of final goods and services is counted in GDP?

2. Which of the following are stock variables, and which are flow variables?
   a. Microsoft's revenues
   b. Microsoft's market value (the total value of shares held by its stockholders)
   c. A household's spending
   d. The value of a household's stock portfolio

3. Using the expenditure approach, which of the following would be directly counted as part of U.S. GDP in 2001? In each case, state whether the action causes an increase in *C*, *I*, *G*, or *NX*.
   a. A new personal computer produced by IBM, which remained unsold at the year's end
   b. A physician's services to a household
   c. Produce bought by a restaurant to serve to customers
   d. The purchase of 1,000 shares of Disney stock
   e. The sale of 50 acres of commercial property
   f. A real estate agent's commission from the sale of property
   g. A transaction in which you clean your roommate's apartment in exchange for his working on your car
   h. An Apple I-Mac computer produced in the United States, and purchased by a French citizen
   i. The government's Social Security payments to retired people

4. How is the word *investment* used differently in economics than in ordinary language? Explain each of the three categories of investment.

5. Describe the different kinds of factor payments.

6. What is the difference between nominal and real variables? What is the main problem with using nominal variables to track the economy?

7. Discuss the value and reliability of GDP statistics in both short-run and long-run analyses of the economy.

8. Real GDP was measured at around $8.8 trillion in 1999. Was the actual value of goods and services produced in the United States in 1999 likely to have been higher or lower than that? Why?

9. What, if anything, could the government do to reduce frictional and structural unemployment?

10. Categorize each of the following according to the type of unemployment it reflects. Justify your answers.
   a. Workers are laid off when a GM factory closes due to a recession.
   b. Workers selling software in a store are laid off when the store goes bankrupt due to competition from on-line software dealers.
   c. Migrant farm workers' jobs end when the harvest is finished.
   d. Lost jobs result from the movement of textile plants from Massachusetts to the South and overseas.

11. Can unemployment ever be good for the economy? Explain.

12. What are some of the different types of costs associated with unemployment?

13. Discuss some of the problems with the way the Bureau of Labor Statistics computes the unemployment rate. In what ways do official criteria lead to an overestimate or underestimate of the actual unemployment figure?

## P R O B L E M S   A N D   E X E R C I S E S

1. Calculate the total change in a year's GDP for each of the following scenarios:
   a. A family sells a home, without using a broker, for $150,000. They could have rented it on the open market for $700 per month. They buy a 10-year-old condominium for $200,000; the broker's fee on the transaction is 6 percent of the selling price. The condo's owner was formerly renting the unit at $500 per month.
   b. General Electric uses $10 million worth of steel, glass, and plastic to produce its dishwashers. Wages and salaries in the dishwasher division are $40 million; the division's only other expense is $15 million in interest that it pays on its bonds. The division's revenue for the year is $75 million.
   c. On March 31, you decide to stop throwing away $50 a month on convenience store nachos. You buy $200 worth of equipment, cornmeal, and cheese, and make your own nachos for the rest of the year.
   d. You win $25,000 in your state's lottery. Ever the entrepreneur, you decide to open a Ping Pong ball washing service, buying $15,000 worth of equipment from SpiffyBall Ltd. of Hong Kong and $10,000 from Ball-B-Kleen of Toledo, Ohio.
   e. Tone-Deaf Artists, Inc. produces 100,000 new White Snake CDs that it prices at $15 apiece. Ten thousand CDs are sold abroad, but, alas, the rest remain unsold on warehouse shelves.

2. The country of Freedonia uses the same method to calculate the unemployment rate as the U.S. Bureau of Labor Statistics uses. From the data below, compute Freedonia's unemployment rate.

| | |
|---|---|
| Population | 10,000,000 |
| Under 16 | 3,000,000 |
| Over 16 | |
| In military service | 500,000 |
| In hospitals | 200,000 |
| In prison | 100,000 |
| Worked one hour or more in previous week | 4,000,000 |
| Searched for work during previous four weeks | 1,000,000 |

## C H A L L E N G E   Q U E S T I O N

Suppose, in a given year, someone buys a General Motors automobile for $30,000. That same year, GM produced the car in Michigan, using $10,000 in parts imported from Japan. However, the parts imported from Japan themselves contained $3,000 in components produced in the United States.

a. By how much does U.S. GDP rise?
b. Using the expenditure approach, what is the change in each component (*C, I, G,* and *NX*) of U.S. GDP?
c. What is the change in Japan's GDP and each of its components?

## E X P E R I E N T I A L   E X E R C I S E S

1. One criticism of the U.S. national income accounts is that they ignore the effects of environmental pollution. The World Bank's group on environmental economics has been investigating ways of assessing environmental degradation. Take at look at their work on "green accounting" at *http://wbln0018.Worldbank.org/environment/EEI.nsf/all/Green+Accounting?OpenDocument*. What kinds of problems have they identified, and what proposals have they made to deal with those problems?

   http://

2. Data on the Consumer Price Index are released near the middle of each month. (You can find the exact date by consulting the online calendar at *http://www.leggmason.com/CAL/calendar.html*) Data on GDP are released on the last Friday of each month (in preliminary, revised, and then final form). Analysis of these data appears in the first section of the following weekday's *Wall Street Journal*. Look in the "Economy" section to find the story. What do the latest available data tell you about the current rate of inflation and the current rate of GDP growth? Is the economy expanding or contracting?

   http://

# 6

# THE MONETARY SYSTEM, PRICES, AND INFLATION

**Unit of value** A common unit for measuring how much something is worth.

**Means of payment** Anything acceptable as payment for goods and services.

Y ou pull into a gas station deep in the interior of the distant nation of Chaotica. The numbers on the gas pump don't make sense to you, and you can't figure out how much to pay. Luckily, the national language of Chaotica is English, so you can ask the cashier how much the gas costs. He replies, "Here in Chaotica, we don't have any standard system for measuring quantities of gas, and we don't have any standard way to quote prices. My pump here measures in my own unit, called the Slurp, and I will sell you 6 Slurps for that watch you are wearing, or a dozen Slurps for your camera." You spend the next half hour trying to determine how many Slurps there are in a gallon and what form of payment you can use besides your watch and camera.

Life in the imaginary nation of Chaotica would be difficult. People would spend a lot of time figuring out how to trade with each other, time that could otherwise be spent producing things or enjoying leisure activities. Fortunately, in the real world, virtually every nation has a *monetary system* that helps to organize and simplify our economic transactions.

## THE MONETARY SYSTEM

A monetary system establishes two different types of standardization in the economy. First, it establishes a **unit of value**—a common unit for measuring how much something is worth. A standard unit of value permits us to compare the costs of different goods and services and to communicate these costs when we trade. The dollar is the unit of value in the United States. If a college textbook costs $75, while a one-way airline ticket from Phoenix to Minneapolis costs $300, we know immediately that the ticket has the same value in the marketplace as four college textbooks.

The second type of standardization concerns the **means of payment**—the things we can use as payment when we buy goods and services. In the United States, the means of payment include dollar bills, personal checks, money orders, credit cards like Visa and American Express, and, in some experimental locations, prepaid cash cards with magnetic strips.

These two functions of a monetary system—establishing a unit of value and a standard means of payment—are closely related, but they are not the same thing.

The unit-of-value function refers to the way we *think* about and record transactions; the means-of-payment function refers to how payment is actually made.

The unit of value works in the same way as units of weight, volume, distance, and time. In fact, the same sentence in Article I of the U.S. Constitution gives Congress the power to create a unit of value along with units of weights and measures. All of these units help us determine clearly and precisely what is being traded for what. Think about buying gas in the United States—you exchange dollars for gallons. The transaction will go smoothly and quickly only if there is clarity about both the unit of fluid volume (gallons) *and* the unit of purchasing power (dollars).

The means of payment can be different from the unit of value. For example, in some countries where local currency prices change very rapidly, it is common to use the U.S. dollar as the unit of value—to specify prices in dollars—while the local currency remains the means of payment. Even in the United States, when you use a check to buy something, the unit of value is the dollar, but the means of payment is a piece of paper with your signature on it.

In the United States, the dollar is the centerpiece of our monetary system. It is the unit of value in virtually every economic transaction, and dollar bills are very often the means of payment as well. How did the dollar come to play such an important role in the economy?

## HISTORY OF THE DOLLAR

Prior to 1790, each colony had its own currency. It was named the "pound" in every colony, but it had a different purchasing power in each of them. In 1790, soon after the Constitution went into effect, Congress created a new unit of value called the dollar. Historical documents show that merchants and businesses switched immediately to the new dollar, thereby ending the chaos of the colonial monetary systems. Prices began to be quoted in dollars, and accounts were kept in dollars. The dollar rapidly became the standard unit of value.

But the primary means of payment in the United States until the Civil War was paper currency issued by private banks. Just as the government defined the length of the yard, but did not sell yardsticks, the government defined the unit of value, but let private organizations provide the means of payment.

During the Civil War, however, the government issued the first federal paper currency, the greenback. It functioned as both the unit of value and the major means of payment until 1879. Then the government got out of the business of money creation for a few decades. During that time, currency was once again issued by private banks. Then, in 1913, a new institution called the **Federal Reserve System** was created to be the national monetary authority in the United States. The Federal Reserve was charged with creating and regulating the nation's supply of money, and it continues to do so today.

**Federal Reserve System** The central bank and national monetary authority of the United States.

## WHY PAPER CURRENCY IS ACCEPTED AS A MEANS OF PAYMENT

You may be wondering why people are willing to accept paper dollars as a means of payment. Why should a farmer give up a chicken, or a manufacturer give up a new car, just to receive a bunch of green rectangles with words printed on them? In fact, paper currency is a relatively recent development in the history of the means of payment.

The earliest means of payment were precious metals and other valuable commodities such as furs or jewels. These were called *commodity money* because they had important uses other than as a means of payment. The nonmoney use is what

Today, dollars are not backed by gold or silver, but we accept them as payment because we know that others will accept them from us.

**Fiat money** Anything that serves as a means of payment by government declaration.

gave commodity money its ultimate value. For example, people would accept furs as payment because furs could be used to keep warm. Similarly, gold and silver had a variety of uses in industry, as religious artifacts, and for ornamentation.

Precious metals were an especially popular form of commodity money. Eventually, to make it easier to identify the value of precious metals, they were minted into coins whose weight was declared on their faces. Because gold and silver coins could be melted down into pure metal and used in other ways, they were still commodity money.

Commodity money eventually gave way to paper currency. Initially, paper currency was just a certificate representing a certain amount of gold or silver held by a bank. At any time, the holder of a certificate could go to the bank that issued it and trade the certificate for the stated amount of gold or silver. People were willing to accept paper money as a means of payment for two reasons. First, the currency could be exchanged for a valuable commodity like gold or silver. Second, the issuer—either a government or a bank—could only print new money when it acquired additional gold or silver. This put strict limits on money printing, so people had faith that their paper money would retain its value in the marketplace.

But today, paper currency is no longer backed by gold or any other physical commodity. If you have a dollar handy, put this book down and take a close look at the bill. You will not find on it any promise that you can trade your dollar for gold, silver, furs, or anything else. Yet we all accept it as a means of payment. Why? A clue is provided by the statement in the upper left-hand corner of every bill: *This note is legal tender for all debts, public and private.* The statement affirms that the piece of paper in your hands will be accepted as a means of payment (you can "tender" it to settle any "debt, public or private") by any American because the government says so. This type of currency is called **fiat money.** *Fiat,* in Latin, means "let there be," and fiat money serves as a means of payment by government declaration.

The government need not worry about enforcing this declaration. The real force behind the dollar—and the reason that we are all willing to accept these green pieces of paper as payment—is its long-standing acceptability by *others.* As long as you have confidence that you can use your dollars to buy goods and services, you won't mind giving up goods and services for dollars. And because everyone else feels the same way, the circle of acceptability is completed.

But while the government can declare that paper currency is to be accepted as a means of payment, it cannot declare the terms. Whether 10 gallons of gas will cost you 1 dollar, 10 dollars, or 20 dollars is up to the marketplace. The value of the dollar—its purchasing power—does change from year to year, as reflected in the changing prices of the things we buy. In the rest of this chapter, we will discuss some of the problems created by the dollar's changing value and the difficulty economists have measuring and monitoring the changes. We postpone until later chapters the question of *why* the value of the dollar changes from year to year.

## MEASURING THE PRICE LEVEL AND INFLATION

One hundred years ago, you could buy a pound of coffee for 15 cents, see a Broadway play for 40 cents, buy a new suit for $6, and attend a private college for $200 in yearly tuition.[1] Needless to say, the price of each of these items has gone up considerably since then. Microeconomic causes—changes in individual markets—can

---

1    Scott Derks, ed., *The Value of the Dollar: Prices and Incomes in the United States: 1860–1989* (Detroit, MI: Gale Research Inc., 1994), various pages.

explain only a tiny fraction of these price changes. For the most part, these price rises came about because of an ongoing rise in the **price level**—the average level of dollar prices in the economy. In this section, we begin to explore how the price level is measured, and how this measurement is used.

**Price level** The average level of dollar prices in the economy.

## INDEX NUMBERS

Most measures of the price level are reported in the form of an **index**—a series of numbers, each one representing a different period. Index numbers are meaningful only in a *relative* sense: We compare one period's index number with that of another period and can quickly see which one is larger and by how much. The actual number for a particular period has no meaning in and of itself.

In general, an index number for any measure is calculated as

**Index** A series of numbers used to track a variable's rise or fall over time.

$$\frac{\text{Value of measure in current period}}{\text{Value of measure in base period}} \times 100.$$

Let's see how index numbers work with a simple example. Suppose we want to measure how violence on TV has changed over time, and we have data on the number of violent acts shown in each of several years. We could then construct a TV-violence index. Our first step would be to choose a *base period*—a period to be used as a benchmark. Let's choose 1996 as our base period, and suppose that there were 10,433 violent acts on television in that year. Then our violence index in any current year would be calculated as

$$\frac{\text{Number of violent acts in current year}}{10,433} \times 100.$$

In 1996—the base year—the index will have the value $(10,433/10,433) \times 100 = 100$. Look again at the general formula for index numbers, and you will see that this is always true: *An index will always equal 100 in the base period.*

Now let's calculate the value of our index in another year. If there were 14,534 violent acts in 2000, then the index that year would have the value

$$\frac{14,534}{10,433} \times 100 = 139.3.$$

Index numbers compress and simplify information so that we can see how things are changing at a glance. Our media violence index, for example, tells us at a glance that the number of violent acts in 2000 was 139.3 percent of the number in 1996. Or, more simply, TV violence grew by 39.3 percent between 1996 and 2000.

## THE CONSUMER PRICE INDEX

The most widely used measure of the price level in the United States is the **Consumer Price Index (CPI)**. This index—which is designed to track the prices paid by the typical consumer—is compiled and reported by the Bureau of Labor Statistics (BLS).

Measuring the prices paid by the typical consumer is not easy. Two problems must be solved before we even begin. The first problem is to decide which goods and services we should include in our average. The CPI tracks only *consumer* prices; it excludes goods and services that are not directly purchased by consumers. More specifically, the CPI excludes goods purchased by businesses (such as capital

**Consumer Price Index** An index of the cost, through time, of a fixed market basket of goods purchased by a typical household in some base period.

equipment, raw materials, or wholesale goods), goods and services purchased by government agencies (such as fighter-bombers and the services of police officers) and goods and services purchased by foreigners (U.S. exports). The CPI *does* include newly produced consumer goods and services that are part of consumption spending in our GDP—things such as new clothes, new furniture, new cars, haircuts, and restaurant meals. It also includes some things that are *not* part of our GDP but that are part of the typical family's budget. For example, the CPI includes prices for *used* goods such as used cars or used books, and imports from other countries—for example, French cheese, Japanese cars, and Mexican tomatoes.

The second problem is how to combine all the different prices into an average price level. In any given month, different prices will change by different amounts. The average price of doctor's visits might rise by 1 percent, the price of blue jeans might rise by a tenth of a percent, the price of milk might fall by half a percent, and so on. When prices change at different rates, and when some are rising while others are falling, how can we track the change in the *average* price level? We would not want to use a simple average of all prices—adding them up and dividing by the number of goods. A proper measure would recognize that we spend very little of our incomes on some goods—such as Tabasco sauce—and much more on others—like car repairs or rent.

The CPI's approach is to track the cost of the *CPI market basket*—the collection of goods and services that the typical consumer bought in some base period. If the market basket's cost rises by 10 percent over some period, then the price level, as reported by the CPI, will rise by 10 percent. This way, goods and services that are relatively unimportant in the typical consumer's budget will have little weight in the CPI. Tabasco sauce could triple in price and have no noticeable impact on the cost of the complete market basket. Goods that are more important—such as auto repairs or rent—will have more weight.

In recent years, the base year[2] for the CPI has been 1983, so, following our general formula for price indexes, the CPI is calculated as

$$\frac{\textbf{Cost of market basket in current year}}{\textbf{Cost of market basket in 1983}} \times 100.$$

The appendix to this chapter discusses the calculation of the CPI in more detail.

http://

You can find the latest information on the CPI at http://stats.bls.gov/newsrels.htm—the Bureau of Labor Statistics Web site.

## HOW THE CPI HAS BEHAVED

Table 1 shows the actual value of the CPI for December of selected years. Because it is reported in index number form, we can easily see how much the price level has changed over different time intervals. In December 1999, for example, the CPI had a value of 168.3, telling us that the typical market basket in that year cost 68.3 percent more than it would have cost in the July 1983 base period. In December 1960, the CPI was 29.8, so the cost of the market basket in that year was only 29.8 percent of its cost in July 1983. In July 1983 (not shown), the CPI's value was 100.

[2] To be more specific: The market basket currently used by the Bureau of Labor Statistics reflects purchasing patterns over the period 1993–95. However, the *base period* used in calculations is July 1983. Thus, a more detailed version of our formula is: CPI in current year = Cost of 1993–95 market basket in current year/Cost of 1993–95 market basket in July 1983 × 100. The denominator requires some careful interpretation: It is what the 1993–95 market basket *would* have cost at July 1983 prices. As you can verify, with this formula, the CPI in July 1983 will be equal to 100. In official BLS statistics, the July 1983 base period is still referred to as the "1982–1984 base period" because a survey of consumer spending patterns had been conducted from 1982 to 1984.

| | | TABLE 1 |
| --- | --- | --- |
| Year | Consumer Price Index | CONSUMER PRICE INDEX, DECEMBER, SELECTED YEARS, 1960–1999 |
| 1960 | 29.8 | |
| 1965 | 31.8 | |
| 1970 | 39.8 | |
| 1975 | 55.5 | |
| 1980 | 86.3 | |
| 1985 | 109.3 | |
| 1990 | 133.8 | |
| 1995 | 153.5 | |
| 1999 | 168.3 | |

## FROM PRICE INDEX TO INFLATION RATE

The Consumer Price Index is a measure of the price *level* in the economy. The **inflation rate** measures how fast the price level is changing, as a percentage rate. When the price level is rising, as it almost always is, the inflation rate is positive. When the price level is falling, as it did during the Great Depression, we have a negative inflation rate, which is called **deflation.**

Figure 1 shows the U.S. rate of inflation—as measured by the CPI—since 1950. For each year, the inflation rate is calculated as the percentage change in the CPI from December of the previous year to December of that year. For example, the CPI in December 1998 was 163.9, and in December 1999 it was 168.3. The inflation rate for 1999 was $(168.3 - 163.9)/163.9 = 0.027$ or 2.7 percent. Notice that inflation was low in the 1950s and 1960s, was high in the 1970s and early 1980s, and has been low since then. In later chapters, you will learn what causes the inflation rate to rise and fall.

> **Inflation rate** The percent change in the price level from one period to the next.

> **Deflation** A *decrease* in the price level from one period to the next.

## HOW THE CPI IS USED

The CPI is one of the most important measures of the performance of the economy. It is used in three major ways:

*As a Policy Target.* In the introductory macroeconomics chapter, we saw that price stability—or a low inflation rate—is one of the nation's important macroeconomic goals. The measure most often used to gauge our success in achieving low inflation is the CPI.

*To Index Payments.* A payment is **indexed** when it is set by a formula so that it rises and falls proportionally with a price index. An indexed payment makes up for the loss in purchasing power that occurs when the price level rises. It raises the nominal payment by just enough to keep its purchasing power unchanged. In the United States, millions of government retirees and Social Security recipients have their benefit payments

> **Indexation** Adjusting the value of some nominal payment in proportion to a price index, in order to keep the real payment unchanged.

DANGEROUS CURVES

People often confuse the statement "prices are rising" with the statement "inflation is rising," but they do not mean the same thing. Remember that the inflation rate is the rate of *change* of the price level. To have rising inflation, the price level must be rising by a greater and greater percentage each period. But we can also have rising prices and *falling* inflation. For example, from 1996 to 1998, the CPI rose each year—"prices were rising." But they rose by a smaller percentage each year than the year before, so "inflation was falling"—from 3.3 percent, to 2.7 percent, and, finally, to 1.6 percent in 1998.

**FIGURE 1**

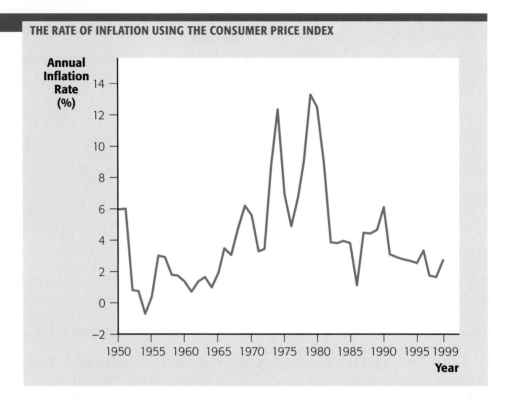

**THE RATE OF INFLATION USING THE CONSUMER PRICE INDEX**

indexed to the CPI. About one-quarter of all union members—more than 5 million workers—have labor contracts that index their wages to the CPI. Since the 1980s, the U.S. income tax has been indexed as well—the threshold income levels at which tax rates change automatically rise at the same rate as the CPI. And the government now sells bonds that are indexed to the CPI. The owner of an indexed bond receives a payment each year to make up for the loss of purchasing power when the CPI rises.

*To Translate from Nominal to Real Values.* In order to compare economic values from different periods, we must translate **nominal variables**—measured in the number of dollars—into **real variables,** which are adjusted for the change in the dollar's purchasing power. The CPI is often used for this translation. Since calculating real variables is one of the most important uses of the CPI, we devote the next section to that topic.

**Nominal variable**  A variable measured in current dollars.

**Real variable**  A variable measured in terms of purchasing power.

## REAL VARIABLES AND ADJUSTMENT FOR INFLATION

Suppose that from December 2001 to December 2002, your nominal wage—what you are paid in dollars—rises from $15 to $30 per hour. Are you better off? That depends. You are earning twice as many dollars. But you should care not about how many green pieces of paper you earn, but how many goods and services you can buy with that paper. How, then, can we tell what happened to your purchasing power? By focusing not on the *nominal wage*—the number of *dollars* you earn—but on the *real wage*—the *purchasing power* of your wage. To track your real wage, we need to look at the number of dollars you earn *relative to the price level.*

Since the "typical worker" and the "typical consumer" are pretty much the same, the CPI is usually the price index used to calculate the real wage. The real-wage formula is as follows:

$$\text{Real wage in any year} = \frac{\text{Nominal wage in that year}}{\text{CPI in that year}} \times 100.$$

To see that this formula makes sense, let's go back to our fictional example: From 2001 to 2002, your nominal wage doubles from $15 to $30. Now, suppose the price of everything that you buy doubles at the same time. It is easy to see that in this case, your purchasing power would remain unchanged. And that is just what our formula tells us: If prices double, the CPI doubles as well. With 2001 as our base year, the CPI would increase from 100 in 2001 to 200 in the year 2002. The *real* wage would be ($15/100) $\times$ 100 = $15 in 2001 and ($30/200) $\times$ 100 = $15 in 2002. The real wage would remain unchanged.

Now suppose that prices doubled between 2001 and 2002, but your nominal wage remained unchanged at $15. In this case, your purchasing power would be cut in half. You'd have the same number of dollars, but each one would buy half as much as it did before. Our formula gives us a real wage of ($15/100) $\times$ 100 = $15 in 2001 and ($15/200) $\times$ 100 = $7.50 in 2002. The real wage falls by half.

Now look at Table 2, which shows the average hourly earnings of wage earners over the past four decades. In the first two columns, you can see that the average American wage earner was paid $4.67 per hour in December 1975, and almost triple that—$13.46—in December 1999. Does this mean the average hourly worker was paid more in 1999 than in 1975? In *dollars,* the answer is clearly yes. But what about in *purchasing power?* Or, using the new terminology you've learned: What happened to the *real wage* over this period?

Let's see. We know that the *nominal wage* rose from $4.67 in 1975 to $13.46 in 1999. But—from the table—we also know that the CPI rose from 55.5 to 168.3 over the same period. Using our formula, we find that

$$\text{Real wage in 1975} = \frac{\$4.67}{55.5} \times 100 = \$8.41.$$

$$\text{Real wage in 1999} = \frac{\$13.46}{168.3} \times 100 = \$7.99.$$

Thus, although the average worker earned more *dollars* in 1999 than in 1975, when we use the CPI as our measure of prices, her purchasing power seems to have fallen

| | | | | TABLE 2 |
|---|---|---|---|---|
| Year | Nominal Wage, Dollars per Hour | CPI | Real Wage in 1983 Dollars per Hour | **NOMINAL AND REAL WAGES** |
| 1960 | 2.05 | 29.8 | 6.88 | |
| 1965 | 2.50 | 31.8 | 7.86 | |
| 1970 | 3.31 | 39.8 | 8.32 | |
| 1975 | 4.67 | 55.5 | 8.41 | |
| 1980 | 6.94 | 86.3 | 8.04 | |
| 1985 | 8.72 | 109.3 | 7.98 | |
| 1990 | 10.17 | 133.8 | 7.60 | |
| 1995 | 11.60 | 153.5 | 7.56 | |
| 1999 | 13.46 | 168.3 | 8.00 | |

over those years. *Why* this apparent decline in purchasing power? This is an interesting and important question, and one we'll begin to answer later in the chapter. The important point to remember here is that

> *when we measure changes in the macroeconomy, we usually care not about the number of dollars we are counting, but the purchasing power those dollars represent. Thus, we translate nominal values into real values using the formula*
>
> $$\text{real value} = \frac{\text{nominal value}}{\text{price index}} \times 100.$$

This formula, usually using the CPI as the price index, is how most real values in the economy are calculated. But there is one important exception: To calculate real GDP, the government uses a different procedure, to which we now turn.

### INFLATION AND THE MEASUREMENT OF REAL GDP

In the previous chapter, we discussed the difference between nominal GDP and real GDP. After reading this chapter, you might think that real GDP is calculated just like the real wage: dividing nominal GDP by the consumer price index. But the consumer price index is *not* used to translate nominal GDP figures into real GDP figures. Instead, a special price index—which we can call the **GDP price index**—is calculated for GDP.

**GDP price index** An index of the price level for all final goods and services included in GDP.

The most important differences between the CPI and the GDP price index are in the types of goods and services covered by each index. First, the GDP price index *includes* some prices that the CPI ignores. In particular, while the CPI tracks only the prices of goods bought by American *consumers,* the GDP price index must also include the prices of goods and services purchased by the government, investment goods purchased by businesses, and exports, which are purchased by foreigners.

Second, the GDP price index *excludes* some prices that are part of the CPI. In particular, the GDP price index leaves out used goods and imports, both of which are included in the CPI. This makes sense, because while used goods and imports are part of the typical consumer's market basket, they do not contribute to current U.S. GDP.

We can summarize the chief difference between the CPI and the GDP price index this way:

> *The GDP price index measures the prices of all goods and services that are included in U.S. GDP, while the CPI measures the prices of all goods and services bought by U.S. households.*[3]

### THE COSTS OF INFLATION

A high or even moderate rate of inflation—whether it is measured by the CPI or the GDP price index—is never welcome news. What's so bad about inflation? As we've seen, it certainly makes your task as an economics student more difficult: Rather than taking nominal variables at face value, you must do those troublesome calculations to convert them into real variables.

---

[3] The technical name for the GDP price index is the *chain-type annual weights GDP price index.* It differs from the CPI not only in goods covered, but also in its mathematical formula.

But inflation causes much more trouble than this. It can impose costs on society, and on each of us individually. Yet when most people are asked *what* the cost of inflation is, they come up with an incorrect answer.

## THE INFLATION MYTH

Most people think that inflation—merely by making goods and services more expensive—erodes the average purchasing power of income in the economy. The reason for this belief is easy to see: The higher the price level, the fewer goods and services a given income will buy. It stands to reason, then, that inflation—which raises prices—must be destroying the purchasing power of our incomes. Right?

Actually, this statement is mostly wrong.

To see why, remember that every market transaction involves *two* parties—a buyer and a seller. When a price rises, buyers of that good must pay more, but sellers get more revenue when they sell it. The loss in buyers' real income is matched by the rise in sellers' real income. Inflation may *redistribute* purchasing power among the population, but it does not change the *average* purchasing power, when we include both buyers and sellers in the average.

In fact, most people in the economy participate on both sides of the market. On the one hand, they are consumers—as when they shop for food or clothing or furniture. On the other hand, they work in business firms that *sell* products, and may benefit (in the form of higher wages or higher profits) when their firms' incomes rise. Thus, when prices rise, a particular person may find that her purchasing power has either risen or fallen, depending on whether she is affected more as a seller or as a buyer. But regardless of the outcome for individuals, our conclusion remains the same:

> *Inflation can redistribute purchasing power from one group to another, but it cannot—by itself—decrease the average real income in the economy.*

Why, then, do people continue to believe that inflation robs the average citizen of real income? Largely because real incomes sometimes do decline—for *other* reasons. Inflation—while not the *cause* of the decline—will often be the *mechanism* that brings it about. Just as we often blame the messenger for bringing bad news, so too, we often blame inflation for lowering our purchasing power when the real cause lies elsewhere.

Let's consider an example. In Table 2, notice the decline in real wages during the late 1970s. The real wage fell from $8.41 in 1975 to $8.04 in 1980—a decline of more than 4 percent. During this period, not only wage earners, but also salaried workers, small-business owners, and corporate shareholders all suffered a decline in their real incomes. What caused the decline?

There were several reasons, but one of the most important was the dramatic rise in the price of imported oil—from $3 per barrel in 1973 to $34 in 1981, an increase of more than 1,000 percent. The higher price for oil meant that oil-exporting countries, like Saudi Arabia, Kuwait, and Iraq, got more goods and services for each barrel of oil they supplied to the rest of the world, including the United States. But with these nations claiming more of America's output, less remained for the typical American. That is, the typical American family had to suffer a decline in real income. As always, a rise in price shifted income from buyers to sellers. But in this case, the sellers were foreigners, while the buyers were Americans. Thus, the rise in the price of foreign oil caused average purchasing power in the United States to decline.

But what was the mechanism that brought about the decline? Since real income is equal to (nominal income/price index) × 100, it can decrease in one of two ways: a fall in the numerator (nominal income) or a rise in the denominator (the price index).

The decline in real income in the 1970s was all from the denominator. Look back at Figure 1. You can see that this period of declining real wages in the United States was also a period of unusually high inflation; at its peak in 1979, the inflation rate exceeded 13 percent. As a result, most workers blamed *inflation* for their loss of purchasing power. But inflation was not the *cause*; it was just the *mechanism*. The cause was a change in the terms of trade between the United States and the oil exporting countries—a change that resulted in higher oil prices.

To summarize, the common idea that inflation imposes a cost on society by decreasing average real income in the economy is incorrect. But inflation *does* impose costs on society, as the next section shows.

## THE REDISTRIBUTIVE COST OF INFLATION

One cost of inflation is that it often redistributes purchasing power *within* society. But because the winners and losers are chosen haphazardly—rather than by conscious social policy—the redistribution of purchasing power is not generally desirable. In some cases, the shift in purchasing power is downright perverse—harming the needy and helping those who are already well off.

How does inflation sometimes redistribute real income? An increase in the price level reduces the purchasing power of any payment that is specified in nominal terms. For example, some workers have contracts that set their nominal wage for two or three years, regardless of any future inflation. The nationally set minimum wage, too, is set for several years and specified in nominal dollars. Under these circumstances, inflation can harm ordinary workers, since it erodes the purchasing power of their pre-specified nominal wage. Real income is redistributed from these workers to their employers, who benefit by paying a lower real wage. But the effect can also work the other way: benefiting ordinary households and harming businesses. For example, many homeowners sign fixed-dollar mortgage agreements with a bank. These are promises to pay the bank the same nominal sum each month. Inflation can reduce the *real* value of these payments, thus redistributing purchasing power away from the bank and toward the average homeowner.

In general,

> *inflation can shift purchasing power away from those who are awaiting future payments specified in dollars, and toward those who are obligated to make such payments.*

But does inflation *always* redistribute income from one party in a contract to another? Actually, no; if the inflation is *expected* by both parties, it should not redistribute income. The next section explains why.

**Expected *Inflation* Need Not *Shift Purchasing Power.*** Suppose a labor union is negotiating a three-year contract with an employer, and both sides agree that each year, workers should get a 3-percent increase in their real wage. Labor contracts, like most other contracts, are usually specified in nominal terms: The firm will agree to give workers so many additional *dollars per hour* each year. If neither side anticipates any inflation, they should simply negotiate a 3-percent *nominal* wage hike. With an unchanged price level, the *real* wage would then also rise by the desired 3 percent.

But suppose instead that both sides anticipate 10-percent inflation each year for the next three years. Then, they must agree to *more* than a 3-percent nominal wage increase in order to raise the real wage by 3 percent. How much more?

We can answer this question with a simple mathematical rule:

> *Over any period, the percentage change in a real value (%∆Real) is approximately equal to the percentage change in the associated nominal value (%∆Nominal) minus the rate of inflation:*
>
> **%∆Real = %∆Nominal − Rate of inflation.**

If the inflation rate is 10 percent, and the real wage is to rise by 3 percent, then the change in the nominal wage must satisfy the equation

**3 percent = %∆Nominal − 10 percent ⟹ %∆Nominal = 13 percent.**

The required nominal wage hike is 13 percent.

You can see that as long as both sides correctly anticipate the inflation, and no one stops them from negotiating a 13-percent nominal wage hike, inflation will *not* affect either party in real terms:

> *If inflation is fully anticipated, and if both parties take it into account, then inflation will* not *redistribute purchasing power.*

We come to a similar conclusion about contracts between lenders and borrowers. When you lend someone money, you receive a reward—an interest payment—for letting that person use your money instead of spending it yourself. The annual *interest rate* is the interest payment divided by the amount of money you have lent. For example, if you lend someone $1,000 and receive back $1,040 one year later, then your interest payment is $40, and the interest *rate* on the loan is $40/$1,000 = 0.04, or 4 percent.

But there are actually *two* interest rates associated with every loan. One is the **nominal interest rate**—the percentage increase in the lender's *dollars* from making the loan. The other is the **real interest rate**—the percentage increase in the lender's *purchasing power* from making the loan. It is the *real* rate—the change in purchasing power—that lenders and borrowers should care about.

In the absence of inflation, real and nominal interest rates would always be equal. A 4-percent increase in the lender's *dollars* would always imply a 4-percent increase in her purchasing power. But if there is inflation, it will reduce the purchasing power of the money paid back. Does this mean that inflation redistributes purchasing power? Not if the inflation is correctly anticipated, and if there are no restrictions on making loan contracts.

For example, suppose both parties anticipate inflation of 5 percent and want to arrange a contract whereby the lender will be paid a 4-percent *real* interest rate. What *nominal* interest rate should they choose? Since an interest rate is the *percentage change* in the lender's funds, we can use our approximation rule,

**%∆Real = %∆Nominal − Rate of inflation**

which here becomes

**%∆ in Lender's purchasing power = %∆ in Lender's dollars − Rate of inflation**

or

**Real interest rate = Nominal interest rate − Rate of inflation.**

**Nominal interest rate** The annual percent increase in a lender's *dollars* from making a loan.

**Real interest rate** The annual percent increase in a lender's *purchasing power* from making a loan.

In our example, where we want the real interest rate to equal 4 percent when the inflation rate is 5 percent, we must have

$$4 \text{ percent} = \text{Nominal interest rate} - 5 \text{ percent}$$

or

$$\text{Nominal interest rate} = 9 \text{ percent.}$$

Once again, we see that as long as both parties correctly anticipate the inflation rate, and face no restrictions on contracts (that is, they are free to set the nominal interest rate at 9 percent), then no one gains or loses.

When inflation is *not* correctly anticipated, however, our conclusion is very different.

### *Unexpected Inflation* Does *Shift Purchasing Power.*

Suppose that, expecting no inflation, you agree to lend money at a 4-percent nominal interest rate for one year. You and the borrower think that this will translate into a 4-percent real rate. But it turns out you are both wrong: The price level actually rises by 3 percent, so the *real* interest rate ends up being $4\% - 3\% = 1\%$. As a lender, you have given up the use of your money for the year, expecting to be rewarded with a 4-percent increase in purchasing power. But you get only a 1-percent increase. Your borrower was willing to pay 4 percent in purchasing power, but ends up paying only 1 percent. *Unexpected* inflation has led to a better deal for your borrower and a worse deal for you.

That will not make you happy. But it could be even worse. Suppose the inflation rate is higher—say, 6 percent. Then your real interest rate ends up at $4\% - 6\% = -2\%$—a negative real interest rate. You get back *less* in purchasing power than you lend out—*paying* (in purchasing power) for the privilege of lending out your money. The borrower is *rewarded* (in purchasing power) for borrowing!

Negative real interest rates like this are not just a theoretical possibility. In the late 1970s, when inflation turned out to be higher than expected for several years in a row, many borrowers ending up paying negative rates to lenders.

Now, let's consider one more possibility: Expected inflation is 6 percent, so you negotiate a 10-percent nominal rate, thinking this will translate to a 4 percent real rate. But the actual inflation rate turns out to be zero, so the real interest rate is 10 percent − 0 percent = 10 percent. In this case, inflation turns out to be *less* than expected, so the *real* interest rate is higher than either of you anticipated. The borrower is harmed, and you (the lender) benefit.

These examples apply, more generally, to any agreement on future payments: to a worker waiting for a wage payment and the employer who has promised to pay it; to a doctor who has sent out a bill and the patient who has not yet paid it; or to a supplier who has delivered goods and his customer who hasn't yet paid for them.

> *When inflationary expectations are inaccurate, purchasing power is shifted between those obliged to make future payments and those waiting to be paid. An inflation rate higher than expected harms those awaiting payment and benefits the payers; an inflation rate lower than expected harms the payers and benefits those awaiting payment.*

# THE RESOURCE COST OF INFLATION

In addition to its possible redistribution of income, inflation imposes another cost upon society. To cope with inflation, we are forced to use up time and other resources as we go about our daily economic activities (shopping, selling, saving) that we could otherwise have devoted to productive activities. Thus, inflation imposes an *opportunity cost* on society as a whole and on each of its members:

> *When people must spend time and other resources coping with inflation, they pay an opportunity cost—they sacrifice the goods and services those resources could have produced instead.*

Let's first consider the resources used up by *consumers* to cope with inflation. Suppose you shop for clothes twice a year. You've discovered that both The Gap and Banana Republic sell clothing of similar quality and have similar service, and you naturally want to shop at the one with the lower prices. If there is no inflation, your task is easy: You shop first at The Gap and then at Banana Republic; thereafter, you rely on your memory to determine which is less expensive.

With inflation, however, things are more difficult. Suppose you find that prices at Banana Republic are higher than you remember them to be at The Gap. It may be that Banana Republic is the more expensive store, or it may be that prices have risen at *both* stores. How can you tell? Only a trip back to The Gap will answer the question—a trip that will cost you extra time and trouble. If prices are rising very rapidly, you may have to visit both stores on the same day to be sure which one is cheaper. Now, multiply this time and trouble by all the different types of shopping you must do on a regular or occasional basis—for groceries, an apartment, a car, concert tickets, compact discs, restaurant meals, and more. Inflation can make you use up valuable time—time you could have spent earning income or enjoying leisure activities. True, if you shop for some of these items on the Internet, you can compare prices in less time, but not zero time. And most shopping is *not* done over the Internet.

Inflation also forces *sellers* to use up resources. First, remember that sellers of goods and services are also buyers of resources and intermediate goods. They, too, must do comparison shopping when there is inflation, and use up hired labor time in the process. Second, each time sellers raise prices, labor is needed to put new price tags on merchandise, to enter new prices into a computer scanning system, to update the HTML code on a web page, or to change the prices on advertising brochures, menus, and so on.

Finally, inflation makes us all use up resources managing our financial affairs. We'll try to keep our funds in accounts that pay high nominal interest rates, in order to preserve our purchasing power, and minimize what we keep as cash or in low-interest checking accounts. Of course, this means more frequent trips to the bank or the automatic teller machine, to transfer money into our checking accounts or get cash each time we need it.

All of these additional activities—inspecting prices at several stores or Web sites, changing price tags or price entries, going back and forth to the automatic teller machine—use up not only time, but other resources too, such as gasoline, paper, or the wear and tear on your computer. From society's point of view, these resources could have been used to produce *other* goods and services that we'd enjoy.

You may not have thought much about the resource cost of inflation, because in recent years, U.S. inflation has been so low—under 3 percent per year in the 1990s. Such a low rate of inflation is often called *creeping inflation*—from week to week

http://

To learn more about the strengths and weaknesses of the CPI, read Allison Wallace and Brian Motley, "A Better CPI" (http://www.frbsf.org/econrsrch/wklyltr/wklytr99/el99-05.html).

or month to month, the price level creeps up so slowly that we hardly notice the change. The cost of coping with creeping inflation is negligible.

But it has not always been this way. Three times during the last 50 years, we have had double-digit inflation—about 14 percent during 1947–48, 12 percent in 1974, and 13 percent during 1979 and 1980. Going back farther, the annual inflation rate reached almost 20 percent during World War I and rose above 25 percent during the Civil War.

And as serious as these episodes of American inflation have been, they pale in comparison to the experiences of other countries. In Germany in the early 1920s, the inflation rate hit thousands of percent *per month*. And more recently—in the late 1980s—several South American countries experienced inflation rates in excess of 1,000 percent annually. For a few weeks in 1990, Argentina's annual inflation rate even reached 400,000 percent! Under these conditions, the monetary system breaks down almost completely. Economic life is almost as difficult as in Chaotica.

## IS THE CPI ACCURATE?

The Bureau of Labor Statistics spends millions of dollars gathering data to ensure that its measure of inflation is accurate. To determine the market basket of the typical consumer every 10 years or so, the BLS randomly selects thousands of households and analyzes their spending habits. In the last household survey—completed in 1993–95—each of about 15,000 families kept diaries of their purchases for two weeks.

But that is just the beginning. Every month, the bureau's shoppers visit 23,000 retail stores, 7,000 rental apartments, and 18,000 owner-occupied homes to record 71,000 different prices. Finally, all of the prices are combined to determine the cost of the typical consumer's market basket for the current month.

The BLS is a highly professional agency, typically headed by an economist. Billions of dollars are at stake for each 1-percent change in the CPI, and the BLS deserves high praise for keeping its measurement honest and free of political manipulation. Nevertheless, conceptual problems and resource limitations make the CPI fall short of the ideal measure of inflation. Economists—even those who work in the BLS—widely agree that the CPI overstates the U.S. inflation rate. By how much?

According to a report by an advisory committee of economists appointed by the Senate Finance Committee in 1996, the overall bias has been at least 1.1 percent annually in recent years.[4] That is, in a typical year, the reported rise in the CPI has been about 1 percentage point greater than the true rise in the price level. The BLS has been working hard to reduce this upward bias, and—especially in the late 1990s—it made some progress. But significant bias remains.

### SOURCES OF BIAS IN THE CPI

There are several reasons for the upward bias in the CPI.

**Substitution Bias.** Until recently, the CPI almost completely ignored a general principle of consumer behavior: People tend to *substitute* goods that have become

---

[4]  See *Toward a More Accurate Measure of the Cost of Living,* Report to the Senate Finance Committee from the Advisory Commission to Study the Consumer Price Index, December 1996.

relatively cheaper in place of those that have become relatively more expensive. For example, in the seven years from 1973 to 1980, the retail price of oil-related products—like gasoline and home heating oil—increased by more than 300 percent, while the prices of most other goods and services rose by less than 100 percent. As a result, people found ways to conserve on oil products. They joined carpools, used public transportation, insulated their homes, and in many cases moved closer to their workplaces to shorten their commute. Yet throughout this period, the CPI basket—based on a survey of buying patterns in 1972–73—assumed that consumers were buying unchanged quantities of oil products.

The treatment of oil products is an example of a more general problem that has plagued the CPI for decades. Until recently, the CPI strictly followed a procedure of using fixed *quantities* to determine the relative importance of each item. That is, it assumed that households continued to buy each good or service in the same quantities at which they bought it during the last household survey. Compounding the problem, the survey to determine spending patterns—and to update the market basket—was taken only about once every 10 years or so. So by the end of each 10-year period, the CPI's assumptions about spending habits could be far off the mark, as they were in the case of oil in the 1970s.

The BLS has *partially* fixed this problem, in two ways.[5] First, beginning in 2002, it will update the market basket with a household survey every *two* years instead of every 10 years. This is widely considered an important improvement in CPI measurement.

Second, as of January 1999, the CPI no longer assumes that the typical consumer continues to buy the same *quantity* of each good that he bought in the last household "market basket" survey. Instead, the CPI assumes that when a good's relative price rises by 10 percent, typical consumers buy 10 percent less of it, and switch their purchases to other goods whose prices are rising more slowly.

However, this is only a partial fix. The CPI still only recognizes the possibility of such substitution *within* categories of goods, and *not among* them. For example, if the price of steak rises relative to the price of hamburger meat, the CPI now assumes that consumers will substitute away from steak and toward hamburger meat, since both are in the same category: *beef*. However, if the price of all beef products rises relative to chicken and pork, the CPI assumes that there is *no* substitution at all from beef toward chicken and pork. As a result, beef products will be overweighted in the CPI until the next survey.

> *Although the BLS has partially fixed the problem, the CPI still suffers from substitution bias. That is, categories of goods whose prices are rising most rapidly tend to be given exaggerated importance in the CPI, and categories of goods whose prices are rising most slowly tend to be given too little importance in the CPI.*

**New Technologies.** Brand-new technologies are another source of upward bias in the CPI. One problem is that goods using new technologies are introduced into the BLS market basket only after a lag. These goods often drop rapidly in price after they are introduced, helping to balance out price rises in other goods. By excluding

---

[5]    For a discussion of these and other recent changes in the CPI, see "Planned Change in the Consumer Price Index Formula," Bureau of Labor Statistics, April 16, 1998 (*http://stats.bls.gov/cpigm02.htm*) and "Future Schedule for Expenditure Weight Updates in the Consumer Price Index," Bureau of Labor Statistics, December 18, 1998 (*http://stats.bls.gov/cpiupdt.htm*).

a category of goods whose prices are dropping, the CPI overstates the rate of inflation. For example, even though many consumers were buying and using cellular phones throughout the 1990s, they were not included in the BLS basket of goods until 1998. As a result, the CPI missed the rapid decline in the price of cell phones. Updating the market basket every two years—instead of every 10—should reduce this source of bias after 2002.

But there is another issue with new technologies: They often offer consumers a lower-cost alternative for obtaining the same service. For example, the introduction of cable television lowered the cost of entertainment significantly by offering a new, cheaper alternative to going out to see movies. This should have registered as a drop in the price of "seeing movies." But the CPI does not have any good way to measure this reduction in the cost of living. Instead, it treats cable television as an entirely separate service.

> *The CPI excludes new products that tend to drop in price when they first come on the market. When included, the CPI regards them as entirely separate from existing goods and services, instead of recognizing that they lower the cost of achieving a given standard of living. The result is an overestimate of the inflation rate.*

### Changes in Quality.

Many products are improving over time. Cars are much more reliable than they used to be and require much less routine maintenance. They have features like air bags and antilock brakes that were unknown in the early 1980s. The BLS struggles to deal with these changes. It knows that when cars become more expensive, some of the rise in price is not really inflation, but rather charging more because the consumer is *getting* more. In addition to cars, the BLS has recently developed sophisticated statistical techniques to account for quality improvements in computers and peripherals, clothing, and rental apartments. In January 1999, televisions were added to the list, and in coming years, the BLS hopes to extend the techniques to even more categories. Thus, slowly but surely, the BLS is planning to chip away at the upward bias in inflation caused by unmeasured quality improvements.

But in the meantime, many improvements in quality are still ignored by the CPI. When food prices rise due to better nutritional quality, when VCR prices rise due to better performance and convenience, or when the cost of surgery rises due to more sophisticated techniques that have greater success rates, the CPI merely records a price increase, as if the same thing is costing more.

> *The CPI still fails to recognize that, in many cases, prices rise because of improvements in quality, not because the cost of living has risen. This causes the CPI to overstate the inflation rate.*

### Growth in Discounting.

The CPI treats toothpaste bought at a high-priced drugstore and toothpaste bought at Wal-Mart or Drugstore.com as different products. And it assumes that we continue to buy from high- and low-priced stores in unchanged proportions. But that is not what has been happening. In fact, Americans are buying more and more of their toothpaste and other products from discounters, but the CPI does not consider this in measuring inflation. The purchasing power you have lost from inflation is not as great as the CPI says if you, like most Americans, are stretching your dollar by going more often to discount outlets, warehouse stores, and Web sites with low prices.

*The CPI omits reductions in the prices people pay from more frequent shopping at discount stores and so overstates the inflation rate.*

## THE CONSEQUENCES OF OVERSTATING INFLATION

The impact of overstating the inflation rate is both serious and wide ranging. First, it means that many real variables have been rising more rapidly than the official numbers suggest. For example, look again at Table 2. It tells us that, from 1975 to 1995, the average real wage *fell* from $8.41 to $7.56, a decrease of about 10 percent. This calculation is based on the official CPI. But suppose the CPI overstated the inflation rate by just 1.1 percentage points per year over this period, as the government's advisory commission has suggested. Then the real wage did not fall at all over this period, but actually *rose* by about 11 percent. (See Challenge Question #3 at the end of this chapter.)

Second, remember that low inflation is an important macroeconomic goal. As you'll learn in future chapters, this goal is not always easy to achieve and may require large—if temporary—sacrifices. If the CPI overstates inflation—and continues to do so in the future—we may be making these sacrifices unnecessarily: We may take painful steps to bring inflation down when the real problem is that our official inflation measure is exaggerating the problem.

Finally, since many payments are indexed to the CPI, an overstatement of inflation results in *over*indexing—payments that rise *faster* than the true price level. For example, suppose a Social Security recipient's payment of $1,000 per month is indexed to the CPI in order to keep the real payment constant as prices rise. Suppose, too, that over 10 years, the CPI reports annual inflation of 3 percent. By the end of the period, the CPI will rise by 35 percent, and the nominal payment will rise to $1,350.[6] But what if the CPI is wrong, and the actual inflation rate is just 1.9 percent per year during the period? Then, using the initial year as the base period, an accurate price index will rise from 100 to 120.7. This tells us that the *real* Social Security payment will rise from $1,000 to ($1,350/120.7) $\times$ 100 = $1,118—an increase of about 11 percent. This "overpayment" of $118 per month at the end of the period may suit the Social Security recipient just fine. But remember that the rest of society pays for the retired person's gain through higher real tax payments. The same general principle applies to union workers, government pensioners, or anyone else who is overindexed due to errors in the CPI:

*When a payment is indexed, and the price index overstates inflation, inflation will increase the real payment, shifting purchasing power toward those who are indexed and away from the rest of society.*

## THE FUTURE OF THE CPI

In the past, the CPI has mostly tracked the cost of a fixed basket of goods, and it has done a reasonably good job of doing so. But it has *not* done a good job tracking what many people call the *cost of living*—the number of dollars a person must pay in order to enjoy a given level of economic satisfaction. When people substitute cheaper goods, take advantage of new technologies, and enjoy quality improvements, they are trying to get more satisfaction for a given cost, or else trying to

---

6    Over 10 years, 3 percent annual inflation raises the CPI by a factor of $(1.03)^{10} = 1.35$.

maintain their level of satisfaction in spite of price hikes. And to some extent, they are successful. In the past, the CPI has ignored our ability to increase and preserve our satisfaction from a given amount of spending; it has *not* tried to tell us what is happening to the cost of *living*.

But this is changing. The repairs that have already been made to the CPI—and others that many economists believe the BLS should make—are moving the index closer to a *cost of living* indicator. Once we try to measure the cost of living, however, we enter into some nebulous territory. How is the cost of living affected when our medical care is provided by an HMO that lowers the price, but gives us fewer options in choosing our own doctors? When the price of new textbooks rises, how much satisfaction do people lose when they substitute cheaper, used textbooks? How should we incorporate falling crime rates that enable us to protect our lives and property at lower cost? And what about other aspects of our society that affect the quality of our lives: leisure time, the state of the environment, the safety of our workplaces, the quality of our culture, and so on? Do we want changes in these aspects of life to affect our cost-of-living measure?

For all of these reasons, fixing the CPI is controversial. Further, some groups—including Social Security recipients, union workers, and pensioners—stand to lose from any fix that will reduce the reported inflation rate. After all, these groups gain from any overestimate of inflation, because their benefits are indexed to the CPI. In fact, many Social Security recipients view suggestions to correct the CPI as a backdoor effort to reduce their benefits.

Thus, the CPI has entered the realm of politics. The voices arguing for continued changes to the CPI are getting stronger, but so are the voices of those opposed.

## S U M M A R Y

Money serves two important functions. First, it is a *unit of value* that helps us measure how much something is worth and compare the costs of different goods and services. Second, it is a *means of payment* by being generally acceptable in exchange for goods and services. Without money, we would be reduced to barter, a very inefficient way of carrying out transactions.

The value of money is its purchasing power, and this changes as the prices of the things we buy change. The overall trend of prices is measured using a price index. Like any index number, a price index is calculated as: (value in current period/value in base period) × 100. The most widely used price index in the United States is the *Consumer Price Index (CPI)*, which tracks the prices paid for a typical consumer's "market basket." The percent change in the CPI is the inflation rate.

The most common uses of the CPI are for indexing payments, as a policy target, and to translate from nominal to real variables. Many nominal variables, such as the nominal wage, can be corrected for price changes by dividing by the CPI and then multiplying by 100. The result is a real variable,

such as the real wage, that rises and falls only when its purchasing power rises and falls. Another price index in common use is the GDP price index. It tracks prices of all final goods and services included in GDP.

Inflation—a rise over time in a price index—is costly to our society. One of inflation's costs is an arbitrary redistribution of income. Unanticipated inflation shifts purchasing power away from those awaiting future dollar payments and toward those obligated to make such payments. Another cost of inflation is the resource cost: People use valuable time and other resources trying to cope with inflation.

It is widely agreed that the CPI has overstated inflation in recent decades—probably by more than one percentage point per year. As a result, the official statistics on real variables may contain errors, and people who are indexed to the CPI have been actually overindexed, enjoying an increase in real income that is paid for by the rest of society. The Bureau of Labor Statistics has been trying to eliminate the upward bias in the CPI, but so far, it has only eliminated part of the problem. Meanwhile, fixing the CPI has become a political issue—and a controversial one.

## K E Y   T E R M S

| | | | |
|---|---|---|---|
| unit of value | price level | deflation | GDP price index |
| means of payment | index | indexation | nominal interest rate |
| Federal Reserve System | Consumer Price Index | nominal variable | real interest rate |
| fiat money | inflation rate | real variable | |

## R E V I E W   Q U E S T I O N S

1. Distinguish between the *unit-of-value* function of money and the *means-of-payment* function. Give examples of how the U.S. dollar has played each of these two roles.

2. How does the price level differ from, say, the price of a haircut or a Big Mac?

3. Explain how you might construct an index of bank deposits over time. What steps would be involved?

4. What is the CPI? What does it measure? How can it be used to calculate the inflation rate?

5. Can the inflation rate be decreasing at the same time the price level is rising? Can the inflation rate be increasing at the same time the price level is falling? Explain.

6. What are the main uses of the CPI? Give an example of each use.

7. Explain the logic of the formula that relates real values to nominal values.

8. What are the similarities between the CPI and the GDP price index? What are the differences?

9. What are the costs of inflation?

10. Under what circumstances would inflation redistribute purchasing power? How? When would it *not* redistribute purchasing power?

11. How is a nominal interest rate different from a real interest rate? Which do you think is the better measure of the rate of return on a loan?

## P R O B L E M S   A N D   E X E R C I S E S

1. Both gold and paper currency have served as money in the United States. What are some of the advantages of paper currency over gold?

2. Which would be more costly—a steady inflation rate of 3 percent per year, or an inflation rate that was sometimes high and sometimes low, but that averaged 3 percent per year? Justify your answer.

3. Given the following *year-end* data, calculate the inflation rate for years 2, 3, and 4. Calculate the real wage in each year:

| Year | CPI | Inflation Rate | Nominal Wage | Real Wage |
|---|---|---|---|---|
| 1 | 100 | — | $10.00 | _____ |
| 2 | 110 | _____ | $12.00 | _____ |
| 3 | 120 | _____ | $13.00 | _____ |
| 4 | 115 | _____ | $12.75 | _____ |

4. This chapter discusses the costs of inflation. Would there be any costs to a *deflation*—a period of falling prices? If so, what would they be? Give examples.

5. Given the following data, calculate the real interest rate for years 2, 3, and 4. (Assume that each CPI number tells us the price level at the *end* of each year.)

| Year | CPI | Nominal Interest Rate | Real Interest Rate |
|---|---|---|---|
| 1 | 100 | — | — |
| 2 | 110 | 15% | _____ |
| 3 | 120 | 13% | _____ |
| 4 | 115 | 8% | _____ |

If you lent $200 to a friend at the beginning of year 2 at the prevailing nominal interest rate of 15 percent, and your friend returned the money—with the interest—at the end of year 2, did you benefit from the deal?

6. Your friend asks for a loan of $100 for one year and offers to pay you 5 percent interest. Your friend expects the inflation rate over that one-year period to be 6 percent; you expect it to be 4 percent. You agree to make the loan, and the actual inflation rate turns out to be 5 percent. Who benefits and who loses?

7. If there is 5 percent inflation each year for eight years, what is the *total* amount of inflation (i.e., the total percentage rise in the price level) over the entire eight-year period? (*Hint:* The answer is *not* 40 percent.)

## CHALLENGE QUESTIONS

1. Inflation is sometimes said to be a tax on nominal money holdings. If you hold $100 and the price level increases by 10 percent, the purchasing power of that $100 falls by about 10 percent. Who benefits from this inflation tax?

2. During the late nineteenth and early twentieth centuries, many U.S. farmers favored inflationary government policies. Why might this have been the case? (*Hint:* Do farmers typically pay for their land in full at the time of purchase?)

3. Look again at the first paragraph under the heading, "The Consequences of Overstating Inflation." It says that if the CPI overstated the inflation rate by 1.1 percentage points each year from 1975 to 1995, then the average real wage did not fall by 10 percent as reported, but actually grew by 11 percent. Prove this statement true, using numbers (as needed) from Table 2.

## EXPERIENTIAL EXERCISE

1. How has the U.S. inflation rate compared with rates in other industrial economies in recent years? To explore this question, go to the international economic trends Web page of the Federal Reserve Bank of St. Louis (*http://www.stls.frb.org/publications/iet*). Choose two nations and compare their recent inflation experiences to that of the United States. Why should we be careful in comparing inflation rates internationally?

# APPENDIX

## CALCULATING THE CONSUMER PRICE INDEX

The Consumer Price Index (CPI) is the government's most popular measure of inflation. It tracks the cost of the collection of goods—called the *CPI market basket*—bought by a typical consumer in some *base period*. This appendix demonstrates how the Bureau of Labor Statistics (BLS) calculates the CPI. To help you follow the steps clearly, we'll do the calculations for a very simple economy with just two goods: hamburger meat and oranges (not a pleasant world, but a manageable one). Table 3 shows prices for each good, and the quantities produced and consumed, in two different periods: December 2002 (the base period) and December 2003. The market basket (measured in the base period) is given in the third column of the table: In December 2002, the typical consumer buys 30 pounds of hamburger and 50 pounds of oranges. Our formula for the CPI in any period $t$ is

CPI in period $t$

$$= \frac{\text{Cost of market basket at prices in period } t}{\text{Cost of market basket at 2002 prices}} \times 100,$$

where each year's prices are measured in December of that year.

**TABLE 3**

### PRICES AND WEEKLY QUANTITIES IN A TWO-GOOD ECONOMY

|  | December 2002 | | December 2003 | |
| --- | --- | --- | --- | --- |
|  | Price (per lb.) | Quantity (lbs.) | Price (per lb.) | Quantity (lbs.) |
| Hamburger Meat | $5.00 | 30 | $6.00 | 10 |
| Oranges | $1.00 | 50 | $1.10 | 100 |

Table 4 shows the calculations we must do to determine the CPI in December 2002 and December 2003. In the table, you can see that the cost of the 2002 market basket at 2002 prices is $200. The cost of the *same* market basket at 2003's higher prices is $235.

**TABLE 4**

### CALCULATIONS FOR THE CPI

|  | At December 2002 Prices | At December 2003 Prices |
| --- | --- | --- |
| Cost of 30 lbs. of Hamburger | $5.00 × 30 = $150 | $6.00 × 30 = $180 |
| Cost of 50 lbs. of Oranges | $1.00 × 50 = $50 | $1.10 × 50 = $55 |
| Cost of Entire Market Basket | $150 × $50 = $200 | $180 + $55 = $235 |

To determine the CPI in December 2002—the base period—we use the formula with period $t$ equal to 2002, giving us

CPI in 2002

$$= \frac{\text{Cost of 2002 basket at 2002 prices}}{\text{Cost of 2002 basket at 2002 prices}} \times 100$$

$$= \frac{\$200}{\$200} \times 100 = 100.$$

That is, the CPI in December 2002—the base period—is equal to 100. (The formula, as you can see, is set up so that the CPI will always equal 100 in the base period, regardless of which base period we choose.)

Now let's apply the formula again, to get the value of the CPI in December 2003:

CPI in 2003

$$= \frac{\text{Cost of 2002 basket at 2003 prices}}{\text{Cost of 2002 basket at 2002 prices}} \times 100$$

$$= \frac{\$235}{\$200} \times 100 = 117.5.$$

From December 2002 to December 2003, the CPI rises from 100 to 117.5. The rate of inflation over the year 2003 is therefore 17.5 percent.

Notice that the CPI gives more weight to price changes of goods that are more important in the consumer's budget. In our example, the percentage rise in the CPI (17.5 percent) is closer to the percentage rise in the price of hamburger (20 percent) than it is to the percentage price rise of oranges (10 percent). This is because a greater percentage of our budget is *spent* on hamburger than on oranges, so hamburger carries more weight in the CPI.

But one of the CPI's problems, discussed in the body of the chapter, is *substitution bias*. The CPI recognizes that consumers substitute *within* categories of goods. For example, if we had a third good—steak—the CPI would recognize that consumers will buy more steak if the price of hamburger rises faster than the price of steak. But the CPI assumes there is no substitution *among* categories—between beef products and fruit, for example. No matter how much the relative price of beef products like hamburger rises, the CPI assumes that people will continue to buy the same quantity of it, rather than substitute goods in other categories like oranges. Therefore, as the price of hamburger rises, the CPI assumes that we spend a greater and greater percentage of our budgets on it; hamburger gets *increasing weight* in the CPI. In our example, spending on hamburger is assumed to rise from $150/$200 = 0.75, or 75 percent of the typical weekly budget, to $180/$235 = 0.766, or 76.6 percent. In fact, however, the rapid rise in price would cause people to substitute *away* from hamburger toward other goods whose prices are rising more slowly. This is what occurs in our two-good example, as you can see in the last column of Table 3. In 2003, the quantity of hamburger purchased drops to 10, and the quantity of oranges rises to 100. In an ideal measure, the decrease in the quantity of hamburger would reduce its weight in determining the overall rate of inflation. But the CPI ignores this. Look back at how we've calculated the CPI in this example, and you will see that we have entirely ignored the information in the last column of Table 3, which shows the new quantities purchased in 2003. This failure to correct for substitution bias across categories of goods is one of the reasons the CPI overstates inflation.

# THE CLASSICAL LONG-RUN MODEL

Economists sometimes disagree with each other. In news interviews, class lectures, and editorials, they give differing opinions about even the simplest matters. To the casual observer, it might seem that economics is little more than guesswork, where anyone's opinion is as good as anyone else's. But there is actually much more agreement among economists than there appears to be.

Take the following typical example: Two distinguished economists appear on *CNN Moneyline*. In a somber tone, Willow Bay—the anchor—asks each of them what should be done to maintain the health of the economy. "We need to cut taxes," replies the first economist. "If individuals can keep more of what they earn, they'll have more incentive to work. And if we lower taxes on business, they'll have more incentive to invest and grow." (Don't worry if this chain of logic isn't clear to you yet—it will be by the end of the next chapter.)

"No, no, no," the second economist interrupts. "A tax cut would be the *worst* thing we could do right now. The economy is already pumping out just about as many goods and services as it can. A tax cut—which would put more funds into buyers' hands—would only increase spending, overheat the economy, and lead to inflationary dangers that the U.S. Federal Reserve would have to prevent." (You'll begin learning what's behind this argument a few chapters later.)

Which of these economists is correct? Very likely, *both* of them are correct. But how can this be? Aren't the two responses contradictory? Not really, because each economist is hearing—and answering—a different question. The first economist is addressing the *long-run* impact of a cut in taxes—the impact we can expect after several years have elapsed. The second economist is focusing on the *short-run* impact—the effects we'd see over the next year.

Once the distinction between the long run and the short run becomes clear, many apparent disagreements among macroeconomists dissolve. If Willow Bay had asked our two economists about the long-run impact of cutting taxes, both may well have agreed that it would lead to more jobs and more investment by business firms. If asked about the short-run impact, both may have agreed about the potential danger of inflation. If no time horizon is specified, however, an economist is likely to focus on the horizon he or she feels is most important—something about which economists sometimes *do* disagree. The real dispute, though, is less over how the economy *works* and more about what our priorities should be in guiding it.

Ideally, we would like our economy to do well in both the long run and the short run. Unfortunately, there is often a trade-off between these two goals: Doing better in the short run can require some sacrifice of long-run goals, and vice versa. The problem for policymakers is much like that of the captain of a ship sailing through the North Atlantic. On the one hand, he wants to reach his destination (his long-run goal); on the other hand, he must avoid icebergs along the way (his short-run goal). As you might imagine, avoiding icebergs may require the captain to deviate from an ideal long-run course. At the same time, reaching port might require risking the occasional iceberg.

The same is true of the macroeconomy. If you flip back two chapters and look at Figure 4, you will see that there are two types of movements in total output—the long-run trajectory showing the growth of potential output and the short-run movements around that trajectory, which we call economic fluctuations or business cycles. Macroeconomists are concerned with both types of movements. But, as you will see, policies that can help us smooth out economic fluctuations may prove harmful to growth in the long run, while policies that promise a high rate of growth might require us to put up with more severe fluctuations in the short run.

## MACROECONOMIC MODELS: CLASSICAL VERSUS KEYNESIAN

**Classical model** A macroeconomic model that explains the long-run behavior of the economy, assuming that all markets clear.

The **classical model,** developed by economists in the nineteenth and early twentieth centuries, was an attempt to explain a key observation about the economy: Over periods of several years or longer, the economy performs rather well. That is, if we step back from current conditions and view the economy over a long stretch of time, we see that it operates reasonably close to its potential output. And even when it deviates, it does not do so for very long. Business cycles may come and go, but the economy eventually returns to full employment. Indeed, if we think in terms of decades rather than years or quarters, the business cycle fades in significance much like the waves in a choppy sea disappear when viewed from a jet plane.

In the classical view, this behavior is no accident: Powerful forces are at work that drive the economy toward full employment. Many of the classical economists went even further, arguing that these forces operated within a reasonably short period of time. And even today, an important group of macroeconomists continues to believe that the classical model is useful even in the shorter run.

Until the Great Depression of the 1930s, there was little reason to question these classical ideas. True, output fluctuated around its trend, and from time to time there were serious recessions, but output always returned to its potential, full-employment level within a few years or less, just as the classical economists predicted. But during the Great Depression, output was stuck far below its potential for many years. For some reason, the economy wasn't working the way the classical model said it should.

In 1936, in the midst of the Great Depression, the British economist John Maynard Keynes offered an explanation for the economy's poor performance. His new model of the economy—soon dubbed the *Keynesian model*—changed many economists' thinking.[1] Keynes and his followers argued that, while the classical model

---

[1]  Keynes's attack on the classical model was presented in his book *The General Theory of Employment, Interest and Money* (1936). Unfortunately, it's a very difficult book to read, though you may want to try. Keynes's assumptions were not always clear, and some of his text is open to multiple interpretations. As a result, economists have been arguing for decades about what Keynes really meant.

might explain the economy's operation in the long run, the long run could be a very long time in arriving. In the meantime, production could be stuck below its potential, as it seemed to be during the Great Depression.

Keynesian ideas became increasingly popular in universities and government agencies during the 1940s and 1950s. By the mid-1960s, the entire profession had been won over: Macroeconomics *was* Keynesian economics, and the classical model was removed from virtually all introductory economics textbooks. You might be wondering, then, why we are bothering with the classical model here. After all, it's an older model of the economy, one that was largely discredited and replaced, just as the Ptolemaic view that the sun circled the earth was supplanted by the more modern, Copernican view. Right?

Not really. The classical model is still important, for two reasons. First, in recent decades, there has been an active counterrevolution against Keynes's approach to understanding the macroeconomy. Many of the counterrevolutionary new theories are based largely on classical ideas. In some cases, the new theories are just classical economics in modern clothing, but in other cases significant new ideas have been added. By studying classical macroeconomics, you will be better prepared to understand the controversies centering on these newer schools of thought.

The second—and more important—reason for us to study the classical model is its usefulness in understanding the economy over the long run. Even the many economists who find the classical model inadequate for understanding the economy in the short run find it extremely useful in analyzing the economy in the long run.

> *While Keynes's ideas and their further development help us understand economic fluctuations—movements in output around its long-run trend—the classical model has proven more useful in explaining the long-run trend itself.*

This is why we will use the terms "classical view" and "long-run view" interchangeably in the rest of the book; in either case, we mean "the ideas of the classical model used to explain the economy's long-run behavior."

## ASSUMPTIONS OF THE CLASSICAL MODEL

Remember from Chapter 1 that all models begin with *assumptions* about the world. The classical model is no exception. Many of the assumptions are merely simplifying—they make the model more manageable, enabling us to see the broad outlines of economic behavior without getting lost in the details. Typically, these assumptions involve aggregation, such as ignoring the many different interest rates in the economy and instead referring to a single interest rate, or ignoring the many different types of labor in the economy and analyzing instead a single aggregate labor market. These simplifications are usually harmless—adding more detail would make our work more difficult, but would not add much insight, nor would it change any of the central conclusions of the classical view.

There is, however, one assumption in the classical view that goes beyond mere simplification. This is an assumption about how the world works, and it is critical to the conclusions we will reach in this and the next chapter. We can state it in two words: *markets clear.*

> *A critical assumption in the classical model is that **markets clear**: The price in every market will adjust until quantity supplied and quantity demanded are equal.*

**Market clearing** Adjustment of prices until quantities supplied and demanded are equal.

Does the market-clearing assumption sound familiar? It should: It was the basic idea behind our study of supply and demand. When we look at the economy through the classical lens, we assume that the forces of supply and demand work fairly well throughout the economy and that markets do reach equilibrium. An excess supply of anything traded will lead to a fall in its price; an excess demand will drive the price up.

The market-clearing assumption, which permeates classical thinking about the economy, provides an early hint about why the classical model does a better job over longer time periods (several years or more) than shorter ones. In many markets, prices might not fully adjust to their equilibrium values for many months or even years after some change in the economy. An excess supply or excess demand might persist for some time. Still, if we wait long enough, an excess supply in a market will eventually force the price down, and an excess demand will eventually drive the price up. That is, *eventually*, the market will clear. Therefore, when we are trying to explain the economy's behavior over the long run, market clearing seems to be a reasonable assumption.

In the remainder of the chapter, we'll use the classical model to answer a variety of important questions about the economy in the long run, such as:

- How is total employment determined?
- How much output will we produce?
- What role does total spending play in the economy?
- What happens when things change?

Keep in mind that, in our discussion of the classical model, we will focus on *real* variables: real GDP, the real wage, real saving, and so on. These variables are typically measured in the dollars of some base year, and their numerical values change only when their *purchasing power* changes.

## HOW MUCH OUTPUT WILL WE PRODUCE?

Over the last decade, on average, the U.S. economy produced about $7.5 trillion worth of goods and services per year (valued in 1996 dollars). How was this average level of output determined? Why didn't we produce $10 trillion per year? Or just $2 trillion? There are so many things to consider when answering this question—variables you constantly hear about in the news—wages, interest rates, investment spending, government spending, taxes, and more. Each of these concepts plays an important role in determining total output, and our task in this chapter is to show how they all fit together.

But what a task! How can we disentangle the complicated web of economic interactions we see around us? Our starting point will be the first step of our *four-step procedure*, introduced toward the end of Chapter 3. To review, that first step was to *characterize the market*—to decide which market or markets best suit the problem being analyzed, and then identify the buyers and sellers who interact in that market.

But which market should we start with?

The classical approach is to start at the beginning, with the *reason* for all this production in the first place. In the classical view, all production arises from one source: our desires for goods and services. Of course, we cannot buy goods and services if we don't have income. And with that fact comes an important implication:

*In order to earn income so we can buy goods and services, we must supply labor and other resources to firms.*

**FIGURE 1**

**THE LABOR MARKET**

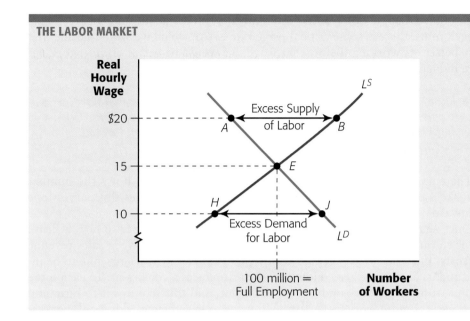

The equilibrium wage rate of $15 per hour is determined at point *E,* where the upward-sloping labor supply curve crosses the downward-sloping labor demand curve. At any other wage, an excess demand or excess supply of labor will cause an adjustment back to equilibrium.

Thus, a logical place to start is with the markets for resources—markets for labor, land, and capital. To keep things simple, however, we'll concentrate our attention on just one type of resource—labor. In our classical world, we assume that firms are making use of all the capital and land that are available in the economy. The only question is: How much *labor* will firms employ to produce goods and services? Moreover, since we are building a *macroeconomic* model, we'll aggregate all the different types of labor—office workers, construction workers, teachers, taxi drivers, waiters, writers, and more—into a single variable, called labor.

## THE LABOR MARKET

The classical labor market is illustrated in Figure 1. The number of workers is measured on the horizontal axis, and the real hourly wage rate is measured on the vertical axis. Remember that the *real wage*—which is measured in the dollars of some base year—tells us the amount of goods that workers can buy with an hour's earnings.

Now look at the two curves in the figure. These are supply and demand curves, similar to the supply and demand curves for maple syrup, but there is one key difference: For a *good* such as maple syrup, households are the demanders and firms the suppliers. But for labor, the roles are reversed: Households supply labor, and firms demand it.

The curve labeled $L^S$ is the **labor supply curve** in this market; it tells us how many people will want to work at each wage. The upward slope tells us that the greater the real wage, the greater the number of people who will want to work. Why does the labor supply curve slope upward?

The answer comes from Key Step #2, in which we identify the goals and constraints of decision makers in a market.

Think about your own decision about whether to work—to supply labor. Your goal—at the most general level—is to be as well off as possible. You value both income and leisure time, and in the best of all possible worlds, you'd have a lot of both. However, in the real world, you face a constraint: To earn income, you must go to work and give up leisure. Thus, each of us will want to work only if the income we will earn *at least* compensates us for the leisure that we will give up.

 Characterize the Market

**Labor supply curve** Indicates how many people will want to work at various wage rates.

 Identify Goals and Constraints

Of course, people differ in the way that they value income and leisure. Thus, for each of us, there is some critical wage rate above which we would decide that we're better off working. Below that wage, we would be better off not working. Thus, in Figure 1,

> *the labor supply curve slopes upward because—as the wage rate increases— more and more individuals are better off working than not working. Thus, a rise in the wage rate increases the number of people in the economy who want to work—to supply their labor.*

The curve labeled $L^D$ is the **labor demand curve,** which shows the number of workers firms will want to hire at any real wage. Why does this curve slope downward?

Identify Goals and Constraints

Once again, we use Key Step #2. In deciding how much labor to hire, a firm's goal is to earn the greatest possible profit—the difference between sales revenue and costs. If a firm's owners could choose, they'd like the firm's revenue to be in-finite and its costs to be zero. However, each firm faces a constraint: To earn more revenue, it must produce and sell more output, and this requires it to hire (and pay wages to) more workers. A firm will want to keep hiring additional workers as long as the output produced by those workers adds more to revenue than it adds to costs.

**Labor demand curve** Indicates how many workers firms will want to hire at various wage rates.

Now think about what happens as the wage rate rises. Some workers that added more to revenue than to cost at the lower wage will now cost more than they add in revenue. Accordingly, the firm will not want to employ these workers at the higher wage.

> *As the wage rate increases, each firm in the economy will find that—to maxi-mize profit—it should employ fewer workers than before. When all firms behave this way together, a rise in the wage rate will decrease the quantity of labor demanded in the economy. This is why the economy's labor demand curve slopes downward.*

Find the Equilibrium

In the classical view, *all markets clear*—including the market for labor. That is, the classical model tells us to apply Key Step #3 in a particular way: The real wage adjusts until the quantities of labor supplied and demanded are equal. In the labor market in Figure 1, the market-clearing wage is $15 per hour, since that is where the labor supply and labor demand curves intersect. While every worker would prefer to earn $20 rather than $15, at $20 there would be an excess supply of labor equal to the distance *AB*. With not enough jobs to go around, competition among workers would drive the wage downward. Similarly, firms might prefer to pay their workers $10 rather than $15, but at $10, the excess demand for labor (equal to the distance *HJ*) would drive the wage upward. When the wage is $15, however, there is neither an excess demand nor an excess supply of labor, so the wage will neither increase nor decrease. Thus, $15 is the equilibrium wage in the economy. Reading along the hori-zontal axis, we see that at this wage, 100 million people will be working.

Notice that, in the figure, labor is fully employed; that is, the number of work-ers that firms want to hire is equal to the number of people who want jobs. There-fore, everyone who wants a job at the market wage of $15 should be able to find one. Small amounts of frictional unemployment might exist, since it takes some time for new workers or job switchers to find jobs. And there might be structural unemployment, due to some mismatch between those who want jobs in the market and the types of jobs available. But there is no *cyclical* unemployment of the type we discussed two chapters ago.

Full employment of the labor force is an important feature of the classical model. As long as we can count on markets (including the labor market) to clear, government action is not needed to ensure full employment; it happens automatically:

> *In the classical view, the economy achieves full employment on its own.*

Automatic full employment may strike you as odd, since it contradicts the cyclical unemployment we sometimes see around us. For example, in the recession of the early 1990s, millions of workers around the country, in all kinds of professions and labor markets, were unable to find jobs for many months. Remember, though, that the classical model takes the long-run view, and over long periods of time, full employment is a fairly accurate description of the U.S. labor market. Cyclical unemployment, by definition, lasts only as long as the current business cycle itself; it is not a permanent, long-run problem.

## DETERMINING THE ECONOMY'S OUTPUT

So far, we've focused on the labor market to determine the economy's level of employment. In our example, 100 million people will have jobs. Now we ask: How much output will these 100 million workers produce? The answer depends on two things: (1) the amount of other resources (land and capital) available for labor to use; and (2) the state of *technology*, which determines how much output we can produce with given inputs, as well as the types of inputs available (horse-drawn wagons or trucks; pencil and paper or a laptop computer).

In the classical model, we treat the quantities of land and capital, as well as the state of technology, as fixed during the period we are analyzing. This certainly makes sense in the case of land: Total acreage is pretty much fixed in a country, and there is little that anyone can do to increase it. But what about technology and capital? The state of technology changes with each new invention or discovery. We can already predict, for example, that over the next decade, genetic engineering will lead to completely new drugs and other medical treatments and change the way many existing drugs are produced. And our capital stock changes rapidly as well, since we are constantly producing new capital—more tractors, fiber-optic cable, computers, and factory buildings. How can we treat these as fixed, especially since the classical model is a long-run model?

The answer is: We assume that technology and the capital stock are constant *not* because we believe that they really are, but because doing so helps us understand what happens when they change. We divide our classical analysis of the economy into two questions: (1) What would be the long-run equilibrium of the macroeconomy for a *given* state of technology and a *given* capital stock? and (2) What happens to this equilibrium when capital or technology *changes*? In this chapter, we focus on the first question only. In the next chapter, on economic growth, we'll address the second question. Since we are assuming, for now, a given state of technology, as well as given quantities of land and capital, there is only one variable left that can affect total output: labor. So it's time to explore how changes in total employment affect total production.

**The Production Function.** The relationship between the quantity of labor employed in the economy and the total quantity of output produced is called the **aggregate production function:**

**Aggregate production function**
The relationship showing how much total output can be produced with different quantities of labor, with land, capital, and technology held constant.

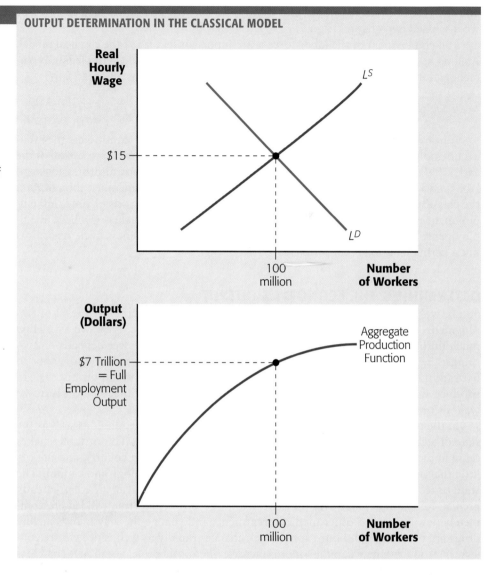

**FIGURE 2**

In the labor market, the demand and supply curves intersect to determine an employment level of 100 million workers. Given the stock of capital and the current level of technology, the production function shows that those 100 million workers can produce $7 trillion of real GDP.

**OUTPUT DETERMINATION IN THE CLASSICAL MODEL**

*The aggregate production function shows the total output the economy can produce with different quantities of labor, given constant amounts of land and capital and the current state of technology.*

The bottom panel of Figure 2 shows what a nation's aggregate production function might look like. The upward slope tells us that an increase in the number of people working will increase the quantity of output produced. But notice the shape of the production function: It flattens out as we move rightward along it.

The declining slope of the aggregate production function is the result of *diminishing returns to labor:* Output rises when another worker is added, but the rise is smaller and smaller with each successive worker. Why does this happen? For one thing, as we keep adding workers, gains from specialization are harder and harder to come by. Moreover, as we continue to add workers, each one will have less and less capital and land to work with.

Figure 2 also illustrates how the aggregate production function, together with the labor market, determines the economy's total output or real GDP. In our example, the labor market (upper panel) automatically generates full employment of 100 million workers, and the production function (lower panel) tells us that 100 million workers—together with the available capital and land and the current state of technology—can produce $7 trillion worth of output. Since $7 trillion is the output produced by a fully employed labor force, it is also the economy's potential output level.

> *In the classical, long-run view, the economy reaches its potential output automatically.*

This last statement is an important conclusion of the classical model and an important characteristic of the economy in the long run: Output tends toward its potential, full-employment level *on its own,* with no need for government to steer the economy toward it. And we have arrived at this conclusion merely by assuming that the labor market clears and observing the relationship between employment and output.

# THE ROLE OF SPENDING

Something may be bothering you about the classical view of output determination—a potential problem we have so far carefully avoided: What if business firms are unable to sell all the output produced by a fully employed labor force? Then the economy would not be able to sustain full employment for very long. Business firms will not continue to employ workers who produce output that is not being sold. Thus, if we are asserting that potential output is an equilibrium for the economy, we had better be sure that *total spending* on output is equal to *total production* during the year. But can we be sure of this?

In the classical view, the answer is, absolutely yes! We'll demonstrate this in two stages: first, in a very simple (but very unrealistic) economy, and then, under more realistic conditions.

## TOTAL SPENDING IN A VERY SIMPLE ECONOMY

Imagine a world much simpler than our own, a world with just two types of economic units: households and business firms. In this world, households spend all of their income on goods and services. They do not save any of their income, nor do they pay taxes. Such an economy is illustrated in the **circular flow** diagram of Figure 3.

The arrows on the right-hand side show that resources—labor, land, and capital—are supplied by households, and purchased by firms, in *factor markets*. In return, households receive payments—wages, rent, interest, and profit. For example, if you were working part time in a restaurant while attending college, you would be supplying a resource (labor) in a factor market (the market for waiters). In exchange, you would earn a wage. Similarly, the owner of the land on which the restaurant sits is a supplier in a factor market (the market for land) and will receive a payment (rent) in return. The payments received by resource owners are called *factor payments*.

On the left side of the diagram, the outer arrows show the flow of goods and services—food, new clothes, books, movies, and more—that firms supply, and households buy, in various *goods* markets. Of course, households must pay for these goods and services, and their payments provide revenue to firms—as shown by the inner arrows.

**Circular flow** A diagram that shows how goods, resources, and dollar payments flow between households and firms.

**FIGURE 3**

**THE CIRCULAR FLOW**

The outer loop of the diagram shows the flows of goods and resources. Households supply resources to firms, which use them to produce goods. The inner loop shows money flows. Firms' factor payments become income to households. Households use the income to purchase goods from firms.

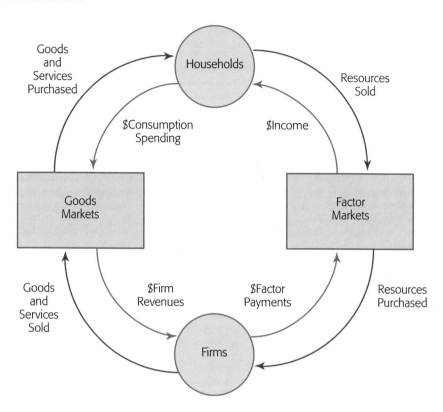

Now comes an important insight. As you learned two chapters ago, the total output of firms is equal to the total income of households. For example, if the economy is producing $7 trillion worth of output, then it also creates $7 trillion in household income. And in this simple economy—in which households spend all of their income—spending would equal $7 trillion as well.

In general,

> *In a simple economy with just households and firms, in which households spend all of their income, total spending must be equal to total output.*

**Say's law** The idea that total spending will be sufficient to purchase the total output produced.

This simple proposition is called **Say's law,** after the classical economist Jean Baptiste Say (1767–1832), who popularized the idea. Say noted that each time a good or service is produced, an equal amount of income is created. This income is spent—it comes back to the business sector to purchase its goods and services. In Say's own words:

> *A product is no sooner created than it, from that instant, affords a market for other products to the full extent of its own value. . . . Thus, the mere circumstance of the creation of one product immediately opens a vent for other products.*[2]

---

2    J. B. Say, *A Treatise on Political Economy*, 4th ed. (London: Longman, 1821), Vol. I, p. 167.

For example, each time a shirt manufacturer produces a $25 shirt, it creates $25 in factor payments to households. (Forgot why? Go back two chapters.) But $25 in factor payments will lead to $25 in total spending—just enough to buy the very shirt produced. Of course, those households who receive the $25 in factor payments will not necessarily buy a shirt with it: The shirt manufacturer must still worry about selling its own output. But in the aggregate, we needn't worry about there being sufficient demand for the *total* output produced. Business firms—by producing output—also create a demand for goods and services equal to the value of that output. Or, to put it most simply, *supply creates its own demand:*

> Say's law states that by producing goods and services, firms create a total demand for goods and services equal to what they have produced.

Say's law is crucial to the classical view of the economy. Why? Remember that market clearing in resource markets assures us that firms will produce potential output. Say's law then assures us that, in the aggregate, firms will be able to *sell* this output, so that full employment can be sustained.

## TOTAL SPENDING IN A MORE REALISTIC ECONOMY

The real world is more complicated than the imaginary one we've just considered. In the real world,

1. Households don't spend *all* their income. Rather, some of their income is saved or goes to *pay taxes*.
2. Households are not the only spenders in the economy. Rather, businesses and the government buy some of the final goods and services we produce.
3. In addition to markets for goods and resources, there is also a *loanable funds* market where household saving is made available to borrowers in the business or government sectors.

All of these details complicate our picture of the economy. Can we have confidence that Say's law will hold under these more realistic conditions?

As you are about to see, yes, we can.

Let's consider the economy of Classica—a fictional economy that behaves according to the classical model. Classica's economy in 2002 is described in Table 1. Notice that total output and total income are both equal to $7 trillion ($7,000 billion), which is assumed to be the potential output level.

Two entries in the table require a bit of explaining. First, **net taxes** are total tax revenue minus government transfer payments such as unemployment insurance, welfare payments, and Social Security benefits. As discussed two chapters ago, these transfer payments are the part of tax revenue that the government takes from one set of households and gives right back to another set of households. Since transfer

**Net taxes** Government tax revenues minus transfer payments.

| TABLE 1 |
|---|
| **FLOWS IN THE ECONOMY OF CLASSICA, 2002** |

| | |
|---|---|
| Total Output | $7 trillion |
| Total Income | $7 trillion |
| Consumption Spending ($C$) | $4 trillion |
| Investment Spending ($I^P$) | $1 trillion |
| Government Spending ($G$) | $2 trillion |
| Net Tax Revenue ($T$) | $1.25 trillion |
| Household Saving ($S$) | $1.75 trillion |

payments stay within the household sector as a whole, we can treat them as if they were never paid to the government at all. Net taxes, then, are the funds that flow from the household sector as a whole to the government in any given year. Letting $T$ represent net taxes, we have

$$T = \text{Total taxes} - \text{Transfer payments.}$$

**(Household) saving** The portion of after-tax income that households do not spend on consumption goods.

Second, **household saving** (often, just **saving**) is the part of the household sector's income that is left after deducting what it pays to the government in taxes and what it spends on consumption. Using the symbol $S$ for household saving, $Y$ for total income, and $C$ for consumption spending, we can write

$$S = Y - T - C.$$

## LEAKAGES AND INJECTIONS

As you can see in Table 1, Classica's households earn $7 trillion in income during the year, but they spend only $4 trillion. That leaves $3 trillion left over from their income after we deduct their consumption spending. Part of this remaining $3 trillion goes to pay net taxes ($1.25 trillion), and whatever is left is, by definition, saved ($1.75 trillion).

**Leakages** Income earned, but not spent, by households during a given year.

Saving and net taxes are called **leakages** out of the income–spending stream— income that households earn but do not spend. Leakages are important because they seem to threaten Say's law—the classical idea that total spending will always equal output. To see why, look at the rectangles in Figure 4. Total output (the first

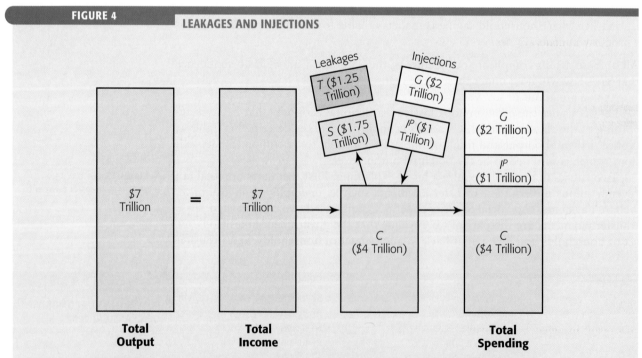

**FIGURE 4**     **LEAKAGES AND INJECTIONS**

By definition, total output equals total income. Leakages—net taxes and saving—reduce consumption spending below total income. Injections—government purchases plus investment spending— contribute to total spending. When leakages equal injections, total spending equals total output.

rectangle) is, by definition, always equal in value to total income (the second rectangle). As we've seen in Figure 3, if households spent all of this income, then consumption spending would equal total output. But leakages reduce consumption spending below total income, as you can see in the third, lower rectangle. In Classica, total leakages = $1.75 trillion + $1.25 trillion = $3 trillion, and this must be subtracted from income of $7 trillion to get consumption spending of $4 trillion. Thus, if consumption spending were the only spending in the economy, business firms would be unable to sell their entire potential output of $7 trillion.

Fortunately, in addition to leakages, there are **injections**—spending from sources *other* than households. Injections boost total spending, and enable firms to produce and sell a level of output greater than just consumption spending.

There are two types of injections in the economy. First is the government's purchases of goods and services. When government agencies—federal, state, or local—buy aircraft, cleaning supplies, cellular phones, or computers, they are buying a part of the economy's output.

The other injection is business firms' investment spending on new capital. We call this **planned investment spending** (or sometimes, just *investment spending*), and represent it with the symbol $I^P$. Recall, from two chapters ago, that actual investment ($I$) consists not just of planned investment in new capital, but also the unplanned changes in inventories. While *some* of the change in inventories in any year might be desired and planned by firms, we'll assume that most of the change in inventories comes as a surprise. More specifically, an increase in inventories is usually an unwelcome surprise, while a decrease in inventories is a pleasant surprise. For example, if Calvin Klein produces $40 million in clothing during the year, but actually ships and sells only $35 million, the $5 million in unsold output will be an unplanned increase in inventories—a surprise that will not make Calvin Klein's owners very happy. But if the company sells $45 million one year—more that it produced—it must have sold some goods out of the inventories it had previously built up. This will generally be good news for the firm.

Why, when we define injections, do we only count *planned* investment spending ($I^P$), rather than actual investment ($I$)? Why do we exclude the change in inventories? Because changes in inventories, being unplanned surprises, are basically one-time events. They do not represent a sustainable source of spending for the economy, and therefore do not help us determine the economy's equilibrium.

Injections are the opposite of leakages: Whereas leakages reduce total spending in the economy, injections increase it. In Figure 4, the last rectangle shows how total injections—investment and government purchases—are added to consumption to obtain total spending. As you can see, total spending is the sum of consumption, planned investment, and government purchases.[3] In Classica, using Table 1, we find that consumption spending ($C$) is $4 trillion, investment spending ($I$) is $1 trillion, and government purchases ($G$) are $2 trillion, giving us total spending of $7 trillion.

This may strike you as suspiciously convenient: Total spending is exactly equal to total output, just as we would like it to be if we want firms to continue producing their potential output level of $7 trillion. And, of course, we have cooked the numbers to make them come out that way. But do we have any reason to *expect* this result in an economy over the long run? Actually, we do.

**Injections** Spending from sources other than households.

**Planned investment spending** Business purchases of plant and equipment.

---

3    There is one more source of spending in the economy that we are not considering here: spending by foreigners, on Classica's exports. But as long as exports (an injection) and imports (a leakage) are equal, none of the conclusions that follow are affected in important ways. We'll focus more directly on exports and imports in our short-run macro model, which begins two chapters after this one.

Take another look at the rectangles in Figure 4. Notice that in going from total output to total spending, leakages are subtracted and injections are added. Clearly, total output and total spending will be equal only when leakages and injections are equal as well:

> *Total spending will equal total output if and only if total leakages in the economy are equal to total injections—that is, only if the sum of saving and net taxes is equal to the sum of investment spending and government purchases.*

And here is a surprising result: This condition will automatically be satisfied. To see why, we must first take a detour through another important market. Then we'll come back to the all-important equality between leakages and injections.

## THE LOANABLE FUNDS MARKET

Characterize the Market

**Loanable funds market** Arrangements through which households make their saving available to borrowers.

The **loanable funds market** is where households make their saving available to those who need additional funds. When you save—that is, when you have income left over after paying taxes and buying consumption goods—you can put your surplus funds in a bank, buy a bond or a share of stock, or use the funds to buy a variety of other assets. In each of these cases, you would be a supplier in the loanable funds market.

Households supply funds because they receive a reward for doing so. But the reward comes in different forms. When the suppliers *lend* out funds, the reward is *interest payments*. When the funds are provided through the stock market, the suppliers become part owners of the firm and their payment is called *dividends*. To keep our discussion simple, we'll assume that all funds transferred are *loaned* and that the payment is simply *interest*.

On the other side of the market are those who want to obtain funds—demanders in this market. Business firms are important demanders of funds. When Avis wants to add cars to its automobile rental fleet, when McDonald's wants to build a new beef-processing plant, or when the local dry cleaner wants to buy new dry cleaning machines, it will likely raise the funds in the loanable funds market. It may take out a bank loan, sell bonds, or sell new shares of stock. In each of these cases, a firm's planned investment spending would be equal to the funds it obtains from the loanable funds market.

Aside from households and business firms, the other major player in the loanable funds market is the government. Government participates in the market whenever it runs a budget deficit or a budget surplus.

**Budget deficit** The excess of government purchases over net taxes.

**Budget of surplus** The excess of net taxes over government purchases.

> *When government purchases of goods and services (G) are greater than net taxes (T), the government runs a **budget deficit** equal to G − T. When government purchases of goods and services (G) are less than net taxes (T), the government runs a **budget surplus** equal to T − G.*

In our example in Table 1, Classica's government is running a budget deficit: Government purchases are $2 trillion, while net taxes are $1.25 trillion, giving us a deficit of $2 trillion − $1.25 trillion = $0.75 trillion. This deficit is financed by borrowing in the loanable funds market. In any year, the government's demand for funds is equal to its deficit.

But surpluses, too, involve the government in the loanable funds market. When the government runs a surplus, it pays back debts that it incurred while running deficits in previous years. For example, the federal government's total unpaid debt is called the **national debt**. When the federal government runs a surplus, it pays back

**National debt** The total amount of government debt outstanding.

part of the national debt, buying back government bonds that it issued in previous years when it ran deficits. In this sense, it becomes a *supplier* of loanable funds, because it is putting funds into the market, where they can be borrowed by others.

> *State and local governments, like the federal government, can run deficits and surpluses, requiring them to participate in the loanable funds market. In our classical model, we aggregate all of these levels of government together, and refer only to the government. When the government runs a budget deficit, it demands loanable funds equal to its deficit. When the government runs a budget surplus, it supplies loanable funds equal to its surplus.*

We can summarize our view of the loanable funds market so far with these two points:

- The supply of funds is the sum of household saving and the government's budget surplus, if any.
- The demand for funds is the sum of the business sector's planned investment spending and the government sector's budget deficit, if any.

In Classica, the government is running a deficit, not a surplus, so for now, we'll analyze the loanable funds market with a budget deficit only. Then, in the "Using the Theory" section, we'll take up the case of a budget surplus.

## THE SUPPLY OF FUNDS CURVE
When the government is running a budget deficit rather than a surplus, households are the only suppliers of funds. Since interest is the reward for saving and supplying funds to the financial market, a rise in the interest rate *increases* the quantity of funds supplied (household saving), while a drop in the interest rate decreases it. This relationship is illustrated by Classica's upward-sloping **supply of funds curve** in Figure 5. If the interest rate is 3 percent, households save $1.5 trillion, and if the interest rate rises to 5 percent, people save more and the quantity of funds supplied rises to $1.75 trillion.

When the Stop & Shop Corporation opens a new supermarket, it very likely obtains the funds from the loanable funds market, by issuing bonds, taking out bank loans, or issuing new shares of stock.

 Identify Goals and Constraints

**Supply of funds curve** Indicates the level of household saving at various interest rates.

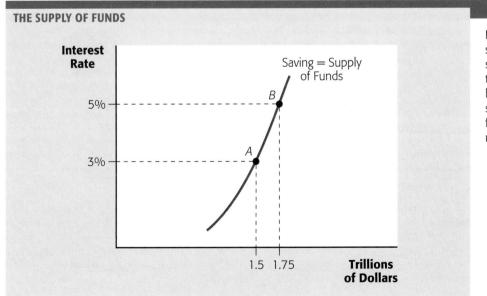

**FIGURE 5**

Interest is the reward for saving. The upward-sloping supply of funds curve shows that at higher interest rates, households consume less, save more, and supply more funds to the loanable funds market.

> *The quantity of funds supplied to the financial market depends positively on the interest rate. This is why the saving, or supply of funds, curve slopes upward.*

Of course, other things can affect saving besides the interest rate—tax rates, expectations about the future, and the general willingness of households to postpone consumption, to name a few. In drawing the supply of funds curve, we assume each of these variables is constant. In the next chapter, we'll explore what happens when some of these variables change.

Identify Goals and Constraints

## THE DEMAND FOR FUNDS CURVE

**Investment demand curve** Indicates the level of investment spending firms plan at various interest rates.

Like saving, investment also depends on the interest rate. This is because businesses buy plant and equipment when the expected benefits of doing so exceed the costs. Since businesses obtain the funds for their investment spending from the loanable funds market, a key cost of any investment project is the interest rate that must be paid on borrowed funds. As the interest rate rises and investment costs increase, fewer projects will look attractive, and investment spending will decline. This is the logic of the downward-sloping **investment demand curve** in Figure 6. At a 5 percent interest rate, firms would borrow $1 trillion and spend it on capital equipment; at an interest rate of 3 percent, business borrowing and investment spending would rise to $1.5 trillion.

> *When the interest rate falls, investment spending and the business borrowing needed to finance it rise. The investment demand curve slopes downward.*

What about the government's demand for funds? Will it, too, be influenced by the interest rate? Probably not very much. Government seems to be cushioned from the cost–benefit considerations that haunt business decisions. Any company president who ignored interest rates in deciding how much to borrow would be quickly out of a job. U.S. presidents and legislators have often done so with little political cost.

For this reason, when government is running a budget deficit, our classical model treats government borrowing as independent of the interest rate: No matter

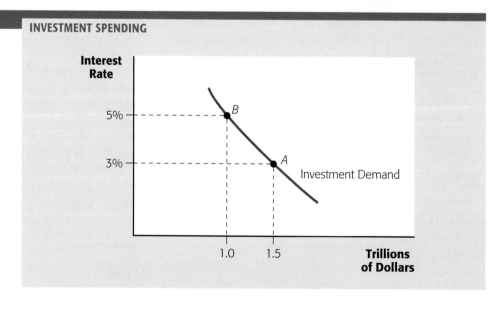

**FIGURE 6**

Businesses borrow in order to finance new investment, and the interest rate measures the cost of borrowing. The downward-sloping investment demand curve shows that more new projects will be financially attractive at low interest rates than at high rates.

**INVESTMENT SPENDING**

**FIGURE 7**

## THE DEMAND FOR FUNDS

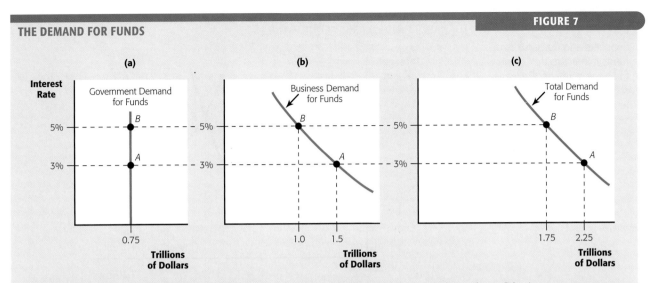

In panel (a), the government's demand for funds—to finance the budget deficit—is independent of the interest rate. Businesses' demand for funds—for investment—is inversely related to the interest rate in panel (b). The total demand for funds in panel (c) is the horizontal sum of government and business demand. At lower interest rates, more funds are demanded than at higher rates.

what the interest rate, the government sector's deficit—and its borrowing—remain constant. This is why we have graphed the **government's demand for funds curve** as a vertical line in panel (a) of Figure 7.

> *The government sector's deficit and, therefore, its demand for funds are independent of the interest rate.*

In the figure, the government deficit—and hence the government's demand for funds—is equal to $0.75 trillion at any interest rate.

In Figure 7, the **total demand for funds curve** is found by horizontally summing the government demand curve (panel (a)) and the business demand curve (panel (b)). For example, if the interest rate is 5 percent, firms demand $1 trillion in funds, and the government demands $0.75 trillion, so that the total quantity of loanable funds demanded is $1.75 trillion. A drop in the interest rate—to 3 percent—increases business borrowing to $1.5 trillion, while the government's borrowing remains at $0.75 trillion, so the total quantity of funds demanded rises to $2.25 trillion.

> *As the interest rate decreases, the quantity of funds demanded by business firms increases, while the quantity demanded by the government remains unchanged. Therefore, the total quantity of funds demanded rises.*

**Government demand for funds curve** Indicates the amount of government borrowing at various interest rates.

**Total demand for funds curve** Indicates the total amount of borrowing at various interest rates.

## EQUILIBRIUM IN THE LOANABLE FUNDS MARKET

 Find the Equilibrium

In the classical view, the loanable funds market—like all other markets—is assumed to clear: The interest rate will rise or fall until the quantities of funds supplied and demanded are equal. Figure 8 illustrates the financial market of Classica, our fictional economy. Equilibrium occurs at point *E*, with an interest rate of

**FIGURE 8**

Suppliers and demanders of funds interact to determine the interest rate in the loanable funds market. At an interest rate of 5%, quantity supplied and quantity demanded are both equal to $1.75 trillion.

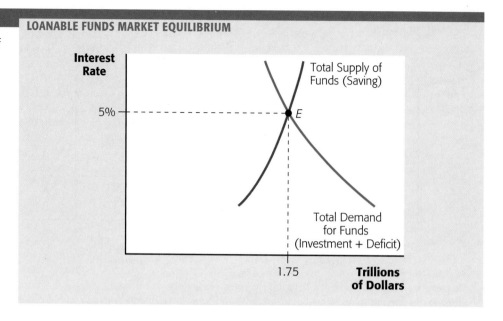

**LOANABLE FUNDS MARKET EQUILIBRIUM**

5 percent and total saving equal to $1.75 trillion. Of the total saved, $1 trillion goes to business firms for capital purchases, and $0.75 trillion goes to the government to cover its deficit.

So far, our exploration of the loanable funds market has shown us how three important variables in the economy are determined: the interest rate, the level of saving, and the level of investment. But it really tells us more. Remember the question that sent us on this detour into the loanable funds market in the first place: Can we be sure that all of the output produced at full employment will be purchased? We now have the tools to answer this question.

## THE LOANABLE FUNDS MARKET AND SAY'S LAW

In Figure 4 (flip back 6 pages), you saw that total spending will equal total output if and only if *total leakages* in the economy (saving plus net taxes) are equal to *total injections* (planned investment plus government purchases). Now we can see how this requirement is satisfied automatically. Because the loanable funds market clears, we know that the interest rate—the price in this market—will rise or fall until the quantities of funds supplied (saving) and funds demanded (investment plus the deficit) are equal. Letting $S$ stand for saving, $I^P$ for investment, and $G - T$ for the deficit, we can state that the interest rate will adjust until

$$\underbrace{S}_{\substack{\text{Quantity of} \\ \text{funds supplied}}} = \underbrace{I^P + G - T}_{\substack{\text{Quantity of} \\ \text{funds demand}}}$$

Rearranging this equation by moving $T$ to the left side, we find that, when the loanable funds market clears,

$$\underbrace{S + T}_{\text{Leakages}} = \underbrace{I^P + G}_{\text{Injections}}$$

In other words, market clearing in the loanable funds market *assures us* that total leakages in the economy will equal total injections, which in turn *assures us* that there will be enough spending in the economy to purchase whatever output level is produced. Thus,

> *as long as the loanable funds market clears, Say's law holds even in a more realistic economy with saving, taxes, investment, and a government deficit.*

To see the logic of this conclusion another way, go back again to Figure 4. There, we saw that households spend only part of their income; the rest is either saved or paid as taxes. Now, taxes and saving do not just disappear from the economy: Tax payments go to the government, which spends them. Saving goes to the loanable funds market, where it will be passed along to the government or to business firms. In each case, the funds that households do not spend are simply passed along to another sector of the economy that *does* spend them. As long as the loanable funds market is working properly, income never escapes from the economy. Instead, every dollar in leakages is recycled back into the spending stream in the form of injections.

Figure 9 shows how leakages are transformed into injections. The dollar amounts are for the economy of Classica. In the figure, you can see that by producing $7 trillion in output, firms create $7 trillion in payments to inputs. Of this total,

---

**AN EXPANDED CIRCULAR FLOW**

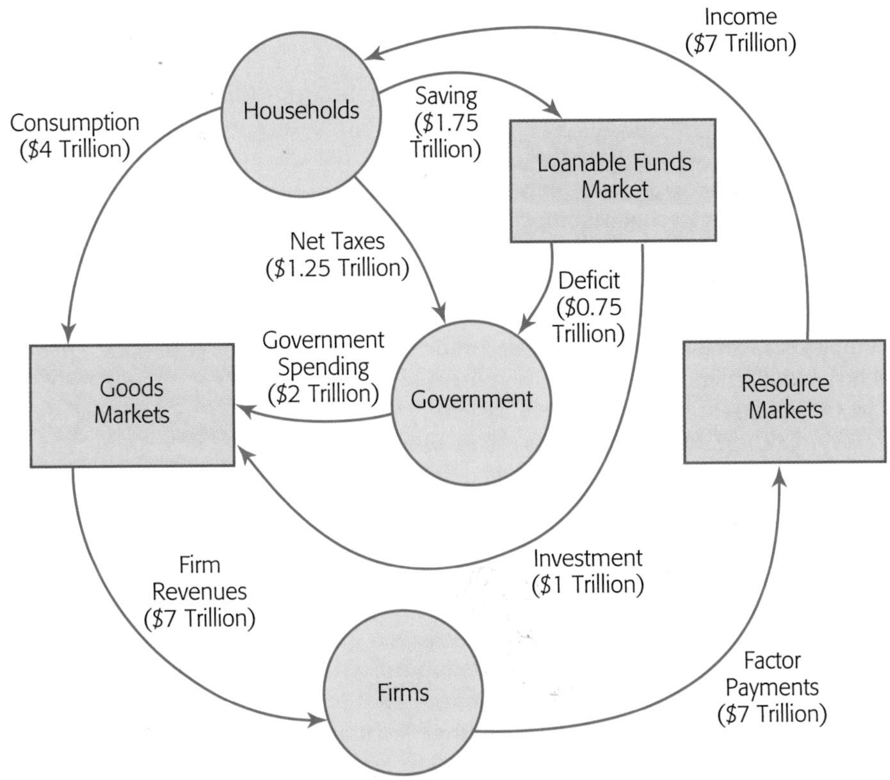

**FIGURE 9**

Saving is transformed into business and government spending in the loanable funds market. The interest rate adjusts to guarantee that saving plus net taxes will equal government purchases plus investment. As a result, total income will equal total spending. (The dollar numbers—which come from Table 2—are for our hypothetical economy, Classica.)

households spend $4 trillion. The rest goes to pay net taxes ($1.25 trillion) or is saved ($1.75 trillion). But taxes and saving do not escape from the economy: The tax payments of $1.25 trillion and part of the saving ($0.75 trillion) are spent by the government, whose purchases are $2 trillion. The rest of the saving ($1 trillion) is spent by business firms on new capital. In the end, the entire $7 trillion in output is purchased, just as Say's law asserts.

Say's law is a powerful concept. But be careful not to overinterpret it. Say's law shows that the *total* value of spending in the economy will equal the *total* value of output, which rules out a general overproduction or underproduction of goods in the economy. It does not promise us that each firm in the economy will be able to sell all of its output. It is perfectly consistent with Say's law that there be excess supplies in some markets, as long as they are balanced by excess demands in other markets.

But lest you begin to think that the classical economy might be a chaotic mess, with excess supplies and demands in lots of markets—don't forget about the *market-clearing* assumption. In each market, prices adjust until supplies and demands are equal. For this reason, the classical, long-run view rules out over- or underproduction in individual markets, as well as the generalized overproduction ruled out by Say's law.

## THE CLASSICAL MODEL: A SUMMARY

You've just completed a first tour of the classical model, our framework for understanding the economy in the long run. Before we begin to use this model, this is a good time to go back and review what we've done.

We began with a critical assumption: All markets clear. We then used the first three Key Steps of our four-step procedure to organize our thinking about the economy. First, we focused on an important market—the labor market—and identified the buyers and sellers in that market. We identified the goals and constraints of these buyers and sellers. And then we found the equilibrium in that market by applying the market-clearing assumption.

We went through a similar process with the loanable funds market, identifying the suppliers and demanders, examining how each would be affected by changes in the interest rate, and finding the equilibrium in that market as well. Then, we saw how market clearing in the loanable funds market assures us that total spending will be just sufficient to purchase the potential output level.

In our excursion through the classical model, we've come to some important conclusions. First, we've seen that *the economy will achieve and sustain potential output on its own*. We have also reached an interesting conclusion about the role of spending in the economy: *We need never worry about there being too little or too much spending; Say's law assures us that total spending is always just right to purchase the economy's total output.*

All of this tells us that the government needn't worry much about the economy's level of production: It reaches the right level on its own. But suppose the government wanted to stimulate the economy, and raise the level of economic activity in order to increase employment and output. Could the government accomplish this by engineering an *increase* in total spending? We'll answer that question in our "Using the Theory" section.

# FISCAL POLICY IN THE CLASSICAL MODEL

Can the government raise output by raising spending in the economy? It seems like it could, and two ideas come readily to mind. First, the government could simply spend more itself—purchasing more goods, like tanks and police cars, and more services, like those provided by high school teachers and judges. Alternatively, the government could cut taxes so that households would keep more of their income, causing them to spend more on food, clothing, furniture, travel, movies, new cars, and so on. When the government either increases its spending or reduces taxes in order to influence the level of economic activity, it is engaging in *fiscal policy:*

*Using the*
# THEORY

> *Fiscal policy is a change in government purchases or in net taxes de-signed to change total spending in the economy and thereby influence the levels of employment and output.*

A fiscal policy of increasing government purchases or decreasing net taxes should cause spending to rise, and business firms—able to sell more—would surely hire more workers and produce more goods and services. Right?

In the classical model, this is dead wrong. Fiscal policy is completely in-effective. It cannot change total output or employment in the economy, pe-riod. It cannot even change total spending. Moreover, fiscal policy is *unnec-essary*, since the economy achieves and sustains full employment on its own.

> *In the classical view, fiscal policy is both ineffective and unnecessary.*

Here, we'll demonstrate this conclusion for the case of an increase in government spending. In a challenge question at the end of this chapter, you are invited to demonstrate the same conclusion for the case of a tax cut.

Let's see what would happen if the government of Classica attempted to in-crease employment and output by increasing its own purchases. More specifically, suppose its purchases rise from the current $2 trillion to $2.5 trillion annually, while net taxes remain unchanged. What will happen?

To answer this, we must first answer another question: Where will Classica's government get the additional $0.5 trillion it spends? If net taxes are unchanged (as we are assuming), then the government must dip into the loanable funds market to borrow the additional funds. Figure 10 illustrates the effects. Initially, with govern-ment purchases equal to $2 trillion, the demand for funds curve is $D_1$, and equilib-rium occurs at point A with the interest rate equal to 5 percent. If government pur-chases increase by $0.5 trillion, with no change in taxes, the budget deficit increases by $0.5 trillion, and so does the government's demand for funds. The demand for funds curve shifts rightward by $0.5 trillion to $D_2$, since total borrowing will now be $0.5 trillion greater at *any* interest rate. After the shift, there would be an excess demand for funds at the original interest rate of 5 percent. The total quantity of funds demanded would be $2.25 trillion (point H), while the quantity supplied would continue to be $1.75 trillion (point A). Thus, the excess demand for funds would be equal to the distance AH in the figure, or $0.5 trillion. This excess demand drives up the interest rate to 7 percent. As the interest rate rises, two things happen.

First, a higher interest rate chokes off some investment spending, as business firms decide that certain investment projects no longer make sense. For example,

**Fiscal policy** A change in gov-ernment purchases or net taxes designed to change total spending and total output.

## FIGURE 10

Beginning from equilibrium at point A, an increase in the budget deficit created to finance additional government purchases shifts the demand for funds curve from $D_1$ to $D_2$. At point H, the quantity of funds demanded exceeds the quantity supplied, so the interest rate begins to rise. As it rises, households are led to save more, and business firms invest less. In the new equilibrium at point B, both consumption and investment spending have been completely crowded out by the increased government spending.

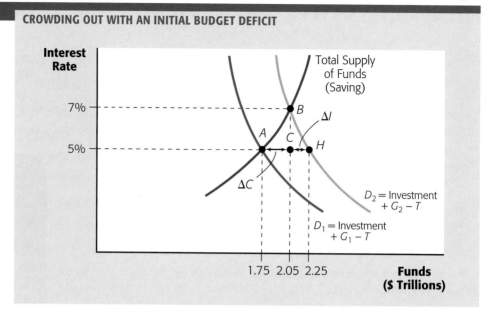

**CROWDING OUT WITH AN INITIAL BUDGET DEFICIT**

the local dry cleaner might wish to borrow funds for that new machine at an interest rate of 5 percent, but not at 7 percent. In the figure, as we move along the new demand-for-funds curve $D_2$, from point H to point B, investment declines by $0.2 trillion (from $2.25 trillion to $2.05 trillion). (Question: How do we know that only business borrowing, and not also government borrowing, adjusts as we move from point H to point B?) Thus, one consequence of the rise in government purchases is a *decrease in investment spending.*

But that's not all: The rise in the interest rate also causes saving to increase. Of course, when people save more of their incomes, they spend less, so another consequence of the rise in government purchases is a *decrease in consumption spending.* In the figure, we move from point A to point B along the saving curve, as saving increases (and consumption decreases) by $0.3 trillion—rising from $1.75 trillion to $2.05 trillion.

Let's recap: As a result of the increase in government purchases, both investment spending and consumption spending decline. The government's purchases have *crowded out* the spending of households (C) and businesses (I).

**Crowding out**  A decline in one sector's spending caused by an increase in some other sector's spending.

> *Crowding out is a decline in one sector's spending caused by an increase in some other sector's spending.*

But we are not quite finished. If we sum the drop in C and the drop in I, we find that total private sector spending has fallen by $0.3 trillion + $0.2 trillion = $0.5 trillion. That is, the drop in private sector spending is precisely equal to the rise in public sector spending, G. Not only is there crowding out, there is **complete crowding out**—each dollar of government purchases causes private sector spending to decline by a full dollar. The net effect is that total spending (C + I + G) does not change at all!

**Complete crowding out**  A dollar-for-dollar decline in one sector's spending caused by an increase in some other sector's spending.

> *In the classical model, a rise in government purchases completely crowds out private sector spending, so total spending remains unchanged.*

A closer look at Figure 10 shows that this conclusion always holds, regardless of the particular numbers used or the shapes of the curves. When $G$ increases, the demand-for-funds curve shifts rightward by the same amount that $G$ rises, or the distance from point $A$ to point $H$. Then the interest rate rises, causing two things to happen. First, the movement along the supply of funds curve, from point $A$ to point $B$, shows that saving rises (consumption falls) by the distance $AC$. Second, the movement along the demand for funds curve, from point $H$ to point $B$, shows that investment spending falls by the amount $CH$. The impact can be summarized as follows:

- Increase in $G = AH$
- Decrease in $C = AC$
- Decrease in $I = CH$

And since $AC + CH = AH$, we know that the combined decrease in $C$ and $I$ is precisely equal to the increase in $G$.

Because there is complete crowding out in the classical model, a rise in government purchases cannot change total spending. And the logic behind this result is straightforward. Each additional dollar the government spends is obtained from the financial market, where it would have been spent by someone else if the government hadn't borrowed it. How do we know this? Because the financial market funnels every dollar of household saving—no more and no less—to either the government or business firms. If the government borrows more, it just removes funds that would have been spent by businesses (the drop in $I$) or by consumers (the drop in $C$).

> *An increase in government purchases has no impact on total spending and no impact on total output or total employment.*

Of course, the opposite sequence of events would happen if government purchases decreased: The drop in $G$ would shrink the deficit. The interest rate would decline, and private sector spending ($C$ and $I$) would rise by the same amount that government purchases had fallen. (See if you can draw the graphs to prove this to yourself.) Once again, total spending and total output would remain unchanged.

## FISCAL POLICY WITH A BUDGET SURPLUS

Fiscal policy has the same macroeconomic effects whether the government is initially running a budget deficit or a budget surplus. However, in the case of a budget surplus, the graphical analysis is a bit different.

Figure 11 shows equilibrium in the loanable funds market with a budget surplus. Remember that, with a budget surplus, the government *supplies* loanable funds, rather than demands them. Therefore, the total demand for loanable funds in Figure 11 is equal to business investment spending alone. The supply of loanable funds, however, now consists of household saving *plus* the budget surplus. That is, because of the surplus, the total supply of funds curve $S_1$ lies further to the right than it otherwise would by the amount of the surplus.

In the initial equilibrium at point $A$, the interest rate is 5 percent, and the total quantity of funds supplied and demanded are equal, at $1.75 trillion. If government spending rises by $0.5 trillion, with no change in taxes, the budget surplus will shrink by $0.5 trillion, shifting the supply of funds curve leftward by that amount to $S_2$. In new equilibrium at point $B$, the interest rate is higher (7 percent) and the quantity of funds supplied and demanded is lower ($1.55 trillion).

But that's not all: The rise in the interest rate also causes saving to increase, and consumption spending to decrease. This is represented by the movement from point $H$

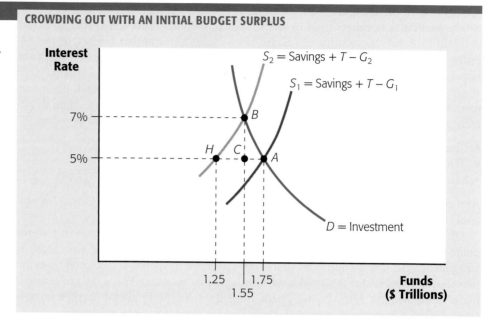

**FIGURE 11**

Beginning from equilibrium at point A, an increase in government purchases causes a decrease in the budget surplus, shifting the supply of funds curve from $S_1$ to $S_2$. At point H, the quantity of funds demanded exceeds the quantity supplied, so the interest rate begins to rise. As it rises, households are led to save more, and business firms invest less. In the new equilibrium at point B, both consumption and investment spending have been completely crowded out by the increased government spending.

**CROWDING OUT WITH AN INITIAL BUDGET SURPLUS**

to point B along the new supply of funds curve, which causes saving to rise (consumption to decrease) by $0.3 trillion, or the distance HC. The rise in the interest rate also causes investment spending to decrease along the total demand for funds curve, from point A to point B. Investment spending falls by $0.2 trillion, or the distance AC. Once again, we see that the rise in government spending has completely crowded out consumption and investment spending: A $0.5 trillion rise in government spending has caused consumption and investment spending to decrease by a total of $0.5 trillion. Total spending remains unchanged, and the fiscal policy is completely ineffective.

Our exploration of fiscal policy shows us that, in the long run, government efforts to change total output by changing government spending or taxes are not only unnecessary, but also ineffective. What, then, *should* a government do to help manage the macroeconomy in the long run? And what *can* it do? These are questions we explore in the next chapter, where we use the classical model to analyze how the economy grows and what governments can do to help or hinder that growth.

## SUMMARY

The classical model is an attempt to explain the behavior of the economy over long time periods. Its most critical assumption is that markets clear—that prices adjust in every market to equate quantities demanded and supplied. The labor market is perhaps the most important part of the classical model. When the labor market clears, we have full employment, and the economy produces the potential level of output.

Another important concept is the production function. It shows the total output the economy can produce with different quantities of labor and for given amounts of land and capital and a given state of technology. When the labor market is at full employment, the production function can be used to determine the economy's potential level of output.

According to Say's law, total spending in the economy will always be just sufficient to purchase the amount of total output produced. By producing and selling goods and services, firms create a total demand equal to what they have produced. If households do not spend their entire incomes, the excess is channeled—as saving—into the loanable funds market, where it is borrowed and spent by businesses and government.

In the loanable funds market, the quantity of funds supplied equals household saving, which depends positively on the interest rate, plus the government budget surplus, if there is one. The quantity of funds demanded equals business investment, which depends negatively on the interest rate, and any government budget deficit, if there is one. The interest rate adjusts so that the quantity of funds supplied always equals the quantity demanded. Equivalently, it adjusts so that saving ($S$) equals the sum of investment spending ($I$) and the government budget deficit ($G - T$).

Fiscal policy cannot affect total output in the classical model. An increase in government purchases results in complete crowding out of investment and consumption spending, leaving total spending and total output unchanged.

## KEY TERMS

| | | | |
|---|---|---|---|
| classical model | Say's law | loanable funds market | government demand for |
| market clearing | net taxes | budget deficit | funds curve |
| labor supply curve | (household) saving | budget surplus | total demand for funds curve |
| labor demand curve | leakages | national debt | fiscal policy |
| aggregate production function | injections | supply of funds curve | crowding out |
| circular flow | planned investment spending | investment demand curve | complete crowding out |

## REVIEW QUESTIONS

1. Discuss the critical assumption on which the classical model is based. How does it relate to the length of time over which we are analyzing the economy?

2. Describe how, in the classical model, the economy reaches full employment automatically. Is this a "realistic" depiction of how the economy behaves?

3. Why does the classical model treat technology and the capital stock as constant?

4. Explain why the slope of the aggregate production function diminishes as more labor is employed.

5. "According to Say's law, all markets always clear." True or false? Explain.

6. What is the difference between net taxes and total tax revenue? Why is the distinction important?

7. Who are the two major groups on the demand side of the loanable funds market? Why does each seek funds there? What is the "price" of these funds?

8. What is the source of funds supplied to the loanable funds market? Explain why the supply of funds curve slopes upward, and why the curve depicting business demand for funds slopes downward.

9. How will the slope of the demand for funds curve be affected if the government runs a budget deficit? Why?

10. Why does Say's law hold even after household saving and taxes are taken into account?

11. Explain the implications of the classical model for government economic policy. What are the two consequences of an increase in government spending that the model predicts?

12. A senator asserts that deficit spending reduces business investment dollar for dollar—every dollar the government borrows means that business investment must fall by a dollar. Is he correct? Why or why not?

## PROBLEMS AND EXERCISES

1. Use a diagram similar to Figure 2 to illustrate the effect—on aggregate output and the real hourly wage—of (a) an increase in labor demand, and (b) an increase in labor supply.

2. The following data give a complete picture of the household, business, and government sectors for 2001 in the small nation of Sylvania. (All dollar figures are in billions.)

| | |
|---|---|
| Consumption spending | $50 |
| Capital stock (end of 2000) | $100 |
| Capital stock (end of 2001) | $103 |
| Government welfare payments | $5 |
| Government unemployment insurance payments | $2 |
| Government payroll | $3 |
| Government outlays for equipment and material | $2 |
| Depreciation rate | 7% |
| Interest rate | 6% |

a. Assuming the government budget for 2001 was in balance, calculate total investment, government purchases, real GDP, total saving, and net taxes for this economy.

b. Calculate total leakages and total injections.

c. Now suppose, instead, that the government increased its spending by $2 billion for the year with no change in taxes. Explain how the variables from (a) will be affected (i.e., will they increase or decrease?).

d. Draw a graph depicting the situation in the loanable funds market and reflecting the assumption of a balanced budget. Clearly label the equilibrium interest rate, saving, and demand for funds. Now, add another curve reflecting any change that occurs when the government runs a deficit; show what happens to the variables you discussed in (c).

e. Under the assumption in (c), suppose Sylvania has a usury law that prohibits interest rates from going above 6 percent. Explain what will happen now in the loanable funds market, and in the economy as a whole.

3. Using a three-panel graph similar in style to Figure 7, illustrate how the *supply* of funds curve is obtained when the government is running a budget surplus.

4. Show that Say's law still holds when the government is running a surplus, rather than a deficit. (*Hint:* Use an argument similar to the one in the section titled "The Loanable Funds Market and Say's Law.")

5. Use graphs to depict the effect on saving, investment, and the interest rate of a *decrease* in government spending when the government is running a budget surplus.

## C H A L L E N G E   Q U E S T I O N S

1. Using an analysis similar to the one in the "Using the Theory" section, show that a tax cut cannot increase total spending in the economy, under each of the following two assumptions:

a. Initially, *none* of the tax cut is saved, so that consumption spending rises by an amount equal to the tax cut.

b. Initially, the *entire* tax cut is saved, causing the supply of funds curve to shift rightward by an amount equal to the tax cut.

2. Assume the loanable funds market is in equilibrium. Influential media pundits begin to warn about impending economic doom—recession, layoffs, and so forth. Using graphs, discuss what might happen to the equilibrium interest rate and the equilibrium quantity of funds. Assume that the government budget is in balance—neither a deficit nor a surplus. (*Hint:* How would these warnings separately affect household and business behavior in the loanable funds market?)

## E X P E R I E N T I A L   E X E R C I S E

1. Use the *Wall Street Journal,* or Infotrac, to locate a recent article about U.S. fiscal policy. More specifically, look for an article that mentions both the interest rate and the rate of economic growth. Once you have found such an article, try to translate the argument into graphs similar to those you have encountered in this chapter. Is the story consistent with what you have learned? If yes, explain how. If not, how might you account for the discrepancy?

# ECONOMIC GROWTH AND RISING LIVING STANDARDS

Economist Thomas Malthus, writing in 1798, came to a striking conclusion: "Population, when unchecked, goes on doubling itself every twenty-five years, or increases in a geometrical ratio. . . . The means of subsistence . . . could not possibly be made to increase faster than in an arithmetic ratio."[1] From this simple logic, Malthus forecast a horrible fate for the human race. There would be repeated famines and wars to keep the rapidly growing population in balance with the more slowly growing supply of food and other necessities. The prognosis was so pessimistic that it led Thomas Carlyle, one of Malthus's contemporaries, to label economics "the dismal science."

But history has proven Malthus wrong . . . at least in part. In the industrialized nations, living standards have increased beyond the wildest dreams of anyone alive in Malthus's time. Economists today are optimistic about these nations' long-run material prospects. At the same time, living standards in many of the less-developed countries have remained stubbornly close to survival level and, in some cases, have fallen below it.

What are we to make of this? Why have living standards steadily increased in some nations but not in others? And what, if anything, can governments do to speed the rise in living standards? These are questions about economic growth—the long-run increase in an economy's output of goods and services.

In this chapter, you will learn what makes economies grow. Our approach will make use of the classical model, focusing on Key Step #4: What Happens When Things Change? As you'll see, growth arises from *shifts* of the curves of the classical model. And by the end of this chapter, you will know why increasing the rate of economic growth is not easy. While nations can take measures to speed growth, each measure carries an opportunity cost. More specifically,

*achieving a higher rate of growth in the long run generally requires some sacrifice in the short run.*

---

[1]  Thomas Robert Malthus, *Essay on the Principle of Population*, 1798.

# THE IMPORTANCE OF GROWTH

Why should we be concerned about economic growth? For one simple reason:

> *When output grows faster than the population, GDP per capita—which we call the **average standard of living**—will rise. When output grows more slowly than the population, the average standard of living will fall.*

**Average standard of living** Total output (real GDP) per person.

Measuring the standard of living by GDP per capita may seem limiting. After all, as we saw two chapters ago, many important aspects of our quality of life are not captured in GDP. Leisure time, workplace safety, good health, a clean environment—we care about all of these. Yet they are not considered in GDP.

Still, many aspects of our quality of life *are* counted in GDP: food, housing, medical care, education, transportation services, and movies and video games, to name a few. It is not surprising, then, that economic growth—measured by increases in GDP—remains a vital concern in every nation.

Economic growth is especially important in countries with income levels far below those of Europe, Japan, and the United States. The average standard of living in some third-world nations is so low that many families can barely acquire the basic necessities of life, and many others perish from disease or starvation. Table 1 lists GDP per capita, infant mortality rates, life expectancies, and adult literacy rates for some of the richest and poorest countries. The statistics for the poor countries are grim enough, but even they capture only part of the story. Unsafe and unclean workplaces, inadequate housing, and other sources of misery are part of daily life for most people in these countries. Other than emigration, economic growth is their only hope.

Growth is a high priority in prosperous nations, too. As we know, resources are scarce, and we cannot produce enough of everything to satisfy all of our desires simultaneously. We want more and better medical care, education, vacations, enter-

| TABLE 1 | | | | |
|---|---|---|---|---|
| **SOME INDICATORS OF ECONOMIC WELL-BEING IN RICH AND POOR COUNTRIES, 1997** | **Real GDP per Capita** | **Infant Mortality Rate (per 1,000 Live Births)** | **Life Expectancy at Birth** | **Adult Literacy Rate** |
| **Country** | | | | |
| **RICH COUNTRIES** | | | | |
| United States | $29,010 | 6.6 | 76.7 | Greater than 99% |
| Japan | $24,070 | 4.4 | 80.0 | Greater than 99% |
| France | $22,030 | 6.0 | 78.1 | Greater than 99% |
| United Kingdom | $20,730 | 6.3 | 77.2 | Greater than 99% |
| Italy | $20,290 | 6.8 | 78.2 | 98.3% |
| **POOR COUNTRIES** | | | | |
| Ghana | $1,640 | 78.9 | 60.0 | 66.4% |
| Pakistan | $1,560 | 95.1 | 64.0 | 40.9% |
| Azerbaijan | $1,550 | 73.9 | 69.9 | 96.3% |
| Cambodia | $1,290 | 106.0 | 53.4 | 66.0% |
| Sierra Leone | $   410 | *na* | 37.2 | 33.3% |

*Sources:* United Nations Development Programme, *Human Development Report 1999* (available at **http://www.undp.org/hdro/report.html**), Table 1; U.S. Bureau of the Census, *Statistical Abstract of the United States, 1997* (available at **http://www.census.gov/prod/www/statistical-abstract-us.html**), Table 1336.

tainment . . . the list is endless. When output per capita is growing, it's at least *possible* for everyone to enjoy an increase in material well-being without anyone having to cut back. We can also accomplish important social goals—helping the poor, improving education, cleaning up the environment—by asking those who are doing well to sacrifice part of the rise in their material well-being, rather than suffer a drop.

But when output per capita stagnates, material gains become a fight over a fixed pie: The more purchasing power my neighbor has, the less is left for me. With everyone struggling for a larger piece of this fixed pie, conflict replaces cooperation. Efforts to help the less fortunate, wipe out illiteracy, reduce air pollution—all are seen as threats, rather than opportunities.

In the 1950s and 1960s, economic growth in the wealthier nations seemed to be taking care of itself. Economists and policy makers focused their attention on short-run movements around full-employment output, rather than on the growth of full-employment output itself. The real payoff for government seemed to be in preventing recessions and depressions—in keeping the economy operating as close to its potential as possible.

All of that changed starting in the 1970s, and economic growth became a national and international preoccupation. Like most changes in perception and thought, this one was driven by experience. Table 2 tells the story. It gives the average yearly growth rates of real GDP per capita for the United States and some of our key trading partners.

Over most of the postwar period, output in the more prosperous industrialized countries (such as the United States, the United Kingdom, and Canada) grew by 2 or 3 percent per year, while output in the less wealthy ones—those with some catching up to do—grew even faster. But beginning in the mid-1970s, all of these nations saw their growth rates slip.

In the late 1990s, only the United States and the United Kingdom returned to their previous high rates of growth, while the other industrialized countries continued to grow more slowly than their historical averages.

Looking at the table, you might think that this slowing in growth was rather insignificant. Does the tiny difference between the pre-1972 and the post-1972 growth rates in the United States really matter? Indeed, it does. Recall our example a few chapters ago in which an increase in the growth rate of around 1 percentage point over the past 26 years would mean that, today, our GDP per capita would be $10,000 greater. Seemingly small differences in growth rates matter a great deal.

| Country | 1948–1972 | 1972–1988 | 1988–1995 | 1995–1999 |
|---|---|---|---|---|
| United States | 2.2% | 1.7% | 1.0% | 2.6% |
| United Kingdom | 2.4 | 2.1 | 0.9 | 2.1 |
| Canada | 2.9 | 2.6 | 0.6 | 1.9 |
| France | 4.3 | 2.1 | 1.2 | 2.1 |
| Italy | 4.9 | 2.8 | 1.6 | 1.4 |
| West Germany | 5.7 | 2.2 | 1.3 | 0.9 |
| Japan | 8.2 | 3.3 | 2.1 | 1.5 |

**TABLE 2**

**AVERAGE ANNUAL GROWTH RATE OF OUTPUT PER CAPITA**

*Sources:* Angus Maddison, *Phases of Capitalist Development* (Oxford: Oxford University Press, 1982); U.S. Census Bureau IDB Summary Demographic Data (**http://www.census.gov/ipc/www/idbsum.html**); and *Economic Report of the President*, 2000, Table B-110, and various World Bank publications. *Note:* Data for Germany includes West Germany only through 1995, and all of Germany from 1995–1999.

## WHAT MAKES ECONOMIES GROW?

Today we understand much more about economic growth than we did in the days of Thomas Malthus. Yet virtually all of our modern ideas about growth are based on the classical model you studied in the previous chapter—and for good reason: Economic growth is a *long-run* phenomenon. The classical model is particularly well suited to analyze long-run economic problems, including the problem of growth.

From the classical model, we know that the economy tends to operate at its full-employment output level over the long run. When we think about the causes of economic growth, then, we should think about changes that would cause full-employment output to increase. In virtually all countries enjoying economic growth, the three most important causes are increases in employment, increases in the capital stock, and changes in technology. In the next several pages, we'll look at each of these in turn.

*What Happens When Things Change?*

## GROWTH IN EMPLOYMENT

In the long run, as the classical model shows, the economy tends to generate a job for just about everyone who wants to work at prevailing wage rates. Therefore, total employment will rise whenever the *labor force*—the number of people who have or want jobs—increases. But what causes the labor force to increase?

One possibility is an increase in labor *supply:* a rise in the number of people who would like to work at any given wage. This is illustrated in Figure 1 by a rightward shift in the labor supply curve. We'll discuss *why* the labor supply curve might shift later; here, we'll concentrate on the consequences of the shift.

Before the shift, the labor supply curve is $L_1^S$, the market clears at a wage of $15 per hour, and the fully employed labor force is 100 million workers. The aggregate production function tells us that, with the given amounts of capital and land in the economy, and the given state of technology, 100 million workers can produce $7 trillion in goods and services—the initial value of full-employment output. When the labor supply curve shifts to $L_2^S$, the market-clearing wage drops to $12. Business firms—finding labor cheaper to hire—increase the number of workers employed along the labor demand curve, from point A to point B. The labor force increases to 120 million workers, and full-employment output rises to $8 trillion.

But growth in employment can also arise from an increase in labor demand: a rise in the number of workers firms would like to hire at any given wage. Once again, we'll consider the *causes* of labor demand changes momentarily; here, we focus on the *consequences.*

Graphically, an increase in labor demand is represented by a rightward shift in the labor demand curve, as in Figure 2. As the wage rate rises from $15 to its new equilibrium of $17, we move along the labor supply curve from point A to point B. More people decide they want to work as the wage rises. Equilibrium employment once again rises from 100 million to 120 million workers, and full-employment output rises from $7 trillion to $8 trillion. Thus,

> *growth in employment can arise from an increase in labor supply (a rightward shift in the labor supply curve) or an increase in labor demand (a rightward shift of the labor demand curve).*

You may have noticed one very important difference between the labor market outcomes in Figures 1 and 2: When labor *supply* increases, the wage rate falls (from $15 to $12 in Figure 1); when labor *demand* increases, the wage rate rises (from

**AN INCREASE IN LABOR SUPPLY**

**FIGURE 1**

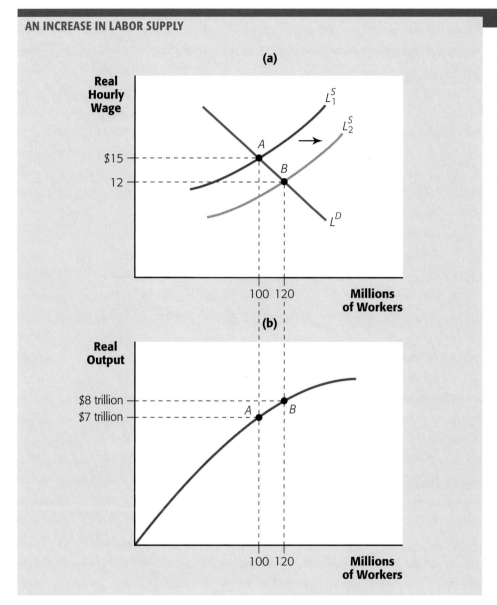

**(a)**

**(b)**

At point *A*, labor supply and demand determine an employment level of 100 million workers, and real GDP of $7 trillion. An increase in labor supply will raise employment to 120 million (at point *B*), although with a lower wage rate. With more people working, real GDP rises to $8 trillion.

$15 to $17 in Figure 2). Which of the figures describes the actual experience of the U.S. labor market?

Actually, a combination of both: Over the past 50 years, the U.S. labor supply curve has shifted steadily rightward, sometimes slowly, sometimes more rapidly. Why the shift in labor supply? In part, the reason has been steady population growth: The more people there are, the more will want to work at any wage. But another reason has been an important change in tastes: an increase in the desire of women (especially married women) to work.

Over the past 50 years, as the labor supply curve has shifted rightward, the labor demand curve has shifted rightward as well. Why? Throughout this period, firms have been acquiring more and better capital equipment for their employees to use. Managers and accountants now keep track of inventories and other important accounts with lightning-fast computer software instead of account ledgers,

**FIGURE 2**

If firms demand more labor, employment will increase—from 100 million to 120 million—while the wage rate rises. With more people working, real GDP increases from $7 trillion to $8 trillion.

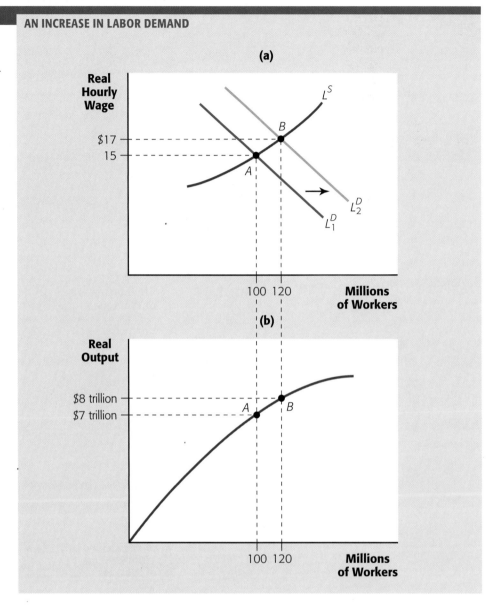

**AN INCREASE IN LABOR DEMAND**

supermarket clerks use electronic scanners instead of hand-entry cash registers, and college professors or their research assistants now gather data by searching for a few hours on the Web instead of a few weeks in the library. At the same time, workers have become better educated and better trained. These changes have increased the amount of output a worker can produce in any given period, so firms have wanted to hire more of them at any wage.[2]

In fact, over the past century, increases in labor demand have outpaced increases in labor supply, so that, on balance, the average wage has risen and employment has increased. This is illustrated in Figure 3, which shows a shift in the labor supply curve from $L_1^S$ to $L_2^S$, and an even greater shift in the labor demand curve from $L_1^D$ to $L_2^D$.

---

[2]    These changes in physical and human capital have also shifted the economy's production function, but we'll consider that in the next section.

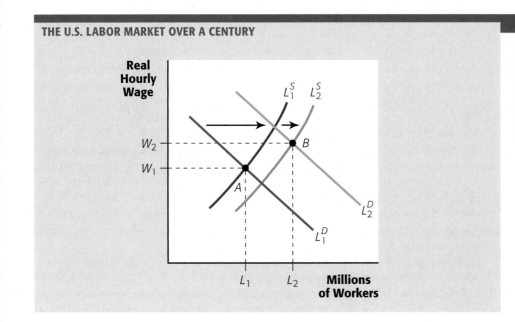

**THE U.S. LABOR MARKET OVER A CENTURY**

**FIGURE 3**

Over the past century, increases in labor demand have outpaced increases in supply. As a result, both the level of employment and the average wage have risen.

The impact of these changes on total employment has been dramatic. Between 1947 and 1999, the *labor force participation rate*—the fraction of the adult population that is either working or looking for work—rose from 58.3 percent to 67.1 percent. The increased participation rate was due partly to women's increased tastes for working, as mentioned, and partly to the increase in the average wage rate that made work more rewarding. Together, growth in the population and in the participation rate have increased the U.S. labor force from 59.4 million workers in 1947 to 139.4 million workers in 1999.

Currently, the U.S. Bureau of Labor Statistics predicts employment growth of 1 percent per year until the year 2010. Is there anything we can do to make employment grow even faster, and thus increase our rate of economic growth? Can we speed up the rightward shifts in labor supply and labor demand? Yes, we can. But as you read on, keep in mind that these measures to increase employment are not necessarily socially desirable. These measures would, most likely, accomplish the goal, but they would also have costs—costs that Americans may or may not be willing to pay. Later, we'll discuss these costs.

## HOW TO INCREASE EMPLOYMENT

One set of policies to increase employment focuses on changing labor supply. And an often-proposed example of this type of policy is a decrease in income tax rates. Imagine that you have a professional degree in accounting, physical therapy, or some other field, and you are considering whether to take a job. Suppose the going rate for your professional services is $30 per hour. If your average tax rate is 33 percent, then one-third of your income will be taxed away, so your take-home pay would be only $20 per hour. But if your tax rate were cut to 20 percent, you would take home $24 per hour. Since you care about your take-home pay, you will respond to a tax cut in the same way you would respond to a wage increase—even if the wage your potential employer pays does not change at all. If you would be willing to take a job that offers a take-home pay of $24, but not one that offers $20, then the tax cut would be just what was needed to get you to seek work.

When we extend your reaction to the population as a whole, we can see that a cut in the income tax rate can convince more people to seek jobs at any given wage, shifting the labor supply curve rightward. This is why economists and politicians who focus on the economy's long-run growth often recommend lower taxes on labor income to encourage more rapid growth in employment. They point out that many American workers must pay combined federal, state, and local taxes of more than 40 cents out of each additional dollar they earn, and that this may be discouraging work effort in the United States.

In addition to tax rate changes, some economists advocate changes in government transfer programs to speed the growth in employment. They argue that the current structure of many government programs creates disincentives to work. For example, families receiving welfare payments, food stamps, unemployment benefits, and Social Security retirement payments all face steep losses in their benefits if they go to work or increase their work effort. Redesigning these programs might therefore stimulate growth in labor supply.

This reasoning was an important motive behind the sweeping reforms in the U.S. welfare system passed by Congress, and signed by President Clinton, in August 1996. Among other things, the reforms reduced the number of people who were eligible for benefits, cut the benefit amount for many of those still eligible, and set a maximum coverage period of five years for most welfare recipients. Later in this chapter, we'll discuss some of the costs of potentially growth-enhancing measures like this. Here, we only point out that changes in benefit programs have the potential to change labor supply.

> *A cut in tax rates increases the reward for working, while a cut in benefits to the needy increases the hardship of* not *working. Either policy can cause a greater rightward shift in the economy's labor supply curve than would otherwise occur and speed the growth in employment and output.*

Government policies can also affect the labor demand curve. In recent decades, subsidies for education and training, such as government-guaranteed loans for college students or special training programs for the unemployed, have helped to increase the skills of the labor force and made workers more valuable to potential employers. Government also subsidizes employment more directly—by contributing part of the wage when certain categories of workers are hired—the disabled, college work-study participants, and, in some experimental programs, inner-city youth. By enlarging these programs, government could increase the number of workers hired at any given wage and thus shift the labor demand curve to the right:

> *Government policies that help increase the skills of the workforce or that subsidize employment more directly shift the economy's labor demand curve to the right, increasing employment and output.*

Efforts to speed employment growth are controversial. In recent decades, those who prefer an activist government have favored policies to increase labor *demand* through government-sponsored training programs, more aid to college students, employment subsidies to firms, and similar programs. Those who prefer a more *laissez-faire* approach have generally favored policies to increase the labor *supply* by *decreasing* government involvement—lower taxes or a less generous social safety net.

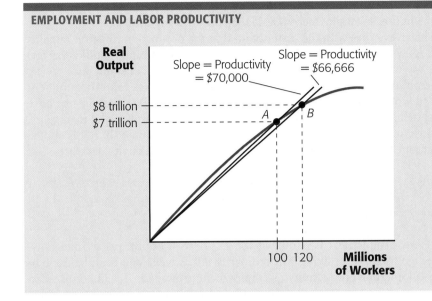

**FIGURE 4**

**EMPLOYMENT AND LABOR PRODUCTIVITY**

Real Output

Slope = Productivity = $70,000

Slope = Productivity = $66,666

$8 trillion

$7 trillion

A    B

100  120   **Millions of Workers**

At any level of employment, labor productivity can be calculated by dividing total output by total employment. This is also shown by the slope of a line from the origin to a point on the production function. At point *A*, productivity is $70,000 per worker. With more employment at point *B*, productivity is lower—$66,666 per worker.

## EMPLOYMENT GROWTH AND PRODUCTIVITY

Increases in employment have been an important source of economic growth in the United States and many other countries. But growth from this source has a serious drawback: It does not necessarily raise a nation's standard of living. Indeed, it can even cause living standards to fall. Why? Because living standards are closely tied to **labor productivity** (sometimes just called **productivity**)—the nation's total output divided by the total number of workers that produce it. Productivity is the output produced by the average worker in a year.[3]

**Labor productivity** Total output (real GDP) per worker.

Figure 4 illustrates the relationship between labor productivity and the economy's production function. At any level of employment, productivity is calculated by dividing total yearly output (on the vertical axis) by the total number of workers (on the horizontal axis):

$$\text{Productivity} = \frac{\text{output}}{\text{employment}} = \frac{\text{vertical measure}}{\text{horizontal measure}}.$$

For example, in the figure, 100 million workers can produce $7 trillion in output. Productivity at this level of employment is thus $7 trillion/100 million = $70,000 per worker, which is the slope of the line drawn from the origin to point *A* on the production function.[4]

Now look at what happens when employment rises to 120 million workers: Labor productivity falls to $8 trillion/120 million = $66,666 per worker, the slope of

[3]   Productivity is more often defined as total output divided by total *labor hours*—the output produced by the average worker in an hour. But our calculations will be easier if we use the definition given in the text. As long as the typical worker's hours remain unchanged, the two definitions of productivity—output per hour or output per worker per year—will rise or fall by the same percentage.

[4]   The slope of a straight line is always "rise over run," or the change along the vertical axis divided by the change along the horizontal axis between any two points. Since our straight line begins at the origin, we can use the origin as our first point, so that the change in the vertical axis is just total output and the change in the horizontal axis is total employment. This gives us total output/total employment as the slope of the line.

http://

Paul Bauer's "Are We in a Productivity Boom?" provides a more in-depth exploration of recent U.S. productivity experience. It's available at http://www.clev.frb.org/research/com99/index.htm.

the line drawn from the origin to point *B* on the production function. In fact, as you can see in the figure, as employment rises, labor productivity drops.

Why? The answer lies with the assumption that the production function remains unchanged. As we move rightward along a given production function, like the one in Figure 4, we are assuming that the nation's capital stock is constant. As a consequence, as employment increases, each worker has less and less capital equipment with which to work, and the average worker's output falls. If 100 ditchdiggers have 100 shovels, then each has his own shovel. If we double the number of ditchdiggers, but hold constant the number of shovels, then each worker must share his shovel with another and digs fewer ditches in any period. Labor productivity decreases.

> *When employment increases, while the capital stock remains constant, the amount of capital available to the average worker will decrease, and labor productivity will fall.*

Falling labor productivity is bad news for a society. If output per worker falls, then the average standard of living will ordinarily fall as well. What can be done to prevent the fall in labor productivity as employment grows? Or—even better—can anything be done to *increase* labor productivity even as more people are working? The answer is yes, as you'll see in the next section.

*What Happens When Things Change?*

## GROWTH OF THE CAPITAL STOCK

The key to increasing labor productivity is to increase the nation's stock of capital. Has your college or university acquired more computers, desks, or campus-patrol vehicles in the past year? Did it install a new phone system? Build a new classroom or dormitory? If the answer to any of these questions is yes, then your school has helped create growth of the U.S. capital stock. With more capital—more assembly lines, bulldozers, computers, factory buildings, and the like—a given number of workers can produce more output than before, so the production function will *shift upward*.

Figure 5 shows the shift. With the initial amount of capital, the economy operates at point *A* on the lower aggregate production function, where 100 million workers produce $7 trillion in output. The increase in capital shifts the production function upward, and—with the same employment level—the economy now operates at point *D*, where 100 million workers produce $8 trillion in output.[5]

Looking back to Figure 4, and comparing it with Figure 5, you'll notice that output increases by the same amount in both cases; but the consequences for productivity are very different. In Figure 4, an increase in employment causes labor productivity to fall; in Figure 5, an increase in capital causes labor productivity to rise. (How do we know that productivity rises in Figure 5? *Hint*: Compare the slopes of the line through point *A* and the line through point *D*.)

> *An increase in the capital stock causes labor productivity and living standards to increase.*

---

[5]   In order to focus on the pure effects of an increase in capital, Figure 5 holds the level of employment constant. But as you learned earlier in this chapter, an increase in capital will make workers more productive, and firms will want to hire more of them at any given wage. Thus, a complete analysis of capital growth would show the labor demand curve shifting rightward at the same time as the production function shifts upward.

**FIGURE 5**

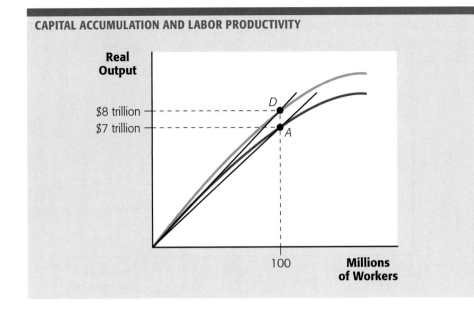

**CAPITAL ACCUMULATION AND LABOR PRODUCTIVITY**

An increase in the capital stock shifts the production function upward. At point *A*, 100 million workers could produce $7 trillion of real GDP; labor productivity is $70,000 per worker. With more capital, those same workers could produce $8 trillion of real GDP; productivity is then higher, at $80,000 per worker.

To summarize, when the labor force grows (with a constant capital stock), labor productivity falls; and when the capital stock grows (with a constant labor force), productivity rises. These are interesting hypothetical cases. But in the real world, both the capital stock and the labor force grow from year to year. What happens to labor productivity when both changes occur simultaneously? That depends on what happens to **capital per worker**—the total quantity of capital divided by total employment. Greater capital per worker means greater productivity: You can dig more ditches with a shovel than with your bare hands, and even more with a backhoe.

**Capital per worker** The total capital stock divided by total employment.

> *If the capital stock grows faster than employment, then capital per worker will rise, and labor productivity will increase along with it. But if the capital stock grows more slowly than employment, then capital per worker will fall, and labor productivity will fall as well.*

In the United States and most other developed countries, the capital stock has grown more rapidly than the labor force. As a result, labor productivity has risen over time. But in some developing countries, the capital stock has grown at about the same rate as, or even more slowly than, the population, and labor productivity has remained stagnant or fallen. We will return to this problem in the "Using the Theory" section of this chapter.

## INVESTMENT AND THE CAPITAL STOCK

Now you can see why an increase in the capital stock plays such a central role in economists' thinking about growth: It works by raising labor productivity and thus unambiguously helps to raise living standards. But how does a nation's capital stock grow?

To answer this question, it's important to realize that capital is a *stock variable.* As you learned a few chapters ago, a stock variable measures a quantity at a moment in time. More specifically, the capital stock is a measure of total plant and equipment in the economy at any moment. Planned investment, on the other hand, is a *flow variable*—it measures a process that takes place over a period of time. In this case, the flow is the rate at which we are producing *new* plant and equipment over some period. The

**FIGURE 6**

Government policies that make investment more profitable will increase investment spending at each interest rate. The resulting rightward shift of the investment demand curve leads to a higher level of investment spending, at point *B*.

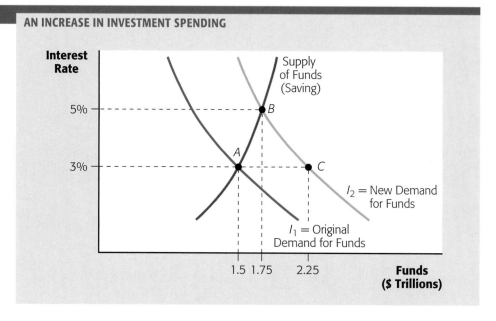

**AN INCREASE IN INVESTMENT SPENDING**

relationship between the capital stock and the flow of investment is similar to that between the flow of water into a bathtub and the total amount of water in the tub itself. As long as investment is greater than depreciation (more water flows into the tub than drains out), the total stock of capital (the quantity of water in the tub) will rise. Moreover, the greater the flow of investment, the faster will be the rise in the capital stock.

## HOW TO INCREASE INVESTMENT

A government seeking to spur investment has more than one weapon in its arsenal. It can direct its efforts toward businesses themselves, toward the household sector, or toward its own budget.

**Targeting Businesses: Increasing the Incentive to Invest.**   One kind of policy to increase investment targets the business sector itself, with the goal of increasing planned investment spending. Figure 6 shows how this works. The figure shows a simplified view of the loanable funds market where—to focus on investment—we assume that there is no budget deficit, so there is no government demand for funds. The initial equilibrium in the market is at point *A*, where household saving (the supply of funds) and investment (the demand for funds) are both equal to $1.5 trillion and the interest rate is 3 percent. Now suppose that the government takes steps to make investment more profitable, so that—at any interest rate—firms will want to purchase $0.75 trillion more in capital equipment than before. Then the investment curve would shift rightward by $0.75 trillion—from $I_1$ to $I_2$, and the interest rate would rise from 3 percent to 5 percent. Note that, as the interest rate rises, some—but not all—of the original increase in planned investment is choked off. In the end, investment rises from $1.5 trillion to $1.75 trillion, and so each year $0.25 trillion more is added to the capital stock than would otherwise be added.

These are the mechanics of a rightward shift in the investment curve. But what government measures would *cause* such a shift in the first place? That is, how could the government help to make investment spending more profitable for firms?

One such measure would be a reduction in the **corporate profits tax**, which would allow firms to keep more of the profits they earn from investment projects.

**Corporate profits tax**   A tax on the profits earned by corporations.

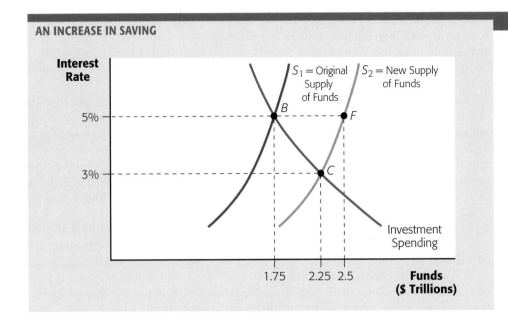

**AN INCREASE IN SAVING**

*Interest Rate*

$S_1$ = Original Supply of Funds   $S_2$ = New Supply of Funds

5%

3%

Investment Spending

1.75   2.25  2.5

**Funds ($ Trillions)**

B   F   C

**FIGURE 7**

If households decide to save more of their incomes, the supply of funds will increase. With more funds available, the interest rate will fall. Businesses will respond by increasing their borrowing, and investment will increase from $1.75 trillion to $2.25 trillion.

Another, even more direct, policy is an **investment tax credit**, which subsidizes corporate investment in new capital equipment.

> *Reducing business taxes or providing specific investment incentives can shift the investment curve rightward, thereby speeding growth in physical capital, and increasing the growth rate of living standards.*

Of course, the same reasoning applies in reverse: An *increase* in the corporate profits tax or the *elimination* of an investment tax credit would shift the investment curve to the left, slowing the rate of investment, the growth of the capital stock, and the rise in living standards.

**Investment tax credit** A reduction in taxes for firms that invest in certain favored types of capital.

### Targeting Households: Increasing the Incentive to Save.

While firms make decisions to purchase new capital, it is largely households that supply the firms with funds, via personal saving. Thus, an increase in investment spending can originate in the household sector, through an increase in the desire to save. This is illustrated in Figure 7. If households decide to save more of their incomes at any given interest rate, the supply of funds curve will shift rightward, from $S_1$ to $S_2$. The increase in saving drives down the interest rate, from 5 percent to 3 percent, which, in turn, causes investment to increase. With a lower interest rate, NBC might decide to borrow funds to build another production studio, or the corner grocery store may finally decide to borrow the funds it needs for a new electronic scanner at the checkout stand. In this way, an increase in the desire to save is translated—via the financial market—into an increase in investment and faster growth in the capital stock.

What might cause households to increase their saving? The answer is found in the reasons people save in the first place. And to understand these reasons, you needn't look farther than yourself or your own family. You might currently be saving for a large purchase (a car, a house, a vacation, college tuition) or to build a financial cushion in case of hard times ahead. You might even be saving to support yourself during retirement, though this is a distant thought for most college students. Given these motives, what would make you save more? Several things: greater uncertainty about your economic future, an increase in your life expectancy, anticipation of an earlier retirement, a change in tastes toward big-ticket items, or even just a change in your attitude about saving. Any of these changes—if they occurred in many households simultaneously—would shift the saving curve (the supply of funds curve) to the right, as in Figure 7.

But government policy can increase household saving as well. One often-proposed idea is to decrease the **capital gains tax.** A capital gain is the profit you earn when you sell an asset, such as a share of stock or a bond, at a higher price than you paid for it. By lowering the special tax rate for capital gains, households would be able to keep more of the capital gains they earn. As a result, stocks and bonds would become more rewarding to own, and you might decide to reduce your current spending in order to buy them. If other households react in the same way, total saving would rise, and the supply of funds to the financial market would increase.

Another frequently proposed measure is to switch from the current U.S. income tax—which taxes all income whether it is spent or saved—to a **consumption tax,** which would tax only the income that households spend. A consumption tax could work just like the current income tax, except that you would deduct your saving from your income and pay taxes on the remainder. This would increase the reward for saving since, by saving, you would earn additional interest on the part of your income that would have been taxed away under an income tax. Individual retirement accounts, or IRAs, allow households to deduct limited amounts of saving from their incomes before paying taxes. A general consumption tax would go much further and allow *all* saving to be deducted.

Another proposal to increase household saving is to restructure the U.S. Social Security system, which provides support for retired workers who have contributed funds to the system during their working years. Because Social Security encourages people to rely on the government for income during retirement, they have less incentive to save for retirement themselves. The proposed restructuring would link workers' Social Security benefits to their actual contributions to the system, whereas under the current system some people receive benefits worth far more than the amount they have contributed.

> *Government can alter the tax and transfer system to increase incentives for saving. If successful, these policies would make more funds available for investment, speed growth in the capital stock, and speed the rise in living standards.*

(Do any of these methods of increasing saving disturb you? Remember, we are not advocating any measures here; rather, we are merely noting that such measures would increase saving and promote economic growth. We'll discuss the *costs* of growth-promoting measures later.)

**Shrinking the Government's Budget.**  A final pro-investment measure is directed at the government sector itself. The previous chapter showed that an increase in government purchases, financed by borrowing in the financial market, completely crowds out consumption and investment. A *decrease* in government purchases has the opposite effect: raising consumption and investment.

Figure 8 reintroduces the government to the financial market to show how this works. Initially, the government is running a deficit of $0.75 trillion, equal to the distance *EA.* The total demand for funds is now the sum of investment and the government's budget deficit, given by the curve labeled "Investment Spending + Deficit." The demand for funds curve intersects the supply of funds curve at point *A,* creating an equilibrium interest rate of 5 percent and equilibrium saving of $1.75

**Capital gains tax**  A tax on profits earned when a financial asset is sold at more than its acquisition price.

**Consumption tax**  A tax on the part of their income that households spend.

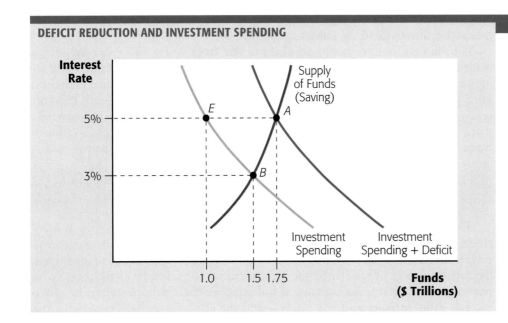

**DEFICIT REDUCTION AND INVESTMENT SPENDING**

**FIGURE 8**

Eliminating the government's budget deficit will reduce government borrowing in the loanable funds market. As a result, the total demand for funds will fall, as will the interest rate. At a lower interest rate, businesses will increase their investment spending from $1 trillion (point *E*) to $1.5 trillion (point *B*).

trillion. At this interest rate, investment spending is only $1 trillion. The part of saving not going to finance investment spending ($1.75 trillion − $1 trillion = $0.75 trillion) is being used to finance the budget deficit.

Now consider what happens if the government eliminates the deficit—say, by reducing its purchases by $0.75 trillion. The demand for funds would consist of investment spending only. Since there would be no other borrowing, the new equilibrium would be point *B*, with an interest rate of 3 percent and investment equal to $1.5 trillion—greater than before. By balancing its budget, the government no longer needs to borrow in the loanable funds market, which frees up funds to flow to the business sector instead. Initially, this creates a surplus of funds. But—as the loanable funds market clears—the interest rate drops, and the surplus of funds disappears. (Why does a drop in the interest rate make the surplus disappear? *Hint:* What happens to saving and to investment as the interest rate declines?)

The link between the government budget, the interest rate, and investment spending is the major reason why the U.S. government, and governments around the world, try to reduce and, if possible, eliminate budget deficits. They have learned that

*a shrinking deficit or a rising surplus tends to reduce interest rates and increase investment, thus speeding the growth in the capital stock.*

In the 1990s, Congress set strict limits on the growth of government spending, and the budget deficit began shrinking. In 1998, the federal budget turned from deficit to surplus, and was projected to remain in surplus for at least a decade. These surpluses are helping to keep interest rates low, which in turn leads to greater business investment spending. The hope is that this will lead to a higher capital stock and greater productivity than we would have without the budget surpluses.

### An Important Proviso About the Government Budget.
A reduction in the deficit or an increase in the surplus—even if they stimulate private investment—are not *necessarily* pro-growth measures. It depends on *how* the budget changes. By an increase in taxes? A cut in government spending? And if the latter, which government

programs will be cut? Welfare? National defense? Highway repair? The answers can make a big difference to the impact on growth.

For example, in our discussions of the capital stock so far, we've ignored government capital—roads, communication lines, bridges, and dams. To understand the importance of government capital, just imagine what life would be like without it. How would factories obtain their raw materials or distribute their goods if no one repaired the roads? How would contracts between buyers and sellers be enforced if there were no public buildings to house courts and police departments? Government capital supports private economic activity in more ways than we can list here.

> *Government investment in new capital and in the maintenance of existing capital makes an important contribution to economic growth.*

This important observation complicates our view of deficit reduction. It is still true that a decrease in government spending will lower the interest rate and increase private investment. But if the budget cutting falls largely on government investment, the negative effect of smaller public investment will offset some of the positive impact of greater private investment. Shrinking the deficit will then alter the *mix* of capital—more private and less public—and the effect on growth could go either way. A society rife with lawlessness, deteriorating roads and bridges, or an unreliable communications network might benefit from a shift toward public capital. For example, a study of public budgets in African nations—which have poor road conditions—found that each one-dollar-per-year cut in the road-maintenance budget increased vehicle operating costs by between $2 and $3 per year, and in one case, by as much as $22 per year.[6] This is an example where a cut in government spending—even if it reduces the deficit—probably hinders growth. By contrast, a stable society (Sweden comes to mind) with a fully developed and well-maintained public infrastructure might be able to have faster growth by shifting the mix away from public and toward private capital.

> *The impact of deficit reduction on economic growth depends on which government programs are cut. Shrinking the deficit by cutting government investment will not stimulate growth as much as would cutting other types of government spending.*

## HUMAN CAPITAL AND ECONOMIC GROWTH

So far, the only type of capital we've discussed is physical capital—the plant and equipment workers use to produce output. But when we think of the capital stock most broadly, we include *human capital* as well. **Human capital**—the skills and knowledge possessed by workers—is as central to economic growth as is physical capital. After all, most types of physical capital—computers, CAT scanners, and even shovels—will contribute little to output unless workers know how to use them. And when more workers gain skills or improve their existing skills, output rises just as it does when workers have more physical capital:

**Human capital** Skills and knowledge possessed by workers.

> *An increase in human capital works like an increase in physical capital to increase output: It causes the production function to shift upward, raises productivity, and increases the average standard of living.*

---

[6]    This World Bank study was cited in *The Economist,* June 10, 1995, p. 72.

There is another similarity between human and physical capital: Both are *stocks* that are increased by *flows* of investment. The stock of human capital increases whenever investment in new skills during some period, through education and training, exceeds the depreciation of existing skills over the same period, through retirement, death, or deterioration. Therefore, greater investment in human capital will speed the growth of the human capital stock, the growth in productivity, and the growth in living standards.

Human capital investments are made by business firms (when they help to train their employees), by government (through public education and subsidized training), and by households (when they pay for general education or professional training). Human capital investments have played an important role in recent U.S. economic growth. Can we do anything to increase our rate of investment in human capital?

In part, we've already answered this question: Some of the same policies that increase investment in *physical* capital also work to raise investment in human capital. For example, a decrease in the budget deficit would lower the interest rate and make it cheaper for households to borrow for college loans and training programs. A change in the tax system that increases the incentive to save would have the same impact, since this, too, would lower interest rates. And an easing of the tax burden on business firms could increase the profitability of *their* human capital investments, leading to more and better worker training programs.

But there is more: Human capital, unlike physical capital, cannot be separated from the person who provides it. If you own a building, you can rent it out to one firm and sell your labor to another. But if you have training as a doctor, your labor and your human capital must be sold together, as a package. Moreover, your wage or salary will be payment for both your labor and your human capital. This means that income tax reductions—which we discussed earlier as a means of increasing labor supply—can also increase the profitability of human capital to households, and increase their rate of investment in their own skills and training. For example, suppose an accountant is considering whether to attend a course in corporate financial reporting, which would increase her professional skills. The course costs $4,000, and will increase the accountant's income by $1,000 per year for the rest of her career. With a tax rate of 40 percent, her take-home pay would increase by $600 per year, so her annual rate of return on her investment would be $600/$4,000 = 15 percent. But with a lower tax rate—say, 20 percent—her take-home pay would rise by $800 per year, so her rate of return would be $800/$4,000 = 20 percent. The lower the tax rate, the greater is the rate of return on our accountant's human capital investment, and the more likely she will be to acquire new skills. Thus,

> *many of the pro-growth policies discussed earlier—policies that increase employment or increase investment in physical capital—are also effective in promoting investment in human capital.*

College-level courses are one important way that countries increase the stock of human capital and shift up their production function.

# TECHNOLOGICAL CHANGE

What Happens When Things Change?

So far, we've discussed how economic growth arises from greater quantities of resources—more labor, more physical capital, or more human capital. But another important source of growth is **technological change**—the invention or discovery of new inputs, new outputs, or new methods of production. Indeed, it is largely because of

**Technological change** The invention or discovery of new inputs, new outputs, or new production methods.

technological change that Malthus's horrible prediction (cited at the beginning of this chapter) has not come true. In the last 60 years, for example, the inventions of synthetic fertilizers, hybrid corn, and chemical pesticides have enabled world food production to increase faster than population.

New technology affects the economy in much the same way as do increases in the capital stock. Flip back 7 pages to Figure 5. There, you saw that an increase in the capital stock would shift the production function upward and increase output. New technology, too, shifts the production function upward, since it enables any given number of workers to produce more output. In many cases, the new technology requires the acquisition of physical and human capital before it can be used. For example, a new technique for destroying kidney stones with ultrasound, rather than time-consuming surgery, can make doctors more productive—but not until they spend several thousand dollars to buy the ultrasound machine and take a course on how to use it. In other cases, a new technology can be used without any additional equipment or training, as when a factory manager discovers a more efficient way to organize workers on the factory floor. In either case, technological change will shift the production function upward and increase productivity. It follows that

> *the faster the rate of technological change, the greater the growth rate of productivity, and the faster the rise in living standards.*

It might seem that technological change is one of those things that just happens. Thomas Edison invents electricity, or Steve Jobs and Steve Wozniak develop the first practical personal computer in their garage. But the pace of technological change is not as haphazard as it seems. The transistor was invented as part of a massive research and development effort by AT&T and intended to improve the performance of communications electronics. Similarly, the next developments in computer technology, transportation, and more will depend on how much money is spent on research and development (R&D) by the leading technology firms:

> *The rate of technological change in the economy depends largely on firms' total spending on R&D. Policies that increase R&D spending will increase the pace of technological change.*

What can the government do to increase spending on R&D? First, it can increase its own direct support for R&D by carrying out more research in its own laboratories or increasing funding for universities and tax incentives to private research labs.

**Patent protection**  A government grant of exclusive rights to use or sell a new technology.

Second, the government can enhance **patent protection**, which increases rewards for those who create new technology by giving them exclusive rights to use it or sell it. For example, when the DuPont Corporation discovered a unique way to manufacture Spandex, it obtained a patent to prevent other firms from copying its technique. This patent has enabled DuPont to earn millions of dollars from its invention. Without the patent, other firms would have copied the technique, competed with DuPont, and taken much of its profit away. Hundreds of thousands of new patents are issued every year in the United States: to pharmaceutical companies for new prescription drugs, to telecommunications companies for new cellular technologies, and to the producers of a variety of household goods ranging from can openers to microwave ovens.

Since patent protection increases the rewards that developers can expect from new inventions, it encourages them to spend more on R&D. By broadening patent protection—issuing patents on a wider variety of discoveries—or by lengthening patent protection—increasing the number of years during which the developer has exclusive rights to market the invention—the government could increase the expected profits from new technologies. That would increase total spending on R&D and increase the pace of technological change. Currently in the United States, patents give inventors and developers exclusive marketing rights over their products for a period of about 20 years. Increasing patent protection to 30 years would certainly increase R&D spending at many firms.

Finally, R&D spending is in many ways just like other types of investment spending: The funds are drawn from the financial market, and R&D programs require firms to buy something now (laboratories, the services of research scientists, materials to build prototypes) for the uncertain prospect of profits in the future. Therefore, almost any policy that stimulates investment spending in general will also increase spending on R&D. Cutting the tax rate on capital gains or on corporate profits, or lowering interest rates by encouraging greater saving or by reducing the budget deficit, can each help to increase spending on R&D and increase the rate of technological change.

## THE COST OF ECONOMIC GROWTH

So far in this chapter, we've discussed a variety of policies that could increase the rate of economic growth and speed the rise in living standards. Why don't all nations pursue these policies and push their rates of economic growth to the maximum? For example, why did the U.S. standard of living (output per capita) grow by 2.6 percent per year between 1995 and 1999? Why not 4 percent per year? Or 6 percent? Or even more?

The answer hinges on one of the basic principles of economics:

> *Government policy is constrained by the reactions of private decision makers. As a result, policy makers face trade-offs: Making progress toward one goal often requires some sacrifice of another goal.*

Economics is famous for making the public aware of policy trade-offs. One of the most important things you will learn in your introductory economics course is that there are no costless solutions to society's problems. Just as individuals face an opportunity cost when they take an action (they must give up something else that they value), so, too, policy makers face an opportunity cost whenever they pursue a policy: They must compromise on achieving some other social goal.

Economic models can help us identify the trade-offs associated with different policy choices. Although confronting a trade-off is rarely pleasant, doing so helps us formulate wiser policies and avoid unpleasant surprises. In this section, you will see that while a variety of policies can increase a nation's rate of economic growth, each of these policies involves a trade-off: It imposes a cost on some group or requires some sacrifice of other social goals.

> *Promoting economic growth involves unavoidable trade-offs: It requires some groups, or the nation as a whole, to give up something else that is valued. In order to decide how fast we want our economy to grow, we must consider growth's costs as well as its benefits.*

What are the costs of growth?

## BUDGETARY COSTS

If you look back over this chapter, you'll see that many of the pro-growth policies we've analyzed involve some kind of tax cut. Cutting the income tax rate will likely increase the labor supply. Cutting taxes on capital gains or corporate profits will increase investment directly. And cutting taxes on saving will increase household saving, lower interest rates, and thus increase investment spending indirectly. Unfortunately, implementing any of these tax cuts would force the government to choose among three unpleasant alternatives: increase some other tax to regain the lost revenue, cut government spending, or permit the budget deficit to rise.

Who will bear the burden of this budgetary cost? That depends on which alternative is chosen. Under the first option—increasing some other tax—the burden falls on those who pay the other tax. For example, if income taxes are cut, real estate taxes might be increased. A family might pay lower income taxes, but higher property taxes. Whether it comes out ahead or behind will depend on how much income the family earns relative to how much property it owns.

The second option, cutting government spending, imposes the burden on those who currently benefit from government programs. These include not only those who directly benefit from a program—like welfare recipients or farmers—but also those who benefit from government spending more indirectly. Even though you may earn your income in the private sector, if government spending is cut, you may suffer from a deterioration of public roads, decreased police protection, or poorer schools for your children.

The third option—a larger budget deficit or a smaller budget surplus—is more complicated. Suppose a tax cut causes the government to end up with a larger deficit. Then greater government borrowing will increase the total amount of government debt outstanding—called the national debt—and lead to greater interest payments to be made by future generations, in the form of higher taxes. The same is true even if the government is running a budget surplus. In that case, a tax cut will *reduce* the size of the surplus, and reduce the amount of the national debt the government pays back each year. Once again, the tax cut raises the interest payments that future generations must bear.

But that is not all. From the previous chapter, we know that a rise in the budget deficit (by increasing the demand for funds) or a drop in the budget surplus (by decreasing the supply of funds) drives up the interest rate. The higher interest rate will reduce investment in physical capital by businesses, as well as investment in human capital by households, and both effects will work to decrease economic growth. It is even possible that so much private investment will be crowded out that the tax cut, originally designed to boost economic growth, ends up slowing growth instead. At best, the growth-enhancing effects of the tax cut will be weakened. This is why advocates of high growth rates usually propose one of the other options—a rise in some other tax or a cut in government spending—as part of a pro-growth tax cut.

In sum,

> *properly targeted tax cuts can increase the rate of economic growth, but will force us to either redistribute the tax burden or cut government programs.*

## CONSUMPTION COSTS

Any pro-growth policy that works by increasing investment—private or government, in physical capital, human capital, or R&D—requires a sacrifice of current consumption spending. The land, labor, and capital we use to produce new cloth-

**FIGURE 9**

**CONSUMPTION, INVESTMENT, AND ECONOMIC GROWTH**

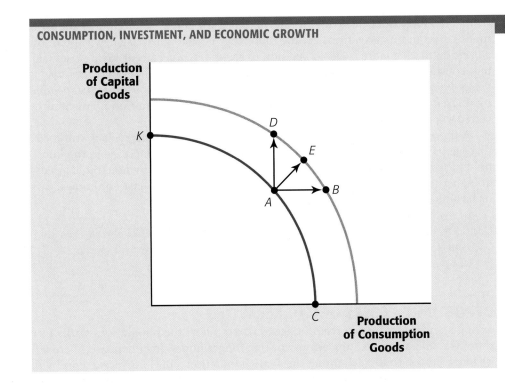

In the current period, a nation can choose to produce only consumer goods (point C), or it can produce some capital goods by sacrificing some current consumption, as at point A. If investment at point A exceeds capital depreciation, the capital stock will grow, and the production possibilities frontier will shift outward. After it does, the nation can produce more consumption goods (point B), more capital goods (point D), or more of both (point E).

cutting machines, oil rigs, assembly lines, training facilities, college classrooms, or research laboratories could have been used instead to produce clothing, automobiles, video games, and other consumer goods. In other words, we face a trade-off: The more capital goods we produce in any given year, the fewer consumption goods we can enjoy in that year.

The role of this trade-off in economic growth can be clearly seen with a familiar tool from Chapter 2: the production possibilities frontier (PPF). Figure 9 shows the PPF for a nation with some given amount of land, labor, and capital that must be allocated to the production of two types of output: capital goods and consumption goods. At point K, the nation is using all of its resources to produce capital goods and none to produce consumption goods. Point C represents the opposite extreme—all resources used to produce consumption goods and none for capital goods. Ordinarily, a nation will operate at an intermediate point such as A, where it is producing both capital and consumption goods.

Now, as long as capital production at point A is greater than the depreciation of existing capital, the capital stock will grow. In future periods, the economy—with more capital—can produce more output, as shown by the outward shift of the PPF in the figure. If a nation can produce more output, then it can produce more consumption goods for the same quantity of capital goods (moving from point A to point B) or more capital goods for the same quantity of consumption goods (from point A to point D) or more of both (from point A to point E).

Let's take a closer look at how this sacrifice of current consumption goods might come about. Suppose that some change in government policy—an investment tax credit or a lengthening of the patent period for new inventions—successfully shifts the investment curve to the right. (Go back to Figure 6.) What will happen? Businesses—desiring more funds for investment—will drive up the interest rate, and households all over the country will find that saving has become more attractive.

As families increase their saving, we move rightward along the economy's supply of funds curve. In this way, firms get the funds they need to purchase new capital. But a decision to *save more* is also a decision to *spend less*. As current saving rises, current consumption spending necessarily falls. By driving up the interest rate, *the increase in investment spending causes a voluntary decrease in consumption spending by households.* Resources are freed from producing consumption goods and diverted to producing capital goods instead.

Although this decrease in consumption spending is voluntary, it is still a cost that we pay. And in some cases, a painful cost: Some of the increase in the household sector's net saving results from a decrease in borrowing by households that—at higher interest rates—can no longer afford to finance purchases of homes, cars, or furniture. In sum,

> *greater investment in physical capital, human capital, or R&D will lead to faster economic growth and higher living standards in the future, but we will have fewer consumer goods to enjoy in the present.*

## OPPORTUNITY COSTS OF WORKERS' TIME

Living standards will also rise if a greater fraction of the population works or if those who already have jobs begin working longer hours. In either case, there will be more output to divide among the same population.[7] But this increase in living standards comes at a cost: a decrease in time spent in nonmarket activities. For example, with a greater fraction of the population working, a smaller fraction is spending time at home. This might mean that more students have summer jobs instead of studying, more elderly workers are postponing their retirement, or more previously nonworking spouses are entering the labor force. Similarly, an increase in average working hours means that the average worker will have less time for other activities—less time to watch television, read novels, garden, fix up the house, teach his or her children, or do volunteer work.

Thus, when economic growth comes about from increases in employment, we face a trade-off: On the one hand, we can enjoy higher incomes and more goods and services; on the other hand, we will have less time to do things other than work in the market. In a market economy, where choices are voluntary, the value of the income gained must be greater than the value of the time given up. No one forces a worker to re-enter the labor force or to increase her working hours. Any worker who takes either of these actions must be better off for doing so. Still, we must recognize that *something* of value is always given up when employment increases:

> *An increase in the fraction of the population with jobs or a rise in working hours will increase output and raise living standards, but also requires us to sacrifice time previously spent in nonmarket activities.*

## SACRIFICE OF OTHER SOCIAL GOALS

Rapid economic growth is an important social goal, but it's not the only one. Some of the policies that quicken the pace of growth require us to sacrifice other goals that we

---

[7]    You might be wondering how a rise in average hours would be represented in the classical model we've been using. This is left to you as an exercise. But here's a hint: An increase in average hours enables the same number of workers to produce more output.

care about. For example, you've seen that restructuring Social Security benefits would increase saving, leading to more investment and faster growth. But such a move would cut the incomes of those who benefit from the current system and increase the burden on other social programs, such as welfare and food stamps. Extending patent protection would increase incentives for research and development. But it would also extend the monopoly power exercised by patent holders and force consumers to pay higher prices for drugs, electronic equipment, and even packaged foods.

Of course, the argument cuts both ways: Just as government policies to stimulate investment require us to sacrifice other goals, so, too, can the pursuit of other goals impede investment spending and economic growth. Most of us would like to see a cleaner environment and safer workplaces. But government safety and environmental regulations have increased in severity, complexity, and cost over time, reducing the rate of profit on new capital and shrinking investment spending.

Does this mean that business taxes and government regulations should be reduced to the absolute minimum? Not at all. As in most matters of economic policy, we face a trade-off:

> *We can achieve greater worker safety, a cleaner environment, and other social goals, but we may have to sacrifice some economic growth along the way. Alternatively, we can achieve greater economic growth, but we will have to compromise on other things we care about.*

When values differ, people will disagree on just how much we should sacrifice for economic growth or how much growth we should sacrifice for other goals.

# ECONOMIC GROWTH IN THE LESS-DEVELOPED COUNTRIES

*Using the* **THEORY**

In most countries, Malthus's dire predictions have not come true. An important part of the reason is that increases in the capital stock have raised productivity and increased the average standard of living. Increases in the capital stock are even more important in the less-developed countries (LDCs), which have relatively little capital to begin with and where even small increases in capital formation can have dramatic effects on living standards.

But how does a nation go about increasing its capital stock? As you've learned, there are a variety of measures, all designed to accomplish the same goal: shifting resources away from consumer-goods production toward capital-goods production. A very simple formula.

Some countries that were once LDCs—like the four Asian tigers (Hong Kong, Singapore, South Korea, and Taiwan)—have applied the formula very effectively. Output per capita in these counties has grown by an average of 6 percent per year over the past two decades. They were able to shift resources from consumption goods into capital goods in part by pursuing many of the growth-enhancing measures discussed in this chapter: large subsidies for human and physical capital investments, pro-growth tax cuts to encourage saving and investment, and the willingness to sacrifice other social goals—especially a clean environment—for growth.[8] These economies gave up large amounts of potential consumption during a period of intensive capital formation.

---

[8]     The Asian tigers also had some special advantages—such as a high level of human capital to start with.

**TABLE 4**

**ECONOMIC GROWTH IN
SELECTED POOR
COUNTRIES**

| Country | Average Annual Growth Rate of Output per Capita | |
|---|---|---|
| | 1975–85 | 1985–1997 |
| Pakistan | 3.5% | 2.9% |
| Bangladesh | 2.1% | 2.8% |
| Ghana | −2.2% | 1.8% |
| Kenya | 0.6% | 0.5% |
| Benin | 1.9% | −0.3% |
| Democratic Republic of the Congo | −3.1% | −6.8% |
| Sierra Leone | −1.2% | −3.5% |

*Source:* United Nations Development Programme, *Human Development Report 1999* (available at **http://www.undp.org/hdro/report.html**), Table 6.

But other LDCs have had great difficulty raising living standards. Table 4 shows growth rates for several of them. In some cases—such as Pakistan, Bangladesh, and more recently, Ghana—slow but consistent growth has given cause for optimism. In other cases—such as Kenya and Benin—living standards have barely budged over the past few decades. In still other cases—for example, the Democratic Republic of the Congo and Sierra Leone—output per capita has been falling steadily. Why do some LDCs have such difficulty achieving economic growth?

Much of the explanation for the low growth rates of many LDCs lies with three characteristics that they share:

1. *Very low current output per capita.* Living standards are so low in some LDCs that they cannot take advantage of the trade-off between producing consumption goods and producing capital goods. In these countries, pulling resources out of consumption would threaten the survival of many households. In the individual household, the problem is an inability to save: Incomes are so low that households must spend all they earn on consumption.

2. *High population growth rates.* Low living standards and high population growth rates are linked together in a cruel circle of logic. On the one hand, population growth by itself tends to reduce living standards; on the other hand, a low standard of living tends to increase population growth. Why? First, the poor are often uneducated in matters of family planning. Second, high mortality rates among infants and children encourage families to have many offspring, to ensure the survival of at least a few to care for parents in their old age. As a result, while the average woman in the United States will have fewer than two children in her lifetime, the average woman in Haiti will have about five children, and the average woman in Rwanda will have more than six.

3. *Poor infrastructure.* Political instability, poor law enforcement, corruption, and adverse government regulations make many LDCs unprofitable places to invest. Low rates of investment mean a smaller capital stock and lower productivity. Infrastructure problems also harm worker productivity in another way: Citizens must spend time guarding against thievery and trying to induce the government to let them operate businesses—time they could otherwise spend producing output.

These three characteristics—low current production, high population growth, and poor infrastructure—interact to create a vicious circle of continuing poverty, which we can understand with the help of the familiar PPF between capital goods and consumption goods. Look back at Figure 9, and now imagine that it applies to

**http://**

The World Bank Economic Growth Project's Web site is a comprehensive source of information about economic growth (http://www.world bank.org/html/prdmg/ grthweb/growth_t.htm).

a poor, developing country. In this case, an outward shift of the PPF does not, in itself, guarantee an increase in the standard of living. In the LDCs, the population growth rate is often very high, and—with a constant labor force participation ratio—employment grows at the same rate as the population. If employment grows more rapidly than the capital stock, then even though the PPF is shifting outward, capital per worker will decline. The result is falling labor productivity and a general decline in living standards.

> *In order to have a rising living standard, a nation's stock of capital must not only grow, but grow faster than its population.*

Point N in Figure 10 shows the minimum amount of investment needed to increase capital per worker, labor productivity, and living standards for a given rate of population growth. For example, if the population is growing at 4 percent per year, then point N indicates the investment needed to increase the total capital stock by 4 percent per year. If investment is just equal to N, then capital per worker—and living standards—remains constant. If investment exceeds N, then capital per worker—and living standards—will rise. Of course, the greater the growth in population, the higher point N will be on the vertical axis, since greater investment will be needed just to keep up with population growth.

The PPF in Figure 10 has an added feature: Point S shows the minimum acceptable level of consumption—the amount of consumer goods the economy *must* produce in a year. For example, S might represent the consumption goods needed to prevent starvation among the least well off, or to prevent unacceptable social consequences, such as violent revolution.

Now we can see the problem faced by the most desperate of the less-developed economies. Output is currently at a point like H in Figure 10, with investment just equal to N. The capital stock is not growing fast enough to increase capital per worker, and so labor productivity and living standards are stagnant. In this situation, the PPF shifts outward each year, but not quickly enough to improve people's

**LDC GROWTH AND LIVING STANDARDS**

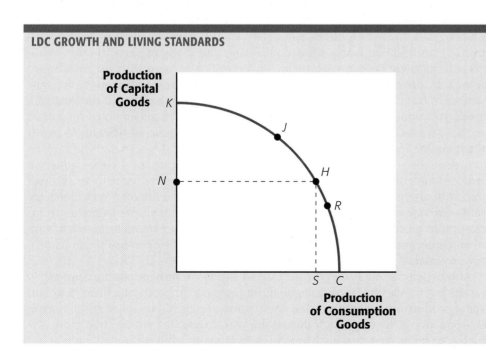

**FIGURE 10**

In order to increase capital per worker when population is growing, yearly investment spending must exceed some minimum level N. In any year, there is a minimum level of consumption, S, needed to support the population. If output is currently at point H, capital per worker and living standards are stagnant. But movement to a point like J would require an unacceptably low level of consumption.

lives. It could be even worse: Convince yourself that, at a point like *R*, the average standard of living declines even though the capital stock is growing—that is, even though the PPF will shift outward in future periods.

The solution to this problem appears to be an increase in capital production beyond point *N*—a movement *along* the PPF from point *H* to a point such as *J*. As investment rises above *N*, capital per worker rises, and the PPF shifts outward rapidly enough over time to raise living standards. In a wealthy country, like the United States, such a move could be engineered by changes in taxes or other government policies. But in the LDCs depicted here, such a move would be intolerable: At point *H*, consumption is already equal to *S*, the lowest acceptable level. Moving to point *J* would require reducing consumption *below S*.

> The poorest LDCs are too poor to take advantage of the trade-off between consumption and capital production in order to increase their living standards. Since they cannot reduce consumption below current levels, they cannot produce enough capital to keep up with their rising populations.

In recent history, countries have attempted several methods to break out of this vicious circle of poverty. During the 1930s, the dictator Joseph Stalin simply *forced* the Soviet economy from a point like *H* to one like *J*. His goal was to shift the Soviet Union's PPF outward as rapidly as possible. But, as you can see, this reduced consumption below the minimum level *S*, and Stalin resorted to brutal measures to enforce his will. Many farmers were ordered into the city to produce capital equipment. With fewer people working on farms, agricultural production declined, and there was not enough food to go around. Stalin's solution was to confiscate food from the remaining farmers and give it to the urban workforce. Of course, this meant starvation for millions of farmers. Millions more who complained too loudly, or who otherwise represented a political threat, were rounded up and executed.

A less-brutal solution to the problem of the LDCs is to make the wealthy bear more of the burden of increasing growth. If the decrease in consumption can be limited to the rich, then total consumption can be significantly reduced—freeing up resources for investment—without threatening the survival of the poor. This, however, is not often practical, since the wealthy have the most influence with government in LDCs. Being more mobile, they can easily relocate to other countries, taking their savings with them. This is why efforts to shift the sacrifice to the wealthy are often combined with restrictions on personal liberties, such as the freedom to travel or to invest abroad. These moves often backfire in the long run, since restrictions on personal and economic freedom are remembered long after they are removed and make the public—especially foreigners—hesitant to invest in that country.

A third alternative—and the one used increasingly since the 1940s—is *foreign investment* or *foreign assistance*. If the wealthier nations—individually or through international organizations such as the World Bank or the International Monetary Fund—provide the LDCs with capital, then the capital *available* to them can increase, with *no* cutbacks in consumption. This permits an LDC to make *use* of capital and consumption goods at a point like *F* in Figure 11(a), even though its *production* remains—for the moment—at point *H*.

A variation on this strategy is for foreign nations to provide consumer goods so that the poorer nation can shift its *own* resources out of producing them (and into capital production) without causing consumption levels to fall. Once again, if capital production exceeds point *N* during the year, capital per worker will grow, setting the stage for continual growth to higher standards of living.

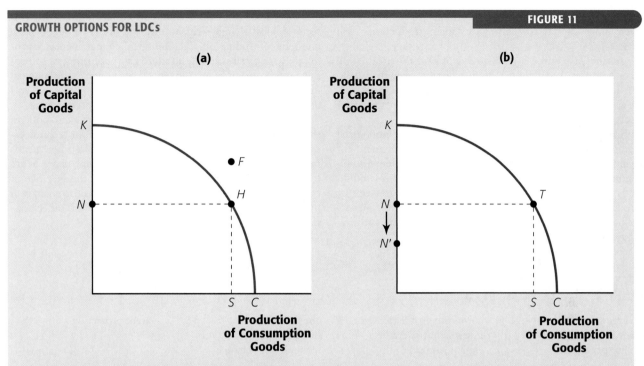

**GROWTH OPTIONS FOR LDCs**                                    **FIGURE 11**

**(a)**                                                       **(b)**

Panel (a) shows an LDC producing at point *H,* where the available consumption goods are just sufficient to meet minimum standards (point *S*). If the nation can obtain goods externally—through foreign investment or foreign assistance—it can *make use* of capital and consumption goods at a point like *F*—outside of its PPF.

Panel (b) shows a case where capital production at point *T* is just sufficient to keep up with a rising population, but not great enough to raise capital per worker and living standards. If this nation can reduce its population growth rate, then the same rate of capital production will increase capital per worker and raise the standard of living.

Finally, there is a fourth alternative. Consider a nation producing at point *T* in Figure 11(b). Capital production is just sufficient to keep up with a rising population, so the PPF shifts outward each year, but not rapidly enough to raise living standards. If this nation can reduce its population growth rate, however, then less capital production will be needed just to keep up with population growth. In the figure, point *N* will move downward to *N'*. If production remains at point *T,* the PPF will continue to shift outward as before, but now—with slower population growth—productivity and living standards will rise. Slowing the growth in population has been an important (and successful) part of China's growth strategy, although it has required severe restrictions on the rights of individual families to have children. Policy trade-offs, once again.

## S U M M A R Y

The growth rate of real GDP is a key determinant of economic well-being. If output grows faster than the population, then the average standard of living will rise. Output can grow because of increases in employment, increases in capital, and improvements in technology.

Employment will increase if there is an increase in either labor supply or labor demand. Labor supply is determined by the size of the working-age population and by individuals'

willingness to forego leisure in return for a wage. Population growth is something that occurs naturally, but the amount of work effort supplied by a given population is sensitive to after-tax labor earnings. A decrease in the income tax rate would stimulate labor supply.

Labor demand is influenced by productivity. Any factor that makes labor more productive will increase the demand for labor, raise employment, and contribute to economic growth. If employees become better trained, or if they are given more capital to work with, their productivity will increase.

An increase in the capital stock will shift the production function upward and contribute to economic growth. Whenever investment exceeds depreciation, the capital stock will grow. And if the capital stock grows faster than the labor force, then labor productivity will rise.

Investment can be encouraged by government policies. If the government reduces its budget deficit, the demand for loanable funds will fall, the interest rate will decline, and investment will increase. Investment can also be stimulated directly through reductions in the corporate profits tax or through subsidies to new capital. Finally, policies that encourage household saving can also lower the interest rate and contribute to capital formation.

The third factor that contributes to economic growth is technological change—the application of new inputs or new methods of production. Technological change increases productivity and raises living standards by permitting us to produce more output from a given set of inputs. Technological improvements can be traced back to spending on research and development, either by the government or by private firms.

Economic growth is not costless. Government policies that stimulate employment, capital formation, or technological progress require either tax increases, cuts in other spending programs, or an increase in the national debt. More broadly, any increase in investment requires the sacrifice of consumption today. Any increase in employment from a given population requires a sacrifice of leisure time and other nonmarket activities.

## K E Y   T E R M S

| | | | |
|---|---|---|---|
| average standard of living | corporate profits tax | consumption tax | patent protection |
| labor productivity | investment tax credit | human capital | |
| capital per worker | capital gains tax | technological change | |

## R E V I E W   Q U E S T I O N S

1. Discuss the three ways a country can increase its equilibrium level of output.

2. Why can population growth be a mixed blessing in terms of economic growth?

3. Explain how a tax cut could lead to *slower* economic growth.

4. If a country's PPF is shifting outward, is it necessarily the case that the country's standard of living is rising? Why or why not?

5. Why did Malthus's dire prediction fail to materialize? Do you think it could still come true? Explain your reasoning.

6. "Faster economic growth can benefit everyone and need not harm anyone. That is, there is no policy trade-off when it comes to economic growth." True or false? Explain.

7. Explain the following statement: "In some LDCs, it can be said that a significant cause of continued poverty is poverty itself."

8. Describe four ways in which LDCs might improve their growth performance. Discuss the opportunity cost that must be borne in each case and identify the group that is most likely to bear it.

## P R O B L E M S   A N D   E X E R C I S E S

1. Discuss the effect (holding everything else constant) each of the following would have on full-employment output, productivity, and the average standard of living. Use the appropriate graphs (e.g., labor market, loanable funds market, production function), and state your assumptions when necessary.

   a. Increased immigration
   b. An aging of the population with an increasing proportion of retirees
   c. A baby boom
   d. A decline in the tax rate on corporate profits
   e. Reduction of unemployment compensation benefits

g. Expanding the scope of the federal student loan program

h. Easier access to technical information on the Internet

2. Below are GDP and growth data for the United States and four other countries:

| | 1950 per Capita GDP (in Constant Dollars) | 1990 per Capita GDP (in Constant Dollars) | Average Yearly Growth Rate |
|---|---|---|---|
| United States | $9,573 | $21,558 | 2.0% |
| France | $5,221 | $17,959 | 3.0% |
| Japan | $1,873 | $19,425 | 5.7% |
| Kenya | $ 609 | $ 1,055 | 1.3% |
| India | $ 597 | $ 1,348 | 2.0% |

*Source:* Angus Maddison, *Monitoring the World Economy, 1820–1992.* Paris, OECD, 1995.

a. For both years, calculate each country's per capita GDP as a percentage of U.S. per capita GDP. Which countries appear to be catching up to the United States, and which are lagging behind?

b. If these countries continue to grow at the average growth rates given, how long will it take France to catch up to the United States? How long will it take India? Kenya?

3. Below are data for the country of Barrovia, which has long been concerned with economic growth.

| | Population (Millions) | Employment (Millions) | Labor Productivity | Total Output |
|---|---|---|---|---|
| 1997 | 100 | 50 | $ 9,500 | _____ |
| 1998 | 104 | 51 | $ 9,500 | _____ |
| 1999 | 107 | 53 | $ 9,750 | _____ |
| 2000 | 108 | 57 | $ 9,750 | _____ |
| 2001 | 110 | 57 | $10,000 | _____ |

a. Fill in the entries for total output in each of the five years.

b. Calculate the following for each year (except 1997):
(1) Population growth rate (from previous year)
(2) Growth rate of output (from previous year)
(3) Growth rate of per capita output (from previous year)

## CHALLENGE QUESTIONS

1. Economist Amartya Sen has argued that famines in underdeveloped countries are not simply the result of crop failures or natural disasters. Instead, he suggests that wars, especially civil wars, are linked to most famine episodes in recent history. Using a framework similar to Figure 11, discuss the probable effect of war on a country's PPF. Explain what would happen if the country were initially operating at or near a point like *S,* the minimum acceptable level of consumption.

2. All else equal, why might someone prefer to invest in physical capital in a less-developed country with a small capital stock than in a more developed country that already has much capital? When wealth holders look for a place to invest and compare prospects in these two types of countries, is all else (other than existing capital stock) really equal? Explain.

## EXPERIENTIAL EXERCISES

1. Technological change is an important drive of economic growth. Refer to the "Technology" column in the Marketplace section of a recent *Wall Street Journal.* Find a story about some technological innovation that seems interesting to you. How will this innovation affect the U.S. production function? Does it seem likely to affect employment as well? If so, which types of workers will benefit, and which will be harmed?

2. Investment in computing technology is an oft-cited source of economic growth. To learn more, read Adam Zaretsky's "Have Computers Made Us More Productive? A Puzzle." It's available from the Federal Reserve Bank of St. Louis at *http://www.stls.frb.org/publications/re/1998/d/re19998d3.html.* Based on what you've learned, use the model developed in this chapter to show how improvements in information technology will affect the U.S. economy in the long run. Then, make a list of who will benefit and who will be harmed by these changes. How would you expect each group to respond to the changes?

# ECONOMIC FLUCTUATIONS

**Boom** A period of time during
which real GDP is above potential GDP.

If you are like most college students, you will be looking for a job when you grad-
uate, or you will already have one and want to keep it for a while. In either case,
your fate is not entirely in your own hands. Your job prospects will depend, at
least in part, on the overall level of economic activity in the country.

If the classical model of the previous two chapters described the economy at
every point in time, you'd have nothing to worry about. Full employment would be
achieved automatically, so you could be confident of getting a job at the going wage
for someone with your skills and characteristics. Unfortunately, this is not how the
world works: Neither output nor employment grows as smoothly and steadily as
the classical model predicts. Instead, as far back as we have data, the United States
and similar countries have experienced *economic fluctuations*.

In Figure 1, look first at the red line in panel (a). It shows full-employment or potential output since 1960—the level of real GDP predicted by the classical model. As
a result of technological change and growth in the capital stock and population, full-
employment output rises steadily. But now look at the blue line, which shows *actual*
output. You can see that actual GDP fluctuates above and below the classical model's
predictions. During *recessions,* which are shaded in the figure, output declines, occasionally sharply. During *expansions* (the unshaded periods) output rises quickly—
usually faster than potential output is rising. Indeed, in the later stages of an expansion, output often *exceeds* potential output—a situation that economists call a **boom.**

Panel (b) shows another characteristic of expansions and contractions: fluctuations in employment. During expansions, such as the period from 1983 to 1990,
employment grows rapidly. During recessions (shaded), such as 1990–91, employment declines. Moreover, as we go through a cycle, the causal relationship between
output and employment seems to go in the opposite direction to what the classical
model predicts. Instead of changes in employment causing changes in output, it
seems that—over the business cycle—it is changes in output that cause firms to
change their employment levels. For example, in a recession, many business firms
lay off workers. If asked why, they would answer that they are reducing employment *because* they are producing less output.

Finally, look at Figure 2, which presents the unemployment rate over the same
period as in Figure 1. Figure 2 shows a critical aspect of fluctuations—the bulge of
unemployment that occurs during each recession. When GDP falls, the unemploy-

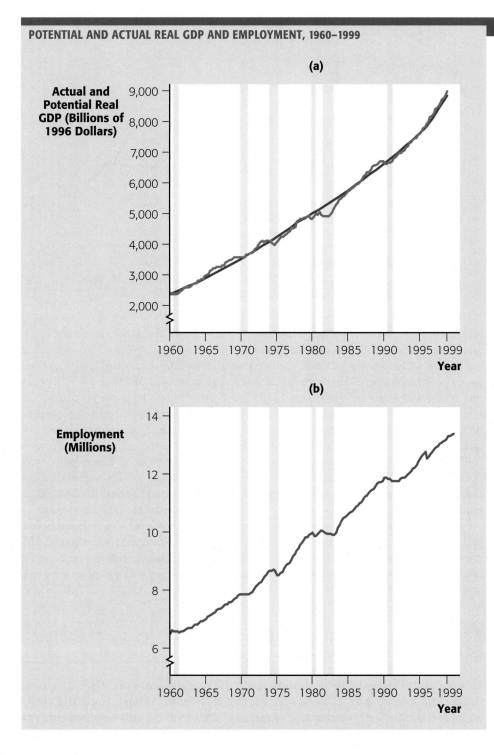

**POTENTIAL AND ACTUAL REAL GDP AND EMPLOYMENT, 1960–1999**

**(a)**

Actual and Potential Real GDP (Billions of 1996 Dollars)

9,000
8,000
7,000
6,000
5,000
4,000
3,000
2,000

1960  1965  1970  1975  1980  1985  1990  1995  1999
**Year**

**(b)**

Employment (Millions)

14
12
10
8
6

1960  1965  1970  1975  1980  1985  1990  1995  1999
**Year**

**FIGURE 1**

In panel (a), the red line shows full-employment (or potential) real GDP since 1960. It indicates how much output would be produced if the economy were always at full employment. The blue line shows actual real GDP. During recessions (shaded), output declines; during expansions, it rises quickly.

Panel (b) shows how employment fluctuates over the business cycle. During expansions, employment grows rapidly. During recessions, employment declines.

ment rate increases. In the last few decades, the worst bulge in unemployment occured in 1982, when more than 10 percent of the labor force was looking for work. In expansions, on the other hand, the unemployment rate falls. In our most recent expansion—which is still continuing as this is being written—unemployment dropped to 4 percent. In some expansions, the unemployment rate can drop even lower than the full-employment level. In the sustained expansion of the late 1960s,

**FIGURE 2**

The unemployment rate—the fraction of the labor force without a job—rises during recessions and falls during expansions.

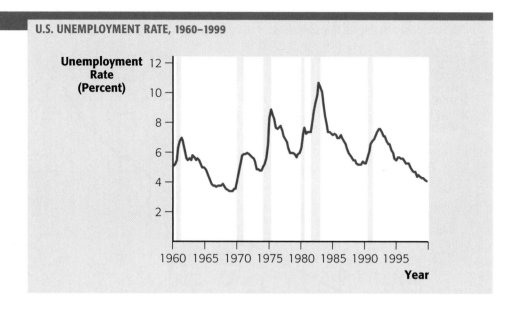

**U.S. UNEMPLOYMENT RATE, 1960–1999**

http://

Carl Walsh explores recent economic fluctuations in his "Changes in the Business Cycle," available at http://www.frbsf.org/econrsrch/wklyltr/wklyltr99/e199-16.html.

for example, it reached a low of just over 3 percent. At the same time, output exceeded its potential, as you can verify in Figure 1.

Figure 1 also shows something else: Expansions and recessions don't last forever. Indeed, sometimes they are rather brief. The recession of 1990–91, for example, ended within a year.

But if you look carefully at the figure, you'll see that the back-to-back recessions of the early 1980s extended over three full years. And during the Great Depression of the 1930s (not shown), it took more than a decade for the economy to return to full employment. Expansions can last for extended periods, too. The expansion of the 1980s lasted about seven years, from 1983 to 1990. And as this is being written (March 2000), the expansion that began in March 1991 had become the longest expansion in U.S. economic history—already nine years old and still going strong.

If we are to explain economic fluctuations, then, we have three things to explain: (1) *why* they occur in the first place, (2) why they do not last forever, and (3) why they sometimes last so long. Our first step is to see whether the macroeconomic model you've already studied—the classical, long-run model—can explain why economic fluctuations occur.

## CAN THE CLASSICAL MODEL EXPLAIN ECONOMIC FLUCTUATIONS?

Can the classical model help us understand the facts of economic fluctuations, as shown in Figures 1 and 2? Or do we need to modify the model to explain them? More specifically, can the classical model explain why GDP and employment typically fall *below* potential during a recession and often rise above it in an expansion? Let's see.

### SHIFTS IN LABOR DEMAND

One idea, studied by a number of economists, is that a recession might be caused by a leftward shift of the labor demand curve. This possibility is illustrated in Figure 3, in which a leftward shift in the labor demand curve would move us down and to the

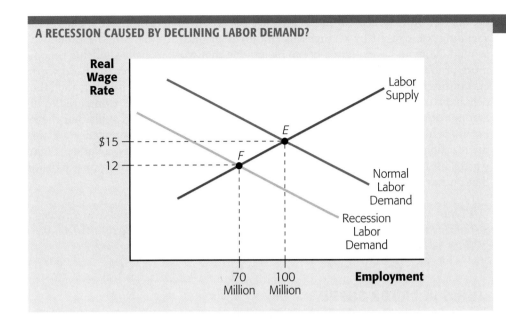

**A RECESSION CAUSED BY DECLINING LABOR DEMAND?**

**FIGURE 3**

If a recession were caused by a leftward shift of the labor demand curve, both employment and the real wage would fall—as in the movement from point *E* to point *F*. In fact, large, sudden shifts in labor demand are an unlikely explanation for real-world fluctuations.

left along the labor supply curve. In the diagram, as the labor market equilibrium moves from point *E* to point *F*, employment falls and so does the real wage rate. Is this a reasonable explanation for recessions? Most economists feel that the answer is no, and for a very good reason.

The labor demand curve tells us the number of workers the nation's firms want to employ at each real wage rate. A leftward shift of this curve would mean that firms want to hire *fewer* workers at any given wage than they wanted to hire before. What could make them come to such a decision? One possibility is that firms are suddenly unable to sell all the output they produce. Therefore, the story would go, they must cut back production and hire fewer workers at any wage.

But as you've learned, total spending is *never* deficient in the classical model. On the contrary, from the classical viewpoint, total spending is automatically equal to whatever level of output firms decide to produce. A decrease in spending by one sector of the economy would cause an equal *increase* in spending by another sector, with no change in total spending. While it is true that a decrease in output and employment could cause total spending to decrease (because Say's law tells us total spending is always equal to total output), the causation cannot go the other way in the classical model. In that model, changes in total spending cannot arise on their own. Therefore, if we want to explain a leftward shift in the labor demand curve using the classical model, we must look for some explanation other than a sudden change in spending.

Another possibility is that the labor demand curve shifts leftward because workers have become less *productive* and therefore less valuable to firms. This might happen if there were a sudden decrease in the capital stock, so that each worker had less equipment to work with. Or it might happen if workers suddenly forgot how to do things—how to operate a computer or use a screwdriver or fix an oil rig. Short of a major war that destroys plant and equipment, or an epidemic of amnesia, it is highly unlikely that workers would become less productive so suddenly. Thus, a leftward shift of the labor demand curve is an unlikely explanation for recessions.

What about booms? Could a *rightward* shift of the labor demand curve (not shown in Figure 3) explain them? Once again, a change in total spending cannot be the answer. In the classical model, as discussed a few paragraphs ago, changes in spending are caused by changes in employment and output, not the other way around. Nor can we explain a boom by arguing that workers have suddenly become more productive. While it is true that the capital stock grows over time and workers continually gain new skills—and that both of these movements shift the labor demand curve to the right—such shifts take place at a glacial pace. Compared to the amount of machinery already in place, and to the knowledge and skills that the labor force already has, annual increments in physical capital or knowledge are simply too small to have much of an impact on labor demand. Thus, a sudden rightward shift of the labor demand curve is an unlikely explanation for an expansion that pushes us beyond potential output.

> *Because shifts in the labor demand curve are not very large from year to year, the classical model cannot explain real-world economic fluctuations through shifts in labor demand.*

## SHIFTS IN LABOR SUPPLY

A second way the classical model might explain a recession is through a shift in the labor supply curve. Figure 4 shows how this would work. If the labor supply curve shifts to the left, the equilibrium moves up and to the left along the labor demand curve, from point *E* to point *G*. The level of employment falls, and output falls with it.

This explanation of recessions has almost no support among economists. First, remember that the labor supply schedule tells us, at each real wage rate, the number of people who would like to work. This number reflects millions of families' preferences about working in the market rather than pursuing other activities, such as taking care of children, going to school, or enjoying leisure time. A leftward shift in labor supply would mean that fewer people want to work at any given wage—that preferences have changed toward these other, nonwork activities. But in reality, preferences tend to change very slowly, and certainly not rapidly enough to explain recessions.

---

| **FIGURE 4** |
| --- |

If a recession were caused by a leftward shift of the labor supply curve, employment would fall, but the real wage would rise—as in the movement from point *E* to point *G*. In fact, shifts in labor supply occur very slowly, so they cannot explain economic fluctuations.

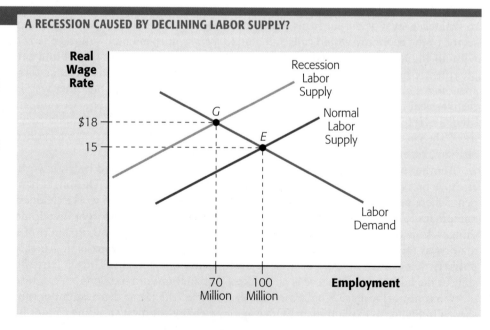

**A RECESSION CAUSED BY DECLINING LABOR SUPPLY?**

Second, even if such a shift in preferences did occur, it could not explain the facts of real-world downturns. Recessions are times when unusually large numbers of people are looking for work (see Figure 2). It would be hard to square that fact with a shift in preferences away from working.

The same arguments could be made about expansions: To explain them with labor supply shifts, we would have to believe that preferences suddenly change *toward* market work and away from other activities—an unlikely occurrence. And, in any case, expansions are periods when the unemployment rate typically falls to unusually low levels; *fewer*—not more—people are seeking work.

> *Because sudden shifts of the labor supply curve are unlikely to occur, and because they could not accurately describe the facts of the economic cycle, the classical model cannot explain fluctuations through shifts in the supply of labor.*

## VERDICT: THE CLASSICAL MODEL CANNOT EXPLAIN ECONOMIC FLUCTUATIONS

In earlier chapters, we stressed that the classical model works well in explaining the movements of the economy in the longer run. Now, we see that it does a rather poor job of explaining the economy in the short run. Why is this? Largely because the classical model involves assumptions about the economy that make sense in the longer run, but not in the short run. Chief among these is the assumption that the labor market clears—that is, that the labor market operates at the point of intersection of the labor supply and labor demand curves. As long as this assumption holds, a boom or recession would have to arise from a sudden, significant *movement* in that intersection point, caused by a sudden and significant *shift* in either the labor demand curve or the labor supply curve.

But now, we've seen that such sudden shifts are very unlikely. Moreover, even if they did occur, they could not explain the changes in job-seeking activity that we observe in real-world recessions. And this, in a nutshell, is why we must reject the classical model when we turn our attention to the short run.

> *We cannot explain the facts of short-run economic fluctuations with a model in which the labor market always clears. This is why the classical model, which assumes that the market always clears, does a poor job of explaining the economy in the short run.*

## ECONOMIC FLUCTUATIONS: A MORE REALISTIC VIEW

Booms and recessions are two of the most interesting and persistent facets of the economy. Earlier in this book, you learned that recessions can be very costly to society, and in future chapters you'll learn why even booms—the periods during which output exceeds its potential—present serious problems. Yet in spite of determined and often heroic efforts, no economy has been able to eradicate economic fluctuations. In universities and government agencies, economists are conducting research to better understand economic fluctuations. And while there is not yet complete agreement on every feature of them, there is a growing consensus on many aspects. In this and the next several chapters, we will present some of the key ideas behind that consensus. These ideas are based on the concept of **disequilibrium**—the term used to describe a market that does not clear. In particular, we will focus on

**Disequilibrium** A situation in which a market does not clear—quantity supplied is not equal to quantity demanded.

The labor supply curve tells us the wage that must be offered to attract any given number of workers. For example, point *E* indicates that, in order to attract 100 million workers, the real wage must be at least $15 per hour. This is because the opportunity cost of working for the 100-millionth worker is $15 per hour.

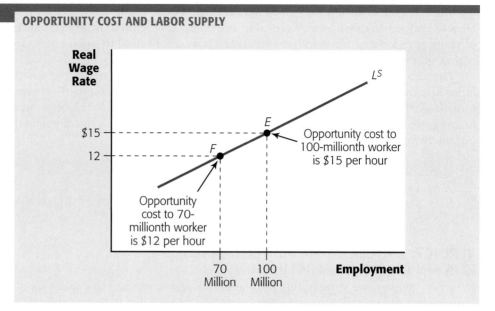

**OPPORTUNITY COST AND LABOR SUPPLY**

disequilibrium in the labor market—situations in which the level of employment is *not* where the supply and demand curves intersect.

We begin by taking a closer look at the labor supply and labor demand curves themselves.

## OPPORTUNITY COST AND LABOR SUPPLY

So far in this book, we've viewed the labor supply curve as telling us the number of people who want to work at any given real wage. For example, the labor supply curve in Figure 5 tells us that if the wage is $15 per hour, 100 million people would wish to have jobs (point *E*). But we can also interpret the curve in another way: It tells us the wage that must be offered to attract any given number of workers into the labor market. For example, point *E* shows us that, in order to attract 100 million workers, the real wage must be at least $15 per hour.

How can we interpret that wage? Each of the 100 million individuals who would work at $15 would be deciding that it is better to work in the market than to spend time at home or in school. For those workers, $15 exceeds the *opportunity cost* of working—the value of the other activities sacrificed by going to work.

Now consider the 100-millionth worker—the *last* worker to be attracted into the labor force when the wage is $15. For this person, the opportunity cost of working must be *exactly* $15—at any wage greater than $15, he will choose to work; at any lower wage, his choice will be to stay home or go to school. More generally,

> *at every point along the labor supply curve, the wage rate tells us the opportunity cost of working for the last worker to enter the labor force.*

## FIRMS' BENEFITS FROM HIRING: THE LABOR DEMAND CURVE

Now let's take a look at the labor demand curve. We've been viewing this curve as telling us the number of workers firms want to hire at any real wage. But it also tells us the highest wage firms would be willing to pay to hire any given number of

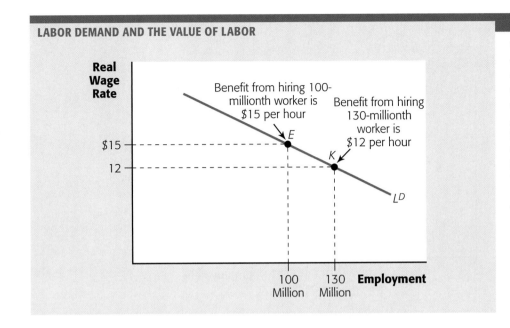

**FIGURE 6**

**LABOR DEMAND AND THE VALUE OF LABOR**

The labor demand curve tells us the highest wage firms would be willing to pay to hire any given number of workers. For example, point E indicates that, for firms to be willing to hire 100 million workers, the real wage can be no higher than $15 per hour. This is because the 100-millionth worker benefits the firm by $15 per hour.

workers. For example, look at the labor demand curve in Figure 6. Point E shows that, in order for firms to employ 100 million workers, the wage can be no greater than $15 per hour. Each of those 100 million workers must benefit firms by $15 or more per hour, or else he or she would not be hired. And the 100-millionth worker—the one that would be hired at a wage of $15, but not at any greater wage—must benefit some firm by exactly $15. In general,

*at every point along the labor demand curve, the wage rate tells us the benefit obtained by some firm from the last worker hired.*

## THE MEANING OF LABOR MARKET EQUILIBRIUM

Now look at Figure 7, and for the moment, focus on point E, the equilibrium. The idea that the labor market must be at this equilibrium point is essential to the classical model. Point E is on both the labor supply and the labor demand curves. This tells us that the opportunity cost for the last worker hired—the 100-millionth—is just equal to the benefit some firm receives from hiring that worker. In ordinary circumstances, as you've learned, the labor market will settle at point E, with 100 million people working and a real wage equal to $15 per hour. Moreover, at this equilibrium point, workers and firms are exploiting all available opportunities for mutual gain. How do we know this?

We can reason as follows: At any employment level less than 100 million, there are workers whose opportunity cost of working is less than the benefit firms would get from hiring them. For example, if employment were 70 million, the opportunity cost of the *next* worker—who would *not* be working—would be just a tiny bit more than $12 per hour, as shown by point F. But some firm could enjoy benefits from that person's work of just under $18 per hour, as shown by point G. At any wage between $12 and $18, both parties would gain if that worker were hired. For example, if the firm hired the worker for $15 per hour, the worker would gain: Her opportunity cost of working is only about $12, but she would actually get $15. The

FIGURE 7

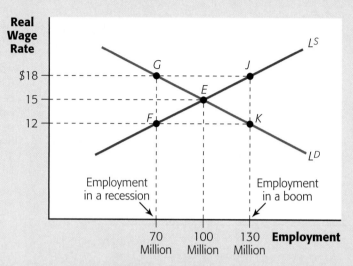

**FIGURE 7**

**LABOR MARKET EQUILIBRIUM**

The labor supply and labor demand curves intersect at point *E* to determine an equilibrium employment of 100 million and an equilibrium real wage of $15 per hour. At any lower level of employment, such as 70 million, the benefit some firm would enjoy from hiring an additional worker exceeds the opportunity cost to that worker. For example, the 70-millionth worker would benefit some firm by $18 per hour, but her opportunity cost of working is only $12 per hour. Mutually beneficial gains are possible for both worker and firm. Only at equilibrium (*E*) are there no further gains to be exploited.

If employment *exceeds* the equilibrium at point *E*, firms would be hiring workers whose opportunity cost exceeded firms' benefit from hiring them. For example, the 130-millionth worker would benefit some firm by only $12 per hour, but her cost of working is $18 per hour. Employment has increased beyond the level of mutual gain, and there are incentives to reduce it.

firm would also gain, since the benefit of hiring the worker is about $18, but the firm would pay only $15. Similar gains would be possible for any increase in hiring, until total employment reached 100 million.

Now suppose that employment has already reached 100 million. What would happen if the *next* worker (the 100,000,001st) were hired? This person would have an opportunity cost a tiny bit more than $15 per hour, but the benefit from hiring him would be a bit less than $15 per hour. There is no wage at which this worker could be hired for mutual gain. The same would be true of all other workers beyond 100 million. For example, if employment were to rise all the way to 130 million, the opportunity cost for the 130-millionth worker would be $18 (point *J*), but a firm could benefit by only $12 (point *K*) from hiring him.

In sum, there is only one level of employment that exhausts all of the mutually beneficial opportunities for trade among workers and firms, and this is where the labor supply and demand curves intersect:

> *At the equilibrium level of employment, all opportunities for mutually beneficial trade in the labor market have been exploited.*

## THE LABOR MARKET WHEN OUTPUT IS BELOW POTENTIAL

Now we can see what happens in the labor market during a recession. When employment falls below the classical, full-employment level at point *E*, both firms and workers could gain if employment increased. But employment *doesn't* increase.

Something in the overall economic system isn't working right, and the opportunities for mutual gain are not exploited as they should be. In Figure 7, for example, employment might fall to 70 million, where the opportunity cost for the next worker would be just $12, while the benefit to some firm from hiring this worker would be $18. A mutually beneficial deal between them is certainly possible . . . but it doesn't happen. The labor market is in *disequilibrium:*

> *During a recession, the labor market is in disequilibrium, and the benefit from hiring another worker exceeds the opportunity cost to that worker.*

What *causes* disequilibrium in the labor market? We'll discuss that a bit later in this chapter. But our analysis so far helps us understand why recessions—once they occur—do not last forever. There are strong incentives for the labor market to return to equilibrium, namely, the benefits workers and firms would enjoy from an increase in employment. Until employment returns to the level at which the labor demand and supply curves intersect, these opportunities for mutual gain are not being fully exploited.

> *In recessions, there are incentives to increase the level of employment because the benefit to firms from additional employment exceeds the opportunity cost to workers. These incentives help explain why recessions do not last forever.*

## THE LABOR MARKET WHEN OUTPUT IS ABOVE POTENTIAL

What about booms? They are just as temporary as are recessions and recoveries. Once again, Figure 7 shows why. Suppose the economy is experiencing a boom in which 130 million people are working. Then there are workers whose opportunity cost of working exceeds the benefit of their work to firms. The 130-millionth worker, for example, has an opportunity cost of $18, but his firm benefits by only $12. No matter what wage we choose, one side of the deal—either the worker or the firm—loses out if that worker is hired. Suppose the 130-millionth worker is paid $18 in order to convince him to take a job. Then the firm has an incentive to let that worker go. The same is true for every level of employment beyond 100 million workers: If workers are paid their opportunity cost, firms will have an incentive to reduce employment.

> *In booms, there are incentives to decrease the level of employment because the benefit to firms from some who have been hired is smaller than the opportunity cost to those workers. These incentives help explain why booms do not last forever.*

Now you can understand one of the observations about expansions and recessions that we set out to explain: that they do not last forever. But why do they occur in the first place?

## WHAT TRIGGERS ECONOMIC FLUCTUATIONS?

Recessions that bring output below potential and expansions that drive output above potential are periods during which the economy is going a bit haywire: Opportunities for mutual gain are not being exploited. But why? In particular, why does the labor market move away from its equilibrium in the short run? Let's start to answer this question by looking at a world that is much simpler than our own.

## A VERY SIMPLE ECONOMY

Imagine an economy with just two people: Yasmin and Pepe. Yasmin is especially good at making popcorn, but she eats only yogurt. Pepe, by contrast, is very good at making yogurt, but eats only popcorn. If things are going well, Yasmin and Pepe will make suitable amounts of popcorn and yogurt and trade with each other. Because of the gains from specialization, their trade will make them both better off than if they tried to function without trading. And under ordinary circumstances, Yasmin and Pepe will take advantage of all mutually beneficial opportunities for trading. Our two-person economy will thus operate at full employment, since both individuals will be fully engaged in making products for the other. You can think of their trading equilibrium as being like the labor market equilibrium in the classical model (such as point *E* in Figure 7), where workers and firms are taking advantage of all mutually beneficial opportunities for hiring and producing.

Now, suppose there is a breakdown in communication. For example, Yasmin may get the impression that Pepe is not going to want as much popcorn as before. She would then decide to make less popcorn for Pepe. At their next trading session, Pepe will be offered less popcorn, so he will decide to produce less yogurt. The result: Total production in the economy declines, and our two traders will lose some of the benefits of trading. This corresponds to a recession.

In reading the previous paragraph, you might be thinking, "Wait a minute. If either Yasmin or Pepe got the impression that the other might want less of the other's product, wouldn't a simple conversation between them straighten things out?" If these are your thoughts, you are absolutely right. A breakdown in communication and a drop in production would be extremely unlikely . . . *in a simple economy with just two people.* And therein lies the problem: The real-world economy is much more complex than the world of Yasmin and Pepe.

## THE REAL-WORLD ECONOMY

Think about the U.S. economy, with its millions of businesses producing goods and services for hundreds of millions of people. In many cases, production must be planned long before goods are actually sold. For example, from inception to final production, it takes nearly a year to build a house and two years to develop a new automobile model or produce a Hollywood film. If one firm—say, General Motors—believes that consumers will buy fewer of its cars next year, it cannot simply call a meeting of all potential customers and find out whether its fears are justified. Nor can it convince people, as Yasmin can convince Pepe, that their own jobs depend on their buying a GM car. Most potential car buyers do *not* work for General Motors and don't perceive any connection between buying a car and keeping their own job. Under the circumstances, it may be entirely logical for General Motors to plan for a lower production level and lay off some of its workers.

Of course, this would not be the end of the story. By decreasing its workforce, GM would create further problems for the economy. The workers it has laid off, who will earn less income or none at all, will cut back on *their* spending for a variety of consumer goods—restaurant meals, movies, vacation travel—and they will certainly postpone any large purchases they'd been planning, such as a new large-screen television or that family trip to Disney World. This will cause other firms—the firms producing these consumer goods and services—to cut back on *their* production, laying off *their* workers, and so on. In other words, what began as a perceived decrease in spending in one sector of the economy can work its way through other sectors, causing a full-blown recession.

This example illustrates a theme that we will revisit in the next chapter: The interdependence between production and income. When people spend their incomes, they give firms the revenue they need to hire workers . . . and pay the workers' income! If any link in this chain is broken, output and income may both decline. In our example, the link was broken because of incorrect expectations by firms in one sector of the economy. But there are other causes of recessions as well, also centering on the interdependence between production and income, and a failure to coordinate the decisions of millions of firms and households.

The classical model, however, waves these potential problems aside. It assumes that workers and firms, with the aid of markets, can work things out—like Yasmin and Pepe—and enjoy the benefits of producing and trading. And the classical model is right: People *will* work things out . . . eventually. But in the short run, we need to look carefully at the problems of coordinating production, trade, and consumption in an economy with hundreds of millions of people and tens of millions of businesses.

A boom can arise in much the same way as a recession. It might start because of an increase in production in one sector of the economy—say, the housing sector. With more production and more workers earning higher incomes, spending increases in other sectors as well, until output rises above the classical, full-employment level.

## SHOCKS THAT PUSH THE ECONOMY AWAY FROM EQUILIBRIUM

In our discussion above, General Motors decided to cut back on its production of cars because its managers believed, rightly or wrongly, that the demand for GM cars had decreased. Often, many firms will face a real or predicted drop in spending at the same time. We call this a **spending shock** to the economy—a change in spending that initially affects one or more sectors and ultimately works its way through the entire economy.

In the real world, the economy is constantly buffeted by shocks, and they often cause full-fledged macroeconomic fluctuations. Table 1 lists some of the recessions and expansions of the last 50 years, along with the events and spending shocks that are thought to have caused them, or at least contributed heavily. You can see that each of these shocks first affected spending and output in one or more sectors of the economy. For example, several recessions have been set off by increases in oil prices, which caused a decrease in spending on products that depend on oil and energy, such as automobiles, trucks, and new factory buildings. Other recessions were precipitated by military cutbacks. Still others came about when the Federal Reserve caused sudden increases in interest rates that led to decreased spending on new homes and other goods. (You'll learn about the Federal Reserve and its policies a few chapters from now.) Expansions, on the other hand, have been caused by military buildups, and by falling oil prices that stimulated spending on energy-related products. The expansion of the mid- and late-1990s began when the development of the Internet, and improvements in computers more generally, led to an increase in investment spending. Once the economy began expanding, it was further spurred by other factors, such as a rise in stock prices and consumer optimism, both of which led to an increase in consumption spending.

In addition to these identifiable spending shocks, the economy is buffeted by other shocks whose origins are harder to spot. For example, consumption was higher than expected in the late 1980s, contributing to the rapid expansion that occurred in those years. In the early 1990s, consumption fell back to normal, helping

**Spending shock** A change in spending that ultimately affects the entire economy.

Katherine Bradbury's "Job Creation and Destruction in Massachusetts" http://www.bos.frb.org/economic/pdf/neer599c.pdf provides a case study of how the labor market adjusts.

**TABLE 1**

**EXPANSIONS, RECESSIONS, AND SHOCKS THAT CAUSED THEM**

| Period | | Event | Spending Shock |
|---|---|---|---|
| Early 1950s | Expansion | Korean War | Defense Spending ↑ |
| 1953 | Recession | End of Korean War | Defense Spending ↓ |
| Late 1960s | Expansion | Vietnam War | Defense Spending ↑ |
| 1970 | Recession | Change in Federal Reserve Policy | Spending on New Homes ↓ |
| 1974 | Recession | Dramatic Increase in Oil Prices | Spending on Cars and Other Energy-using Products ↓ |
| 1980 | Recession | Dramatic Increase in Oil Prices | Spending on Cars and Other Energy-using Products ↓ |
| 1981–82 | Recession | Change in Federal Reserve Policy | Spending on New Homes, Cars and Business Investment ↓ |
| Early 1980s | Expansion | Military Buildup | Defense Spending ↑ |
| Late 1980s | Expansion | Huge Decline in Oil Prices | Spending on Energy-using Products ↑ |
| 1990 | Recession | Large Increase in Oil Prices; Collapse of Soviet Union | Spending on Cars and Other Energy-using Products ↓; Defense Spending ↓ |
| 1991–2000 | Expansion | Technological Advances in Computers; Development of the Internet; High Wealth Creation | Spending on Capital Equipment ↑; Consumption ↑ |

Half of our recessions since the early 1950s have been caused, at least in part, by rapid rises in oil prices.

to cause the recession of that period. There was no obvious event that caused these changes in consumption.

As you can see in Table 1, the economy barely has time to adjust to one shock before it is hit by another. But we can usually see the beginnings of the adjustment process, and sometimes we can follow it through to its end. In the case of an adverse shock, large numbers of workers lose their jobs. The shock puts the labor market into the situation like that depicted a few pages earlier in Figure 7, with employment at 70 million workers. At recession levels of employment, the benefit from working exceeds the opportunity cost of working, providing an incentive for firms to increase their hiring. This incentive guides the economy through a long and gradual period of recovery, during which output and employment rise to their equilibrium levels. Unemployed workers are gradually reabsorbed into the economy until full employment is restored.

But notice the word *gradually*. The process of adjustment back to equilibrium in the labor market can take surprisingly long. This is in sharp contrast to what happens in other markets. In most microeconomic markets, like the one for maple syrup, or macroeconomic markets, like the stock market, there are strong incentives to return to equilibrium, and the response to these incentives is rapid. If quantity supplied does not equal quantity demanded, equilibrium will be restored within hours, days, or weeks. In the labor market, the *incentives* to get to equilibrium are similar to those in other markets, but the process of getting there takes much longer. It can take—and has taken—years for the economy to return to full employment after a recession, as we saw in Figures 1 and 2. For example, the unemployment rate exceeded 10 percent in 1982 and did not fall below 6 percent until 1986.

A positive shock triggers an expansion, and may push the economy into a boom. This puts the labor market in the situation like the one in Figure 7 in which employment rises to 130 million. Again, there is an incentive to return to normal conditions. In this case, cutting the workforce releases workers whose opportunity cost of working is greater than the benefits firms get from their work. As firms respond to these incentives, employment and output will gradually fall back to their full-employment levels. But once again, the process of adjustment back to equilibrium can take years.

Why does it take so long for employment and output to return to normal after a shock?

# THE ECONOMICS OF SLOW ADJUSTMENT

To see why the economy does not adjust immediately and fully to a shock, let's take a close look at a representative firm—say, a hotel. Imagine that you manage a hotel with 100 rooms. You would learn, as do most hotel operators, that you do *not* want to fill all 100 rooms night after night. Instead, you do better with some excess capacity—enough vacant rooms to enable some early arrivals to move in when they first show up, to permit some flexibility in case of problems like broken telephones or leaky faucets, and to accommodate the occasional surge in demand without turning away your regular customers and losing their business to another hotel. We'll suppose that you try to manage your operation so that, on an average night, you will fill 70 of the 100 rooms. (In fact, the hotel industry, like the airline industry, tends to operate at around 70 percent of capacity.)

Of course, if you are aiming to fill 70 percent of your rooms, on average, then you will hire the appropriate number of workers to clean the rooms, provide room service, wash dishes and towels, and so on. This is your normal employment level.

## ADJUSTMENT IN A BOOM

Now suppose the economy experiences a boom. Output is above its potential, income is high, and so there is an increase in the number of travelers who want to stay at your hotel. As a result, you begin to find that all 100 rooms are filled. What will you do? Eventually, you will take steps to restore normal utilization, such as reducing the amount of advertising or changing your directory listings to show higher prices. But these changes take time, and it would not make sense to make them until you were sure they were necessary. After all, the jump in utilization may not last more than a few weeks. Reversing any changes you make would be costly, and you might regret having made them in haste. For a while, therefore, you will likely hold off making changes. That is, in the short run, you would probably accept unusually high utilization of your hotel.

But what about the additional work that must be done with higher occupancy? For a day or two, you might get your employees to work longer hours and work harder on the job, but you cannot expect them to do so for very long. Soon you will have to hire more workers, even if just temporarily. As we saw earlier, it will take time to bring utilization down to normal levels. In the meantime, your best choice is to increase employment above its normal level. Thus, in the short run, the increase in demand for rooms will lead to higher-than-normal employment.

What is true for your hotel will also be true of other firms in the economy. As they experience the immediate effects of a positive spending shock, they will temporarily operate their factories, stores, or offices at above-normal rates of utilization. As a consequence, they will increase employment to higher-than-normal levels. At these employment levels, the benefits firms get from hiring the additional workers will be smaller than the opportunity cost of their work, but—when all options are considered—this is the sensible thing for firms to do.

> *When a positive shock causes a boom, firms operate—temporarily—at above-normal rates of utilization. As a consequence, employment rises above its normal, full-employment level.*

Now let's go back to your hotel. Suppose that the increase in demand turns out to be long lasting: Month after month, you find yourself filling all 100 rooms. Eventually, you will decide to start making the changes that will restore your normal rate of utilization. You might raise prices, cut back on your advertising, offer fewer frills, or take some combination of steps to get you back to your normal 70-percent occupancy rate.

As your occupancy rate falls back to normal, you will lay off those additional employees you hired, so your level of employment, too, will fall back to normal. Of course, you are not the only firm in the economy behaving this way. Other firms, too, are laying off workers as they bring their businesses back to normal operating ranges. When these adjustments are completed, employment in the nation as a whole will be back at its normal, full-employment level:

> *Over time, firms that have experienced an increase in demand will return to normal utilization rates, and employment will fall back to its normal, full-employment level.*

## ADJUSTMENT IN A RECESSION

Now consider a quite different situation. The economy enters a recession, and you begin to find that only 30 of your rooms are rented. Do you take action on the spot to get to your normal 70 guests? Probably not, for two reasons. First, you cannot immediately bring your utilization rate back to normal: Most of the steps you could take to make your hotel more attractive (offer lower prices, more frills, and so on) will benefit the 30 guests who are renting your rooms already, but it takes time for the word to get out and attract *additional* guests. Second, you don't want to change your policies in haste, only to make costly reversals in a few weeks. You will probably wait a while, operating at below-normal capacity for several weeks or even months, meanwhile laying off some of your workers because they are no longer needed. As a result, you—and managers at thousands of other firms—will find yourself laying off some workers whose benefits to you are ordinarily greater than their opportunity cost of working. Yet, considering all of your options, it's a sensible thing to do.

> *When an adverse shock causes a recession, firms operate—temporarily—at below-normal rates of utilization. As a consequence, employment drops below its normal, full-employment level.*

But what if the decrease in demand turns out to be long lasting? After several months, you—and other firms—will realize that it is time to make the changes necessary to bring rates of utilization back up. This might mean lowering prices, offering better amenities, stepping up advertising, and more. As you take these steps, and your occupancy rate rises back to normal, you will hire additional employees, since the benefits of hiring them exceed the opportunity cost of their work. Your employment level will rise back to normal. As other firms behave the same way, employment in the nation will rise back to its normal, full-employment level.

> *Over time, firms that have experienced a decrease in demand will return to normal utilization rates, and employment will rise back to its normal, full-employment level.*

## THE SPEED OF ADJUSTMENT

The way we have told our story, it seems that the labor market should adjust fully to a shock—and return to full employment—in a few weeks or months, not the years it often actually takes in the real world. What accounts for the slow adjustment of employment? There is some controversy about this issue, but one of the likely explanations has to do with a realistic view of how jobs are destroyed and created.

Think about what happens in a recession: Workers are laid off, and employment decreases until firms decide to return to normal capacity. But unemployed workers don't necessarily wait around for their original employers to rehire them. Instead, many will look for other jobs, and some will find them. In fact, the rate of new hiring remains high in a recession, suggesting that many of those whose jobs are lost in contracting sectors find jobs in other sectors, even during a recession. This means that when you, as hotel manager, decide to return to normal employment levels, many of those you laid off will have found jobs elsewhere. You will have to search once again for people suitable for hotel work, and you will have to train them. This searching and training is both costly *and time consuming*. We shouldn't be surprised, then, that it can take considerable time—even a few years—for employment to recover fully from a recession.

Job-searching behavior by firms and workers is just one explanation for the slow pace of adjustment back to full employment. In later chapters, we'll carefully examine other explanations that involve the behavior of wages and prices.

## WHERE DO WE GO FROM HERE?

The classical model that you've learned in previous chapters is certainly useful: It helps us understand economic growth over time, and how economic events and economic policies affect the economy over the long run. But in trying to understand expansions and recessions—where they come from, and why they last for one or more years—we've had to depart from the strict framework of the classical model. In particular, you've seen that *the labor market will not always clear in the short run,* and you've learned why. As we saw with our hotel example, in order to maintain normal employment at every moment in time—which would add up nationally to the classical, market-clearing employment level—firms would have to adjust more quickly than it makes sense for them to do.

You've also seen how a shock to the economy can affect spending and production in one sector and spread to other sectors, causing a recession or a boom. And you've seen why it can take a year or more to return to full employment after a shock.

One theme of our discussion has been the central role of spending in understanding economic fluctuations. In the classical model, spending could be safely ignored. First, Say's law assured us that total spending would always be sufficient to buy the output produced at full employment. Second, a change in spending—for example, a decrease in military spending by the government—causes other categories of spending to rise by just the right amount to use the resources being freed up by the government. In the long run, we can have faith in the classical perspective on spending.

But in the short run, we've seen that spending shocks to the economy affect production—usually in one specific sector. When employment changes in that sector, the spending of workers *there* will change as well, affecting demand in still other sectors. Clearly, if we want to understand fluctuations, we need to take a close look at spending. This is what we will do in the next chapter, when we study the *short-run macro model*.

## S U M M A R Y

The classical model does not always do a good job of describing the economy over short time periods. Over periods of a few years, national economies experience economic fluctuations in which output rises above or falls below its long-term growth path. Periods of rapidly rising output are referred to as expansions, while periods of falling output are called recessions. When real GDP fluctuates, it causes the level of employment and the unemployment rate to fluctuate as well.

The classical model cannot explain economic fluctuations because it assumes that the labor market always clears—that is, it always operates at the point where the labor supply and demand curves intersect. Evidence suggests that this market-clearing assumption is not always valid over short time periods. Instead, the labor market is sometimes characterized by *disequilibrium*, in which employment is above or below the level at which the supply and demand curves intersect.

Whenever the labor market—or any market—is out of equilibrium, there are forces that tend to drive it back to equilibrium. If employment is below equilibrium, then there are opportunities for mutually beneficial deals between employers and unemployed workers. If these deals go through, then employment—and output—will increase. But sometimes it takes time for these mutually beneficial agreements to be discovered and negotiated. During that time period, the economy can continue to operate below potential. When employment is above equilibrium, firms have incentives to cut back employment, and eventually they will do so. But in the meantime, the economy will experience a boom.

Deviations from the full-employment level of output are often caused by *spending shocks*—changes in spending that initially affect one sector, and then work their way through the entire economy. Negative shocks can cause recessions, while positive shocks can cause expansions that lead to booms. Eventually, output will return to its long-run equilibrium level, but it does not do so immediately. The return to full employment takes time because of the costs of adjusting back to normal output levels, and also because of time-consuming job search by workers and firms. Workers laid off in a recession, for example, will seek work elsewhere—a process that takes time. Similarly, it takes time for employers to find new employees to replace those laid off. The origins of economic fluctuations can be understood more fully with the short-run macro model, which we will study in the next chapter.

## K E Y   T E R M S

| boom | disequilibrium | spending shock |
|------|----------------|----------------|

## R E V I E W   Q U E S T I O N S

1.  How does a *recession* differ from an *expansion?* Describe the typical behavior of GDP and the unemployment rate during each of these periods.

2.  Why can't a recession be explained in terms of a reduction in labor demand? In terms of a reduction in labor supply?

3.  In an economy with just two people, economic fluctuations would be unlikely to occur. Why? What is the key difference in the real-world economy that makes economic fluctuations more likely?

4.  "During the last half-century economic fluctuations in the United States have been caused entirely by changes in military spending." True or false? Explain.

5.  Suppose the economy is disturbed by a negative spending shock. Describe a typical pattern of adjustment to that shock. What will happen to real GDP and the unemployment rate over time?

6.  In what sense are mutual opportunities for gain not being exploited during a recession?

## PROBLEMS AND EXERCISES

1. Use the following data to construct a labor demand and supply diagram.

| Wage Rate | Quantity of Labor Demanded | Quantity of Labor Supplied |
|---|---|---|
| $ 9 | 95 million | 65 million |
| 10 | 90 | 70 |
| 11 | 85 | 75 |
| 12 | 80 | 80 |
| 13 | 75 | 85 |
| 14 | 70 | 90 |

a. What are the equilibrium wage rate and level of employment?
b. Explain the opportunity for mutually beneficial trade that exists if employment is 70 million.

2. Suppose you run a photocopy shop and for one month you experience a surge in business above normal levels. What steps would you take during the month? What additional steps would you take if the surge lasted for two years? How do your answers help explain why booms occur and why they are temporary?

# THE SHORT-RUN MACRO MODEL

E very December, newspapers and television news broadcasts focus their attention on spending. You might see a reporter standing in front of a Toys-"R"-Us outlet, warning that unless holiday shoppers loosen their wallets and spend big on toys, computers, vacation trips, dishwashers, and new cars, the economy is in for trouble.

Of course, spending matters during the rest of the year, too. But holiday spending attracts our attention because the normal forces at work during the rest of the year become more concentrated in late November and December. Factories churn out merchandise and stores stock up at higher than normal rates. If consumers are in Scrooge-like moods, unsold goods will pile up in stores. In the months that follow, these stores will cut back on their orders for new goods. As a result, factories will decrease production and lay off workers.

And the story will not end there. The laid-off workers—even those who collect some unemployment benefits—will see their incomes decline. As a consequence, they will spend less on a variety of consumer goods. This will cause other firms—the ones that produce those consumer goods—to cut back on *their* production.

This hypothetical example reinforces a conclusion we reached in the last chapter: Spending is very important in the short run. And it points out an interesting circularity: The more income households have, the more they will spend. That is, *spending depends on income*. But the more households spend, the more output firms will produce—and the more income they will pay to their workers. Thus, *income depends on spending*.

> *In the short run, spending depends on income, and income depends on spending.*

In this chapter, we will explore this circular connection between spending and income. We will do so with a very simple macroeconomic model, which we'll call the *short-run macro model*. Many of the ideas behind the model were originally developed by the British economist John Maynard Keynes in the 1930s. The **short-run macro model** focuses on the role of spending in explaining economic fluctuations. It explains how shocks that initially affect one sector of the economy quickly influence other sectors, causing changes in total output and employment.

To keep the model as simple as possible, we will—for the time being—ignore all influences on production *besides* spending. As a result, the short-run model may appear strange to you at first, like a drive along an unfamiliar highway. You may wonder: Where is all the scenery you are used to seeing along the classical road? Where are the labor market, the production function, the loanable funds market, and the market-clearing assumption? Rest assured that many of these concepts are still with us, lurking in the background and waiting to be exposed, and we will come back to them in later chapters. But in this chapter, we assume that spending—and *only* spending—determines how much output the economy will produce.

**Thinking About Spending.**  Before we begin our analysis of spending, we have some choices to make.

First, spending on *what*? People spend on food, clothing, furniture, and vacations. They also spend to buy stocks and bonds, to buy homes, to buy used goods, and to buy things produced in foreign countries. In order to know what kind of spending we are going to discuss, we need to use Key Step #1 of our four-step procedure. That is, we need to decide which market's spending to analyze. How should we choose?

Remember our main purpose in building the short-run macro model: to explain fluctuations in real GDP that the long-run, classical model cannot explain. Accordingly, we will ignore spending on things that are *not* part of our GDP, like stocks and bonds and real estate and goods produced abroad. Instead,

> *in the short-run macro model, we focus on spending in markets for currently produced U.S. goods and services—that is, spending on things that are included in U.S. GDP.*

Next, to fully characterize our market, we must also identify the *participants* in that market. We know who the sellers are: U.S. firms. But there are so many different types of buyers of U.S. goods and services: city dwellers and suburbanites; government agencies like the Department of Defense and the local school board; businesses of all types, ranging from the corner convenience store to a huge corporation such as AT&T; and foreigners from nearby Canada and distant Fiji. How should we organize our thinking about all of these different types of buyers?

Macroeconomists have found that the most useful approach is to divide them into four broad categories:

- Households, whose spending is called consumption spending ($C$)
- Business firms, whose spending is called investment spending ($I^P$)
- Government agencies, whose spending on goods and services is called government purchases ($G$)
- Foreigners, whose spending we measure as net exports ($NX$)

These categories should seem familiar to you. They were the same ones we used to break down GDP in the expenditure approach. In the first part of this chapter, we'll take another look at each of these types of buyers. Then, we'll add their purchases together to explore the behavior of *total* spending in the economy.

Finally, one more choice: Should we look at *nominal* or *real* spending? (Recall that a nominal variable is measured in current dollars, while a real variable is measured in the constant dollars of some base year.) Ultimately, we care more about real variables, such as real output and real income, because they are the more closely related to our economic well-being. For example, a rise in *nominal* output might

**Short-run macro model**  A macroeconomic model that explains how changes in spending can affect real GDP in the short run.

 Characterize the Market

mean that we are producing more goods and services, or it might just mean that prices have risen and production has remained the same or fallen. But a rise in *real* output always means that production has increased. For this reason, we will think about real variables right from the beginning. When we discuss "consumption spending," we mean "real consumption spending," "investment spending" means "real investment spending," and so on.

## CONSUMPTION SPENDING

A natural place for us to begin our look at spending is with its largest component: *consumption spending*. In all, household spending on consumer goods—groceries, restaurant meals, rent, car repairs, movies, telephone calls, and furniture—is about two-thirds of total spending in the economy. Total consumption spending in the economy is the sum of spending by over a hundred million U.S. households. Each household is trying to achieve the highest level of economic well-being attainable, given the constraints that they face. Because we are interested in the macroeconomy, we don't concern ourselves with the differences between one consumer good and another. Instead, we want to know: What determines the *total* amount of consumption spending?

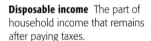

Identify Goals and Constraints

The answer is, many different things. Think about yourself: What determines how much you spend in a given year? The most obvious determinant is your income, or—more precisely—your **disposable income**, the part of your income left over after you pay taxes:[1]

**Disposable income** The part of household income that remains after paying taxes.

$$\text{Disposable Income} = \text{Income} - \text{Taxes}.$$

Each of us—in trying to pursue our goal of economic satisfaction—is faced with a constraint: We only have so much disposable income. And when that constraint is relaxed or tightened—when we find ourselves with more or less disposable income—our consumption spending changes. All else equal, you'd certainly spend more on consumer goods with a disposable income of $50,000 per year than with a disposable income of $20,000 per year. (Here, as elsewhere, we are speaking about *real* variables: *real* consumption and *real* disposable income.)

But other factors besides your disposable income influence how much you spend. For example, suppose your disposable income is $50,000 per year. How much of that sum will you spend, and how much will you save? Since the *interest rate* determines your reward for saving, you would probably save more at a higher interest rate like 10 percent than at a lower interest rate like 2 percent. But since you'd be saving more, you'd be spending less. So we can expect consumption spending to be smaller at higher interest rates, and larger at lower interest rates.

Another determinant of consumption is *wealth*—the total value of your assets (home, stocks, bonds, bank accounts, and the like) minus your outstanding liabilities (mortgage loans, credit card debt, student loans, and so on). Even if your disposable income stayed the same, an increase in your wealth—say, because your stocks or bonds became more valuable—would probably induce you to spend more.

---

[1]   Strictly speaking, we deduct *net* taxes from income to obtain disposable income. Net taxes are the taxes households pay *minus* the transfer payments households receive from the government.

*Expectations* about your future would affect your spending as well. If you become more optimistic about your job security or expect a big raise, you might spend more of your income now. Similarly, increased pessimism, such as greater worries about losing your job, would lead you to decrease spending now.

We could list many other variables that would influence your consumption spending—how long you expect to live, inheritances you expect to receive over your lifetime, and more.

What do these personal observations tell us about *aggregate* consumption spending? Just as your own consumption spending would be influenced by a variety of variables in the economy, so, too, would the consumption spending of other households. Each of the variables we've discussed will therefore influence aggregate consumption spending in predictable ways. We would expect a rise in aggregate disposable income—the total of every household's disposable income in the economy—to cause a rise in aggregate consumption spending. Similarly, a rise in the overall level of interest rates should cause a decrease in aggregate consumption spending.

Figure 1 summarizes some of the important variables that influence consumption spending, and the direction of their effects. A plus sign indicates that consumption spending moves in the same direction as the variable; for example, a rise in disposable income will cause a rise in consumption. A minus sign indicates that the variables are negatively related—a rise in the interest rate will cause consumption spending to fall.

## CONSUMPTION AND DISPOSABLE INCOME

Of all the factors that might influence consumption spending, the most important is disposable income. Figure 2 shows the relationship between real consumption spending and real disposable income in the United States from 1960 to 1999. Each point in the diagram represents a different year. For example, the point labeled "1982" represents a disposable income in that year of $3,773 billion and consumption spending of $3,260 billion. Notice that as disposable income rises, consumption spending rises as well. Indeed, almost all of the variation in consumption spending from year to year can be explained by variations in disposable income. Although the other factors in Figure 1 do affect consumption spending, their impact appears to be relatively minor.

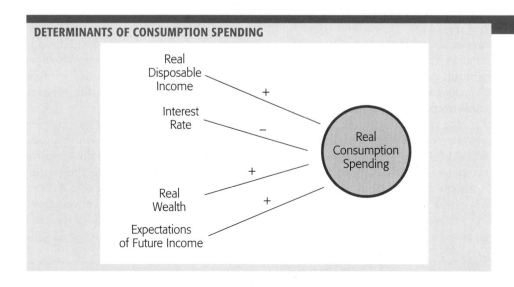

**FIGURE 1**

**DETERMINANTS OF CONSUMPTION SPENDING**

Real Disposable Income → + → Real Consumption Spending
Interest Rate → −
Real Wealth → +
Expectations of Future Income → +

**FIGURE 2**

When real consumption expenditure is plotted against real disposable income, the resulting relationship is almost perfectly linear: As real disposable income rises, so does real consumption spending.

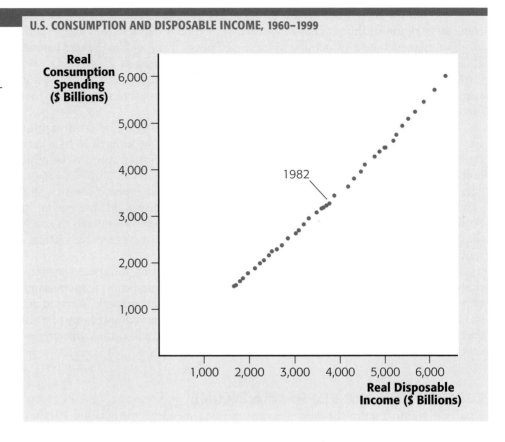

**U.S. CONSUMPTION AND DISPOSABLE INCOME, 1960–1999**

There is something even more interesting about Figure 2: The relationship between consumption and disposable income is almost perfectly *linear*—the points lie remarkably close to a straight line. This almost-linear relationship between consumption and disposable income has been observed in a wide variety of historical periods and a wide variety of nations. This is why, when we represent the relationship between disposable income and consumption with a diagram or an equation, we use a straight line.

Our discussion will be clearer if we move from the actual data in Figure 2 to the hypothetical example in Table 1. Each row in the table represents a combination of real disposable income and consumption we might observe in an economy. For example, the table shows us that if disposable income were equal to $7,000 billion in some year, consumption spending would equal $6,200 billion in that year. When we plot this data on a graph, we obtain the straight line in Figure 3. This line is called the **consumption function**, because it illustrates the functional relationship between consumption and disposable income.

**Consumption function** A positively sloped relationship between real consumption spending and real disposable income.

Like every straight line, the consumption function in Figure 3 has two main features: a vertical intercept and a slope. Mathematically, the intercept—in this case, $2,000 billion—tells us how much consumption spending there would be in the economy if disposable income were zero. However, the real purpose of the vertical intercept is not to identify what would actually happen at zero disposable income, but rather to help us determine which particular line represents consumption spending in the diagram. After all, there are many lines we could draw that have the same slope as the one in the figure. But only one of them has a vertical intercept of $2,000.

**TABLE 1**

**HYPOTHETICAL DATA ON DISPOSABLE INCOME AND CONSUMPTION**

| Real Disposable Income (Billions of Dollars per Year) | Real Consumption Spending (Billions of Dollars per Year) |
|---|---|
| 0 | 2,000 |
| 1,000 | 2,600 |
| 2,000 | 3,200 |
| 3,000 | 3,800 |
| 4,000 | 4,400 |
| 5,000 | 5,000 |
| 6,000 | 5,600 |
| 7,000 | 6,200 |
| 8,000 | 6,800 |

The vertical intercept in the figure also has a name: **autonomous consumption spending.** It represents the combined impact on consumption spending of everything *other than* disposable income. For example, if household wealth were to increase, or the interest rate were to decrease, consumption would be greater at any level of disposable income. The entire consumption function in the figure would shift upward, so its vertical intercept would increase. We would call this *an increase*

**Autonomous consumption spending** The part of consumption spending that is independent of income; also, the vertical intercept of the consumption function.

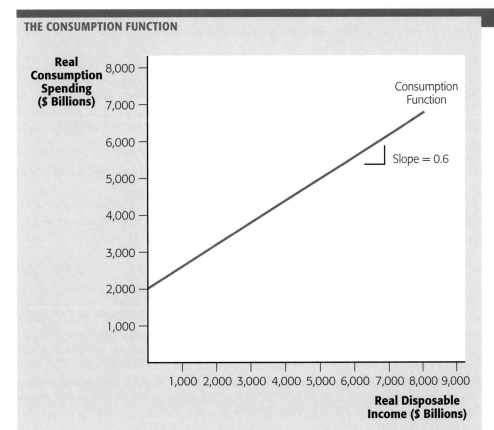

**THE CONSUMPTION FUNCTION**

**FIGURE 3**

Real consumption spending is linearly related to real disposable income. The vertical axis intercept of the line, $a$ = $2,000 billion, shows autonomous consumption expenditure. The slope of the line, $b$ = 0.6, is the marginal propensity to consume.

*in autonomous consumption spending.* Similarly, a decrease in wealth, or a rise in interest rates, would cause a *decrease in autonomous consumption spending,* and shift the consumption function downward.

The second important feature of Figure 3 is the slope, which shows the change along the vertical axis divided by the change along the horizontal axis as we go from one point to another on the line. If we use $\Delta C$ to represent the change in real consumption spending, and $\Delta Y_D$ to represent the change in real disposable income, then the slope of the consumption function is given by

$$\text{slope} = \frac{\Delta C}{\Delta Y_D}.$$

As you can see in the table, each time disposable income rises by $1,000 billion, consumption spending rises by $600 billion, so that the slope is $\Delta C/\Delta Y_D = \$600$ billion/$1,000 billion = 0.6.

The slope in Figure 3 is an important feature not just of the consumption function itself, but also of the macroeconomic analysis we will build from it. This is why economists have given this slope a special name, the *marginal propensity to consume,* abbreviated *MPC.* In our example, the *MPC* is 0.6.

We can think of the *MPC* in three different ways, but each of them has the same meaning:

**Marginal propensity to consume**
The amount by which consumption spending rises when disposable income rises by one dollar.

> *The **marginal propensity to consume** (MPC) is (1) the slope of the consumption function; (2) the change in consumption divided by the change in disposable income ($\Delta C/\Delta Y_D$); or (3) the amount by which consumption spending rises when disposable income rises by one dollar.*

Logic suggests that the *MPC* should be larger than zero (when income rises, consumption spending will rise), but less than 1 (the rise in consumption will be *smaller* than the rise in disposable income). This is certainly true in our example: With an *MPC* of 0.6, each one-dollar rise in disposable income causes spending to rise by 60 cents. It is also observed to be true in economies throughout the world. Accordingly,

> *we will always assume that* $0 < \text{MPC} < 1$.

**Representing Consumption with an Equation.** Sometimes, we'll want to use an equation to represent the straight-line consumption function. The most general form of the equation is

$$C = a + b\, Y_D.$$

The term *a* is the vertical intercept of the consumption function. It represents the theoretical level of consumption spending at $Y_D = 0$, which you've learned is called *autonomous consumption spending.* In the equation, you can see clearly that autonomous consumption (*a*) is the part of consumption that does *not* depend on disposable income. In our example in Figure 3, *a* is equal to $2,000 billion.

The other term, *b,* is the slope of the consumption function. This is our familiar marginal propensity to consume (*MPC*), telling us how much consumption *increases* each time disposable income rises by a dollar. In our example in Figure 3, *b* is equal to 0.6.

## CONSUMPTION AND INCOME

The consumption function is an important building block of our analysis. Consumption is the largest component of spending, and disposable income is the most important determinant of consumption. But there is one limitation of the line as we've drawn it in Figure 3: It shows us the value of consumption at each level of *disposable* income, whereas we will need to know the value of consumption spending at each level of *income*. Disposable income, you remember, is the income that people have left over after taxes: $Y_D = Y - T$. How can we convert the line in Figure 3 into a relationship between consumption and income?

If the government collected no taxes, total income and disposable income would be equal, so that the relationship between consumption and income on the one hand, and consumption and disposable income on the other hand, would be identical. In that case, the line in Figure 3 would show the relationship between consumption and income. But what about when taxes are not zero?

Table 2 illustrates the consumption–income relationship when households must pay taxes. In the table, we treat taxes as a fixed amount—in this case, $2,000 billion. Some taxes are, indeed, fixed in this way, such as the taxes assessed on real estate by local governments. Other taxes, like the personal income tax and the sales tax, rise and fall with income in the economy. Treating all taxes as if they are independent of income, as in Table 2, will simplify our discussion without changing our results in any important way.

Notice that the last two columns of the table are identical to the columns in Table 1: In both tables, we assume that the relationship between consumption spending and disposable income is the same. For example, both tables show us that, when disposable income is $7,000 billion, consumption spending is $6,200 billion. But in Table 2, we see that a disposable income of $7,000 is associated with an income of $9,000. Thus, when income is $9,000, consumption spending is $6,200. By comparing the first and last columns of Table 2, we can trace out the relationship between consumption and income. This relationship—which we call the **consumption–income line**—is graphed in Figure 4.

If you compare the consumption–income line in Figure 4 with the line in Figure 3, you will notice that both have the same slope of 0.6, but the consumption–income

**Consumption–income line** A line showing aggregate consumption spending at each level of income or GDP.

| | | | | | TABLE 2 |
| Income or GDP (Billions of Dollars per Year) | Tax Collections (Billions of Dollars per Year) | Disposable Income (Billions of Dollars per Year) | Consumption Spending (Billions of Dollars per Year) | | THE RELATIONSHIP BETWEEN CONSUMPTION AND INCOME |
|---|---|---|---|---|---|
| 2,000 | 2,000 | 0 | 2,000 | | |
| 3,000 | 2,000 | 1,000 | 2,600 | | |
| 4,000 | 2,000 | 2,000 | 3,200 | | |
| 5,000 | 2,000 | 3,000 | 3,800 | | |
| 6,000 | 2,000 | 4,000 | 4,400 | | |
| 7,000 | 2,000 | 5,000 | 5,000 | | |
| 8,000 | 2,000 | 6,000 | 5,600 | | |
| 9,000 | 2,000 | 7,000 | 6,200 | | |
| 10,000 | 2,000 | 8,000 | 6,800 | | |

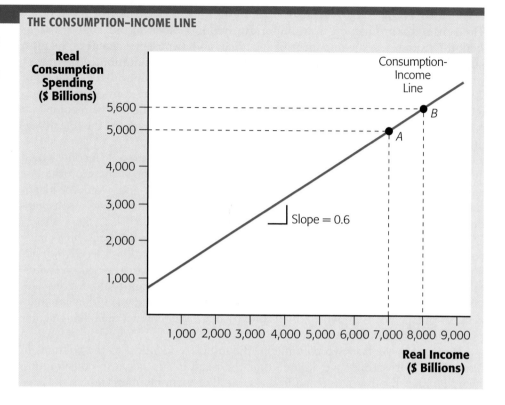

**FIGURE 4**

Real consumption spending is linearly related to real income. The slope of the line, $b = 0.6$, is the marginal propensity to consume.

**THE CONSUMPTION–INCOME LINE**

line is lower by $1,200 billion. This raises three important questions. First, why do taxes lower the consumption–income line? Because at any level of income, taxes reduce disposable income and therefore reduce consumption spending.

Second, why is the consumption–income line lower by precisely $1,200 billion? Because any decrease in taxes ($T$) will cause consumption spending to fall by $MPC \times \Delta T$. In our example, when we impose taxes of $2,000 billion on the population, disposable income will drop by $2,000 billion at any level of income. With an $MPC$ of 0.6, consumption at any level of income falls by $0.6 \times \$2,000$ billion = $1,200 billion.

Finally, why is the *slope* of the consumption–income line unaffected by taxes? Because when taxes are a fixed amount, disposable income rises dollar-for-dollar with income. With an $MPC$ of 0.6, consumption spending will rise by 60 cents each time income rises by a dollar, just as it would if there were no taxes at all. In other words, while a fixed amount of taxes affects the relationship between the *level* of income and the *level* of consumption spending, it does not affect the relationship between a *change* in income and a *change* in consumption spending. You can verify this in Table 2: Each time income rises by $1,000 billion, consumption spending rises by $600 billion, giving a slope of $\Delta C/\Delta Y$ = $600 billion/$1,000 billion = 0.6, just as in the case with no taxes. More generally,

> *when the government collects a fixed amount of taxes from households, the line representing the relationship between consumption and income is shifted downward by the amount of the tax times the marginal propensity to consume (MPC). The slope of this line is unaffected by taxes, and is equal to the MPC.*

# SHIFTS IN THE CONSUMPTION–INCOME LINE

As you've learned, consumption spending depends positively on income: If income increases and taxes remain unchanged, disposable income will rise, and consumption spending will rise along with it. The chain of causation can be represented this way:

In Figure 4, this change in consumption spending would be represented by a *movement along* the consumption–income line. For example, a rise in income from $7,000 billion to $8,000 billion would cause consumption spending to increase from $5,000 billion to $5,600 billion, moving us from point *A* to point *B* along the consumption–income line.

But consumption spending can also change for reasons other than a change in income, causing the consumption–income line itself to shift. For example, a decrease in taxes will increase disposable income at each level of income. Consumption spending will then increase at any income level, shifting the entire line upward. The mechanism works like this:

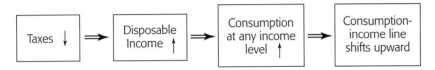

In Figure 5, a decrease in taxes from $2,000 billion to $500 billion increases disposable income at each income level by $1,500 billion, and causes consumption at each income level to increase by $0.6 \times \$1,500$ billion = $900 billion. This means that the consumption line shifts upward, to the upper line in the figure.

Other changes besides increases or decreases in taxes can shift the consumption–income line as well. All of these other changes work by changing *autonomous consumption*—the vertical intercept of the consumption function in Figure 3. By shifting the relationship between consumption and disposable income, we shift the relationship between consumption and income as well. For example, an increase in household wealth would increase autonomous consumption, and shift the consumption–income line upward, as in Figure 5. Increases in autonomous consumption could also occur if the interest rate decreased, if households developed a taste for spending more of their disposable incomes, or if they became more optimistic about the future. In general, increases in autonomous consumption work this way:

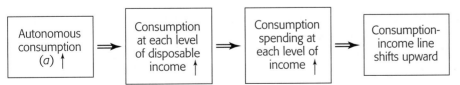

We can summarize our discussion of changes in consumption spending as follows:

*When a change in income causes consumption spending to change, we move* along *the consumption–income line. When a change in anything else besides income causes consumption spending to change, the line will shift.*

A change in any non-income determinant of consumption spending causes the consumption–income line to shift. A decrease in taxes, for example, increases disposable income and leads to increased consumption spending at any level of income. This is reflected in the upward shift of the consumption–income line. In addition to a tax cut, an increase in autonomous consumption—due to higher wealth, greater optimism, or a lower interest rate—would also lead to an upward shift of the line.

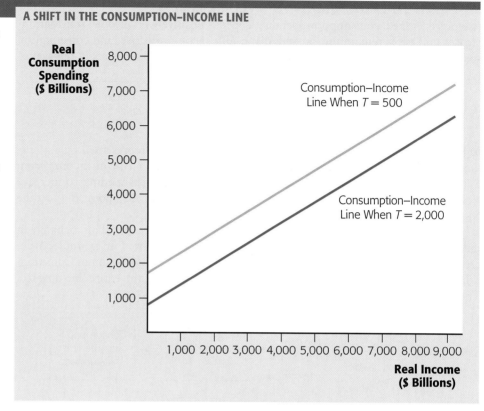

**A SHIFT IN THE CONSUMPTION–INCOME LINE**

Table 3 provides a more specific summary of how different types of changes in consumption spending are represented with the consumption–income line. Remember that all of the changes that *shift* the line—other than a change in taxes—work by increasing or decreasing autonomous consumption (*a*).

## GETTING TO TOTAL SPENDING

In addition to household consumption spending, there are three other types of spending on goods and services produced by American firms: investment, government purchases, and purchases by foreigners. Let's consider each of these types of spending in turn.

**CHANGES IN CONSUMP-TION SPENDING AND THE CONSUMPTION–INCOME LINE**

| Rightward Movement Along the Line | Leftward Movement Along the Line | Entire Line Shifts Upward | Entire Line Shifts Downward |
|---|---|---|---|
| When | When | When | When |
| Income ↑ | Income ↓ | Taxes ↓ | Taxes ↑ |
| | | Household wealth ↑ | Household wealth ↓ |
| | | Interest rate ↓ | Interest rate ↑ |
| | | Greater optimism | Greater pessimism |

## INVESTMENT SPENDING

Remember that in the definition of GDP, *investment* ($I$) consists of three components: (1) business spending on plant and equipment; (2) purchases of new homes; and (3) accumulation of unsold inventories. In this chapter, as we did when we studied the classical model, we focus not on actual investment, but on *planned investment* or *investment spending* (we'll use these two terms interchangeably). Planned investment ($I^p$) is business purchases of plant and equipment, and construction of new homes.

Why do we focus on planned investment and leave out inventory accumulation? When we look at how spending influences the economy, we are interested in the purchases households, firms, and the government *want* to make. But some inventory changes, as you learned a few chapters ago, are an *unplanned* and *undesired* occurrence that firms try to avoid. While firms want to have *some* inventories on hand, sudden *changes* in inventories are typically not desirable. To keep the model simple, we treat *all* inventory changes as temporary, unplanned occurrences for the firm, and we exclude them when we measure spending in the economy. But even though they are excluded from spending, inventory changes will play an important part in our analysis, as you will see below.

> *In the short-run macro model, we define investment spending as plant and equipment purchases by business firms, and new home construction. Inventory investment is treated as unintentional and undesired, and is therefore excluded from our definition of investment spending.*

What determines the level of investment spending in a given year? In this chapter, we will regard investment spending as a *fixed value*, determined by forces outside of our analysis. This may seem surprising. After all, aren't there variables that affect investment spending in predictable ways? Indeed, there are.

For example, in the classical model, you learned that planned investment is likely to be affected by the interest rate. Indeed, in the real world, the investment–interest rate relationship is quite strong. Investment is also influenced by the general level of optimism or pessimism about the economy and by new technological developments. But if we introduced all of these other variables into our analysis, we would find ourselves working with a very complex framework, and much too soon. In future chapters, we'll explore some of the determinants of investment spending, but in this chapter, to keep things simple, we assume that investment spending is some given amount. We'll explore what happens when that amount changes, but we will not, in this chapter, try to explain what *causes* investment spending to change.

> *For now, we regard investment spending as a given value, determined by forces outside of our model.*

## GOVERNMENT PURCHASES

Government purchases include all of the goods and services that government agencies—federal, state, and local—buy during the year. We treat government purchases in the same way as investment spending: as a given value, determined by forces outside of our analysis. Why?

The relationship between government purchases and other macroeconomic variables—particularly income—is rather weak. In recent decades, the biggest changes in government purchases have involved military spending. These changes have been based on world politics, rather than macroeconomic conditions. So when we assume that government spending is a given value, independent of the other variables in our model, our assumption is actually realistic.

> *In the short-run macro model, government purchases are treated as a given value, determined by forces outside of the model.*

As with investment spending, we'll be exploring what happens when the "given value" of government purchases changes. But we will not try to explain what causes it to change.

## NET EXPORTS

If we want to measure total spending on U.S. output, we must also consider the international sector. About 11 percent of U.S.-produced goods are sold to *foreign* consumers, *foreign* businesses, and *foreign* governments. These are U.S. *exports*, and they are as much a part of total spending on U.S. output as the other types of spending we've discussed so far. Thus, exports must be included in our measure of total spending.

But international trade in goods and services also requires us to make an adjustment to the other components of spending. A portion (about 14 percent) of the output bought by *American* consumers, firms, and government agencies was produced abroad. From the U.S. point of view, these are *imports*—spending on foreign, rather than U.S., output. These imports are included in our measures of consumption, investment, and government spending, giving us an exaggerated measure of spending on *American* output. But we can easily correct for this overcount by simply deducting imported consumption goods from our measure of consumption, deducting imported investment goods from our measure of investment, and deducting imported government purchases from our measure of government purchases. Of course, this means we will be deducting total imports from our measure of total spending.

In sum, to incorporate the international sector into our measure of total spending, we must add U.S. exports, and subtract U.S. imports. These two adjustments can be made together by simply including *net exports* (NX) as the foreign sector's contribution to total spending.

$$\text{Net Exports} = \text{Total Exports} - \text{Total Imports.}$$

By including net exports, we simultaneously ensure that we have included U.S. output that is sold to foreigners, and excluded consumption, investment, and government spending on output produced abroad.

Net exports can change for a variety of reasons: changes in tastes toward or away from a particular country's goods, changes in the price of foreign currency on world foreign exchange markets, and more. In the final chapter of this book, we'll discuss in more detail how and why net exports change. But in this chapter, to keep things simple, we assume that net exports—like investment spending and government purchases—are some given amount. We'll explore what happens when that amount changes, but we will not, in this chapter, try to explain what causes net exports to change.

> *For now, we regard net exports as a given value, determined by forces outside of our analysis.*

It's important to remember that net exports can be *negative*, and—in the United States—they have been negative since 1982. Negative net exports means that our imports are greater than our exports. Or, equivalently, Americans are buying more foreign goods and services than foreigners are buying of ours. In that case, net exports contribute *negatively* to total spending on U.S. output.

## SUMMING UP: AGGREGATE EXPENDITURE

Now that we've discussed all of the components of spending in the economy, we can be more precise about measuring total spending. First, we'll use the phrase *aggregate expenditure* to mean total spending on U.S. output over some period of time. More formally,

*Aggregate expenditure is the sum of spending by households, businesses, the government, and the foreign sector on final goods and services produced in the United States.*

**Aggregate expenditure (AE)** The sum of spending by households, business firms, the government, and foreigners on final goods and services produced in the United States.

Remembering that $C$ stands for household consumption spending, $I^p$ for investment spending, $G$ for government purchases, and $NX$ for net exports, we have

$$\text{Aggregate expenditure} = C + I^p + G + NX.$$

Aggregate expenditure spending plays a key role in explaining economic fluctuations. Why? Because over several quarters or even a few years, business firms tend to respond to changes in aggregate expenditure by changing their level of output. That is, a rise in aggregate expenditure leads firms throughout the economy to raise their output level, while a drop in aggregate expenditure causes a decrease in output throughout the economy. While these changes are temporary, they persist long enough to create the kinds of economic fluctuations that you saw in the previous chapter's Figures 1 and 2. In the next section, we'll explore just how changes in spending create these economic fluctuations.

## INCOME AND AGGREGATE EXPENDITURE

As we discussed earlier, the relationship between income and spending is circular: Spending depends on income, and income depends on spending. In Table 4, we take up the first part of that circle: how total spending depends on income. In the table, column 1 lists some possible income levels, and column 2 shows the level of consumption spending we can expect at each income level. These two columns are just the consumption–income relationship we introduced earlier, in Table 2.

Column 3 shows that business firms in this economy buy $700 billion per year in plant and equipment, regardless of the level of income. Government purchases are also fixed in value, as shown by column 4: At every level of income, the government buys $500 billion in goods and services. And net

**DANGEROUS CURVES**

The definition of aggregate expenditure looks very similar to the definition of GDP presented in the chapter entitled "Production, Income, and Employment." Does this mean that aggregate expenditure and total output are always the same number? Not at all. There is a slight—but important—difference in the definitions. GDP is defined as $C + I + G + NX$. Aggregate expenditure, by contrast, is defined as $C + I^p + G + NX$. The difference is that GDP adds actual investment ($I$), which includes business firms' inventory investment. Aggregate expenditure adds just planned investment ($I^p$), which *excludes* inventory investment. The two numbers will not be equal unless inventory investment is zero. (And we'll use this fact to help us find the equilibrium GDP in the next section.)

| TABLE 4 | | | | | | |
| --- | --- | --- | --- | --- | --- | --- |
| **THE RELATIONSHIP BETWEEN INCOME AND AGGREGATE EXPENDITURE** | | | | | | |
| **(1)** Income or GDP (Billions of Dollars per Year) | **(2)** Consumption Spending (Billions of Dollars per Year) | **(3)** Investment Spending (Billions of Dollars per Year) | **(4)** Government Purchases (Billions of Dollars per Year) | **(5)** Net Exports (Billions of Dollars per Year) | **(6)** Aggregate Expenditure (*AE*) (Billions of Dollars per Year) | **(7)** Change in Inventories (Billions of Dollars per Year) |
| 2,000 | 2,000 | 700 | 500 | 400 | 3,600 | −1,600 |
| 3,000 | 2,600 | 700 | 500 | 400 | 4,200 | −1,200 |
| 4,000 | 3,200 | 700 | 500 | 400 | 4,800 | −800 |
| 5,000 | 3,800 | 700 | 500 | 400 | 5,400 | −400 |
| **6,000** | **4,400** | **700** | **500** | **400** | **6,000** | **0** |
| 7,000 | 5,000 | 700 | 500 | 400 | 6,600 | 400 |
| 8,000 | 5,600 | 700 | 500 | 400 | 7,200 | 800 |
| 9,000 | 6,200 | 700 | 500 | 400 | 7,800 | 1,200 |
| 10,000 | 6,800 | 700 | 500 | 400 | 8,400 | 1,600 |

exports, in column 5, are assumed to be $400 billion at each level of income. Finally, if we add together the entries in columns 2, 3, and 4, we get $C + I^p + G + NX$, or aggregate expenditure, shown in column 6. (For now, ignore column 7.)

Notice that aggregate expenditure increases as income rises. But notice also that the rise in aggregate expenditure is *smaller* than the rise in income. For example, you can see that when income rises from $5,000 billion to $6,000 billion (column 1), aggregate expenditure rises from $5,400 billion to $6,000 billion (column 6). Thus, a $1,000 billion increase in income is associated with a $600 billion increase in aggregate expenditure. This is because, in our analysis, consumption is the only component of spending that depends on income, and consumption spending always increases according to the marginal propensity to consume, here equal to 0.6. More generally,

> when income increases, aggregate expenditure (AE) *will rise by the* MPC *times the change in income:* $\Delta AE = MPC \times \Delta Y$.

Find the Equilibrium

# FINDING EQUILIBRIUM GDP

Table 4 shows how spending depends on income. In this section, you will see how income depends on spending—that is, how the spending behavior of households, firms, and government agencies determines the economy's *equilibrium income* or *equilibrium GDP*—a level of GDP that represents, at least in the short run, a point of rest for the economy. That is, we are about to use Key Step #3 of our four-step procedure. As always, the equilibrium will be a point of rest of the economy: a value for GDP that remains the same until something we've been assuming constant begins to change. That part of Key Step #3 will be familiar to you.

However, be forewarned: Our method of *finding* equilibrium in the short run is very different from anything you've seen before in this text.

Our starting point in finding the economy's short-run equilibrium is to ask ourselves what would happen, hypothetically, if the economy were operating at different levels of output. Let's start with a GDP of $9,000 billion. Could this be the equilibrium GDP we seek? That is, if firms were producing this level of output, would they keep doing so? Let's see.

Table 4 tells us that when GDP is equal to $9,000 billion, aggregate expenditure is equal to $7,800 billion. Business firms are *producing* $1,200 billion more than they

DANGEROUS CURVES

You may be wondering why, in the short-run macro model, a firm that produces more output than it sells wouldn't just lower the price of its goods. That way, it could sell more of them, and not have to lower its output as much. Similarly, a firm whose sales exceeded its production could take advantage of the opportunity to raise its prices, which would result in lower sales. To some extent, firms *do* change prices—even in the short run. But they change their output levels, too. To remain as simple as possible, the short-run macro model assumes that firms adjust *only* their output to match aggregate expenditure. That is, *in the short-run macro model, prices don't change at all.* In a later chapter, we'll make the more realistic assumption that firms adjust both prices and output.

are *selling*. Since firms will certainly not be willing to continue producing output they cannot sell, we can infer that, in future periods, they will slow their production. Thus, if the economy finds itself at a GDP of $9,000 billion, it will not stay there. In other words, $9,000 billion is *not* where the economy will settle in the short run, so it is *not* our equilibrium GDP. More generally,

> *when aggregate expenditure is less than GDP, output will decline in the future. Thus, any level of output at which aggregate expenditure is less than GDP cannot be the equilibrium GDP.*

Now let's consider the opposite case: a level of GDP of $3,000 billion. At this level of output, the table shows aggregate expenditure of $4,200 billion—spending is actually *greater* than output by $1,200 billion. What will business firms do in response? Since they are selling more output than they are currently producing, we can expect them to *increase* their production in future months. Thus, if GDP is $3,000 billion, it will tend to rise in the future. So $3,000 is *not* our equilibrium GDP.

> *When aggregate expenditure is greater than GDP, output will rise in the future. Thus, any level of output at which aggregate expenditure exceeds GDP cannot be the equilibrium GDP.*

Now consider a GDP of $6,000 billion. At this level of output, our table shows that aggregate expenditure is precisely equal to $6,000 billion: Output and aggregate expenditure are equal. Since firms, on the whole, are selling just what they produce—no more and no less—they should be content to produce that same amount in the future. We have found our equilibrium GDP:

> *In the short run, equilibrium GDP is the level of output at which output and aggregate expenditure are equal.*

**Equilibrium GDP** In the short run, the level of output at which output and aggregate expenditure are equal.

## INVENTORIES AND EQUILIBRIUM GDP

When firms *produce* more goods than they sell, what happens to the unsold output? It is added to their inventory stocks. When firms *sell* more goods than they produce, where do the additional goods come from? They come from firms' inventory stocks. You can see that the gap between output and spending determines what will happen to inventories during the year.

More specifically,

> *the change in inventories during any period will always equal output minus aggregate expenditure.*

For example, Table 4 tells us that if GDP is equal to $9,000 billion, aggregate expenditure is equal to $7,800 billion. In this case, we can find that the change in inventories is

$$\Delta \text{Inventories} = GDP - AE$$
$$= \$9{,}000 \text{ billion} - \$7{,}800 \text{ billion} = \$1{,}200 \text{ billion}.$$

When GDP is equal to $3,000 billion, aggregate expenditure is equal to $4,200 billion, so that the change in inventories is

$$\Delta \text{Inventories} = GDP - AE$$
$$= \$3{,}000 \text{ billion} - \$4{,}800 \text{ billion} = -\$1{,}200 \text{ billion}.$$

Notice the negative sign in front of the $1,200 billion; if output is $3,000 billion, then inventory stocks will *shrink* by $1,200 billion.

Only when output and total sales are equal—that is, when GDP is at its equilibrium value—will the change in inventories be zero. In our example, when GDP is at its equilibrium value of $6,000 billion, so that aggregate expenditure is also $6,000 billion, the change in inventories is equal to zero. At this output level, we have

$$\Delta \text{Inventories} = GDP - AE$$
$$= \$6{,}000 \text{ billion} - \$6{,}000 \text{ billion} = \$0.$$

What you have just learned about inventories suggests another way to find the equilibrium GDP in the economy: Find the output level at which the change in inventories is equal to zero. Firms cannot allow their inventories of unsold goods to keep growing for very long (they would go out of business), nor can they continue to sell goods out of inventory for very long (they would run out of goods). Instead, they will desire to keep their production in line with their sales, so that their inventories do not change.

To recap,

$$AE < GDP \implies \Delta \text{Inventories} > 0 \implies GDP \downarrow \text{ in future periods.}$$

$$AE > GDP \implies \Delta \text{Inventories} < 0 \implies GDP \uparrow \text{ in future periods.}$$

$$AE = GDP \implies \Delta \text{Inventories} = 0 \implies \text{No change in } GDP.$$

Now look at the last column in Table 4, which lists the change in inventories at different levels of output. This column is obtained by subtracting column 6 from column 1. The equilibrium output level is the one at which the change in inventories equals zero, which, as we've already found, is $6,000 billion.

## FINDING EQUILIBRIUM GDP WITH A GRAPH

To get an even clearer picture of how equilibrium GDP is determined, we'll illustrate it with a graph, although it will take us a few steps to get there. Figure 6 begins the process by showing how we can construct a graph of aggregate expenditure. The lowest line in the figure, labeled *C*, is our familiar consumption–income line, obtained from the data in the first two columns of Table 4.

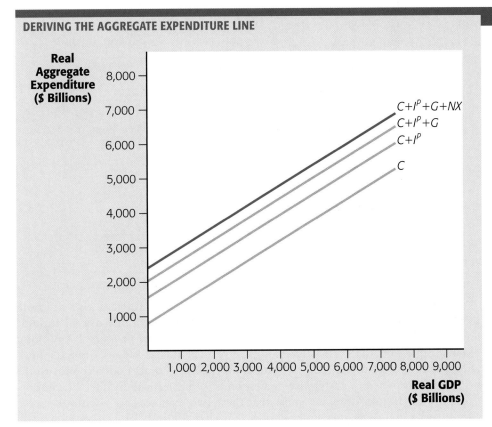

**FIGURE 6**

**DERIVING THE AGGREGATE EXPENDITURE LINE**

Aggregate expenditure is the total of consumption, investment, government purchases, and net exports at a given level of real income. The aggregate expenditure line is derived by adding fixed amounts of investment, government purchases, and net exports to consumption, as determined by the consumption–income line. The slope of the aggregate expenditure line is the marginal propensity to consume.

The next line, labeled $C + I^p$, shows the *sum* of consumption and investment spending at each income level. Notice that this line is parallel to the $C$ line, which means that the vertical distance between them—$700 billion—is the same at any income level. This vertical difference is investment spending, which remains the same at all income levels.

The next line adds government purchases to consumption and investment spending, giving us $C + I^p + G$. The $C + I^p + G$ line is parallel to the $C + I^p$ line. The vertical distance between them—$500 billion—represents government purchases. Like investment, government purchases are the same at all income levels.

Finally, the top line adds net exports, giving us $C + I^p + G + NX$, or aggregate expenditure. The distance between the $C + I^p + G + NX$ line and the $C + I^p + G$ line—$400 billion—represents net exports, which are assumed to be the same at any level of income.

Now look just at the aggregate expenditure line—the top line—in Figure 6. Notice that it slopes upward, telling us that as income increases, so does aggregate expenditure. And the slope of the aggregate expenditure line is less than 1: When income increases, the rise in aggregate expenditure is *smaller* than the rise in income. In fact, the slope of the aggregate expenditure line is equal to the *MPC*, or 0.6 in this example. This tells us that a one-dollar rise in income causes a 60-cent increase in aggregate expenditure. (Question: Which of the four components of aggregate expenditure rises when income rises? Which remain the same?)

Now we're almost ready to use a graph like the one in Figure 6 to locate equilibrium GDP, but first we must develop a little geometric trick.

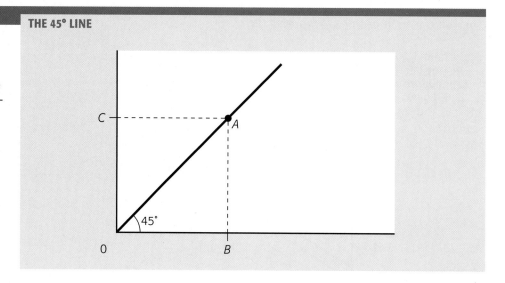

**FIGURE 7**

When both axes are measured in the same units, the 45° line can be used to show all points at which the value measured on the horizontal axis equals the value measured on the vertical axis. In the figure, the distances 0*C*, 0*B*, and *BA* are all equal.

Figure 7 shows a graph in which the horizontal and vertical axes are both measured in the same units, such as dollars. It also shows a line drawn at a 45° angle that begins at the origin. This 45° line has a useful property: Any point along it represents the same value along the vertical axis as it does along the horizontal axis. For example, look at point *A* on the line. Point *A* corresponds to the horizontal distance 0*B*, and it also corresponds to the vertical distance 0*C*. But because the line is a 45° line, we know that these two distances are equal: 0*B* = 0*C*. Moreover, a glance at the figure shows that that 0*B* and *BA* are equal as well. Now we have two choices for measuring the distance 0*B*: We can measure it horizontally, or we can measure it as the vertical distance *BA*. In fact, *any* horizontal distance can also be read vertically, merely by going from the horizontal value (point *B* in our example) up to the 45° line.

> *A 45° line is a translator line: It allows us to measure any horizontal distance as a vertical distance instead.*

Now we can apply this geometric trick to help us find the equilibrium GDP. In our aggregate expenditure diagram, we want to compare output with aggregate expenditure. But output is measured horizontally, while aggregate expenditure is measured vertically. Our 45° line, however, enables us to measure output vertically as well as horizontally, and thus permits us to compare two vertical distances.

Figure 8 shows how this is done. The solid line is the aggregate expenditure line ($C + I^P + G + NX$) from Figure 6. We've dispensed with the other three lines that were drawn in Figure 7 because we no longer need them. The black line is our 45° translator line. Now, let's search for the equilibrium GDP by considering a number of possibilities. For example, could the output level $9,000 billion be our sought-after equilibrium? Let's see. We can measure the output level $9,000 billion as the vertical distance from the horizontal axis up to point *A* on the 45° line. But when output is $9,000 billion, aggregate expenditure is the vertical distance from the horizontal axis to point *H* on the aggregate expenditure line. Notice that, since point *H* lies below point *A*, aggregate expenditure is less than output. If firms *did* produce $9,000 billion worth of output, they would accumulate inventories equal to the vertical distance *HA* (the excess of output over spending). We conclude graphically (as

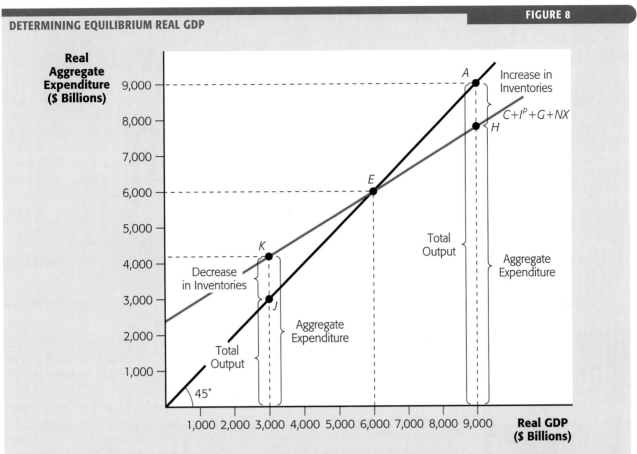

**FIGURE 8**

DETERMINING EQUILIBRIUM REAL GDP

At point *E,* where the aggregate expenditure line crosses the 45° line, the economy is in short-run equilibrium. With real GDP equal to $6,000 billion, aggregate expenditure equals real GDP. At higher levels of real GDP—such as $9,000 billion—total production exceeds aggregate expenditures. At point *A,* firms will be unable to sell all they produce. Unplanned inventory increases equal to *HA* will lead them to reduce production. At lower levels of real GDP—such as $3,000 billion—aggregate expenditure exceeds total production. Firms find their inventories falling, and they will respond by increasing production.

we did earlier, using our table) that if output is $9,000 billion, firms will accumulate inventories of unsold goods and reduce output in the future. Thus, $9,000 billion is not our equilibrium. In general,

> *at any output level at which the aggregate expenditure line lies* below *the 45° line, aggregate expenditure is less than GDP. If firms produce any of these output levels, their inventories will grow, and they will reduce output in the future.*

Now let's see if an output of $3,000 billion could be our equilibrium. First, we read this output level as the vertical distance up to point *J* on the 45° line. Next, we note that when output is $3,000 billion, aggregate expenditure is the vertical distance up to point *K* on the aggregate expenditure line. Point *K* lies *above* point *J,* so aggregate expenditure is greater than output. If firms *did* produce $3,000 billion in output, inventories would *decrease* by the vertical distance *JK.* With declining inventories, firms would want to increase their output in the future, so $3,000 billion is not our equilibrium. More generally,

> *at any output level at which the aggregate expenditure line lies above the 45° line, aggregate expenditure exceeds GDP. If firms produce any of these output levels, their inventories will decline, and they will increase their output in the future.*

Finally, consider an output of $6,000 billion. At this output level, the aggregate expenditure line and the 45° line cross. As a result, the vertical distance up to point $E$ on the 45° line (representing output) is the same as the vertical distance up to point $E$ on the aggregate expenditure line. If firms produce an output level of $6,000 billion, aggregate expenditure and output will be precisely equal, inventories will remain unchanged, and firms will have no incentive to increase or decrease output in the future. We have thus found our equilibrium on the graph: $6,000 billion.

> *Equilibrium GDP is the output level at which the aggregate expenditure line intersects the 45° line. If firms produce this output level, their inventories will not change, and they will be content to continue producing the same level of output in the future.*

## EQUILIBRIUM GDP AND EMPLOYMENT

Now that you've learned how to find the economy's equilibrium GDP in the short run, a question may have occurred to you: When the economy operates at equilibrium, will it also be operating at full employment? The answer is: *not necessarily.* Let's see why.

If you look back over the two methods we've employed to find equilibrium GDP—using columns of numbers as in Table 4, and using a graph as in Figure 8—you will see that in both cases we've asked only one question: How much will households, businesses, the government, and foreigners *spend* on goods produced in the United States? We did not ask any questions about the number of people who want to work. Therefore, it would be quite a coincidence if our equilibrium GDP happened to be the output level at which the entire labor force were employed.

Figure 9 shows how we can find total employment in the economy. In panel (b), we show the economy's production function—the relationship between employment and output for a given capital stock and technology. This production function is similar to the one we used a few chapters ago in the classical model. But there is one important difference: The axes are reversed. Instead of measuring labor on the horizontal axis and output on the vertical axis, the production function in Figure 9 is turned on its side, with labor measured vertically and output measured horizontally. On the vertical axis, $L_{FE}$ is the number of people who *would* be working if the economy were operating at full employment. The production function tells us that, at full employment, GDP would be $Y_{FE}$ (potential output). This is the long-run equilibrium from the classical model.

But will $Y_{FE}$ be the equilibrium in the short run? Not necessarily. One possible outcome is shown in panel (a). Here, the aggregate expenditure line and the 45° line intersect at point $E$. Equilibrium GDP in the short run is $Y_e$. But—according to the production function in panel (b)—to produce an output of $Y_e$ requires employment of only $L_e$. Since $L_e$ is less than $L_{FE}$, we will have abnormally low employment. Or, looked at another way, the level of *un*employment will be higher than normal.

But why? What prevents firms from hiring the extra people who want jobs? After all, with more people working, producing more output, wouldn't there be more income in the economy and therefore more spending? Indeed, there would be. But

During the Great Depression of the 1930s, the economy's short-run equilibrium output fell far below potential, and at least a quarter of the labor force became unemployed.

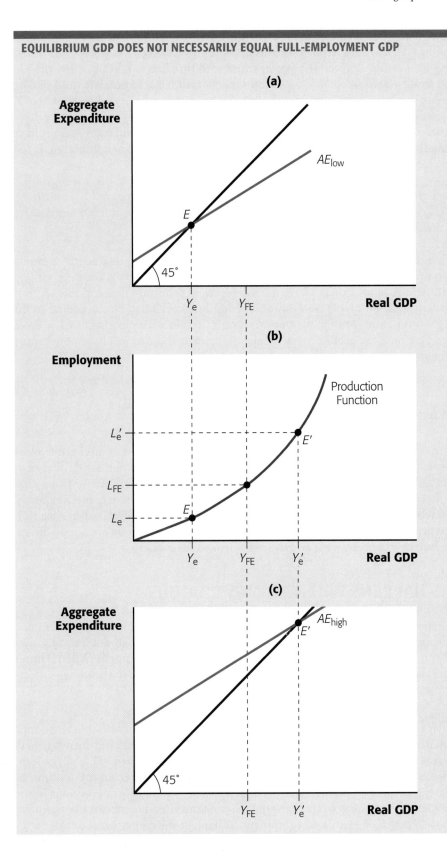

**EQUILIBRIUM GDP DOES NOT NECESSARILY EQUAL FULL-EMPLOYMENT GDP**

**FIGURE 9**

Panel (a) shows that, in the short run, equilibrium GDP can fall short of full employment GDP. This is illustrated by point $E$, where the aggregate expenditure line crosses the 45° line to determine an equilibrium GDP of $Y_e$. This is below full-employment output, $Y_{FE}$. The production func-tion in panel (b) shows that at $Y_e$ employment is $L_e$ which lies below the full-employment level, $L_{FE}$.

Panel (c) shows the opposite case, in which equilibrium GDP exceeds its full-employment level. At point $E'$, the aggregate expenditure line crosses the 45° line to determine an equilibrium GDP of $Y_e'$, which exceeds full-employment output, $Y_{FE}$. The production function in panel (b) shows that with output at $Y_e'$ employment is $L_e'$ which lies above the full-employment level, $L_{FE}$.

not *enough* additional spending to justify the additional employment. To prove this, just look at what would happen if firms *did* hire $L_{FE}$ workers. Output would rise to $Y_{FE}$, but at this output level, the aggregate expenditure line would lie below the 45° line, so *firms would be unable to sell all their output.* Unsold goods would pile up in inventories, and firms would cut back on production until output reached $Y_e$ again, with employment back at $L_e$.

Panel (a) of Figure 9 shows that we can be in short-run equilibrium and yet have abnormally high unemployment. The reason: The aggregate expenditure line is *too low* to create an intersection at full-employment output.

> *In the short-run macro model, cyclical unemployment is caused by insufficient spending. As long as spending remains low, production will remain low, and unemployment will remain high.*

What about the opposite possibility? In the short run, is it possible for spending to be *too high*, causing unemployment to be *too low*? Absolutely. Panel (c) of Figure 9 illustrates such a case. Here, the aggregate expenditure line and the 45° line intersect at point $E'$, giving us a short-run equilibrium GDP at $Y'_e$. According to the production function, producing an output of $Y'_e$ requires employment of $L'_e$. Since $L'_e$ is greater than the economy's normal employment $L_{FE}$, we will have abnormally high employment, and abnormally low *un*employment.

> *In the short-run macro model, the economy can overheat because spending is too high. As long as spending remains high, production will exceed potential output, and unemployment will be unusually low.*

In the previous chapter, we concluded that the classical model could not explain economic fluctuations. The short-run macro model, on the other hand, does provide an explanation: The aggregate expenditure line may be low, meaning that in the short run, equilibrium GDP is below full employment. Or aggregate expenditure may be high, meaning that in the short run, equilibrium GDP is above the full-employment level. (Of course, this is just a first step in explaining economic fluctuations. In later chapters, we'll add more realism to the model.)

What Happens When
Things Change?

## WHAT HAPPENS WHEN THINGS CHANGE?

So far, you've seen how the economy's equilibrium level of output is determined in the short run, and the important role played by spending in determining that equilibrium. But now its time to use Key Step #4 (What Happens When Things Change?) and explore how a spending shock—a sudden change in spending—affects equilibrium output.

### A CHANGE IN INVESTMENT SPENDING

Suppose the equilibrium GDP in an economy is $6,000 billion, and then business firms increase their investment spending on plant and equipment. This might happen because business managers feel more optimistic about the economy's future, or because there is a new "must have" technology (such as Internet connections in the late 1990s), or because government policy has changed and increased the incentive for firms to buy new plant and equipment. Whatever the cause, firms decide to increase yearly planned investment purchases by $1,000 billion above the original level. What will happen?

**FIGURE 10**

**THE EFFECT OF A CHANGE IN INVESTMENT SPENDING**

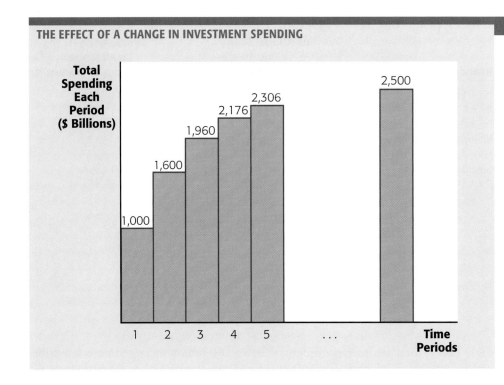

An increase in investment spending sets off a chain reaction, leading to successive rounds of increased spending and income. As shown here, a $1000 billion increase in investment first causes real GDP to increase by $1,000 billion. Then, with higher incomes, households increase consumption spending by the *MPC* times the change in disposable income. In round 2, spending and GDP increase by another $600 billion. In succeeding rounds, increases in income lead to further changes in spending, but in each round the increases in income and spending are smaller than in the preceding round.

First, sales revenue at firms that manufacture investment goods—firms like IBM, Bethlehem Steel, Caterpillar, and Westinghouse—will increase by $1,000 billion. But remember, each time a dollar in output is produced, a dollar of income (factor payments) is created. Thus, the $1,000 billion in additional sales revenue will become $1,000 billion in additional income. This income will be paid out as wages, rent, interest, and profit to the households who own the resources these firms have purchased.[2]

What will households—as consumers—do with their $1,000 billion in additional income? Remember that taxes are fixed, so that households are free to spend or save their additional income as they desire. What they will do depends crucially on the *marginal propensity to consume* (MPC) *in the economy*. If the MPC is 0.6, then consumption spending will rise by 0.6 × $1,000 billion = $600 billion. Households will save the remaining $400 billion.

But that is not the end of the story. When households spend an additional $600 billion, firms that produce consumption goods and services—firms such as Mc-Donald's, Coca-Cola, American Airlines, and Disney—will receive an additional $600 billion in sales revenue, which, in turn, will become income for the households that supply resources to these firms. And when *these* households see *their* incomes rise by $600 billion, they will spend part of it as well. With an *MPC* of 0.6, consumption spending will rise by 0.6 × $600 billion = $360 billion, creating still more sales revenue for firms, and so on and so on. . . .

As you can see, an increase in investment spending will set off a chain reaction, leading to successive rounds of increased spending and income. The process is illustrated in Figure 10. After the $1,000 billion increase in investment spending, there is a

---

2    Some of the sales revenue will also go to pay for intermediate goods, such as raw materials, electricity, and supplies. But the intermediate-goods suppliers will also pay wages, rent, interest, and profit for *their* resources, so that household income will still rise by the full $1,000 billion.

| TABLE 5 | | | |
|---|---|---|---|
| **CUMULATIVE INCREASES IN SPENDING WHEN INVESTMENT INCREASES BY $1,000 BILLION** | **Round** | **Additional Spending in This Round (Billions of Dollars)** | **Additional Spending in All Rounds (Billions of Dollars)** |
| | Initial Increase in Investment | 1,000 | 1,000 |
| | Round 2 | 600 | 1,600 |
| | Round 3 | 360 | 1,960 |
| | Round 4 | 216 | 2,176 |
| | Round 5 | 130 | 2,306 |
| | Round 6 | 78 | 2,384 |
| | Round 7 | 47 | 2,431 |
| | Round 8 | 28 | 2,459 |
| | Round 9 | 17 | 2,476 |
| | Round 10 | 10 | 2,486 |
| | . | . | . |
| | . | . | . |
| | . | . | . |
| | All other rounds | Very close to 14 | Very close to 2,500 |

$600 billion increase in consumption, then a $360 billion increase in consumption, and on and on. Each successive round of additional spending is 60 percent of the round before. Total spending rises from $1,000 billion to $1,600 billion to $1,960 billion and so on. And each time spending increases, output rises to match it. These successive increases in spending and output occur quickly—the process is largely completed within a year. At the end of the process, when the economy has reached its new equilibrium, spending and output will have increased considerably. But by how much?

Table 5 gives us the answer. The second column shows us the additional spending in each round, while the third column shows the cumulative rise in spending. As you can see, the cumulative increase gets larger and larger with each successive round, but it grows by less and less each time. Eventually, the additional spending in a given round is so small that we can safely ignore it. At this point, the cumulative increase in spending and output will be very close to $2,500 billion—so close that we can ignore any difference.

## THE EXPENDITURE MULTIPLIER

Let's go back and summarize what happened in our example: Business firms increased their investment spending by $1,000 billion, and as a result, spending and output rose by $2,500 billion. Equilibrium GDP increased by *more than* the initial increase in investment spending. In our example, the increase in equilibrium GDP ($2,500 billion) was two-and-a-half times the initial increase in investment spending ($1,000 billion). As you can verify, if investment spending had increased by half as much ($500 billion), GDP would have increased by 2.5 times *that* amount ($1,250 billion). In fact, *whatever* the rise in investment spending, equilibrium GDP would increase by a factor of 2.5, so we can write

$$\Delta GDP = 2.5 \times \Delta I^p.$$

In our example, the change in investment spending was *multiplied by* the number 2.5 in order to get the change in GDP that it causes. For this reason, 2.5 is called the *expenditure multiplier* in this example.

*The **expenditure multiplier** is the number by which the change in investment spending must be multiplied to get the change in equilibrium GDP.*

The value of the expenditure multiplier depends on the value of the *MPC* in the economy. If you look back at Table 5, you will see that each round of additional spending would have been larger if the *MPC* had been larger. For example, with an *MPC* of 0.9 instead of 0.6, spending in round 2 would have risen by $900 billion, in round 3 by $810 billion, and so on. The result would have been a larger cumulative change in GDP, and a larger multiplier.

There is a very simple formula we can use to determine the multiplier for *any* value of the *MPC*. To obtain it, let's start with our numerical example in which the *MPC* is 0.6. When investment spending rises by $1,000 billion, the change in equilibrium GDP can be written as follows:

$$\Delta GDP = \$1{,}000 \text{ billion} + \$600 \text{ billion} + \$360 \text{ billion} + \$216 \text{ billion} + \ldots$$

Factoring out the $1,000 billion change in planned investment, this becomes

$$\Delta GDP = \$1{,}000 \text{ billion } [1 + 0.6 + 0.36 + 0.216 + \ldots]$$
$$= \$1{,}000 \text{ billion } [1 + 0.6 + 0.6^2 + 0.6^3 + \ldots]$$

In this equation, $1,000 billion is the change in investment ($\Delta I^p$), and 0.6 is the *MPC*. To find the change in GDP that applies to *any* $\Delta I^p$ and *any* *MPC*, we can write

$$\Delta GDP = \Delta I^p \times [1 + (MPC) + (MPC)^2 + (MPC)^3 + \ldots]$$

Now we can see that the term in brackets—the infinite sum $1 + MPC + (MPC)^2 + (MPC)^3 + \ldots$—is our multiplier. But what is its value?

We can borrow a rule from the mathematics of sums just like this one. The rule tells us that for any variable $H$ that has a value between zero and 1, the infinite sum

$$1 + H + H^2 + H^3 + \ldots$$

always has the value $1/(1 - H)$. So we can replace $H$ with the *MPC*, since the *MPC* is always between zero and 1. This gives us a value for the multiplier of $1/(1 - MPC)$.

*For any value of the* MPC, *the formula for the expenditure multiplier is* $1/(1 - \text{MPC})$.

In our example, the *MPC* was equal to 0.6, so the expenditure multiplier had the value $1/(1 - 0.6) = 1/0.4 = 2.5$. If the *MPC* had been 0.9 instead, the expenditure multiplier would have been equal to $1/(1 - 0.9) = 1/0.1 = 10$. The formula $1/(1 - MPC)$ can be used to find the multiplier for any value of the *MPC* between zero and one.

Using the general formula for the expenditure multiplier, we can restate what happens when investment spending increases:

$$\Delta GDP = \left[ \frac{1}{(1 - MPC)} \right] \times \Delta I^p.$$

The multiplier effect is a rather surprising phenomenon. It tells us that an increase in investment spending ultimately affects GDP by *more* than the initial increase in investment. Moreover, the multiplier can work in the other direction, as you are about to see.

## THE MULTIPLIER IN REVERSE

Suppose that, in Table 5, investment spending had *decreased* instead of increased. Then the initial change in spending would be −$1,000 billion ($\Delta I^p = -\$1,000$ billion). This would cause a $1,000 billion decrease in revenue for firms that produce investment goods, and they, in turn, would pay out $1,000 billion less in factor payments. In the next round, households—with $1,000 billion less in income—would spend $600 billion less on consumption goods, and so on. The final result would be a $2,500 billion *decrease* in equilibrium GDP.

> *Just as increases in investment spending cause equilibrium GDP to rise by a multiple of the change in spending, decreases in investment spending cause equilibrium GDP to fall by a multiple of the change in spending.*

The multiplier formula we've already established will work whether the initial change in spending is positive or negative.

## OTHER SPENDING SHOCKS

Shocks to the economy can come from other sources besides investment spending. In fact, when *any* sector's spending behavior changes, it will set off a chain of events similar to that in our investment example. Let's see how an increase in government spending could set off the same chain of events as an increase in investment spending.

Suppose that government agencies increased their purchases above previous levels. For example, the Department of Defense might raise its spending on new bombers, or state highway departments might hire more road-repair crews, or cities and towns might hire more teachers. If total government purchases rise by $1,000 billion, then, once again, household income will rise by $1,000 billion. As before, households will spend 60 percent of this increase, causing consumption—in the next round—to rise by $600 billion, and so on and so on. The chain of events is exactly like that of Table 5, with one exception: The first line in column 1 would read, "Initial Increase in Government Purchases" instead of "Initial Increase in Investment." Once again, output would increase by $2,500 billion.

Besides planned investment and government purchases, there are two other components of spending that can set off the same process. One is an increase in net exports. This can come about either from an increase in the economy's exports to foreigners, or a *decrease* in imports *from* foreigners. For example, either an increase in exports of $1,000 billion, or a decrease in imports of $1,000 billion, would increase net exports by $1,000 billion and set off the same multiplier process described above.

Finally, a change in *autonomous consumption* can set off the process. For example, after a $1,000 billion increase in autonomous consumption spending we would see further increases in consumption spending of $600 billion, then $360 billion, and so on. This time, the first line in column 1 of Table 5 would read, "Initial Increase in Autonomous Consumption," but every entry in the table would be the same.

> *Changes in planned investment, government purchases, net exports, or autonomous consumption lead to a multiplier effect on GDP. The expenditure multiplier—1/(1 − MPC)—is what we multiply the initial change in spending by in order to get the change in equilibrium GDP.*

The following four equations summarize how we use the expenditure multiplier to determine the effects of different spending shocks in the short-run macro model. Keep in mind that these formulas work whether the initial change in spending is positive or negative.

$$\Delta GDP = \left[ \frac{1}{(1 - MPC)} \right] \times \Delta I^P$$

$$\Delta GDP = \left[ \frac{1}{(1 - MPC)} \right] \times \Delta G$$

$$\Delta GDP = \left[ \frac{1}{(1 - MPC)} \right] \times \Delta NX$$

$$\Delta GDP = \left[ \frac{1}{(1 - MPC)} \right] \times \Delta a$$

## A GRAPHICAL VIEW OF THE MULTIPLIER

Figure 11 illustrates the multiplier using our aggregate expenditure diagram. The darker line is the aggregate expenditure line from Figure 8. The aggregate expenditure line intersects the 45° line at point $E$, giving us an equilibrium GDP of $6,000 billion.

Now, suppose that either autonomous consumption, investment spending, net exports, or government purchases rises by $1,000 billion. Regardless of which of these types of spending increases, the effect on our aggregate expenditure line is the same: It will *shift upward* by $1,000 billion, to the higher line in the figure. The new aggregate expenditure line intersects the 45° line at point $F$, showing that our new equilibrium GDP is equal to $8,500 billion.

What has happened? An initial spending increase of $1,000 billion has caused equilibrium GDP to increase from $6,000 billion to $8,500 billion—an increase of $2,500 billion. This is just what our multiplier of 2.5 tells us. In general,

$$\Delta GDP = \left[ \frac{1}{(1 - MPC)} \right] \times \Delta \text{Spending}$$

and in this case,

$$\text{\$2,500 billion} = 2.5 \times \text{\$1,000 billion.}$$

> *An increase in autonomous consumption spending, investment spending, government purchases, or net exports will shift the aggregate expenditure line upward by the increase in spending, causing equilibrium GDP to rise. The increase in GDP will equal the initial increase in spending times the expenditure multiplier.*

## AN IMPORTANT PROVISO ABOUT THE MULTIPLIER

In this chapter, we've presented a model to help us focus on the central relationship between spending and output. To keep the model as simple as possible, we've ignored many real-world factors that interfere with, and reduce the size of, the

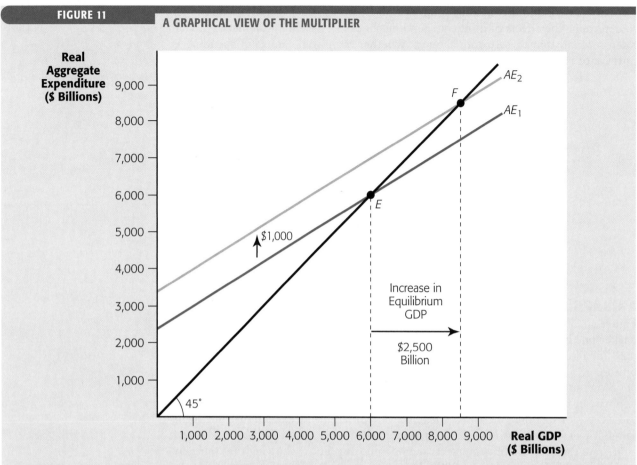

**FIGURE 11**

**A GRAPHICAL VIEW OF THE MULTIPLIER**

The economy starts off at point *E* with equilibrium real GDP of $6,000 billion. A $1,000 billion increase in spending shifts the aggregate expenditure line upward by $1,000 billion, triggering the multiplier process. Eventually, the economy will reach a new equilibrium at point *F*, where the new, higher aggregate expenditure line crosses the 45° line. At *F*, real GDP is $8,500 billion—an increase of $2,500 billion.

**Automatic stabilizers** Forces that reduce the size of the expenditure multiplier and diminish the impact of spending shocks.

multiplier effect. These forces are called **automatic stabilizers** because, with a smaller multiplier, spending shocks will cause a much smaller change in GDP. As a result, economic fluctuations will be milder.

> *Automatic stabilizers reduce the size of the multiplier and therefore reduce the impact of spending shocks on the economy. With milder fluctuations, the economy is more stable.*

How do automatic stabilizers work? They shrink the additional spending that occurs in each round of the multiplier, and thereby reduce the final multiplier effect on equilibrium GDP. In Table 5, automatic stabilizers would reduce each of the numerical entries after the first $1,000 billion, and lead to a final change in GDP smaller than $2,500 billion.

Here are some of the real-world automatic stabilizers we've ignored in the simple, short-run macro model of this chapter:

*Taxes.* We've been assuming that taxes remain constant, so that a rise in income causes an equal rise in disposable income. But some taxes (like the personal income tax) rise with income. As a result, in each round of the multiplier, the increase in disposable income will be smaller than the increase in income. With a smaller rise in disposable income, there will be a smaller rise in consumption spending as well.

*Transfer Payments.* Some government transfer payments fall as income rises. For example, many laid-off workers receive unemployment benefits, which help support them for several months while they are unemployed. But when income and output rise, employment also rises, and newly hired workers must give up their unemployment benefits. As a result, a rise in income will cause a smaller rise in *disposable* income. Consumption will then rise by less in each round of the multiplier.

*Interest Rates.* In a later chapter, you'll learn that an increase in output often leads to rising interest rates as well. This will crowd out some investment spending, making the increase in aggregate expenditure smaller than our simple story suggests.

*Prices.* In a later chapter, you'll learn that the price level tends to rise as spending and production increase. This, in turn, tends to counteract any increase in spending.

*Imports.* Some additional spending is on goods and services imported from abroad. That is, instead of remaining constant, imports often rise as income rises, and net exports therefore fall as income rises. This helps to counteract any increase in spending caused by a rise in income.

*Forward-looking Behavior.* Consumers may be *forward looking*. If they realize that the fluctuations in the economy are temporary, their consumption spending may be less sensitive to changes in their current income. Therefore, any change in income will cause a smaller change in consumption spending, and lead to a smaller multiplier effect.

Remember that each of these automatic stabilizers reduces the size of the multiplier, making it smaller than the simple formulas given in this chapter. For example, the simple formula for the expenditure multiplier is $1/(1 - MPC)$. With an *MPC* of about 0.9—which is in the ballpark for the United States and many other countries—we would expect the multiplier to be about 10 . . . *if the simple formula were accurate.* In that case, a $1,000 billion increase in government spending would cause output to rise by $10,000 billion—quite a large multiplier effect.

**DANGEROUS CURVES**

It's easy to become confused about the relationship between consumption spending and the expenditure multiplier. Does a change in consumption spending *cause* a multiplier effect? Or does the multiplier effect create an increase in consumption spending? Actually, the causation runs in both directions. The key is to recognize that there are *two* kinds of changes in consumption spending.

One kind of change is a change in autonomous consumption spending (the term *a* in the consumption function). This change will *shift* the aggregate expenditure line up or down, telling us that total spending will be greater or smaller at *any* level of income. It is the kind of change that *causes* a multiplier effect.

But consumption also changes when something other than autonomous consumption sets off a multiplier effect. This is because consumption depends on income, and income always increases during the successive rounds of the multiplier effect. Such a change in consumption is represented by a movement *along* the aggregate expenditure line, rather than a shift.

Whenever you discuss a change in consumption spending, make sure you know whether it is a change in autonomous consumption (a shift of the curve) or a change in consumption caused by a change in income (movement along the curve).

But after we take account of all of the automatic stabilizers, the multiplier is considerably smaller. How much smaller? Most of the forecasting models used by economists in business and government predict that the multiplier effect takes about nine months to a year to work its way through the economy. At the end of the process, the multiplier has a value of about 1.5. This means that a $1,000 billion increase in, say, government spending should cause GDP to increase by only about $1,500 billion in a year. This is much less than the $10,000 billion increase predicted by the simple formula $1/(1 - MPC)$ when the $MPC$ is equal to 0.9.

> *In the real world, due to automatic stabilizers, spending shocks have much weaker impacts on the economy than our simple multiplier formulas would suggest.*

Finally, there is one more automatic stabilizer you should know about, perhaps the most important of all: the *passage of time*. Why is this an automatic stabilizer? Because, as you've learned, the impact of spending shocks on the economy are *temporary*. As time passes, the classical model—lurking in the background—stands ready to take over. A few months after a shock, the corrective mechanisms we discussed in the previous chapter begin to operate, and the economy begins to return to full employment. As time passes, the impact of the spending shock gradually disappears. And if we wait long enough—a few years or so—the effects of the shock will be gone entirely. That is, after a shock pulls us away from full-employment GDP, the economy will eventually return to full-employment GDP—right where it started. We thus conclude that

> *in the long run, our multipliers have a value of zero: No matter what the change in spending or taxes, output will return to full employment, so the change in equilibrium GDP will be zero.*

Of course, the year or two we must wait can seem like an eternity to those who are jobless when the economy is operating below its potential. The short run is not to be overlooked. This is why, in the next several chapters, we will continue with our exploration of the short run, building on the macro model you've learned in this chapter. However, we'll make the analysis more complete and more realistic by bringing in some of the real-world features that were not fully considered here.

## COMPARING MODELS: LONG RUN AND SHORT RUN

Before leaving this chapter, it's important to note some startling differences between the long-run classical model you learned about a few chapters ago, and the short-run macro model of this chapter. We've already discussed one of these differences: In the classical model, the economy operates *automatically* at full-employment, or potential, output. In the short-run macro model, by contrast, the economy can operate above its potential or below its potential. The reason for the difference is that, in the short run, spending affects output: A negative spending shock can cause a recession that pushes output below potential GDP; a positive spending shock can cause a rapid expansion that pushes the economy above potential GDP.

There are two other important contrasts between the predictions of the two models. One concerns the role of saving in the economy, and the other concerns the effectiveness of fiscal policy. Let's explore each of these issues in turn.

## THE ROLE OF SAVING

In the long run, saving has positive effects on the economy. This was demonstrated two chapters ago, when—using the classical model—we discussed economic growth. Suppose, for example, that households decide to save more at any level of income. In the long run, the extra saving will flow into the loanable funds market, where it will be borrowed by business firms to purchase new plant and equipment. Thus, an increase in saving automatically leads to an increase in planned investment, faster growth in the capital stock, and a faster rise in living standards. Indeed, we can expect an increase in saving to have precisely these effects . . . in the long run.

But in the short run, the automatic mechanisms of the classical model do not keep the economy operating at its potential. On the contrary, *spending* influences output in the short run. If households decide to save more at each income level, they also—by definition—*spend less* at each income level. Or, putting it another way, an increase in saving is the same as a *decrease* in autonomous consumption spending, *a*. As you've learned in this chapter, a decrease in autonomous consumption spending causes a decrease in output through the multiplier process. If the economy is initially operating at full employment, the increase in saving will push output *below* its potential.

> *In the long run, an increase in the desire to save leads to faster economic growth and rising living standards. In the short run, however, it can cause a recession that pushes output below its potential.*

You can see that there are two sides to the "savings coin." The impact of increased saving is positive in the long run and potentially dangerous in the short run. Are you wondering how we get from the potentially harmful short-run effect of higher saving to the beneficial long-run effect? We'll address this question a few chapters later, when we examine how the economy adjusts from its short-run equilibrium to its long-run equilibrium.

## THE EFFECT OF FISCAL POLICY

In the classical model, you learned that fiscal policy—changes in government spending or taxes designed to change equilibrium GDP—is completely ineffective. More specifically, an increase in government purchases *crowds out* an equal amount of household and business spending: The rise in *G* is exactly matched by the decrease in *C* and *I* . . . in the long run.

But in the short run, once again, we cannot rely on the mechanisms of the classical model that are so effective in the long run. In the short run, *an increase in government purchases causes a multiplied increase in equilibrium GDP.* Therefore, in the short run, fiscal policy can actually change equilibrium GDP!

This important observation suggests that fiscal policy could, in principle, play a role in altering the path of the economy. If output begins to dip below potential, couldn't we use fiscal policy to pull us out of it or even prevent the recession entirely? For example, if investment spending decreases by $100 billion, setting off a negative multiplier effect, couldn't we just increase government purchases by $100 billion to set off an equal, positive multiplier effect? Why wait the many months or years it would take for the classical model to "kick in" and bring the economy back to full employment when we have such a powerful tool—fiscal policy—at our disposal?

Indeed, in the 1960s and early 1970s, this was the thinking of many economists. At that time, the view that fiscal policy could effectively smooth out economic fluctuations—perhaps even eliminate them entirely—was very popular. But very few economists believe this today. Why? In part, because of practical difficulties in executing the right fiscal policy at the right time. But more importantly, the rules of economic policy making have changed: The Federal Reserve now attempts to neutralize fiscal policy changes long before they can affect spending and output in the economy. In later chapters, we'll discuss the practical difficulties of executing fiscal policy and how the Federal Reserve has changed the "rules of the game."

## THE RECESSION OF 1990–1991

*Using the*
# THEORY

Our most recent recession began in the second half of 1990 and continued into 1991. Table 6 tells the story. The second column shows real GDP in 1996 dollars in each of several quarters. For example, "1990:2" denotes the second quarter of 1990, and during that three-month period, GDP was $6,705 billion at an annual rate. (That is, if we had continued producing that quarter's GDP for an entire year, we *would* have produced a total of $6,705 billion worth of goods and services in the year 1990.)

As you can see, real GDP began to fall in the third quarter, and it continued to drop until the second quarter of 1991. In all, GDP fell for three consecutive quarters. During this time, real output fell by $100 billion, a drop of about 1.5 percent. At the same time, the unemployment rate rose, from 5.1 percent in June of 1990 to 7.7 percent in June of 1992. The economy had not completely recovered by the presidential election of November 1992, and many observers believe that the recession and slow recovery were the deciding factors in George Bush's loss to Bill Clinton.

Can our short-run model help us understand what caused this recession? Very much so. In retrospect, we can see that there were two separate spending shocks to the economy in early 1990.

First, for a variety of reasons, a financial crisis had developed, in which some banks and savings and loan associations were near bankruptcy. Many banks, playing it safe, responded by cutting back on loans for new home purchases, as well as for business expansion. The media began to speak of a "credit crunch," in which homebuyers and businesses were forced to pay very high interest rates on loans, or were unable to borrow at all. The consequence was a sizable decrease in the demand for new housing and for plant and equipment—an investment spending

| TABLE 6 | | | | |
|---|---|---|---|---|
| **THE RECESSION OF 1990–1991** | Quarter | Real GDP (Billions of 1996 Dollars) | Change in Real GDP from Previous Quarter (Billions of 1996 Dollars) | Real Investment Spending (Billions of 1996 Dollars) | Consumer Confidence Index |
| | 1990:2 | 6,705 | | 933 | 105 |
| | 1990:3 | 6,695 | −10 | 913 | 90 |
| | 1990:4 | 6,644 | −51 | 850 | 61 |
| | 1991:1 | 6,616 | −28 | 815 | 65 |
| | 1991:2 | 6,658 | +42 | 809 | 77 |

shock. (Remember that investment spending includes new housing construction as well as plant and equipment.)

The second shock resulted from global politics. In the summer of 1990, Iraqi troops invaded and occupied Kuwait. The United States responded by sending troops to Kuwait and, in early 1991, launched an attack on Iraqi troops. Americans began to fear a prolonged and costly war in the Middle East, one that would, among other things, cause a large increase in the price of oil. They remembered that in the early 1970s, the last time that oil prices had risen substantially, the U.S. economy plunged into recession. As a result, American households became less confident about the economy.

The fifth column of Table 6 shows the rapid decline in the *consumer confidence index* that was occurring at the time. The index is based on a survey of about 5,000 households. Each month, these households respond to questions about their job and career prospects in the months ahead, their expected income, their spending plans, and so forth. A drop in consumer confidence makes households spend less at *any* income level. Or, put another way, households wanted to *save more* at any income level. Viewed either way, the drop in consumer confidence caused a decrease in autonomous consumption, *a*. This was the second spending shock to the economy.

In sum, in early 1990, there were two spending shocks to the economy: a decline in planned investment and a decline in autonomous consumption. Each of these shocks had a multiplier effect on the economy, causing income and spending to decline in successive rounds for almost a year. Beginning in 1992, the credit crunch began to subside, increasing investment spending, and the Gulf War ended, increasing consumer confidence. At the same time, the long-run corrective forces of the classical model were beginning to work. Together, all of these factors helped the economy to recover in 1992 and on into 1993.

**http://**
Jennifer Gardner has explored what happened in the labor market during 1990 and 1991. You can find her analysis at http://www.bls.gov/opub/mlr/1994/06/art1full.pdf.

## SUMMARY

In the short run, spending depends on income and income depends on spending. The short-run macro model was developed to explore this circular connection between spending and income.

Total spending is the sum of four aggregates—consumption spending by households, investment spending by firms, government purchases of goods and services, and net exports. Consumption spending ($C$) depends primarily on disposable income—what households have left over after paying taxes. The consumption function is a linear relationship between disposable income and consumption spending. The marginal propensity to consume—a number between zero and 1—indicates the fraction of each additional dollar of disposable income that is consumed. For a given level of income, consumption spending can change as a result of changes in the interest rate, wealth, or expectations about the future. Each of these changes will shift the consumption function.

Investment spending ($I^p$), government purchases ($G$), and net exports ($NX$) are taken as given values, determined by forces outside our analysis. Aggregate expenditure ($AE$) is the sum $C + I^p + G + NX$; it varies with income because consumption spending varies with income.

Equilibrium GDP is the level of output at which aggregate expenditure is just equal to GDP ($Y$). If $AE$ exceeds $Y$, then firms will experience unplanned decreases in inventories. They will respond by increasing production. If $Y$ exceeds $AE$, firms will find their inventories increasing and will respond by reducing production. Only when $AE = Y$ will there be no unplanned inventory changes and no reason for firms to change production. Graphically, this occurs at the point where the aggregate expenditure line intersects the 45° line.

Spending shocks will change the economy's short-run equilibrium. An increase in investment spending, for example, shifts the aggregate expenditure line upward and triggers the multiplier process. The initial increase in investment spending causes income to increase. That, in turn, leads to an increase in consumption spending, a further increase in income, more consumption spending, and so on. The economy eventually reaches a new equilibrium with a change in GDP that is a multiple of the original increase in spending. Other spending shocks would have similar effects. The size of the *expenditure multiplier* is determined by the marginal propensity to consume.

There are several important differences between the short-run macro model and the long-run classical model. In the long run, the economy operates at potential output; in the short run, GDP can be above or below potential. In the long run, saving contributes to economic growth by making funds available for firms to invest in new capital. In the short run, increased saving means reduced spending and a lower level of output. Finally, fiscal policy is completely ineffective in the long run, but can have important effects on total demand and output in the short run.

## K E Y   T E R M S

| | | | |
|---|---|---|---|
| short-run macro model | autonomous consumption | consumption–income line | expenditure multiplier |
| disposable income | spending | aggregate expenditure | automatic stabilizers |
| consumption | marginal propensity to | equilibrium GDP | |
| function | consume | | |

## R E V I E W   Q U E S T I O N S

1. Briefly describe the four main categories of spending.

2. There are three different ways to interpret the marginal propensity to consume. What are they?

3. List, and briefly explain, the main determinants of consumption spending. Indicate whether a change in each determinant causes a movement along, or a shift of, the consumption–income line.

4. What are the main components of *planned investment* or *investment spending*? How does the definition of actual investment differ from planned investment?

5. What conditions must be satisfied in order for GDP to be at its equilibrium value? Is this equilibrium GDP the same as the economy's potential GDP? Why or why not?

6. Suppose that an increase in government purchases disturbs the economy's short-run equilibrium. Describe what happens as the economy adjusts to the change in spending.

7. What is the expenditure multiplier? How is it calculated, and how is it used?

8. What is an automatic stabilizer? List some automatic stabilizers for the U.S. economy. Which of these stabilizers do you think have gotten stronger, and which weaker, over the past several decades? Why?

9. Compare the macroeconomic role of saving in the short run and in the long run.

## P R O B L E M S   A N D   E X E R C I S E S

1.

| Y | C | I | G | NX |
|---|---|---|---|---|
| 3,000 | 2,500 | 300 | 500 | 200 |
| 4,000 | 3,250 | 300 | 500 | 200 |
| 5,000 | 4,000 | 300 | 500 | 200 |
| 6,000 | 4,750 | 300 | 500 | 200 |
| 7,000 | 5,500 | 300 | 500 | 200 |
| 8,000 | 6,250 | 300 | 500 | 200 |

a. What is the marginal propensity to consume implicit in this data?
b. Plot a 45° line, and then use the data to draw an aggregate expenditure line.
c. What is the equilibrium level of real GDP?

2.

| Y | C | I | G | NX |
|---|---|---|---|---|
| 7,000 | 6,100 | 400 | 1,000 | 500 |
| 8,000 | 6,900 | 400 | 1,000 | 500 |
| 9,000 | 7,700 | 400 | 1,000 | 500 |
| 10,000 | 8,500 | 400 | 1,000 | 500 |
| 11,000 | 9,300 | 400 | 1,000 | 500 |
| 12,000 | 10,100 | 400 | 1,000 | 500 |
| 13,000 | 10,900 | 400 | 1,000 | 500 |

a. What is the marginal propensity to consume implicit in this data?
b. What is the numerical value of the multiplier for this economy?
c. What is the equilibrium level of real GDP?

d.  Suppose that government purchases ($G$) decreased from 1,000 to 400 at each level of income. What would happen to the equilibrium level of real GDP?

3.  Use an aggregate expenditure diagram to show the effect of each of the following changes:
    a.  an increase in autonomous consumption spending due, say, to optimism on the part of consumers
    b.  an increase in U.S. exports
    c.  a decreases in taxes
    d.  an increase in U.S. imports

    In each case, be sure to label the initial equilibrium and the new equilibrium.

4.  What would be the effect on real GDP and total employment of each of the following changes?
    a.  As a result of restrictions on imports into the United States, net exports ($NX$) increase.
    b.  The federal government launches a new program to improve highways, bridges, and airports.
    c.  Banks are offering such high interest rates that consumers decide to save a larger proportion of their incomes.

d.  The growth of Internet retailing leads business firms to purchase more computer hardware and software.

5.  Using the data given in Problem 2, construct a table similar to Table 5 in this chapter.
    a.  Show what would happen in the first five rounds following an increase in investment spending from 400 to 800.
    b.  What would be the ultimate effect of that increase in investment spending?
    c.  How much would households spend on consumption goods in the new equilibrium?

6.  Suppose that households become thriftier—that is, they now wish to save a larger proportion of their disposable income and spend a smaller proportion.
    a.  In the table in Problem 2, which column of data would be affected? How is it affected?
    b.  Draw an aggregate expenditure diagram and show how an increase in saving can be measured in that diagram.
    c.  Use your aggregate expenditure diagram to show how an economy that is initially in short-run equilibrium will respond to an increase in thriftiness.

## C H A L L E N G E   Q U E S T I O N S

1.  Read Appendix 1 (if you have not already done so). Then, suppose that $a = 600$, $b = 0.75$, $T = 400$, $I^P = 600$, $G = 700$, and $NX = 200$. Calculate the equilibrium level of real GDP. Then check that the equilibrium value equals the sum $C + I^P + G + NX$.

2.  The short-run equilibrium condition that $Y = C + I^P + G + NX$ can be reinterpreted as follows. First, subtract $C$ from both sides to get $Y - C = I^P + G + NX$. Then

note that all income not spent on consumption goods is either taxed or saved, so that $Y - C = S + T$. Now combine the two equations to obtain $S + T = I^P + G + NX$.

Construct a diagram with real GDP measured on the horizontal axis. Draw two lines—one for $S + T$ and the other for $I^P + G + NX$. How would you interpret the point where the two lines cross? What would happen if investment spending increased?

## E X P E R I E N T I A L   E X E R C I S E S

1.  Read Jane Katz's "When the economy goes south: What happens during a recession?" available from the Federal Reserve Bank of Boston at *http://www.bos.frb. org/economic/nerr/katz99_3.htm*. Also, re-read the "Using the Theory" section in this chapter. Then use a graph to show your interpretation of the 1990–91 recession, using the ideas you've learned in this chapter.

2.  Business investment spending is an important component of aggregate expenditure. Review the "Business Bulletin" column in the Thursday *Wall Street Journal*. What are some recent trends in investment spending? Are these trends likely to cause an increase or a decrease in aggregate expenditure? (*Note:* Purchases of stocks and bonds are *not* investment in the sense described in this chapter!)

# APPENDIX 1

## FINDING EQUILIBRIUM GDP ALGEBRAICALLY

The chapter showed how we can find equilibrium GDP using tables and graphs. This appendix demonstrates an algebraic way of finding the equilibrium GDP.

Our starting point is the relationship between consumption and disposable income given in the chapter,

$$C = a + bY_D$$

where $a$ represents autonomous consumption spending, and $b$ represents the marginal propensity to consume. Remember that disposable income ($Y_D$) is the income that the household sector has left after taxes. Letting $T$ represent taxes, and $Y$ represent total income or GDP, we have

$$Y_D = Y - T.$$

If we now substitute $Y_D = Y - T$ into $C = a + bY_D$, we get an equation showing consumption at each level of income:

$$C = a + b(Y - T).$$

We can rearrange this equation algebraically to read

$$C = (a - bT) + bY.$$

This is the general equation for the consumption–income line. When graphed, the term in parentheses ($a - bT$) is the vertical intercept, and $b$ is the slope. (Figure 5 shows a specific example of this line in which $a = \$2,000$, $b = 0.6$, and $T = \$2,000$.)

As you've learned, total spending or aggregate expenditure ($AE$) is the sum of consumption spending ($C$), investment spending ($I^p$), government spending ($G$) and net exports ($NX$):

$$AE = C + I^p + G + NX.$$

If we substitute for $C$ the equation $C = (a - bT) + bY$, we get

$$AE = a - bT + bY + I^p + G + NX.$$

Now we can use this equation to find the equilibrium GDP. Equilibrium occurs when output ($Y$) and aggregate expenditure ($AE$) are the same. That is,

$$Y = AE$$

or, substituting the equation for $AE$,

$$Y = a - bT + bY + I^p + G + NX.$$

This last equation will hold true only when $Y$ is at its equilibrium value. We can solve for equilibrium $Y$ by first bringing all terms involving $Y$ to the left-hand side:

$$Y - bY = a - bT + I^p + G + NX.$$

Next, factoring out $Y$, we get

$$Y(1 - b) = a - bT + I^p + G + NX.$$

Finally, dividing both sides of this equation by $(1 - b)$ yields

$$Y = \frac{a - bT + I^p + G + NX}{1 - b}.$$

This last equation shows how equilibrium GDP depends on $a$ (autonomous consumption), $b$ (the MPC), $T$ (taxes), $I^p$ (investment spending), $G$ (government purchases), and $NX$ (net exports). These variables are all determined "outside our model." That is, they are given values that we use to determine equilibrium output, but they are not themselves affected by the level of output. Whenever we use actual numbers for these given variables in the equation, we find the same equilibrium GDP we would find using a table or a graph.

In the example we used throughout the chapter, the given values (found in Tables 1, 2, and 4) are, in billions of dollars, $a = 2,000$; $b = 0.6$; $T = 2,000$; $I^p = 700$; $G = 500$; and $NX = 400$. Plugging these values into the equation for equilibrium GDP, we get

$$Y = \frac{2,000 - (0.6 \times 2,000) + 700 + 500 + 400}{1 - 0.6}$$

$$= \frac{2,400}{0.4}$$

$$= 6,000.$$

This is the same value we found in Table 4 and Figure 8.

# APPENDIX 2

## THE SPECIAL CASE OF THE TAX MULTIPLIER

You learned in this chapter how changes in autonomous consumption, investment, and government purchases affect aggregate expenditure and equilibrium GDP. But there is another type of change that can influence equilibrium GDP: a change in taxes. For this type of change, the formula for the multiplier is slightly different from the one presented in the chapter.

Let's suppose that household taxes ($T$) *decrease* by $1,000 billion. The immediate impact is to increase households' *disposable income* ($Y_D$) by $1,000 billion at the current level of income. As a result, consumption spending will increase. But by how much?

The answer is, *less than* $1,000 billion. When households get a tax cut, they increase their spending *not* by the full amount of the cut, but only by a *part* of it. The amount by which spending initially increases depends on the *MPC*. In our example, in which the *MPC* is 0.6, and disposable income rises by $1,000 billion, the initial change in consumption spending is just $600 billion. *This is the first change in spending that occurs after the tax cut.* Of course, once consumption spending rises, every subsequent round of the multiplier will work just as in Table 5: In the next round, consumption spending will rise by $360 billion, and then $216 billion, and so on.

Now let's compare what happens when taxes are cut by $1,000 billion with what happens when spending rises by $1,000 billion. As you can see from Table 5, when investment rises by $1,000 billion, the initial change in spending is, by definition, $1,000 billion. But when taxes are cut by $1,000 billion, the initial change in spending is *not* $1,000 billion, but *$600 billion*.

Thus, the first line of the table is missing in the case of a $1,000 billion tax cut. All subsequent rounds of the multiplier are the same, however. Therefore, we would expect the $1,000 billion tax cut to cause a $1,500 billion increase in equilibrium GDP—not the $2,500 billion increase listed in the table.

Another way to say this is: For each dollar that taxes are cut, equilibrium GDP will increase by $1.50 rather than $2.50—the increase is one dollar less in the case of the tax cut. This observation tells us that the tax multiplier must have a numerical value *1.0 less than* the spending multiplier of the chapter.

Finally, there is one more difference between the spending multiplier of the chapter and the tax multiplier: While the spending multiplier is a positive number (because an increase in spending causes an increase in equilibrium GDP), the tax multiplier is a negative number, since a tax cut (a negative change in taxes) must be multiplied by a *negative* number to give us a *positive* change in GDP. Putting all this together, we conclude that

*the tax multiplier is 1.0 less than the spending multiplier, and negative in sign.*

Thus, if the *MPC* is 0.6 (as in the chapter), so that the spending multiplier is 2.5, then the tax multiplier will have a value of $-(2.5 - 1) = -1.5$.

More generally, since the tax multiplier is 1.0 less than the spending multiplier and is also negative, we can write

$$\text{Tax multiplier} = -(\text{spending multiplier} - 1).$$

Because the spending multiplier is $1/(1 - MPC)$, we can substitute to get

$$\text{Tax multiplier} = -\left[\frac{1}{1 - MPC} - 1\right]$$

$$= -\frac{1 - (1 - MPC)}{1 - MPC}$$

$$= \frac{-MPC}{1 - MPC}.$$

Hence,

*the general formula for the tax multiplier is*

$$\frac{-MPC}{(1 - MPC)}.$$

For any change in taxes, we can use the formula to find the change in equilibrium GDP as follows:

$$\Delta GDP = \frac{-MPC}{1 - MPC} \times \Delta T .$$

In our example, in which taxes were cut by \$1,000 billion, we have $\Delta T = -\$1,000$ billion and $MPC = 0.6$. Plugging these values into the formula, we obtain

$$\Delta GDP = \left[\frac{-0.6}{1 - 0.6}\right] \times -\$1,000 \text{ billion}$$

$$= \$1,500 \text{ billion}.$$

# THE BANKING SYSTEM AND THE MONEY SUPPLY

Everyone knows that money doesn't grow on trees. But where does it actually come from? You might think that the answer is simple: The government just prints it. Right?

Sort of. It is true that much of our money supply is, indeed, paper currency, provided by our national monetary authority. But most of our money is *not* paper currency at all. Moreover, the monetary authority in the United States—the Federal Reserve System—is technically not a part of the executive, legislative, or judicial branches of government. Rather, it is a quasi-independent agency that operates *alongside* of the government.

In future chapters, we'll make our short-run macro model more realistic by bringing in money and its effects on the economy. This will deepen your understanding of economic fluctuations, and help you understand our policy choices in dealing with them. But in this chapter, we focus on money itself, and the institutions that help create it. We will begin, in the next section, by taking a close look at what money is and how it is measured.

## WHAT COUNTS AS MONEY

Money, loosely defined, is the means of payment in the economy. And as you will learn in the next chapter, the amount of money in circulation can affect the macroeconomy. This is why governments around the world like to know how much money is available to their citizens.

In practice, the standard definition of money is *currency, checking account balances,* and *travelers checks.* What do these have in common and why are they included in the definition of money when other means of payment—such as credit cards—are not included?

First, only *assets*—things of value that people own—are regarded as money. Paper currency, travelers checks, and funds held in checking accounts are all examples of assets. But *the right to borrow* is not considered an asset, so it is not part of the money supply. This is why the credit limit on your credit card, or your ability to go into a bank and borrow money, is not considered part of the money supply.

Second, only things that are widely *acceptable* as a means of payment are regarded as money. Currency, travelers checks, and personal checks can all be used to buy things or pay bills. Other assets—such as the funds in your savings account—cannot generally be used to pay for goods and services, and so they fail the acceptability test.

Finally, only highly *liquid* assets are regarded as money.

**Liquidity** The property of being easily converted into cash.

> An asset is considered **liquid** if it can be converted to cash quickly and at little cost. An illiquid asset, by contrast, can be converted to cash only after a delay, or at considerable cost.

Checking account balances are highly liquid because you can convert them to cash at the ATM or by cashing a check. Travelers checks are also highly liquid. But stocks and bonds are *not* as liquid as checking accounts or travelers checks. Stock- and bondholders must go to some trouble and pay brokers' fees to convert these assets into cash.

## MEASURING THE MONEY STOCK

In practice, governments have several alternative definitions of the money stock. These definitions include a selection of *assets* that are (1) generally acceptable as a means of payment and (2) relatively liquid.

Notice the phrase "*relatively* liquid." This does not sound like a hard and fast rule for measuring the money supply, and indeed it is not. This is why there are different measures of the money supply: Each interprets the phrase "relatively liquid" in a different way. To understand this better, let's look at the different kinds of liquid assets that people can hold.

### ASSETS AND THEIR LIQUIDITY

Figure 1 lists a spectrum of assets, ranked according to their liquidity, along with the amounts of each asset in the U.S. public's hands on January 31, 2000. The most liquid asset of all is **cash in the hands of the public.** It takes no time and zero expense to convert this asset into cash, since it's *already* cash. At the beginning of 2000, the public—including residents of other countries—held about $521 billion in cash.

**Cash in the hands of the public** Currency and coins held outside of banks.

Next in line are three asset categories of about equal liquidity. **Demand deposits** are the checking accounts held by households and business firms at commercial banks, including huge ones like the Bank of America or Citibank, and smaller ones like Simmons National Bank in Arkansas. These checking accounts are called "demand" deposits because when you write a check to someone, that person can go into a bank and, on demand, be paid in cash. This is one reason that demand deposits are considered very liquid: The person who has your check can convert it into cash quickly and easily. Another reason is that you can withdraw cash from your own checking account very easily—24 hours a day with an ATM card, or during banking hours if you want to speak to a teller. As you can see in the figure, the U.S. public held $345 billion in demand deposits in early 2000.

**Demand deposits** Checking accounts that do not pay interest.

*Other checkable deposits* is a catchall category for several types of checking accounts that work very much like demand deposits. This includes *automatic transfers from savings accounts,* which are interest-paying savings accounts that automatically transfer funds into checking accounts when needed. On January 31, 2000, the U.S. public held $242 billion of these types of checkable deposits.

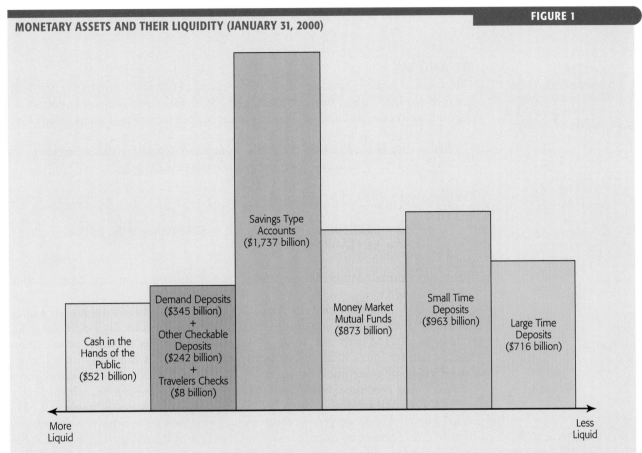

**FIGURE 1**

**MONETARY ASSETS AND THEIR LIQUIDITY (JANUARY 31, 2000)**

Savings Type
Accounts
($1,737 billion)

Demand Deposits
($345 billion)
+
Other Checkable
Deposits
($242 billion)
+
Travelers Checks
($8 billion)

Cash in the
Hands of the
Public
($521 billion)

Money Market
Mutual Funds
($873 billion)

Small Time
Deposits
($963 billion)

Large Time
Deposits
($716 billion)

More
Liquid

Less
Liquid

Assets vary according to their liquidity—the ease with which they can be converted into cash. Assets toward the left side of this figure are more liquid than those toward the right side.

*Travelers checks* are specially printed checks that you can buy from banks or other private companies, like American Express. Travelers checks can be easily spent at almost any hotel or store. You can often cash them at a bank. You need only show an I.D. and countersign the check. In early 2000, the public held about $8 billion in travelers checks.

*Savings-type accounts* at banks and other financial institutions (such as *savings and loan* institutions) amounted to $1,737 billion in early 2000. These are less liquid than checking-type accounts, since they do not allow you to write checks. While it is easy to transfer funds from your savings account to your checking account, you must make the transfer yourself.

Next on the list are deposits in *retail money market mutual funds (MMMFs)*, which use customer deposits to buy a variety of financial assets. Depositors can withdraw their money by writing checks. In early 2000, the general public held about $873 billion in such MMMFs.

*Time deposits* (sometimes called *certificates of deposit,* or *CDs*) require you to keep your money in the bank for a specified period of time (usually six months or longer), and impose an interest penalty if you withdraw early. In January 2000, the public held $963 billion in *small time deposits* (in amounts under $100,000) and $716 billion in *large time deposits* (in amounts over $100,000).

Now let's see how these assets have been used to define "money" in different ways.

## M1 AND M2

**M1** A standard measure of the money supply, including cash in the hands of the public, checking account deposits, and travelers checks.

The standard measure of the money stock is called **M1**. It is the sum of the first four assets in our list: cash in the hands of the public, demand deposits, other checkable deposits, and travelers checks. These are also the four most liquid assets in our list.

> **M1 = cash in the hands of the public + demand deposits + other checking account deposits + travelers checks.**

On January 31, 2000, this amounted to

> **M1 = $521 billion + $345 billion + $242 billion + $8 billion**
> **= $1,116 billion.**

When economists or government officials speak about "the money supply," they usually mean M1.

But what about the assets left out of M1? While savings accounts are not as liquid as any of the components of M1, for most of us there is hardly a difference. All it takes is an ATM card and, *presto*, funds in your savings account become cash. Money market funds held by households and businesses are fairly liquid, even though there are sometimes restrictions or special risks involved in converting them into cash. And even time deposits—if they are not too large—can be cashed in early with only a small interest penalty. When you think of how much "means of payment" you have, you are very likely to include the amounts you have in these types of accounts. This is why another common measure of the money supply, **M2**, adds these and some other types of assets to M1:

**M2** M1 plus savings account balances, noninstitutional money market mutual fund balances, and small time deposits.

> **M2 = M1 + savings-type accounts + retail MMMF balances + small denomination time deposits.**

Using the numbers for January 31, 2000 in the United States:

> **M2 = $1,116 billion + $1,737 billion + $873 billion + $963 billion**
> **= $4,689 billion.**

There are other official measures of the money supply besides M1 and M2 that add in assets that are less liquid than those in M2. But M1 and M2 have been the most popular, and most commonly watched, definitions.

It is important to understand that the M1 and M2 money stock measures exclude many things that people use regularly as a means of payment. Although M1 and M2 give us important information about the activities of the Fed and of banks, they do not measure all the different ways that people hold their wealth or pay for things. Credit cards, for example, are not included in any of the official measures. But for most of us, unused credit is a means of payment, to be lumped together with our cash and our checking accounts. As credit cards were issued to more and more Americans over the last several decades, the available means of payment increased considerably, much more than the increase in M1 and M2 suggests.

Technological advances—now and in the future—will continue the trend toward new and more varied ways to make payments. For example, at the 1996

**http://**

In "The Changing Nature of the Payments System," (http://www. phil.frb.org/files/br/brma00lm.pdf) Loretta Mester explores the effects of technological change on the means of payment.

Olympics, people used electronic cash to make small transactions—smaller than would make sense with credit cards. You could buy a card worth $5, $10, or $20 and use it in place of cash or checks. In 1999, Citibank began testing similar electronic cash cards in the Upper West Side of Manhattan. Electronic cash

> **DANGEROUS CURVES**
>
> In our definitions of money—whether M1, M2, or some other measure—we include cash (coin and paper currency) only if it is *in the hands of the public*. The italicized words are important. Some of the nation's cash is stored in banks' vaults, and is released only when the public withdraws cash from their accounts. Other cash is in the hands of the Federal Reserve, which stores it for future release. But until this cash is released from bank vaults or the Fed, it is *not* part of the money supply. Only the cash possessed by households, businesses, or government agencies (other than the Fed) is considered part of the money supply.

is clearly a means of payment, even though it is not yet included in any measure of the money supply. If electronic cash becomes important in the economy, it will probably be included in M1.

Fortunately, the details and complexities of measuring money are not important for understanding the monetary system and monetary policy. For the rest of our discussion, we will make a simplifying assumption:

> *We will assume the money supply consists of just two components: cash in the hands of the public and demand deposits.*
>
> *Money supply = cash in the hands of public + demand deposits.*

As you will see later, our definition of the money supply corresponds closely to the liquid assets that our national monetary authority—the Federal Reserve—can control. While there is not much that the Federal Reserve can do directly about the amount of funds in savings accounts, MMMFs, or time deposits, or about the development of electronic cash or the ability to borrow on credit cards, it can tightly control the sum of cash in the hands of the public and demand deposits.[1]

We will spend the rest of this chapter analyzing how money is created and what makes the money supply change. Our first step is to introduce a key player in the creation of money: the banking system.

# THE BANKING SYSTEM

Think about the last time you used the services of a bank. Perhaps you deposited a paycheck in the bank's ATM, or withdrew cash to take care of your shopping needs for the week. We make these kinds of transactions dozens of times every year without ever thinking about what a bank really is, or how our own actions at the bank—and the actions of millions of other bank customers—might contribute to a change in the money supply.

## FINANCIAL INTERMEDIARIES

Let's begin at the beginning: What are banks? They are important examples of **financial intermediaries**—business firms that specialize in assembling loanable funds from households and firms whose revenues exceed their expenditures, and channeling those funds to households and firms (and sometimes the government)

**Financial intermediary** A business firm that specializes in brokering between savers and borrowers.

---

[1]   The Fed can also control some other types of checkable deposits. To keep our analysis as simple as possible, we consider only demand deposits.

whose expenditures exceed revenues. Financial intermediaries make the economy work much more efficiently than would be possible without them.

To understand this more clearly, imagine that Boeing, the U.S. aircraft maker, wants to borrow a billion dollars for three years. If there were no financial intermediaries, Boeing would have to make individual arrangements to borrow small amounts of money from thousands—perhaps millions—of households, each of which wants to lend money for, say, three months at a time. Every three months, Boeing would have to renegotiate the loans, and it would find borrowing money in this way to be quite cumbersome. Lenders, too, would find this arrangement troublesome. All of their funds would be lent to one firm. If that firm encountered difficulties, the funds might not be returned at the end of three months.

An intermediary helps to solve these problems by combining a large number of small savers' funds into custom-designed packages and then lending them to larger borrowers. The intermediary can do this because it can predict—from experience—the pattern of inflows of funds. While some deposited funds may be withdrawn, the overall total available for lending tends to be quite stable. The intermediary can also reduce the risk to depositors by spreading its loans among a number of different borrowers. If one borrower fails to repay its loan, that will have only a small effect on the intermediary and its depositors.

Of course, intermediaries must earn a profit for providing brokering services. They do so by charging a higher interest rate on the funds they lend than the rate they pay to depositors. But they are so efficient at brokering that both lenders and borrowers benefit. Lenders earn higher interest rates, with lower risk and greater liquidity, than if they had to deal directly with the ultimate users of funds. And borrowers end up paying lower interest rates on loans that are specially designed for their specific purposes.

The United States boasts a wide variety of financial intermediaries, including commercial banks, savings and loan associations, mutual savings banks, credit unions, insurance companies, and some government agencies. Some of these intermediaries—called *depository institutions*—accept deposits from the general public and lend the deposits to borrowers. There are four types of depository institutions:

1. *Savings and loan associations (S&Ls)* obtain funds through their customers' time, savings, and checkable deposits and use them primarily to make mortgage loans.
2. *Mutual savings banks* accept deposits (called *shares*) and use them primarily to make mortgage loans. They differ from S&Ls because they are owned by their depositors, rather than outside investors.
3. *Credit unions* specialize in working with particular groups of people, such as members of a labor union or employees in a specific field of business. They acquire funds through their members' deposits and make consumer and mortgage loans to other members.
4. *Commercial banks* are the largest group of depository institutions. They obtain funds mainly by issuing checkable deposits, savings deposits, and time deposits and use the funds to make business, mortgage, and consumer loans.

Since commercial banks will play a central role in the rest of this chapter, let's take a closer look at how they operate.

## COMMERCIAL BANKS

A commercial bank (or just "bank" for short) is a private corporation, owned by its stockholders, that provides services to the public. For our purposes, the most important service is to provide checking accounts, which enable the bank's customers to pay bills and make purchases without holding large amounts of cash that could be lost or stolen. Checks are one of the most important means of payment in the economy. Every year, U.S. households and businesses write trillions of dollars' worth of checks to pay their bills, and many wage and salary earners have their pay deposited directly into their checking accounts. And as you saw in Figure 1, the public holds about as much money in the form of demand deposits and other checking-type accounts as it holds in cash.

Banks provide checking account services in order to earn a profit. Where does a bank's profit come from? Mostly from lending out the funds that people deposit and charging interest on the loans, but also by charging for some services directly, such as check-printing fees or that annoying dollar or so sometimes charged for using an ATM.

## A BANK'S BALANCE SHEET

We can understand more clearly how a bank works by looking at its *balance sheet,* a tool used by accountants. A **balance sheet** is a two-column list that provides information about the financial condition of a bank at a particular point in time. In one column, the bank's *assets* are listed—everything of value that it *owns.* On the other side, the bank's *liabilities* are listed—the amounts that the bank *owes.*

**Balance sheet** A financial statement showing assets, liabilities, and net worth at a point in time.

Table 1 shows a simplified version of a commercial bank's balance sheet.

Why does the bank have these assets and liabilities? Let's start with the assets side. The first item, $20 million, is the value of the bank's real estate—the buildings and the land underneath them. This is the easiest to explain, because a bank must have one or more branch offices in order to do business with the public.

Next, comes $25 million in *bonds,* and $65 million in *loans.* **Bonds** are IOUs issued by a corporation or a government agency when it borrows money. A bond promises to pay back the loan either gradually (e.g., each month), or all at once at some future date. **Loans** are IOUs signed by households or noncorporate businesses. Examples are auto loans, student loans, small business loans, and home mortgages (where the funds lent out are used to buy a home). Both bonds and loans generate interest income for the bank.

**Bond** An IOU issued by a corporation or government agency when it borrows funds.

**Loan** An IOU issued by a household or noncorporate business when it borrows funds.

Next come two categories that might seem curious: $2 million in "vault cash," and $8 million in "accounts with the Federal Reserve." Vault cash, just like it sounds, is the coin and currency that the bank has stored in its vault. In addition, banks maintain their own accounts with the Federal Reserve, and they add and

| Assets | | Liabilities and Net Worth | |
|---|---|---|---|
| Property and buildings | $ 20 million | Demand deposit liabilities | $100 million |
| Government and corporate bonds | $ 25 million | Net worth | $ 20 million |
| Loans | $ 65 million | | |
| Cash in vault | $ 2 million | | |
| In accounts with the Federal Reserve | $ 8 million | | |
| Total Assets | $120 million | Total Liabilities plus Net Worth | $120 million |

**TABLE 1**

**A TYPICAL COMMERCIAL BANK'S BALANCE SHEET**

subtract to these accounts when they make transactions with other banks. Neither vault cash nor accounts with the Federal Reserve pay interest. Why, then, does the bank hold them? After all, a profit-seeking bank should want to hold as much of its assets as possible in income-earning form—bonds and loans.

There are two explanations for vault cash and accounts with the Federal Reserve. First, on any given day, some of the bank's customers might want to withdraw more cash than other customers are depositing. The bank must always be prepared to honor its obligations for withdrawals, so it must have some cash on hand to meet these requirements. This explains why it holds vault cash.

**Reserves** Vault cash plus balances held at the Fed.

Second, banks are required by law to hold **reserves,** which are defined as *the sum of cash in the vault and accounts with the Federal Reserve.* The amount of reserves a bank must hold is called **required reserves.** The more funds its customers hold in their checking accounts, the greater the amount of required reserves. The **required reserve ratio,** set by the Federal Reserve, tells banks the fraction of their checking accounts that they must hold as required reserves.

**Required reserves** The minimum amount of reserves a bank must hold, depending on the amount of its deposit liabilities.

For example, the bank in Table 1 has $100 million in demand deposits. If the required reserve ratio is 0.1, this bank's required reserves are $0.1 \times \$100$ million $=$ $10 million in reserves. The bank must hold *at least* this amount of its assets as reserves. Since our bank has $2 million in vault cash, and $8 million in its *reserve account* with the Federal Reserve, it has a total of $10 million in reserves, the minimum required amount.

**Required reserve ratio** The minimum fraction of checking account balances that banks must hold as reserves.

Now skip to the right side of the balance sheet. This bank's only liability is its demand deposits. Why are demand deposits a *liability*? Because the bank's customers have the right to withdraw funds from their checking accounts. Until they do, the bank *owes* them these funds.

Finally, the last entry. When we total up both sides of the bank's balance sheet, we find that it has $120 million in assets, and only $100 million in liabilities. If the bank were to go out of business, selling all of its assets and using the proceeds to pay off all of its liabilities (its demand deposits), it would have $20 million left over. Who would get this $20 million? The bank's owners—its stockholders. The $20 million is called the bank's **net worth.** More generally,

**Net worth** The difference between assets and liabilities.

$$\text{Net worth} = \text{Total assets} - \text{Total liabilities.}$$

We include net worth on the liabilities side of the balance sheet because it is, in a sense, what the bank would owe to its owners if it went out of business. Notice that, because of the way net worth is defined, both sides of a balance sheet must always have the same total: *A balance sheet always balances.*

Private banks are just one of the players that help determine the money supply. Now we turn our attention to the other key player—the Federal Reserve System.

## THE FEDERAL RESERVE SYSTEM

**Central bank** A nation's principal monetary authority.

Every large nation controls its banking system with a **central bank.** Most of the developed countries established their central banks long ago. For example, England's central bank—the Bank of England—was created in 1694. France was one of the latest in Europe, waiting until 1800 to establish the Banque de France. But the United States was even later. Although we experimented with central banks at various times in our history, we did not get serious about a central bank until 1913, when Congress established the *Federal Reserve System.*

## THE GEOGRAPHY OF THE FEDERAL RESERVE SYSTEM

FIGURE 2

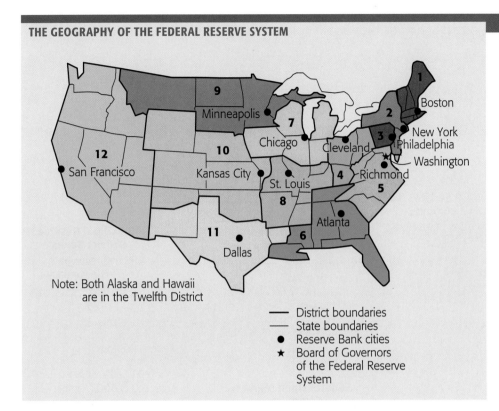

Note: Both Alaska and Hawaii are in the Twelfth District

— District boundaries
— State boundaries
● Reserve Bank cities
★ Board of Governors of the Federal Reserve System

The United States is divided into 12 Federal Reserve districts, each with its own Federal Reserve Bank.

Why did it take the United States so long to create a central bank? Part of the reason is the suspicion of central authority that has always been part of U.S. politics and culture. Another reason is the large size and extreme diversity of our country, and the fear that a powerful central bank might be dominated by the interests of one region to the detriment of others. These special American characteristics help explain why our own central bank is different in form from its European counterparts.

One major difference is indicated in the very name of the institution—the Federal Reserve System. It does not have the word "central" or "bank" anywhere in its title, making it less suggestive of centralized power.

Another difference is the way the system is organized. Instead of a single central bank, the United States is divided into 12 Federal Reserve districts, each one served by its own Federal Reserve Bank. The 12 districts and the Federal Reserve Banks that serve them are shown in Figure 2. For example, the Federal Reserve Bank of Dallas serves a district consisting of Texas and parts of New Mexico and Louisiana, while the Federal Reserve Bank of Chicago serves a district including Iowa and parts of Illinois, Indiana, Wisconsin, and Michigan.

Another interesting feature of the Federal Reserve System is its peculiar status within the government. Strictly speaking, it is not even a *part* of any branch of government. But the *Fed* (as the system is commonly called) was created by Congress, and could be eliminated by Congress if it so desired. Second, both the president and Congress exert some influence on the Fed through their appointments of key officials in the system. Finally, the Fed's mission is not to make a profit like an ordinary corporation, but rather to serve the general public.

The Federal Open Market Committee meets in this room, inside the Fed's headquarters in Washington DC. The meetings are highly secretive. No one from the media, and no one representing Congress or the President, is permitted in the room during the meetings.

Principal decision-making power at the Fed is vested in the Board of Governors, who are appointed by the president and confirmed by the Senate. Monetary policy is set by the Federal Open Market Committee, which consists of the 7 governors plus 5 of the presidents of Federal Reserve Banks.

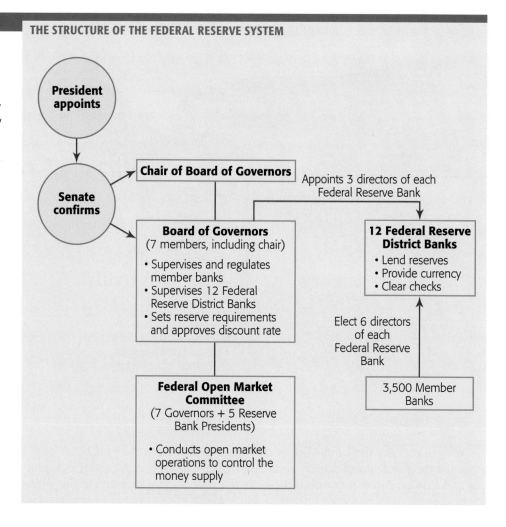

**THE STRUCTURE OF THE FEDERAL RESERVE SYSTEM**

## THE STRUCTURE OF THE FED

Figure 3 shows the organizational structure of the Federal Reserve System. Near the top is the Board of Governors, consisting of seven members who are appointed by the president and confirmed by the Senate for a 14-year term. The most powerful person at the Fed is the chairman of the Board of Governors—one of the seven governors who is appointed by the president, with Senate approval, to a four-year term as chair. In order to keep any president or Congress from having too much influence over the Fed, the four-year term of the chair is *not* coterminous with the four-year term of the president. As a result, every newly elected president inherits the Fed chair appointed by his predecessor, and may have to wait several years before making an appointment of his own.

Each of the 12 Federal Reserve Banks is supervised by nine directors, three of whom are appointed by the Board of Governors. The other six are elected by private commercial banks—the official stockholders of the system. The directors of each Federal Reserve Bank choose a president of that bank, who manages its day-to-day operations.

Notice that Figure 3 refers to "member banks." Only about 3,500 of the 9,000 or so commercial banks in the United States are members of the Federal Reserve

System. But they include all 2,500 *national banks* (those chartered by the federal government) and about 1,000 *state banks* (chartered by their state governments). All of the largest banks in the United States (e.g., Citibank, Bank of America, and BankBoston) are nationally chartered banks and therefore member banks as well.

## THE FEDERAL OPEN MARKET COMMITTEE
Finally, we come to what most economists regard as the most important part of the Fed—the **Federal Open Market Committee (FOMC)**. As you can see in Figure 3, the FOMC consists of all 7 governors of the Fed, along with 5 of the 12 district bank presidents.[2] The committee meets about eight times a year to discuss current trends in inflation, unemployment, output, interest rates, and international exchange rates. After determining the current state of the economy, the FOMC sets the general course for the nation's money supply.

**Federal Open Market Committee** A committee of Federal Reserve officials that establishes U.S. monetary policy.

The word "open" in the FOMC's name is ironic, since the committee's deliberations are private. Summaries of its meetings are published only after a delay of a month or more. In some cases, the committee will release a brief public statement about its decisions on the day they are made. But not even the president of the United States knows the details behind the decisions, or what the FOMC actually discussed at its meeting, until the summary of the meeting is finally released. The reason for the word "open" is that the committee exerts control over the nation's money supply by buying and selling bonds in the public ("open") bond market. Later, we will discuss how and why the FOMC does this.

## THE FUNCTIONS OF THE FEDERAL RESERVE
The Federal Reserve, as the overseer of the nation's monetary system, has a variety of important responsibilities. Some of the most important are:

**Supervising and Regulating Banks.** We've already seen that the Fed sets and enforces reserve requirements, which all banks—not just Fed members—must obey. The Fed also sets standards for establishing new banks, determines what sorts of loans and investments banks are allowed to make, and closely monitors banks' financial activities.

**Acting as a "Bank for Banks."** Commercial banks use the Fed in much the same way that ordinary citizens use commercial banks. For example, we've already seen that banks hold most of their reserves in reserve accounts with the Fed. In addition, banks can borrow from the Fed, just as we can borrow from our local bank. The Fed charges a special interest rate, called the **discount rate,** on loans that it makes to member banks. In times of financial crisis, the Fed is prepared to act as *lender of last resort,* to make sure that banks have enough reserves to meet their obligations to depositors.

**Discount rate** The interest rate the Fed charges on loans to banks.

**Issuing Paper Currency.** The Fed doesn't actually *print* currency; that is done by the government's Bureau of Engraving and Printing. But once printed, it is shipped to the Fed (under *very* heavy guard). The Fed, in turn, puts this currency

---

[2]    Although all Reserve Bank presidents attend FOMC meetings, only 5 of the 12 presidents can vote on FOMC decisions. The president of the Federal Reserve Bank of New York has a permanent vote because New York is such an important financial center. But the remaining four votes rotate among the other district presidents.

into circulation. This is why every U.S. bill carries the label *Federal Reserve Note* on the top.

**Check Clearing.**   Suppose you write a check for $500 to pay your rent. Your building's owner will deposit the check into *his* checking account, which is probably at a different bank than yours. Somehow, your rent payment must be transferred from your bank account to your landlord's account at the other bank—a process called *check clearing*. In some cases, the services are provided by private clearinghouses. But in many other cases—especially for clearing out-of-town checks—the Federal Reserve system performs the service by transferring funds from one bank's reserve account to another's.

**Controlling the Money Supply.**   The Fed, as the nation's monetary authority, is responsible for controlling the money supply. Since this function is so important in macroeconomics, we explore it in detail in the next section.

# THE FED AND THE MONEY SUPPLY

Suppose the Fed wants to change the nation's money supply. (*Why* would the Fed want to do this? The answer will have to wait until the next chapter.) There are many ways this could be done. To increase the money supply, the Fed could print up currency and give it to Fed officials, letting them spend it as they wish. Or it could hold a lottery and give all of the newly printed money to the winner. To decrease the money supply, the Fed could require that all citizens turn over a portion of their cash to Fed officials who would then feed it into paper shredders.

These and other methods would certainly work, but they hardly seem fair or orderly. In practice, the Fed uses a more organized, less haphazard method to change the money supply: *open market operations*.

> When the Fed wishes to increase or decrease the money supply, it buys or sells government bonds *to bond dealers, banks, or other financial institutions. These actions are called* **open market operations.**

**Open market operations**  Purchases or sales of bonds by the Federal Reserve System.

We'll make two special assumptions to keep our analysis of open market operations simple for now.

1.  Households and businesses are satisfied holding the amount of cash they are currently holding. Any additional funds they might acquire are deposited in their checking accounts. Any decrease in their funds comes from their checking accounts.
2.  Banks never hold reserves in excess of those legally required by law.

Later, we'll discuss what happens when these simplifying assumptions do not hold. We'll also assume that the required reserve ratio is 0.1, so that each time deposits rise by $1,000 at a bank, its required reserves rise by $100.

## HOW THE FED INCREASES THE MONEY SUPPLY

To increase the money supply, the Fed will *buy* government bonds. This is called an *open market purchase*. Suppose the Fed buys a government bond worth $1,000 from Salomon Brothers, a bond dealer that has a checking account at First National

Bank.[3] The Fed will pay Salomon Brothers with a $1,000 check, which the firm will deposit into its account at First National. First National, in turn, will send the check to the Fed, which will credit First National's reserve account by $1,000.

These actions will change First National's balance sheet as follows:

**CHANGES IN FIRST NATIONAL BANK'S BALANCE SHEET**

| Action | Changes in Assets | Changes in Liabilities |
|---|---|---|
| Fed buys $1,000 bond from Salomon Brothers, which deposits $1,000 check from Fed into its checking account. | +$1,000 in reserves | +$1,000 in demand deposits |

Notice that here we show only *changes* in First National's balance sheet. Other balance-sheet items—such as property and buildings, loans, government bonds, or net worth—are not immediately affected by the open market purchase, so they are not listed here. As you can see, First National gains an asset—reserves—so we enter "+$1,000 in reserves" on the left side of the table. But there are also additional liabilities—the $1,000 that is now in Salomon Brothers' checking account and which First National owes to that firm. The additional liabilities are represented by the entry "+$1,000 in demand deposits" on the right side. Since First National's balance sheet was in balance before Salomon Brothers' deposit, and since assets and liabilities both grew by the same amount—$1,000—we know that the balance sheet is still in balance. Total assets are again equal to total liabilities plus net worth.

Before we go on, let's take note of two important things that have happened. First, the Fed, by conducting an open market purchase, has injected *reserves* into the banking system. So far, these reserves are being held by First National, in its reserve account with the Fed.

The second thing to notice is something that is easy to miss: *The money supply has increased.* How do we know? Because demand deposits are part of the money supply, and they have increased by $1,000. As you are about to see, even more demand deposits will be created before our story ends.

To see what will happen next, let's take the point of view of First National Bank's manager. He might reason as follows: "My demand deposits have just increased by $1,000. Since the required reserve ratio is 0.1, I must now hold 0.1 × $1,000 = $100 in additional reserves. But my *actual* reserves have gone up by more than $100; in fact, they have gone up by $1,000. Therefore, I have **excess reserves**—reserves above those I'm legally required to hold—equal to $1,000 − $100, or $900. Since these excess reserves are earning no interest, I should lend them out." Thus, we can expect First National, in its search for profit, to lend out $900 at the going rate of interest.

**Excess reserves** Reserves in excess of required reserves.

How will First National actually make the loan? It could lend out $900 in *cash* from its vault. It would be more typical, however, for the bank to issue a $900 *check* to the borrower. When the borrower deposits the $900 check into his own bank account (at some other bank), the Federal Reserve—which keeps track of these transactions for the banking system—will deduct $900 from First National's reserve account and transfer it to the other bank's reserve account. This will cause a further change in First National's balance sheet, as follows:

---

[3]  We'll limit our analysis to commercial banks, which hold demand deposits, although our story would be similar if other types of depository institutions were involved.

**CHANGES IN FIRST NATIONAL BANK'S BALANCE SHEET**

| Action | Changes in Assets | Changes in Liabilities |
|---|---|---|
| Fed buys $1,000 bond from Salomon Brothers, which deposits $1,000 check from Fed into its checking account. | +$1,000 in reserves | +$1,000 in demand deposits |
| First National lends out $900 in excess reserves. | **−$900 in reserves** **+$900 in loans** | |
| The total effect on First National from beginning to end. | +$100 in reserves +$900 in loans | +$1,000 in demand deposits |

Look at the boldface entries in the table. By making the loan, First National has given up an asset—$900 in reserves. This causes assets to change by −$900. But First National also gains an asset of equal value—the $900 loan. (Remember: While loans are liabilities to the borrower, they are assets to banks.) This causes assets to change by +$900. Both of these changes are seen on the assets side of the balance sheet.

Now look at the bottom row of the table. This tells us what has happened to First National from beginning to end. We see that, after making its loan, First National has $100 more in reserves than it started with, and $900 more in loans, for a total of $1,000 more in assets. But it also has $1,000 more in liabilities than it had before—the additional demand deposits that it owes to Salomon Brothers. Both assets and liabilities have gone up by the same amount. Notice, too, that First National is once again holding exactly the reserves it must legally hold. It now has $1,000 more in demand deposits than it had before, and it is holding $0.1 \times \$1,000 = \$100$ more in reserves than before. First National is finished ("loaned up") and cannot lend out any more reserves.

But there is still more to our story. Let's suppose that First National lends the $900 to the owner of a local business, Paula's Pizza, and that Paula deposits her loan check into *her* bank account at Second Federal Bank. Then, remembering that the Fed will transfer $900 in reserves from First National's reserve account to that of Second Federal, we'll see the following changes in Second Federal's balance sheet:

**CHANGES IN SECOND FEDERAL'S BALANCE SHEET**

| Action | Changes in Assets | Changes in Liabilities |
|---|---|---|
| Paula deposits $900 loan check into her checking account. | +$900 in reserves | +$900 in demand deposits |

Second Federal now has $900 more in assets—the increase in its reserve account with the Federal Reserve—and $900 in additional liabilities—the amount added to Paula's checking account.

Now consider Second Federal's situation from its manager's viewpoint. He reasons as follows: "My demand deposits have risen by $900, which means my required reserves have risen by $0.1 \times \$900 = \$90$. But my reserves have *actually* increased by $900. Thus, I have *excess reserves* of $\$900 - \$90 = \$810$, which I will lend out." After making the $810 loan, Second Federal's balance sheet will change once again (look at the boldface entries):

**CHANGES IN SECOND FEDERAL'S BALANCE SHEET**

| Action | Changes in Assets | Changes in Liabilities |
|---|---|---|
| Paula deposits $900 loan check into her checking account. | +$900 in reserves | +$900 in demand deposits |
| Second Federal lends out $810 in excess reserves. | −$810 in reserves<br>+$810 in loans | |
| The total effect on Second Federal from beginning to end. | +$ 90 in reserves<br>+$810 in loans | +$900 in demand deposits |

In the end, as you can see in the bottom row of the table, Second Federal has $90 more in reserves than it started with, and $810 more in loans. Its demand deposit liabilities have increased by $900. Notice, too, that the money supply has increased once again—this time, by $900.

Are you starting to see a pattern? Let's carry it through one more step. Whoever borrowed the $810 from Second Federal will put it into his or her checking account at, say, Third State Bank. This will give Third State excess reserves that it will lend out. As a result, its balance sheet will change as shown.

**CHANGES IN THIRD STATE'S BALANCE SHEET**

| Action | Changes in Assets | Changes in Liabilities |
|---|---|---|
| Borrower from Second Federal deposits $810 loan check into checking account. | +$810 in reserves | +$810 in demand deposits |
| Third State lends out $729 in excess reserves. | −$729 in reserves<br>+$729 in loans | |
| The total effect on Third State from beginning to end. | +$ 81 in reserves<br>+$729 in loans | +$810 in demand deposits |

As you can see, demand deposits increase each time a bank lends out excess reserves. In the end, they will increase by a *multiple* of the original $1,000 in reserves injected into the banking system by the open market purchase. Does this process sound familiar? It should. It is very similar to the explanation of the *expenditure multiplier* in the previous chapter, where in each round, an increase in spending led to an increase in income, which caused spending to increase again in the next round. Here, instead of spending, it is the *money supply*—or more specifically, *demand deposits*—that increase in each round.

## THE DEMAND DEPOSIT MULTIPLIER

By how much will demand deposits increase in total? If you look back at the balance sheet changes we've analyzed, you'll see that each bank creates less in demand deposits than the bank before. When Salomon Brothers deposited its $1,000 check from the Fed at First National, $1,000 in demand deposits was created. This led to an additional $900 in demand deposits created by Second Federal, another $810 created by Third State, and so on. In each round, a bank lent 90 percent of the deposit it received. Eventually the additional demand deposits will become so small that we can safely ignore them. When the process is complete, how much in additional demand deposits have been created?

| TABLE 2 | | | |
|---|---|---|---|
| **CUMULATIVE INCREASES IN DEMAND DEPOSITS AFTER A $1,000 CASH DEPOSIT** | **Round** | **Additional Demand Deposits Created by This Bank** | **Additional Demand Deposits Created by All Banks** |
| | First National Bank | $1,000 | $ 1,000 |
| | Second Federal | $ 900 | $ 1,900 |
| | Third State | $ 810 | $ 2,710 |
| | Bank 4 | $ 729 | $ 3,439 |
| | Bank 5 | $ 656 | $ 4,095 |
| | Bank 6 | $ 590 | $ 4,685 |
| | Bank 7 | $ 531 | $ 5,216 |
| | Bank 8 | $ 478 | $ 5,694 |
| | Bank 9 | $ 430 | $ 6,124 |
| | Bank 10 | $ 387 | $ 6,511 |
| | Bank 11 | $ 349 | $ 6,860 |
| | Bank 12 | $ 314 | $ 7,174 |
| | . . . | | |
| | All Other Banks | very close to $2,826 | |
| | Total | | $10,000 |

Table 2 provides the answer. Each row of the table shows the additional demand deposits created at each bank, as well as the running total. The last row shows that, in the end, $10,000 in new demand deposits has been created.

Let's go back and summarize what happened in our example. The Fed, through its open market purchase, injected $1,000 of reserves into the banking system. As a result, demand deposits rose by $10,000—10 times the injection in reserves. As you can verify, if the Fed had injected twice the amount of reserves ($2,000), demand deposits would have increased by 10 times *that* amount ($20,000). In fact, *whatever* the injection of reserves, demand deposits will increase by a factor of 10, so we can write

$$\Delta DD = 10 \times \text{reserve injection}$$

where "*DD*" stands for demand deposits. The injection of reserves must be *multiplied by* the number 10 in order to get the change in demand deposits that it causes. For this reason, 10 is called the *demand deposit multiplier* in this example.

**Demand deposit multiplier** The number by which a change in reserves is multiplied to determine the resulting change in demand deposits.

> The **demand deposit multiplier** *is the number by which we must multiply the injection of reserves to get the total change in demand deposits.*

The size of the demand deposit multiplier depends on the value of the required reserve ratio set by the Fed. If you look back at Table 2, you will see that each round of additional deposit creation would have been smaller if the required reserve ratio had been larger. For example, with a required reserve ratio of 0.2 instead of 0.1, Second Federal would have created only $800 in deposits, Third State would have created only $640, and so on. The result would have been a smaller cumulative change in deposits, and a smaller multiplier.

Now let's derive the formula we can use to determine the demand deposit multiplier for *any* required reserve ratio. We'll start with our example in which the required reserve ratio is 0.1. If $1,000 in reserves is injected into the system, the total change in deposits can be written as follows:

$$\Delta DD = \$1,000 + \$900 + \$810 + \$729 + \ldots$$

Factoring out $1,000, this becomes

$$\Delta DD = \$1,000 \times [1 + 0.9 + 0.9^2 + 0.9^3 + \ldots]$$

In this equation, $1,000 is the initial injection of reserves ($\Delta$reserves), and 0.9 is the fraction of reserves that each bank loans out, which is 1 minus the required reserve ratio (1 − 0.1 = 0.9). To find the change in deposits that applies to *any* change in reserves and *any* required reserve ratio (*RRR*), we can write

$$\Delta DD = \Delta \text{Reserves} \times [1 + (1 - RRR) + (1 - RRR)^2 + (1 - RRR)^3 + \ldots]$$

Now we can see that the term in brackets—the infinite sum $1 + (1 - RRR) + (1 - RRR)^2 + (1 - RRR)^3 + \ldots$—is our demand deposit multiplier. But what is its value?

Recall from the last chapter that an infinite sum

$$1 + H + H^2 + H^3 + \ldots$$

always has the value $1/(1 - H)$ as long as $H$ is a fraction between zero and 1. In the last chapter, we replaced $H$ with the MPC to get the expenditure multiplier. But here, we will replace $H$ with $1 - RRR$ (which is always between zero and 1) to obtain a value for the deposit multiplier of $1/[1 - (1 - RRR)] = 1/RRR$.

> For *any value of the required reserve ratio* (RRR), *the formula for the demand deposit multiplier is* 1/RRR.

In our example, the *RRR* was equal to 0.1, so the deposit multiplier had the value $1/0.1 = 10$. If the *RRR* had been 0.2 instead, the deposit multiplier would have been equal to $1/0.2 = 5$.

Using our general formula for the demand deposit multiplier, we can restate what happens when the Fed injects reserves into the banking system as follows:

$$\Delta DD = \left(\frac{1}{RRR}\right) \times \Delta \text{Reserves}.$$

Since we've been assuming that the amount of cash in the hands of the public (the other component of the money supply) does not change, we can also write

$$\Delta \text{Money Supply} = \left(\frac{1}{RRR}\right) \times \Delta \text{Reserves}.$$

## THE FED'S INFLUENCE ON THE BANKING SYSTEM AS A WHOLE

We can also look at what happened to total demand deposits and the money supply from another perspective. When the Fed bought the $1,000 bond from Salomon Brothers, it injected $1,000 of reserves into the banking system. That was the only increase in reserves that occurred in our story. Where did the additional $1,000 in reserves end up? If you go back through the changes in balance sheets, you'll see that First National ended up with $100 in additional reserves, Second Federal ended up with $90, Third Savings with $81, and so on. Each of these banks is required to hold more reserves than initially, because its demand deposits have increased. In the end, *the additional $1,000 in reserves will be distributed among different banks in the system as required reserves.*

> *After an injection of reserves, the demand deposit multiplier stops working—and the money supply stops increasing—only when all the reserves injected are being held by banks as* required *reserves.*

This observation helps us understand the demand deposit multiplier in another way. In our example, the deposit-creation process will continue until the entire injection of $1,000 in reserves becomes *required* reserves. But with a *RRR* of 0.1, each dollar of reserves entitles a bank to have $10 in demand deposits. Therefore, by injecting $1,000 of reserves into the system, the Fed has enabled banks, in total, to hold $10,000 in additional demand deposits. Only when $10,000 in deposits has been created will the process come to an end.

Just as we've looked at balance sheet changes for each bank, we can also look at the change in the balance sheet of the *entire banking system*. The Fed's open market purchase of $1,000 has caused the following changes:

**CHANGES IN THE BALANCE SHEET OF THE ENTIRE BANKING SYSTEM**

| Changes in Assets | Changes in Liabilities |
|---|---|
| +$1,000 in reserves<br>+$9,000 in loans | +$10,000 in demand deposits |

In the end, total reserves in the system have increased by $1,000—the amount of the open market purchase. Each dollar in reserves supports $10 in demand deposits, so we know that total deposits have increased by $10,000. Finally, we know that a balance sheet always balances. Since liabilities increased by $10,000, loans must have increased by $9,000 to increase total assets (loans and reserves) by $10,000.

**DANGEROUS CURVES**

Demand deposits are a means of payment, and banks create them. This is why we say that banks "create deposits" and "create money." But don't fall into the trap of thinking that banks create *wealth*. No one gains any additional wealth as a result of money creation.

To see why, think about what happened in our story when Salomon Brothers deposited the $1,000 check from the Fed into its account at First National. *Salomon Brothers* was no wealthier: It gave up a $1,000 check from the Fed and ended up with $1,000 more in its checking account, for a net gain of zero. Similarly, the *bank* gained no additional wealth: It had $1,000 more in cash, but it also *owed* Salomon Brothers $1,000—once again, a net gain of zero.

The same conclusion holds for any other step in the money-creation process. When Paula borrows $900 and deposits it into her checking account at Second Federal, she is no wealthier: She has $900 more in her account, but owes $900 to First National. And once again, the bank is no wealthier: It has $900 more in demand deposits, but owes this money to Paula.

Always remember that while banks can "create money," they cannot create wealth.

## HOW THE FED DECREASES THE MONEY SUPPLY

Just as the Fed can increase the money supply by purchasing government bonds, it can also *decrease* the money supply by *selling* government bonds—an *open market sale.*

Where does the Fed get the government bonds to sell? It has trillions of dollars' worth of government bonds from open market *purchases* it has conducted in the past. Since, on average, the Fed tends to increase the money supply each year, it conducts more open market purchases than open market sales, and its stock of bonds keeps growing. So we needn't worry that the Fed will run out of bonds to sell.

Suppose the Fed sells a $1,000 government bond to a bond dealer, Merrill Lynch, which—like Salomon Brothers in our earlier example—has a checking account at First National Bank. Merrill Lynch pays the Fed for the bond with a $1,000 check drawn on its account at First National. When the Fed gets Merrill Lynch's check, it will present the check to First National and deduct $1,000 from First National's reserve account. In turn, First National will deduct $1,000 from Merrill Lynch's checking account.

After all of this has taken place, First National's balance sheet will show the following changes:

**CHANGES IN FIRST NATIONAL BANK'S BALANCE SHEET**

| Action | Changes in Assets | Changes in Liabilities |
|---|---|---|
| Fed sells $1,000 bond to Merrill Lynch, which pays with a $1,000 check drawn on First National. | −$1,000 in reserves | −$1,000 in demand deposits |

Now First National has a problem. Since its demand deposits have decreased by $1,000, it can legally decrease its reserves by 10 percent of that, or $100. But its reserves have *actually* decreased by $1,000, which is $900 more than they are allowed to decrease. First National has *deficient reserves*—reserves smaller than those it is legally required to hold. How can it get the additional reserves it needs?

First National will have to *call in a loan*—that is, ask for repayment—in the amount of $900.[4] A loan is usually repaid with a check drawn on some other bank. When First National gets this check, the Federal Reserve will add $900 to its reserve account, and deduct $900 from the reserve account at the other bank. This is how First National brings its reserves up to the legal requirement. After it calls in the $900 loan, First National's balance sheet will change as follows:

**CHANGES IN FIRST NATIONAL BANK'S BALANCE SHEET**

| Action | Changes in Assets | Changes in Liabilities |
|---|---|---|
| Fed sells $1,000 bond to Merrill Lynch, which pays with a $1,000 check drawn on First National. | −$1,000 in reserves | −$1,000 in demand deposits |
| First National calls in loans worth $900. | +$ 900 in reserves<br>−$ 900 in loans | |
| The total effect on First National from beginning to end. | −$ 100 in reserves<br>−$ 900 in loans | −$1,000 in demand deposits |

Look at the boldfaced terms. After First National calls in the loan, the composition of its assets will change: $900 more in reserves, and $900 less in loans. The

---

[4] In reality, bank loans are for specified time periods, and a bank cannot actually demand that a loan be repaid early. But most banks have a large volume of loans outstanding, with some being repaid each day. Typically, the funds will be lent out again the very same day they are repaid. But a bank that needs additional reserves will simply reduce its rate of new lending on that day, thereby reducing its total amount of loans outstanding. This has the same effect as "calling in a loan."

last row of the table shows the changes to First National's balance sheet from beginning to end. Compared to its initial situation, First National has $100 less in reserves (it lost $1,000 and then gained $900), $900 less in loans, and $1,000 less in demand deposits.

As you might guess, this is not the end of the story. Remember that whoever paid back the loan to First National did so by a check drawn on another bank. That other bank, which we'll call Second United Bank, will lose $900 in reserves and experience the following changes in its balance sheet:

**CHANGES IN SECOND UNITED BANK'S BALANCE SHEET**

| Action | Changes in Assets | Changes in Liabilities |
|---|---|---|
| Someone with an account at Second United Bank writes a $900 check to First National. | −$900 in reserves | −$900 in demand deposits |

Now Second United Bank is in the same fix that First National was in. Its demand deposits have decreased by $900, so its reserves can legally fall by $90. However, its actual reserves have decreased by $900—which is $810 too much. Now it is Second United's turn to call in a loan. (On your own, fill in the rest of the changes in Second United Bank's balance sheet as it successfully brings its reserves up to the legal requirement.)

As you can see, the process of calling in loans will involve many banks. Each time a bank calls in a loan, demand deposits are destroyed—the same amount as were created in our earlier story, in which each bank *made* a new loan. The total decline in demand deposits will be a multiple of the initial withdrawal of reserves. Keeping in mind that a withdrawal of reserves is a *negative change in reserves,* we can still use our demand deposit multiplier—$1/(RRR)$—and our general formula:

$$\Delta DD = \left(\frac{1}{RRR}\right) \times \Delta\text{Reserves}.$$

Applying it to our example, we have

$$\Delta DD = \left[\frac{1}{0.1}\right] \times (-\$1,000) = -\$10,000.$$

In words, the Fed's $1,000 open market sale causes a $10,000 decrease in demand deposits. Since we assume that the public's cash holdings do not change, the money supply decreases by $10,000 as well.

To the banking system as a whole, the Fed's bond sale has done the following:

**CHANGES IN BALANCE SHEET FOR THE ENTIRE BANKING SYSTEM**

| Changes in Assets | Changes in Liabilities |
|---|---|
| −$1,000 in reserves<br>−$9,000 in loans | −$10,000 in demand deposits |

## SOME IMPORTANT PROVISOS ABOUT THE DEMAND DEPOSIT MULTIPLIER

Although the process of money creation and destruction as we've described it illustrates the basic ideas, our formula for the demand deposit multiplier—$1/RRR$—is oversimplified. In reality, the multiplier is likely to be smaller than our formula suggests, for two reasons.

First, we've assumed that as the money supply changes, the public does *not* change its holdings of cash. But in reality, as the money supply increases, the public typically will want to hold part of the increase as demand deposits, and part of the increase as cash. As a result, in each round of the deposit-creation process, some reserves will be *withdrawn* in the form of cash. This will lead to a smaller increase in demand deposits than in our story.

DANGEROUS CURVES

In this section, you learned how the Fed sells government bonds to decrease the money supply. It's easy to confuse this with another type of government bond sale, which is done by the U.S. Treasury.

The U.S. Treasury is the branch of government that collects tax revenue, disburses money for government purchases and transfer payments, and borrows money to finance any government budget deficit. The Treasury borrows funds by issuing *new* government bonds and *selling* them to the public—to banks, other financial institutions, and bond dealers. What the public pays for these bonds is what they are lending the government.

When the Fed conducts open market operations, however, it does not buy or sell *newly* issued bonds, but "secondhand bonds"—those already issued by the Treasury to finance past deficits. Thus, open market sales are *not* government borrowing; they are strictly an operation designed to change the money supply, and they have no direct effect on the government budget.

Second, we've assumed that banks will always lend out all of their excess reserves. In reality, banks often *want* to hold excess reserves, for a variety of reasons. For example, they may want some flexibility to increase their loans in case interest rates—their reward for lending—rise in the near future. Or they may prefer not to lend the maximum legal amount during a recession, because borrowers are more likely to declare bankruptcy and not repay their loans. If banks increase their holdings of excess reserves as the money supply expands, they will make smaller loans than in our story, and in each round, demand deposit creation will be smaller.

## OTHER TOOLS FOR CONTROLLING THE MONEY SUPPLY

Open market operations are the Fed's primary means of controlling the money supply. But there are two other tools that the Fed can use to increase or decrease the money supply.

- *Changes in the required reserve ratio.* In principle, the Fed can set off the process of deposit creation, similar to that described earlier, by lowering the required reserve ratio. Look back at Table 1, which showed the balance sheet of a bank facing a required reserve ratio of 0.1 and holding exactly the amount of reserves required by law—$10 million. Now suppose the Fed lowered the required reserve ratio to 0.05. Suddenly, the bank would find that its required reserves were only $5 million; the other $5 million in reserves it holds would become excess reserves. To earn the highest profit possible, the bank would increase its lending by $5 million. At the same time, all other banks in the country would find that some of their formerly required reserves were now excess reserves, and they would increase their lending. The money supply would increase.

   On the other hand, if the Fed *raised* the required reserve ratio, the process would work in reverse: All banks would suddenly have reserve deficiencies and be forced to call in loans. The money supply would decrease.

- *Changes in the discount rate.* The discount rate, mentioned earlier, is the rate the Fed charges banks when it lends them reserves. In principle, a lower discount rate—enabling banks to borrow reserves from the Fed more cheaply—might encourage banks to borrow more. An increase in borrowed reserves works just like any other injection of reserves into the banking system: It increases the money supply.

On the other side, a rise in the discount rate would make it more expensive for banks to borrow from the Fed, and decrease the amount of borrowed reserves in the system. This withdrawal of reserves from the banking system would lead to a decrease in the money supply.

Changes in either the required reserve ratio or the discount rate *could* set off the process of deposit creation or deposit destruction in much the same way outlined in this chapter. In reality, neither of these policy tools is used very often. The most recent change in the required reserve ratio was in April 1992, when the Fed lowered the required reserve ratio for most demand deposits from 12 percent to 10 percent. Changes in the discount rate are more frequent, but it is not unusual for the Fed to leave the discount rate unchanged for a year or more.

Why are these other tools used so seldom? Part of the reason is that they can have such unpredictable effects. When the required reserve ratio changes, all banks in the system are affected simultaneously. Even a tiny error in predicting how a typical bank will respond can translate into a huge difference for the money supply.

A change in the discount rate has uncertain effects as well. Many bank managers do not like to borrow reserves from the Fed, since it puts them under closer Fed scrutiny. And the Fed discourages borrowing of reserves unless the bank is in difficulty. Thus, a small change in the discount rate is unlikely to have much of an impact on bank borrowing of reserves, and therefore on the money supply.

Open market operations, by contrast, have more predictable impacts on the money supply. They can be fine-tuned to any level desired. Another advantage is that they are covert. No one knows exactly what the FOMC decided to do to the money supply at its last meeting. And no one knows whether it is conducting more open market purchases or more open market sales on any given day (it always does a certain amount of both to keep bond traders guessing). By maintaining secrecy, the Fed can often change its policies without destabilizing financial markets, and also avoid the pressure that Congress or the president might bring to bear if its policies are not popular.

> While other tools can affect the money supply, open market operations have two advantages over them: precision and secrecy. This is why open market operations remain the Fed's primary means of changing the money supply.

The Fed's ability to conduct its policies in secret—and its independent status in general—is controversial. Some argue that secrecy and independence are needed so that the Fed can do what is best for the country—keeping the price level stable—without undue pressure from Congress or the president. Others argue that there is something fundamentally undemocratic about an independent Federal Reserve, whose governors are not elected and who can, to some extent, ignore the popular will. In recent years, because the Fed has been so successful in guiding the economy, the controversy has largely subsided.

## BANK FAILURES AND BANKING PANICS

*Using the*
**THEORY**

A bank failure occurs when a bank is unable to meet the requests of its depositors to withdraw their funds. Typically, the failure occurs when depositors begin to worry about the bank's financial health. They may believe that their bank has made unsound loans that will not be repaid, so that it does not have enough assets to cover its demand deposit liabilities. In that case, everyone will want to be first in line to withdraw cash, since banks meet requests for withdrawals on a first-come, first-served basis. Those who wait may not be able to get any cash at all. This can lead to a **run on the bank,** with everyone trying to withdraw funds simultaneously.

Ironically, a bank can fail even if it is in good financial health, with more than enough assets to cover its liabilities, just because people *think* the bank is in trouble. Why should a false rumor be a problem for the bank? Because many of its assets are illiquid, such as long-term loans. These cannot be sold easily or quickly enough to meet the unusual demands for withdrawal during a run on the bank.

For example, look back at Table 1, which shows a healthy bank with more assets than liabilities. But notice that the bank has only $2 million in vault cash. Under normal circumstances, that would be more than enough to cover a day of heavy withdrawals. But suppose that depositors hear a rumor that the bank has made many bad loans, and they want to withdraw $40 million. The bank would soon exhaust its $2 million in cash. It could then ask the Federal Reserve for more cash, using the $8 million in its reserve account, and the Fed would likely respond quickly, perhaps even delivering the cash the same day. The bank could also sell its $25 million in government bonds and obtain more cash within a few days. But all together, this will give the bank only $35 million with which to honor requests for withdrawals. What then? Unless the bank is lucky enough to have many of its long-term loans coming due that week, it will be unable to meet its depositors' requests for cash. A false rumor can cause a bank to fail.

**Run on the bank** An attempt by many of a bank's depositors to withdraw their funds.

A **banking panic** occurs when many banks fail simultaneously. In the past, a typical panic would begin with some unexpected event, such as the failure of a large bank. During recessions, for example, many businesses go bankrupt, so fewer bank loans are repaid. A bank that had an unusual number of "bad loans" would be in trouble, and if the public found out about this, there might be a run on that bank. The bank would fail, and many depositors would find that they had lost their deposits.

**Banking panic** A situation in which depositors attempt to withdraw funds from many banks simultaneously.

But that would not be the end of the story. Hearing that their neighbors' banks were short of cash might lead others to question the health of their own banks. Just to be sure, they might withdraw their own funds, preferring to ride out the storm and keep their cash at home. As we've seen, even healthy banks can fail under the pressure of a bank run. They, too, would have to close their doors, stoking the rumor mill even more, and so on.

Banking panics can cause serious problems for the nation. First, there is the hardship suffered by people who lose their accounts when their bank fails. Second, even when banks do not fail, the withdrawal of cash decreases the banking system's reserves. As we've seen, the withdrawal of reserves leads—through the demand deposit multiplier—to a larger decrease in the money supply. In the next chapter, you will learn that a decrease in the money supply can cause a recession. In a banking panic, the money supply can decrease suddenly and severely, causing a serious recession.

There were five major banking panics in the United States from 1863 to 1907. Indeed, it was the banking panic of 1907 that convinced Congress to establish the Federal Reserve System. From the beginning, one of the Fed's primary functions was to act as a lender of last resort, providing banks with enough cash to meet their obligations to depositors.

But the creation of the Fed did not, in itself, solve the problem. Figure 4 shows the number of bank failures each year since 1921. As you can see, banking panics continued to plague the financial system even after the Fed was created. The Fed did

**FIGURE 4**

**BANK FAILURES IN THE UNITED STATES, 1921–1999**

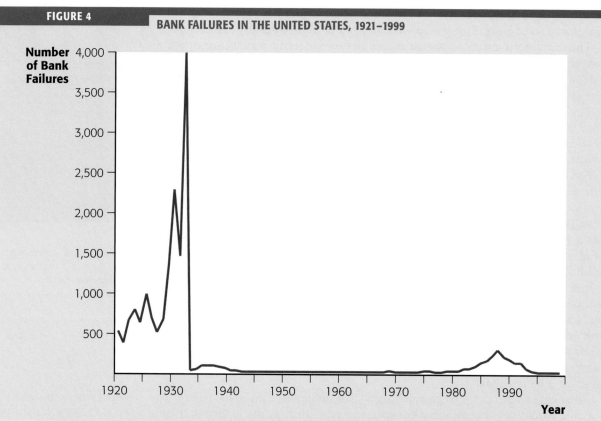

Bank failures continued after the Fed was created in 1913. During the Great Depression, a large number of banks failed. The Fed learned a hard lesson: It needed to inject reserves into the banking system whenever a crisis threatened. The creation of the Federal Deposit Insurance Corporation in 1933 also strengthened faith in the stability of the banking system. Few banks have failed since that time.

not always act forcefully enough or quickly enough to prevent the panic from spreading.

The Great Depression is a good example of this problem. In late 1929 and 1930, many banks began to fail because of bad loans. Then, from October 1930 until March 1933, more than one-third of all banks failed as frantic depositors stormed bank after bank, demanding to withdraw their funds—even from banks that were in reasonable financial health. Many economists believe that the banking panic of 1930–1933 turned what would have been just a serious recession into the Great Depression. Officials of the Federal Reserve System, not quite grasping the seriousness of the problem, stood by and let it happen.[5]

As you can see in Figure 4, banking panics were largely eliminated after 1933. Indeed, except for the moderate increase in failures during the late 1980s and early 1990s, the system has been almost failure free. Why the dramatic improvement?

Largely for two reasons. First, the Federal Reserve learned an important lesson from the Great Depression, and it now stands ready to inject reserves into the system more quickly in a crisis. Moreover, in 1933 Congress created the Federal De-

---

[5]   Milton Friedman and Anna Jacobson Schwartz, *A Monetary History of the United States, 1867–1960* (Princeton University Press, 1963), especially p. 358.

posit Insurance Corporation (FDIC) to reimburse those who lose their deposits. If your bank is insured by the FDIC (today, accounts are covered in 99 percent of all banks) and cannot honor its obligations for any reason—bad loans, poor management, or even theft—the FDIC will reimburse you up to the first $100,000 you lose in each of your bank accounts. (If you have more than $100,000 in a single bank account, you are not insured for the amount over $100,000.)

The FDIC has had a major impact on the psychology of the banking public. Imagine that you hear your bank is about to go under. As long as you have less than $100,000 in your account, you will not care. Why? Because even if the rumor turns out to be true, you will be reimbursed in full. The resulting calmness on your part, and on the part of other depositors, will prevent a run on the bank. This makes it very unlikely that bank failures will spread throughout the system.

FDIC protection for bank accounts has not been costless. Banks must pay insurance premiums to the FDIC, and they pass this cost on to their depositors and borrowers by charging higher interest rates on loans and higher fees for their services. And there is a more serious cost. If you are thoroughly protected in the event of a bank failure, your bank's managers have little incentive to develop a reputation for prudence in lending funds, since you will be happy to deposit your money there anyway. Without government regulations, banks could act irresponsibly, taking great risks with your money, and you would remain indifferent. Many more banks would fail, the FDIC would have to pay off more depositors, and banks—and their customers—would bear the burden of higher FDIC premiums. This is the logic behind the Fed's continuing regulation of bank lending. Someone must watch over the banks to keep the failure rate low, and if the public has no incentive to pay attention, the Fed must do so. Most economists believe that if we want the freedom from banking panics provided by the FDIC, we must also accept the strict regulation and close monitoring of banks provided by the Fed and other agencies.

Look again at Figure 4 and notice the temporary rise in bank failures of the late 1980s and the early 1990s. Most of these failures occurred in state-chartered banks. These banks are less closely regulated by the Fed, and are often insured by state agencies instead of the FDIC. When a few banks went bankrupt because highly speculative loans turned sour, insurance funds in several states were drained. Citizens in those states began to fear that insufficient funds were left to insure their own deposits, and the psychology of banking panics took over. To many observers, the experience of the late 1980s and early 1990s was a reminder of the need for a sound insurance system and close monitoring of the banking system.

http://

Fred Furlong and Simon Kwan, in "Rising Bank Risk?" (http://www.frbsf. org/econrsrch/wklyltr/ wklyltr99/e199-32.html) explore recent developments in bank behavior.

## S U M M A R Y

In the United States, the standard measure of money—M1—includes currency, checking account balances, and travelers checks. Each of these assets is liquid and widely acceptable as a means of payment. Other, broader measures go beyond M1 to include funds in savings accounts and time deposits.

The amount of money circulating in the economy is controlled by the Federal Reserve, operating through the banking system. Banks and other financial intermediaries are profit-seeking firms that collect loanable funds from households and businesses, then repackage them to make loans to other households, businesses, and governmental agencies,

The Federal Reserve injects money into the economy by altering banks' balance sheets. In a balance sheet, assets always equal liabilities plus net worth. One important kind of asset is *reserves*—funds that banks are required to hold in proportion to their demand deposit liabilities. When the Fed wants to increase the money supply, it buys bonds in the open market and pays for them with a check. This is called an *open market purchase*. When the Fed's check is deposited in a bank, the bank's balance sheet changes. On the asset side, reserves increase; on the liabilities side, demand deposits (a form of money) also increase. The bank can lend some of the reserves, and the money loaned will end up in some other banks where it supports creation of still more demand deposits. Eventually, demand deposits, and the M1 money supply, increase by some multiple of the original injection of reserves by the Fed. The *demand deposit multiplier*—the inverse of the required reserve ratio—gives us that multiple.

The Fed can decrease the money supply by selling government bonds—an *open market sale*—causing demand deposits to shrink by a multiple of the initial reduction in reserves. The Fed can also change the money supply by changing either the required reserve ratio or the discount rate it charges when it lends reserves to banks.

## KEY TERMS

| | | | |
|---|---|---|---|
| liquidity | financial intermediary | required reserve ratio | open market operations |
| cash in the hands of the public | balance sheet | net worth | excess reserves |
| | bond | central bank | demand deposit multiplier |
| demand deposits | loan | Federal Open Market | run on the bank |
| M1 | reserves | Committee | banking panic |
| M2 | required reserves | discount rate | |

## REVIEW QUESTIONS

1. Describe the main characteristics of money. What purpose does money serve in present-day economies?

2. Which of the following is considered part of the U.S. money supply?
   a. A $10 bill you carry in your wallet
   b. A $100 travelers check you bought but did not use
   c. A $100 bill in a bank teller's till
   d. The $325.43 balance in your checking account
   e. A share of General Motors stock worth $40

3. Given the following data, calculate the value of the M1 money supply (the data are in billions of dollars):

   | | |
   |---|---|
   | Bank reserves | 50 |
   | Cash in the hands of the public | 400 |
   | Demand deposits | 400 |
   | Noninstitutional MMMF balances | 880 |
   | Other checkable deposits | 250 |
   | Savings-type account balances | 1,300 |
   | Small time deposits | 950 |
   | Travelers checks | 10 |

4. What is a depository institution? Give an example of each of the four types of depository institutions.

5. What are reserves? What determines the amount of reserves that a bank holds? Explain the difference between required reserves and excess reserves.

6. What are the main functions of the Federal Reserve System?

7. Explain how the Federal Reserve can use open market operations to change the level of bank reserves. How does a change in reserves affect the money supply? (Give answers for both an increase and a decrease in the money supply.)

8. Suppose that the money supply is $1 trillion. Decision makers at the Federal Reserve decide that they wish to reduce the money supply by $100 billion, or by 10 percent. If the required reserve ratio is 0.05, what does the Fed need to do to carry out the planned reduction?

9. How does a "run on a bank" differ from a "banking panic"? What are their implications for the economy? What steps have been taken to reduce the likelihood of bank runs and bank panics?

## PROBLEMS AND EXERCISES

1. Suppose the required reserve ratio is 0.2. If an extra $20 billion in reserves is injected into the banking system through an open market purchase of bonds, by how much can demand deposits increase? Would your answer be different if the required reserve ratio were 0.1?

2. Suppose bank reserves are $100 billion, the required reserve ratio is 0.2, and excess reserves are zero. Now suppose that the required reserve ratio is lowered to 0.1 and that banks once again become fully "loaned up" with no excess reserves. What is the new level of demand deposits?

3. For each of the following situations, determine whether the money supply will increase, decrease, or stay the same.
   a. Depositors become concerned about the safety of depository institutions.
   b. The Fed lowers the required reserve ratio.

c. The economy enters a recession and banks have a hard time finding credit-worthy borrowers.

d. The Fed sells $100 million of bonds to First National Bank of Ames, Iowa.

4. Suppose that the Fed decides to increase the money supply. It purchases a government bond worth $1,000 from a private citizen. He deposits the check in his account at First National Bank, as in the chapter example. But now, suppose that the required reserve ratio is 0.2, rather than 0.1 as in the chapter.

a. Trace the effect of this change through three banks— First National, Second Federal, and Third State. Show the changes to each bank's balance sheet as a result of the Fed's action.

b. By how much does the money supply change in each of these first three rounds?

c. What will be the ultimate change in demand deposits in the entire banking system?

## C H A L L E N G E   Q U E S T I O N

1. Sometimes banks wish to hold reserves in excess of the legal minimum. Suppose the Fed makes an open market purchase of $100,000 in government bonds. The required reserve ratio is 0.1, but each bank decides to hold additional reserves equal to 5 percent of its deposits.

a. Trace the effect of the open market purchase of bonds through the first three banks in the money expansion process. Show the changes to each bank's balance sheet.

b. Derive the demand deposit multiplier in this case. Is it larger or smaller than when banks hold no excess reserves?

c. What is the ultimate change in demand deposits in the entire banking system?

## E X P E R I E N T I A L   E X E R C I S E S

1. The *Journal of Internet Banking and Commerce* at *http://www.arraydev.com/ commerce/jibc/current.htm* is a Web-based magazine devoted to online banking and related issues. Take a look at the current edition and see if you can determine any problems that electronic banking might cause the Fed. Also see what you can learn about the status of Internet banking outside the United States.

2. If you have access to the Interactive Edition of *The Wall Street Journal*, you can use the Briefing Books feature to obtain data on over 10,000 public companies. Find the Briefing Book on a large commercial bank in your area. Look at some of its press releases to determine how this bank has been influenced by Federal Reserve regulations and operations.

# THE MONEY MARKET AND THE INTEREST RATE

Which of the following two newspaper headlines might you see in your daily paper?

1. "Motorists Fear Department of Energy Will Raise Gasoline Prices"
2. "Wall Street Expects Fed to Raise Interest Rates"

You probably know the answer—the first headline is entirely unrealistic. The Department of Energy, the government agency that makes energy policy, has no authority to set prices in any market. The Federal Reserve, by contrast, has full authority to influence the interest rate—the price of borrowing money. And it exercises this authority every day. This is why headlines such as the second one appear in newspapers so often.

In this chapter, you will learn how the Fed, through its control of the money supply, also controls the interest rate. We'll continue our focus on the short run, postponing any discussion about longer time horizons until the next chapter.

## THE DEMAND FOR MONEY

Re-read the title of this section. Does it appear strange to you? Don't people always want as much money as possible?

Indeed, they do. But when we speak about the *demand* for something, we don't mean the amount that people would desire if they could have all they wanted, without having to sacrifice anything for it. Instead, economic decision makers always face constraints: They must sacrifice one thing in order to have more of another. Thus, the *demand for money* does not mean how much money people would *like* to have in the best of all possible worlds. Rather, it means *how much money people would like to hold, given the constraints that they face.* Let's first consider the demand for money by an individual, and then turn our attention to the demand for money in the entire economy.

Identify Goals and Constraints

### AN INDIVIDUAL'S DEMAND FOR MONEY
Money is one of the forms in which people hold their wealth. Unfortunately, at any given moment, the total amount of wealth we have is given; we can't just snap our

fingers and have more of it. Therefore, if we want to hold more wealth in the form of money, we must hold less wealth in other forms—savings accounts, money market funds, time deposits, stocks, bonds, and so on. Indeed, people exchange one kind of

> You've been reminded several times, but since it's a very common mistake, another reminder won't hurt. Money and wealth are *stock* variables, not flow variables. They refer to amounts held *at a particular moment in time*. Do not confuse them with flow variables such as *income* or *saving*. Your income is what you earn *over a period of time*. Your saving is the part of your disposable income that you do not spend *over a period of time*.

**DANGEROUS CURVES**

wealth for another millions of times a day—in banks, stock markets, and bond markets. If you sell shares in the stock market, for example, you give up wealth in the form of corporate stock and acquire money. The buyer of your stock gives up money and acquires the stock.

These two facts—that wealth is given, and that you must give up one kind of wealth in order to acquire more of another—determine an individual's **wealth constraint.** Whenever we speak about the demand for money, the wealth constraint is always in the background, as in the following statement:

**Wealth constraint** At any point in time, wealth is fixed.

> *An individual's* quantity of money demanded *is the amount of wealth that the individual chooses to hold as money, rather than as other assets.*

Why do people want to hold some of their wealth in the form of money? The most important reason is that money is a *means of payment;* you can buy things with it. Other forms of wealth, by contrast, are *not* used for purchases. (For example, we don't ordinarily pay for our groceries with shares of stock.) However, the other forms of wealth provide a financial return to their owners. For example, bonds, savings deposits, and time deposits pay interest, while stocks pay dividends and may also rise in value (which is called a *capital gain*). Money, by contrast, pays either very little interest (some types of checking accounts) or none at all (cash and most checking accounts). Thus,

> *when you hold money, you bear an opportunity cost—the interest you could have earned.*

Each of us must continually decide how to divide our total wealth between money and other assets. The upside to money is that it can be used as a means of payment. The more of our wealth we hold as money, the easier it is to buy things at a moment's notice, and the less often we will have to pay the costs (in time, trouble, and commissions to brokers) to change our other assets into money. The downside to money is that it pays little or no interest.

To keep our analysis as simple as possible, we'll use bonds as our representative nonmoney asset. We'll also assume money pays *no* interest at all. In our discussion, therefore, people will choose between two assets that are mirror images of each other. Specifically,

> *individuals choose how to divide wealth between two assets: (1)* money, *which can be used as a means of payment but earns no interest; and (2)* bonds, *which earn interest, but cannot be used as a means of payment.*

This choice involves a clear trade-off: The more wealth we hold as money, the less often we will have to go through the inconvenience of changing our bonds into money . . . but the less interest we will earn on our wealth.

What determines how much money an individual will decide to hold? While tastes vary from person to person, three key variables have rather predictable impacts on most of us.

- *The price level.* The greater the number of dollars you spend in a typical week or month, the more money you will want to have on hand to make your purchases. A rise in the price level, which raises the dollar cost of your purchases, should therefore increase the amount of money you want to hold.
- *Real income.* Suppose the price level remains unchanged, but your income increases. Your purchasing power or *real* income will increase, and so will the number of dollars you spend in a typical week or month. Once again, since you are spending more dollars, you will choose to hold more of your wealth in the form of money.
- *The interest rate.* Interest payments are what you give up when you hold money—the *opportunity cost* of money. The greater the interest rate, the greater the opportunity cost of holding money. Thus, a rise in the interest rate *decreases* your quantity of money demanded.

The effect of the interest rate on the quantity of money demanded will play a key role in our analysis. But before we go any further, you may be wondering whether it is realistic to think that changes in the interest rate—which are usually rather small—would have any effect at all. Here, as in many aspects of economic life, you may not find yourself consciously thinking about the interest rate in deciding how to adjust your money-holding habits. Just as you don't rethink all your habits about using lights and computers every time the price of electricity changes, you may respond to interest rates more casually. But when we add up everybody's behavior, we find a noticeable and stable tendency for people to hold less money when it is more expensive to hold money—that is, when the interest rate is higher.

*Identify Goals and Constraints*

**The Demand for Money by Businesses.** Our discussion of money demand has focused on the typical individual. But some money (not a lot in comparison to what individuals hold) is held by businesses. Stores keep some currency in their cash registers, and firms generally keep funds in business checking accounts. Businesses face the same types of constraints as individuals: They have only so much wealth, and they must decide how much of it to hold as money rather than other assets. The quantity of money demanded by businesses follows the same principles we have developed for individuals: They want to hold more money when real income or the price level is higher, and less money when the opportunity cost (the interest rate) is higher.

## THE ECONOMY-WIDE DEMAND FOR MONEY

When we use the term *demand for money* without the word *individual*, we mean the total demand for money by all wealth holders in the economy—businesses and individuals. And just as each person and each firm in the economy has only so much wealth, so, too, there is a given amount of wealth in the economy as a whole at any given time. In our analysis, this total wealth must be held in one of two forms: money or bonds.

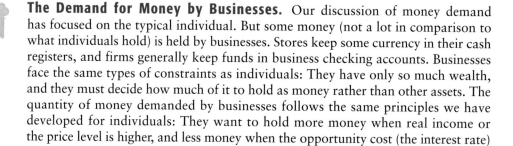

> *The (economy-wide) quantity of money demanded is the amount of total wealth in the economy that all households and businesses, together, choose to hold as money rather than as bonds.*

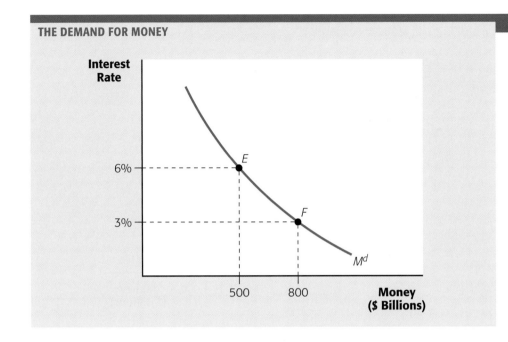

**FIGURE 1**

**THE DEMAND FOR MONEY**

The downward-sloping money demand curve shows that, for given real GDP and a given price level, the amount of money demanded by households and firms is inversely related to the interest rate. At an interest rate of 6 percent, $500 billion of money is demanded; at the lower interest rate of 3 percent, $800 billion is demanded.

The demand for money in the economy depends on the same three variables that we discussed for individuals. In particular, (1) a rise in the price level will increase the demand for money; (2) a rise in real income (real GDP) will increase the demand for money; and (3) a rise in the interest rate will *decrease* the quantity of money demanded.

**The Money Demand Curve.** Figure 1 shows a **money demand curve**, which tells us *the total quantity of money demanded in the economy at each interest rate.* Notice that the curve is downward sloping. As long as the other influences on money demand don't change, a drop in the interest rate—which lowers the opportunity cost of holding money—will increase the quantity of money demanded.

Point *E*, for example, shows that when the interest rate is 6 percent, the quantity of money demanded is $500 billion. If the interest rate falls to 3 percent, we move to point *F*, where the quantity demanded is $800 billion. As we move along the money demand curve, the interest rate changes, but other determinants of money demand (such as the price level and real income) are assumed to remain unchanged.

**Shifts in the Money Demand Curve.** What happens when something *other* than the interest rate changes the quantity of money demanded? Then the curve shifts. For example, suppose that real income increases. Then, at each interest rate, individuals and businesses will want to hold *more* of their wealth in the form of money. The entire money demand curve will shift rightward. This is illustrated in Figure 2, where the money demand curve shifts rightward from $M_1^d$ to $M_2^d$. At an interest rate of 6 percent, the quantity of money demanded rises from $500 billion to $700 billion; if the interest rate were 3 percent, the amount of money demanded would rise from $800 billion to $1,000 billion.

*A change in the interest rate moves us along the money demand curve. A change in money demand caused by something other than the interest rate (such as real income or the price level) will cause the curve to shift.*

**Money demand curve** A curve indicating how much money will be willingly held at each interest rate.

**FIGURE 2**

An increase in real GDP or in the price level will shift the money demand curve to the right. At each interest rate, more money will be demanded.

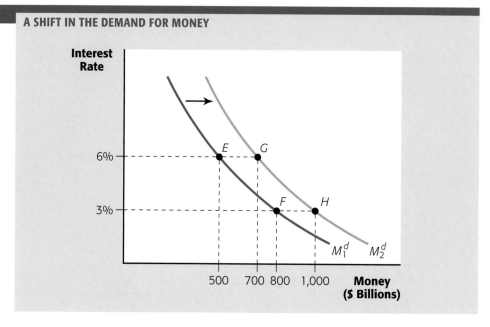

**A SHIFT IN THE DEMAND FOR MONEY**

Figure 3 summarizes how the key variables we've discussed so far affect the demand for money.

## THE SUPPLY OF MONEY

Just as we did for money demand, we would like to draw a curve showing the quantity of money *supplied* at each interest rate. In the previous chapter, you learned how the Fed controls the money supply: It uses open market operations to inject or

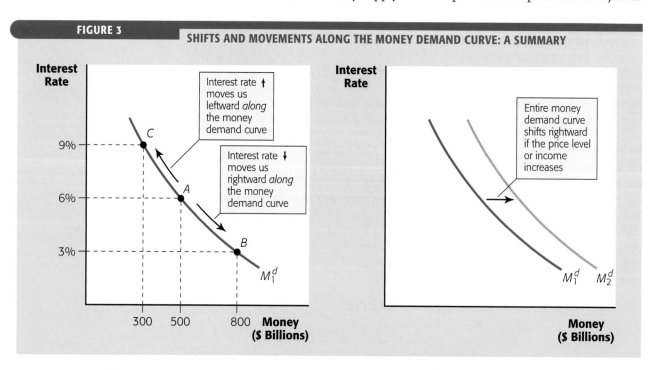

**FIGURE 3**

**SHIFTS AND MOVEMENTS ALONG THE MONEY DEMAND CURVE: A SUMMARY**

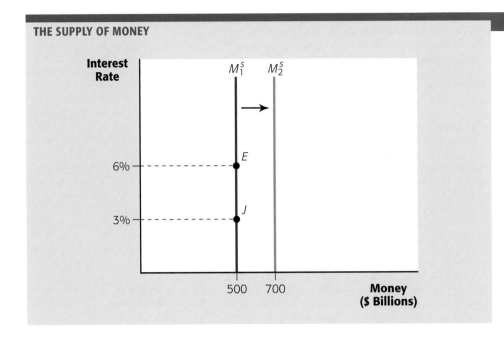

**FIGURE 4**

**THE SUPPLY OF MONEY**

Once the Fed sets the money supply, it remains constant until the Fed changes it. The vertical supply curve labeled $M^s_1$ shows a money supply of $500 billion, regardless of the interest rate. An increase in the money supply to $700 billion is depicted in a rightward shift of the money supply curve to $M^s_2$.

withdraw reserves from the banking system and then relies on the demand deposit multiplier to do the rest. Since the Fed decides what the money supply will be, we treat it as a fixed amount. That is, the interest rate can rise or fall, but the money supply will remain constant unless and until the Fed decides to change it.

Look at the vertical line labeled $M^S_1$ in Figure 4. This is the economy's **money supply curve,** which shows the total amount of money supplied at each interest rate. The line is vertical because once the Fed sets the money supply, it remains constant until the Fed changes it. In the figure, the Fed has chosen to set the money supply at $500 billion. A rise in the interest rate from, say, 3 percent to 6 percent would move us from point $J$ to point $E$ along the solid money supply curve, leaving the money supply unchanged.

**Money supply curve** A line showing the total quantity of money in the economy at each interest rate.

Now suppose the Fed, for whatever reason, were to *change* the money supply. Then there would be a *new* vertical line, showing a different quantity of money supplied at each interest rate. Recall from the previous chapter that the Fed raises the money supply by purchasing bonds in an open market operation. For example, if the demand deposit multiplier is 10, and the Fed purchases government bonds worth $20 billion, the money supply increases by 10 × $20 billion = $200 billion. In this case, the money supply curve shifts rightward, to the vertical line labeled $M^S_2$ in the figure.

> *Open market purchases of bonds inject reserves into the banking system, and shift the money supply curve rightward by a multiple of the reserve injection. Open market sales have the opposite effect: They withdraw reserves from the system and shift the money supply curve leftward by a multiple of the reserve withdrawal.*

## EQUILIBRIUM IN THE MONEY MARKET

 Find the Equilibrium

Now we are ready for Key Step #3: to combine what you've learned about money demand and money supply to find the equilibrium interest rate in the economy. But

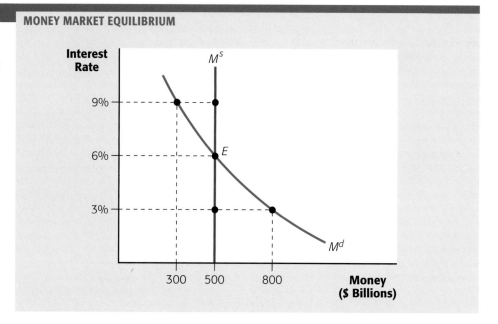

Money market equilibrium occurs when households and firms are content to hold the amount of money they are actually holding. At point *E*—at an interest rate of 6 percent—the quantity of money demanded equals the quantity supplied, and the market is in equilibrium. At a higher interest rate, such as 9 percent, there would be an excess supply of money, and the interest rate would fall. At a lower interest rate, such as 3 percent, there would be an excess demand for money, and the interest rate would rise.

**MONEY MARKET EQUILIBRIUM**

before we do, a question may have occurred to you. Haven't we already discussed how the interest rate is determined? Indeed, we have. The classical model tells us that the interest rate is determined by equilibrium in the *loanable funds market*—where a flow of loanable funds is offered by lenders to borrowers. But remember: The classical model tells us how the economy operates in the *long run*. We can rely on its mechanisms to work only over long periods of time. Here, we are interested in how the interest rate is determined in the *short run*, so we must change our perspective. Toward the end of the chapter, we'll come back to the classical model and explain why its theory of the interest rate does not apply in the short run.

In the short run—our focus here—we look for the equilibrium interest rate in the *money market:* the interest rate at which the quantity of money demanded and the quantity of money supplied are equal. Figure 5 combines the money supply and demand curves. Equilibrium occurs at point *E*, where the two curves intersect. At this point, the quantity of money demanded and the quantity supplied are both equal to $500 billion, and the equilibrium interest rate is 6 percent.

It is important to understand what equilibrium in the money market actually means. First, remember that the money supply curve tells us the quantity of money, determined by the Fed, that *actually exists* in the economy. Every dollar of this money—either in cash or in checking account balances—is held by *someone*. Thus, the money supply curve, in addition to telling us the quantity of money supplied by the Fed, also tells us the quantity of money that people are actually holding at any given moment. The money demand curve, on the other hand, tells us how much money people *want* to hold at each interest rate. Thus, when the quantity of money supplied and the quantity demanded are equal, all of the money in the economy is being *willingly held*. That is, people are *satisfied* holding the money that they are *actually* holding.

> *Equilibrium in the money market occurs when the quantity of money people are* actually *holding (quantity supplied) is equal to the quantity of money they* want *to hold (quantity demanded).*

Can we have faith that the interest rate will reach its equilibrium value in the money market, such as 6 percent in our figure? Indeed we can. In the next section, we explore the forces that drive the money market toward its equilibrium.

## HOW THE MONEY MARKET REACHES EQUILIBRIUM

To understand how the money market reaches its equilibrium, suppose that the interest rate, for some reason, were *not* at its equilibrium value of 6 percent in Figure 5. For example, suppose the interest rate were 9 percent. As the figure shows, at this interest rate the quantity of money demanded would be $300 billion, while the quantity supplied would be $500 billion. Or, put another way, people would *actually* be holding $500 billion of their wealth as money, but they would *want* to hold only $300 billion as money. There would be an **excess supply of money** (the quantity of money supplied would exceed the quantity demanded) equal to $500 billion − $300 billion = $200 billion.

Now comes an important point. Remember that in our analysis, money and bonds are the only two assets available. If people want to hold *less* money than they are currently holding, then, by definition, they must want to hold *more* in bonds than they are currently holding—an **excess demand for bonds**.

> *When there is an excess supply of money in the economy, there is also an excess demand for bonds.*

To understand this more clearly, imagine that instead of the money market, which can seem rather abstract, we were discussing something more concrete: the arrangement of books in a bookcase. Suppose that you have a certain number of books, and you have only two shelves on which to hold all of them—top and bottom. One day, you look at the shelves and decide that, the way you've arranged things, the top shelf has *too many* books. Then, by definition, you must also feel that the bottom shelf has *too few* books. That is, an excess supply of books on the top shelf (it has more books than you want there) is the same as an excess demand for books on the bottom shelf (it has fewer books than you want there).

A similar conclusion applies to the money market. People allocate a given amount of wealth between two different assets: money and bonds. Too much in one asset implies too little in the other.

So far, we've established that if the interest rate were 9 percent, which is higher than its equilibrium value, there would be an excess supply of money, and an excess demand for bonds. What would happen? The public would try to convert the undesired money into bonds. That is, people would try to *buy* bonds. Just as there is a market for money, there is also a market for bonds. And as the public begins to demand more bonds, making them scarcer, *the price of bonds will rise.* We can illustrate the steps in our analysis so far as follows:

We conclude that, when the interest rate is higher than its equilibrium value, the price of bonds will rise. Why is this important? In order to take our story further, we must first take a detour for a few paragraphs.

**Excess supply of money** The amount of money supplied exceeds the amount demanded at a particular interest rate.

**Excess demand for bonds** The amount of bonds demanded exceeds the amount supplied at a particular interest rate.

When bond traders—such as those pictured here—try to buy more bonds, the price of bonds rises, and the interest rate on those bonds falls.

**An Important Detour: Bond Prices and Interest Rates.** A bond, in the simplest terms, is a promise to pay back borrowed funds at a certain date or dates in the future. There are many types of bonds. Some promise to make payments each month or each year for a certain period and then pay back a large sum at the end. Others promise to make just one payment—perhaps 1, 5, 10, or more years from the date the bond is issued. When a large corporation or the government wants to borrow money, it issues a new bond and sells it in the marketplace; the amount borrowed is equal to the price of the bond.

Let's consider a very simple example: a bond that promises to pay to its holder $1,000 exactly one year from today. Suppose that you purchase this bond from the issuer—a firm or government agency—for $800. Then you are lending $800 to the issuer, and you will be paid back $1,000 one year later. What interest rate are you earning on your loan? Let's see: You will be getting back $200 more than you lent, so that is your *interest payment*. The interest *rate* is the interest payment divided by the amount of the loan, or $200/$800 = 0.25 or 25 percent.

Now, what if instead of $800, you paid a price of $900 for this very same bond. The bond still promises to pay $1,000 one year from now, so your interest payment would now be $100, and your interest rate would be $100/$900 = 0.11 or 11 percent—a considerably lower interest rate. As you can see, the interest rate that you will earn on your bond depends entirely on the *price* of the bond. *The higher the price, the lower the interest rate.*

This general principle applies to virtually all types of bonds, not just the simple one-time-payment bond we've considered here. Bonds promise to pay various sums to their holders at different dates in the future. Therefore, the more you pay for any bond, the lower your overall rate of return, or interest rate, will be. Thus:

> *When the price of bonds rises, the interest rate falls; when the price of bonds falls, the interest rate rises.*[1]

The relationship between bond prices and interest rates helps explain why the government, the press, and the public are so concerned about the *bond market,* where bonds issued in previous periods are bought and sold. This market is sometimes called the *secondary* market for bonds, to distinguish it from the *primary* market where newly issued bonds are bought and sold. When you hear that "the bond market rallied" on a particular day of trading, it means that prices rose in the secondary bond market. This is good news for bond holders. But it is also good news for any person or business that wants to borrow money. When prices rise in the secondary market, they immediately rise in the primary market as well, since newly issued bonds and previously issued bonds are almost perfect substitutes for each other. Therefore, a bond market rally not only means lower interest rates in the secondary market, it also means lower interest rates in the primary market, where firms borrow money by issuing new bonds. Sooner or later, it will also lead to a drop in the interest rate on mortgages, car loans, credit card balances, and even many student loans. This is good news for borrowers. But it is bad news for anyone wishing to lend money, for now they will earn less interest.

---

[1]    In our macroeconomic model of the economy, we refer to *the* interest rate. In the real world, there are many types of interest rates—a different one for each type of bond, and still other rates on savings accounts, time deposits, car loans, mortgages, and more. However, all of these interest rates move up and down together, even though some may lag behind a few days, weeks, or months. Thus, when bond prices rise, interest rates *generally* will fall, and vice versa.

Now that you understand the relationship between bond prices and interest rates, let's return to our analysis of the money market.

### Back to the Money Market.

Look back at Figure 5, and let's recap what you've learned so far. If the interest rate were 9 percent, there would be an excess supply of money, and therefore an excess demand for bonds. The public would try to buy bonds, and the price of bonds would rise. Now we can complete the story. As

**DANGEROUS CURVES**

We've shown that when the money market is not in equilibrium, the public *tries* to buy or sell bonds. The word *tries* is important. On any given day, the total number of bonds—like the money stock—is some fixed amount. (We ignore the relatively small number of newly issued bonds added to the market each day.) Therefore, it is impossible for the public as a whole to acquire more bonds, or to get rid of them. A single individual may be able to acquire bonds or money by exchanging with another individual. But the total amount of bonds and money held by the public will remain unchanged.

How, then, does the money market achieve equilibrium? When many people simultaneously try to sell bonds, they cause the price of bonds to fall. The price of bonds stops falling only when the public, as a whole, is happy holding the same bonds they were holding originally. When many people simultaneously try to acquire bonds, they cause the price of bonds to rise until the public is, once again, satisfied holding what it started with. *Individuals* may buy and sell bonds, but the public, as a whole, can only *try* to.

you've just learned, a rise in the price of bonds means a *decrease* in the interest rate. The complete sequence of events is

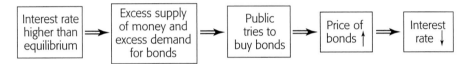

Thus, if the interest is 9 percent in our figure, it will begin to fall. Therefore, 9 percent is *not* the equilibrium interest rate.

How far will the interest rate fall? As long as there continues to be an excess supply of money, and an excess demand for bonds, the public will still be trying to acquire bonds and the interest rate will continue to fall. But notice what happens in the figure as the interest rate falls: The quantity of money demanded *rises*. Finally, when the interest rate reaches 6 percent, the excess supply of money, and therefore the excess demand for bonds, is eliminated. At this point, there is no reason for the interest rate to fall further, so 6 percent is, indeed, our equilibrium interest rate.

We can also do the same analysis from the other direction. Suppose the interest rate were *lower* than 6 percent in the figure. Then, as you can see in Figure 5, there would be an *excess demand for money*, and an *excess supply of bonds*. In this case, the following would happen:

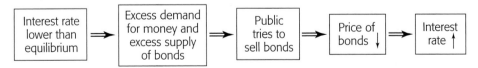

The interest rate would continue to rise until it reached its equilibrium value: 6 percent.

## WHAT HAPPENS WHEN THINGS CHANGE?

What Happens When Things Change?

Now that we have seen how the interest rate is *determined* in the money market, we turn our attention to *changes* in the interest rate. We'll focus on two questions:

If the Fed wishes to lower the interest rate, it can do so by increasing the money supply. At point *E,* the money market is in equilibrium at an interest rate of 6 percent. To lower the rate, the Fed could increase the money supply to $800 billion. At the original interest rate, there would be an excess supply of money (and an excess demand for bonds). Bond prices would rise, and the interest rate would fall until a new equilibrium is established at point *F* with an interest rate of 3 percent.

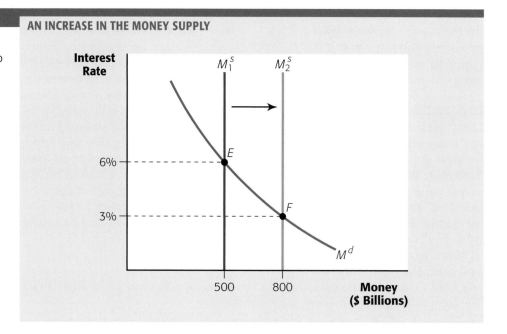

**AN INCREASE IN THE MONEY SUPPLY**

(1) What *causes* the equilibrium interest rate to change? and (2) What are the *consequences* of a change in the interest rate? As you are about to see, the Fed can change the interest rate as a matter of policy, or the interest rate can change on its own, as a by-product of other events in the economy. We'll begin with the Fed.

## HOW THE FED CHANGES THE INTEREST RATE

Changes in the interest rate from day to day, or week to week, are often caused by the Fed. Later in this chapter, you'll learn *why* the Fed often wants to manipulate the interest rate. For now, we'll focus on *how* the Fed does this.

Suppose the Fed wants to *lower* the interest rate. Fed officials cannot just *declare* that the interest rate should be lower. To change the interest rate, the Fed must change the *equilibrium* interest rate in the money market, and it does this by changing the money supply.

Look at Figure 6. Initially, with a money supply of $500 billion, the money market is in equilibrium at point *E,* with an interest rate of 6 percent. To lower the interest rate, the Fed *increases* the money supply through open market purchases of bonds. In the figure, the Fed raises the money supply to $800 billion, shifting the money supply curve rightward. (This is a much greater shift than the Fed would ever actually engineer in practice, but it makes the graph easier to read.) At the old interest rate of 6 percent, there would be an excess supply of money and an excess demand for bonds. This will drive the interest rate down until it reaches its new equilibrium value of 3 percent, at point *F.* The process works like this:

The Fed can *raise* the interest rate as well, through open market *sales* of bonds. In this case, the money supply curve in Figure 6 would shift leftward (not shown), setting off the following sequence of events:

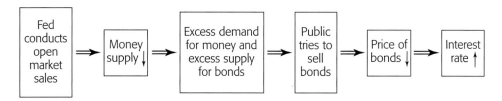

> *If the Fed increases the money supply by buying government bonds, the interest rate falls. If the Fed decreases the money supply by selling government bonds, the interest rate rises. By controlling the money supply through purchases and sales of bonds, the Fed can also control the interest rate.*

## THE FED IN ACTION

When the Fed tries to achieve a macroeconomic goal by controlling or manipulating the money supply, it is conducting *monetary policy*. During periods of economic calm, such as 1993 through 1999, the Fed's monetary policy tends to be stable, and the interest rate remains at about the same level from year to year. Occasionally, however, the Fed sees the need to act dramatically—to adjust the money stock aggressively and engineer large changes in interest rates. Such an episode occurred in the period from mid-1999 to early 2000. In 1999, the Fed believed that the economy was becoming overheated and that it needed to be slowed down by a rise in the interest rate (you'll learn why a higher interest rate slows the economy in the next section).

Figure 7 shows what happened. Starting in June 1999, the Fed began to conduct open market sales of bonds, withdrawing reserves from the banking system. As you can see in panel (a) of the figure, from mid-1999 to early 2000, banking system reserves fell by about $2.9 billion. This, in turn, shrank demand deposits and similar checking account balances by about $29.3 billion—10 times the withdrawal of reserves. (The previous chapter explained why the decrease in checking-type accounts is greater than the decrease in reserves.)

Because checking account balances are part of the money supply, the Fed's action shifted the money supply curve leftward. This, in turn, caused the interest rate to rise. Panel (c) of the figure shows changes in the *federal funds rate*—the interest rate that the Fed watches the most closely when it conducts monetary policy. The **federal funds rate** is the interest rate that banks with excess reserves charge for lending reserves to other banks. Although it is just an interest rate for lending among banks, it varies closely with other interest rates in the economy, so it gives us a good idea of how interest rates in general were changing during this period. As you can see, the federal funds rate rose by a full percentage point, from 4.75 percent to 5.75 percent, over the period. From March to May, 2000 (not shown), after the graphs in Figure 7 were drawn, the Fed continued its tightening of the money supply, and the federal funds rate rose even higher, to 6.5 percent.

The contraction of the money supply and the rise in interest rates from mid-1999 and into 2000 raise some important questions. Why would the Fed feel the need to raise interest rates in the first place? Why does it do so gradually, rather than all at once? And how does the Fed know how much to tighten? We'll be answering

**http://**

You can find recent and historical data on the money supply and interest rates at the Fed's Web site: http://www.bog.frb.fed.us/releases.

**Federal funds rate** The interest rate charged for loans of reserves among banks.

questions like these in the next two chapters. But we can begin to understand the Fed's motives by learning how interest rate changes affect the economy, which is the subject of the next section.

## HOW DO INTEREST RATE CHANGES AFFECT THE ECONOMY?

Suppose the Fed increases the money supply through open market purchases of bonds. The interest rate falls, for the reasons discussed earlier in this chapter, and strongly confirmed by the data shown in Figure 7. But what then? How is the

**FIGURE 7**                    **THE FED IN ACTION**

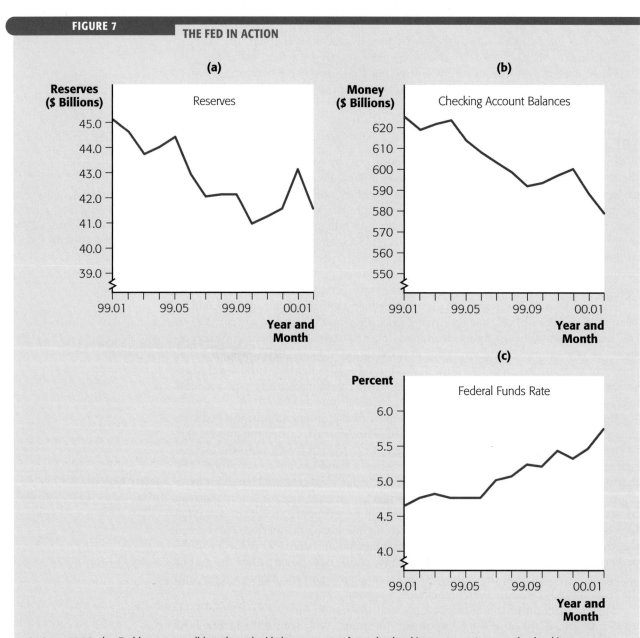

In June 1999, the Fed began to sell bonds and withdraw reserves from the banking system. As a result, checking account balances fell, the federal funds rate increased, and other interest rates in the economy (not shown) increased as well.

macroeconomy affected? The answer is: *A drop in the interest rate will boost several different types of spending in the economy.*

**How the Interest Rate Affects Spending.**  First, a lower interest rate stimulates business spending on plant and equipment. This idea came up a few chapters ago in the classical model, but we will go back over it here.

Remember that the interest rate is one of the key costs of any investment project. If a firm must borrow funds, it will have to pay for them at the going rate of interest—for example, by selling a bond at the going price. If the firm uses its *own* funds, so it doesn't have to borrow, the interest rate *still* represents a cost: Each dollar spent on plant and equipment *could* have been lent to someone else at the going interest rate. Thus, the interest rate is the *opportunity cost* of the firm's own funds when they are spent on plant and equipment.

A firm deciding whether to spend on plant and equipment compares the benefits of the project—the increase in future income—with the costs of the project. With a lower interest rate, the costs of funding investment projects are lower, so more projects will get the go-ahead. Other variables affect investment spending as well. But for given values of these other variables, a drop in the interest rate will cause an increase in spending on plant and equipment.

Interest rate changes also affect another kind of investment spending: spending on new houses and apartments that are built by developers or individuals. Most people borrow to buy houses or condominiums, and most developers borrow to build apartment buildings. The loan agreement for housing is called a *mortgage,* and mortgage interest rates move closely with other interest rates. Thus, when the Fed lowers the interest rate, families find it more affordable to buy homes, and landlords find it more profitable to build new apartments. Total investment in new housing increases.

Finally, in addition to investment spending, the interest rate affects consumption spending on big ticket items such as new cars, furniture, and dishwashers. Economists call these *consumer durables* because they usually last several years. People often borrow to buy consumer durables, and the interest rate they are charged tends to rise and fall with other interest rates in the economy. Spending on new cars, the most expensive durable that most of us buy, is especially sensitive to interest rate changes. When the interest rate falls, consumption spending rises at *any* level of disposable income. It causes a *shift* of the consumption function, not a movement along it. Therefore, we consider this impact on consumption to be a rise in autonomous consumption spending, called *a* in our discussion of the consumption function.

We can summarize the impact of monetary policy as follows:

> *When the Fed increases the money supply, the interest rate falls, and spending on three categories of goods increases: plant and equipment, new housing, and consumer durables (especially automobiles). When the Fed decreases the money supply, the interest rate rises, and these categories of spending fall.*

**Monetary Policy and the Economy.**  Now we can finally see how monetary policy affects the economy overall. The only remaining step is one you learned two chapters ago: how a change in spending affects output and employment. This is what our short-run macro model was all about.

In Figure 8, we revisit the short-run macro model, but we now include the money market in our analysis. In panel (a), the Fed has initially set the money supply at $500 billion. Equilibrium is at point *E,* with an interest rate (*r*) of 6 percent.

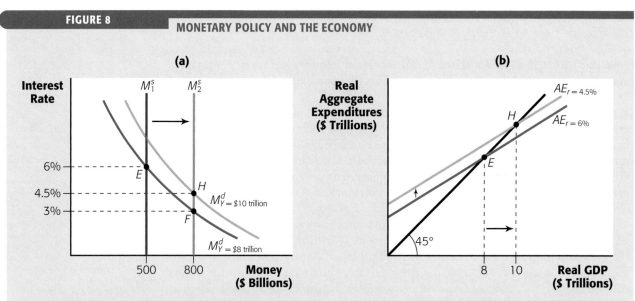

**FIGURE 8**

**MONETARY POLICY AND THE ECONOMY**

Monetary policy involves an interaction between the interest rate and equilibrium real GDP. Initially, the Fed has set the money supply at $500 billion, so the interest rate is 6 percent (point *E*). Given that interest rate, aggregate expenditure is $AE_{r\,=\,6\%}$ in panel (b), and real GDP is $8 trillion (point *E*).

If the Fed increases the money supply to $800 billion, money market equilibrium moves temporarily to point *F* in panel (a). The interest rate falls, stimulating interest-sensitive spending and driving aggregate expenditures upward in panel (b). Through the multiplier process, real GDP increases. As it does, the money demand curve shifts rightward in panel (a). In the new equilibrium, real GDP is $10 trillion and the interest rate is 4.5 percent (point *H*).

Panel (b) shows the familiar short-run aggregate expenditure diagram, with equilibrium at point *E*, and equilibrium GDP equal to $8 trillion.

But notice the new labels in the figure. The aggregate expenditure line has the subscript "*r* = 6%," and the money demand curve has the subscript "*Y* = $8 trillion." These are necessary because of the *interdependence* between the interest rate and equilibrium GDP. Recall that the money demand curve will shift if there is a change in real income. Therefore, our money demand curve is drawn for a particular level of real income—the level determined in panel (b), or $8 trillion. Similarly, as you are about to see, a change in the interest rate will cause the aggregate expenditure line to shift. Therefore, our aggregate expenditure line is drawn for a particular interest rate—the one determined in the money market, or 6 percent. As you can see, the equilibrium in each panel depends on the equilibrium in the other panel.

Now we suppose that the Fed increases the money supply to $800 billion. (Again, this is an unrealistically large change in the money supply, but it makes it easier to see the change in the figure.) In panel (a), the money market equilibrium moves from point *E* to point *F*, and the interest rate begins to drop. (It would drop all the way down to 3 percent, except that the money demand curve will start shifting as well before we are finished.) The drop in the interest rate causes planned investment spending on plant and equipment and on new housing to rise. It also causes an increase in consumption spending—especially on consumer durables like automobiles—to rise at any level of income. This is an increase in autonomous consumption spending (*a*). In panel (b), the rise in spending causes the aggregate expenditure line to shift upward, setting off the multiplier effect and increasing equilibrium GDP. The rise in income causes the money demand curve to shift rightward, since the demand for money is greater when income is higher.

To find the final equilibrium in the economy, we would need quite a bit of information about how sensitive spending is to the drop in the interest rate, as well as how changes in income feed back into the money market to affect the interest rate. In Figure 8, we've illustrated just one possibility, in which the new equilibrium is at point H in both the money market and the aggregate expenditure diagrams. At this new equilibrium, the interest rate ends up at 4.5 percent, so the higher aggregate expenditure line is labeled "$r = 4.5\%$." Equilibrium GDP has risen to $10 trillion, so the new higher money demand curve is labeled "$Y = \$10$ trillion." In the end, we see that the Fed, by increasing the money supply and lowering the interest rate, has increased the level of output.

We've covered a lot of ground to reach our conclusion, so let's review the highlights of how monetary policy works. This is what happens when the Fed conducts open market purchases of bonds:

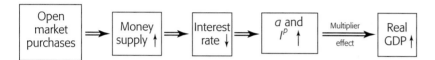

Open market *sales* by the Fed have exactly the opposite effects. In this case, the money supply curve in Figure 8 would shift leftward (not shown), driving the interest rate up. The rise in the interest rate would cause a decrease in interest-sensitive spending ($a$ and $I$), shifting the aggregate expenditure line downward. Equilibrium GDP would fall by a multiple of the initial decrease in spending.

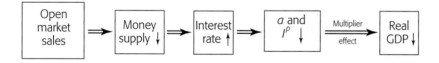

## FISCAL POLICY (AND OTHER SPENDING CHANGES) REVISITED

Two chapters ago, we discussed how fiscal policy affects the economy in the short run. For example, an increase in government purchases causes output to rise, and in successive rounds of the multiplier, spending and output rise still more. Now that we've added the money market to our analysis, it's time to revisit fiscal policy. As you'll see, its effects are now a bit more complicated.

Figure 9 shows the money market and the familiar short-run aggregate expenditure diagram. Initially, we have equilibrium in both panels. In panel (a), the money market equilibrium is point E, with the interest rate at 6 percent. In panel (b), the solid aggregate expenditure line, labeled "$r = 6\%$," is consistent with the interest rate we've found in the money market. As you can see, with this aggregate expenditure line, the equilibrium is at

When thinking about the effects of monetary policy, try not to confuse movements *along* the aggregate expenditure line with *shifts* of the line itself. We move along the line only when a change in *income* causes spending to change. The line shifts when something *other* than a change in income causes spending to change.

When the Fed changes the interest rate, both types of changes occur, but it's important to keep the order straight. *First,* the drop in the interest rate (something other than income) causes interest-sensitive spending to change, *shifting* the aggregate expenditure line. *Then,* increases in income in each round of the multiplier cause further increases in spending, moving us *along* the new aggregate expenditure line.

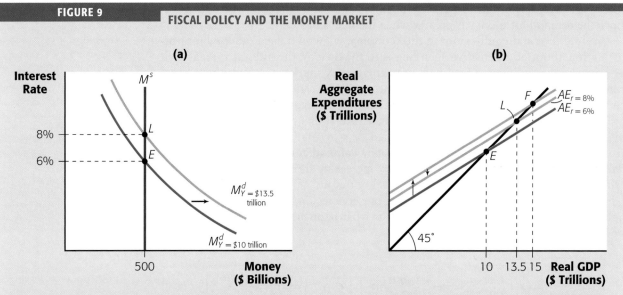

**FIGURE 9**

**FISCAL POLICY AND THE MONEY MARKET**

The economy is initially in equilibrium with an interest rate of 6 percent in panel (a) and real GDP of $10 trillion in panel (b). An increase in government purchases shifts the aggregate expenditure line upward, triggering the multiplier process. If the interest rate did not change, equilibrium would be reestablished at point F in panel (b) with real GDP of $15 trillion. But the increase in GDP stimulates money demand in panel (a), driving the interest rate upward to 8 percent at point L. That reduces interest-sensitive spending, lowering aggregate expenditure to $AE_{r=8\%}$ in panel (b) so that the real GDP at the new equilibrium is $13.5 trillion (point L).

point E, with real GDP equal to $10 trillion, just as we assumed when we drew the money demand curve in panel (a).

**An Increase in Government Purchases.**  Now let's see what happens when the government changes its fiscal policy, say, by increasing government purchases by $2 trillion. Panel (b) shows the initial effect: The aggregate expenditure line shifts upward, by $2 trillion, to the topmost aggregate expenditure line. This new aggregate expenditure line is drawn for the same interest rate as the original line: $r = 6\%$. The shift illustrates what *would* happen if there were no change in the interest rate, as in our analysis of fiscal policy two chapters ago.

As you've learned, the increase in government purchases will set off the multiplier process, increasing GDP and income in each round. *If this were the end of the story,* the result would be a rise in real GDP equal to $[1/(1 - MPC)] \times \Delta G$. In our example, with an MPC of 0.6, the multiplier would be $1/(1 - 0.6) = 2.5$. The new equilibrium would be at point F, with GDP equal to $15 trillion—a rise of $5 trillion.

But point F is *not* the end of our story—not when we include effects in the money market. As income increases, the money demand curve in panel (a) will shift rightward, raising the interest rate. As a result, autonomous consumption (a) and investment spending (I) will decrease and shift the aggregate expenditure line downward. That is,

> *an increase in government purchases, which by itself shifts the aggregate expenditure line upward, also sets in motion forces that shift it downward.*

We can outline these forces as follows:

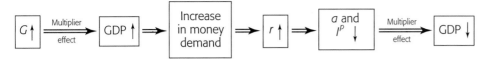

Thus, at the same time as the increase in government purchases has a *positive* multiplier effect on GDP, the decrease in *a* and *I* have *negative* multiplier effects. Which effect dominates? The positive multiplier effect. Why? Because the only force pulling GDP down—a higher interest rate—*depends upon* a rise in GDP. (It is the rise in GDP that shifts the money demand curve and drives up the interest rate.) If the negative effect on GDP were stronger, GDP would actually decrease in the end, so the interest rate would be lower, not higher, and there would be no force pulling GDP down at all.

Thus, we know that an increase in government purchases causes GDP to rise. But the rise is smaller than the simple multiplier formula suggests. That's because the simple multiplier ignores the moderating effect of a rise in the interest rate on GDP.

> *In the short run, an increase in government purchases causes real GDP to rise, but not by as much as if the interest rate had not increased.*

Let's sum up the characteristics of the new equilibrium after an increase in government purchases:

- The aggregate expenditure line is higher, but by less than $\Delta G$.
- Real GDP and real income are higher, but the rise is less than $[1/(1 - MPC)] \times \Delta G$.
- The money demand curve has shifted rightward, because real income is higher.
- The interest rate is higher, because money demand has increased.
- Autonomous consumption and investment spending are lower, because the interest rate is higher.

Figure 9 indicates one possible result that is consistent with all of these requirements. In the figure, the new equilibrium occurs at point *L* in both panels, with the new equilibrium GDP at $13.5 trillion and the new equilibrium interest rate at 8 percent. Notice that real GDP has risen, but by only $3.5 trillion—not the $5 trillion suggested by the simple multiplier formula. Moreover, the two panels of the diagram are consistent with each other. The aggregate expenditure line (labeled *r* = 8%) corresponds to the equilibrium interest rate in the money market. The money demand curve (labeled "*Y* = $13.5 trillion") corresponds to the equilibrium GDP in the aggregate expenditure diagram.

**Crowding Out Once Again.** Our analysis illustrates an interesting by-product of fiscal policy. Comparing our initial equilibrium (point *E* in both panels) to the final equilibrium (point *L*), we see that government purchases increase, but—because of the rise in the interest rate—*investment spending has decreased.*

What about consumption spending? It is influenced by two opposing forces. The rise in the interest rate causes *some* types of consumption spending (e.g., on automobiles) to decrease, but the rise in *income* makes other types of consumption spending *increase*. Thus, an increase in government purchases may increase or decrease consumption spending, depending on which effect is stronger.

Summing up:

> *When effects in the money market are included in the short-run macro model, an increase in government purchases raises the interest rate and* crowds out *some private investment spending. It* may *also crowd out consumption spending.*

This should sound familiar. In the classical, long-run model, an increase in government purchases also causes crowding out. But there is one important difference between crowding out in the classical model and the effects we are outlining here. In the classical model, there is *complete crowding out:* Investment spending and consumption spending fall by the same amount that government purchases rise. As a result, total spending does not change at all, and neither does GDP. This is why, in the long run, we expect fiscal policy to have no effect on equilibrium GDP.

In the short run, however, our conclusion is somewhat different. While we expect *some* crowding out from an increase in government purchases, *it is not complete.* Investment spending falls, and consumption spending *may* fall, but together, they do not drop by as much as the rise in government purchases. In the short run, real GDP rises.

**Other Spending Changes.**    So far, we've focused on the impact on the economy of a change in government purchases. But our analysis extends to *any* shock that shifts the aggregate expenditure line. Positive shocks would shift the aggregate expenditure line upward, just as in Figure 9. More specifically:

> *Increases in government purchases, investment, and autonomous consumption, as well as decreases in taxes, all shift the aggregate expenditure line upward. Real GDP rises, but so does the interest rate. The rise in equilibrium GDP is smaller than if the interest rate remained constant.*

For example, a $2 trillion increase in investment spending shifts the aggregate expenditure line upward by $5 trillion, as in Figure 9. If there were no rise in the interest rate, real GDP would rise according to the simple multiplier of $1/(1 - MPC)$ = 2.5. Applying this multiplier to a $2 trillion increase in investment tells us that real GDP would rise by a full $5 trillion. But once again, the rise in GDP does drive up the interest rate in the money market, which works to decrease investment and interest-sensitive consumption. And once again, GDP will rise, but not by as much as the simple multiplier suggests.

Negative shocks shift the aggregate expenditure line *downward.* More specifically:

> *Decreases in government purchases, investment, and autonomous consumption, as well as increases in taxes, all shift the aggregate expenditure line downward. Real GDP falls, but so does the interest rate. The decline in equilibrium GDP is smaller than if the interest rate remained constant.*

**What About the Fed?**    In our analysis of spending shocks, we've made an implicit but important assumption. Look back at Figure 9. Notice that, from beginning to end, the money supply curve never shifted. This implies that the Fed just stands by, not interfering at all with the changes we've been describing. More specifically, we've been assuming that *the Fed does not change the money supply in response to shifts in the aggregate expenditure line.*

While this assumption has helped us focus on the impact of spending shocks, it is not the way the Fed has conducted policy during the past few decades. Instead, the Fed has usually responded to neutralize the impact of spending shocks. That is, it has used monetary policy to prevent spending shocks from changing GDP at all. You'll learn why, and how, the Fed does this when we revisit monetary policy in the chapter after next.

## ARE THERE TWO THEORIES OF THE INTEREST RATE?

At the beginning of this chapter, you were reminded that you had already learned a different theory of how the interest rate is determined in the economy. In the classical model, the interest rate is determined in the *market for loanable funds*. In this chapter, you learned that the interest rate is determined in the *money market,* where people make decisions about holding their wealth as money and bonds. Which theory is correct?

The answer is: Both are correct. The classical model, you remember, tells us what happens in the economy in the *long run*. Therefore, when we ask what changes the interest rate over long periods of time—many years or even a decade—we should think about the market for loanable funds. But over shorter time periods—days, weeks, or months—we should use the money market model presented in this chapter.

Why don't we use the classical loanable funds model to determine the interest rate in the short run? Because, as you've seen, the economy behaves differently in the short run than it does in the long run. For example, in the classical model, output is automatically at full employment. But in the short run, output changes as the economy goes through booms and recessions. These changes in output affect the loanable funds market in ways that the classical model does not consider. For example, flip back to the chapter on the classical model and look at Figure 9 there. Recessions, which decrease household income, also decrease household saving at any given interest rate: With less income, households will spend less *and* save less. The supply of loanable funds curve would shift leftward in the diagram, and the interest rate would rise. The classical model—because it ignores recessions—ignores these short-run changes in the supply of loanable funds.

The classical model also ignores an important idea discussed in this chapter: that the public continuously chooses how to divide its wealth between money and bonds. In the short run, the public's preferences over money and bonds can change, and this, in turn, can change the interest rate. This idea does not appear in the classical model.

Of course, in the long run, the classical model gives us an accurate picture of how the economy—and the interest rate—behaves. Recessions and booms don't last forever, so the economy returns to full employment. Thus, in the long run we needn't worry about recessions causing shifts in the supply of loanable funds curve. Also, changes in preferences for holding money and bonds are rather short lived. We can ignore these changes when we take a long-run view.

> *Our view of the interest rate depends on the time period we are considering. In the long run, we view the interest rate as determined in the market for loanable funds, where household saving is lent to businesses and the government. In the short run, we view the interest rate as determined in the money market, where wealth holders adjust their wealth between money and bonds, and the Fed participates by controlling the money supply.*

# EXPECTATIONS AND THE FED

*Using the*
## THEORY

So far, we've considered changes in the interest rate engineered by the Fed, or caused by a spending shock that shifts the aggregate expenditure line upward or downward. Here, we discuss one additional source of interest rate changes: a *shift in the money demand curve*. Note that you've already seen what happens when the money demand curve shifts as a by-product of a spending shock (Figure 9). Here, we explore what happens when the *initial shock* to the economy is a shift in the money demand curve. More specifically, we'll look at what happens when a change in expectations about future interest rates shifts the demand for money curve.

## EXPECTATIONS AND MONEY DEMAND

Why should expectations about the future interest rate affect money demand *today*? Because bond prices and interest rates are negatively related. If you expect the interest rate to rise in the future, then you also expect the price of bonds to fall in the future.

To see this more clearly, imagine (pleasantly) that you hold a bond promising to pay you $100,000 in exactly one year and that the going interest rate is currently 5 percent. The price for your bond will be $95,238. Why? At that price, a buyer would earn $100,000 − $95,238 = $4,762 in interest. Since the bond cost $95,238, the buyer's rate of return would be $4,762/$95,238 = 0.05, or 5 percent—the going rate of interest. If you tried to charge more than $95,238 for the bond, its rate of return would be less than 5 percent, so no one would buy it—they could always earn 5 percent by buying another bond that pays the going rate of interest.

Now suppose that you *expect* the interest rate to rise to 10 percent in the near future, say, next week. (This is an unrealistically large change in the interest rate in so short a time, but it makes the point dramatically.) Then next week, the going price for your bond would be only about $90,909. At that price, a buyer would earn $100,000 − $90,909 = $9,091 in interest, so the buyer's rate of return would be $9,091/$90,909 = 0.10, or 10 percent. Thus, if you believe that the interest rate is about to rise from 5 to 10 percent, you also believe the price of your bond is about to fall from $95,238 to $90,909—a drop of over $4,300.

What would you do?

Logically, you would want to sell your bond *now*, before the price drops. If you still want to hold this type of bond later, you can always buy it back next week at the lower price, and gain from the transaction. Thus, if you expect the interest rate to rise in the future, you will want to exchange your bonds for money *today*. Your demand for money will increase.

Of course, if *you* expect the interest rate to drop, and your expectation is reasonable, others will probably feel the same way. They, too, will want to trade in their bonds for money. Thus, if the expectation is widespread, there will be an increase in the demand for money economy-wide.

> *A general expectation that interest rates will rise (bond prices will fall) in the future will cause the money demand curve to shift rightward in the present.*

Notice that when people expect the interest rate to rise, we *shift* the money demand curve, rather than move along it. People will want to hold more money at any *current* interest rate.

**FIGURE 10**

**INTEREST RATE EXPECTATIONS**

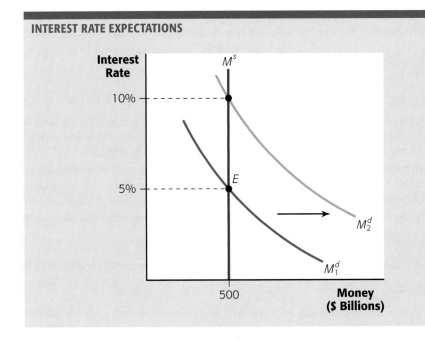

If households and firms expect the interest rate to rise in the future, their demand for money will increase today. Starting from equilibrium at point *E,* an expected increase in the interest rate from 5 percent to 10 percent will increase money demand to $M_2^d$. The result is a self-fulfilling prophecy: The interest rate increases to 10 percent *today.*

Figure 10 shows what will happen in the money market when people expect the interest rate to rise. Initially, with the money supply equal to $500 billion, the equilibrium is at point *E* and the interest rate is 5 percent. But the expected rise in the interest rate shifts the money demand curve rightward. After the shift, there is an excess demand for money and an excess supply of bonds at the original interest rate of 5 percent. As the public attempts to sell bonds, the price of bonds will fall, which means the interest rate will rise.

How far will the interest rate rise? That depends. Imagine a simple case where *everyone* in the economy expected the interest rate to rise to 10 percent next week. Then *no one* would want to hold bonds at any *current* interest rate less than 10 percent. For example, if the interest rate rose to 9 percent, people would still expect it to rise further, so they would still want to sell their bonds. Therefore, to return the money market to equilibrium, the interest rate would rise to exactly the level that people expected. This is the case we've illustrated in Figure 10, where the money demand curve shifts rightward by just enough to raise the interest rate to 10 percent. More generally:

> *When the public as a whole expects the interest rate to rise in the future, they will drive up the interest rate in the present.*

When information comes along that makes people believe that interest rates will rise and bond prices fall in the near future, the result is an immediate rise in the interest rate and a fall in bond prices. This principle operates even if the information is false and there is ultimately no reason for the interest rate to rise. Thus, a general expectation that interest rates will rise can be a *self-fulfilling prophecy:* Because people believe it, it actually happens. Their expectation alone is enough to drive up the interest rate.

This immediate response to information about the future—and the possibility of a self-fulfilling prophecy—works in the opposite direction as well:

> *When the public expects the interest rate to drop in the future, they will drive down the interest rate in the present.*

In this case, the public expects bond prices to rise, so they try to shift their wealth from money to bonds. In Figure 10, the money demand curve would shift leftward (not shown). The price of bonds would rise, and the interest rate would fall, just as was originally expected.

## MANAGING EXPECTATIONS

Changes in interest rates due to changes in expectations can have important consequences. First, fortunes can be won and lost depending on how people bet on the future. For example, suppose you believe the interest rate is about to drop, so you buy bonds, thinking their price is about to rise. But suppose the interest rate actually *rises* instead. Then your bonds will immediately drop in price and be worth less than what you paid for them. In fact, it is not unusual for major bondholders—such as pension funds or money market mutual funds—to gain or lose millions of dollars in a single day based on a good or a bad bet.

Another consequence is one we discussed earlier in this chapter: Changes in the interest rate affect aggregate expenditure, and therefore output. Fortunately, the Fed can counteract these changes with open market purchases or sales of bonds, as needed, and we'll discuss this a bit later.

Still, the public's ever-changing expectations about future interest rates make the Fed's job more difficult. Expectations can change interest rates, and changes in interest rates can affect individual fortunes as well as the economy as a whole. This observation helps explain some seemingly mysterious Fed behavior. Public policy statements made by the Fed's chair (currently Alan Greenspan) or by other Fed officials are remarkably tentative, and sometimes downright confusing. You can read them again and again and still have no idea what the Fed intends to do about interest rates in the future.

For example, on July 9, 1993, the Federal Reserve's Open Market Committee (FOMC) released a summary of the minutes of its May 1993 meeting. Here is the part of the statement explaining the Fed's future intentions regarding the money supply and interest rates. See if you can tell what the Fed planned to do.

> *In the view of a majority of the members . . . developments over recent months were sufficiently worrisome to warrant positioning policy for a move toward restraint should signs of continuing inflation continue to multiply. . . . Slightly greater reserve restraint would or slightly lesser reserve restraint might be acceptable.*[2]

And here is the key sentence from a more recent FOMC statement, released after its May 1999 meeting:

> *. . . [T]he Committee recognizes the need to be alert to developments over coming months that might indicate that financial conditions may no longer be consistent with containing inflation.*[3]

This is the kind of writing that gives English teachers indigestion. But from the Fed's point of view, the obfuscation is understandable. If the officials of the FOMC had given stronger hints about their thinking, the money and bond markets might have gone into overdrive, as people rushed to buy or sell bonds in order to profit (or avoid loss) from the Fed's action. On rare occasions, Fed officials—by speaking

---

[2]    *New York Times*, July 10, 1993.
[3]    Federal Reserve Board Press Release, May 18, 1999 (*http://www.bog.frb.fed.us/BoardDocs/Press/General/1999/19990518/DEFAULT.HTM*).

more clearly—have given unintentionally strong hints and then had to quickly undo the damage with further statements or open market operations.

But secrecy about the Fed's intentions leads to surprises when the Fed finally acts, and surprises, too, create turmoil in the financial markets. In late 1998—after urging by government officials and the financial community—the Fed began an experiment: Immediately after its meetings, the FOMC would reveal if it had any significant "bias" toward either raising or lowering rates at its next meeting. (The Fed had been deciding on such a bias since the 1960s, but—until 1998—had kept the information secret until weeks later.) The idea was to cushion the blow when the interest rate move finally came, so that the financial markets would react more gradually. But the experiment failed because the public reacted as if the Fed's bias was really its *plan* for interest rates, despite Fed statements to the contrary. Thus, each announcement of bias caused a frenzy of activity in financial markets.

In February 2000, the Fed abandoned its experiment with *bias*, and began a new experiment: It would just state how the FOMC viewed *risks* to the economy, rather than hint at future changes in interest rates. This experiment represented a new kind of compromise between clarity and secrecy: The FOMC would inform the public of *which* policy direction was *more likely*, but provide no information on *how likely* the policy was. For example, here is the statement released by the FOMC immediately after its meeting on February 2, 2000, the first such release under the new experiment:

> *Against the background of its long-run goals of price stability and sustainable economic growth and of the information currently available, the Committee believes the risks are weighted mainly toward conditions that may generate heightened inflation pressures in the foreseeable future.*[4]

As you'll see in the chapter after next, the Fed usually responds to inflationary dangers by raising interest rates. By stating that it viewed inflation as a greater danger than recession, the FOMC was informing the public that it was more likely to raise rates than to lower them. However, it was not saying that it *planned* to raise interest rates or even that a rise was likely. That would depend on how *important* the FOMC viewed the inflationary dangers, something that was not revealed in the statement.

The minutes of the most recent FOMC meeting are available at http://www.bog.frb.fed.us/FOMC/minutes.

---

[4]   Federal Reserve Board Press Release, February 2, 2000 (*http://www.bog.frb.fed.us/BoardDocs/Press/General/2000/20000202/DEFAULT.HTM*).

## S U M M A R Y

The interest rate is a key macroeconomic variable. This chapter explores how the supply and demand for money interact to determine the interest rate in the short run, and how the Federal Reserve can adjust the money supply to change the interest rate.

An individual's demand for money indicates the fraction of wealth that person wishes to hold in the form of money, for different interest rates. Money is useful as a means of payment, but holding money means sacrificing the interest that could be earned by holding bonds instead. The higher the interest rate, the larger the fraction of their wealth people will hold in the form of bonds, and the smaller the fraction they will hold as money.

The demand for money is sensitive to the interest rate, but it also depends on the price level, real income, and expecta-

tions. An increase in the price level, higher real income, or an increase in the expected future interest rate can each shift the money demand curve to the right.

The money supply is under the control of the Fed and is independent of the interest rate. Equilibrium in the money market occurs at the intersection of the downward-sloping money demand curve and the vertical money supply curve. The interest rate will adjust so that the quantity of money demanded by households and firms just equals the quantity of money supplied by the Fed and the banking system.

Conditions in the money market mirror conditions in the bond market. If the interest rate is above equilibrium in the money market, there will be an excess supply of money there. People *want to* hold less money than they actually *do* hold, which means that they wish to hold more bonds than they do hold. An excess supply of money means an excess demand for bonds. As people try to obtain more bonds, the price of bonds rises, and the interest rate falls. Thus, an excess supply of money will cause the interest rate to fall. Similarly, an excess demand for money will cause the interest rate to rise.

The Fed can increase the money supply through an open market purchase of bonds, and decrease it through an open market sale. An increase in the money stock creates an excess supply of money. Very quickly, the interest rate will fall so that the public is willing to hold the now-higher money supply. A decrease in the money stock will drive up the interest rate.

Changes in the interest rate affect interest-sensitive forms of spending—firms' spending on plant and equipment, new housing constructions, and households' purchases of "big ticket" consumer durables. By lowering the interest rate, the Fed can stimulate aggregate expenditures and increase GDP through the multiplier process.

Finally, expectations of future interest rate changes can become self-fulfilling prophecies, as well as create undesirable turmoil in financial markets.

## K E Y   T E R M S

wealth constraint
money demand curve

money supply curve
excess supply of money

excess demand for bonds

federal funds rate

## R E V I E W   Q U E S T I O N S

1. Why do individuals choose to hold some of their wealth in the form of money? Besides individual tastes, what factors help determine how much money an individual holds?

2. Why does the money demand curve slope downward? Which of the following result in a shift of the money demand curve and which result in a movement along the curve? If there is a shift, in which direction?
   a. The Fed lowers interest rates.
   b. The Fed raises interest rates.
   c. The price level falls.
   d. The price level rises.
   e. Income increases.
   f. Income decreases.

3. Why is the economy's money supply curve vertical? What causes the money supply curve to shift?

4. What sequence of events brings the money market to equilibrium if there is an excess supply of money? An excess demand for money?

5. The text mentions that starting in June 1999 the Fed began selling government bonds, and as a result, the interest rate rose. Explain how the Fed's sale of bonds led to a lower interest rate.

6. Describe how an increase in the interest rate affects spending on the following:
   a. plant and equipment
   b. new housing
   c. consumer durables

7. Does a change in expectations about the interest rate result in a shift in the money demand curve or a movement along it? Explain what happens in the money market when people expect the interest rate to fall.

8. Why do we have both a short-run and a long-run theory of the interest rate? Briefly, what determines the interest rate in the short run? In the long run?

## P R O B L E M S   A N D   E X E R C I S E S

1. Assume the demand deposit multiplier is 10. For each of the following, state the impact on the money supply curve (the direction it will shift, and the amount of the shift).
   a. The Fed purchases bonds worth $10 billion.
   b. The Fed sells bonds worth $5 billion.

2. A bond promises to pay $500 one year from now. For the following prices, find the corresponding interest payments and interest rates that the bond offers.

| Price | Amount Paid in One Year | Interest Payment | Interest Rate |
|-------|-------------------------|------------------|---------------|
| $375  | $500                    | _____       | _____    |
| $425  | $500                    | _____       | _____    |
| $450  | $500                    | _____       | _____    |
| $500  | $500                    | _____       | _____    |

As the price of the bond rises, what happens to the bond's interest rate?

3.  "A general expectation that the interest rate will fall can be a self-fulfilling prophecy." Explain what this means.

4.  Suppose that, in an attempt to prevent the economy from overheating, the Fed raises the interest rate. Illustrate graphically, using a diagram similar to Figure 8 in this chapter, the effect on the money supply, interest rate, and GDP.

5.  For each of the following events, state (1) the impact on the money demand curve, and (2) whether the Fed should increase or decrease the money supply if it wants to keep the interest rate unchanged. (*Hint:* It will help to draw a diagram of the money market for each case.)
    a.  People start making more of their purchases over the Internet, using credit cards.
    b.  Increasing fear of credit card fraud makes people stop buying goods over the Internet with credit cards, and discourages the use of credit cards in other types of purchases as well.
    c.  A new type of electronic account is created in which your funds are held in bonds up to the second you make a purchase. Then—when you buy something— just the right amount of bonds are transferred to the

ownership of the seller. (*Hint:* Would you want to increase or decrease the amount of your wealth in the form of money after this new type of account were available?)

6.  Determine whether monetary policy is *more* or *less* effective in changing GDP when autonomous consumption and investment spending are very sensitive to changes in the interest rate, and explain your reasoning.

7.  In a later chapter, you will learn that a drop in the interest rate has *another* channel of influence on real GDP: It causes a depreciation of the dollar (that is, it makes the dollar cheaper to foreigners), which, in turn, increases our net exports.
    a.  When we take account of the effect on net exports, does a given change in the money supply have *more* or *less* of an impact on real GDP?
    b.  Suppose that the Fed wants to rein in real GDP as it did in late 1999 and early 2000. Should the Fed raise the interest rate by more or by less when it takes the impact on net exports into account (compared to the case of no impact on net exports)? Explain.

## C H A L L E N G E   Q U E S T I O N S

1.  Determine whether *fiscal policy* is *more* or *less* effective in changing GDP when autonomous consumption and investment spending are very sensitive to changes in the interest rate, and explain your reasoning.

2.  In Problem 7, you were asked how the *net export* effect changes the potency of monetary policy. Answer the same question about fiscal policy (that is, does the net export effect make fiscal policy more or less potent in changing GDP?).

## E X P E R I E N T I A L   E X E R C I S E

1.  A favorite activity of many macroeconomists is "Fed watching." Go to the Federal Reserve System's Web site and look for the most recent Congressional testimony of the board chairman (*http://www.bog.frb.fed.us/ boarddocs/testimony*). Is the Fed currently signalling that it will raise or lower interest rates, or that it will hold them constant? Is the Fed stating its intentions directly, or hiding them with vague language?

http://

# AGGREGATE DEMAND AND AGGREGATE SUPPLY

Economic fluctuations are facts of life. If you need a reminder, look back at Figure 1 in the chapter titled "Economic Fluctuations." There you can see that while potential GDP trends upward year after year—due to economic growth—*actual* GDP tends to rise above and fall below potential over shorter periods.

But the figure also reveals another important fact about the economy: Deviations from potential output don't last forever. When output dips below or rises above potential, the economy returns to potential output after a few quarters or years. True, in some of these episodes, government policy—either fiscal or monetary—helped the economy return to full employment more quickly. But even without corrective policies—such as during long parts of the Great Depression of the 1930s—the economy shows a remarkable tendency to begin moving back toward potential output. Why? And what, exactly, is the mechanism that brings us back to our potential when we have strayed from it? These are the questions we will address in this chapter. And we'll address them by studying the behavior of a variable that we've put aside for several chapters: the price level.

The chapter begins by exploring the relationship between the price level and output. This is a two-way relationship, as you can see in Figure 1 in *this* chapter. On the one hand, changes in the price level cause changes in real GDP. This causal relationship is illustrated by the *aggregate demand curve,* which we will discuss shortly. On the other hand, changes in real GDP cause changes in the price level. This relationship is summarized by the *aggregate supply curve,* to which we will turn later.

Once we've developed the aggregate demand and supply curves, we'll be able to use them to understand how changes in the price level—sometimes gently, other times more harshly—steer the economy back toward potential output.

## THE AGGREGATE DEMAND CURVE

In this section, we'll focus on how changes in the price level affect equilibrium real GDP. We'll postpone until later the question of *why* the price level might change.

**FIGURE 1**

**THE TWO-WAY RELATIONSHIP BETWEEN OUTPUT AND THE PRICE LEVEL**

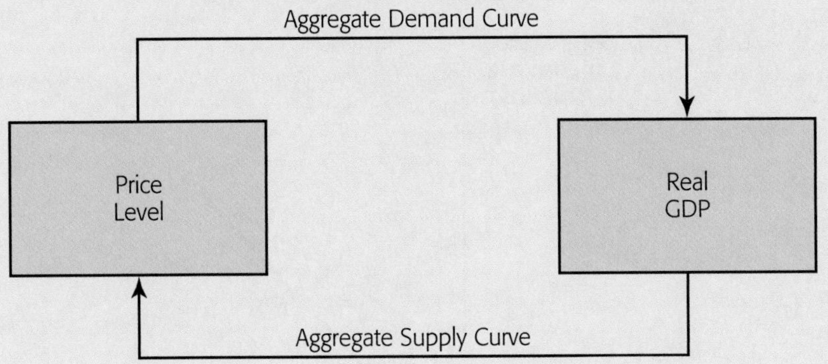

Aggregate Demand Curve

| Price Level |          | Real GDP |

Aggregate Supply Curve

## THE PRICE LEVEL AND THE MONEY MARKET

Our first step in understanding how price level changes affect the economy is their impact in the money market. And this impact is straightforward: When the price level rises, the money demand curve shifts rightward. Why? Remember that the money demand curve tells us how much of their wealth people want to hold as money (as opposed to bonds) at each interest rate. People hold bonds because of the interest they pay; people hold money because of its convenience. Each day, as we make purchases, we need cash or funds in our checking account to pay for them. If the price level rises, and the average purchase becomes more expensive, we'll need to hold more of our wealth as money just to achieve the same level of convenience. Thus, at any given interest rate, the demand for money increases, and the money demand curve shifts rightward.

The shift in money demand, and its impact on the economy, is illustrated in Figure 2. Panel (a) has our familiar money market diagram. We'll assume that, initially, the price level in the economy is equal to 100. With this price level, the money market is in equilibrium at point $E$, with an interest rate of 6 percent.

In panel (b), equilibrium GDP is at point $E$, with output equal to $10 trillion. The aggregate expenditure line is marked "$r = 6\%$," which is the equilibrium interest rate we just found in the money market.

Now let's imagine a rather substantial rise in the price level—from 100 to 140. What will happen in the economy? The initial impact is in the money market. The money demand curve will start to shift rightward, and the interest rate will rise. Next, in panel (b), the higher interest rate decreases interest-sensitive spending—business investment, new housing, and consumer durables. The aggregate expenditure line shifts downward, and equilibrium real GDP decreases. All of these changes continue until we reach a new, consistent equilibrium in both panels. Compared with our initial position, this new equilibrium has the following characteristics:

- The money demand curve has shifted rightward.
- The interest rate is higher.
- The aggregate expenditure line has shifted downward.
- Equilibrium GDP is lower.

Remember that all of these changes are caused by a rise in the price level.

The points labeled $H$ in panels (a) and (b) show one possible new equilibrium consistent with these requirements. In panel (a), the money demand curve has

**FIGURE 2**

**DERIVING THE AGGREGATE DEMAND CURVE**

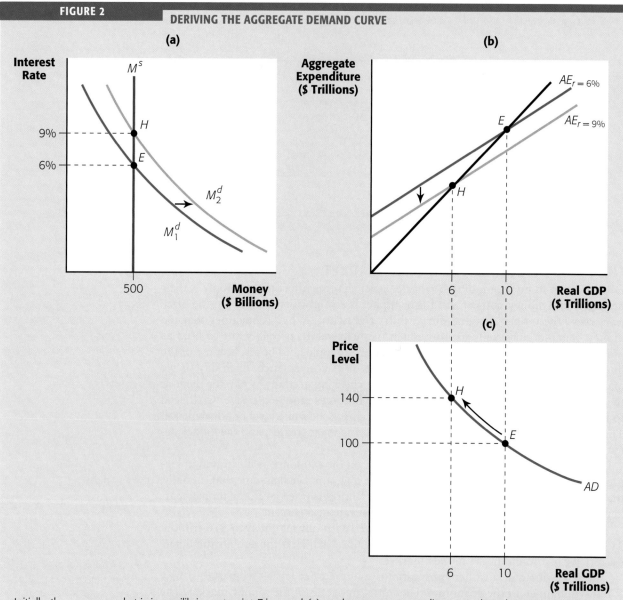

Initially, the money market is in equilibrium at point *E* in panel (a), and aggregate expenditure equals real GDP at point *E* in panel (b). That price-output combination determines point *E* in panel (c). A higher price level—140—increases money demand, raises the interest rate, reduces interest-sensitive spending, and lowers aggregate expenditure. Through the multiplier process, equilibrium real GDP falls to $6 trillion. The new price-output combination determines point *H* in panel (c). Connecting points like *E* and *H* yields the downward-sloping aggregate demand (*AD*) curve.

shifted to $M_2^d$. The interest rate has risen to 9 percent. The aggregate expenditure line has shifted downward, to the one marked "$r = 9\%$." Finally, equilibrium output has fallen to $6 trillion.

Now recall the initial event that caused real GDP to fall: a rise in the price level. We've thus established an important principle:

> *A rise in the price level causes a decrease in equilibrium GDP.*

## DERIVING THE AGGREGATE DEMAND CURVE

In panel (c), we introduce a new curve that summarizes the negative relationship between the price level and equilibrium GDP more directly. In this panel, the price level is measured along the vertical axis, while real GDP is on the horizontal. Point $E$ represents our initial equilibrium, with $P = 100$ and equilibrium GDP = $10 trillion. Point $H$ represents the new equilibrium, with $P = 140$ and equilibrium GDP = $6 trillion. If we continued to change the price level to other values—raising it further to 150, lowering it to 85, and so on—we would find that each different price level results in a different equilibrium GDP. This is illustrated by the downward-sloping curve in the figure, which we call the *aggregate demand curve.*

> The *aggregate demand* (AD) *curve tells us the equilibrium real GDP at any price level.*

**Aggregate demand (AD) curve** A curve indicating equilibrium GDP at each price level.

## UNDERSTANDING THE *AD* CURVE

The *AD* curve is unlike any other curve you've encountered in this text. In all other cases, our curves have represented simple behavioral relationships. For example, the demand curve for maple syrup shows us how a change in price affects the behavior of buyers in a market. Similarly, the aggregate expenditure line shows how a change in income affects total spending in the economy.

But the *AD* curve represents more than just a behavioral relationship between two variables. Each point on the curve represents a short-run *equilibrium* in the economy. For example, point $E$ on the *AD* curve in Figure 2 tells us that when the price level is 100, *equilibrium* GDP is $10 trillion. Thus, point $E$ doesn't just tell us that total spending is $10 trillion; rather, it tells us that when $P = 100$, and when spending and output have the same value, then *both* are equal to $10 trillion.

As you can see, a better name for the *AD* curve would be the "equilibrium output at each price level" curve—not a very catchy name. The *AD* curve gets its name because it *resembles* the demand curve for an individual product. It's a downward-sloping curve, with the price level (instead of the price of a single good) on the vertical axis and *equilibrium total output* (instead of the quantity of a single good demanded) on the horizontal axis. But there the similarity ends. The *AD* curve is not a demand curve at all, in spite of its name.

**DANGEROUS CURVES**

Watch out for two very common mistakes about the aggregate demand curve. The first is thinking that it is simply a "total demand" or "total spending" curve for the economy, telling us the total quantity of output that purchasers want to buy at each price level. This is an oversimplification. Rather, the *AD* curve tells us the *equilibrium real GDP* at each price level. Remember that equilibrium GDP is the level of output at which total spending *equals* total output. Thus, total spending is only part of the story behind the *AD* curve: the other part is the requirement that total spending and total output be equal.

A second, related mistake is thinking that the *AD* curve slopes downward for the same reason that a microeconomic demand curve slopes downward. This, too, is wrong: *microeconomic* demand curves for individual products rely on an entirely different mechanism than the one we've described for the *AD* curve. In the market for maple syrup, for example, a rise in price causes quantity demanded to decrease mostly because people switch to *other* goods that are now relatively cheaper. But along the *AD* curve, a rise in the price level generally causes the prices of all goods to increase *together*. In this case, there are no relatively cheaper goods to switch to!

The *AD* curve works in an entirely different way from microeconomic demand curves. Along the *AD* curve, an increase in the price level raises the interest rate in the money market, which decreases spending on interest-sensitive goods, causing a drop in equilibrium GDP.

## MOVEMENTS ALONG THE *AD* CURVE

As you will see later in this chapter, a variety of events can cause the price level to change, and move us *along* the AD curve. It's important to understand what happens in the economy as we make such a move.

Look again at the AD curve in panel (c) of Figure 2. Suppose the price level rises, and we move from point E to point H along this curve. Then the following sequence of events occurs: The rise in the price level increases the demand for money, raises the interest rate, decreases autonomous consumption (*a*) and investment spending ($I^p$), and works through the multiplier to decrease equilibrium GDP. The process can be summarized as follows:

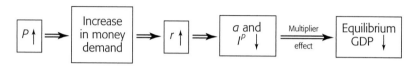

The opposite sequence of events will occur if the price level falls, moving us rightward along the AD curve:

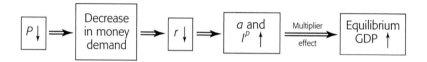

## SHIFTS OF THE *AD* CURVE

When we move along the AD curve in Figure 2, we assume that the price level changes, but that other influences on equilibrium GDP are constant. When any of these other influences on GDP changes, the AD curve will shift. The distinction between movements along the AD curve and shifts of the curve itself is very important. Always keep the following rule in mind:

> *When a change in the price level causes equilibrium GDP to change, we move along the* AD *curve. Whenever anything other than the price level causes equilibrium GDP to change, the* AD *curve itself shifts.*

What are these other influences on GDP? They are the very same changes you learned about in previous chapters. Specifically, equilibrium GDP will change whenever there is a change in any of the following:

- government purchases
- taxes
- autonomous consumption spending
- investment spending
- net exports
- the money supply

Let's consider some examples and see how each causes the AD curve to shift.

**Spending Shocks.**  Spending shocks initially affect the economy by shifting the aggregate expenditure line. Here, we'll see how these spending shocks—which you've encountered several times in this book already—shift the AD curve.

In Figure 3, we assume that the economy begins at a price level of 100. In the money market (not shown), the equilibrium interest rate is 6 percent, and equilib-

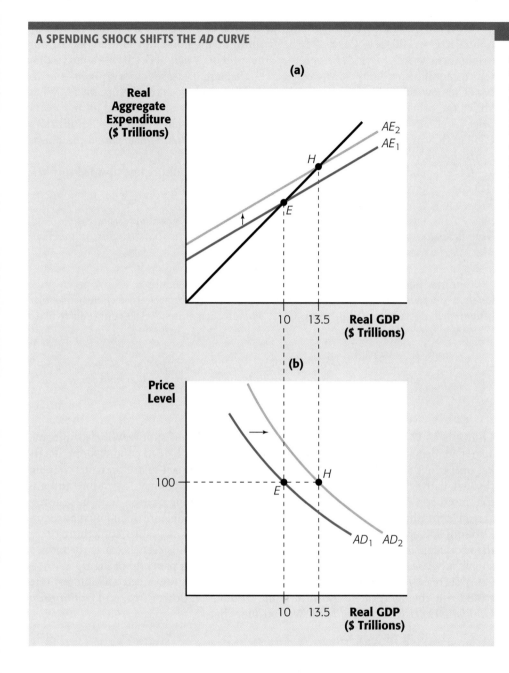

**FIGURE 3**

**A SPENDING SHOCK SHIFTS THE *AD* CURVE**

A positive spending shock, such as an increase in government purchases, shifts the aggregate expenditure line upward in panel (a), leading to a new level of equilibrium GDP. At each price level, GDP is higher than before, indicating that the *AD* curve has shifted to the right.

rium output—given by point $E$ in panel (a)—is $10 trillion. Panel (b) shows the same equilibrium as represented by point $E$ on $AD_1$.

Now let's repeat an experiment from the previous chapter: We'll increase government purchases by $2 trillion and ask what happens if the price level remains at 100. If you flip back to Figure 9 in the previous chapter, you'll see that this rise in government purchases caused the $AE$ line to shift upward, but it also caused the equilibrium interest rate to rise to 8 percent, causing the $AE$ line to shift back downward a bit. The result was that equilibrium GDP rose to $13.5 trillion. This new equilibrium is also shown in panel (a) of Figure 3. The aggregate expenditure line shifts upward to $AE_2$, and the equilibrium moves to point $H$. With the price level remaining at 100, equilibrium GDP increases.

Now look at panel (b) in Figure 3. There, the new equilibrium is represented by point $H$ ($P = 100$, real GDP = $13.5 trillion). This point lies to the right of our original curve $AD_1$. Point $H$, therefore, must lie on a *new AD* curve—a curve that tells us equilibrium GDP at any price level *after the increase in government spending*. The new $AD$ curve is the one labeled $AD_2$, which goes through point $H$. What about the other points on $AD_2$? They tell us that, if we had started at any *other* price level, an increase in government spending would have increased equilibrium GDP at that price level, too. We conclude that *an increase in government purchases shifts the entire AD curve rightward*.

Other spending shocks that shift the aggregate expenditure line upward shift the $AD$ curve rightward, just as in Figure 3. More specifically,

> *the* AD *curve shifts rightward when government purchases, investment spending, autonomous consumption spending, or net exports increase, or when taxes decrease.*

Our analysis also applies in the other direction. For example, at any given price level, a *decrease* in government spending shifts the aggregate expenditure line *downward*, decreasing equilibrium GDP. This in turn shifts the $AD$ curve leftward.

More generally,

> *the* AD *curve shifts leftward when government purchases, investment spending, autonomous consumption spending, or net exports decrease, or when taxes increase.*

**Changes in the Money Supply.**   Changes in the money supply will also shift the aggregate demand curve. To see why, let's imagine that the Fed conducts open market operations to *increase* the money supply. As you learned in the previous chapter, this will cause the interest rate to decrease, increasing investment spending and autonomous consumption spending. Together, these spending changes will shift the aggregate expenditure line upward, just as in the panel (a) of Figure 3, and increase equilibrium GDP. Since this change in equilibrium output is caused by something *other* than a change in the price level, the $AD$ curve shifts. In this case, because the money supply *increased*, the $AD$ curve shifts *rightward*, just as in panel (b) of Figure 3.

A decrease in the money supply would have the opposite effect: The interest rate would rise, the aggregate expenditure line would shift downward, and *equilibrium GDP at any price level would fall.* We conclude that

> *an increase in the money supply shifts the* AD *curve rightward. A decrease in the money supply shifts the* AD *curve leftward.*

**Shifts vs. Movements Along the *AD* Curve: A Summary.**   Figure 4 summarizes how some events in the economy cause a movement along the AD curve, and other events shift the $AD$ curve. You can use the figure as an exercise, drawing diagrams similar to Figures 2 and 3 to illustrate why we move along or shift the $AD$ curve in each case.

Notice that panels (b) and (c) of Figure 4 tell us how a variety of events affect the $AD$ curve, but *not* how they affect *real* GDP. The reason is that, even if we know which $AD$ curve we are on, we could be at *any point* along that curve, depending on the price level.

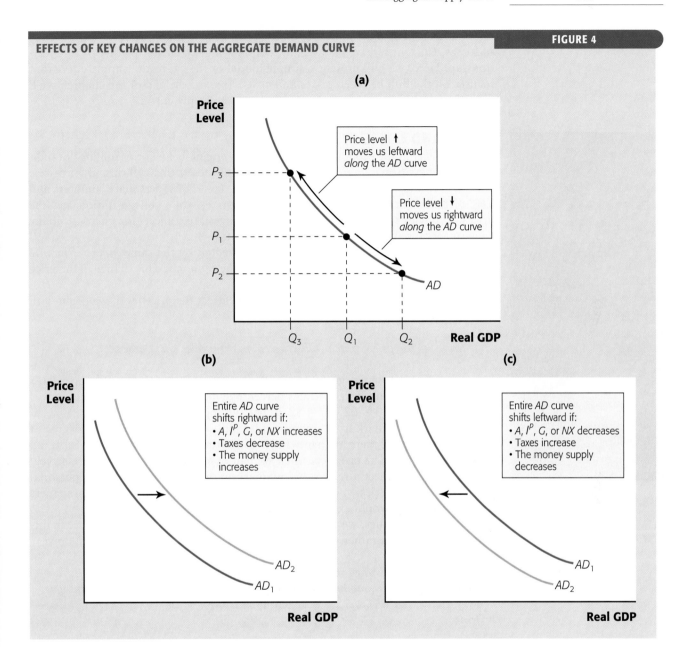

**EFFECTS OF KEY CHANGES ON THE AGGREGATE DEMAND CURVE**          **FIGURE 4**

**(a)**

Price level ↑ moves us leftward *along* the AD curve

Price level ↓ moves us rightward *along* the AD curve

**(b)**

Entire *AD* curve shifts rightward if:
• *A, I^P, G,* or *NX* increases
• Taxes decrease
• The money supply increases

**(c)**

Entire *AD* curve shifts leftward if:
• *A, I^P, G,* or *NX* decreases
• Taxes increase
• The money supply decreases

But how is the price level determined? Our first step in answering that question is to understand the other side of the relationship between GDP and the price level.

## THE AGGREGATE SUPPLY CURVE

Look back at Figure 1, which illustrates the *two-way* relationship between the price level and output. On the one hand, changes in the price level affect output. This is the relationship—summarized by the *AD* curve—that we explored in the previous section. On the other hand, changes in output affect the price level. This relationship—summarized by the *aggregate supply curve*—is the focus of this section.

The effect of changes in output on the price level is complex, involving a variety of forces. Current research is helping economists get a clearer picture of this relationship. Here, we will present a simple model of the aggregate supply curve that focuses on the link between prices and costs. Toward the end of the chapter, we'll discuss some additional ideas about the aggregate supply curve.

## PRICES AND COSTS IN THE SHORT RUN

The price *level* in the economy results from the pricing behavior of millions of individual business firms. In any given year, some of these firms will raise their prices, and some will lower them. For example, during the 1990s, personal computers and long-distance telephone calls came down in price, while college tuition and the prices of movies rose. These types of price changes are subjects for *microeconomic* analysis, because they involve individual markets.

But often, all firms in the economy are affected by the same *macroeconomic* event, causing prices to rise or fall throughout the economy. This change in the price *level* is what interests us in macroeconomics.

To understand how macroeconomic events affect the price level, we begin with a very simple assumption:

> *A firm sets the price of its products as a markup over cost per unit.*

For example, if it costs Burger King $2.00, on average, to produce a Whopper (cost per unit is $2.00), and Burger King's percentage markup is 10 percent, then it will charge $2.00 + (0.10 \times $2.00) = $2.20 per Whopper.[1]

The percentage markup in any particular industry will depend on the degree of competition there. If there are many firms competing for customers in a market, all producing very similar products, then we can expect the markup to be relatively small. Thus, we expect a relatively low markup on fast-food burgers or personal computers. In industries where there is less competition—such as daily newspapers or jet aircraft—we would expect higher percentage markups.

In macroeconomics, we are not concerned with how the markup differs in different industries, but rather with the *average percentage markup* in the economy:

> *The average percentage markup in the economy is determined by competitive conditions in the economy. The competitive structure of the economy changes very slowly, so the average percentage markup should be somewhat stable from year to year.*

But a stable markup does not necessarily mean a stable price level, because unit costs can change. For example, if Burger King's markup remains at 10 percent, but the unit cost of a Whopper rises from $2.00 to $3.00, then the price of a Whopper will rise to $3.00 + (0.10 \times $3.00) = $3.30. Extending this example to all firms in the economy, we can say:

> *In the short run, the price level rises when there is an economy-wide increase in unit costs, and the price level falls when there is an economy-wide decrease in unit costs.*

Burger King, like other firms in the economy, charges a markup over its costs per unit. The average markup in the economy is determined by competitive conditions, and tends to change slowly over time.

---

[1]     In microeconomics, you learn more sophisticated theories of how firms' prices are determined. But our simple markup model captures a central conclusion of those theories: that an increase in costs will result in higher prices.

Our primary concern in this chapter is the impact of *output* on unit costs and, therefore, on the price level. Why should a change in output affect unit costs and the price level? We'll focus on three key reasons.

As total output increases:

***Greater amounts of inputs may be needed to produce a unit of output.*** As output increases, firms hire new, untrained workers who may be less productive than existing workers. Firms also begin using capital and land that are less well suited to their industry. As a result, greater amounts of labor, capital, land, and raw materials are needed to produce each unit of output. Even if the prices of these inputs remain the same, unit costs will rise. For example, imagine that Intel increases its output of computer chips. Then it will have to be less picky about the workers it employs, hiring some who are less well suited to chip production than those already working there. Thus, more labor hours will be needed to produce each chip. Intel may also have to begin using older, less-efficient production facilities, which require more silicon and other raw materials per chip. Even if the prices of all of these inputs remain unchanged, unit costs will rise.

***The prices of non-labor inputs rise.*** This is especially true of inputs like land and natural resources, which may be available only in limited quantities in the short run. An increase in the output of final goods raises the demand for these inputs, causing their prices to rise. Firms that produce final goods experience an increase in unit costs, and raise their own prices accordingly.

***The nominal wage rate rises.*** Greater output means higher employment, leaving fewer unemployed workers looking for jobs. As firms compete to hire increasingly scarce workers, they must offer higher nominal wage rates to attract them. Higher nominal wages increase unit costs, and therefore result in a higher price level. Notice that we use the nominal wage, rather than the real wage we've emphasized elsewhere in this book. That's because we are interested in explaining how firms' prices are determined. Since price is a nominal variable, it will be marked up over *nominal* costs.

A decrease in output affects unit costs through the same three forces, but with the opposite result. As output falls, firms can be more selective in hiring the best, most efficient workers and in choosing other inputs, decreasing input requirements per unit of output. Decreases in demand for land and natural resources will cause their prices to drop. And as unemployment rises, wages will fall as workers compete for jobs. All of these contribute to a drop in unit costs, and a decrease in the price level.

All three of our reasons are important in explaining why a change in output affects the price level. However, they operate within different time frames. When total output increases, new, less-productive workers will be hired rather quickly. Similarly, the prices of certain key inputs—such as lumber, land, oil, and wheat—may rise within a few weeks or months.

But our third explanation—changes in the nominal wage rate—is a different story. While wages in some lines of work might respond very rapidly, we can expect wages in many industries to change very little or not at all for a year or more after a change in output.

> *For a year or so after a change in output, changes in the average nominal wage are less important than other forces that change unit costs.*

Here are some of the more important reasons why wages in many industries respond so slowly to changes in output:

- Many firms have union contracts that specify wages for up to three years. While wage increases are often built into these contracts, a rise in output will not affect the wage increase. When output rises or falls, these firms continue to abide by the contract.
- Wages in many large corporations are set by slow-moving bureaucracies.
- Wage changes in either direction can be costly to firms. Higher wages must be widely publicized in order to raise the number of job applicants at the firm. Lower wages can reduce the morale of workers—and their productivity. Thus, many firms are reluctant to change wages until they are reasonably sure that any change in demand for their output will be long lasting.
- Firms may benefit from developing reputations for paying stable wages. A firm that raises wages when output is high and labor is scarce may have to lower wages when output is low and labor is plentiful. Such a firm would develop a reputation for paying unstable wages, and have difficulty attracting new workers.

In this section, we focus exclusively on the short run—a time horizon of a year or so after a change in output. Since the average wage rate changes very little over the short run, we'll make the following simplifying assumption: *The nominal wage rate is fixed in the short run.* More specifically,

> *we assume that changes in output have no effect on the nominal wage rate in the short run.*[2]

Keep in mind, though, that our assumption of a constant wage holds only in the *short run.* As you will see later, wage changes play a very important role in the economy's adjustment over the long run.

Since we assume a constant nominal wage in the short run, a change in output will affect unit costs through the other two factors we mentioned earlier. Specifically, in the short run, a rise in real GDP raises firms' unit costs because (1) the prices of non-labor inputs rise, and (2) input requirements per unit of output rise. With a constant percentage markup, the rise in unit costs translates into a rise in the price level. Thus,

> *in the short run, a rise in real GDP, by causing unit costs to increase, will also cause a rise in the price level.*

In the other direction, a *drop* in real GDP lowers unit costs because (1) the prices of non-labor inputs fall, and (2) input requirements per unit of output fall. With a constant percentage markup, the drop in unit costs translates into a fall in the price level.

> *In the short run, a fall in real GDP, by causing unit costs to decrease, will also cause a decrease in the price level.*

## DERIVING THE AGGREGATE SUPPLY CURVE

Figure 5 summarizes our discussion about the effect of output on the price level in the short run. Suppose the economy begins at point *A,* with output at $10 trillion

---

[2]    This simplifying assumption is not entirely realistic. In some industries, wages will respond to changes in output, at least somewhat, even in the short run. However, assuming that the nominal wage remains constant in the short run makes our model much simpler, without affecting any of our essential conclusions.

## THE AGGREGATE SUPPLY CURVE

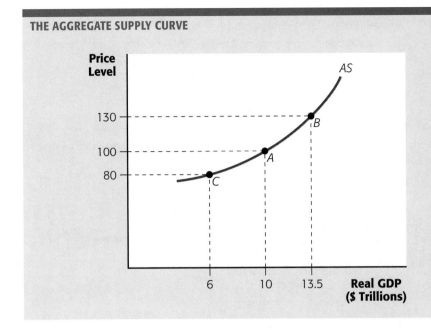

**FIGURE 5**

Beginning at point *A,* an increase in output will raise unit costs. For given percentage markups, firms will raise the prices they charge. An increase in output from $10 trillion to $13.5 trillion might raise the price level from 100 to 130 at point *B.* A decrease in output would lower unit costs and lead firms to lower their prices. The price level might fall to 80 at point *C.* Connecting points such as *A, B,* and *C* traces out the economy's *AS* curve.

and the price level at 100. Now suppose that output rises to $13.5 trillion. What will happen in the short run? Even though wages are assumed to remain constant, the price level will rise because of the other forces we've discussed. In the figure, the price level rises to 130, indicated by point *B.* If, instead, output *fell* to $7 trillion, the price level would fall—to 80 in the figure, indicated by point *C.*

As you can see, each time we change the level of output, there will be a new price level in the short run, giving us another point on the figure. If we connect all of these points, we obtain the economy's *aggregate supply curve:*

> *The aggregate supply curve (or **AS** curve) tells us the price level consistent with firms' unit costs and their percentage markups at any level of output* over the short run.

**Aggregate supply (AS) curve** A curve indicating the price level consistent with firms' unit costs and markups for any level of output over the short run.

A more accurate name for the *AS* curve would be the "short-run-price-level-at-each-output-level" curve, but that is more than a mouthful. The *AS* curve gets its name because it *resembles* a microeconomic market supply curve. Like the supply curve for maple syrup we discussed in Chapter 3, the *AS* curve is upward sloping, and it has a price variable (the price level) on the vertical axis, and a quantity variable (total output) on the horizontal axis. But there, the similarity ends.

### MOVEMENTS ALONG THE *AS* CURVE

When a change in output causes the price level to change, we *move along* the economy's *AS* curve. But what happens in the economy as we make such a move?

Look again at the *AS* curve in Figure 5. Suppose we move from point *A* to point *B* along this curve in the short run. The increase in output raises the prices of raw materials and other (non-labor) inputs and also raises input requirements per unit of output at many firms. Both of these changes increase costs per unit. As long as the markup remains somewhat stable, the rise in unit costs will lead firms to raise their prices, and the price level will increase. Thus, as we move upward along the *AS* curve, we can represent what happens as follows:

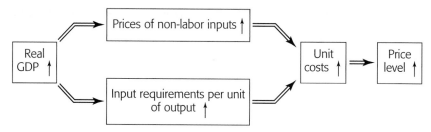

The opposite sequence of events occurs when real GDP falls, moving us downward along the *AS* curve:

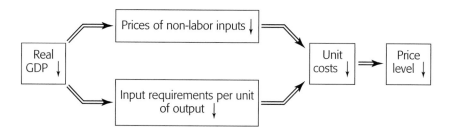

## SHIFTS OF THE *AS* CURVE

When we drew the *AS* curve in Figure 5, we assumed that a number of important variables remained unchanged. In particular, we assumed that the only changes in unit costs were those caused by a change in output. But in the real world, unit costs sometimes change for reasons *other* than a change in output. When this occurs, unit costs—and the price level—will change at *any* level of output, so the *AS* curve will shift.

In general, we distinguish between a movement along the *AS* curve, and a shift of the curve itself, as follows:

> *When a change in real GDP causes the price level to change, we move along the* AS *curve. When anything* other *than a change in real GDP causes the price level to change, the* AS *curve itself shifts.*

A common mistake about the *AS* curve is thinking that it describes the same kind of relationship between price and quantity as a microeconomic supply curve. There are two reasons why this is wrong.

First, the direction of causation between price and output is reversed for the *AS* curve. For example, when we draw the supply curve for maple syrup, we view changes in the price of maple syrup as causing a change in output supplied. But along the *AS* curve, a change in output causes a change in the price level.

Second, the basic assumption behind the *AS* curve is very different from that behind a single market supply curve. When we draw the supply curve for an individual product, we assume that the prices of inputs used in producing the good remain fixed. This is a sensible thing to do, because an increase in production for a single good is unlikely to have much effect on input prices in the economy as a whole.

But when we draw the *AS* curve, we imagine an increase in *real GDP,* in which *all* firms are increasing their output. This will significantly raise the demand for inputs, so it is unrealistic to assume that input prices will remain fixed. Indeed, the rise in input prices as output increases is one of the important reasons for the *AS* curve's upward slope.

Figure 6 illustrates the logic of a shift in the *AS* curve. Suppose the economy's initial *AS* curve is $AS_1$. Now suppose that some economic event *other* than a change in output—for the moment, we'll leave the event unnamed—causes firms to raise their prices. Then the price level will be higher at *any* level of output we might imagine, so the *AS* curve must shift *upward*—for example, to $AS_2$ in the figure. At an output level of $10 trillion, the price level would rise from 100 to 140. At any other output level, the price level would also rise.

DANGEROUS CURVES

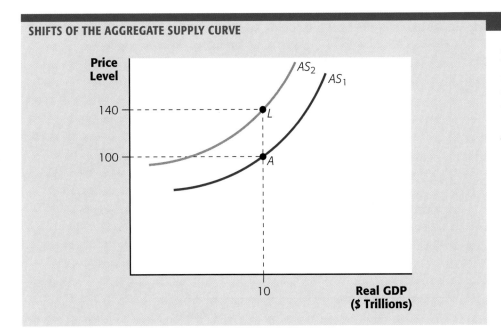

**FIGURE 6**

**SHIFTS OF THE AGGREGATE SUPPLY CURVE**

Any factor that changes firms' unit costs at any output level will shift the *AS* curve. For example, an increase in world oil prices or bad weather would shift the *AS* curve upward; the price level would be higher at each level of real GDP.

What can cause unit costs to change at any given level of output? The following are some important examples:

- *Changes in world oil prices.* Oil is traded on a world market, where prices can fluctuate even while output in the United States does not. And changes in world oil prices have caused major shifts in the *AS* curve. Three events over the past few decades—an oil embargo by Arab oil-producing nations in 1973–74, the Iranian revolution in 1978–79, Iraq's invasion of Kuwait in 1990—all caused large jumps in the price of oil. Each time, costs per unit rose for firms across the country, and they responded by charging higher prices than before for *any* output level they might produce. As in Figure 6, the *AS* curve shifted upward. Conversely, in 1991, the price of oil decreased dramatically. This caused unit costs to decrease at many firms, shifting the *AS* curve downward.
- *Changes in the weather.* Good crop-growing weather increases farmers' yields for any given amounts of land, labor, capital, and other inputs used. This decreases farms' unit costs, and the price of agricultural goods falls. Since many of these goods are final goods (such as fresh fruit and vegetables), the price drop will contribute directly to a drop in the price level, and a downward shift of the *AS* curve. Additionally, agricultural products are important inputs in the production of many other goods. (For example, corn is an input in beef production.) Good weather thus leads to a drop in input prices for many other firms in the economy, causing their unit costs—and their prices—to decrease. For these reasons, we can expect good weather to shift the *AS* curve downward. Bad weather, which decreases crop yields, increases unit costs at any level of output, and shifts the *AS* curve upward.
- *Technological change.* New technologies can enable firms to produce any given level of output at lower unit costs. In recent years, for example, we've seen revolutions in telecommunications, information processing, and medicine. The result has been steady downward shifts of the *AS* curve.
- *Adjustment to the Long Run.* We've assumed that, in the short run, the nominal wage remains unchanged as output changes. But as we extend our time horizon

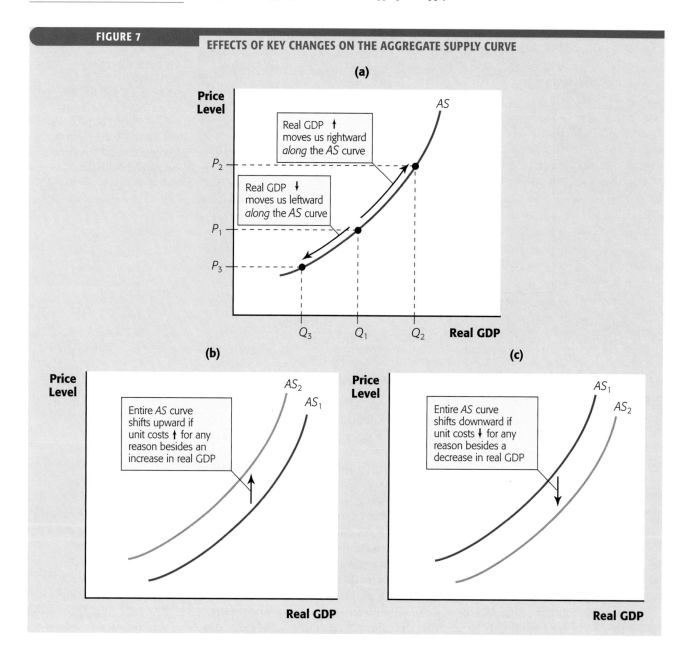

**FIGURE 7**

**EFFECTS OF KEY CHANGES ON THE AGGREGATE SUPPLY CURVE**

**(a)**

Real GDP ↑ moves us rightward *along* the AS curve

Real GDP ↓ moves us leftward *along* the AS curve

**(b)**

Entire *AS* curve shifts upward if unit costs ↑ for any reason besides an increase in real GDP

**(c)**

Entire *AS* curve shifts downward if unit costs ↓ for any reason besides a decrease in real GDP

beyond the first year after a change in output, our assumption of a constant wage becomes increasingly unrealistic. As you will see a bit later, when output is above its full-employment level, we can expect nominal wage rates to rise. This is part of the long-run adjustment process in the economy. Similarly, if output is below potential, wage rates will eventually fall. These adjustments in wages shift the *AS* curve, since we assumed a constant wage when we drew the curve.

Figure 7 summarizes how different events in the economy cause a movement along, or a shift in, the *AS* curve. But the *AS* curve tells only half of the economy's story: It shows us the price level *if* we know the level of output. The *AD* curve tells the other half of the story: It shows us the level of output *if* we know the economy's price level. In the next section, we finally put the two halves of the story together, allowing us to determine both the price level and output.

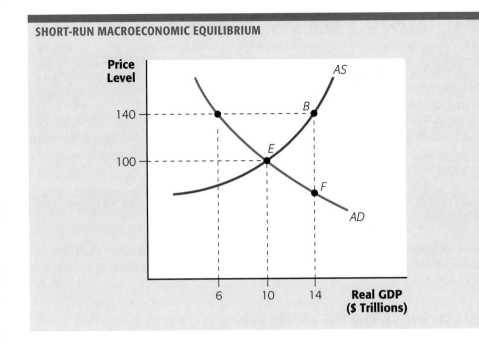

**SHORT-RUN MACROECONOMIC EQUILIBRIUM**

**FIGURE 8**

Short-run equilibrium occurs where the *AD* and *AS* curves intersect. At point *E,* the price level of 100 is consistent with an output of $10 trillion along the *AD* curve. The output level of $10 trillion is consistent with a price level of 100 along the *AS* curve. At any other combination of price level and output, such as point *F,* at least one condition for equilibrium will not be satisfied.

## *AD* AND *AS* TOGETHER: SHORT-RUN EQUILIBRIUM

Find the Equilibrium

Where will the economy settle in the short run? That is, where is our **short-run macroeconomic equilibrium?** Figure 8 shows how to answer that question, using both the *AS* curve and the *AD* curve. If you suspect that the equilibrium is at point *E,* the intersection of these two curves, you are correct. At that point, the price level is 100, and output is $10 trillion. But it's worth thinking about *why* point *E*—and only point *E*—is our short-run equilibrium.

First, we know that the economy must be at some point on the *AD* curve. Otherwise, real GDP would not be at its equilibrium value. For example, suppose the economy were at point *B*, which lies to the right of the *AD* curve. At this point, the price level is 140, and output is $14 trillion. But the *AD* curve tells us that with a price level of 140, *equilibrium* output is $6 trillion. Thus, at point *B*, real GDP would be greater than its equilibrium value. As you learned several chapters ago, this situation cannot persist for long, since inventories would pile up, and firms would be forced to cut back on their production. Thus, point *B* cannot be our short-run equilibrium.

Second, short-run equilibrium requires that the economy be operating on its *AS* curve. Otherwise, firms would not be charging the prices dictated by their unit costs and the average percentage markup in the economy. For example, point *F* lies *below* the *AS* curve. But the *AS* curve tells us that if output is $14 trillion, based on the average percentage markup and unit costs, the price level should be 140 (point *B*), not something lower. That is, the price level at point *F* is *too low* for equilibrium. This situation will not last long either.

We could make a similar argument for other points that are off the *AS* and *AD* curves, always coming to the same conclusion: Unless the economy is on *both* the *AS* and the *AD* curves, the price level and the level of output will change. Only when the economy is at point *E*—on *both* curves—will we have reached a sustainable level of real GDP and the price level.

**Short-run macroeconomic equilibrium** A combination of price level and GDP consistent with both the *AD* and *AS* curves.

# WHAT HAPPENS WHEN THINGS CHANGE?

Now that we know how the short-run equilibrium is determined, and armed with our knowledge of the *AD* and *AS* curves, we are ready to put the model through its paces. In this section, we'll explore how different types of events cause the short-run equilibrium to change.

Our short-run equilibrium will change when either the *AD* curve, the *AS* curve, or both, *shift*. Since the consequences for the economy are very different for shifts in the *AD* curve as opposed to shifts in the *AS* curve, economists have developed a shorthand language to distinguish between them:

> *An event that causes the* AD *curve to shift is called a **demand shock**. An event that causes the* AS *curve to shift is called a **supply shock**.*

In this section, we'll first explore the effects of demand shocks, both in the short run and during the adjustment process to the long run. Then, we'll take up the issue of supply shocks.

**Demand shock**  Any event that causes the *AD* curve to shift.

**Supply shock**  Any event that causes the *AS* curve to shift.

What Happens When
Things Change?

## DEMAND SHOCKS IN THE SHORT RUN

Demand shocks can be caused by spending shocks or by changes in monetary policy. In both cases, the *AD* curve shifts. Figure 4, which lists the reasons for a shift in the *AD* curve, also serves as a list of demand shocks to the economy. Let's consider some examples.

**An Increase in Government Purchases.**  You've learned that an increase in government purchases shifts the *AD* curve rightward. Now we can see how it affects the economy in the short run. Figure 9 shows the initial equilibrium at point *E,* with the price level equal to 100 and output at $10 trillion. Now, suppose that government purchases rise by $2 trillion. Figure 4 (b) tells us that the *AD* curve will shift rightward. What will happen to equilibrium GDP?

In our example in the previous chapter, a $2 trillion rise in government purchases increased output to $13.5 trillion, and also raised the interest rate in the money market to 8 percent. (Flip back to Figure 9 in that chapter to refresh your memory.) But nowhere in our previous analysis did we consider any change in the price level. Thus, the rise in GDP to $13.5 trillion in the previous chapter makes sense *only if the price level does not change.* Here, in Figure 9, this *would* be a movement rightward, from point *E* to point *J*. However, *point* J *does not describe the economy's short-run equilibrium.* Why not? Because it ignores two facts that you've learned about in this chapter: The rise in output will change the price level, and the change in the price level will, in turn, affect equilibrium GDP.

To see this more clearly, let's first suppose that the price level did *not* rise when output increased, so that the economy actually *did* arrive at point *J* after the *AD* shift. Would we stay there? Absolutely not. Point *J* lies below the *AS* curve, telling us that when GDP is $13.5 trillion, the price level consistent with firms' unit costs, and average markup is 130, not 100. Firms would soon raise prices, and this would cause a movement upward along $AD_2$. The price level would keep rising, and output would keep falling, until we reached point *H*. At that point—with output at $12 trillion—we would be on both the *AS* and *AD* curves, so there would be no reason for a further rise in the price level and no reason for a further fall in output.

**FIGURE 9**

**THE EFFECT OF A DEMAND SHOCK**

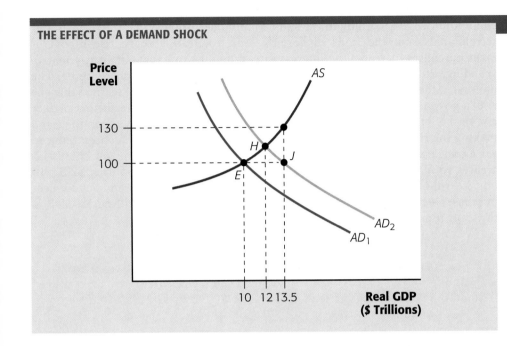

Starting at point *E,* an increase in government purchases would shift the *AD* curve rightward to *AD*₂. Point *J* illustrates where the economy would move if the price level remained constant. But as output increases, the price level rises. Thus, the economy moves along the *AS* curve from point *E* to point *H.*

However, the process we've just described is not entirely realistic. It assumes that when government purchases rise, *first* output increases (the move to point *J*), and *then* the price level rises (the move to point *H*). In reality, output and the price level tend to rise *together*. Thus, the economy would likely *slide along* the *AS* curve from point *E* to point *H*. As we move along the *AS* curve, output rises, increasing unit costs and the price level. At the same time, the rise in the price level *reduces equilibrium GDP—the level of output toward which the economy is heading on the* AD *curve*—from point *J* to point *H*.

We can summarize the impact of a rise in government purchases this way:

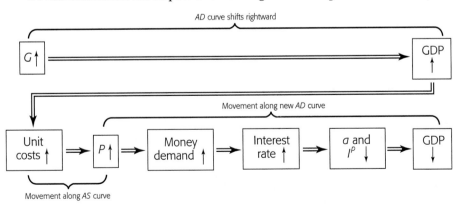

Net Effect: GDP ↑, but by less due to effect of *P* ↑

Let's step back a minute and get some perspective about this example of fiscal policy. This is the third time in this text that we've considered fiscal policy in the short run. Each time, the discussion became more realistic, and we've seen that the effect of fiscal policy becomes weaker. In our first analysis, we ignored any increase in the interest rate, and found that a rise in government purchases increased equilibrium GDP according to the simple multiplier formula $1/(1 - MPC)$. In our second analysis, in the chapter before this one, you learned that a rise in government purchases increases the interest rate, crowding out some interest-sensitive spending, thus making the rise in GDP smaller than it would otherwise be. The multiplier, therefore, was smaller than $1/(1 - MPC)$. Now you've learned that the rise in government purchases *also* increases the price level. This leads to a *further* rise in the interest rate, crowding out still *more* interest-sensitive spending, and making the rise in GDP smaller still. The size of the multiplier has been reduced yet again. (In our example, a \$2 trillion increase in government purchases increases equilibrium GDP by \$2.5 trillion, so the multiplier would be \$2.5 trillion/\$2 trillion = 1.25.) However, as you can see in Figure 9, a rise in government purchases—even when we include the rise in the price level—still raises GDP in the short run.

We can summarize the impact of price-level changes this way:

> *When government purchases increase, the horizontal shift of the* AD *curve measures how much real GDP would* increase *if the price level remained constant.* But because the price level does rise, real GDP rises by *less than the horizontal shift in the* AD *curve.*

Now let's switch gears into reverse: How would we illustrate the effects of a *decrease* in government purchases? In this case, the AD curve would shift *leftward*, causing the following to happen:

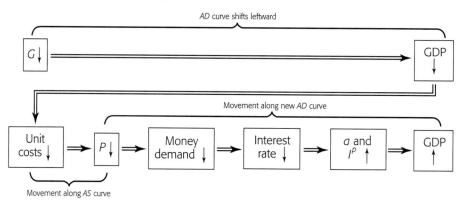

Net Effect: GDP↓, but by less due to effect of P↓

As you can see, the same sequence of events occurs in the same order, but each variable moves in the opposite direction. A decrease in government purchases decreases equilibrium GDP, but the multiplier effect is smaller because the price level falls.

**An Increase in the Money Supply.** Although monetary policy stimulates the economy through a different channel than fiscal policy, once we arrive at the AD and AS diagram, the two look very much alike. For example, an increase in the money supply, which reduces the interest rate, will stimulate interest-sensitive consumption and investment spending. Real GDP then increases, and the AD curve shifts rightward, just as in Figure 9. Once output begins to rise, we have the same sequence of events as in fiscal policy: The price level rises, so the increase in GDP will be smaller. We can represent the situation as follows:

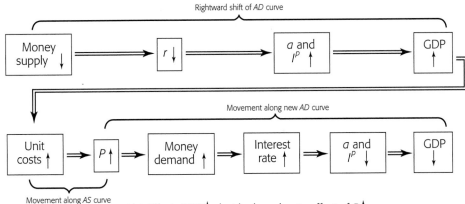

Net Effect: GDP ↑, but by less due to effect of P ↑

### Other Demand Shocks.

On your own, try going through examples of different demand shocks (see the list in Figures 4 (b) and (c)) and explain the sequence of events in each case that causes output and the price level to change. This will help you verify the following general conclusion about demand shocks:

> *A positive demand shock—one that shifts the AD curve rightward—increases both real GDP and the price level in the short run. A negative demand shock—one that shifts the AD curve leftward—decreases both real GDP and the price level in the short run.*

### An Example: The Great Depression.

As mentioned at the beginning of the chapter, the U.S. economy collapsed far more seriously during the period 1929 through 1933—the onset of the Great Depression—than it did at any other time in the country's history. Because the price level fell during this time, we know that the contraction was caused by an adverse demand shock. An adverse supply shock would have caused the price level to *rise* as GDP fell.

What do we know about the demand shocks that caused the depression? This question has been debated by economists almost continuously over the past 70 years. The candidates are numerous, and it appears that a combination of events was responsible. The 1920s were a period of optimism—with high levels of investment by businesses and spending by families on houses and cars. The stock market soared. In the fall of 1929, the bubble of optimism burst. The stock market crashed, and investment and consumption spending plummeted. Similar events occurred in other countries, and the demand for products exported by the United States fell. The Fed—then only 16 years old—reacted by cutting the money supply sharply, which added an adverse monetary shock to all of the cutbacks in spending. Each of these events contributed to a leftward shift of the *AD* curve, causing both output and the price level to fall.

### DEMAND SHOCKS: ADJUSTING TO THE LONG RUN

In Figure 9, point *H* shows the new equilibrium after a positive demand shock *in the short run*—a year or so after the shock. But point *H* is not necessarily where the economy will end up in the long run. For example, suppose full-employment output is $10 trillion, and point *H*—representing an output of $12 trillion—is above full-employment output. Then—with employment unusually high and

What Happens When
Things Change?

unemployment unusually low—business firms will have to compete to hire scarce workers, driving up the wage rate. It might take a year or more for the wage rate to rise significantly—recall our earlier list of reasons that wages adjust only slowly. But when we extend our horizon to several years or more, we must recognize that if output is above its potential, the wage rate will rise. Since the AS curve is drawn for a *given wage*, a rise in the wage rate will *shift* the curve upward, changing our equilibrium.

Alternatively, we could imagine a situation in which short-run equilibrium GDP was *below* its potential. In this case, with abnormally high unemployment, workers would compete to get scarce jobs, and eventually the wage rate would fall. Then the AS curve would shift downward, once again changing our equilibrium GDP.

> *In the short run, we treat the wage rate as given. But in the long run, the wage rate can change. When output is above full employment, the wage rate will rise, shifting the AS curve upward. When output is below full employment, the wage rate will fall, shifting the AS curve downward.*

Now we are ready to explore what happens over the long run in the aftermath of a demand shock. Figure 10 shows an economy in equilibrium at point E. We assume that the initial equilibrium is at full-employment output ($Y_{FE}$), since—as you are about to see—this is where the economy always ends up after the long-run adjustment process is complete. To make our results as general as possible, we'll use symbols, rather than numbers, to represent output and price levels.

Now suppose the AD curve shifts rightward due to, say, an increase in government purchases. In the short run, the equilibrium moves to point H, with a higher price level ($P_2$) and a higher level of output ($Y_2$). Point H tells us where the economy will be about a year after the increase in government purchases, before the

---

**FIGURE 10**

Beginning at point E, a positive demand shock would shift the aggregate demand curve to $AD_2$, raising both output and the price level. At point H, output is above the full-employment level, $Y_{FE}$. Firms will compete to hire scarce workers, thereby driving up the wage rate. The higher wage rate will shift the AS curve to $AS_2$. Only when the economy returns to full-employment output at point K will there be no further shifts in AS.

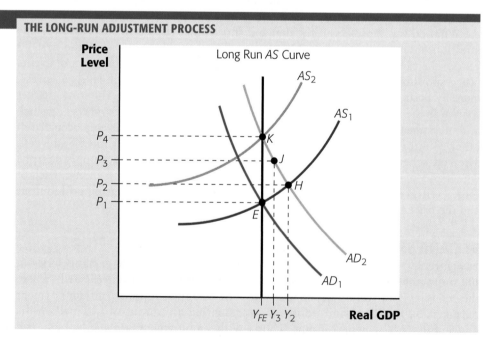

**THE LONG-RUN ADJUSTMENT PROCESS**

wage rate has a chance to adjust. (Remember, along any given $AS$ curve, the wage rate is assumed to be constant.)

But now let's extend our analysis beyond a year. Notice that $Y_2$ is greater than $Y_{FE}$. The wage will begin to rise, raising unit costs at any given output level and causing firms to raise prices. In the figure, the $AS$ curve would begin shifting upward. Point $J$ shows where the shifting aggregate supply curve might be two years after the shock, after the long-run adjustment process has begun. (You might want to pencil this intermediate $AS$ curve into the figure, so that it intersects $AD_2$ at point $J$.) At this point, output would be at $Y_3$, and the rise in the price level has moved us along the new aggregate demand curve, $AD_2$.

Now, is point $J$ our final, long-run equilibrium? No, it cannot be. At $Y_3$, output is *still* greater than $Y_{FE}$, so the wage rate will continue to rise, and the $AS$ curve will continue to shift upward. At point $J$, the long-run adjustment process is not yet complete. When will the process end? Only when the wage rate stops rising—that is, only when output has returned to $Y_{FE}$. This occurs when the $AS$ curve has shifted all the way to $AS_2$, moving the economy to point $K$—our new, long-run equilibrium.

As you can see, the increase in government purchases has no effect on equilibrium GDP in the long run: The economy returns to full employment, which is just where it started. This is why the long-run adjustment process is often called the economy's **self-correcting mechanism.** And this mechanism applies to any demand shock, not just an increase in government purchases:

> *If a demand shock pulls the economy away from full employment, changes in the wage rate and the price level will eventually cause the economy to correct itself and return to full-employment output.*

**Self-correcting mechanism** The adjustment process through which price and wage changes return the economy to full-employment output in the long run.

For a positive demand shock that shifts the $AD$ curve rightward, the self-correcting mechanism works like this:

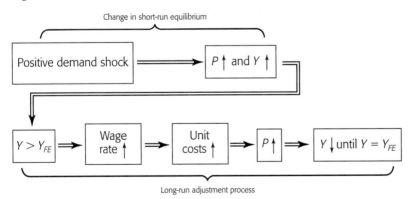

Figure 11 illustrates the case of a negative demand shock, in which the $AD$ curve shifts leftward. In this case, the short-run equilibrium GDP is *below* $Y_{FE}$—at point N. Over the long run, however, the unusually high unemployment drives the wage rate down, shifting the $AS$ curve down as well. The price level decreases, causing equilibrium GDP to rise along the $AD_2$ curve. The process comes to a halt only when output returns to $Y_{FE}$. Thus, in the long run, the economy moves from point $E$ to point $M$, and the negative demand shock causes no change in equilibrium GDP.

The complete sequence of events after a negative demand shock looks like this:

Starting from point *E,* a negative demand shock shifts the *AD* curve to *AD₂,* lowering GDP and the price level. At point *N,* output is below the full-employment level. With unemployed labor available, wages will fall, enabling firms to lower their prices. The *AS* curve shifts downward until full employment is regained at point *M,* with a lower price level.

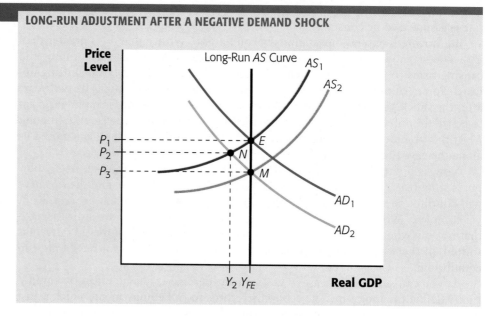

**LONG-RUN ADJUSTMENT AFTER A NEGATIVE DEMAND SHOCK**

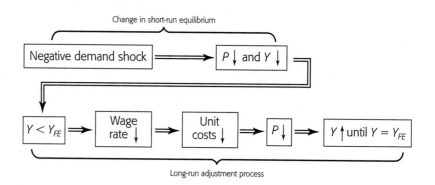

Pulling all of our observations together, we can summarize the economy's self-correcting mechanism as follows:

> *Whenever a demand shock pulls the economy away from full employment, the self-correcting mechanism will eventually bring it back. When output exceeds its full-employment level, wages will eventually rise, causing a rise in the price level and a drop in GDP until full employment is restored. When output is less than its full-employment level, wages will eventually fall, causing a drop in the price level and a rise in GDP until full employment is restored.*

## THE LONG-RUN AGGREGATE SUPPLY CURVE

The self-correcting mechanism provides an important link between the economy's long-run and short-run behaviors. It helps us understand why deviations from full employment don't last forever. Often, however, we are primarily interested in the long-run effects of a demand shock. In these cases, we may want to skip over the self-correcting mechanism and go straight to its end result. A new version of the *AS* curve helps us do this.

Look again at Figure 10, which illustrates the impact of a positive demand shock. The economy begins at full employment at point *E*, then moves to point *H* in the short run (before the wage rate rises), and then goes to point *K* in the long run (after the rise in wages). If we skip over the short-run equilibrium, we find that the positive demand shock has moved the economy from *E* to *K*, which is vertically above *E*. That is, in the long run, the price level rises, but output remains unchanged.

Now look at the vertical line in Figure 10, which shows another way of illustrating this long-run result. In the figure, the vertical line is the economy's **long-run aggregate supply curve**. It summarizes all possible output and price-level combinations at which the economy could end up in the long run. It is vertical because, in the long run, GDP will be the same—full-employment output—*regardless* of the position of the *AD* curve. The price level, however, will depend on the position of the *AD* curve. In the long run, a positive demand shock shifts the *AD* curve rightward, moving the economy from *E* to *K*: a higher price level, but the same level of output. Similarly, in Figure 11, a negative demand shock—which shifts the *AD* curve leftward—moves the economy from *E* to *M* in the long run: a lower price level with the same level of output.[3]

The long-run aggregate supply curve in Figures 10 and 11 tell us something very important about the economy: In the long run, after the self-correcting mechanism has done its job, *the economy behaves as the classical model predicts*. In particular, the classical model tells us that demand shocks cannot change equilibrium GDP in the long run. The figure brings us to the same conclusion: While demand shocks shift the *AD* curve, this only moves the economy up or down along a vertical long-run *AS* curve, leaving output unchanged.

The long-run aggregate supply curve also illustrates another classical conclusion. In the classical model, an increase in government purchases causes *complete crowding out*—the rise in government purchases is precisely matched by a drop in consumption and investment spending, leaving total output and total spending unchanged. In Figure 10, the same result holds in the long run. How do we know? The figures tell us that, in the long run, the rise in government purchases causes no change in GDP. But if GDP is the same, and government purchases are higher, then the other components of GDP—consumption and investment—must decrease by the amount that government purchases increased.

> *The self-correcting mechanism shows us that, in the long run, the economy will eventually behave as the classical model predicts.*

But notice the word *eventually* in the previous statement. It can take several years before the economy returns to full employment after a demand shock. This is why governments around the world are reluctant to rely on the self-correcting mechanism alone to keep the economy on track. Instead, they often use fiscal and monetary policies in an attempt to return the economy to full employment more quickly. We'll explore fiscal and monetary policies in more detail in the next two chapters.

## SUPPLY SHOCKS

In recent decades, supply shocks have been important sources of economic fluctuations. The most dramatic supply shocks have resulted from sudden changes in

**Long-run aggregate supply curve**
A vertical line indicating all possible output and price-level combinations at which the economy could end up in the long run.

What Happens When Things Change?

---

[3]    Of course, full-employment output can increase from year to year, as you learned in the chapter on economic growth. When the economy is growing, the long-run *AS* curve will shift rightward. In that case, the level of output at which the economy will eventually settle increases from year to year.

**FIGURE 12**

An adverse supply shock would shift the *AS* curve upward from $AS_1$ to $AS_2$. In the short-run equilibrium at point *R*, the price level is higher and output is below $Y_{FE}$. Eventually, wages will fall, causing unit costs to fall, and the *AS* curve will shift back to its original position. A positive supply shock would have just the opposite effect.

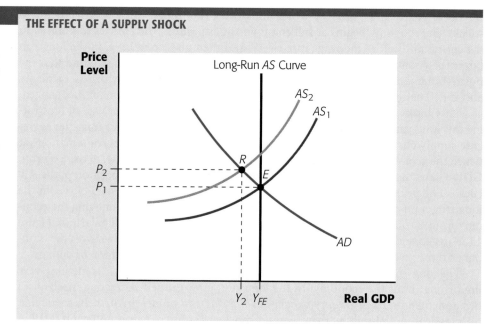

**THE EFFECT OF A SUPPLY SHOCK**

world oil prices. As you are about to see, supply shocks affect the economy differently from demand shocks.

### Short-Run Effects of Supply Shocks.

Figure 12 shows an example of a supply shock: an increase in world oil prices that shifts the aggregate supply curve upward, from $AS_1$ to $AS_2$. As rising oil prices increase unit costs, firms will begin raising prices, and the price level will increase. The rise in the price level decreases equilibrium GDP along the *AD* curve. In the short run, the price level will continue to rise, and the economy will continue to slide upward along its *AD* curve, until we reach the $AS_2$ curve at point *R*. At this point, the price level is consistent with firms' unit costs and average markup (we are on the *AS* curve), and total output is equal to total spending (we are on the *AD* curve). As you can see, the short-run impact of higher oil prices is a rise in the price level and a fall in output. We call this a *negative* supply shock, because of the negative effect on output.

> *In the short run, a* negative *supply shock shifts the* AS *curve upward, decreasing output and increasing the price level.*

Notice the sharp contrast between the effects of negative supply shocks and negative demand shocks in the short run. After a negative demand shock (see, for example, Figure 11), both output and the price level fall. After a negative supply shock, however, output falls, but the price level rises. Economists and journalists have coined the term **stagflation** to describe a *stag*nating economy experiencing in*flation*.

**Stagflation** The combination of falling output and rising prices.

> *A negative supply shock causes* stagflation *in the short run.*

Stagflation caused by increases in oil prices is not just a theoretical possibility. Three of our recessions in the last quarter century—in 1973–74, 1980, and 1990–91—followed increases in world oil prices. And each of these three recessions also saw jumps in the price level.

A *positive supply shock* would increase output by shifting the *AS* curve downward. As you can see if you draw such a shift on your own,

> *a positive supply shock shifts the* AS *curve downward, increasing output and decreasing the price level.*

Examples of positive supply shocks include unusually good weather, a drop in oil prices, and a technological change that lowers unit costs. In addition, a positive supply shock can sometimes be caused by government policy. A few chapters ago, we discussed how the government could use tax incentives and other policies to increase the rate of economic growth. These policies work by shifting the *AS* curve downward, thus increasing output while tending to decrease the price level.

Another type of policy tries to deal directly with negative supply shocks. For example, after the oil price shocks of the 1970s, the federal government built a strategic reserve of oil in huge underground storage areas. The idea was to release oil from the reserve if another oil price shock hit, in order to stabilize the price. The reserve was used in this way, but not enough to make much difference in the world price of oil.

**Long-Run Effects of Supply Shocks.** What about the effects of supply shocks in the long run? In some cases, we need not concern ourselves with this question, because some supply shocks are temporary. For example, except in unusual cases, periods of rising oil prices are followed by periods of falling oil prices. Similarly, supply shocks caused by unusually good or bad weather, or by natural disasters, are always short lived. A temporary supply shock causes only a temporary shift in the *AS* curve; over the long run, the curve simply returns to its initial position, and the economy returns to full employment. In Figure 12, the *AS* curve would shift back from $AS_2$ to $AS_1$, the price level would fall, and the economy would move from point *R* back to point *E*.

In other cases, however, a supply shock can last for an extended period. One example was the rise in oil prices during the 1970s, which persisted for several years. In cases like this, is there a self-correcting mechanism that brings the economy back to full employment after a long-lasting supply shock? Indeed, there is, and it is the same mechanism that brings the economy back to full employment after a demand shock.

Look again at Figure 12. At point *R*, output is below full-employment output. In the long run, as workers compete for scarce jobs, the wage rate will decline. This will cause the *AS* curve to shift *downward*. The wage will continue to fall until the economy returns to full employment—that is, until we are back at point *E*.

> *In the long run, the economy self-corrects after a supply shock, just as it does after a demand shock. When output differs from its full-employment level, the wage rate changes, and the* AS *curve shifts until full employment is restored.*

## SOME IMPORTANT PROVISOS ABOUT THE *AS* CURVE

The upward-sloping aggregate supply curve we've presented in this chapter gives a realistic picture of how the economy behaves after a demand shock. In the short run, positive demand shocks that increase output also raise the price level. Negative demand shocks that decrease output generally put downward pressure on prices.

However, the story we have told about what happens as we move along the *AS* curve is somewhat incomplete.

First, we made the assumption that prices are completely flexible—that they can change freely over short periods of time. In fact, however, some prices take time to adjust, just as wages take time to adjust. Firms print catalogs containing prices that are good for, say, six months. The public utility commission in your state may set the prices of electricity, gas, water, and basic telephone service in advance for a year or more.

Second, we assumed that wages are completely *inflexible* in the short run. But in *some* industries, wages respond quickly. For example, in the construction industry, contractors hire workers for projects lasting a few months. When they can't find the workers they want, they immediately offer higher wages—they don't wait a year.

Third, there is more to the process of recovering from a shock than the adjustment of prices and wages. During a recession, many workers lose their jobs at the same time. It takes time for those workers to become re-established in new jobs. As time passes, and job losers become job finders, the economy tends to recover. This process, in addition to the changes in wages and prices we've discussed, is part of the long-run adjustment process and helps to bring the economy back to full employment after a shock.

## *Using the* THEORY

# THE RECESSION AND RECOVERY OF 1990–92

The aggregate demand and aggregate supply curves are not just graphs; they are tools that help us understand important economic events. In this section, we'll look at how we can use these tools to understand our most recent recession.

Our story begins in mid-1990, when Iraq invaded Kuwait, a major oil producer. During this conflict, Kuwait's oil was taken off the world market, and so was Iraq's. The reduction in oil supplies resulted in an immediate and substantial increase in the price of oil, a key input to many industries. Panel (a) of Figure 13 shows that the price of oil rose from a low of $14 to a high of $27 per barrel in 1990.

Figure 14 shows our *AS–AD* analysis of the shock. Initially, the economy is on both $AD_1$ and $AS_1$, with equilibrium at point *E*, and output at its full-employment level. Then, the oil price shock shifts the *AS* curve upward, to $AS_2$. As the short-run equilibrium moves to point *R*, real GDP falls and the price level rises. Going back to Figure 13, we see that this is indeed what happened. Panel (b) shows that real GDP did fall in the period after the shock, from $6.7 trillion in mid-1990 to about $6.6 trillion in early 1991. Although the fall was not large, the economy was well below potential by 1992, because potential continued to grow. In panel (c), you can see that the Consumer Price Index rose especially rapidly during this period. Late 1990 through early 1991 was clearly a period of stagflation.

Now let's return to our *AS–AD* analysis in Figure 14. At point *R*, output is below its full-employment level. If the price of oil had remained high, our theory tells us, the self-correcting mechanism would have begun to work: Falling wages would have decreased unit costs. However, the self-correcting mechanism wasn't needed in this case: As you can see in Figure 13, the oil price shock was temporary. Oil prices fell back down in early 1991, shifting the *AS* curve back to $AS_1$ without the self-correcting mechanism. In panel (b) of Figure 13, you can see that real GDP began to recover in early 1991, and continued moving back to its full-employment level in the succeeding years.

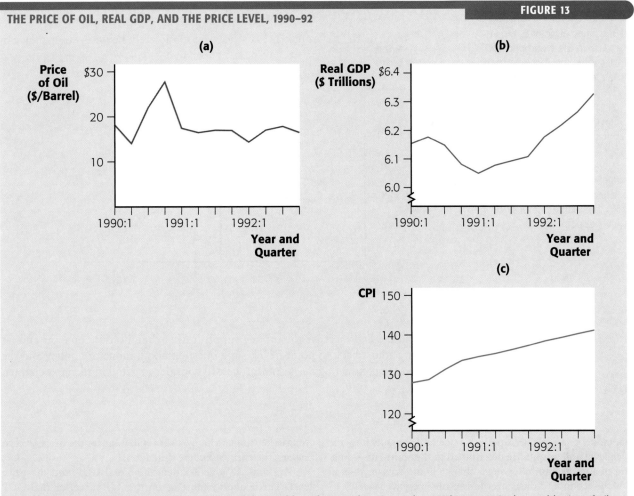

**THE PRICE OF OIL, REAL GDP, AND THE PRICE LEVEL, 1990–92**

**FIGURE 13**

In mid-1990, Kuwaiti and Iraqi oil was taken off the world market, resulting in a substantial increase in the world price of oil, as shown in panel (a). U.S. GDP fell, and the consumer price index rose. When oil prices fell in 1991, GDP recovered.

But something looks fishy here. In our *AS–AD* analysis, the price level should rise when the negative supply shock hits and then gradually *fall* back to its original level when the shock proves temporary. But panel (c) of Figure 13 shows that this prediction was not borne out by the experience of 1990–92. While the price level did rise rapidly in the year after the shock, it *continued to rise* in the next two years as the economy self-corrected. Have we missed something?

Yes, we have. In our analysis of demand and supply shocks in this chapter, we've been focusing on only one change at a time. And here, too, we've been looking at the events of 1990–92 by considering *only* the shift of the *AS* curve. In particular, as the *AS* curve shifts upward and then downward, we've assumed that the *AD* curve stays put.

But that is not what happened in the early 1990s. Instead, in the period after the shock, the Fed increased the money supply, shifting the *AD* curve rightward. Thus, instead of moving from point *R* back to *E*, the economy moved from *R* to *T*. (You can draw in the new *AD* curve to help you see the move.) Output rose, but the price level rose as well.

**FIGURE 14**

Beginning at point *E,* the increase in the world price of oil shifted the *AS* curve from $AS_1$ to $AS_2$. Output fell and the price level rose. When oil prices fell in 1991, the *AS* curve shifted back to $AS_1$. Because the Fed simultaneously increased the money supply, the *AD* curve shifted rightward (not shown). By 1992, output was back to $Y_{FE}$, but with a higher price level at point *T.*

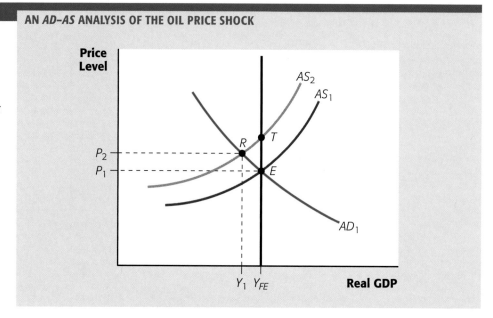

**AN *AD–AS* ANALYSIS OF THE OIL PRICE SHOCK**

Why did the Fed increase the money supply, rather than hold it constant and let the economy adjust back to point *E*? This is a question about monetary policy and the Fed's motives in conducting it—a subject we will consider in detail in the next chapter.

## S U M M A R Y

The model of aggregate supply and demand explains how the price level and output are determined in the short run—a period of a year or so following a change in the economy—and how the economy adjusts over longer time periods as well.

The aggregate demand (*AD*) curve shows how changes in the price level affect equilibrium real GDP. A change in the price level shifts the money demand curve and alters the interest rate in the money market. The change in the interest rate, in turn, affects interest-sensitive forms of spending, shifts the aggregate expenditure curve, triggers the multiplier process, and leads to a new level of equilibrium real GDP. A lower price level means a higher equilibrium real GDP, and a higher price level means lower GDP. The downward-sloping *AD* curve is drawn for given values of government spending, taxes, autonomous consumption spending, investment spending, the money supply, and the public's preferences for holding money and bonds. Changes in any of those factors will cause the *AD* curve to shift.

The aggregate supply (*AS*) curve summarizes the way changes in output affect the price level. To draw the *AS* curve, we assume that firms set the price of individual products as a markup over their costs per unit, and that the economy's average markup is determined by competitive conditions. We also assume that the nominal wage rate is fixed in the short run. As we move upward along the *AS* curve, a rise in real GDP, by raising unit costs, causes the price level to increase. When any-

thing other than a change in real GDP causes the price level to change, the entire *AS* curve shifts.

*AD* and *AS* together determine real GDP and the price level. The economy must be on the *AD* curve, or real GDP would not be at its equilibrium level. It must be on the *AS* curve or firms would not be charging prices dictated by their unit costs and markups. Both conditions are satisfied at the intersection of the two curves.

The *AD/AS* equilibrium can be disturbed by a demand shock. An increase in government purchases, for example, shifts the *AD* curve rightward. As a result, the price level rises, and so does real GDP. In the long run, if GDP is above potential, wages will rise. This causes unit costs to rise and shifts the *AS* curve upward. Eventually, GDP will return to potential and the only long-run result of the demand shock is a higher price level. This implies that the economy's long-run aggregate supply curve is vertical at potential output.

The short-run *AD/AS* equilibrium can also be disturbed by a supply shock, such as an increase in world oil prices. With unit costs higher at each level of output, the *AS* curve shifts upward, decreasing real GDP and increasing the price level. Eventually, the shock will be self-correcting: With output below potential, the wage rate will fall, unit costs will decrease, and the *AS* curve will shift back downward until full employment is restored.

## K E Y   T E R M S

aggregate demand (AD)
  curve
aggregate supply (AS) curve

short-run macroeconomic
  equilibrium
demand shock

supply shock
self-correcting
  mechanism

long-run aggregate
  supply curve
stagflation

## R E V I E W   Q U E S T I O N S

1. What causal relationship does the aggregate demand curve describe? Why does the *AD* curve slope downward? What does each point on the *AD* curve represent?

2. "Only spending shocks can shift the aggregate demand curve." True or false? Explain.

3. List three reasons why a change in output affects unit costs and subsequently the price level.

4. What causal relationship does the aggregate supply curve describe? Why does the *AS* curve slope upward?

5. Why does equilibrium occur only where the *AD* and *AS* curves intersect?

6. What is the economy's *self-correcting mechanism*, and how does it work?

7. What is the long-run aggregate supply curve? Why is it vertical?

8. Does the vertical shape of the long-run aggregate supply curve support the predictions of the classical model with regard to the effectiveness of fiscal policy and crowding out? Explain.

9. How does an economy recover from a negative supply shock?

## P R O B L E M S   A N D   E X E R C I S E S

1. With a three-panel diagram—one panel showing the money market, one showing the aggregate expenditure diagram, and one showing the *AD* curve—show how a *decrease* in the money supply shifts the *AD* curve leftward.

2. Using a diagram showing the aggregate expenditure line, the money market, and the *AD* curve, describe how an increase in taxes affects the interest rate, real aggregate expenditure, and the aggregate demand curve. (Assume that the price level does not change.) What other changes would result in these same effects?

3. Suppose firms become pessimistic about the future and consequently investment spending falls. With an *AD* and

*AS* graph, describe the short-run effects on GDP and the price level. If the price level were constant, how would your answer change?

4. With an *AD* and *AS* diagram, explain the short-run effect of a decrease in the money supply on GDP and the price level. What is the effect in the long run? Assume the economy begins at full employment.

5. A new government policy successfully lowers firms' unit costs. What are the short-run and the long-run effects of such a policy? (Assume that full-employment output does not change.)

## C H A L L E N G E   Q U E S T I O N S

1. Suppose that wages are slow to adjust downward but rapidly adjust upward. What would the *AS* curve look like? How would this affect the economy's adjustment to spending shocks (compared to the analysis given in the chapter)?

2. In recent years, because of technological change, the *AS* curve has been shifting downward, but the price level has not fallen. Why? (*Hint:* What has the Fed been doing?)

## EXPERIENTIAL EXERCISE

1.  Net exports are an important influence on aggregate demand. Find a story in today's *Wall Street Journal* that describes an event that will affect U.S. imports or exports. A good place to look is in the "International" page in the first section of the *Journal*. Analyze the story you have chosen, and illustrate the event using the aggregate expenditure model and the aggregate demand and supply model.

# INFLATION AND MONETARY POLICY

In the late 1970s, the annual inflation rate in the United States reached 13 percent. At the time, polls showed that the public considered inflation the most serious economic problem facing the country. In the nine years following 1991, however, the annual inflation rate never exceeded 3.5 percent, and the problem receded as a matter of public concern. Keeping the inflation rate low has been one of the solid victories of national economic policy.

How did the Fed achieve this victory? Why was it less successful in earlier periods? Are there costs, as well as benefits, to a lower inflation rate? And how should the Fed respond to economic disturbances as it faces the future?

In this chapter, we'll be addressing these and other questions as we take a closer look at the Fed's conduct of monetary policy. Our earlier discussions of monetary policy were somewhat limited, because we lacked the tools—aggregate demand and aggregate supply—to explain changes in the price level. In this chapter, we'll explore monetary policy more fully, making extensive use of the *AD* and *AS* curves.

## THE OBJECTIVES OF MONETARY POLICY

The Fed's objectives have changed over the years. When the Fed was first established in 1913, its chief responsibility was to ensure the stability of the banking system. By acting as a *lender of last resort*—injecting reserves into the banking system in times of crisis—the Fed was supposed to alleviate financial panics.

By the 1950s, the stability of the banking system was no longer a major concern, largely because the United States had not had a banking panic in decades. (Deposit insurance programs had effectively eliminated panics.) Accordingly, the Fed's objective in the 1950s and 1960s changed to keeping the interest rate low and stable. In the 1970s, the Fed's objectives shifted once again. As stated in the Federal Reserve Banking Act of 1978, which is still in force, the Fed is now responsible for achieving a low, stable rate of inflation, and full employment of the labor force. Let's consider each of these goals in turn.

## LOW, STABLE INFLATION

Why is a low rate of inflation important? Several chapters ago, we reviewed the social costs of inflation. When the inflation rate is high, society uses up resources coping with it—resources that could have been used to produce goods and services. Among these resources are the labor needed to update prices at stores and factories, as well as the additional time spent by households and businesses to manage their wealth and protect it from a loss of purchasing power.

In addition to keeping the inflation rate low, the Fed tries to keep it *stable* from year to year. For example, the Fed would prefer a steady yearly inflation rate of 3 percent to an inflation rate of 5 percent half the time, and 1 percent the other half, even though the average inflation rate would be 3 percent in both cases. The reason is that unstable inflation is difficult to predict accurately; it will often turn out higher or lower than people expected. As you learned several chapters ago, an inflation rate higher than expected redistributes real income from lenders to borrowers, while an inflation rate lower than expected has the opposite effect. Thus, unstable inflation adds to the risk of lending and borrowing, and interferes with long-run financial planning.

The Fed, as a public agency, chooses its policies with the costs of inflation in mind. And the Fed has another concern: Inflation is very unpopular with the public. Surveys show that most people associate high rates of inflation with a general breakdown of government and the economy.[1] A Fed chairman who delivers low rates of inflation is seen as popular and competent, while one who tolerates high inflation goes down in history as a failure.

## FULL EMPLOYMENT

"Full employment" means that unemployment is at normal levels. But what, exactly, is a *normal* amount of employment?

Recall that there are different types of unemployment. Some of the unemployed in any given month will find jobs after only a short time of searching. This *frictional* unemployment is part of the normal working of the labor market, and is not a serious social problem. Other job seekers will spend many months or years out of work because they lack the skills that employers require, or because they lack information about available jobs. While this *structural* unemployment is a serious social problem, it is best solved with *micro*economic policies, such as job-training programs or improved information flows.

*Cyclical* unemployment, by contrast, is a *macro*economic problem. It occurs during a recession, in which millions of workers lose their jobs and remain unemployed as they seek new ones. This is why macroeconomists use the term "full employment" to mean *the absence of cyclical employment*. When the economy achieves full employment according to this definition, macroeconomic policy has done all that it can do.

The Fed is concerned about cyclical unemployment for two reasons. First is its *opportunity cost*: the output that the unemployed could have produced if they were working. Part of this opportunity cost is paid by the unemployed themselves, in the form of lost earnings, and part is paid by people who remain employed, but pay higher taxes to provide unemployment benefits to job losers. By maintaining full employment, the Fed can help society avoid this cost.

Second, cyclical unemployment represents a social failure. In a recession, people who have the right skills and who could be working actually *lose* their jobs. Excess

---

[1]     Robert J. Shiller, "Public Resistance to Inflation: A Puzzle," *Brookings Papers on Economic Activity,* 1997.

unemployment lingers for several years after a recession strikes. Thus, cyclical unemployment caused by a recession is a partial breakdown of the system. The economy is not doing what it should do: provide a job for anyone who wants to work and who has the needed skills.

But why should the Fed try to eliminate only *cyclical* unemployment? Why not go further—pushing output above its full-employment level? After all, at higher levels of output, business firms would be more willing to hire *any* available workers. The frictionally unemployed would find jobs more easily, and some of the structurally unemployed would be hired as well. If unemployment is a bad thing, shouldn't the Fed aim for the lowest possible unemployment rate possible?

The answer is no. If the unemployment rate falls too low, GDP rises beyond its potential, full-employment level. As you learned in the last chapter, this causes the economy's self-correcting mechanism to kick in: The *AS* curve shifts upward, increasing the price level. Thus, unemployment that is too low compromises the Fed's other chief goal by creating inflation. And, as you will see later in the chapter, the Fed could not keep the economy operating above full employment for more than a short time anyway. In the long run, its attempts to push the economy too hard would only create more inflation and would not succeed in lowering unemployment.

The unemployment rate at which GDP is at its full-employment level—that is, with no cyclical unemployment—is sometimes called the **natural rate of unemployment.**

> *When the unemployment rate is below the natural rate, GDP is greater than potential output. The economy's self-correcting mechanism will then create inflation. When the unemployment rate is above the natural rate, GDP is below potential output. The self-correcting mechanism will then put downward pressure on the price level.*

**Natural rate of unemployment**
The unemployment rate when there is no cyclical unemployment.

The word *natural* must be interpreted with care. The natural unemployment rate is not etched in stone, nor is it the outcome of purely natural forces that can't be influenced by public policy. But it is determined by rather slow-moving forces in the economy: how frequently workers move from job to job, how efficiently the unemployed can search for jobs and firms can search for new workers, and how well the skills of the unemployed match the skills needed by employers. The natural rate can also be influenced by government policies that provide incentives or disincentives for workers to find jobs quickly, or for employers to hire them. The natural rate can change when any of these underlying conditions change. Indeed, economists generally believe that over the past decade, the natural rate has decreased in the United States—from 6 or 6.5 percent in the mid-1980s to 4 or 4.5 percent today. Meanwhile, in many European countries, the natural rate of unemployment has increased in recent years—exceeding 10 percent in France and close to 20 percent in Spain. The causes of these changes in the natural rate, as well as the *extent* of the changes, are hotly debated by economists. But there is general agreement about the direction: down in the United States, up in Europe.

Why use the term *natural* for such a changeable feature of the economy? The term makes sense only from the perspective of *macroeconomic* policy. Simply put, there isn't much that macroeconomic policy can do about the natural rate. Stimulating the economy with fiscal or monetary policy may bring the *actual* unemployment rate down for a time, but it will not change the natural rate itself. And pushing unemployment below the natural rate would cause inflation. Thus, the natural rate of unemployment can be seen as a kind of goalpost for the Fed. The location of the goalpost may change over the years, but during any given year, it tells us where the Fed is aiming.

**FIGURE 1**

Panel (a) shows the annual inflation rate since 1950. The United States suffered periods of high inflation in the 1970s and early 1980s. Since then, the inflation rate has been much lower. Panel (b) shows the quarterly unemployment rate. Unemployment was particularly high during the early 1980s, and dropped dramatically during the 1990s.

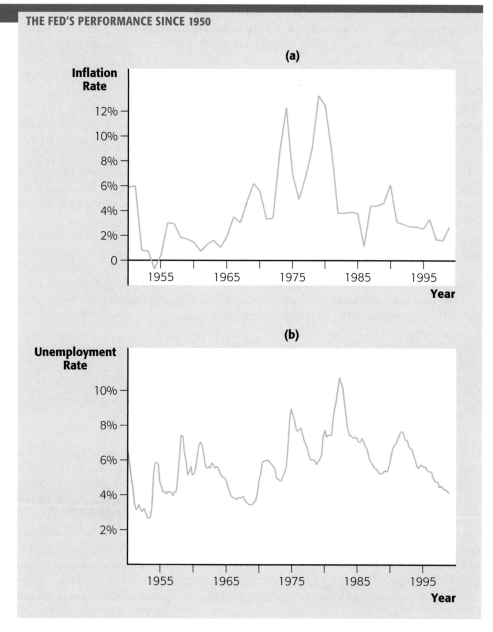

**THE FED'S PERFORMANCE SINCE 1950**

## THE FED'S PERFORMANCE

How well has the Fed achieved its goals? Panel (a) of Figure 1 shows the annual inflation rate since 1950, as measured by the Consumer Price Index. You can see that monetary policy permitted extended periods of high inflation in the 1970s and early 1980s. You can also see, as noted at the beginning of the chapter, that the Fed has achieved great success in controlling inflation since then. Indeed, in the 16 years from 1984 to 1999, the annual inflation rate exceeded 4.6 percent only once—in 1990, during the supply shock caused by higher oil prices. And in recent years, inflation at or below 3 percent has become the norm.

Panel (b) shows the quarterly rate of unemployment since 1950. Over the last decade or so, the Fed's performance on unemployment has been somewhat mixed. From 1984 to 1999, the unemployment rate was 7 percent or greater—significantly above its natural rate—slightly more than one-fourth of the time. The most recent period of high unemployment was during the recession of the early 1990s, when the unemployment rate stayed above 7.5 percent for half a year. But notice the remarkable improvement in unemployment from mid-1992 and after. Through 1997, the Fed kept the unemployment rate hovering very close to 5 percent, and after 1997, it slowly inched the unemployment rate down to 4 percent, which it finally reached in January 2000. And this reduction in unemployment was accomplished *without* heating up inflation.

As you can see, the Fed has had a good—and improving—record in recent years. The inflation rate has been kept low and relatively stable, and—especially in the last few years—unemployment has been near and even below most estimates of the natural rate. How has the Fed done it? Are there any general conclusions we can reach about how a central bank should operate to achieve the twin goals of full employment and a stable, low inflation rate? Indeed there are, as you'll see in the next section.

## FEDERAL RESERVE POLICY: THEORY AND PRACTICE

So far in this text, we've assumed that the Fed's response to spending shocks is a **passive monetary policy.** That is, in the face of spending shocks, the Fed conducts neither open market purchases nor open market sales of bonds, and just keeps the money supply constant. While this was useful for understanding how different events can affect the economy, it is not a realistic description of the Fed's actions. In recent years, the Fed has tried to maintain a stable level of real GDP, rather than a stable money supply. Ideally, the Fed would like to keep the economy operating as close to its potential output as possible. If output falls below potential, there is painful and wasteful unemployment; if output rises above potential, there is a danger of inflation.

**Passive monetary policy** When the Fed keeps the money supply constant regardless of shocks to the economy.

In order to keep real GDP as close as possible to its potential, the Fed must pursue an **active monetary policy,** in which it responds to events in the economy by *changing* the money supply. As you'll see, the required change in the money supply depends on what type of event the Fed is responding to.

**Active monetary policy** When the Fed changes the money supply to achieve some objective.

In some cases, the proper response is easy to determine, because the same action that maintains full employment also helps maintain low inflation. But in other cases, the Fed must trade off one goal for another: Responses that maintain full employment will worsen inflation, and responses that alleviate inflation will create more unemployment.

We'll make a temporary simplifying assumption in this section: that the Fed's goal for the inflation rate is *zero.* In reality, the Fed's goal is *low,* but not zero, inflation. Later, we'll discuss why the Fed prefers a low inflation rate to a zero rate, and how this modifies our analysis.

### RESPONDING TO CHANGES IN MONEY DEMAND

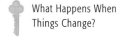 What Happens When Things Change?

Potential disturbances to the economy sometimes arise from a shift in the money demand curve. For example, two chapters ago, you learned about the effects of expectations on money demand. If people expect the interest rate to rise (the price of bonds to fall) in the near future, they will want to hold less wealth in the form of

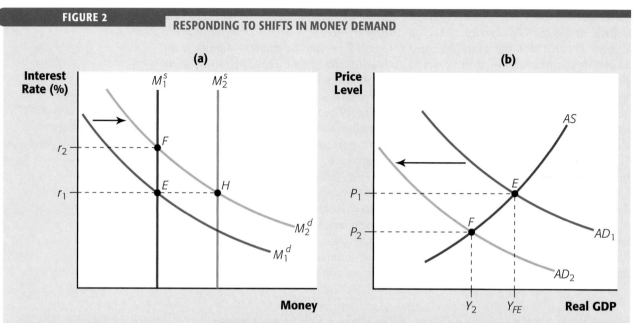

**FIGURE 2**

**RESPONDING TO SHIFTS IN MONEY DEMAND**

Beginning at point *E* in panel (a), an increase in money demand drives the interest rate up to $r_2$ (point *F*). Under a passive monetary policy, this would cause interest-sensitive spending to decrease. In panel (b), the aggregate demand curve would shift to $AD_2$, decreasing GDP from $Y_{FE}$ (at point *E*) to $Y_2$ (at point *F*). The economy would suffer a recession. To maintain full employment, the Fed could increase the money supply to $M_2^s$, preventing any change in the interest rate and any shift in *AD*.

bonds and more in money, so the money demand curve will shift rightward. Larger and longer-lasting shifts in the money demand curve may occur for reasons that are not well understood, although leading suspects are the development of new types of financial assets and new methods of making payments.

How should the Fed respond to shifts in the money demand curve? Figure 2 shows the effect of a rightward shift of the money demand curve. Look first at panel (a). Initially, the money market is in equilibrium at point *E*, with the interest rate equal to $r_1$. When the money demand curve shifts rightward, to $M_2^d$, the equilibrium moves to point *F*, with the higher interest rate $r_2$. With a passive monetary policy— leaving the money supply unchanged—the rise in the interest rate would cause interest-sensitive spending to fall. This, in turn, would decrease equilibrium GDP at any given price level.

Panel (b) shows another way to view the effect of the change in money demand: the *AD* curve shifts leftward, from $AD_1$ to $AD_2$. With a passive monetary policy, the economy would slide down the *AS* curve from point *E* to point *F*, causing a recession. Since the economy began at full-employment output ($Y_{FE}$), the passive monetary policy would cause unemployment to rise above the natural rate, and the price level would decrease.

If the Fed wants to maintain full employment with zero inflation—an unchanged price level—then a passive monetary policy is clearly the wrong response. Is there a better policy?

Indeed there is—an *active* monetary policy. By increasing the money stock— shifting the money supply curve from $M_1^s$ to $M_2^s$—the Fed moves the money market to a new equilibrium at point *H*, *preventing any rise in the interest rate*. If the Fed acts quickly enough, there will be no decrease in interest-sensitive spending and no shift in the *AD* curve. In panel (b), the economy remains at point *E*, and the Fed maintains full employment with zero inflation.

As you can see, shifts in the money demand curve present the Fed with a no-lose situation: By adjusting the money supply to prevent changes in the interest rate, the Fed can achieve both price stability and full employment. During most periods, when the economy is not affected by any shocks other than money demand shifts, the constant interest rate policy will keep the economy on an even keel. This is why, in its day-to-day operations, the Fed sets and maintains an **interest rate target** and then adjusts the money supply to achieve that target.

> To deal with money demand shocks, the Fed sets an interest rate target and changes the money supply as needed to maintain the target. In this way, the Fed can achieve its goals of price stability and full employment simultaneously.

### How the Fed Keeps the Interest Rate on Target.
A quick review of the day-to-day mechanics of Fed policy making shows how it sets and maintains its interest rate target in practice. Fed officials meet each morning to determine that day's monetary policy, based on information gathered the previous afternoon and earlier that morning. A key piece of information is what actually happened to the interest rate since the morning before. A rise in the interest rate means that the money demand curve has shifted rightward; a drop in the interest rate means the curve has shifted leftward.

Using this and other information about the banking system and the economy, the Fed decides what to do. At 11:30 A.M., if the interest rate is above target, the Fed buys government bonds. This increases the money supply and brings the interest rate back down to its target level, as in Figure 2. If, instead, the interest rate is below target, the Fed sells government bonds, decreasing the money supply and raising the interest rate back up to its target level.

## RESPONDING TO SPENDING SHOCKS

The Fed has a somewhat more difficult job responding to spending shocks than to shifts in money demand. Figure 3 illustrates why. In panel (a) the money market is initially in equilibrium at point *E*, with the interest rate at its initial target level of $r_1$. In panel (b) the economy's short-run equilibrium is at point *E*, with output at full employment.

Now suppose that there is a positive spending shock. The shock might originate with the government—an increase in government purchases or a decrease in taxes—or in the private sector—an increase in investment or autonomous consumption or net exports. Whatever the source, the impact in panel (b) is the same: The *AD* curve will shift rightward—from $AD_1$ to $AD_2$—and output will rise. Back in panel (a), the rise in output will shift the money demand curve rightward to $M_2^d$, raising the interest rate. Now let's consider three possible responses by the Fed.

First, the Fed could follow a *passive* monetary policy, leaving the money supply unchanged. In this case, the interest rate would be allowed to rise above its target. In panel (b), the economy would slide upward along the *AS* curve, moving to point *F*. Both output and the price level would rise.

As you can see, the Fed would not want to respond to a spending shock with a passive monetary policy. Output would rise, bringing the unemployment rate below the natural rate. The price level would rise as well—to $P_2$. And in the long run, the price level would rise further—to $P_3$—as the self-correcting mechanism returned the economy to full employment at point *H*.

**Interest rate target** The interest rate the Federal Reserve aims to achieve by adjusting the money supply.

What Happens When Things Change?

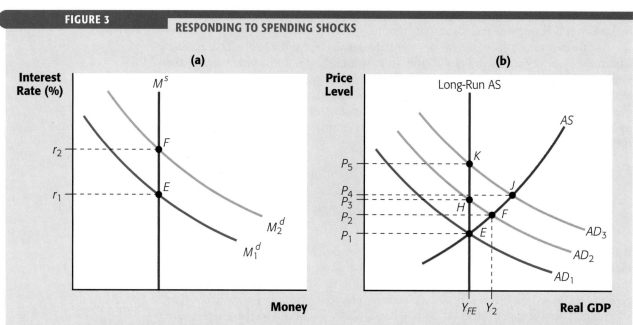

**FIGURE 3**

**RESPONDING TO SPENDING SHOCKS**

A positive spending shock would shift the *AD* curve rightward to $AD_2$ in panel (b), causing both the price level and output to rise. Under a passive monetary policy, that rise in income would cause the money demand curve to shift to $M_2^d$ in panel (a), driving the interest rate upward from $r_1$ to $r_2$.

An active policy of maintaining the interest rate at $r_1$ would make matters worse. To maintain the interest rate target, the Fed would have to increase the money supply, causing an additional rightward shift of the *AD* curve to $AD_3$ and pushing the economy even further above full employment. The price level would increase to $P_4$ in the short run and $P_5$ in the long run.

Would the active policy described earlier—maintaining an interest rate target—be an improvement? Actually, no—it would be even worse. To maintain the interest rate at $r_1$, the Fed would have to *increase* the money supply (not shown). But with no rise in the interest rate to crowd out some consumption and investment spending, the spending shock would shift the *AD* curve rightward even further—say, to $AD_3$. The new short-run equilibrium would then be at point *J*. As you can see, maintaining the interest rate target would push the economy even further beyond its potential output, and increase the price level even more—both in the short run (to $P_4$) and in the long run ($P_5$).

How, then, should the Fed respond to the spending shock? To maintain full employment and a stable price level, the Fed must pursue an active policy, but one that shifts the *AD* curve back to $AD_1$. And it can, indeed, do so. Look at Figure 4. Once again, the figure shows a spending shock that shifts the *AD* curve rightward to $AD_2$, increasing both output and the price level. In the money market, the higher price level and higher income shift the money demand curve rightward, raising the interest rate to $r_2$. But, as you saw in Figure 3, the rise to $r_2$ is not enough to choke off the increase in spending; it causes *some* crowding out of consumption and investment, but not *complete* crowding out. In order to shift the *AD* curve back to $AD_1$, the Fed must raise the interest rate *further*, enough to cause *complete* crowding out. That is, it must raise the interest rate by just enough so that consumption and investment spending decline by an amount equal to the initial spending shock. In the figure, we assume that an interest rate of $r_3$ will do the trick (point *H*). The Fed must decrease the money supply to $M_2^s$. If the Fed acts

**THE BEST RESPONSE TO A SPENDING SHOCK**                                                    **FIGURE 4**

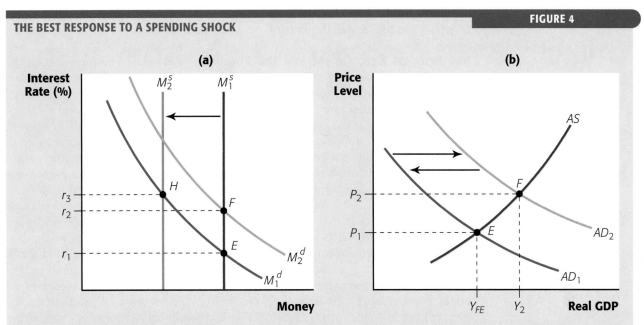

A spending shock that shifts the $AD$ curve to $AD_2$ threatens to raise output beyond its full-employment level, and increase the price level as well. The Fed can neutralize that shift by decreasing the money supply to $M_2^s$. The resulting rise in the interest rate (to $r_3$) would reduce interest-sensitive spending and return the $AD$ curve to $AD_1$.

quickly enough, it can prevent the spending shock from shifting the $AD$ curve at all.[2]

> *To maintain full employment and price stability after a spending shock, the Fed must change its interest rate target. A positive spending shock requires an increase in the target; a negative spending shock requires a decrease in the target.*

In recent years, the Fed has changed its interest rate target as frequently as needed to keep the economy on track. If the Fed observes that the economy is overheating—and that the unemployment rate has fallen below its natural rate—it will raise its target. The Fed—believing that the AD curve was shifting rightward too rapidly—reacted this way in 1999 and early 2000, raising its interest rate target four times in just nine months. When the Fed raises its target, it responds to forces that shift the $AD$ curve rightward by creating an opposing force—a higher interest rate—to shift it leftward again.

When the Fed observes that the economy is sluggish—and the unemployment rate has risen above its natural rate—the Fed will lower its target. This tends to neutralize leftward shifts of the $AD$ curve.

As you can see, spending shocks present the Fed with another no-lose situation: The same policy that helps to keep unemployment at its natural rate also helps to maintain a stable price level. However, spending shocks present a challenge to the Fed that it doesn't face during other, less-eventful periods. To change the interest rate target by just the right amount, the Fed needs accurate information about how

---

[2]   Notice that the new money market equilibrium is along the original money demand curve $M_1^d$, since the policy will return both the price level and income to their original values.

the economy operates. We'll return to this and other problems in conducting monetary policy in the "Using the Theory" section of this chapter.

### The Interest Rate Target and the Financial Markets.

The members of the Open Market Committee think very hard before they vote to change the interest rate target. In addition to its effects on the level of output and the price level, changes in the interest rate target can create turmoil in the stock and bond markets.

Why? Recall that the interest rate and the price of bonds are negatively related. Thus, when the Fed moves the interest rate to a higher target level, the price of bonds drops. Because the public holds trillions of dollars in government and corporate bonds, even a small rise in the interest rate—say, a quarter of a percentage point—causes the value of the public's bond holdings to drop by billions of dollars.

The stock market is often affected in a similar way. People hold stocks because they entitle the owner to a share of a firm's profits, and because stock prices are usually expected to rise as the economy grows and firms become more profitable. But stocks must remain competitive with bonds, or else no one would hold them. The lower the price of a stock, the more attractive the stock is to a potential buyer.

When the Fed raises the interest rate, the rate of return on bonds increases, so bonds become more attractive. As a result, stock prices must fall, so that stocks, too, will become more attractive. And that is typically what happens. Unless other changes are affecting the stock market, a rise in the interest rate causes people to try to sell their stocks in order to acquire the suddenly-more-attractive bonds. This causes stock prices to fall, until stocks are once again as attractive as bonds. Thus, a rise in the interest rate causes stock prices, as well as bond prices, to fall:

> *The stock and bond markets move in the opposite direction to the Fed's interest rate target: When the Fed raises its target, stock and bond prices fall; when it lowers its target, stock and bond prices rise.*

The destabilizing effect on stock and bond markets is one reason the Fed prefers not to change its interest rate target very often. Frequent changes in the target would make financial markets less stable, and the public more hesitant to supply funds to business firms by buying stocks and bonds.

Importantly, financial markets are also affected by *expected* changes in the interest rate target—whether or not they occur. If you expect the Fed to raise its target, you also expect stock and bond prices to fall. Therefore, you would want to dump these assets *now*, before their price drops. Similarly, an expectation of a drop in the interest rate target would make you want to buy stocks and bonds now, before their prices rise. Thus, *changes in expectations* about the Fed's future actions can be as destabilizing as the actions themselves.

This is why the financial press speculates constantly about the likelihood of changes in the interest rate target. Most of the time, the news is of the dog that didn't bark—the Federal Open Market Committee meets and decides to keep the target unchanged. Still, interest rates and stock prices often jump around in the days leading up to meetings of the Open Market Committee.

Once you understand the Fed's logic in changing its interest rate target, you can understand a phenomenon that—at first glance—appears mystifying: Stock and bond prices often fall when good news about the economy is released, and rise when bad news is released. For example, if the Bureau of Labor Statistics announces that jobs are plentiful and the unemployment rate has dropped, or the Commerce Department announces that real GDP has grown rapidly in the previous quarter, the stock and bond markets may plummet. Why? Because owners of stocks and bonds

Financial Markets react when people expect—as they did in early May, 2000—that the Fed may change its interest rate target.

**FIGURE 5**

## RESPONDING TO SUPPLY SHOCKS

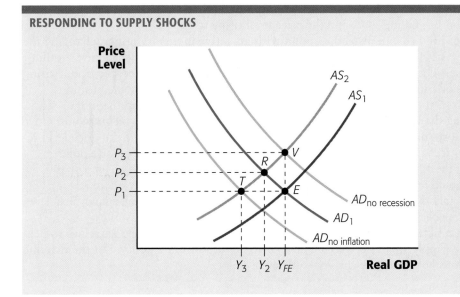

Starting at point $E$, a negative supply shock shifts the $AS$ curve upward to $AS_2$. Under a passive monetary policy, a new short-run equilibrium would be established at point $R$, with a higher price level ($P_2$) and a lower level of output ($Y_2$). The Fed could prevent inflation by decreasing the money supply and shifting $AD$ to $AD_{no\ inflation}$, but output would fall to $Y_3$. At the other extreme, it could increase the money supply and shift the $AD$ curve to $AD_{no\ recession}$. This would keep output at the full-employment level, but at the cost of a higher price level, $P_3$.

know that the Open Market Committee might interpret the good news as evidence that the economy is overheating. They expect the Committee to raise its interest rate target, so they try to sell their stocks and bonds before the committee even meets.

> *Good news about the economy sometimes leads to expectations that the Fed—fearing inflation—will raise its interest rate target. This is why good economic news sometimes causes stock and bond prices to fall. Similarly, bad news about the economy sometimes leads to expectations that the Fed—fearing recession—will lower its interest rate target. This is why bad economic news sometimes causes stock and bond prices to rise.*[3]

## RESPONDING TO SUPPLY SHOCKS

 What Happens When Things Change?

So far in this chapter, you've seen that demand shocks, in general, present the Fed with easy policy choices. By sticking to its interest rate target, it can neutralize any demand shocks that arise from shifts in money demand. And by changing its interest rate target from time to time, it can deal with demand shocks caused by changes in spending. In each of these cases, the very policy that maintains a stable price level also helps to maintain full employment.

But adverse or negative *supply* shocks present the Fed with a true dilemma: If the Fed tries to preserve price stability, it will worsen unemployment; if it tries to maintain high employment, it will worsen inflation. And even though supply shocks are usually temporary, the shocks themselves—and the Fed's response—can affect the economy for several quarters or even years.

Figure 5 illustrates the Fed's dilemma when confronting an adverse supply shock. Initially, the economy is at point $E$ (full employment). Then, a supply shock—say, a rise in world oil prices—shifts the $AS$ curve up to $AS_2$. Under a passive monetary policy, the Fed would not change the money stock, keeping the $AD$ curve at $AD_1$. The short-run equilibrium would then move from point $E$ to point $R$,

---

[3] For a more complete discussion of the stock market, see the Using All the Theory chapter at the end of this book.

http://

For more information about supply shocks, download Bharat Trehan's "Supply Shocks and the Conduct of Monetary Policy," available at http://www.frbsf.org/econrsrch/wklyltr/wklyltr99/el99-21.html.

and the economy would experience stagflation—both inflation and a recession—with output falling to $Y_2$ and the price level rising to $P_2$.

But the Fed can instead respond with an active monetary policy, changing the money stock in order to alter the short-run equilibrium. Which policy should it choose? The answer will depend on whether it is mostly concerned about rising prices or rising unemployment. Let's start by imagining two extreme positions.

First, the Fed could prevent inflation entirely by decreasing the money stock, shifting the $AD$ curve leftward to the curve labeled $AD_{\text{no inflation}}$. This would move the short-run equilibrium to point $T$. Notice, though, that while the price level remains at $P_1$, output decreases to $Y_3$—even lower than under the passive policy.

At the other extreme, the Fed could prevent any fall in output. To accomplish this, the Fed would *increase* the money stock and shift the $AD$ curve rightward, to $AD_{\text{no recession}}$. The equilibrium would then move to point $V$, keeping output at its full-employment level. But this policy causes more inflation, raising the price level all the way to $P_3$.

In practice, the Fed is unlikely to choose either of these two extremes to deal with a supply shock, preferring instead some intermediate policy. But the extreme positions help illustrate the Fed's dilemma:

> *An adverse supply shock presents the Fed with a short-run trade-off: It can limit the recession, but only at the cost of more inflation; and it can limit inflation, but only at the cost of a deeper recession.*

The choice between the two policies is a hard one. After supply shocks, there are often debates within the Fed—and in the public arena—about how best to respond. Inflation *hawks* lean in the direction of price stability, and are willing to tolerate more unemployment in order to achieve it. In the face of an adverse supply shock, hawks would prefer a response that shifts the $AD$ curve closer to $AD_{\text{no inflation}}$, even though it means higher unemployment. Inflation *doves* lean in the direction of a milder recession, and are more willing to tolerate the cost of higher inflation. They would prefer a response that brings the $AD$ curve closer to $AD_{\text{no recession}}$.

**Choosing Between Hawk and Dove Policies.**  When a supply shock hits, should the Fed use a hawk policy, should it employ a dove policy, or should it keep the $AD$ curve unchanged? That depends. Over time, as the economy is hit by supply shocks, the hawk policy maintains more stability in the price level, but less stability in output and employment. The dove policy gives the opposite result: more stability in output and less stability in the price level. The Fed should choose a hawkish policy if it cares more about price stability, and a dovish policy if it cares more about the stability of output and employment. Or it can pick an intermediate policy—one that balances price and employment stability more evenly.

The proper choice depends on how the Fed weights the harm caused by unemployment against the harm caused by inflation. And since the Fed is a public institution, its views should reflect the assessment of society as a whole. This is why supply shocks present such a challenge to the Fed: The public itself is divided between hawks and doves. Both inflation and unemployment cause harm, but of very different kinds. Inflation imposes a more general cost on society—the resources used up to cope with it. If the inflation is unexpected, it will also redistribute income between borrowers and lenders. The costs of unemployment are borne largely by the unemployed themselves—who suffer the harm of job loss—but partly by taxpayers, who provide funds for unemployment insurance. Balancing the gains and losses from hawk and dove policies is no easy task.

In recent years, some officials at the Fed have argued that having two objectives—stable prices *and* full employment—is unrealistic when there are supply shocks. The current chair of the Board of Governors, Alan Greenspan, has asked Congress to change the Fed's mandate to one of controlling inflation, period. But it would be difficult for the Fed to ignore the costs of higher unemployment, even if it was legally permitted to do so. Regardless of any future change in the Fed's mandate, the debate between hawks and doves is destined to continue.

Some income-distributional aspects of monetary policy are explored by Christina and David Romer in "Monetary Policy and the Well-Being of the Poor." It is available at http://www.kc.frb. org/publicat/econrev/PDF/ lq99romr.pdf.

# EXPECTATIONS AND ONGOING INFLATION

So far in this chapter, we've assumed that the Fed strives to maintain *zero* inflation, and that the price level remains constant when the economy reaches its long-run, full-employment equilibrium. But as we discussed earlier, this is not entirely realistic. Look again at panel (a) of Figure 1. There you can see that the U.S. economy has been characterized by *ongoing inflation*. Even in the 1990s—with unemployment at its natural rate—the annual inflation rate has hovered around 2 to 3 percent. That means that, even though the economy is at full employment, prices are *continually rising*.

Why should the price level continue to rise when unemployment is at its natural rate? And how does ongoing inflation change our analysis of the effects of monetary policy, or the guidelines that the Fed should follow? We'll consider these questions next.

## HOW ONGOING INFLATION ARISES

The best way to begin our analysis of ongoing inflation is to explore how it arises in an economy. We can do this by revisiting the 1960s, when the inflation rate rose steadily, and ongoing inflation first became a public concern.

What was special about the economy in the 1960s? First, it was a period of exuberance and optimism, for both businesses and households. Business spending on plant and equipment rose, and household spending on new homes and automobiles rose as well. At the same time, government spending rose—both military spending for the war in Vietnam and social spending on programs to help alleviate poverty. These increases in spending all contributed to rightward shifts of the *AD* curve—they were positive demand shocks. The unemployment rate fell below the natural rate—hovering around 3 percent in the late 1960s. And, as expected, the economy's self-correcting mechanism kicked in: Higher wages shifted the *AS* curve upward, causing the price level to rise.

As you've learned in this chapter, the Fed could have neutralized the positive demand shocks by raising its interest rate target (as in Figure 4), shifting the *AD* curve back to its original position. Alternatively, the Fed could have done nothing, allowing the self-correcting mechanism to bring the economy back to full employment with a higher—but stable—price level (as in the move from point *F* to point *H* in Figure 3). But in the late 1960s, the Fed made a different choice: It maintained its low interest rate target. This required the Fed to increase the money supply, thus adding its *own* positive demand shock to the spending shocks already hitting the economy. In Figure 3, this was the equivalent of moving the *AD* curve all the way out to $AD_3$, preventing any rise in interest rates but overheating the economy even more.

Why did the Fed act in this way? No one knows for sure, but one likely reason is that, in the 1960s, the Fed saw its job differently than it does today. The Fed's goal was to keep the interest rate stable and low, both to maintain high investment spending and to avoid instability in the financial markets. This is what it had been doing for years, with good effect: Americans had prospered in the previous decade, the 1950s, and financial markets were, indeed, stable.

But while this policy worked well in the 1950s, it did not serve the economy well during and after the demand shocks of the 1960s. That's because the Fed's policy—year after year—prevented the self-correcting mechanism from bringing the economy back to full employment. Instead, each time the price level began rising, and the economy began to self-correct, the Fed would increase the money supply *again*, causing output to remain *continually* above its potential output. And that, in turn, meant that the price level would continue to rise, year after year.

Now comes a crucial part of the story: As the price level continued to rise in the 1960s, the public began to *expect* it to rise at a similar rate in the future. This illustrates a more general principle:

> *When inflation continues for some time, the public develops expectations that the inflation rate in the future will be similar to the inflation rates of the recent past.*

Why are expectations of inflation so important? Because when managers and workers expect inflation, it gets built into their decision-making process. Union contracts that set wages for the next three years will include automatic increases to compensate for the anticipated loss of purchasing power caused by future inflation. Nonunion wages will tend to rise each year as well, to match the wages in the unionized sector. And contracts for future delivery of inputs—like lumber, cement, and unfinished goods—will incorporate the higher prices everyone expects by the date of delivery.

> *A continuing, stable rate of inflation gets built into the economy. The built-in rate is usually the rate that has existed for the past few years.*

Once there is built-in inflation, the economy continues to generate continual inflation even *after* the self-correcting mechanism has finally been allowed to do its job and bring us back to potential output. To see why, look at Figure 6. It shows what might happen over three years in an economy with built-in inflation. In the figure, output is at its full-employment level. Each year, the *AS* curve shifts upward, and the *AD* curve shifts rightward, so the price level rises from $P_1$ to $P_2$ to $P_3$. Why does all this happen when there is built-in inflation?

Let's start with the reason for the upward shift of the *AS* curve. Unemployment is at its natural rate, so the self-correction mechanism is no longer contributing to any rise in wages or unit costs. But something else *is* causing unit costs to increase: inflationary expectations. Based on recent experience, the public expects the price level to rise as it has been rising in the past, so wages and input prices will continue to increase, *even though output remains unchanged at full employment.* Thus,

> *in an economy with built-in inflation, the* AS *curve will shift upward each year, even when output is at full employment and unemployment is at its natural rate. The upward shift of the* AS *curve will equal the built-in rate of inflation.*

For example, if the public expects inflation of 3 percent per year, then contracts will call for wages and input prices to rise by 3 percent per year. This means that unit costs will increase by 3 percent. Firms—marking up prices over unit costs—will raise their prices by 3 percent as well, and the *AS* curve will shift upward by 3 percent each year.

Explaining why the *AS* curve shifts upward is only half the story of the long-run equilibrium in Figure 6. We must also explain why the *AD* curve continues to shift rightward. The simple answer is: The *AD* curve shifts rightward because the Fed continues to increase the money supply. But *why* does the Fed shift the *AD* curve rightward, when it knows that doing so only prolongs inflation? One reason is that reducing inflation is *costly* to the economy.

**FIGURE 6**

**LONG-RUN EQUILIBRIUM WITH BUILT-IN INFLATION**

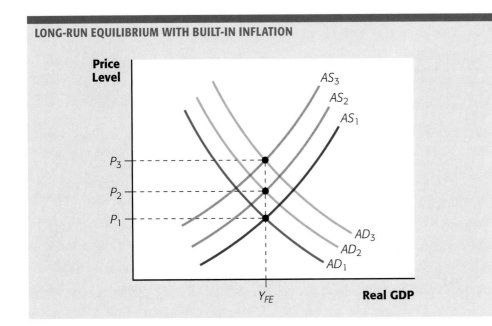

Each year, the aggregate supply curve shifts upward by the built-in rate of inflation. To keep the economy at full employment, the Fed shifts the *AD* curve rightward each year by increasing the money supply.

Imagine what would happen if, one year, the Fed decided *not* to shift the *AD* curve rightward as it had done in the past. During the year, the *AS* curve will shift upward anyway, by a percentage shift equal to the built-in rate of inflation. This will happen *no matter what the Fed does,* because the shift is based on wage and price decisions that, in turn, are based on past experiences of inflation. There is nothing the Fed can do today to affect what has happened in the past, so each year, it must accept the upward shift of the *AS* curve as a given.

But now suppose the Fed decides to reduce inflation by *not* shifting the *AD* curve as it has in the past. Instead, it will just leave the *AD* curve where it was the year before. For example, as the *AS* curve shifts from $AS_2$ to $AS_3$, the Fed might keep the *AD* curve at $AD_2$. See if you can draw the new, temporary equilibrium that the Fed will achieve for the economy. (*Hint:* It's at the intersection of $AD_2$ and $AS_3$). If you've identified the point correctly, you'll see that the Fed would achieve its goal of bringing down inflation this year. The price level would rise from $P_2$ to something less than $P_3$, instead of all the way to $P_3$. But the reduction in inflation is not without cost: The economy's output will decline—a recession.

> *In the short run, the Fed can bring down the rate of inflation by reducing the rightward shift of the* AD *curve, but only at the cost of creating a recession.*

Would the Fed ever purposely create a recession to reduce inflation? Indeed it would, and it has—more than once. By far the most important episode occurred during the early 1980s. As Figure 1 shows, inflation reached the extraordinary level of 14.8 percent in early 1980. Soon after, with the support of the newly elected President Reagan, the Fed embarked on an aggressive campaign to bring inflation down. The Fed stopped increasing the money supply, stopped shifting the *AD* curve rightward, and a recession began in July of 1981. Unemployment peaked, as shown in Figure 1, at 10.7 percent at the end of 1982. With tremendous slack in the economy, the inflation rate fell rapidly, to below 4 percent in 1982. The Fed deliberately created a serious recession, but it brought down the rate of inflation.

The Phillips curve illustrates possible combinations of inflation and unemployment for the economy in the short run, with a given built-in inflation rate. Point $E$ represents a long-run equilibrium, with the economy at the natural rate of unemployment, $U_N$, and inflation at the built-in rate of 6%. If the Fed wishes to decrease the inflation rate to 3%, it must accept a higher short-run unemployment rate—$U_1$ at point $F$.

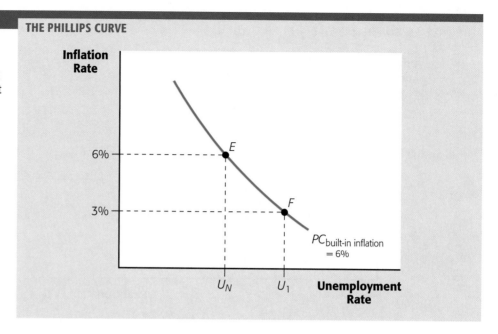

**THE PHILLIPS CURVE**

Creating a recession is not a decision that the Fed takes lightly. Recessions are costly to the economy and painful to those who lose their jobs. The desire to avoid a recession is one reason that the Fed tolerates ongoing inflation and continues to play its role by shifting the $AD$ curve rightward. We'll discuss other reasons for the Fed's tolerance of ongoing inflation a bit later.

## ONGOING INFLATION AND THE PHILLIPS CURVE

Ongoing inflation changes our analysis of monetary policy. For one thing, it forces us to recognize a subtle, but important, change in the Fed's objectives: While the Fed still desires full employment, its other goal—price stability—is not zero inflation, but rather a *low and stable inflation rate.*

Another difference is in the graphs we use to illustrate the Fed's policy choices. Instead of continuing to analyze the economy with $AS$ and $AD$ graphs, when there is ongoing inflation, we usually use another powerful tool.

This tool is the *Phillips curve*—named after the late economist A. W. Phillips, who did early research on the relationship between inflation and unemployment. The **Phillips curve** illustrates the Fed's choices between inflation and unemployment in the short run, for a given built-in inflation rate.

Figure 7 shows a Phillips curve for the U.S. economy. The inflation rate is measured on the vertical axis, the unemployment rate on the horizontal. Point $E$ shows the long-run equilibrium in the economy when the built-in inflation rate is 6 percent. At point $E$, unemployment is at its natural rate—$U_N$—and inflation remains constant from year to year at the built-in rate of 6 percent.

Notice that the Phillips curve is downward sloping. Why? Because it tells the same story we told earlier—with $AD$ and $AS$ curves—about the Fed's options in the short run. If the Fed wants to decrease the rate of inflation from 6 percent to 3 percent, it must slow the rightward shifts of the $AD$ curve. This would cause a movement *along* the Phillips curve from point $E$ to point $F$. As you can see, in moving to point $F$, the economy experiences a recession: Output falls, and unemployment rises above the natural rate.

**Phillips curve**  A curve indicating the Fed's choice between inflation and unemployment in the short run.

**FIGURE 8**

**THE SHIFTING PHILLIPS CURVE**

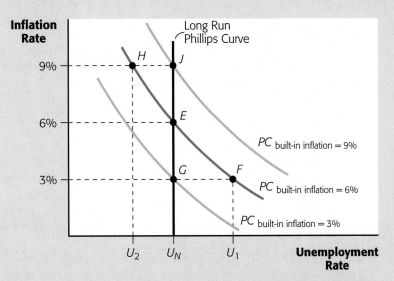

Initially, the economy is at point *E*, with inflation equal to the built-in rate of 6%. If the Fed moves the economy to point *F* and keeps it there, the public will eventually come to expect 3% inflation in the future. At that point, the built-in inflation rate will fall and the curve will shift down to $PC_{\text{built-in inflation} = 3\%}$. The economy will move to point *G* in the long run, with unemployment at the natural rate and an actual inflation rate equal to the built-in rate of 3%.

Starting again at point *E*, a demand shock that was not neutralized by the Fed would move the economy to point *H*; the inflation rate would rise to 9 percent, and the unemployment rate would fall to $U_2$. If the Fed then held the economy at point *H*, the built-in inflation rate would rise to 9%, and the Phillips curve would shift up to $PC_{\text{built-in inflation} = 9\%}$. Eventually, the economy would move to point *J*. The vertical line connecting points *E*, *G*, and *J* is the long-run Phillips curve.

*In the short run, the Fed can move along the Phillips curve by adjusting the rate at which the AD curve shifts rightward. When the Fed moves the economy downward and rightward along the Phillips curve, the unemployment rate increases, and the inflation rate decreases.*

Now suppose the Fed keeps the economy at point *F*. In the long run, the public—observing a 3-percent inflation rate—will come to expect 3-percent inflation in the future. Thus, in the long run, 3 percent will become the economy's built-in rate of inflation. Figure 8 shows the effect on the Phillips curve: It shifts downward, to the lower curve. At any unemployment rate, the inflation rate will be lower, now that the public expects inflation of only 3 percent, rather than 6 percent.

*In the long run, a decrease in the actual inflation rate leads to a lower built-in inflation rate, and the Phillips curve shifts downward.*

Once the Fed has reduced the built-in inflation rate, it can locate anywhere on the new Phillips curve by adjusting how rapidly it lets the money supply grow (and therefore, how rapidly the AD curve shifts rightward each year). Therefore, the Fed can choose to bring the economy back to full employment (point *G*), with a new, lower inflation rate of 3 percent, rather than the previous 6 percent.

**Riding Up the Phillips Curve.** The process we've described—moving down the Phillips curve and thereby causing it to shift downward—also works in reverse: Moving *up* the Phillips curve will cause it to shift *upward*. Figure 8 also illustrates this case. Once again, the economy begins at point *E,* with a built-in inflation rate of 6 percent and unemployment at its natural rate. Now suppose the Fed begins to increase the money supply *more rapidly* than in the past, and—in Figure 6—begins shifting the *AD* curve further rightward than before. In the short run, the economy would move *along* the Phillips curve from point *E* to point *H* in Figure 8. The inflation rate would rise to 9 percent, and the unemployment rate would fall below its natural rate—in the short run.

But suppose the Fed keeps the economy at point *H* for some time—continuing to shift the *AD* curve rightward at a faster rate than before. Then, in the long run, the public will begin to expect 9-percent inflation, and that will become the new built-in rate of inflation. The Phillips curve will then shift upward. At this point, if the Fed returns the economy to full employment, we end up at point *J*. The economy will be back in long-run equilibrium—but with a higher built-in inflation rate.

**The Long-Run Phillips Curve.** In Figure 8, you can see that the Fed's policy choices are different in the short run and in the long run. In the short run, the Fed can move along the Phillips curve, exploiting the trade-off between unemployment and inflation. But in the long run—once the public expectations of inflation adjust to the new reality—the built-in inflation rate will change, and the Phillips curve will shift. Indeed, the Phillips curve will *keep* shifting whenever the unemployment rate is kept above or below the natural rate. (To see why, ask yourself what would happen in the future if the Fed tried to keep the unemployment rate *permanently* at a level like $U_2$—below the natural rate?) Thus, in the long run, the unemployment must eventually return to the natural rate, and output must go back to its potential level. In the long run, the Fed can only choose *which* Phillips curve the economy will be on at that time. That is,

> *in the short run, there is a trade-off between inflation and unemployment: The Fed can choose lower unemployment at the cost of higher inflation, or lower inflation at the cost of higher unemployment. But in the long run, since unemployment always returns to its natural rate, there is no such trade-off.*

Now let's reconsider what we've learned about the Fed's options in the long run. Figure 8 shows us that, when the Fed slows the rightward shifts of the *AD* curve, unemployment returns to the natural rate, but the inflation rate is lower. The figure also shows us that, when the Fed allows the *AD* curve to shift rightward more rapidly than in the past, unemployment returns once again to the natural rate, but the inflation rate is higher. As you can see,

> *in the long run, monetary policy can change the rate of inflation, but not the rate of unemployment.*

Now look at the vertical line in Figure 8. It tells us how monetary policy affects the economy in the long run, without the distractions of the short-run story. The vertical line is the economy's **long-run Phillips curve**, which tells us the combinations of unemployment and inflation that the Fed can choose in the long run. No matter what the Fed does, unemployment will always return to the natural rate, $U_N$, in the long run. However, the Fed can use monetary policy to select any rate of inflation it wants:

**Long-run Phillips curve** A vertical line indicating that in the long run, unemployment must equal its natural rate, regardless of the rate of inflation.

> *The long-run Phillips curve is a vertical line at the natural rate of unemployment. The Fed can select any point along this line in the long run, by using monetary policy to speed or slow the rate at which the AD curve shifts rightward.*

## WHY THE FED ALLOWS ONGOING INFLATION

Since the Fed can choose any rate of inflation it wants, and since inflation is costly to society, we might think that the Fed would aim for an inflation rate of zero. But a look back at panel (a) of Figure 1 shows that this is not what the Fed has chosen to do. In recent years, with unemployment very close to its natural rate, the Fed has maintained annual inflation at around 2 or 3 percent. Why doesn't the Fed eliminate inflation from the economy entirely?

One reason is a widespread belief that the Consumer Price Index (CPI) and other measures of inflation actually *overstate* the true rate of inflation in the economy. As you've learned, many economists believe that the CPI has overstated the true inflation rate by 1 to 2 percent per year. Although the Bureau of Labor Statistics has been working hard to correct the problem, some significant upward bias remains. If the Fed forced the *measured* rate of inflation down to zero, the result would be a true rate of inflation that was negative—prices would actually *fall* each year. But negative rates of inflation can be as costly to society as positive rates: People are as likely to make errors in financial planning when the price level is falling at 2 percent per year as they are when the price level is rising at the same rate. And if the price level drops by more or less than expected, real income will be shifted between borrowers and lenders.

Some economists have offered another explanation for the Fed's behavior: Low, stable inflation makes the labor market work more smoothly. The argument goes as follows: While no one wants a cut in their *real* wage rate, people seem to react differently, depending on *how* the real wage is decreased. For example, suppose there is an excess supply of manufacturing workers, and a wage cut of 3 percent is needed to bring that labor market back to equilibrium. Workers would strongly resist a 3-percent cut in the nominal wage. But they would more easily tolerate a freeze in the nominal wage while the price level rises by 3 percent, even though in both scenarios, the real wage falls by 3 percent. If this argument is correct, then a low or modest inflation rate would help wages adjust in different markets. In some labor markets, real wages can be raised by increasing nominal wages faster than prices. In other labor markets, real wages can be cut by increasing nominal wages more slowly than prices, or not at all.

But the strongest reason for the Fed's tolerance of low inflation is one we've already discussed: Once inflation is built into the economy, it is costly to reduce it. For example, to reduce the built-in inflation rate from its current 2 or 3 percent, the Fed would have to engineer a recession. Even if the Fed believed that the economy would be better off with lower inflation, it would not necessarily choose to pursue this goal. In fact, as a result of the Fed's success in controlling inflation for the past several years, popular concern about inflation has practically disappeared. Since a further reduction in inflation is not valued highly by the public, it is not politically worthwhile to pay the costs of achieving it.

> *The Fed has tolerated measured inflation at 2 to 3 percent per year because it knows that the true rate of inflation is lower, because low rates of inflation may help labor markets adjust more easily, and because there is not much payoff to lowering inflation further.*

*Using the*
# THEORY

# CONDUCTING MONETARY POLICY IN THE REAL WORLD

So far in this chapter, we've described some clear-cut guidelines the Fed *can* and *does* follow in conducting monetary policy. We've seen that the proper policy for dealing with day-to-day changes in money demand is to set and maintain an interest rate target. The proper response to a spending shock is a change in the interest rate target. Dealing with a supply shock is more problematic, since it requires the Fed to balance its goal of low, stable inflation with its goal of full employment. But even here, once the Fed decides on the proper balance, its policy choice is straightforward: Shift the *AD* curve to achieve the desired combination of inflation and unemployment in the short run, and then bring the economy back to full employment in the long run.

In most of our discussion, we've assumed that the Fed has all of the information it needs to determine where the economy *is* operating, where it *should* be operating, and what change in monetary policy will get it there. Unfortunately, the real world is not that simple: The information available to the Federal Open Market Committee is far from perfect. As a result, the Fed's selection and execution of policy are sometimes more complicated than we've suggested so far. In this section, we'll consider some of the problems of monetary policy, and how the Fed has adapted to them.

## INFORMATION ABOUT THE MONEY DEMAND CURVE

The easiest job facing the Fed is responding to shifts in the money demand curve. As you saw in Figure 2, the Fed can stop money demand shocks from affecting output or the price level by adjusting the money stock to keep the interest rate unchanged. If the money demand curve shifts to $M_2^d$, the interest rate rises, so the Fed knows it must increase the money supply to keep the interest rate at $r_1$. The Fed maintains the interest rate by moving *along* the new money demand curve.

But Figure 2 also reveals a potential problem: The Fed cannot know how much to increase the money stock unless it knows the *slope* of the new money demand curve. For example, if the money demand curve has become flatter, the Fed will have to increase the money supply beyond $M_2^s$ in order to maintain its interest rate target.

How does the Fed deal with this problem? In two ways. First, the Fed's research staff tries to estimate the changes in the position and slope of the money demand curve from available data. While the techniques are not perfect, they enable the Fed to make reasonable guesses about the required change in the money supply on any given day.

Second, the Fed uses the trial-and-error procedure that we discussed earlier. For example, suppose the interest rate rises and Fed officials underestimate the required change in the money supply. Then the interest rate will remain above its target rate, and the Fed can try again the next day, increasing the money supply further. In recent years, using a combination of research on the one hand and trial and error on the other, the Fed has been quite successful in reaching and maintaining its interest rate target.

## INFORMATION ABOUT THE SENSITIVITY OF SPENDING TO THE INTEREST RATE

The proper response to spending shocks presents the Fed with a more significant problem. Look back at Figure 3, in which a positive spending shock shifts the *AD* curve rightward to $AD_2$. The Fed will want to neutralize the shock by shifting the

*AD* curve back to $AD_1$. To do so, it will raise its interest rate target. But by how much? That depends on the sensitivity of consumption and investment spending to the interest rate. If spending is *very* sensitive to interest rate changes, only a small rise in the target is needed; if spending is less sensitive, the Fed will need to raise its target rate by more.

Once again, the Fed addresses this problem with both research and trial-and-error methods. The research in this case focuses on how households and businesses change their spending plans when the interest rate rises and falls. This enables the Fed to make reasonable guesses about the required change in the interest rate target.

Trial and error helps the Fed get even closer. Suppose, for example, that there is a positive spending shock that the Fed wants to neutralize. Suppose, too, that the Fed makes an error, and selects an interest rate target that is too low. Then the economy will begin to overheat. As output rises beyond full employment, the price level (or the inflation rate) will rise. The Fed then observes the changes in output and prices, and adjusts its interest rate target again.

There is one major drawback to this procedure, however: It may take many months for the Fed's error to show up. GDP is measured only once each quarter. The Consumer Price Index is released each month, but prices may be slow to adjust to the increase in output. Thus, in contrast to the case of money-demand shifts—where the Fed can correct its errors within days—spending shocks often require the Fed to "wing it" for many months.

## UNCERTAIN AND CHANGING TIME LAGS

We've just seen that it can take many months before the Fed observes how a change in its interest rate target is affecting output and the price level. More importantly, the Fed does not know precisely *how many* months it will take. This presents a serious challenge for monetary policy. Suppose Fed officials believe that the economy is beginning to overheat, and they raise the interest rate target. The new, higher interest rate might not reduce spending for some time. Business firms will finish building the new plants and new homes that they've already started, even at higher interest rates. Investment spending will finally come down only at the point when canceled investment projects *would* have entered the pipeline, many months later. By the time the higher interest rate target has its maximum effect, the economy may be returning to full employment on its own, or it may be hit by a negative demand shock. In this case, the Fed—by raising its interest rate target—will be reining in the economy at just the wrong time, causing a recession.

Economists often use an analogy to describe this problem. Imagine that you are trying to drive a car with a special problem: When you step on the gas, the car will go forward . . . but not until five minutes later. Similarly, when you step on the brake, the car will slow, but also with a five-minute lag. It would be very difficult to maintain an even speed with this car: You'd step on the gas, and when nothing happened, you'd be tempted to step on it harder. By the time the car begins to move, you will have given too much gas and find yourself speeding down the road. So you try to slow down, but once again, hitting the brakes makes nothing happen. So you brake harder, and when the car finally responds, you come to a dead halt.

The Fed can make—and, in the past, has made—a similar mistake. When it tries to cool off an overheated economy, it may find that nothing is happening. Is it just a long time lag, or has the Fed not hit the brakes hard enough? If it hits the brakes harder, it runs the risk of braking the economy too much; if it doesn't, it runs the risk of continuing to allow the economy to overheat. Even worse, the time lag before monetary policy affects prices and output can change over the years: Just when the Fed may think it has mastered the rules of the game, the rules change.

## THE NATURAL RATE OF UNEMPLOYMENT

Finally, we come to the most controversial information problem facing the Fed: uncertainty over the natural rate of unemployment. While there is wide agreement that the natural rate rose in the 1970s and has fallen since the late 1980s, economists remain uncertain about its value during any given period. Many economists believe that today the natural rate is between 4 and 4.5 percent, but no one is really sure.

Why is this a problem? It's very much like the two mountain climbers who become lost. One of them pulls out a map. "Do you see that big mountain over there," he says, pointing off into the distance. "Yes," says the other. "Well," says the first, "according to the map, we're standing on top of it." In order to achieve its twin goals of full employment and a stable, low rate of inflation, the Fed tries to maintain the unemployment rate as close to the natural rate as possible. If its estimate of the natural rate is wrong, it may believe it has succeeded when, in fact, it has not.

For example, suppose the Fed believes the natural rate of unemployment is 4.5 percent, but the rate is really 4 percent. Then—at least for a time—the Fed will be steering the economy toward an unemployment rate that is unnecessarily high, and an output level that is unnecessarily low. We've already discussed the costs of cyclical unemployment; and an overestimate of the natural rate makes society bear these costs needlessly. On the other hand, if the Fed believes the natural rate is 4 percent when it is really 4.5 percent, it will overheat the economy. This will raise the inflation rate—and a costly recession may be needed later in order to reduce it.

Trial and error can help the Fed determine the true natural rate. If the Fed raises unemployment above the true natural rate, the inflation rate will drop. If unemployment falls below the true natural rate, the inflation rate will rise. But—as we discussed earlier—trial and error works best when there is continual and rapid feedback. It can take some time for the inflation rate to change—six months, a year, or even longer. In the meantime, the Fed might believe it has been successful, even while causing avoidable unemployment, or planting the seeds for a future rise in the inflation rate.

Estimating the natural rate of unemployment is made even more difficult because the economy is constantly buffeted by shocks of one kind or another. If the Fed observes that the inflation rate is rising, does that mean that unemployment is below the natural rate? Or is the higher inflation being caused by a negative supply shock? Or by the Fed's response to an earlier, negative demand shock? This information is difficult to sort out, although the Fed has become increasingly sophisticated in its efforts to do so.

As you can see, conducting monetary policy is not easy. The Fed has hundreds of economists carrying out research and gathering data to improve its information about the status of the economy and its understanding of how the economy works. And the effort seems to have paid off, especially over the last decade. But years from now, this period may be seen as the golden age of successful monetary policy. After all, the 1950s also seemed to be a period of good policy, but then the 1960s and especially the 1970s turned into disasters for monetary policy. Because we don't know what kinds of shocks will hit the economy in the future (oil price shocks came out of the blue in the 1970s) or how the Fed will respond to them, we cannot say that monetary policy will necessarily continue to work well in the future.

## SUMMARY

As the nation's central bank, the Federal Reserve bears primary responsibility for maintaining a low, stable rate of inflation and for maintaining full employment of the labor force as the economy is buffeted by a variety of shocks. The money demand curve, for example, may shift, causing a change in the interest rate, a shift in the AD curve, and a change in output and employment. The Fed can neutralize such money demand shocks by setting an interest rate target. To maintain the target, it increases the money supply whenever money demand increases, and decreases the money supply when money demand decreases. This policy enables the Fed to stabilize both inflation and unemployment.

Spending shocks—spontaneous shifts in aggregate expenditures—can also shift the AD curve, causing output to deviate from its full-employment level. The Fed can neutralize spending shocks by adjusting its interest rate target—changing the money supply to shift the AD curve back to its original position.

The Fed's most difficult problem is responding to supply shocks. A negative supply shock—an upward shift of the AS curve—presents the Fed with a dilemma. In the short run, it must choose a point along that new AS curve. If it wishes to maintain price stability, it must shift the AD curve to the left and accept higher unemployment. If the Fed wishes to maintain full employment, it must shift the AD curve to the right and accept a higher rate of inflation. A "hawk" policy puts greater emphasis on price stability, while a "dove" policy emphasizes lower unemployment.

If Fed policy leads to ongoing inflation, then businesses and households come to expect the prevailing inflation rate to continue. As a result, the AS curve continues to shift at that built-in expected inflation rate. To maintain full employment, the Fed must shift the AD curve rightward, creating an inflation rate equal to the expected rate.

If the Fed wishes to change the built-in inflation rate, it must first change the expected inflation rate. For example, to lower the expected inflation rate, the Fed will slow down the rightward shifts of the AD curve. The actual inflation rate will fall, and expectations will eventually adjust downward. While they do so, however, the economy will experience a recession. The Fed's short-run choices between inflation and unemployment can be illustrated with the Phillips curve. In the short run, the Fed can move the economy along the downward-sloping Phillips curve by adjusting the rate at which the AD curve shifts. If the Fed moves the economy to a new point on the Phillips curve and holds it there, the built-in inflation rate will eventually adjust and the Phillips curve will shift. In the long run, the economy will return to the natural rate of unemployment with a different inflation rate. This is why we draw the long-run Phillips curve as a vertical line at the natural rate of unemployment.

## KEY TERMS

| | | | |
|---|---|---|---|
| natural rate of unemployment | passive monetary policy | interest rate target | long-run Phillips curve |
| | active monetary policy | Phillips curve | |

## REVIEW QUESTIONS

1. "The Fed should aim for the lowest possible unemployment rate." True or false? Explain.

2. What effect does a change in the Fed's interest rate target have on financial markets? How do changes in expectations regarding the Fed's position on the interest rate target affect financial markets?

3. "The Fed should respond to any shift in the AD curve by maintaining its interest rate target." True or false? Explain.

4. Explain the trade-off that the Fed faces with regard to negative supply shocks. What do "hawks" and "doves" have to do with this trade-off?

5. Why do expectations of inflation have a significant impact on the economy? What is the impact?

6. What relationship does the Phillips curve illustrate? How does the Fed control movements along the Phillips curve? Why is the long-run Phillips curve vertical?

7. List and explain three reasons why the Fed tolerates some ongoing inflation.

## P R O B L E M S   A N D   E X E R C I S E S

1. Suppose that a law required the Fed to do everything possible to keep the inflation rate equal to zero. Using *AD* and *AS* curves, illustrate and explain how the Fed would deal with (a) a positive money demand shock, (b) a spending shock, and (c) an aggregate supply shock. What would the costs and benefits of such a law be?

2. Suppose that, in a world with *no* ongoing inflation, the government raises taxes. Using *AD* and *AS* curves, describe the effects on the economy if the Fed decides to practice a passive monetary policy. Alternatively, how could the Fed use active policy to neutralize the spending shock?

3. Suppose the economy has been experiencing a low inflation rate. A new chair of the Federal Reserve is named, and she is known to be highly sympathetic to dove policies. Explain the possible effects on the Phillips curve.

4. Using a graph, illustrate why the Fed, if it practices interest rate targeting, is concerned about the slope of the money demand curve. What are the implications of incorrectly estimating the slope?

5. Suppose that initially the price level is $P_1$ and GDP is $Y_1$, with no built-in inflation. The Fed reacts to a negative spending shock by shifting the aggregate demand curve. The next time the Fed receives data on GDP and the price level, it finds that the price level is above $P_1$ and GDP is above $Y_1$. Give two possible explanations for this finding.

## C H A L L E N G E   Q U E S T I O N S

1. Suppose the economy is experiencing ongoing inflation. The Fed wants to reduce expected inflation, so it *announces* that in the future it will tolerate less inflation. How does the Fed's credibility affect the success of the reduction? How can the Fed build its credibility? Are there costs to building credibility? If so, what are they?

2. This chapter mentioned what would happen if the Fed over- or underestimated the natural rate of unemployment. Using the *AD-AS* model, suppose the economy is at the true natural rate of unemployment, so that GDP is at its potential level. Suppose, too, that the Fed wrongly believes that the natural rate of unemployment is higher (potential GDP is lower), and acts to bring the economy back to its supposed potential. What will the Fed do? What will happen in the short run? If the Fed continues to maintain output below potential, what will happen over the long run?

## E X P E R I E N T I A L   E X E R C I S E

The Federal Reserve Bank of Cleveland's monthly publication *Economic Trends* is available online at *http://www.clev.frb.org/research*. Choose a recent issue and click on "Monetary Policy." What are some current developments in U.S. monetary policy? See if you can illustrate them using the *AD-AS* model. A good source for the latest information regarding monetary policy is the Economy column that appears daily in *The Wall Street Journal*. Take a look at today's issue. What is the Fed's current policy stance? Is it focusing more on controlling inflation, or does it seem to be more concerned with the unemployment rate?

# FISCAL POLICY: TAXES, SPENDING, AND THE FEDERAL BUDGET

Almost every year throughout the 1970s, 1980s, and early 1990s, a best-selling book would be published that predicted economic disaster for the United States and the world. In most of these books, the U.S. federal government played a central role. Arguments and statistics were offered to show that federal government spending—which was growing by leaps and bounds—was out of control, causing us to run budget deficits year after year. As a result, the United States was facing a growing debt burden that would soon swallow up all of our incomes, sink the United States economy, and bring about a worldwide depression.

During the late 1990s, as the federal budget picture improved, these disaster books quietly disappeared. In their place came news articles and public statements describing an economic future so bright that it would have been unimaginable just a few years earlier. And the situation faced by the federal government seemed to have flipped on its head. Instead of trying to bring down the ever-growing budget deficit, the key question became: What shall we do with our mounting budget *surpluses*?

What should we make of this flip-flop of public sentiment? Is it realistic? Were we really headed toward disaster until just a few years ago? And have all of our budget problems really been solved so suddenly? In this chapter, we'll take a close look at the government's role in the macroeconomy. You'll learn how to interpret trends in the government's budget, and how to identify the causes and effects of those trends. You'll see that while the United States did, indeed, face a growing budget problem over the last few decades—one that justified some concern—we were *not* on the brink of a disaster. You'll also see that while the U.S. fiscal picture has improved in the early 2000s, it is not as secure as is often suggested.

## THINKING ABOUT SPENDING, TAXES, AND THE BUDGET

Let's start with some simple numbers. In 1959, the federal government's total spending—its outlays for goods and services, transfer payments, and interest on its debt—was $81 billion. By 1999, the total had grown to $1,806 billion, an increase of 2,130 percent. Government spending is out of control—right?

Or consider the national debt—the total amount that the government owes to the public from past borrowing in years in which it ran a budget deficit. In 1959, the national debt was $235 billion; by the end of 1997—at its peak— it had grown to $3,771 billion.[1] That amounted to about $14,500 for every man, woman, and child in the United States—a sum that would have been very painful for each of us, individually, to repay. Wasn't this a crushing burden on the economy?

Actually, these figures are highly misleading. The first problem is that they are *nominal* values, and between 1959 and 1999, the price level rose. Even if the government had continued to spend the same amount or owe the same amount in *purchasing power* terms, the nominal figures would still have more than quintupled over the period. Thus, increases in nominal figures tell us very little.

But if we translate from nominal values into *real values,* we find much smaller increases: From 1959 to the late 1990s, *real* government spending and the *real* national debt each roughly tripled (compare this to the nominal values, which increased more than fifteenfold). Thus,

> *when examining budget-related figures over time, it is grossly misleading to use nominal figures, since the price level rises over time.*

But even if we use real values to make our comparisons, we are still making a serious mistake. From 1959 to 1999, the U.S. population grew, the labor force grew, and the average worker became more productive. As a result, real GDP and real income tripled during this period. Why is that important? Because *spending and debt should be viewed in relation to income.*

We automatically recognize this principle when we think about an individual family or business. Suppose you are told that a family is spending $50,000 each year on goods and services, and has a total debt—a combination of mortgage debt, car loans, student loans, and credit card balances—of $200,000. Is this family acting responsibly? Or is its spending and borrowing out of control? That depends. If the income of the household is $40,000 per year and is expected to remain roughly constant, there is serious trouble. This family would be spending more than it is earning, and its debt would grow each year until it could not handle the monthly interest payments.

But what if the family's income is $800,000 per year? Then our conclusion would change dramatically: We'd wonder, why does this family spend so *little*? And if it owed $200,000, we would not think it irresponsible at all. After all, the family could pay the interest on its debt—or even many times that interest—with a small fraction of its income.

What is true for an individual family is also true for the nation. Spending and debt are important only as *relative* concepts. As a country's total income grows, it will want more of the things that government can provide—education, high environmental standards, police protection, programs to help the needy, and more. Therefore, we expect government spending to rise as a nation becomes richer.

---

[1]    There are many ways to measure the national debt. Some measures include amounts that the U.S. Treasury owes to other government agencies. But this part of the debt, since it is owed by one branch of government to another, could be canceled out at the stroke of a pen. Other measures include unfunded liabilities of U.S. government for Social Security, Medicare, and other benefits in future years. (Unfunded liabilities are the extent to which promises that the government has made to pay out benefits exceed expected revenue sources for those payments.) While unfunded liabilities are a concern for policy makers, they are not yet actual government debt. In this chapter, the national debt is defined as U.S. government bonds currently held outside of U.S. government agencies.

Moreover, as its income grows, a country can *handle* higher interest payments on its debt. Government spending and the total national debt, considered in isolation, tell us nothing about how responsibly or irresponsibly the government is behaving.

> *Budget-related figures such as government spending or the national debt should be considered relative to a nation's total income. This is why we should always look at these figures as percentages of GDP.*

When we take this last step in adjusting our figures, we discover that both government spending and the national debt were not dramatically higher in the late 1990s than in the late 1950s. In 1959, government spending as a fraction of GDP was 16 percent. Over the next four decades, government spending fluctuated between 16 and 23 percent of GDP, but—by 1999—it had returned to 19 percent. Similarly, the national debt was 46 percent of GDP in 1959, and reached a peak of 50 percent in 1993. It ended the century at 40 percent of GDP—lower than in 1959. Thus, the story about federal spending and the federal debt is *not* the story suggested by the unadjusted figures.

In the rest of this chapter, as we explore recent trends in fiscal behavior and their effects on the economy, we'll do so with these lessons in mind. Accordingly, we'll look at fiscal variables as *percentages of GDP*.[2]

## SPENDING, TAXES, AND THE BUDGET: SOME BACKGROUND

Our ultimate goal in this chapter is to understand how fiscal changes have affected, and continue to affect, the macroeconomy. But before we do this, some background will help. What has happened to the *composition* of government spending in recent decades? How does the U.S. tax system work, and what has happened to the government's tax revenues? Why has the national debt risen slowly in some periods, and more rapidly in other periods? And why—in recent years—has the national debt been falling? This section provides answers to these and other questions about the government's finances. Although state and local spending also play an important role in the macroeconomy, most of the significant macroeconomic changes in recent decades have involved the *federal* government. This is why we'll focus on spending, taxing, and borrowing at the federal level.

### GOVERNMENT SPENDING

The federal government's *spending*—the total amount spent or disbursed by the federal government in all of its activities—can be divided into three categories:

- *government purchases*—the total value of the goods and services that the government buys
- *transfer payments*—income supplements the government provides to people, such as Social Security benefits, unemployment compensation, and welfare payments
- *interest on the national debt*—the interest payments the government must make to those who hold government bonds

---

[2]  It makes no difference whether we use nominal or real figures when dividing by GDP, as long as we're consistent. For example, we get the same fraction whether we divide nominal government spending by nominal GDP, or real government spending by real GDP.

The federal government's purchases have declined dramatically (relative to GDP) over the past 40 years. Non-military purchases have always been a stable, small percentage of GDP. Military purchases have declined, except for temporary buildups during the Vietnam War in the late 1960s and during the Reagan administration in the early 1980s.

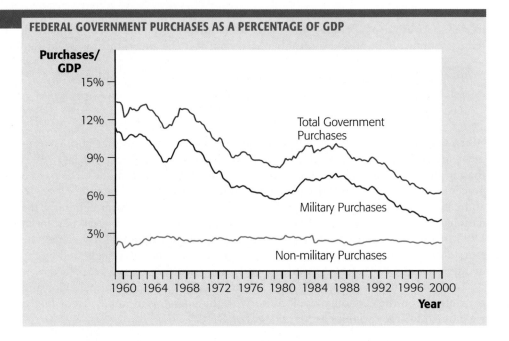

**FEDERAL GOVERNMENT PURCHASES AS A PERCENTAGE OF GDP**

### Government Purchases.

Until the 1980s, government purchases of goods and services were the largest component of government spending. To understand how these purchases have changed over time, it's essential to divide them into two categories: military and non-military. Figure 1 shows total federal purchases, as well as federal military and non-military purchases, from 1959 to 1999.

One fact stands out from the figure: The federal government uses up only a tiny fraction of our national resources for non-military purposes. These non-military purchases include the salaries paid to all government workers outside the Defense Department (for example, federal judges, legislators, and the people who run federal agencies), as well as purchases of buildings, equipment, and supplies. Added together, all the different kinds of non-military government purchases account for a stable, low fraction of GDP—about 2 percent.

This strongly contradicts a commonly held notion: that government spending is growing by leaps and bounds because of bloated federal bureaucracies. Those who believe that government spending has become a growing concern must look somewhere besides non-military purchases for the reason.

> *As a percentage of GDP, non-military government purchases have remained very low and stable. They have not contributed to growth in total government spending.*

What about military purchases? Here, we come to an even stronger conclusion:

> *As a percentage of GDP, military purchases have* declined dramatically *over the past several decades. Like non-military purchases, they have not contributed to any growth in government spending.*

The decline in military purchases is shown by the middle line in Figure 1. They were around 11 percent of GDP in 1959 and fell almost continuously to about

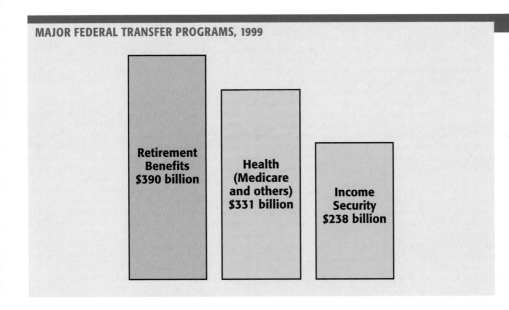

**MAJOR FEDERAL TRANSFER PROGRAMS, 1999**

Retirement Benefits $390 billion

Health (Medicare and others) $331 billion

Income Security $238 billion

**FIGURE 2**

Approximately equal amounts of transfer payments were made for Social Security retirement benefits, health programs such as Medicare and Medicaid, and income security programs such as food stamps and welfare.

4 percent recently. Two buildups interrupted the decline, one associated with the Vietnam War in the late 1960s and the other during the Reagan administration in the 1980s. But both of these buildups were temporary.

The decline of military spending freed up resources amounting to 7 percent of GDP over the span shown in Figure 1. There are debates about whether U.S. defense spending can be cut even more, but given the current U.S. role in global politics, it is unlikely that any future cuts would be substantial. The implications are tremendously important for thinking about the recent past and the future of the federal government's role in the economy:

> *The decline in military spending in relation to GDP since the early 1960s has made* huge *amounts of resources available for other purposes. Because military spending is now only 4 percent of GDP and probably cannot drop much further, there cannot be any similar freeing up of resources in coming decades.*

The resources released from military spending eased many otherwise tough decisions about resource allocation in the economy. In particular, they made it easy for the federal government to provide huge increases in resources to some parts of the population, through transfer payments.

**Social Security and Other Transfers.**  Transfer programs provide cash and in-kind benefits to people whom the federal government designates as needing help. Figure 2 shows the three major categories of transfers. As you can see, they are roughly equal in size.

The largest category is retirement benefits—the payments made by the Social Security system to retired people. Although the benefits are loosely related to past contributions to the Social Security

DANGEROUS CURVES

Don't confuse government spending with government purchases, which are just one component of the government's spending. The other components are transfer payments and interest on the debt.

**FIGURE 3**

Until about 1980, transfers grew rapidly as a fraction of GDP; thereafter, growth slowed. Transfers jumped upward during recessions (shaded), as in 1974, 1981, and 1991.

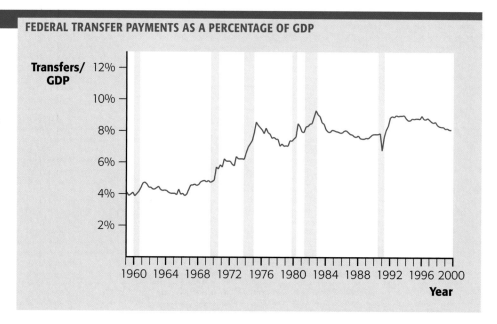

**FEDERAL TRANSFER PAYMENTS AS A PERCENTAGE OF GDP**

system, workers whose earnings are low receive benefits that are worth far more than their contributions. And after age 72, even someone with no history of contributions receives the minimum benefit.

The second-largest category of transfers occurs in health programs. The Social Security system provides health-related benefits to everyone aged 62 and over through Medicare. This is a health insurance plan in which people can go to any doctor they choose, as often as they want, and Medicare will pay 80 percent of the bills. Reform of Medicare to reduce its rapidly growing cost has been proposed, but little reduction in growth has been achieved so far. In addition to funding Medicare, the federal government helps finance state-operated health plans for the poor, through a program called Medicaid. The costs of these programs have been rising rapidly as well.

The third and smallest of the three categories of transfers is *income security*—programs to help poor families. Within this category, the largest component is the food stamp program, which gives coupons or special credit cards—good only for buying food—to qualified families. Welfare payments to poor families are also in this category, but these payments are much smaller than outlays on food stamps.

Have transfer payments been growing as a fraction of GDP? Indeed, they have. All three categories of transfer programs have grown rapidly in recent decades. And Figure 3 shows that total transfer payments as a percentage of GDP have trended upward as well.

> *In recent decades, transfers have been the fastest-growing part of federal government spending and are currently equal to about 8 percent of GDP.*

Growth in transfers relative to GDP was most rapid in the 1970s during the Nixon administration. During this period, government-financed retirement benefits became much more generous, food stamps were introduced, and Medicare expanded. Since then, transfers have remained high, but they have not shown any long-term growth in relation to GDP.

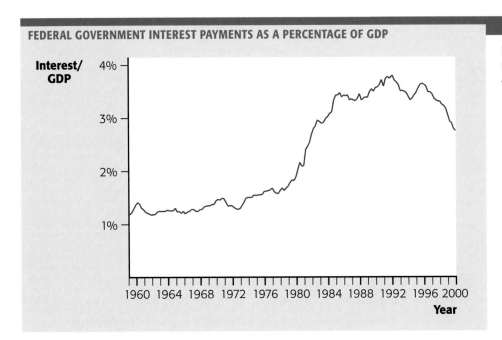

**FIGURE 4**

FEDERAL GOVERNMENT INTEREST PAYMENTS AS A PERCENTAGE OF GDP

Interest payments on the national debt grew rapidly during the early 1980s.

Notice, however, that transfers are sensitive to the ups and downs of the economy. Transfers as a fraction of GDP rise during recessions, as in 1974, 1981, and 1991. This is for two reasons. First, the number of needy recipients rises in a recession, so transfer payments—the numerator of the fraction—increase. Second, GDP—the denominator—falls in a recession. Similarly, transfers as a fraction of GDP fall during expansions, such as our most recent, long expansion that began in 1991. During expansions, the numerator of this fraction falls (why?), and the denominator rises. We will come back to these movements in transfers toward the end of the chapter.

**Interest on the National Debt.** Figure 4 shows the behavior of the third and smallest category of government spending: interest on the national debt. As you can see, interest as a percentage of GDP grew rapidly in the early 1980s, when the debt was growing and interest rates were rising. We'll discuss the reasons for the rise in debt a bit later.

**Total Government Spending.** Figure 5 shows total spending in relation to GDP over the past several decades. There are two important things to notice in the figure. The first is the *fluctuations* in government spending over the period. There was a sharp increase in spending in each recession (shaded) due to the jump in transfers that we saw in Figure 3. The recession of 1981–82 is a striking example. Also visible is the increase in military spending for the Vietnam War in the late 1960s.

The second thing to notice is the *upward trend* of federal spending as a percentage of GDP that lasted until recently:

*Over the past several decades, and until the early 1990s, federal government spending as a percentage of GDP rose steadily. The main causes were increases in transfer payments and increases in interest on the national debt that exceeded the decreases in military spending.*

Federal spending tends to rise relative to GDP during wartime and during recessions; it falls during good times. Over the past several decades, the ratio of federal spending to GDP has trended upward.

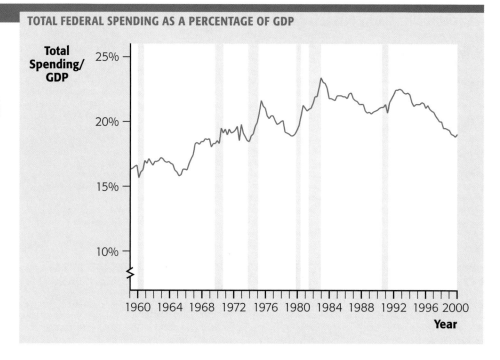

**TOTAL FEDERAL SPENDING AS A PERCENTAGE OF GDP**

Finally, notice the important *downward* trend in the mid and late 1990s:

> *From 1992 to 1999, federal government spending as a percentage of GDP fell steadily, although it remained a higher percentage of GDP than in 1959. The main causes of the decline have been the continued sharp decreases in military spending, and more modest decreases in transfer payments relative to GDP.*

The rise and recent fall in government spending relative to GDP have been important long-run trends. But in order to understand their impact on the macroeconomy, we must look at the other side of the budget: tax revenue.

## FEDERAL TAX REVENUES

The federal government obtains most of its revenue from two sources: the personal income tax and the social security tax. Table 1 breaks down the revenue from these and the other less-important sources.

**SOURCES OF FEDERAL REVENUE, 1999**

| Source | Revenue (Billions of Dollars) |
|---|---|
| Personal income taxes | 879 |
| Corporate income taxes | 185 |
| Social Security taxes | 612 |
| Excise taxes | 70 |
| Other sources | 81 |
| Total | 1,827 |

*Source: Economic Report of the President, 1999, Table B-79.*

| Income | Tax | Average Tax Rate | Marginal Tax Rate |
|---|---|---|---|
| $ 10,000 | $      0 | 0% | 0% |
| 20,000 | 272 | 1.4 | 15 |
| 30,000 | 1,766 | 5.9 | 15 |
| 50,000 | 4,766 | 9.5 | 15 |
| 75,000 | 10,315 | 13.8 | 28 |
| 150,000 | 32,140 | 21.4 | 31 |
| 250,000 | 66,802 | 26.7 | 36 |
| 400,000 | 128,710 | 32.2 | 39.6 |

*Source:* Calculated from the 1999 Form 1040 tax table with the standard deduction of $6,700.

**The Personal Income Tax.** The personal income tax is the most important source of revenue for the federal government and also the most conspicuous and painful. Almost every adult has to file Form 1040 or one of its shorter cousins. One of the signs of success as an American is seeing your federal tax return swell to the size of a magazine. Proposals to reduce both the amount of taxes people pay and the complexity of the tax forms are immensely popular.

The personal income tax is designed to be **progressive**—to tax those at the higher end of the income scale at higher rates than those at the lower end of the scale, and to excuse the poorest families from paying any tax at all. Table 2 shows how the income tax works, in theory, by computing the amount of tax a family of four should have paid in 1999 if it took the standard deduction.[3] The table also shows the **average tax rate**—the fraction of total income a family pays in taxes—and the **marginal tax rate**—the tax rate paid on *each additional dollar* of income.

**Progressive tax** A tax whose rate increases as income increases.

**Average tax rate** The fraction of a given income paid in taxes.

**Marginal tax rate** The fraction of an additional dollar of income paid in taxes.

We can see from Table 2 that the income tax is designed to be quite progressive. In principle, a family in the middle of the income distribution, earning $50,000 per year, should have paid 9.5 percent of its income in taxes, while a family at the top should have paid 32.2 percent of its income in taxes. The table also shows that marginal tax rates on families with the highest income are in the range of 28 to 40 percent.

But the tax system shown in the table does not reflect the ways that people can avoid tax. Many people have deductions far above the standard deduction. Some people earn income that they never report to the government, thereby evading taxes entirely. And people can shelter income in their employer's retirement plan or in a plan of their own. Studies have shown that higher-income households avoid more taxes than poorer families and that the tax system—while still progressive—is much less progressive than suggested by Table 2.

In addition to making the tax system less progressive, tax avoidance reduces the total tax revenues of the federal government. If we use Table 2—along with the incomes people actually earn—to estimate tax revenue, we'd predict that the government would collect between 15 and 20 percent of total personal income. But in reality, income tax revenues amount to only about 10 percent of total personal income.

---

[3]    The federal government allows households to deduct certain expenses (like medical care or the costs of moving to a new job) from their income before calculating the tax that they owe. Alternatively, they may deduct a standard amount (the *standard deduction*) from their income, regardless of their spending patterns.

The Congressional Budget Office maintains historical data on the U.S. federal budget. You can find it at http://www.cbo.gov/showdoc. cfm?index=1821&sequence=0& from=7#1.

**The Social Security Tax.** The Social Security tax applies to wage and salary income only. It was put in place in 1936, to finance the Social Security system created in that year. Whereas the personal income tax is a nightmare of complex forms and rules, the Social Security tax is remarkably simple. The current tax rate is a flat 15.3 percent,[4] except for one complication: The tax is applied only on earnings below a certain amount ($76,200 per year in 2000, although that salary cap rises each year).

The Social Security tax is actually the largest tax paid by many Americans, especially those with lower incomes. These families pay little or no income tax, but pay the Social Security tax on all of their wage earnings. For example, a family with $30,000 of earnings in Table 2 would pay $1,766 in federal income tax, but Social Security taxes on those earnings would be $4,590.

**Other Federal Taxes.** Table 1 shows that the federal government also collects a little more than $336 billion annually from other taxes. The most important of these is the *corporate profits tax,* which raises $185 billion by taxing the profits earned by corporations at a rate of 35 percent.

The corporate profits tax is widely criticized by economists because of two important problems. First, it only applies to corporations. Thus, a business owner can avoid it completely by setting up a sole proprietorship or partnership instead of a corporation. As a result, the tax causes many businesses to forego the benefits of being corporations because of the extra tax they would have to pay.

Second, the corporation tax results in *double taxation* on the portion of corporate profits that corporations pay to their owners. This portion of profits is taxed once when the corporation is taxed and again when the profits are included as part of personal income. The corporation tax is thus a prime target for tax reform. Almost all reform proposals put forward by economists involve integrating the taxation of corporations into the tax system in a way that avoids these two distortions.

The federal government also taxes the consumption of certain products, such as gasoline, alcohol, tobacco, and air travel. These are called *excise taxes.* Excise taxes raise additional revenue for the government, but they are usually put in place for other, nonrevenue reasons as well. The excise tax on gasoline is seen, in part, as a fee on drivers for the use of federal highways. The taxes on alcohol and tobacco are intended to discourage consumption of these harmful products.

**Trends in Federal Tax Revenue.** The top line in Figure 6 shows total federal government revenue, as a percentage of GDP, from all of the taxes we've discussed. Over the 37 years shown in the figure,

> *federal revenue has trended upward from around 17 percent of GDP in 1959 to around 20 percent in 1999.*

While the upward trend in total federal revenue as a fraction of GDP has been rather mild, its *composition* has changed dramatically. The lower two lines in Figure 6 show the part of federal revenue that comes from Social Security taxes and all other taxes. Notice the steady upward trend in Social Security tax revenue. Also notice that all other sources of revenue have remained roughly constant over the same period.

Why have Social Security taxes grown in importance? First, a little background. The Social Security system operates on a pay-as-you-go principle—it taxes people

---

[4]    If you look at your own paycheck, it may seem that the Social Security tax is only 7.65 percent instead of the 15.3 percent we've just mentioned. The reason is that your employer pays half the tax and you pay the other half. But the amount paid on your earnings is the sum, 15.3 percent.

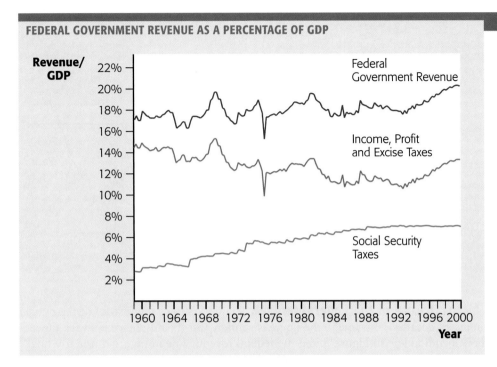

**FIGURE 6**

**FEDERAL GOVERNMENT REVENUE AS A PERCENTAGE OF GDP**

In recent decades, federal government revenue has trended upward to about 20 percent of GDP. This is because total revenue from the personal income tax, corporate profits tax, and excise taxes has remained stable relative to GDP, while Social Security tax revenue has increased.

who are working now in order to pay benefits to those who worked earlier and are now retired. But it also pays more benefits to those who have worked longer. Over the years, the system has benefited from a number of favorable circumstances. In its early decades, most retirees who received benefits had started working before the system began, so their benefits were small in relation to the earnings of those at work. Then, for the past several decades, the system benefited from two favorable demographic factors: first, a relatively small number of retirees (due to very low birth rates during the 1930s); and second, a large number of taxpayers (due to the baby boomers of the 1950s entering and remaining in the labor force).

But now, some demographic trends are working against the system. First, improved health is allowing people to spend a larger fraction of their lives in retirement. That is good from a human perspective, but from an accounting point of view, it means that the average retiree is drawing more benefits. At the same time, the baby boomers will soon begin retiring en masse, which means greater *numbers* of people drawing benefits. Finally, these increased benefits will be funded by a smaller number of working taxpayers. As a result of these trends, *the government has been raising Social Security tax rates* to keep the system solvent. Moreover, the government has been thinking about the future: It has increased the tax rate above the pay-as-you-go level in order to build up reserves, to cover higher expected benefit payouts.

## THE FEDERAL BUDGET AND THE NATIONAL DEBT

Finally, we can bring together what we've learned about the government's tax revenue (from the Social Security tax, personal income tax, corporate profits tax, and other sources) with what we've learned about the government's spending (on purchases, transfers, and net interest). And our first step is straightforward: When total tax revenue exceeds total government spending in any year, the government runs a budget surplus in that year. When the reverse occurs, and total government spending is greater than total tax revenue, the government runs a budget deficit.

Until about 1970, the federal government's budget deficit averaged around zero. Since then, and until very recently, there were deficits in most years—sometimes as high as 6 percent of GDP. The deficit increases (or the surplus decreases) during recessions as transfers rise and tax revenue falls.

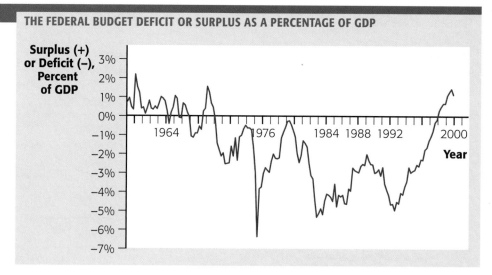

**THE FEDERAL BUDGET DEFICIT OR SURPLUS AS A PERCENTAGE OF GDP**

### Recent History of the Federal Budget.

Figure 7 shows the history of the budget in recent decades. This line in the figure is actually just the difference between the federal spending line in Figure 5 and the federal revenue line in Figure 6 (the top line).[5] The budget graph looks much choppier because the scale of the diagram is different here. But you can see that there was a dramatic change in the behavior of the budget around 1975. Until that year, the government mostly ran deficits, but rarely more than 2 percent of GDP. But from 1975 until 1993, the deficit grew significantly. During that period, it was usually greater than 3 percent of GDP, and often more than 4 percent. Notice, for example, the especially large rise in the deficit that occurred in the early 1980s. This was the combined result of a severe recession, which caused transfers to rise as shown in Figure 3, the buildup in military spending shown in Figure 1, and a large cut in income taxes during President Reagan's first term in office.

But then, in the mid-1990s, the deficit began to come down, and finally, in the late 1990s, the federal government began running budget surpluses for the first time in 30 years. Why did the budget shift from large deficits to surpluses during the 1990s? We'll answer this question in the "Using the Theory" section at the end of this chapter.

### The National Debt.

Before we consider the government's budget further, we need to address some common confusion among three related, but very different, terms: the federal *deficit,* the federal *surplus,* and the national *debt.* The federal deficit and surplus are *flow* variables—they measure the difference between government spending and tax revenue *over a given period,* usually a year. The national debt, by contrast, is a *stock* variable—it measures the total amount that the federal government owes *at a given point in time.* (See the second macroeconomics chapter if you need a refresher on stocks and flows.)

The relationship between these terms is this: Each year that the government runs a deficit, it must borrow funds to finance it, *adding to the national debt.* For

---

[5]    To measure the deficit or surplus, we have included all sources of revenue, and all types of federal spending, whether they are part of the official federal budget or not. In particular, Social Security taxes and social security payments are *officially* considered "off budget" in U.S. government statistics. In this chapter, however, we include the Social Security system in our budget calculations.

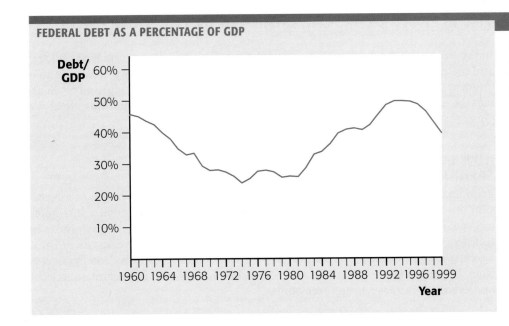

**FEDERAL DEBT AS A PERCENTAGE OF GDP**

**FIGURE 8**

Until about 1980, the debt was shrinking as a fraction of GDP. For the next 15 years, it increased relative to GDP, until the ratio turned down again recently.

example, in 1996, the federal government ran a deficit of $108 billion. During that year, it issued about $108 billion in new government bonds, adding that much to the national debt. On the other hand, each year the government runs a surplus, it uses the surplus to *pay back* some of the national debt. For example, in 1999, the federal government ran a surplus of about $125 billion. That year, it purchased about that much in government bonds it had issued in the past, thus reducing the national debt.[6]

We can measure the national debt as the total value of government bonds held by the public. Thus,

> *deficits—which add to the public's holdings of government bonds—add to the national debt. Surpluses—which decrease the public's bond holdings—subtract from the national debt.*

Since the cumulative total of the government's deficits has been greater than its surpluses, the national debt has grown over the past several decades. For most of this period, it has also grown relative to GDP, as shown in Figure 8.

The rise in the national debt also explains another trend we discussed earlier: the rise in *interest payments* the government must make to those who hold government bonds. The larger the national debt, the greater will be the government's yearly interest payments on the debt. As you saw in Figure 4, total interest payments rose rapidly during the 1980s—the same period in which the national debt zoomed upward. In the 1990s, as the national debt decreased relative to GDP, so did interest payments on the debt.

Now that we've outlined the recent history of federal government spending, taxes, and debt, we can turn our attention to how fiscal changes affect the economy.

---

[6]    The increase or decrease in the national debt is never exactly the same as the annual deficit or surplus, because of accounting details.

What Happens When
Things Change?

# THE EFFECTS OF FISCAL CHANGES IN THE SHORT RUN

In the short run, there is a two-way relationship between the government's budget and the macroeconomy. On the one hand, changes in the economy affect the government's spending and taxes; on the other hand, changes in spending and taxes affect the economy. Let's begin by considering how economic fluctuations affect the government's budget.

## HOW ECONOMIC FLUCTUATIONS AFFECT SPENDING, TAXES, AND THE FEDERAL BUDGET

Economic fluctuations affect both transfer payments and tax revenues. In a recession, in which many people lose their jobs, the federal government contributes larger amounts to state-run unemployment insurance systems and pays more in transfers to the poor, since more families qualify for these types of assistance. Thus, a recession causes transfer payments to rise. Recessions also cause a drop in tax revenue, because household income and corporate profits—two important sources of tax revenue—decrease during recessions.

> *In a recession, because transfers rise and tax revenue falls, the federal budget deficit increases (or the surplus decreases).*

An expansion has the opposite effects on the federal deficit: With lower unemployment and higher levels of output and income, federal transfers decrease and tax revenues increase. Thus,

> *in an expansion, because transfers decrease and tax revenue rises, the budget deficit decreases (or the surplus increases).*

**Cyclical deficit**  The part of the federal budget deficit that varies with the business cycle.

Because the business cycle has systematic effects on spending and revenue, economists find it useful to divide the deficit into two components. The **cyclical deficit** is the part that can be attributed to the current state of the economy. It turns positive (a cyclical deficit) when output is below potential GDP, and negative (a cyclical surplus) when output is above potential. When the economy is operating just at full employment, the cyclical deficit is, by definition, zero.

**Structural deficit**  The part of the federal budget deficit that is independent of the business cycle.

The **structural deficit** is the part of the deficit that is not caused by economic fluctuations. As the economy recovers from a recession, for example, the cyclical deficit goes away, but any structural deficit in the budget will remain.

Cyclical changes in the budget are not a cause for concern, because they average out to about zero, as output fluctuates above and below potential output. Thus, the cyclical deficit should not contribute to a long-run rise in the national debt.

Moreover, changes in the cyclical deficit are actually a good thing for the economy: They help to make economic fluctuations milder than they would otherwise be. Recall that spending shocks have a multiplier effect on output. The larger the multiplier, the greater will be the fluctuations in output caused by any given spending shock. But changes in the cyclical deficit make the multiplier *smaller*, and thus act as an *automatic stabilizer*. How?

Let's use unemployment insurance as an example. In normal times, with the unemployment rate at around, say, 4.5 percent or lower, federal transfers for unemployment insurance are modest. But when a negative spending shock hits the economy, and output and income begin to fall, the unemployment rate rises. Federal transfers for unemployment insurance rise *automatically*. Without assistance from the government, many of the newly unemployed would have to cut back their consumption spending substantially. But unemployment insurance cushions the blow for many such families, allowing them to make smaller cutbacks in consumption. As a result, the total decline in consumption is smaller, and GDP declines by less. Unemployment insurance thus reduces the multiplier.

Other transfer programs have a similar stabilizing effect on output. More people receive food stamps during recessions. Consequently, their consumption falls by less than it would if they did not have this help. And the tax system contributes to economic stability in a similar way. Income tax payments, for example, fall during a recession. With the government siphoning off a smaller amount of income from the household sector, the drop in consumption is smaller than it would be if tax revenues remained constant.

The same principle applies when a positive spending shock hits the economy. Transfer payments automatically decline, as the unemployed find jobs and fewer families qualify for government assistance. And tax revenues automatically rise, since income rises. As a result, the spending shock causes a smaller rise in GDP than would otherwise occur.

> *Many features of the federal tax and transfer systems act as automatic stabilizers. As the economy goes into a recession, these features help to reduce the decline in consumption spending, and they also cause the cyclical deficit to rise. As the economy goes into an expansion, these features help to reduce the rise in consumption spending, and they also cause the cyclical deficit to fall.*

## COUNTERCYCLICAL FISCAL POLICY?

In the previous section, you learned that changes in government spending and taxes that occur automatically during expansions and recessions help to stabilize the economy. This immediately raises a question: Can the government *purposely* change its spending or tax policy to make the economy even more stable? For example, suppose the *AD* curve shifts leftward, and the economy enters a recession. Perhaps the government could increase its purchases of goods and services, or cut income tax rates, thereby shifting the *AD* curve rightward again. If a government changes its spending or taxes in this way, specifically to prevent output from rising above or falling below its potential, it is engaging in **countercyclical fiscal policy.**

In the 1960s and early 1970s, many economists and government officials believed that countercyclical fiscal policy could be an effective tool to counteract the business cycle. Today, however, very few economists hold this position. Instead, they would put the Fed in charge of stabilizing the economy and reserve fiscal policy for addressing long-run issues of resource allocation. Indeed, the last clear use of countercyclical fiscal policy occurred in 1975, when the government gave tax rebates in the depths of a serious recession in order to stimulate consumption. (In Figure 7, you can see the especially large downward spike in tax revenue relative to GDP in that year.)

Why do economists recommend against using countercyclical fiscal policy, and why does Washington follow their advice? There are several reasons.

**Countercyclical fiscal policy**
Changes in taxes or government spending designed to counteract economic fluctuations.

**Timing Problems.** It takes many months or even longer for a fiscal change to be enacted. Consider, for example, a decision to change taxes in the United States. A tax bill originates in the House of Representatives and then goes to the Senate,

Before tax laws or tax rates can be changed, both the U.S. Senate and the U.S. House of Representatives must approve. This can cause long delays.

where it is usually modified. Then a conference committee irons out the differences between the House and Senate versions, and the tax bill goes back to each chamber for a vote. Once legislation is passed, the president must sign it. Even if all goes smoothly, this process can take many months.

But in most cases, it will *not* go smoothly: The inevitable political conflicts will cause further delays. First, there is the thorny question of distributing the cost of a tax hike, or the benefits of a tax cut, among different groups within the country. Each party may argue for changes in the tax bill in order to please its constituents. And some senators and representatives will see the bill as an opportunity to improve the tax system in more fundamental ways, causing further political debate.

All of these problems create the danger that the tax change will take effect long after it is needed. And changes in transfer payments or government purchases would suffer from similar delays. As a result, a fiscal stimulus might take effect after the economy has recovered from a recession and is beginning to overheat; or a fiscal contraction might take effect just as the economy is entering a recession. Fiscal changes would then be a *destabilizing* force in the economy—stepping on the gas when we should be hitting the brakes, or vice versa.

The Fed, by contrast, can increase or decrease the money supply *on the very day it decides that the change is necessary.* While there are time lags in the *effectiveness* of monetary policy (see the "Using the Theory" section in the previous chapter), the ability to execute the policy in short order gives monetary policy an important advantage over fiscal policy for stabilizing the economy.

**Irreversibility.**  A second reason for favoring monetary rather than fiscal policy to stabilize the economy is the difficulty of reversing changes in government spending or taxes. Spending programs that create new government departments or expand existing ones tend to become permanent, or at least difficult to terminate. Many temporary tax changes become permanent as well—the public is never happy to see a tax cut reversed, and the government is often reluctant to reverse a tax hike that has provided additional revenue for government programs.

Reversing monetary policy, while not always painless, is easier to do. For one thing, the Fed makes its decisions secretly—neither government officials nor the public knows for sure what course the Fed has set until six weeks after the Federal Open Market Committee meets. Thus, the Fed is somewhat insulated from the political process in making its decisions. While there are limits to the Fed's independence (Congress could change the Fed's charter, or even eliminate the Fed entirely if it became too unhappy with its performance), these limits do not affect the Fed's ability to act quickly when it sees the need.

**The Fed's Reaction.**  Even if the government attempted to stabilize the economy with fiscal policy, it could not do so very effectively, because—to put it simply—the Fed will not allow it. The Fed views a change in fiscal policy just as it views other spending shocks: as a shift in the *AD* curve that needs to be neutralized. For example, suppose the Fed believes that the *AD* curve is shifting leftward and the economy is entering a recession. Then the Fed will increase the money supply to shift the *AD* curve rightward by the amount it thinks necessary, long before any fiscal change takes effect. The fiscal change, when it is finally enacted, will simply be counteracted with an offsetting change in the money supply. As long as the Fed is free to set its own course, and as long as it continues to see its goal as stabilizing the economy at the natural rate of unemployment and low inflation, there is simply no opportunity—and no need—for countercyclical fiscal policy.

# THE EFFECTS OF FISCAL CHANGES IN THE LONG RUN

 What Happens When Things Change?

Because the Fed acts to neutralize them, fiscal changes have little short-run effect on the macroeconomy. But fiscal changes do have important long-run effects. And to analyze them, we use the model best suited for long-run analysis: the classical model.

We've already considered some of the long-run effects of fiscal policy in this book. In the chapter titled "The Classical, Long-Run Model," we discussed the long-run impact of changes in government purchases. In the chapter titled "Economic Growth and Rising Living Standards," we discussed how government tax and transfer policies can affect the incentives of workers and firms, in turn affecting the economy's long-run growth rate.

Here, we just reiterate the main conclusions of fiscal policy for the long run. First, we can summarize the impact of large and continuing budget deficits—such as occurred during the 1970s and 1980s—as follows:

- Large and continuing budget deficits cause the government to continually demand loanable funds, resulting in higher interest rates and lower investment spending than with a balanced budget.
- Lower investment spending causes the capital stock to grow more slowly. In this way, large budget deficits may contribute to slower growth in the average standard of living.
- Large and continuing budget deficits can harm living standards in another way: they cause the national debt—and annual interest payments on the national debt—to grow. Unless some other form of government spending decreases, tax rates will ultimately have to be raised to pay the higher interest. But higher tax rates, in turn, reduce incentives to work, to invest, and to save.

We can also summarize the impact of large and continuing budget surpluses—such as occurred in the later 1990s and early 2000s—as follows:

- Continual budget surpluses cause the government to *supply* loanable funds (to repay some of the national debt), resulting in lower interest rates and higher investment spending than with a balanced budget.
- Higher investment spending causes the capital stock to grow more rapidly. In this way, budget surpluses may contribute to faster growth in the average standard of living.
- Continuing budget surpluses can benefit living standards in another way: they cause the national debt—and annual interest payments on the national debt—to shrink. This drop in interest payments allows other components of government spending to rise, or else enables the government to lower tax rates. Lower tax rates, in turn, can increase incentives to work, to invest, and to save.

In the rest of this chapter, we will get more specific about the long-run effects of recent fiscal policies. But before you read on, this might be a good time to take out a pencil and paper, and do some active studying. See if you can use the graphs you've learned in this text to illustrate the impact of fiscal policy in the long

DANGEROUS CURVES

This section has argued that rising deficits come at the cost of lower investment spending and therefore reduce the rate of economic growth. But this is not *always* the case. It depends on what *causes* the deficit. In particular, suppose the deficit arises from an increase in government spending to improve the legal, financial, and physical infrastructure of the economy, or to improve education. All of these types of spending contribute to economic growth themselves. Thus, even if the deficits caused by this higher government spending crowd out private investment, their net effect on growth could be favorable.

run. In particular, see if you can use the graphs of the classical model—the loanable funds market, the labor market, and the production function—to illustrate each of the conclusions in the bulleted list on the previous page.

## WERE WE HEADED FOR A DEBT DISASTER?

On a billboard in midtown Manhattan, a giant clock-like digital display tracks the U.S. national debt and how it changes each minute. Through the mid-1990s, as the publicly held debt soared beyond $3 trillion and headed toward $4 trillion, the clock showed the debt growing by about $240,000 per minute. The last four digits on the display changed so rapidly that they appeared as a blur.

The national debt clock was one of several public relations campaigns that spread fear among the American public. How could we ever hope to repay all of this debt? Surely, we were speeding toward a debt disaster, right?

Actually, this was not quite right. True, many economists were *concerned* about budget deficits and growing debt—because of their effects on resource allocation and growth that we discussed in the previous section. But there is a big difference between deficits that are costly to society, and deficits that will bring us rapidly toward crises. In fact, most economists believed that—even when deficits were at their worst—we were *not* on the brink of a debt disaster, and only small budgetary adjustments were needed to change our course and avoid a disaster entirely.

Why?

First, it's important to realize that although we might *choose* to repay the national debt, we do not have to. *Ever.* Moreover, there is nothing automatically wrong with a national debt that *grows* every year. That may sound surprising. How could a government keep borrowing funds without every paying them back? Surely, no business could behave that way.

But actually, many successful businesses *do* behave that way, and continue to prosper. For example, the debt of many major corporations—like AT&T and General Motors—continues to grow, year after year. While they continue to pay interest on their debt, they have no plans to pay back the amount originally borrowed in the foreseeable future. As these companies' bonds become due, they simply *roll them over*—they issue new bonds to pay back the old ones.

Why don't these firms pay back their debt? Because they believe they have a better use for their funds: investing in new capital equipment and research and development to expand their businesses. This will lead to higher future profits. And as long as their profits continue to grow, they can continue to increase their debt.

Of course, this does not mean that *any* size debt would be prudent. Recall the important principle we discussed earlier in the chapter: *Debt and interest payments have meaning only in relation to income.* If a firm's income is growing by 5 percent each year, but its interest payments are growing by 10 percent per year, it would eventually find itself in trouble. Each year, its interest payments would take a larger and larger fraction of its income, and at some point interest payments would exceed total income. But even *before* this occurred, the firm would find itself in trouble. Lenders, anticipating the firm's eventual inability to pay interest, would cut the firm off. At that point, the firm would reach its *credit limit*—the maximum amount it can borrow based on lenders' willingness to lend. Since it could no longer roll over its existing debt with further borrowing, it would have to pay back any bonds coming due, until its debt was comfortably below its credit limit.

All of these observations apply to the federal government as well. As long as the nation's total income is rising, the government can safely take on more debt. More specifically, if the nation's income is growing at least as fast as total interest payments, the debt can continue to grow indefinitely, without putting the government in danger.

The federal government *could* pay back the national debt—by running budget surpluses for many years. But if the government chooses *not* to pay back its debt, it would be acting just like corporations, which behave in similar fashion: It believes it has better uses for its revenue than debt repayment.

But how fast could the government continue to accumulate debt? Or, equivalently, how large could the federal deficit be without making the national debt a greater and greater burden for our citizens to bear?

Let's see. As long as total national income grows at least as fast as interest payments on the debt, the ratio of interest payments to income will not grow. In that case, we could continue to pay interest without increasing the average tax rate on U.S. citizens. Let's use some round numbers to make this clearer. Suppose that the nominal GDP is $10 trillion and the national debt is $5 trillion. Suppose, too, that interest payments average out to 10 percent of the national debt, or $500 billion. Then the ratio of interest payments to nominal GDP would be $500 billion/$10 trillion = 0.05. Now suppose that, over some period of time, both nominal GDP and the national debt double, to $20 trillion and $10 trillion, respectively. Then interest payments would double as well, to $1 trillion. But the ratio of interest payments to nominal GDP would remain constant, at $1 trillion/$20 trillion = 0.05.

More generally,

> as long as the debt grows by the same percentage as nominal GDP, the ratios of debt to GDP and interest payments to GDP will remain constant. In this case, the government can continue to pay interest on its rising debt without increasing the average tax rate in the economy.

This establishes an important *minimal guideline for responsible government*: The debt should grow no faster than nominal GDP. Was the U.S. government within these guidelines when many commentators feared a debt disaster? Not quite . . . but almost. During the 1970s and 1980s, nominal GDP was growing at about 9 percent per year—about 3.2-percent growth in real GDP, plus a little less than 6-percent increase in the price level. So the debt could have grown by an average of about 9 percent per year without any rise in the average tax rate. In fact, over these two decades, the debt grew by an average of 11 percent per year—higher than the guideline. If the debt had continued to grow that much faster than GDP indefinitely, interest payments on the debt would have gradually taken a greater and greater share of our national income, requiring gradually higher tax rates or cuts in other government programs.

However, to prevent a long-term disaster, we didn't have to run surpluses. In fact, we didn't have to stop running deficits. Rather, we had to *decrease the growth rate of the debt* back to, or below, the growth rate of nominal GDP. At the time, this required that we shrink annual deficits by about one percent of GDP. And as we entered the 1990s, we accomplished this and more. True, concern about the mounting debt was instrumental in helping lawmakers shrink the deficit—by creating a political climate in which tax rates could be raised and the growth of government spending slowed down. But while there was certainly cause for concern, and that concern served us well, we were, in truth, far from a debt disaster.

But what about the ratio of debt to GDP—which hit around 0.50 at its peak in 1993? Could the United States have been dangerously close to its credit limit—the amount of debt that would make lenders worry about the government's ability to continue paying interest? If so, we would indeed have been flirting with disaster—a tiny increase in the ratio would have led to a cutoff of further lending and required the budget to be balanced immediately. It might also have caused a financial panic, if everyone tried to sell their U.S. government bonds at the same time, causing bond prices to fall and household wealth to plummet. This was a common scenario in the disaster books discussed at the beginning of the chapter. Were we facing this danger?

Not really. There is, indeed, some credit limit for the U.S. government, but we were probably far from it in 1993. At the conclusion of World War II, the ratio of federal debt to GDP was 1.08—more than twice as high as the recent peak. And at that time, there was little concern that the government would not honor its debt obligations, and in fact, the debt–GDP ratio was brought down dramatically. Thirty years after the end of the war, in 1975, the debt was down to about 23 percent of GDP. From this experience, we might guess that ratio of debt to GDP could exceed 1.0 before the federal government would reach its credit limit. And in recent decades, we did not even come close to this.

*Using the*

# THEORY

ANALYTICAL PERSPECTIVES
BUDGET OF THE UNITED STATES GOVERN

ANALYTICAL PERSPECTIVES
ET OF THE UNITED STATES GOVERNMENT

ANALYTICAL PERSPECTIVES
BUDGET OF THE UNITED STATES GOVERNM

ANALYTICAL PERSPECTIVES
BUDGET OF THE UNITED STATES GOVERNME

ANALYTICAL PERSPECTIVES
UDGET OF THE UNITED STATES GOVERNMENT

# UNDERSTANDING THE NEW BUDGET SURPLUSES

Beginning in 1998, as the U.S. federal government ran its first budget surplus in 30 years, government officials, politicians, and the media began speaking of "surpluses as far as the eye can see." The reason for the optimism was long-term predictions by government agencies that the 1998 surplus was not a one-time affair. Instead, both the President's Office of Management and Budget and the non-partisan Congressional Budget Office (CBO) projected that the budget would continue to be in surplus—and that the surpluses would grow—at least through 2010, and most likely even further into the future. Over the next two years, each time the projections were updated, it seemed that the future surpluses were getting even larger. And in January 2000, newspaper headlines blared that, over the next 10 years, the government would generate a total of $4.2 trillion in surpluses.

Then began the debate: what to *do* with this startlingly large sum. The choices were all pleasant. Some political leaders advocated *spending* the funds: to improve education, to repair our aging roads and bridges, or to build up our defenses against terrorist threats. Others wanted to set the surpluses aside and reserve them for future Social Security benefits, to ensure that the Social Security system would remain solvent forever. Still another option was to give a tax cut to U.S. households, increasing their incentives to work and save, and create an even wealthier economy. Or we could use the surpluses to pay back the national debt—all of it—so as to finally free taxpayers from the interest burden they had shouldered for so many years. Even comedians got into the act: In early 2000, Dennis Miller suggested that we could set aside the next 10 years' worth of surpluses as prize money for a new TV show called *Who Wants to Be a Trillionaire?*

Whatever choice or combination of choices we would ultimately make, one thing seemed certain as we entered the 2000s: the U.S. economy—and the federal budget—was in for a pleasant ride. Was this a valid expectation?

In large part, yes. In early 2000, a close look at the budget predictions showed a mostly rosy future. But it also showed a highly *uncertain* future. In this section, we'll explore the new budget surpluses in more detail. But first, let's address an important issue surrounding the budget surplus: how it is measured.

## MEASURING THE BUDGET SURPLUS

There are two ways to measure the budget surplus or deficit, and—confusingly enough—the media sometimes focuses on one, and sometimes on the other. For years, the standard measure was the *on-budget surplus or deficit*. This is the difference between the government's total tax revenues and its total spending—with one important exception: *It excludes tax revenue and spending associated with the Social Security system.*[7]

Why have a budget measure that excludes Social Security? Largely because the Social Security system was set

**DANGEROUS CURVES**

Several times in this text, you've read that whenever the government runs a budget surplus, it pays down the national debt by the amount of the surplus. And this is true. But in the media, you will often hear someone speak about "spending the surplus" or "using the surplus for tax cuts." This seems to contradict the view that surpluses automatically lead to debt reduction. But actually, the speakers are misusing the word "surplus." What they are really speaking about is different ways of using a *potential surplus*—funds that *would* lead to a surplus if not spent and not given back to taxpayers. Always remember that a surplus is the extent to which tax revenue exceeds government spending. If the government raises its spending or reduces taxes, then, by definition, it is reducing the surplus it will run that year, and reducing the funds it will use that year to pay back the national debt.

up in the 1930s as a separate trust fund. True, the government was to *administer* the collection of Social Security taxes and the payment of benefits, but the system was thought of as separate from the government's other functions. Moreover, it was understood—from the beginning—that keeping the Social Security system solvent might require it to run deficits in some periods and surpluses in other periods. Government accountants felt that these temporary imbalances should not reflect on how the rest of the government was doing. In particular, a Social Security surplus or deficit should not influence our view of whether the government was living within its means, or beyond them. Thus, the on-budget surplus or deficit—which excludes the Social Security system—was the right measure for judging the fiscal behavior of the government.

To gauge the macroeconomic impact of the budget, however, we need to *include* the Social Security system. This is why macroeconomists prefer to look at the *unified budget surplus or deficit*—the difference between the government's total tax revenues (including Social Security taxes) and its total spending (including Social Security benefits).

Why is the unified budget a better measure of the macroeconomic impact of government? First, in the short run, we know that the government's budget affects the macroeconomy primarily through its effect on spending. It makes little difference whether a dollar in taxes is collected from households as income tax or Social Security tax: Either way, disposable income is reduced by the same dollar amount. Similarly, it makes little difference whether a dollar in transfer payments is paid out as welfare payments, educational assistance, Medicare, or Social Security benefits: It still puts a dollar of disposable income into a household's hands. Thus, when measuring the short-run impact of the government's fiscal policy on spending, it makes no sense to isolate Social Security from other government programs.

Second, the unified budget is the best measure to tell us about changes in the national debt over time, and changes in the interest burden of that debt. For example, if the unified budget is in deficit by $10 billion in some year, then the government must borrow $10 billion that year by issuing new bonds, adding $10 billion to the national debt. Indeed, the debt grows by the same $10 billion whether the government has to borrow for the Social Security system or any other reason: Borrowing is borrowing. Similarly, if the unified budget is in surplus by $10 billion, the government will use the surplus to buy back $10 billion of the government bonds it has issued in the past, thus reducing the debt by $10 billion. Once again, it makes no

---

[7]    The U.S. postal service is also excluded from the official budget. However, the difference between the postal services revenue and its spending is so small that excluding it hardly makes a difference.

difference whether the surplus comes from Social Security or other parts of government: Paying back debt is paying back debt.

Throughout this chapter, whenever we have referred to the budget deficit or surplus, we've been using the *unified* budget or surplus. We'll continue to do so here.

## FROM DEFICIT TO SURPLUS: WHY?

The new budget surpluses—those that we experienced in 1998 and 1999, as well as those projected through 2010—have arisen for two separate reasons. The first is the economic expansion that began 1991 and was still going strong in early 2000—the longest expansion on record. Part of the expansion is associated with a rapid rise in *potential GDP*. Technological changes—particularly the use of computers and, more recently, the Internet—have increased the productivity of the U.S. labor force much faster than previously, leading to more rapid growth in our capacity to produce goods and services. But there has also been a cyclical change: From 1991, the economy has moved from recession to expansion. With each passing year, the economy has operated closer and closer to its potential and—in the late 1990s—output may even have exceeded its potential level.

What has this expansion got to do with the budget? As you learned earlier in this chapter, in any expansion, transfers decrease as a fraction of GDP, and tax revenue grows as a fraction of GDP. The growth in tax revenue relative to GDP has been particularly strong in the most recent expansion for two reasons: (1) the rise in stock market values, which increased capital gains tax revenues—a part of the personal income tax; and (2) especially rapid income growth among high income taxpayers, who pay higher tax rates to begin with, and who were pushed into still higher marginal tax brackets as their incomes grew.

But changes in the economy explain only a part of the current and projected surpluses. A second and very important force has been caps on the government's *discretionary* spending—basically, all government spending except for interest on the debt, and transfer programs that are mandated by law (Social Security, Medicare, Medicaid, etc.). Thus, discretionary spending—which in 1999 amounted to $575 billion or 6.3 percent of GDP—includes all spending on national defense, law enforcement, the environment, and the general operations of government. Congress first legislated *caps* on discretionary spending—and devised an effective system to enforce the caps—when it passed the Budget Enforcement Act of 1990. The Omnibus Budget Reconciliation Act of 1993 extended the caps through 1998, and the Balanced Budget Act of 1997 extended them again through 2002. These caps have been very effective in controlling growth in discretionary spending, and actually shrinking this component of spending as a fraction of GDP.

## FUTURE SURPLUSES: HOW LARGE?

One of the startling things about the surpluses projected over the next 10 years is their size. For example, under the CBO's official projections, the cumulative surpluses through 2010 would be between $3.2 and $4.2 trillion. Either of these totals would be large enough to pay back the entire national debt in the hands of the public. (Whether we *do* pay back the national debt depends on whether we choose to actually *run* those surpluses, rather than cut taxes or increase spending instead. See the Dangerous Curves box earlier in this section.)

Figure 9 shows two projections by the CBO. Both are based on common assumptions about the behavior of the economy over the next 10 years (discussed below), but on two different assumptions about discretionary government spending. The upper line, labeled "tighter budget," tracks the surplus as a percentage of GDP

**FIGURE 9**

**CBO PROJECTED ANNUAL SURPLUS AS PERCENTAGE OF GDP**

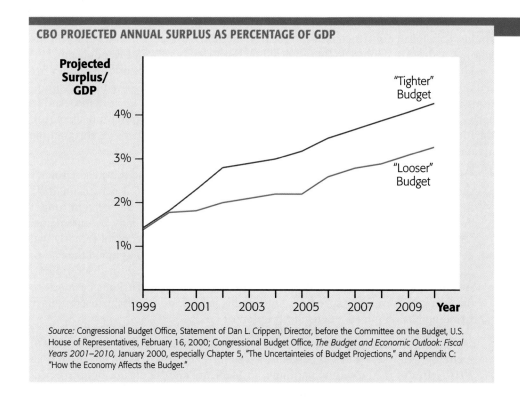

*Source:* Congressional Budget Office, Statement of Dan L. Crippen, Director, before the Committee on the Budget, U.S. House of Representatives, February 16, 2000; Congressional Budget Office, *The Budget and Economic Outlook: Fiscal Years 2001–2010,* January 2000, especially Chapter 5, "The Uncertainteies of Budget Projections," and Appendix C: "How the Economy Affects the Budget."

assuming that discretionary government spending stays within the official budget caps until 2002, and thereafter grows at the rate of inflation. Under this scenario, the annual budget surplus would reach $633 billion, or 4.3 percent of GDP in 2010. The lower line, labeled "looser budget," shows what would happen if discretionary spending is freed from the cap and permitted to grow at the rate of inflation after 2000. Under this scenario, the budget surplus would not be as great—reaching about $489 billion, or 3.3 percent of GDP in 2010. This difference—1 percent of GDP—might not seem like much, but it makes a big difference. Remember that that is the difference in just *one year's* surplus. Looked at cumulatively, the tighter budget assumptions yield a total surplus through 2010 that is $1 trillion greater.

## THE BRIGHT BUDGETARY FUTURE: HOW CERTAIN?

How much faith can we have in the CBO's projections of a bright budgetary future, ones in which we rack up huge potential surpluses year after year? The answer to this question is important. Suppose we decide to use up all or most of the potential surpluses by giving tax cuts, or setting up ambitious new government programs that raise discretionary spending above currently projected levels. And what if we are wrong about the future, and the potential surpluses never materialize. In that case, we will have inadvertently put the budget back into deficit, adding to our national debt. Further, it is difficult to cut government programs once they are put in place, and even more difficult to raise taxes after they have been cut. So a mistake that leads to deficits might not be corrected for years. The economy would then experience all of the effects of deficits and a growing national debt outlined earlier in this chapter (see "The Effects of Fiscal Changes in the Long Run").

So how much faith can we have in the CBO's projections? One thing we do know: The projections are *not* politically motivated. The CBO is a very well respected organization whose purpose is to give background information to members

**http://**

Try your hand at managing the budget by using the National Budget Simulation (http://socrates.berkeley.edu:3333/budget/budget.html).

of Congress, not to take positions in political debates. Although some of the CBO's studies have been controversial, its research methods and conclusions are—on the whole—widely used and widely respected by both Democrats and Republicans.

However, just because the CBO's projections are honest does not mean they are reliable. Projections—especially those made over long periods—require assumptions about the economy and the budget that may or may not be realistic. And in early 2000, as politicians and pundits debated how to *use* the potential surpluses, the uncertain assumptions behind them were rarely discussed. Let's go through the assumptions behind the CBO's projections.

• *Discretionary spending:* All of the CBO's projections assume that discretionary spending will continue to fall as a fraction of GDP—from 6.3 percent in 1999 to either 4.7 percent (under the tighter budget scenario), or 5.3 percent (under the looser budget scenario). But both of these assumptions may be unrealistic. One reason that discretionary spending has been so easy to control recently will be hard to repeat: the decrease in defense spending that accompanied the end of the cold war. In fact, since 1990, almost all of the decrease in discretionary spending as a fraction of GDP (from 8.7 percent to 6.3 percent) has been due to the decrease in military spending. During this period, non-military discretionary spending has remained a constant fraction of GDP.

• *Mandatory transfer payments:* The CBO projections assume that this category of spending will rise, from 9.9 percent of GDP in 1999 to 10.9 percent of GDP in 2010. Most of the growth is attributed to Medicare and Medicaid. But these projections assume a slight *deceleration* of growth in these programs, compared to their rates of growth from 1962 to 1999. Whether this proves to be accurate depends on trends in health care costs, as well as the overall state of the economy. (Only the poor are eligible for Medicaid, so slower economic growth could mean higher than projected eligibility, and greater than projected Medicaid spending.)

• *Tax revenues:* The CBO expects total tax revenue to grow by roughly 4 percent annually from 2001 to 2004, then 4.5 percent per year from 2005 to 2010. But—as you've learned—the behavior of tax revenues depends on the behavior of the economy. Thus, the tax revenue assumptions are only as realistic as are the assumptions about the economy, which we'll address now.

• *Macroeconomic Assumptions:* The three assumptions just discussed refer to the budget, but the behavior of the budget depends on the behavior of the macroeconomy. Among the CBO's critical macroeconomic assumptions over the period 2000 to 2010 are the following:

1. Real GDP growth of 2.8 percent per year
2. Growth in the GDP price index of 1.6 percent per year
3. Growth in the CPI of 2.5 percent per year
4. Unemployment rising steadily from 4.0 percent to 5.2 percent (the CBO's very conservative estimate of the natural rate of unemployment)
5. A roughly constant interest rate on ten-year treasury bonds of 5.7 percent (which was their average interest rate in 1999)

This is a long list of assumptions, and there are others not even listed here. But as you can imagine, we already have a picture that plenty could go wrong with. For example, suppose GDP grows just 0.1 percent slower each year than projected. Then transfers as a fraction of GDP would be higher than projected, and tax revenue lower than projected, leading to a $46 billion shrinkage in the annual surplus by 2010—about half a percentage point of GDP.

Or, for another example, suppose that inflation heats up, because unemployment has fallen below its natural rate. (As you've learned, no one—not even the Fed—knows what the natural rate of unemployment is.) Then the Fed, to slow growth and bring the inflation rate down, would raise its interest rate target. But higher interest rates mean higher interest costs on the debt. And, according to CBO calculations, if the interest rate on 10-year Treasury bonds ends up at 8.7 percent— three percentage points higher than the CBO projects—that would wipe out about a fifth of the potential surplus.

As you can see, plenty can go wrong with the projected surpluses. So it seems natural to ask: How well have such projections done in the past? Unfortunately, the CBO has been making 10-year projections only since 1992, which is not enough time to gauge their accuracy. However, the CBO has been making shorter projections since 1986, and two things stand out about them: (1) There are significant deviations of actual budget numbers from projected numbers; and (2) these deviations grow worse as projections are made further out into the future. For example, since 1986, looking at all of the CBO's projections for just *one* year ahead, the average deviation of the actual deficit or surplus from the projected amount was 1.6 percent of GDP. Going *four* years out, the average deviation from actual was 2.4 percent of GDP. You might think that the deviations were caused by unexpected changes in legislation, like changes in tax laws or changes in government programs. But in fact, almost all of the deviations were caused by unexpected macroeconomic changes. No doubt, if the CBO had been making 10-year projections throughout this period, we would by now have discovered an average deviation substantially larger than 2.4 percentage points of GDP. After all, just a few years ago, the CBO was projecting *deficits* as far as the eye can see.

The CBO is fully aware of the possibility of error. So it has also come up with what it calls a "pessimistic projection"—a not unlikely scenario that could change the budget picture substantially. The pessimistic projection assumes that the pleasant changes in the economy from 1996–1999—faster growth and a deceleration in spending on health care—were temporary, and that the economy will return to more normal patterns from 2000 to 2010. Under this scenario, the surpluses disappear entirely in 2003, turning into growing deficits that approach 3 percent of GDP by 2010.

If the CBO's pessimistic scenario turns out to be accurate, then future spending hikes or tax cuts would have profound implications for the economy. Instead of spending future surpluses, we would be pushing the deficits even *beyond 3 percent* of GDP by 2010, and we'd once again have a rapidly rising national debt. This—as well as concerns over the future of social security—explain why many economists urged caution in early 2000.

## SUMMARY

The U.S. federal government finances its spending through a combination of taxes and borrowing. When government spending exceeds tax revenue, the government runs a budget deficit. It finances that deficit by selling bonds, thereby adding to the national debt. When government spending is less than tax revenue, the government runs a budget surplus. It uses that surplus to buy back bonds it has issued in the past, thus shrinking the national debt.

Federal government spending consists of three broad categories: government purchases of goods and services, transfer payments, and interest on the national debt. Non-military government purchases have traditionally accounted for a stable, low 2 percent of real GDP. Military purchases vary according to global politics; in recent years, they have declined dramatically relative to GDP. Transfer programs—such as Social Security, Medicare, and welfare—have been the fastest-growing part of government spending. They currently equal about 8 percent of GDP.

On the revenue side, the government relies on personal and corporate income taxes, Social Security taxes, and some smaller excise taxes and user fees. In recent decades, federal revenue has been trending upward, and is currently about 20 percent of GDP.

From 1970 through the mid-1990s, federal spending exceeded federal revenues every year, so that the government ran budget deficits. Particularly large deficits occurred in the early 1980s. But in the 1990s, the deficit declined, and in 1998 the government began running yearly budget surpluses.

In the short run, there is a two-way relationship between government spending and taxes on the one hand, and the level of output on the other. First, changes in output affect government spending and taxes. In recessions, for example, government tax revenues fall and transfer payments rise. In this way, the tax and transfer system acts as an automatic stabilizer, helping to smooth out fluctuations.

Second, changes in government spending and taxes affect output. In principle, the government could use countercyclical fiscal policy—changing taxes and spending in order to offset economic fluctuations. However, because of practical problems, countercyclical fiscal policy is seldom used.

In the long run, fiscal changes do have important effects. All else equal, we can expect larger budget deficits to slow growth in living standards, and smaller budget deficits or surpluses to speed the growth of living standards.

Over the 1970s and especially the 1980s, the average federal budget deficit was so large, and the national debt was growing so rapidly, that interest payments on the debt were rising relative to GDP. However, we were not on the brink of a debt disaster, and public concern helped to shrink deficits to more stable levels. By early 2000, the budget picture has turned upside down: Official projections showed growing surpluses through 2010, although these projections were fraught with uncertainty.

## KEY TERMS

| | | | |
|---|---|---|---|
| progressive tax | marginal tax rate | structural deficit | countercyclical fiscal policy |
| average tax rate | cyclical deficit | | |

## REVIEW QUESTIONS

1. Why is it misleading to compare the national debt of $235 billion in 1959 with the national debt of $3,771 billion in 1999?

2. List the three broad categories of federal government spending. According to the most recent data in the chapter, which is the largest category? Have any of the categories decreased relative to GDP over the past 8 years? If so, which ones?

3. What is a *progressive* income tax?

4. List the main sources of federal revenue. How and why has the composition changed recently?

5. Explain the difference between the federal deficit and the national debt. Explain the *relationship* between the federal budget surplus and the national debt.

6. Define the cyclical deficit and the structural deficit. Why are changes in the cyclical deficit not a major long-run concern?

7. What is countercyclical fiscal policy? Is it an effective tool? Explain.

8. "A decrease in the national debt as a fraction of GDP requires the federal government to run budget surpluses." True or false? Explain.

9. While the national debt has been an important concern, most economists don't believe we were truly headed for disaster in the 1980s. Explain.

10. "The United States can count on large budget surpluses for the next 10 years." True or false? Explain.

## PROBLEMS AND EXERCISES

1. Use the following statistics, in billions of units, to calculate the real national debt and the debt relative to GDP in 1990 and 2000 for this hypothetical country. Which figures would you use to compare the national debt in the two years?

| | |
|---|---|
| National Debt in 1990: | 1.2 |
| National Debt in 2000: | 13.84 |
| Nominal GDP in 1990: | 101.7 |
| Nominal GDP in 2000: | 552.2 |
| Price Index in 1990: | 35.2 |
| Price Index in 2000: | 113.3 |

2. Suppose there is a country with 30 households divided into three categories (A, B, and C), with 10 households of each type. If a household earns 20,000 zips (the country's currency) or more in a year, it must pay 15 percent in tax to the government. If the household earns less than 20,000 zips, it doesn't pay any tax. When the economy is operating at full employment, household income is 250,000 zips per year for each type A household, 50,000 zips for type B households, and 20,000 zips for type C households.

  a. If the economy is operating at full employment, how much revenue does the government collect in taxes for the year?

  b. Suppose a recession hits and household income falls for each type of household. Type A households now earn 150,000 zips, type B households earn 30,000 zips, and type C households earn 10,000 zips for the year. How much does the government collect in tax revenue for the year? Assume the government spends all of the revenue it *would* have collected if the economy had been operating at full employment. Under this assumption, what is the effect of the recession on the government budget deficit?

  c. Suppose instead that the economy expanded and household incomes rose to 400,000 zips, 75,000 zips, and 30,000 zips, respectively, for the year. How much tax would the government collect for the year?

What is the effect on the government deficit (assume again that the government spends exactly the amount of revenue it collects when household income is at the values in part (a))?

What does this problem tell you about the relationship between shocks to the economy and the budget deficit?

3. According to the minimal guideline for responsible government outlined in the text, is either of the following two countries having a national debt crisis?

| Country A (Figures in Billions of $) | | |
| --- | --- | --- |
| | *Debt* | *GDP* |
| 1999 | 1 | 100 |
| 2000 | 2 | 110 |
| 2001 | 3 | 150 |

| Country B (Figures in Billions of $) | | |
| --- | --- | --- |
| | *Debt* | *GDP* |
| 1999 | 1236 | 1400 |
| 2000 | 1346 | 1550 |
| 2001 | 1406 | 1707 |

## CHALLENGE QUESTION

Suppose the United States decides to dissipate potential future surpluses by either cutting taxes or increasing government spending.

  a. Compared to a policy of just accruing surpluses and paying down the national debt, what will this policy do to U.S. real GDP and interest rates in the *short run*? Illustrate your answer graphically. (*Hint:* Which macro model, and which graphs, should you use to illustrate effects on output and interest rates in the short run?)

  b. Compared to a policy of just accruing surpluses and paying down the national debt, what will this policy do to U.S. real GDP and interest rates in the *long run*? Illustrate your answer graphically.

  c. Going back to the short run, suppose the Fed responds by neutralizing the impact of the fiscal change in part (a) above. What will happen to real GDP and interest rates?

## EXPERIENTIAL EXERCISE

Use a search engine such as google.com, yahoo.com, or goto.com to find data for: (a) the most recent year's growth rate of output; (b) the most recent month's inflation rate; (c) the most recent month's unemployment rate; and (d) the most recent trading day's interest rate on 10-year treasury bonds.

    For each of these numbers, how does the reality compare with the CBO's early 2000 forecast (given in the "Using the Theory" section of this chapter)? For each number, state whether the deviation from the

forecast tends to make the budget surplus larger or smaller than the forecast. Do all of the deviations tend to influence the budget in the same way? Or do they push the budget in different directions?

    Finally, find the most recent year's *actual* budget surplus or deficit as a fraction of GDP. What is the deviation from the CBO's early 2000 projection? Is the deviation what you'd expect from your analysis of deviations from the macro projection? If not, what might explain the inconsistency?

# 16

# EXCHANGE RATES AND MACROECONOMIC POLICY

If you've ever traveled to a foreign country, you were a direct participant in the **foreign exchange market**—a market in which one country's currency is traded for that of another. For example, if you traveled to Mexico, you might have stopped near the border to exchange some dollars for Mexican pesos.

Even if you have never traveled abroad, you've been involved, at least indirectly, in all kinds of foreign exchange dealings. For example, suppose you buy some Mexican-grown tomatoes at a store in the United States, where you pay with dollars. Except for shipping and retailing services, the resources used to produce those tomatoes were Mexican. A Mexican farmer grew the tomatoes; Mexican truckers transported them to the distribution center in the nearest large city; and Mexican workers, machinery, and raw materials were used to package them. All of these people want to be paid in Mexican pesos, regardless of who buys the final product. After all, they live in Mexico, so they need pesos to buy things there. But you, as an American, want to pay for your tomatoes with dollars.

Let's think about this for a moment. You want to pay for the tomatoes in dollars, but the Mexicans who produced them want to be paid in pesos. How can this happen?

The answer: *Someone,* here or abroad, must use the foreign exchange market to exchange dollars for pesos. For example, it might work like this: You pay dollars to your supermarket, which pays them to a U.S. importer, who sends a check in dollars to the distributor in Mexico, who—finally—turns the check over to a Mexican bank in exchange for pesos. That is how the Mexican distributor is able to pay the Mexican farmer in pesos. In this case, the actual changing of dollars into pesos takes place in a Mexican bank. But why is the Mexican bank willing to accept dollars for pesos? Because the bank is a participant in the market for foreign exchange.

In this chapter, we'll look at the markets in which dollars are exchanged for foreign currency. We'll also expand our macroeconomic analysis to consider the effects of changes in exchange rates. As you'll see, what happens in the foreign exchange market affects the economy, and changes in the economy affect the foreign exchange market. This has implications for the Fed as it tries to use monetary policy to steer the economy and keep it growing smoothly. Finally, in the "Using the Theory" section, you'll see how the tools of the chapter can help us understand why the United States has such a large and persistent trade deficit.

**Foreign exchange market** The market in which one country's currency is traded for another country's.

# FOREIGN EXCHANGE MARKETS AND EXCHANGE RATES

Every day, all over the world, more than a hundred different national currencies are exchanged for one another in banks, hotels, stores, and kiosks in airports and train stations. Traders exchange dollars for Mexican pesos, Japanese yen, European euros, Indian rupees, Chinese yuan, and so on. In addition, traders exchange each of these foreign currencies for one another: pesos for euros, yen for yuan, euros for yen. . . . There are literally thousands of combinations. How can we hope to make sense of these markets—how they operate and how they affect us?

Our basic approach is to treat each pair of currencies as a separate market. That is, there is one market in which dollars are exchanged for euros, another in which Angolan kwanzas trade for yen, and so on. The physical locations where the trading takes place do not matter: Whether you exchange your dollars for yen in France, Germany, the United States, or even in Ecuador, you are a trader in the same dollar–yen market.

 Characterize the Market

In any foreign exchange market, the rate at which one currency is traded for another is called the **exchange rate** between those two currencies. For example, if you happened to trade dollars for British pounds on March 7, 2000, each British pound would have cost you $1.58. On that day, the exchange rate was $1.58 per pound.

**Exchange rate** The amount of one country's currency that is traded for one unit of another country's currency.

## DOLLARS PER POUND OR POUNDS PER DOLLAR?

Table 1 lists exchange rates between the dollar and various foreign currencies on a particular day in 2000. But notice that we can think of any exchange rate in two ways: as so many units of foreign currency per dollar, or so many dollars per unit of foreign currency. For example, the table shows the exchange rate between the British pound and the dollar as 0.6330 pounds per dollar, or 1.5798 dollars per pound. We can always obtain one form of the exchange rate from the other by taking its reciprocal: 1/0.6330 = 1.5798, and 1/1.5798 = 0.6330.

| Country | Name of Currency | Symbol | Units of Foreign Currency per Dollar | Dollars per Unit of Foreign Currency |
|---|---|---|---|---|
| Brazil | real | R | 1.7455 | $0.5729 |
| China | yuan | Y | 8.2784 | 0.1208 |
| European Monetary Union Countries | euro | € | 1.0422 | 0.9595 |
| Great Britain | pound | £ | 0.6330 | 1.5798 |
| India | rupee | R | 43.565 | 0.02295 |
| Japan | yen | ¥ | 105.62 | 0.009468 |
| Mexico | peso | P | 9.2800 | 0.1078 |
| Russia | ruble | R | 28.575 | 0.03500 |

**TABLE 1**

**FOREIGN EXCHANGE RATES, MARCH 7, 2000**

In this chapter, we'll always define the exchange rate as "dollars per unit of foreign currency," as in the last column of the table. That way, from the American point of view, the exchange rate is just another *price*. The same way you pay a certain number of dollars for a gallon of gasoline (the price of gas), so, too, you pay a certain number of dollars for a British pound (the price of pounds).

> The exchange rate is the price of foreign currency in dollars.

Table 1 raises some important questions: Why, in early 2000, did a pound cost $1.58? Why not $1? Or $5? Why did one Japanese yen cost a little less than a penny? And a Russian ruble about three cents?

The answers to these questions certainly affect Americans who travel abroad. Suppose you are staying in a hotel in London that costs 100 pounds per night. If the price of the pound is $1, the hotel room will cost you $100, but if the price is $5, the room will cost you $500. And exchange rates affect Americans who stay at home, too. They influence the prices of many goods we buy in the United States, they help determine which of our industries will expand and which will contract, and they affect the wages and salaries that we earn from our jobs.

How are all these exchange rates determined? In most cases, they are determined by the familiar forces of supply and demand. As in other markets, each foreign exchange market reaches an equilibrium at which the quantity of foreign exchange demanded is equal to the quantity supplied.

In the next several sections, we'll build a model of supply and demand for a representative foreign exchange market: the one in which U.S. dollars are exchanged for British pounds. Taking the American point of view, we'll call this simply "the market for pounds." The other currency being traded—the dollar—will always be implicit.

## THE DEMAND FOR BRITISH POUNDS

To analyze the demand for pounds, we start with a very basic question: *Who* is demanding them? The simple answer is, anyone who has dollars and wants to exchange them for pounds. But the most important buyers of pounds in the pound–dollar market will be American households and businesses. When Americans want to buy things from Britain, they will need to acquire pounds. To acquire them, they will need to offer U.S. dollars. To keep our analysis simple, we'll focus on just these American buyers. We'll also—for now—ignore any demand for pounds by the U.S. government.

> In our model of the market for pounds, we assume that American households and businesses are the only buyers.

*Identify Goals and Constraints*

Why do Americans want to buy pounds? There are two reasons:

- *To buy goods and services from British firms.* Americans buy sweaters knit in Edinburgh, airline tickets sold by Virgin Airways, and insurance services offered by Lloyd's. American tourists also stay in British hotels, use British taxis, and eat at British restaurants. To buy goods and services from British firms, Americans need to acquire pounds in order to pay for them.

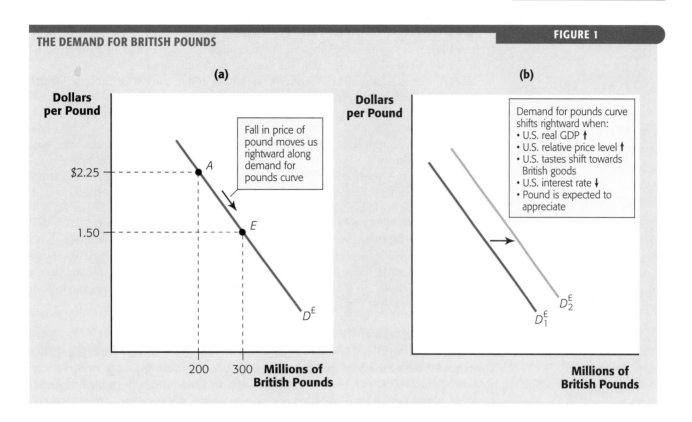

**THE DEMAND FOR BRITISH POUNDS**

**FIGURE 1**

**(a)**

Dollars per Pound

Fall in price of pound moves us rightward along demand for pounds curve

$2.25 ---- A

1.50 ---- E

$D^£$

200  300  **Millions of British Pounds**

**(b)**

Dollars per Pound

Demand for pounds curve shifts rightward when:
• U.S. real GDP ↑
• U.S. relative price level ↑
• U.S. tastes shift towards British goods
• U.S. interest rate ↓
• Pound is expected to appreciate

$D_2^£$

$D_1^£$

**Millions of British Pounds**

- *To buy British assets.* Americans buy British stocks, British corporate or government bonds, and British real estate. In each case, the British seller will want to be paid in pounds, so the American buyer will have to acquire them.

## THE DEMAND FOR POUNDS CURVE

Panel (a) of Figure 1 shows an example of a **demand curve for foreign currency,** in this case, the demand curve for pounds. The curve tells us *the quantity of pounds Americans will want to buy in any given period, at each different exchange rate.* Notice that the curve slopes downward: The lower the exchange rate, the greater the quantity of pounds demanded. For example, at an exchange rate of $2.25 per pound, Americans would want to purchase £200 million (point *A*). If the exchange rate fell to $1.50 per pound, Americans would want to buy £300 million (point *E*).

Why does a lower exchange rate—a lower price for the pound—make Americans want to buy more of them? Because the lower the price of the pound, the less expensive British goods are to American buyers. Remember that Americans think of prices in dollar terms. A British compact disc that sells for £8 will cost an American $18 at an exchange rate of $2.25 per pound, but only $12 if the exchange rate is $1.50 per pound.

Thus, as we move rightward *along* the demand for pounds curve, as in the move from point *A* to point *E*:

**Demand curve for foreign currency**
A curve indicating the quantity of a specific foreign currency that Americans will want to buy, during a given period, at each different exchange rate.

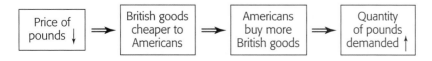

Price of pounds ↓ ⟹ British goods cheaper to Americans ⟹ Americans buy more British goods ⟹ Quantity of pounds demanded ↑

## SHIFTS IN THE DEMAND FOR POUNDS CURVE

In panel (a), you saw that a change in the exchange rate moves us *along* the demand for pounds curve. But other variables besides the exchange rate influence the demand for pounds. If any of these other variables changes, the entire curve will shift. As we consider each of these variables, keep in mind that we are assuming that only one of them changes at a time; we suppose the rest to remain constant.

**U.S. Real GDP.** Suppose real GDP and real income in the United States rise—say, because of continuing economic growth or a recovery from a recession. Then, Americans will buy more of everything, including goods and services from Britain. Thus, at any given exchange rate, Americans will demand more pounds. This is illustrated, in panel (b), as a rightward shift of the demand curve from $D_1^£$ to $D_2^£$.

**Relative Price Levels.** Suppose that the U.S. price level rises by 8 percent, while that in Britain rises by 5 percent. Then U.S. prices will rise *relative* to British prices. Americans will shift from buying their own goods toward buying the relatively cheaper British goods, so their demand for pounds will rise. That is, the demand for pounds curve will shift rightward.

**Americans' Tastes for British Goods.** All else being equal, would you prefer to drive a General Motors Aurora or a Jaguar? Do you prefer British-made films, like *Mansfield Park* or *Hillary and Jackie,* or America's offerings, such as *American Beauty* or *Galaxy Quest*? These are matters of taste, and tastes can change. If Americans develop an increased taste for British cars, films, tea, or music, their demand for these goods will increase, and the demand for pounds curve will shift rightward.

**Relative Interest Rates.** Because financial assets must remain competitive in order to attract buyers, the rates of return on different financial assets—such as stocks and bonds—tend to rise and fall together. Thus, when one country's interest rate is high relative to that of another country, the first country's assets, *in general,* will have higher rates of return.

Now, suppose you're an American trying to decide whether to hold some of your wealth in British financial assets or in American financial assets. You will look very carefully at the rate of return you expect to earn in each country. All else being equal, a lower U.S. interest rate, relative to the British rate, will make British assets more attractive to you. Accordingly, as you and other Americans demand more British assets, you will need more pounds to buy them. The demand for pounds curve will shift rightward.

**Expected Changes in the Exchange Rate.** Once again, imagine you are an American deciding whether to buy an American or a British bond. Suppose British bonds pay 10 percent interest per year, while U.S. bonds pay 5 percent. All else equal, you would prefer the British bond, since it pays the higher rate of return. You would then exchange dollars for pounds at the going exchange rate and buy the bond.

But what if the price of the pound falls before the British bond becomes due? Then, when you cash in your British bond for pounds, and convert the pounds back into dollars, you'll be *selling your pounds at a lower price* than you bought them for. While you'd benefit from the higher interest rate on the British bond, you'd lose on the foreign currency transaction—buying pounds when their price is high, and selling them when their price is low. If the foreign currency loss is great enough, you would be better off with U.S. bonds, even though they pay a lower interest rate.

As you can see, it is not just relative interest rates that matter to wealth holders; it is also *expected changes in the exchange rate.* An expectation that the price of the pound will fall will make British assets less appealing to Americans, since they will expect a foreign currency loss. In this case, the demand for pounds curve will shift leftward.

The opposite holds as well. If Americans expect the price of the pound to *rise,* they will expect a foreign currency *gain* from buying British assets. This will cause the *demand for pounds curve to shift rightward.*

## THE SUPPLY OF BRITISH POUNDS

The demand for pounds is one side of the market for pounds. Now we turn our attention to the other side: the supply of pounds. And we'll begin with our basic question: *Who* is supplying them?

In the real world, pounds are supplied from many sources. Anyone who has pounds and wants to exchange them for dollars can come to the market and supply pounds. But the most important sellers of pounds are British households and businesses—who naturally have pounds and need dollars in order to make purchases from Americans. To keep our analysis simple, we'll focus on just these British sellers, and we'll ignore—for now—any pounds supplied by the British government:

> *In our model of the market for pounds, we assume that British households and firms are the only sellers.*

The British supply pounds in the dollar–pound market for only one reason: because they want dollars. Thus, to ask why the British supply pounds is to ask why they want dollars. We can identify two separate reasons:

 Identify Goals and Constraints

- *To buy goods and services from American firms.* The British buy airline tickets on United Airlines, computers made by IBM and Apple, and the rights to show films made in Hollywood. British tourists stay in American hotels and eat at American restaurants. The British demand dollars—and supply pounds—for all of these purchases.
- *To buy American assets.* The British buy American stocks, American corporate or government bonds, and American real estate. In each case, the American seller will want to be paid in dollars, and the British buyer will acquire dollars by offering pounds.

### THE SUPPLY OF POUNDS CURVE

Panel (a) of Figure 2 shows an example of a **supply curve for foreign currency**— here, British pounds. The curve tells us *the quantity of pounds the British will want to sell in any given period, at each different exchange rate.* Notice that the curve slopes upward: The higher the exchange rate, the greater is the quantity of pounds supplied. For example, at an exchange rate of $1.50 per pound, the British would want to supply £300 million (point *E*). If the exchange rate rose to $2.25 per pound, they would supply £400 million (point *F*).

Why does a higher exchange rate—a higher price for the pound—make the British want to sell more of them? Because the higher the price for the pound, the

**Supply curve for foreign currency**
A curve indicating the quantity of a specific foreign currency that will be supplied, during a given period, at each different exchange rate.

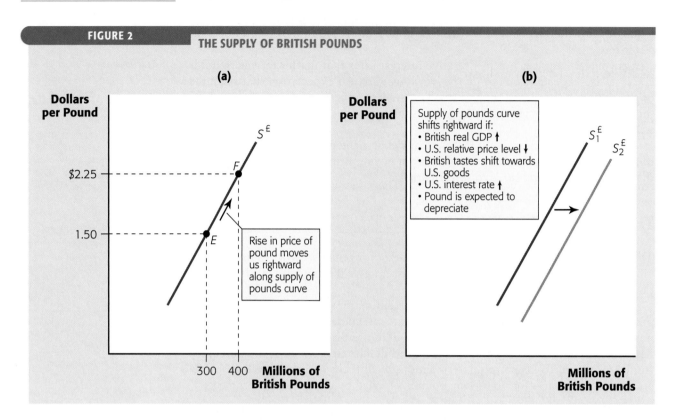

**FIGURE 2**

**THE SUPPLY OF BRITISH POUNDS**

**(a)**

**(b)**

more dollars someone gets for each pound sold. This makes U.S. goods and services less expensive to British buyers, who will want to buy more of them—and who will therefore need more dollars.[1]

To summarize, as we move rightward *along* the supply of pounds curve, such as the move from point *E* to point *F*:

### SHIFTS IN THE SUPPLY OF POUNDS CURVE

When the exchange rate changes, we *move along* the supply curve for pounds, as in panel (a) of Figure 2. But other variables can affect the supply of pounds besides the exchange rate. When any of these variables change, the supply of pounds curve will shift, as shown in panel (b). What are these variables?

**Real GDP in Britain.** If real GDP and real income rise in Britain, British residents will buy more goods and services, including those produced in the United States.

---

[1]    Actually, it is not a logical necessity for the supply of pounds curve to slope upward. Why not? When the price of the pound rises, it is true that the British will buy more U.S. goods and need more dollars to buy them. However, each dollar they buy costs *fewer pounds*. It might be that—even though the British obtain more dollars—they actually supply fewer pounds to get them at the higher exchange rate. In this case, the supply of pounds curve would slope downward. Economists believe, however, that a downward-sloping supply curve for foreign currency—while theoretically possible—is very rare.

Since they will need more dollars to buy U.S. goods, they will supply more pounds. In panel (b) this causes a rightward shift of the supply curve, from $S_1^£$ to $S_2^£$.

**Relative Price Levels.**  Earlier, you learned that a rise in the relative price level in the United States makes British goods more attractive to Americans. But it also makes *American* goods *less* attractive to the British. Since the British will want to buy fewer U.S. goods, they will want fewer dollars and will supply fewer pounds. Thus, a rise in the relative U.S. price level shifts the supply of pounds curve leftward.

**British Tastes for U.S. Goods.**  Recall our earlier discussion about the effect of American tastes on the demand for pounds. The same reasoning applies to the effect of British tastes on the *supply* of pounds. The British could begin to crave things American—or recoil from them. A shift in British tastes toward American goods will shift the supply of pounds curve rightward. A shift in tastes *away* from American goods will shift the curve leftward.

**Relative Interest Rates.**  You've already learned that a rise in the relative U.S. interest rate makes U.S. assets more attractive to Americans. It has exactly the same effect on the British. As the U.S. interest rate rises, and the British buy more U.S. assets, they will need more dollars and will supply more pounds. The supply of pounds curve will shift rightward.

**Expected Change in the Exchange Rate.**  In deciding where to hold their assets, the British have the same concerns as Americans. They will look, in part, at rates of return; but they will *also* think about possible gains or losses on foreign currency transactions. Suppose the British *expect the price of the pound to fall.* Then, by holding U.S. assets, they can anticipate a foreign currency gain—selling pounds at a relatively high price and buying them back again when their price is relatively low. The prospect of foreign currency gain will make U.S. assets more attractive, and the British will buy more of them. *The supply of pounds curve will shift rightward.*

## THE EQUILIBRIUM EXCHANGE RATE

 Find the Equilibrium

**Floating exchange rate**  An exchange rate that is freely determined by the forces of supply and demand.

Now we will make an important—and in most cases, realistic—assumption: that the exchange rate between the dollar and the pound *floats*. A **floating exchange rate** is one that is freely determined by the forces of supply and demand, without government intervention to change it or keep it from changing. Indeed, many of the world's leading currencies, including the Japanese yen, the British pound, the 11-nation euro, and the Mexican peso, do float freely against the dollar most of the time.

In some cases, however, governments do not allow the exchange rate to float freely, but instead manipulate its value by intervening in the market, or even *fix* it at a particular value. We'll discuss government intervention in foreign exchange markets later. In this section, we assume that both the British and U.S. governments leave the dollar–pound market alone.

When the exchange rate floats, the price will settle at the level where quantity supplied and quantity demanded are equal. Here, buyers and sellers are trading British pounds, and the price is the exchange rate—the *price of the pound.*

Look at panel (a) of Figure 3. The equilibrium in the market for pounds occurs at point $E$, where the supply and demand curves intersect. The equilibrium price is $1.50 per pound. As you can verify, if the exchange rate were higher, say, $2.25 per pound,

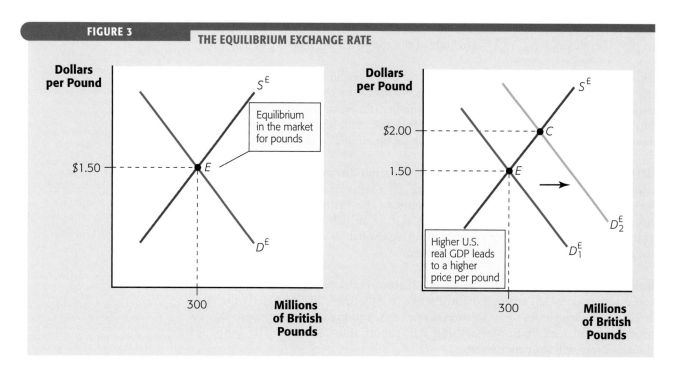

**FIGURE 3**

**THE EQUILIBRIUM EXCHANGE RATE**

there would be an *excess supply* of pounds, forcing the price of the pound back down to $1.50. If the exchange rate were *lower* than the equilibrium price of $1.50, there would be an *excess demand* for pounds, driving the price back up to $1.50.

> *When the exchange rate floats—that is, when the government does not intervene in the foreign currency market—the equilibrium exchange rate is determined at the intersection of the demand curve and the supply curve.*

What Happens When
Things Change?

## WHAT HAPPENS WHEN THINGS CHANGE?

What would cause the price of the pound to rise or fall? The simple answer to this question is, anything that shifts the demand for pounds curve, or the supply of pounds curve, or both curves together. Have another look at the right-hand panels of Figures 1 and 2. They summarize the major factors that can shift the demand and supply curves for pounds and therefore change the floating exchange rate.

Let's illustrate with a simple example. In panel (b) of Figure 3, the initial equilibrium in the market for pounds is at point *E,* with an exchange rate of $1.50 per pound. Now suppose that real GDP rises in the United States. As you've learned (see Figure 1), this rise in U.S. GDP will shift the demand for pounds curve rightward, from $D_1^£$ to $D_2^£$ in the figure. At the old exchange rate of $1.50 per pound, there would be an excess demand for pounds, which would drive the price of the pound higher. The new equilibrium—where the quantities of pounds supplied and demanded are equal—occurs at point *C,* and the new equilibrium exchange rate is $2.00 per pound.

To recap, the increase in American GDP causes the price of the pound to rise from $1.50 to $2.00. When the price of any floating foreign currency rises because

**FIGURE 4**

**THE EXCHANGE RATE IN THE POUND–DOLLAR MARKET**

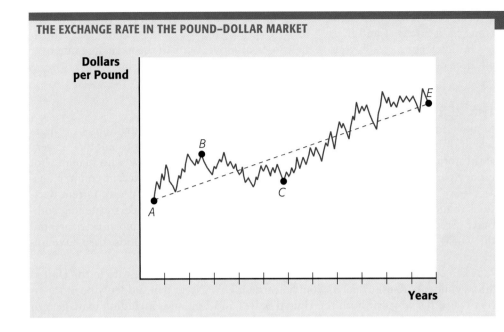

These hypothetical data show typical patterns of exchange rate fluctuations. Over the course of a few minutes, days, or weeks, the exchange rate can experience sharp up-and-down spikes. Over several months or a year or two, the exchange rate may rise or fall, as in the appreciation of the pound from points *A* to *B* and the depreciation from *B* to *C*. Over the long run, there may be a general upward or downward trend, like the appreciation of the pound illustrated by the dashed line connecting points *A* and *E*.

of a shift in the demand curve, the supply curve, or both, we call it an **appreciation** of the currency. In our example, the pound appreciates against the dollar. At the same time, there has been a **depreciation** of the dollar—a fall in its price in terms of pounds. (To see this, calculate the price of the dollar in terms of pounds before and after the shift in demand.)

**Appreciation**  An increase in the price of a currency in a floating-rate system.

**Depreciation**  A decrease in the price of a currency in a floating-rate system.

> *When a floating exchange rates changes, one country's currency will appreciate (rise in price) and the other country's currency will depreciate (fall in price).*

As you've learned, there are many other variables besides U.S. GDP that can change and affect the exchange rate. We could analyze each of these changes, using diagrams similar to panel (b) of Figure 3. However, we'll organize our discussion of exchange rate changes in a slightly different way.

## HOW EXCHANGE RATES CHANGE OVER TIME

When we examine the actual behavior of exchange rates over time, we find three different kinds of movements. Look at Figure 4, which graphs the exchange rate in the pound–dollar market over time. The figure is based on hypothetical data, designed to make these three kinds of movement stand out more clearly than they usually do in practice.

Notice first the sharp up-and-down spikes. These fluctuations in exchange rates occur over the course of a few weeks, a few days, or even a few minutes—periods of time that we call the *very short run*.

Second, we see a gradual rise and fall of the exchange rate over the course of several months or a year or two. An example is the appreciation of the pound from point *A* to *B* and the depreciation of the pound from point *B* to *C*. These are *short-run* movements in the exchange rate.

Finally, notice that while the price of the pound fluctuates in the very short run and the short run, we can also discern a general *long-run* trend: The pound seems to be appreciating in the figure. This long-run trend is illustrated by the dashed line connecting points *A* and *E*.

In this section, we'll explore the causes of movements in the exchange rate over all three periods: the very short run, the short run, and the long run.

## THE VERY SHORT RUN: "HOT MONEY"

Banks and other large financial institutions collectively have trillions of dollars worth of funds that they can move from one type of investment to another at very short notice. These funds are often called "hot money." If those who manage hot money perceive even a tiny advantage in moving funds to a different country's assets—say, because its interest rate is slightly higher—they will do so. Often, decisions to move billions of dollars are made in split seconds, by traders watching computer screens showing the latest data on exchange rates and interest rates around the world. Because these traders move such large volumes of funds, they have immediate effects on exchange rates.

Let's consider an example. Suppose that the relative interest rate in the United States suddenly rises. Then, as you've learned, U.S. assets will suddenly be more attractive to residents of both the United States and England, including managers of hot-money accounts in both countries. As these managers shift their funds from British to United States assets, they will be dumping billions of pounds on the foreign exchange market in order to acquire dollars to buy U.S. assets. This will cause a significant rightward shift of the supply of pounds curve.

In addition to affecting managers of hot-money accounts, the higher relative interest rate in the United States will affect ordinary investors. British investors will want to buy more American assets, helping to shift the supply of pounds curve further rightward. And American investors will want to buy fewer British assets than before, causing some decrease in the *demand* for pounds. Thus, in addition to the very large rightward shift in the supply of pounds, there will be a more moderate leftward shift in the demand for pounds.

Both of these shifts are illustrated in Figure 5: The supply of pounds curve shifts from $S_1^£$ to $S_2^£$, and the demand for pounds curve shifts from $D_1^£$ to $D_2^£$. The result is easy to see: The equilibrium in the market for pounds moves from point *E* to point *G*, and the price of the pound *falls* from \$1.50 to \$1.00. The pound depreciates and the dollar appreciates.

Expectations about future exchange rates can also trigger huge shifts of hot money, and Figure 5 also illustrates what would happen if American and British residents suddenly *expect* the pound to depreciate against the dollar. In this case, it would be the anticipation of foreign currency gains from holding U.S. assets, rather than a higher U.S. interest rate, that would cause the supply and demand curves to shift. As you can see in Figure 5, the expectation that the pound will depreciate actually *causes* the pound to depreciate—a self-fulfilling prophecy.

Sudden changes in relative interest rates, as well as sudden expectations of an appreciation or depreciation of a nation's currency, occur frequently in foreign exchange markets. They can cause massive shifts of hot money from the assets of one country to those of another in very short periods of time. For this reason,

> *relative interest rates and expectations of future exchange rates are the dominant forces moving exchange rates in the very short run.*

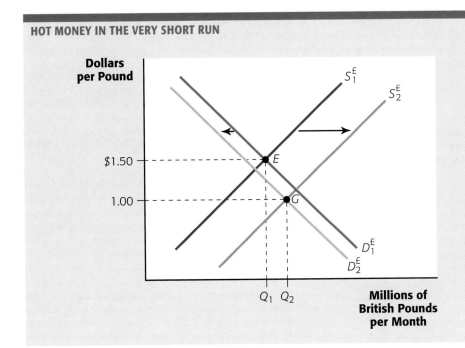

**FIGURE 5**

**HOT MONEY IN THE VERY SHORT RUN**

The market for pounds is initially in equilibrium at point *E,* with an exchange rate of $1.50 per pound. A rise in the U.S. interest rate relative to the British rate will make U.S. assets more attractive to both Americans and Britons. Hot-money managers in both countries will shift funds from British to U.S. assets, causing a rightward shift of the supply of pounds curve. American investors will want to buy fewer British assets, causing a decrease in the demand for pounds. The net effect is a lower exchange rate—$1.00 per pound at point *G.*

## THE SHORT RUN: MACROECONOMIC FLUCTUATIONS

Look again at Figure 4. What explains the movements in the *short run* rate—the changes that occur over several months or a few years? In most cases, the causes are economic fluctuations taking place in one or more countries.

Suppose, for example, that both Britain and the United States are in a recession, and the U.S. economy begins to recover while the British slump continues. As real GDP rises in the United States, so does Americans' demand for foreign goods and services, including those from Britain. The demand for pounds curve will shift rightward, and—as shown in panel (a) of Figure 6—the pound will appreciate.

A year or so later, when Britain recovers from *its* recession, its real GDP will rise. British residents will begin to buy more U.S. goods and services, and supply more pounds so they can acquire more dollars. The supply of pounds curve will shift rightward, and—as shown in panel (b) of Figure 6—the pound will depreciate. Thus,

*in the short run, movements in exchange rates are caused largely by economic fluctuations. All else equal, a country whose GDP rises relatively rapidly will experience a depreciation of its currency. A country whose GDP falls more rapidly will experience an appreciation of its currency.*

This observation contradicts a commonly held myth: that a strong (appreciating) currency is a sign of economic health, and a weak (depreciating) currency denotes a sick economy. The truth may easily be the opposite. Over the course of several quarters or a few years, the dollar could appreciate because the U.S. economy is *weakening*—entering a serious recession. This would cause Americans to cut back spending on domestic *and* foreign goods, and decrease the demand for foreign currency. Similarly, a *strengthening* U.S. economy—in which Americans are earning

**FIGURE 6**

**EXCHANGE RATES IN THE SHORT RUN**

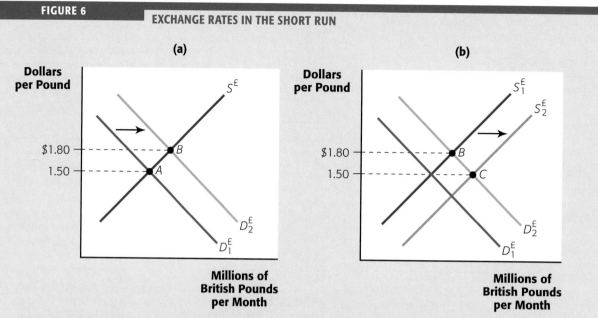

Panel (a) shows a situation in which the United States recovers from a recession first. U.S. demand for foreign goods and services increases, shifting the demand for pounds curve to the right. The result is an appreciation of the pound. Panel (b) shows Britain's subsequent recovery from its recession. As the British begin to buy more U.S. goods and services, the supply of pounds curve shifts rightward, causing the pound to depreciate.

and spending more—would increase the U.S. demand for foreign currency and—all else equal—cause the dollar to depreciate.

Keep in mind, though, that other variables can change over the business cycle besides real GDP, including interest rates and price levels in the two countries. For example, a recession can be caused by a monetary contraction that raises the relative interest rate in a country. Or a monetary stimulus in the midst of a recession could result in a relatively low interest rate. These changes, too, will influence exchange rates over the business cycle.

## THE LONG RUN: PURCHASING POWER PARITY

In mid-1992, you could buy about 100 Russian rubles for one dollar. In mid-1998, that same dollar would get you more than 6,000 rubles—so many that the Russian government that year created a new ruble that was worth 1,000 of the old rubles. (The ruble exchange rate in Table 1 is for the new ruble.) What caused the ruble to depreciate so much against the dollar during those six years?

This is a question about exchange rates over many years—the long run. Movements of hot money—which explain sudden, temporary movements of exchange rates—cannot explain this kind of long-run trend. Nor can business cycles, which are, by nature, temporary. What, then, causes exchange rates to change over the long run?

In general, long-run trends in exchange rates are determined by *relative price levels* in two countries. We can be even more specific:

> *According to the **purchasing power parity (PPP) theory**, the exchange rate between two countries will adjust in the long run until the average price of goods is roughly the same in both countries.*

**Purchasing power parity (PPP) theory** The idea that the exchange rate will adjust in the long run so that the average price of goods in two countries will be roughly the same.

To see why the PPP theory makes sense, imagine a basket of goods that costs $750 in the United States and £500 in Britain. If the prices of the goods themselves do not change, then, according to the PPP theory, the exchange rate will adjust to $750/£500 = $1.5 dollars per pound. Why? Because at this exchange rate, $750 can be exchanged for £500, so the price of the basket is the same to residents of either country—$750 for Americans, and £500 for the British.

Now, suppose the exchange rate was *below* its PPP rate of $1.50 per pound— say, $1 per pound. Then a trader could take $500 to the bank, exchange it for £500, buy the basket of goods in Great Britain, and sell it in the United States for $750. She would earn a profit of $250 on each basket of goods traded. In the process, however, traders would be increasing the demand for pounds and raising the exchange rate. When the price of the pound reached $1.50, purchasing power parity would hold, and special trading opportunities would be gone. As you can see, trading activity will tend to drive the exchange rate toward the PPP rate. (An end-of-chapter review question asks you to explain the adjustment process when the exchange rate starts *higher* than the PPP rate.)

The PPP theory has an important implication:

> *In the long run, the currency of a country with a higher inflation rate will depreciate against the currency of a country whose inflation rate is lower.*

Why? Because in the country with the higher inflation rate, the relative price level will be rising. As that country's basket of goods becomes relatively more expensive, only a depreciation of its currency can restore purchasing power parity. And traders—taking advantage of opportunities like those just described—would cause the currency to depreciate.

### Purchasing Power Parity: Some Important Caveats.

While purchasing power parity is a good general guideline for predicting long-run trends in exchange rates, it does not work perfectly. For a variety of reasons, exchange rates can deviate from their PPP values for many years.

First, some goods—by their very nature—are difficult to trade. Suppose a haircut costs £5 in London and $30 in New York, and the exchange rate is $1.50 per pound. Then British haircuts are cheaper for residents of both countries. Could traders take advantage of this? Not really. They cannot take $30 to the bank in exchange for £20, buy four haircuts in London, ship them to New York, and sell them for a total of $120 there. Haircuts and most other personal services are nontradable.

Second, high transportation costs can reduce trading possibilities even for goods that *can* be traded. Our earlier numerical example would have quite a different ending if moving the basket of goods between Great Britain and the United States involved $500 of freight and insurance costs.

Third, artificial barriers to trade, such as the special taxes or quotas on imports can hamper traders' ability to move exchange rates toward purchasing power parity.

Still, the purchasing power parity theory is useful in many circumstances. Under floating exchange rates, a country whose relative price level is rising rapidly will almost always find that the price of its currency is falling rapidly. If not, all of its tradeable goods would soon be priced out of the world market.

Indeed, we often observe that countries with very high inflation rates have currencies depreciating against the dollar by roughly the amount needed to preserve purchasing power parity. For example, we've already mentioned the sharp depreciation of the Russian ruble from 1992 to 1998. During those six years, the number of rubles that exchanged for a dollar rose from around 100 to about 6,000. Over the same period, the annual inflation rate averaged about 200 percent in Russia, but only about 3 percent in the United States. As a result, the relative price level in Russia skyrocketed, leading to a dramatic depreciation of the ruble against the dollar. Another recent example is Turkey: From mid-1996 to mid-1997, its price level almost doubled, while the dollar price of its currency was cut in half.

## INTERDEPENDENT MARKETS: THE ROLE OF ARBITRAGE

The market for pounds—like any other foreign exchange market—is not a centralized market in a single location. Rather, pounds and dollars are exchanged at tens of thousands of locations—at banks, hotels, airports, and train stations in hundreds of cities and towns around the world. How do we know that the equilibrium exchange rate, such as the one we found back in Figure 3 (a), will be the exchange rate in *all* of these locations? Couldn't it be that in New York pounds sell for $1.50 each, while in London they sell for $1.60, and in Paris, for $1.35?

Actually, no. An exchange rate between two currencies will be the same in every location, except for tiny differences that will exist for only a few seconds. Why? Because of the process of **arbitrage**—the simultaneous buying and selling of a foreign currency in order to profit from any difference in exchange rates.

Figure 7 can help us visualize how **bilateral arbitrage**—in which only one pair of currencies is traded—drives an exchange rate to the same equilibrium value around the world. Suppose that in New York (panel (a)) the equilibrium price of the pound was $1.20, while in London (panel (b)) the price was $1.80. Then astute traders could make fortunes in minutes. American and British traders could buy pounds in New York for $1.20 each, while simultaneously selling them in London for $1.80 each. On each pound traded, they would make a profit of 60 cents. This may not sound like much, but in the foreign exchange market, a professional trader can easily buy and sell millions of dollars' worth of currency in a matter of seconds, with a few keystrokes on a computer. In our example, someone buying $10 million worth of pounds in New York and selling them in London would make a nice profit of $6 million—not bad for the few seconds it took to make the trade.

But before you decide to quit college and become a foreign exchange trader, you should know that differences in exchange rates as large as the one in Figure 7 never actually occur. Why not? Because traders—by taking advantage of even the tiniest differences in exchange rates—wipe out those differences entirely.

Let's go back to Figure 7 and see how bilateral arbitrage equalizes exchange rates in different locations. As traders buy pounds in New York, the demand curve there shifts rightward, from $D_1^\pounds$ to $D_2^\pounds$, thereby increasing the price of the pound in New York. As traders sell pounds in London, the supply curve there shifts rightward, from $S_1^\pounds$ to $S_2^\pounds$, thereby decreasing the price of pounds in London. The process continues until the exchange rate reaches the same value of $1.50 in both markets and there are no more profit opportunities for traders.

**Arbitrage** Simultaneous buying and selling of a foreign currency in order to profit from a difference in exchange rates.

**Bilateral arbitrage** Arbitrage involving one pair of currencies.

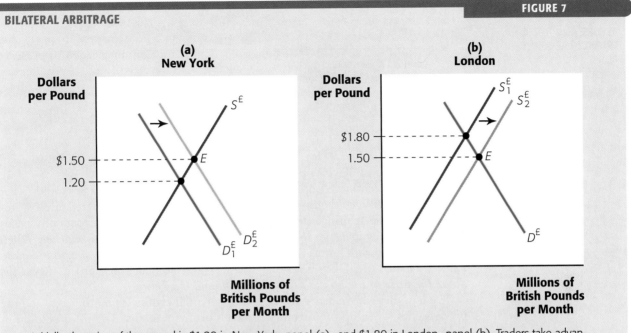

**FIGURE 7**

**BILATERAL ARBITRAGE**

Initially, the price of the pound is $1.20 in New York—panel (a)—and $1.80 in London—panel (b). Traders take advantage of this exchange rate differential by buying pounds in New York and simultaneously selling them in London. As they do so, the demand curve shifts rightward in New York, and the supply curve shifts rightward in London. Arbitrage continues until the exchange rate attains the same value—$1.50 per pound—in both locations.

> *Bilateral arbitrage ensures that the exchange rate between any two currencies is the same everywhere in the world.[2]*

**Triangular Arbitrage.** Another form of arbitrage—called **triangular arbitrage**—involves trades among *three* (or more) countries' currencies. Triangular arbitrage ensures that the number of dollars that exchange for one pound is the same whether you make the trade *directly*—in the dollar–pound market—or *indirectly*, by buying and selling a third currency.

To see how triangular arbitrage works, suppose that the exchange rates among the U.S. dollar, the British pound, and the Mexican peso are as shown in the left-hand column of Table 2: The price of a pound in dollars is $1.80, the price of a peso in dollars is $0.10, and the price of a pound in pesos is 10 pesos.

With these exchange rates, the *direct* price of the pound to Americans is $1.80. But the *indirect* price is $1.00. Why? Because an American, starting with $1.00, could purchase 10 pesos in the dollar–peso market and then use those 10 pesos to purchase 1 pound in the peso–pound market. This difference between the direct and indirect prices for the pound would allow traders to make huge profits. They could

**Triangular arbitrage** Arbitrage involving trades among three (or more) currencies.

---

2  Exchange rates will sometimes *appear* to be different in different locations because a commission for the broker is often built into the rate. These commissions can differ by location, depending on the cost structure and degree of competition among brokers. For example, if you buy pounds in a small-town bank, which faces little competition and may have higher costs, you may pay more for them than if you bought them in a big-city bank. But this is only because the small-town bank is charging a higher commission.

| TABLE 2 | | Exchange Rate Before Arbitrage | Exchange Rate After Arbitrage |
|---|---|---|---|
| **BEFORE AND AFTER TRIANGULAR ARBITRAGE** | Price of pound in dollar–pound market | $1.80 | $1.50 |
| | Price of peso in dollar–peso market | $0.10 | $0.125 |
| | Price of pound in pound–peso market | 10 pesos | 12 pesos |

acquire pounds *indirectly* for $1.00 each and then sell them *directly* for $1.80 each, for a huge profit of 80 cents per pound sold.

However, such large potential profits from triangular arbitrage would never arise in practice. Even the tiniest potential profits would be eliminated, almost immediately, by the arbitrage process itself. In our example, when traders buy pesos with dollars, they *drive up the price of the peso in the dollar–peso market*. When they buy pounds with pesos, they *drive up the price of the pound in the pound–peso market*. Finally, when they buy dollars with pounds to make their profit, they *drive down the price of the pound in the dollar–pound market*.

Each of these movements decreases the potential profits from arbitrage, and the process ends when no opportunity for such profits remains. The third column in Table 2 shows where the exchange rates might end up after the arbitrage process is completed. With these exchange rates, the direct price of the pound is $1.50. And this is also what it would cost to buy a pound *indirectly*: $1.50 gets you 12 pesos, and 12 pesos gets you one pound. There are no more opportunities for arbitrage, because arbitrage has eliminated them.

> *Triangular arbitrage ensures that the price of a foreign currency is the same whether it is purchased directly—in a single foreign exchange market—or indirectly, by buying and selling a third currency.*[3]

## GOVERNMENT INTERVENTION IN FOREIGN EXCHANGE MARKETS

As you've seen, when exchange rates float, they can rise and fall for a variety of reasons. But a government may not be content to let the forces of supply and demand change its exchange rate. If the exchange rate rises, the country's goods will become much more expensive to foreigners, causing harm to its export-oriented industries. If the exchange rate falls, goods purchased from other countries will rise in price. Since many imported goods are used as inputs by U.S. firms (such as oil from the Middle East and Mexico, or computer screens from Japan), a drop in the exchange rate will cause a rise in the U.S. price level. Finally, if the exchange rate is too volatile, it can make trading riskier or require traders to acquire special insurance against foreign currency losses, which costs them money, time, and trouble. For all of these reasons, governments sometime *intervene* in foreign exchange markets involving their currency.

---

[3]     Because brokerage commissions are sometimes built into the price of foreign currency, small differences between the direct and indirect price may remain, even after arbitrage has eliminated all possibilities of profit. This is because two commissions are paid when a person buys indirectly, but only one commission is paid when buying directly.

## MANAGED FLOAT

Many governments let their exchange rate float *most of the time,* but will intervene on occasion when the floating exchange rate moves in an undesired direction or becomes too volatile. For example, look back at Figure 5, where the price of the British pound falls to $1 as hot money is shifted out of British assets. Suppose the British government does not want the pound to depreciate. Then its central bank—the Bank of England—could begin trading in the dollar–pound market itself. It would buy British pounds with dollars, thereby shifting the demand for pounds curve rightward. If it buys just the right amount of pounds, it can prevent the pound from depreciating at all. Alternatively, the U.S. government might not be happy with the *appreciation* of the dollar in Figure 5. In that case, the Federal Reserve can enter the market and buy British pounds with dollars, once again shifting the demand for pounds curve rightward.

The central banks of many countries—including the Federal Reserve—will sometimes intervene in this way in foreign exchange markets. When a government buys or sells its own currency or that of a trading partner to influence exchange rates, it is engaging in a "managed float" or a "dirty float."

> Under a **managed float,** a country's central bank actively manages its exchange rate, buying its own currency to prevent depreciations, and selling its own currency to prevent appreciations.

**Managed float** A policy of frequent central bank intervention to move the exchange rate.

Managed floats are used most often in the very short run, to prevent large, sudden changes in exchange rates. For example, on a single day—March 8, 2000—the Bank of Japan (Japan's central bank) sold over 200 billion yen (about $2 billion worth) in order to stop a rapid appreciation of the yen against the dollar. On the other side, during 1998, the central bank of Guatemala bought almost 2 billion quetzals (about $300 million worth) in order to slow the depreciation of that currency.

That last example raises a question. When a country—such as Guatemala—wants to prevent or slow a depreciation against the dollar, it has to buy its own currency with dollars. Where does it get those dollars? Unfortunately for Guatemala, it is not legally permitted to print dollars—only the U.S. Federal Reserve can do that. Instead, Guatemala must use its *reserves* of dollars—the dollars its central bank keeps on hand specifically to intervene in the dollar–quetzal market.

Almost every nation holds reserves of dollars—as well as euros, yen, and other key currencies—just so it can enter the foreign exchange market and sell them for its own currency when necessary. Under a managed float, periods of selling dollars are usually short-lived, and alternate with periods of buying dollars. Thus, countries rarely use up all of their dollar reserves when they engage in managed floats.

Managed floats are controversial. Some economists believe they help to avoid wide swings in exchange rates, and thus reduce the risks for international traders and investors. But others are critical of how managed floats often work out in practice. They point out that countries often intervene when the forces behind an appreciation or depreciation are strong. In these cases, the intervention only serves to delay inevitable changes in the exchange rate—sometimes, at great cost to a country's reserves of dollars and other key currencies.

http://

If you are interested in learning more about exchange rate systems, read "The International Financial Architecture" by Jeffrey Frankel at http://www.brook. edu/comm/PolicyBriefs/pb051/ pb51.htm.

## FIXED EXCHANGE RATES

A more extreme form of intervention is a **fixed exchange rate,** in which a government declares a particular value for its exchange rate with another currency. The

**Fixed exchange rate** A government-declared exchange rate maintained by central bank intervention in the foreign exchange market.

FIGURE 8

## A FIXED EXCHANGE RATE FOR THE BAHT

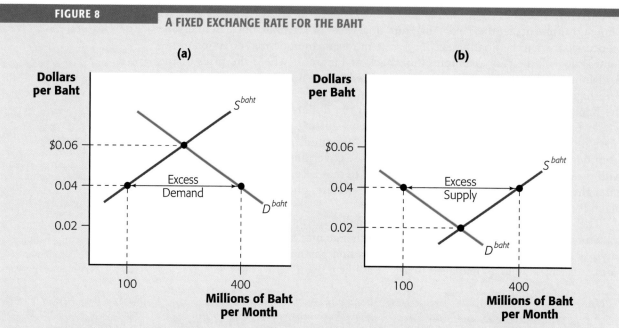

In both panels, Thailand's central bank fixes the exchange rate at $0.04 per baht. In panel (a), the equilibrium exchange rate is $0.06 per baht—higher than the fixed rate. The central bank must sell 300 million baht per month—an amount equal to the excess demand. In panel (b), which shows a different set of supply and demand curves, the equilibrium exchange rate is $0.02 per baht—lower than the fixed rate. The central bank must buy up the excess supply of 300 million baht.

government, through its central bank, then commits itself to intervene in the foreign exchange market any time the *equilibrium* exchange rate differs from the *fixed* rate.

For example, from 1987 to 1997, the government of Thailand fixed the value of its currency—the *baht*—at $0.04 per baht. The two panels of Figure 8 show the different types of intervention that might be necessary in the baht–dollar market to maintain this fixed exchange rate. Each panel shows a different set of supply and demand curves—and a different equilibrium exchange rate that might exist for the baht. Look first at panel (a). Here, we assume that the equilibrium exchange rate is $0.06 per baht, so that the fixed rate is *lower* than the equilibrium rate. At the fixed rate of $0.04 per baht, 400 million baht would be demanded each month, but only 100 million would be supplied. There would be an *excess demand* of 300 million baht, which would ordinarily drive the exchange rate back up to its equilibrium value of $0.06. But the Thai government prevents this by entering the market and *selling* just enough baht to cover the excess demand. In panel (a), the Central Bank of Thailand would sell 300 million baht per month to maintain the fixed rate.

> *When a country fixes its exchange rate below the equilibrium value, the result is an excess demand for the country's currency. To maintain the fixed rate, the country's central bank must sell enough of its own currency to eliminate the excess demand.*

Panel (b) shows another possibility, where the equilibrium exchange rate is $0.02, so that the same fixed exchange rate of $0.04 per baht is now *above* the equilibrium rate. There is an excess *supply* of 300 million baht. In this case, to pre-

**FIGURE 9**

**A FOREIGN CURRENCY CRISIS**

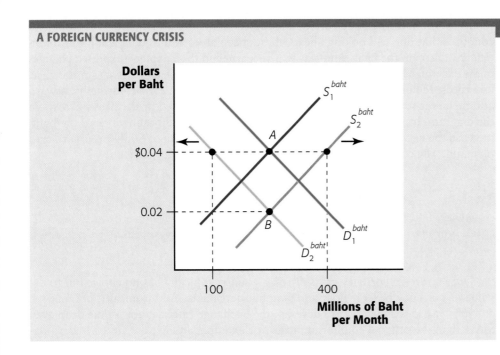

Initially, the baht is fixed at the equilibrium rate of $0.04. When the supply and demand curves shift to $D_2$ and $S_2$, the equilibrium exchange rate falls to $0.02. If Thailand continues to fix the rate at $0.04, it will have to buy up the excess supply of 300 million baht per month, using dollars. As its dollar reserves dwindle, traders will anticipate a drop in the value of the baht, shifting the curves out further, as indicated by the heavy arrows.

vent the excess supply from driving the exchange rate down, the Central Bank of Thailand must *buy* the excess baht.

> *When a country fixes its exchange rate above the equilibrium value, the result is an excess supply of the country's currency. To maintain the fixed rate, the country's central bank must buy enough of its own currency to eliminate the excess supply.*

Fixed exchange rates present little problem for a country as long as the exchange rate is fixed at or very close to its equilibrium rate. But when the equilibrium exchange rate moves away from the fixed rate—as in the two panels of Figure 8—governments often try to maintain their fixed rate anyway, sometimes for long periods. This can create problems, especially when the exchange rate is fixed *above* the equilibrium rate.

To see why, look at Figure 9. Initially, the supply and demand curves for baht are given by $S_1$ and $D_1$, respectively, so that the equilibrium exchange rate, $0.04, is equal to the fixed exchange rate. At this point, the central bank is neither selling nor buying baht. Now, suppose that, for some reason (we'll be more specific in a few paragraphs), the supply and demand curves shift to $S_2$ and $D_2$, respectively. The equilibrium rate falls, so the fixed rate of $0.04 is above the equilibrium rate of $0.02. The Central Bank of Thailand must now *buy* its own currency with dollars—at the rate of 300 million baht per month. Each baht costs the central bank 4 cents, so as the months go by, its dollar reserves are being depleted at the rate of 300 million × $0.04 = $12 million per month. Once those reserves are gone, Thailand will have only two choices: to let its currency float (which means an immediate depreciation to the lower, equilibrium rate), or to declare a new, lower fixed rate—a **devaluation** of its currency.

Of course, at a certain point, foreign exchange speculators and traders would see that Thailand doesn't have many dollars left. (Most countries' central banks regularly

**Devaluation** A change in the exchange rate from a higher fixed rate to a lower fixed rate.

report their holdings of key currencies, and economists can estimate the holdings of countries that don't.) Looking ahead, these speculators and traders will begin to *anticipate* a drop in the baht. And—as you've learned in this chapter—expected changes in the exchange rate *shift* supply and demand curves for foreign currency. In this case, an expected fall in the baht causes the supply curve for baht to shift further rightward and the demand curve to shift further leftward, as indicated by the heavy arrows in the diagram. In Figure 9, these shifts will *decrease* the equilibrium value of the baht, increase the *excess supply* of baht, and make the fixed rate of $0.04 even harder to maintain. The country is now experiencing a *foreign currency crisis*.

> *A **foreign currency crisis** arises when people no longer believe that a country can maintain a fixed exchange rate above the equilibrium rate. As a consequence, the supply of the currency increases, demand for it decreases, and the country must use up its reserves of dollars and other key currencies even faster in order to maintain the fixed rate.*

Once a foreign currency crisis arises, a country typically has no choice but to devalue its currency or let it float and watch it depreciate. And ironically, because the country waited for the crisis to develop, the exchange rate may for a time drop even lower than the original equilibrium rate. For example, in Figure 9, an early devaluation to $0.02 per dollar might prevent a crisis from occurring at all. But once the crisis begins, and the supply and demand curves shift out further than $S_2$ and $D_2$, the currency will have to drop *below* $0.02 to end the rapid depletion of dollar reserves.

### The Asian Financial Crisis.

In 1997, several Asian countries came very close to complete financial collapse. And fixed exchange rates and foreign currency crises—as just described—played a central role. The crisis had its roots in a practice that was common in Asia, especially in the five "frontline" countries most directly affected by the crisis—Thailand, Indonesia, South Korea, Malaysia, and the Philippines.

In these countries, banks borrowed dollars or yen in world markets, and then lent to domestic businesses in the local currency. Thus, banks were vulnerable to declines in exchange rates. For example, if the baht fell, a Thai bank would need more baht to pay back its own loans, while collecting the same number of baht from the local firms it had lent to.

Moreover, in these countries, exchange rates were managed by the government. If foreign exchange traders believed that a government was short of reserves, the exchange rate could fall dramatically. Furthermore, foreign exchange traders knew that these governments were guaranteeing the obligations of their banks. Therefore, any decline in the exchange rate would drain government reserves, making it that much harder to stabilize the exchange rate. This explains why Thailand and the other frontline countries didn't just devalue, or let their currencies float at the first sign of trouble. Even a modest devaluation would have caused their banks to fail.

But a drop in the exchange rate was inevitable. And Thailand's currency was the first to go. In July 1997, the Thai central bank—having defended its fixed rate down to almost its last dollar of reserves—had no choice but to let its currency float. The baht immediately depreciated from $0.04 to $0.02, and Thailand's banks were immediately in trouble.

The baht's depreciation then led to fears of depreciation or devaluation in *other* Asian countries, and served to worsen *their* crises. And there was another impact: In country after country, bank lending to businesses dried up. After all, who wants to put funds into a Korean bank when the Korean won is about to be devalued? Without sufficient funding, many businesses were forced to shut down, others lan-

**Foreign currency crisis** A loss of faith that a country can prevent a drop in its exchange rate, leading to a rapid depletion of its foreign currency (e.g., dollar) reserves.

**http://**

Professor Nouriel Roubini of New York University maintains an excellent Web page devoted to global financial crises. You can find it at http://www.stern.nyu.edu/~nroubini/asia/AsiaHomepage.html

guished, and millions of workers lost their jobs. Here is one way to measure the impact of the crisis: From 1990 to 1996, the average growth rate of the five Asian frontline countries was 7 percent per year. In 1998, the output of these countries *fell* by an average of 7 percent.

The Asian financial crisis lasted more than a year. Before it ended, investors—who had been awakened to the realities of devaluations and other risks—spread the crisis from country to country, and even to several Latin American countries.

In retrospect, the central cause of the crisis was the instability of banks that borrowed in dollars, yen, and other more stable currencies, and lent in their local currency. But government attempts to protect these banks by fixing or managing exchange rates proved to be a costly, and—ultimately—a losing, battle.

## THE EURO

One answer to the problems that countries have encountered in managing their own currencies is to adopt another country's currency or an international currency. For example, Argentina has a currency that is locked to the U.S. dollar. In the 11 Euroland countries, including Germany, France, Italy, and Spain, national exchange rates have already been fixed to a new European currency—the euro.

The Euro—the new common European currency—wasn't yet in circulation when this chapter was being written. But this advertisement shows prototypes of the bills that people in France, Italy, Germany, Spain, and seven other nations will carry in their wallets, beginning in 2002.

But the European nations are going even further: In 2002, their national currencies will cease to exist entirely, to be replaced by the euro. At that time, the European Central Bank will have sole authority for changing the supply of euros. It will determine a single monetary policy for all of Euroland, replacing the separate monetary policies of the different countries.

Why have these 11 European countries decided to do away with their national currencies?

There are several advantages. First, a single currency means that European firms—when they buy or sell across borders—will no longer have to pay commissions on the exchange of currency, or face the risk that exchange rates might change before accounts are settled. This should increase the volume of trade among the Euroland nations. Second, the elimination of exchange rate risk makes it easier for European firms to sell stocks and bonds to residents anywhere in Euroland. This will help ensure that funds are channeled to the most profitable firms throughout the area. Third, adopting a single currency makes cross-country comparison shopping easier. This should help increase competition among firms, and help keep prices down to European consumers. Finally, some of these countries—such as Italy—have had a history of loose monetary policy that has generated high rates of inflation, and high expected inflation. By giving up the right to run an independent monetary policy, and leaving it to the (presumably stricter) European Central Bank, the high-inflation countries of Europe will benefit from lower inflation rates.

There are, however, downsides to the euro. In fact, some economists believe that—at least for a while—the euro will create significant problems for the Euroland countries. Why? With a single currency, there must be a single monetary policy, making it impossible to adjust the money supply and interest rates to the problems of individual nations. For example, suppose Spain goes into a recession. In the old days before the euro, its central bank would increase the Spanish money supply and lower interest rates. But now, what if Spain's recession is accompanied by full employment or even a boom in the rest of Europe? Then, the European central bank will be tightening the money supply and raising interest rates, which will worsen conditions in Spain. Spain could always use fiscal policy. But, as you've learned, countercyclical fiscal policy is fraught with problems. Moreover, membership in

**Optimum currency area** A region whose economies perform better with a single currency than with separate national currencies.

Euroland requires countries to maintain strict fiscal discipline that might prevent them from using a fiscal stimulus when it is needed.

The economists who worry about these problems question whether Europe is an **optimum currency area**—a region whose economies will perform better with a single currency rather than separate national currencies. To be an optimum currency area, the different nations in a region should face common, rather than national, shocks, so that they tend to go into booms and recessions together. In that case, a single monetary policy will be appropriate, because all nations will need stimulus or restraint at the same time. In Europe, unfortunately, the shocks are often national: Different countries are dominated by different industries, face different types of labor unions, and have different institutional frameworks and laws. They are therefore susceptible to national as well as regional shocks.

Another requirement for an optimum currency area is that labor is highly mobile from one country to another. That way, if one country is experiencing a negative shock and goes into a recession that can't be addressed with monetary or fiscal policy (for the reasons discussed earlier), at least its unemployed workers can find work in other countries whose economies are performing better. Indeed, this is what happens in the United States, where labor is highly mobile among states.

But at present, labor is much less mobile across European borders than across the American states. And if unemployed workers stay within a country, its government may feel pressure to abandon the euro so that it can use expansionary fiscal and monetary policy.

In the very long run, the abolition of national currencies—and the creation of the euro—may work to increase labor mobility across Europe, especially if it changes the attitudes of European firms and workers toward cross-national employment. Europe may then move closer to being an optimum currency area in the future.

## EXCHANGE RATES AND THE MACROECONOMY

Exchange rates can have important effects on the macroeconomy—largely through their effect on net exports. And although we've included net exports in our short-run macro model, we haven't yet asked how exchange rates affect them. That's what we'll do now.

### EXCHANGE RATES AND SPENDING SHOCKS

What Happens When Things Change?

Suppose that the dollar depreciates against the foreign currencies of its major trading partners. (We'll discuss *why* that might happen in a later section.) Then U.S. goods would become cheaper to foreigners, and net exports would rise at each level of output. This increase in net exports is a positive spending shock to the economy—it increases aggregate expenditure. And, as you've learned, positive spending shocks increase GDP in the short run.

> *A depreciation of the dollar causes net exports to rise—a positive spending shock that increases real GDP in the short run. An appreciation of the dollar causes net exports to drop—a negative spending shock that decreases real GDP in the short run.*

The impact of net exports on equilibrium GDP—often caused by changes in the exchange rate—helps us understand one reason why governments are often concerned about their exchange rates. An unstable exchange rate can result in repeated shocks to the economy. At worst, this can cause fluctuations in GDP; at best, it makes the central bank's job more difficult as it tries to keep the economy on an even keel.

## EXCHANGE RATES AND MONETARY POLICY

What Happens When Things Change?

In several earlier chapters, we've explored how the Fed tries to keep the U.S. economy on an even keel with monetary policy. The central banks around the world are engaged in a similar struggle, and face many of the same challenges as the Fed. One challenge to central banks is that monetary policy causes changes in exchange rates, and thus has additional effects on real GDP that we have not yet considered.

To understand this, let's run through an example. Suppose the United States is in a recession, and the Fed decides to increase equilibrium GDP. As you've learned, the Fed—by increasing the money supply—brings down the interest rate. Interest-sensitive spending rises, and so does aggregate expenditure. When we consider the foreign exchange market, however, there is an additional effect on aggregate expenditure.

By lowering the U.S. interest rate, the Fed makes foreign financial assets more attractive to Americans, which raises their demand for foreign currency. In the market for pounds, for example, this will shift the demand for pounds curve rightward. At the same time, U.S. financial assets become less attractive to foreigners, which decreases the supply of foreign exchange (in the market for pounds, a leftward shift in the supply of pounds curve). If you sketch out these shifts right now, you'll see that—as long as the exchange rate floats—the result is a *depreciation of the dollar* against the pound.

Now let's see how the depreciation of the dollar affects the economy. With dollars now cheaper to foreigners, they will buy more U.S. goods, raising U.S. exports. At the same time, with foreign goods and services more expensive to Americans, U.S. imports will decrease. Both the increase in exports and the decrease in imports contribute to a rise in net exports, NX. This, in turn, increases aggregate expenditure.

Thus, as you can see, the expansionary monetary policy causes aggregate expenditures to rise in two ways: first, by increasing interest-sensitive spending, and second, by increasing net exports. As a result, equilibrium GDP rises by more—and monetary policy is more effective—when the effects on exchange rates are included.

The channels through which monetary policy works are summarized in the following schematic:

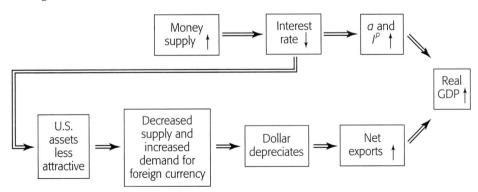

**Net Effect: GDP ↑ by more when the exchange rate's effect on net exports is included**

The top line shows the familiar effect on interest-sensitive spending: An increase in the money supply causes a drop in the interest rate, which increases autonomous consumption spending ($a$) and investment spending ($I^p$). The bottom line shows the *additional* effect on net exports through changes in the exchange rate—the effects we've been discussing.

The analysis of contractionary monetary policy is the same, but in reverse. A decrease in the money supply will not only decrease interest-sensitive spending, it will also cause the dollar to appreciate and net exports to drop. Thus, it will cause equilibrium GDP to fall by more than in earlier chapters, where we ignored the foreign exchange market.

The channel of monetary influence through exchange rates and the volume of trade is an important part of the full story of monetary policy in the United States. And in countries where exports are relatively large fractions of GDP—such as those of Europe—the trade channel is even more important. It is the main channel through which monetary policy affects the economy.

> *Monetary policy has a stronger effect when we include the impact on exchange rates and net exports, rather than just the impact on interest-sensitive consumption and investment spending.*

*Using the* 
# THEORY

Port of Seattle

**Trade deficit** The excess of a nation's imports over its exports during a given period.

**Trade surplus** The excess of a nation's exports over its imports during a given period.

# THE STUBBORN U.S. TRADE DEFICIT

The U.S. trade deficit is often in the news. But what, exactly, is it?

The trade deficit is the extent to which a country's imports exceed its exports:

$$\text{Trade deficit} = \text{imports} - \text{exports}.$$

On the other hand, when exports exceed imports, a nation has a trade surplus:

$$\text{Trade surplus} = \text{exports} - \text{imports}.$$

As you can see, the trade surplus is nothing more than a nation's net exports ($NX$). And when net exports are negative, we have a trade deficit.

The United States has had large trade deficits with the rest of the world since the early 1980s. In 1999, the trade deficit hit an all-time high of $268 billion. Simply put, Americans bought $268 billion more goods and services from other countries than their residents bought from the United States.

Why does the United States have a trade deficit with the rest of the world? A variety of explanations have been offered in the media, including the relatively low quality of U.S. goods (compared to, say, Japan), poor U.S. marketing savvy in selling to foreigners, and a greater degree of protectionism in foreign markets.

But economists believe that there is a much more important reason. In this section, we'll use what you've learned about floating exchange rates to show how the U.S. trade deficit arose and why it continues. To keep our analysis simple, we'll look at the U.S. trade deficit with just one country—Japan—but our results will hold more generally to the trade deficit with other countries as well.

Before we analyze the causes of the trade deficit, we need to do a little math. Let's begin by breaking down the total quantity of yen demanded by Americans ($D^¥$) into two components: the yen demanded to purchase Japanese goods and services (U.S. imports from Japan) and the yen demanded to buy Japanese assets:

$D^¥$ = U.S. imports from Japan + U.S. purchases of Japanese assets.

Similarly, we can divide the total quantity of yen supplied by the Japanese ($S^¥$) into two components: the yen exchanged for dollars to purchase American goods (U.S. exports to Japan), and the yen exchanged for dollars to purchase American assets like stocks, bonds, or real estate:

$S^¥$ = U.S. exports to Japan + Japanese purchases of U.S. assets.

As long as the yen floats against the dollar without government intervention—which it does during most periods—we know that the exchange rate will adjust until the quantities of yen supplied and demanded are equal, or $D^¥ = S^¥$. Substituting the foregoing breakdowns into this equation, we have

U.S. imports from Japan + U.S. purchases of Japanese assets

= U.S. exports to Japan + Japanese purchases of U.S. assets.

Now let's rearrange this equation—subtracting U.S. exports from both sides, and subtracting American purchases of Japanese assets from both sides, to get

U.S. imports from Japan − U.S. exports to Japan

= Japanese purchases of U.S. assets − U.S. purchases of Japanese assets.

The term on the left should look familiar: It is the U.S. trade deficit with Japan. And since a similar equation must hold for every country, we can generalize it this way:

U.S. imports from other countries − U.S. exports to other countries

= foreign purchases of U.S. assets − U.S. purchases of foreign assets.

But what is the expression on the right? It tells us the extent to which foreigners are buying more of our assets than we are buying of theirs. It is often called the **net capital inflow** into the United States, because when the residents of other countries buy U.S. assets, funds flow into the U.S. financial market, where they are made available to U.S. firms and the U.S. government. Thus, the equation we've derived—which must hold true when exchange rates float—can also be expressed as

**Net capital inflow** An inflow of funds equal to a nation's trade deficit.

**U.S. trade deficit = U.S. net capital inflow.**

Why have we bothered to derive this equation? Because it tells us two very important things about the U.S. trade deficit. First, it tells us how the trade deficit is *financed*. Think about it: If the United States is running a trade deficit with, say, Japan, it means that the Japanese are providing more goods and services to Americans—more automobiles, VCRs, memory chips, and other goods—than Americans are providing to them. The Japanese are not doing this out of kindness. They must be getting *something* in return for the extra goods we are getting, and the equation tells us just what that is: U.S. assets. This is one reason why the trade deficit concerns U.S. policy makers: It results in a transfer of wealth from Americans to foreign residents.

The second important insight provided by the equation is that a trade deficit can arise *because* of forces that cause a capital inflow. That is, if forces in the global economy make the right side of the equation positive, then the left side must be positive as well, and we will have a trade deficit. Indeed, economists believe this

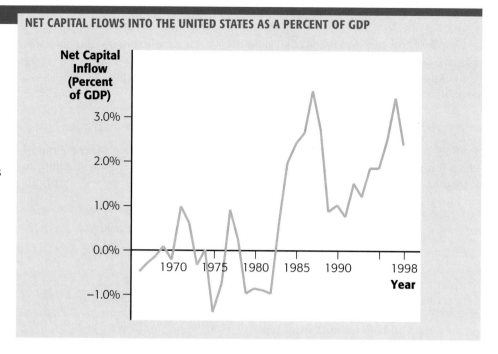

**FIGURE 10**

Beginning in the early 1980s, and continuing today, a massive capital inflow has caused a U.S. trade deficit. The capital inflow was originally caused by high U.S. interest rates relative to interest rates abroad. But in the 1990s and early 2000s, the capital inflow has been sustained by the favorable investment climate in the United States, and by the explosive growth of the Internet sector.

is just what has happened to the United States: that the U.S. trade deficit has been caused by the desire of foreigners to invest in the United States. The result was a massive capital inflow and trade deficit that arose in the early 1980s, as illustrated in Figure 10. That capital inflow was unprecedented in size and duration, and it reversed a long-standing pattern of ownership between the United States and other countries. For decades, American holdings of foreign assets far exceeded foreign holdings of U.S. assets. But the capital inflows of the 1980s changed that: By 1988, foreigners held about $500 billion more in U.S. assets than Americans held in foreign assets. Ten years later, the difference in asset holdings had tripled to about $1.5 trillion.

But how do the forces that create a capital inflow also *cause* a trade deficit? When foreigners start buying more of our assets than we are buying of theirs, the dollar will appreciate above the value it would have if there were no net capital inflow. This makes U.S. goods more expensive to foreigners, and foreign goods cheaper to Americans. Thus,

> *an increase in the desire of foreigners to invest in the United States contributes to an appreciation of the dollar. As a result, U.S. exports—which become more expensive for foreigners—decline. Imports—which become cheaper to Americans—increase. The result is a rise in the trade deficit.*

How can we explain the huge capital inflow that began in the 1980s, and has grown larger over the past decade? In the 1980s, an important part of the story was *a rise in U.S. interest rates relative to interest rates abroad*, which made U.S. assets more attractive to foreigners, and foreign assets less attractive to Americans. In the 1990s, however, U.S. interest rates were low relative to rates in other countries, yet the inflow continued. Why?

Even when U.S. interest rates are the same or lower than abroad, it seems that residents of other countries have a strong preference for holding American assets.

In part, this is because of a favorable investment climate. The United States is a stable country with a long history of protecting individual property rights. People know that if they buy American stocks or bonds, the U.S. government is very unlikely to confiscate these assets or suddenly impose punitive taxes when foreigners want to repatriate the funds to their home countries. The United States also has a stable legal and financial system, reassuring foreign investors that they will be treated fairly and on equal footing with U.S. citizens.

And in the late 1990s, there was another reason for the growing capital inflow: American companies took the lead in exploiting the Internet. New businesses—with the prospect of high future profits—sprang up daily, issuing shares of stock to anyone in the world who wanted to buy them. Thus, an asymmetry developed: The U.S. was offering assets that foreigners found attractive, while no foreign country was offering assets that Americans found nearly as attractive. As we entered the early 2000s, the attractiveness of U.S. stock was continuing to feed the U.S. capital inflow, with no end in sight.

Remember that, under floating exchange rates, the capital inflow equals the trade deficit. Thus, the story of the U.S. capital inflow of the 1980s and 1990s is also the story of the U.S. trade deficit:

> *We can trace the rise in the trade deficit during the 1980s and 1990s to two important sources: first, relatively high interest rates in the 1980s; and second, a long-held preference for American assets that grew stronger in the 1990s. Each of these contributed to a large capital inflow, a higher value for the dollar, and a trade deficit.*

# S U M M A R Y

When residents of two countries trade with one another, one party ordinarily makes use of the foreign exchange market to trade one national currency for another. In this market, suppliers of a currency interact with demanders to determine an exchange rate—the price of one currency in terms of another.

In the market for U.S. dollars and British pounds, for example, demanders are mostly Americans who wish to obtain pounds in order to buy goods and services from British firms, or to buy British assets. A higher dollar price for the pound will lead Americans to demand fewer pounds—the demand curve slopes downward. Changes in U.S. real GDP, the U.S. price level relative to the British price level, Americans' tastes for British goods, interest rates in the United States relative to Britain, or expectations regarding the exchange rate, can each cause the demand curve to shift.

Suppliers of pounds are mostly British residents who wish to buy American goods, services, or assets. A higher dollar price for the pound will lead Britons to supply more pounds— the supply curve slopes upward. The supply curve will shift in response to changes in British real GDP, prices in Britain relative to the United States, British tastes for U.S. goods, the British interest rate relative to the U.S. rate, and expectations regarding the exchange rate.

When the exchange rate floats, the equilibrium rate is determined where the supply and demand curves cross. If the equilibrium is disturbed by, say, a rightward shift of the demand curve, then the currency being demanded will appreciate—the exchange rate will rise. (The other country's currency will depreciate.) In a similar way, a rightward shift of the supply curve will cause the currency being supplied to depreciate.

In practice, each country's currency is traded in a variety of markets around the world. Currency traders, in search of profits, engage in arbitrage whenever the exchange rate differs between two markets. This activity—buying low and selling high—serves to eliminate any exchange rate differentials. A more complex form of arbitrage ensures that the direct and indirect prices of one currency in terms of another will be the same.

Governments often intervene in foreign exchange markets. Many countries manage their float—buying and selling their own currency to alter the exchange rate. Some countries fix their exchange rate to the dollar or the currency of a major trading partner. And in Europe, 11 national governments are on the way to eliminating their national currency, and replacing it with the Euro. Although these 11 nations may not yet be an optimum currency area, they are moving closer to one.

When a currency depreciates, its net exports rise—a positive spending shock. Monetary policy, in addition to its impact on interest-sensitive spending—also changes the exchange rate and net exports, adding to changes in output. This monetary policy is more effective in changing GDP when its effects on net exports are included.

## KEY TERMS

| | | | |
|---|---|---|---|
| foreign exchange market | floating exchange rate | bilateral arbitrage | optimum currency area |
| exchange rate | appreciation | triangular arbitrage | trade deficit |
| demand curve for foreign currency | depreciation | managed float | trade surplus |
| supply curve for foreign currency | purchasing power parity (PPP) theory | fixed exchange rate | net capital inflow |
| | arbitrage | devaluation | |
| | | foreign currency crisis | |

## REVIEW QUESTIONS

1. Why do Americans demand foreign currency? Why does the demand curve for foreign currency slope downward? What factors shift the demand curve for foreign currency to the right? What factors shift it to the left?

2. Why do foreigners supply foreign currency? Why does the supply of foreign currency curve slope upward? What factors shift the supply curve for foreign currency to the right? What factors shift it to the left?

3. Explain how an expected appreciation of a foreign currency can become a self-fulfilling prophecy.

4. What forces move exchange rates in the very short run? In the short run?

5. "A weak currency is a sign of a sick economy." True or false? Explain.

6. What is purchasing power parity? Why might exchange rates deviate from purchasing power parity?

7. Suppose the purchasing power parity exchange rate between the dollar and the pound is $1.50 per pound but, the actual exchange rate is $2 per pound. Explain how a trader could profit by buying a basket of goods in one country (which country?) and selling it in the other. How would such actions by traders affect the exchange rate?

8. What is a managed float and why would a government use it?

9. What is the difference between bilateral arbitrage and triangular arbitrage? What would be different about foreign exchange markets if neither type of arbitrage took place?

10. How does an appreciation of the dollar affect U.S. real GDP?

11. According to economists, what caused the U.S. trade deficit in the 1980s? Why does the trade deficit persist?

## PROBLEMS AND EXERCISES

1. Do the following events cause the dollar to appreciate against the French franc or to depreciate?
   a. Health experts discover that red wine, especially French red wine, lowers cholesterol.
   b. France's GDP falls.
   c. The United States experiences a higher inflation rate than France does.
   d. The United States runs a large budget deficit.

2. Let the demand for British pounds and the supply of British pounds be described by the following equations:

$$\text{Demand for pounds} = 10 - 2e$$
$$\text{Supply of pounds} = 4 + 3e,$$

   where the quantities are in millions of pounds and $e$ is dollars per pound.
   a. Find the equilibrium exchange rate.

   b. Suppose the U.S. government intervenes in the foreign currency market and uses U.S. dollars to buy 2 million pounds. What happens to the exchange rate? Why might the U.S. government do this?

3. Suppose the following are the exchange rates among the U.S. dollar, the Mexican peso, and the Euro:

   $$\text{Dollars per peso} = 0.2.$$
   $$\text{Dollars per euro} = 0.5.$$
   $$\text{Euros per peso} = 0.3.$$

   Is there an opportunity for triangular arbitrage? If so, how would it work?

4. Suppose the United States and Mexico are each other's sole trading partners. The Fed, afraid that the economy is about to overheat, decreases the U.S. money supply.

a. Will the dollar appreciate or depreciate against the Mexican peso? Illustrate with a diagram of the dollar–peso foreign exchange market.

b. What will happen to equilibrium GDP in the United States?

c. How would your analyses in (a) and (b) change if, at the same time that the Fed was increasing the U.S. interest rate, the Mexican central bank increased the Mexican interest rate by an equivalent amount?

## CHALLENGE QUESTIONS

1. It is often stated that the U.S. trade deficit with Japan results from Japanese trade barriers against U.S. goods.

   a. Suppose that Japan and the U.S. trade goods but not assets. Show—with a diagram of the dollar–yen market—that a trade deficit is impossible. (*Hint:* With no trading in assets, the quantity of yen demanded at each exchange rate is equal in value to U.S. imports, and the quantity of yen supplied at each exchange rate is equal in value to U.S. exports.)

   b. In the diagram, illustrate the impact of a reduction in Japanese trade barriers. Would the dollar appreciate or depreciate against the yen? What would be the impact on U.S. net exports?

   c. Now suppose that the United States and Japan also trade assets, but that the Japanese buy more U.S. assets than we buy of theirs. Could the elimination of Japanese trade barriers wipe out the U.S. trade deficit with Japan? Why, or why not? (*Hint:* What is the relationship between the U.S. trade deficit and U.S. net capital inflow?)

2. Suppose that the U.S. government raises spending without increasing taxes. Will there be any effects on the foreign exchange market? (*Hint:* What does this policy do to U.S. interest rates?) When we take the foreign exchange market and net exports into account, will this policy be more effective or less effective in changing equilibrium GDP in the short run?

## EXPERIENTIAL EXERCISES

1. Trade among European nations will be bolstered by the introduction of the euro—a common European currency. Not surprisingly, there are special Web pages devoted to the euro. The official European Union Web site—*http://europa.eu.int/euro/html/entry.html*—is one of them. Go to this Web page to review the latest developments.

2. The latest data on exchange rates appear in the Currency Trading column in the *Wall Street Journal*. You can find it in the Money & Investing section. Try tracking a particular currency over the course of several weeks. Has the dollar been appreciating or depreciating relative to that currency? Try to explain the behavior of the exchange rate based on what you've learned in this chapter.

# Using All the
# THEORY

## THE STOCK MARKET AND THE MACROECONOMY

In December 1996, Alan Greenspan—the chair of the Federal Reserve Board—uttered two sentences that caught the world's attention. Speaking to a Washington research organization, he asked, "How do we know when irrational exuberance has unduly escalated asset values which then become the subject of unexpected and prolonged contractions . . . ? And how do we factor that assessment into monetary policy?"

Greenspan was referring to the rapid rise in stock prices that had occurred over the previous several years. By one broad measure, the average stock's price had doubled over this period—a very rapid rise by historical standards. But when the markets opened for trading at 9:30 A.M. on the morning after Greenspan's speech, stock prices dropped by about 2 percent almost immediately.

That evening, on *Larry King Live* and *ABC News Nightline* and *CNN Moneyline,* pundits debated the meaning and wisdom of Greenspan's remarks. Everyone agreed that the purpose of Greenspan's remarks was to bring down stock prices, and that he had succeeded somewhat. But there were two opposing reactions to what the Fed chair had done. One group of commentators believed that Greenspan was making a mistake, that government officials have no business deciding when stock prices are too high or too low, and should leave the market alone. The other group believed that stock prices had, indeed, risen too high and too fast, and that Greenspan was entirely justified in trying to bring them down.

The debate that took place at the end of December 1996—and continued for the next several years—raises a number of questions. *Why* does the stock market matter? What is its role in the economy? Why should public officials worry when stock prices are too high? And why should two little words—"irrational exuberance"—uttered by one man rock the stock market and drive down share prices? In this chapter—after providing some basic background about the stock market—we'll answer all these questions.

## BASIC BACKGROUND

Let's start with the most basic question of all: What is a share of stock?

First, a share of stock is a private financial asset, like a corporate bond. In fact, stocks and corporate bonds are alike in two ways. Both are issued by corporations to raise funds for investment projects, and both offer future payments to their owners.

But there is also an important difference between these two types of assets. When a corporation issues a bond, it is *borrowing* funds; the bond is just a promise to pay back the loan. A share of stock, by contrast, is a share of *ownership* in a corporation. When a firm issues new shares of stock, those who pay for those shares provide the firm with new funds, and in return, the firm owes them—at some future date or dates—a share of the firm's profits.

When a firm issues new shares of stock—in what is called a *public offering*—the sale of stock generates funds for the firm. Once the newly issued shares are sold, however, the buyer is free to sell them to someone else. Indeed, virtually all of the shares traded in the stock market are previously issued shares, and this trading does not involve the firm that issued the stock.

But a firm is still *concerned* about the price of its previously issued shares for two reasons. First, the firm's owners—its stockholders—want high share prices because that is the price they can sell at. A management team that ignores the desires of stockholders for too long might find itself replaced by other managers who will pay more attention.

Moreover, the price of previously issued shares has an important impact on firms that are planning new public offerings. That's because previously issued shares are perfect substitutes for the firm's new shares, so the firm cannot expect to receive a higher price for its new shares than the going price on its old shares. The higher the price for previously issued shares, the higher the price the firm will receive for *new* shares, and the more funds it will obtain from any given public offering.

## WHY DO PEOPLE HOLD STOCK?

Stock ownership in the United States is growing rapidly. In 1983, only 19 percent of Americans owned shares of stock either directly or through mutual funds—companies that invest in a variety of stocks for their clients. By early 2000, the percentage of Americans who owned stock in these two ways had increased dramatically, to 48 percent. If we included stocks in employer-managed retirement accounts, the percentage of Americans with a stake in the stock market would be much higher. And the stakes are significant. By early 2000, the average U.S. household held more wealth in the stock market than in real estate, including the value of their own home.

Why do so many individuals choose to hold their wealth in stocks? You already know part of the answer: When you own a share of stock, you own part of the corporation. The fraction of the corporation that you own is equal to the fraction of the company's total stock that you own. For example, in April 2000, there were 497,476,000 shares outstanding in Southwest Airlines corporation (no relation to the publisher of this book). If you owned 10,000 shares of Southwest stock, then you owned 10,000/497,476,000 = 0.00002, or about two-thousandths of a percent of the company. That means that you are, in a sense, entitled to two-thousandths of a percent of the firm's after-tax profits.

In practice, however, most firms do not pay out *all* of their profit to shareholders. Instead, some is kept as *retained earnings*, for later use by the firm. The part of profit that is distributed to shareholders is called *dividends*. A firm's dividend payments benefit stockholders in much the same way that interest payments benefit bondholders, providing a source of steady income. Of course, as part owner of a firm, you are part owner of any retained earnings as well, even if you will not benefit from them until later.

Aside from dividends, a second—and usually more important—reason that people hold stocks is that they hope to enjoy *capital gains*. A capital gain is the return someone gets when they sell an asset at a higher price than they paid for it. For example, if you buy shares of Southwest at $15 per share, and later sell them at $19 per share, your capital gain is $4 per share. This is in addition to any dividends you earned while you owned the stock.

Some stocks pay no dividends at all, because the management believes that stockholders are best served by reinvesting all profits within the firm so that *future* profits will be even higher. The idea is to increase the value of the stock, and create capital gains for the shareholders when the stock is finally sold. New or fast-growing companies—such as Yahoo, America Online, and Microsoft—typically pay no dividends at all.

Over the past century, corporate stocks have generally been a good investment. Holding stocks was especially rewarding during the 1990s, as you'll see in the next section.

## TRACKING THE STOCK MARKET

In the United States, financial markets are so important that stock and bond prices are monitored on a continuous basis. If you wish to know the value of a stock, you can find out instantly by checking with a broker or logging onto a Web site (such as Yahoo.com, Morningstar.com, or thomsoninvest.com). In addition, stock prices and other information are reported daily in local newspapers and in specialized financial publications such as the *Wall Street Journal* and the *Financial Times*.

In addition to monitoring individual stocks, the media keep a close watch on many stock market indices or averages. These averages track movements in stock prices as a whole, or movements in particular types of stocks. The oldest and most popular average is the *Dow Jones Industrial Average (DJIA)*, which tracks the prices of 30 of the largest companies in the United States, including AT&T, IBM, and Wal-Mart. Another popular average is the much broader *Standard & Poor's 500 (S&P 500)*, which tracks stock prices of 500 corporations chosen to represent all stocks in the market. Finally, the *NASDAQ* index tracks share prices of about 5,000 mostly newer companies whose shares are traded on the Nasdaq stock exchange—an association of stockbrokers who execute trades electronically. The companies in the NASDAQ include most of the new high-tech companies that are closely connected to the Internet sector.

Often, the three stock market averages will rise and fall at the same time, sometimes by the same percentage. That's because many of the shocks that hit the stock market affect most share prices *together*. But the indices can and do behave differently—sometimes very differently. For example, in early 2000, Internet stocks fluctuated wildly from day to day, as new information changed public opinion about the future of industry. There were many days on which the NASDAQ rose substantially while the Dow and the Standard & Poor's 500 fell, and vice versa.

Table 1 shows how the three averages performed over different lengths of time ending in December 31, 1999. The entries in the table tell us the average annual increase in each index over the period. For example, the entry 15.3 percent in the table (be sure you can find it) tells us that—over the period January 1, 1990 to December 31, 1999—the S&P 500 rose an average of 15.3 percent per year.

As you can see, while the S&P 500 and the DJIA have moved in tandem, NASDAQ has moved upward much more rapidly over the decade. You can also see that the 1990s were a good decade for stocks. Someone who invested $10,000 in a typical group of S&P 500 stocks on January 1, 1990 would have been able to

| | | Average Annual Increase, | Average Annual Increase, | Average Annual Increase, | TABLE 1 |
| | Increase, 1 Year Ending December 31, 1999 | 3 Years Ending December 31, 1999 | 5 Years Ending December 31, 1999 | 10 Years Ending December 31, 1999 | THE PERFORMANCE OF THREE STOCK MARKET INDEXES |
| Index | | | | | |
|---|---|---|---|---|---|
| Dow Jones Industrial Average | 25.2% | 21.3% | 24.6% | 15.4% | |
| Standard & Poor's 500 | 19.5% | 25.6% | 26.2% | 15.3% | |
| NASDAQ | 85.6% | 46.6% | 40.2% | 24.5% | |

*Source:* Dow Jones Web site (*http://averages.dowjones.com/dja_fact.html*), accessed April 17, 2000, and author's calculations.

sell them for $41,523 on December 31, 1999. And someone who had invested $10,000 in a typical collection of NASDAQ stocks would have $89,473 at the end of the period.

## EXPLAINING STOCK PRICES

Why do stock prices change? And why do they change so often?

We can answer these questions—as we answer most questions about the economy—by using our four-step process.

### KEY STEP #1: CHARACTERIZE THE MARKET

The price of a share of stock—like any other price—is determined in a market. But which market? Initially, we'll be focusing on price changes for shares of a particular stock, so the most useful way to organize our thinking is to look at the market for a single corporation's shares. That is, we'll view the "stock market" as a collection of *individual* markets, one for shares of stock in America Online, another for shares in Kmart, another for shares in Starbucks, and so on.

Further, we'll characterize the market for a company's shares as perfectly competitive. Indeed, markets for shares *do* satisfy the three requirements of perfect competition rather closely. There are many buyers and sellers (so many that no one of them can do much to change the market price of the stock).[1] There is a standardized product (it makes no difference to the buyer whether her Kmart shares are being sold to her by Smith or by Jones). And there is easy entry (virtually anyone with funds to invest can open up a brokerage account and buy or sell any publicly traded stock).

In sum,

 Characterize the Market

> *we'll view the stock market as a collection of individual, perfectly competitive markets for particular corporations' shares.*

---

[1]    In some cases, a single buyer or seller holds such a large fraction of a company's shares that his or her decisions have a significant impact on market price. But these exceptions are rare for publicly traded shares.

# KEY STEP #2: IDENTIFY THE GOALS AND CONSTRAINTS

In each market for shares, the buyers and sellers are both individuals and institutions (money market funds, insurance companies, and retirement funds). In either case, a high rate of return is a primary goal. Since most of the return on stocks comes from capital gains, we can state this goal very simply: Buyers will want to buy and hold shares in a company when they believe the stock price will rise, and sell shares in a company when they believe the price will fall.

In addition, stockholders are concerned about risk. All else equal, most of us would prefer to hold financial assets with relatively stable prices, rather than those whose prices fluctuate widely from day to day or month to month. Thus, when people choose *between* stocks and other financial assets, and when they choose *which* companies' shares to hold, they will look at risk as well as the expected rise in price.

In many cases, there is a trade-off between risk and return: The stocks that offer the highest expected return are also subject to the greatest risk. (If that weren't the case, few people would want to hold the riskier stocks.) Therefore, a part of every stockholder's goal is to strike the right balance between risk and return, based on their own attitudes toward risk.

What about constraints? Since stock holding is one way of holding wealth, individuals and institutions are constrained by the amount of wealth at their disposal. For a household, the constraint is the household's net worth. For a mutual fund, the constraint is the total amount of funds that households have contributed.

> *Stockholders are concerned about both the rate of return and the risk associated with stocks. In practice, they try to allocate their total wealth among a collection of assets—including stocks—that strikes the right balance between risk and return.*

# KEY STEP #3: FIND THE EQUILIBRIUM

Like all prices in competitive markets, stock prices are determined by supply and demand. However, in stock markets, our supply and demand curves require careful interpretations.

Figure 1 presents a supply and demand diagram for the shares of Southwest Airlines. Unlike most supply curves you've studied in this book—which show the quantity of something that suppliers want to *sell* over a given period of time—the supply curve in Figure 1 is somewhat different. It tells us the quantity of shares of Southwest stock *in existence* at any moment in time. This is the number of shares that people are *actually* holding.

On any given day, the number of Southwest shares in existence is just the number that the firm has issued previously. Therefore, no matter what happens to the price of the stock, the number of shares remains unchanged, and so does the quantity supplied. This is why the supply curve in the figure is a vertical line at 497 million: Over the time period we're analyzing, there are 497 million shares in existence regardless of the price.

Now, just because 497 million shares of Southwest stock exist, that does not mean that this is the number of shares that people *want* to hold. The desire to hold Southwest shares is given by the downward-sloping demand curve. As you can see, all else equal, the lower the price of the stock, the more shares of Southwest that people will want to hold. Why is this?

First, people have different expectations about the firm's future profits. Some may believe that Southwest will continue to grow as it has in the past. Others will think it is poised for a spurt of higher growth, while still others—more pessimistic—

**FIGURE 1**

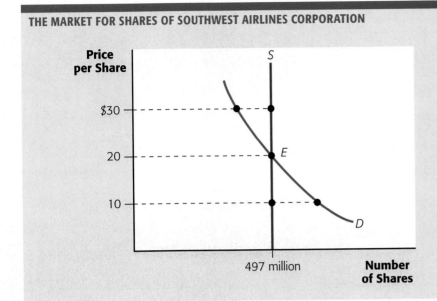

**THE MARKET FOR SHARES OF SOUTHWEST AIRLINES CORPORATION**

The supply curve shows the number of shares of Southwest Airlines stock people *are* holding. The curve is vertical at the number of shares outstanding—which was 497 million in early 2000. The demand curve tells us how many shares people *want* to hold. It slopes downward—the lower the price, the more shares people want to hold. At any price other than the equilibrium price of $20, there would be either an excess supply or an excess demand for shares.

may believe that Southwest's best days are behind it. There will also be different opinions about the *risk* of those future profits. Thus, at any given moment, with an array of opinions about the company's future, each person will have a different price in mind that would make the stock an attractive buy. As the price per share falls, more and more people will find the stock to be a bargain, and want to hold it. This is what the downward-sloping demand curve tells us.

In the figure, you can see that at any price other than $20 per share, the number of shares people *are* holding (on the supply curve) will differ from the number they *want* to hold (on the demand curve). For example, at a price of $10 per share, people would want to hold more shares than they are currently holding. Many would try to buy the stock, and the price would be bid up. At $30 per share, the opposite occurs: People find themselves holding more shares than they want to hold, and they will try to get rid of the excess by selling them. The sudden sales would cause the price to drop. Only at the *equilibrium price* of $20—where the supply and demand curves intersect—are people satisfied holding the number of shares they are *actually* holding.

Stocks achieve their equilibrium prices almost instantly. There are so many stock traders—both individuals and professional fund managers—poised at their computers, ready to buy or sell a particular firm's shares at a moment's notice, that any excess supply or excess demand will cause the price to move within seconds. Thus, we can have confidence that the price of a share at any time is the equilibrium price.

But why do stock prices *change* so often? To answer that question, we need Key Step #4.

## KEY STEP #4: WHAT HAPPENS WHEN THINGS CHANGE?

 What Happens When Things Change?

The *supply* curve for a corporation's shares, like the one in Figure 1, shifts rightward whenever there is a public offering. Can this explain changes in share prices? Not really. Public offerings occur only occasionally and with great fanfare. Moreover, most public offerings by existing companies are for a relatively small number of shares. They shift the supply curve only a little, and therefore have little impact on the

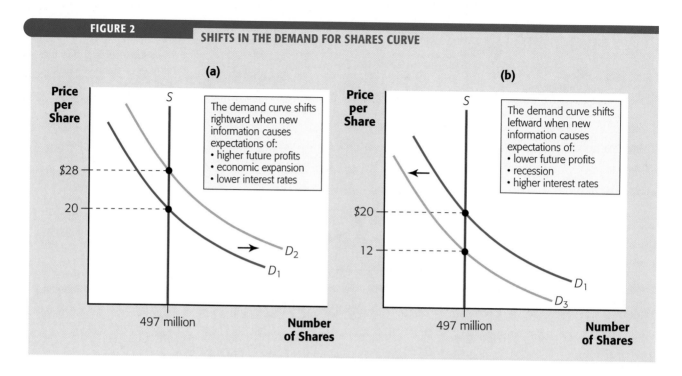

**FIGURE 2**

**SHIFTS IN THE DEMAND FOR SHARES CURVE**

**(a)**

Price per Share

$28

20

$S$

The demand curve shifts rightward when new information causes expectations of:
• higher future profits
• economic expansion
• lower interest rates

$D_2$

$D_1$

497 million

**Number of Shares**

**(b)**

Price per Share

$S$

The demand curve shifts leftward when new information causes expectations of:
• lower future profits
• recession
• higher interest rates

$20

12

$D_1$

$D_3$

497 million

**Number of Shares**

market price of the stock. Thus, the changes in equilibrium prices we observe for most stocks are *not* caused by shifts of the supply curve.

That leaves only one explanation: shifts in *demand*.

> *The changes we observe in a stock's price—over a few minutes, a few days, or a few years—are virtually always caused by shifts in the demand curve.*

Panel (a) of Figure 2 shows how a rightward shift of the demand curve for shares of Southwest Airlines could cause the equilibrium price to rise to $28 per share. Indeed, on rare occasions, the demand curve for a firm's shares has shifted so far rightward in a single day that the share price doubled or even tripled.

But what causes these sudden changes in demand for a share of stock?

In almost all cases, it is one or more of the following three factors:

1. *Changes in expected future profits of the firm.* At any given time, people have an idea about the expected profits of every firm. But these ideas can change as new information becomes available. The new information can pertain to a scientific discovery, a corporate takeover or merger with another company, or a new government policy. Even information that suggests that one of these events *might* occur can change the attractiveness of stocks. After all, a stock in a company that has a 50 percent chance of making huge profits from a new invention is more attractive than a stock that has only a 20 percent chance of such profits.

New information can be positive—shifting the demand curve rightward and increasing the price of the stock. But it can also be negative, shifting the demand curve leftward. A dramatic example of the latter occurred on March 14, 2000. On that day, President Clinton and British Prime Minister Blair issued a joint statement that they would work to make data from the human genome publicly available. Some observers interpreted the statement to indicate a possible tilt in public policy. Perhaps the government was suggesting that it would work to eliminate or shorten the duration of gene-based patents, vastly reducing the future profits of biomedical research companies that held those patents. Within minutes of the statement, demand curves for shares of biotech companies shifted leftward, and share prices plummeted—some by as much as 30 percent.

> *Any new information that* increases *expectations of firms' future profits—including announcements of new scientific discoveries, business developments, or changes in government policy—will shift the demand curves of the affected stocks rightward. New information that* decreases *expectations of future profits will shift the demand curves leftward.*

2. *Macroeconomic fluctuations.* When the economy is expanding, and real GDP is rising, firms *in general* tend to earn higher profits, and these profits are less risky. By contrast, in a recession, sales and profits decrease. For this reason,

> *any news that suggests the economy will enter an expansion, or that an expansion will continue, will shift the demand curves for most stocks rightward. Any news that suggests an economic slowdown or a coming recession shifts the demand curves for most stocks leftward.*

3. *Changes in the interest rate.* Stocks are not the only way that people can hold their wealth. They can also hold money and—more importantly—they can hold interest-earning assets like certificates of deposit or bonds. If the interest rate rises, these other assets become more attractive, and many people will want to shift their wealth *out* of stocks so they can buy them. Thus,

> *a rise in the interest rate in the economy will shift the demand curves for most stocks to the left. Similarly, a drop in the interest rate will shift the demand curves for most stocks to the right.*[2]

Even *expectations* of a future interest rate change can shift demand curves for stocks. This can create some rather convoluted—but logical—explanations for movements in stock prices. For example, suppose that a report comes out suggesting that real GDP is growing very rapidly. All else equal, this makes stocks more attractive. But . . . all else may *not* remain equal. In fact, you may surmise that the U.S. Federal Reserve and its influential chair—currently Alan Greenspan—want to prevent inflation at almost any cost. You might then *anticipate* that the Fed—concerned about the economy overheating—will raise interest rates in the near future to slow down the growth in real GDP. You also know that—if the interest rate *does* rise—stock prices will fall, for the reasons we've just discussed. What should you do? *Dump your stocks now,* to avoid a capital loss later. Since you and many others will no doubt have access to the same information, and feel the same way, the announcement of rapid economic growth could lead—almost immediately—to a *decrease* in stock prices.

Similarly, bad news about economic growth—if it leads to an expected decrease in interest rates—can cause stock prices to rise.

> *News that causes people to anticipate a rise in the interest rate will shift the demand curves for stocks leftward. Similarly, news that suggests a future drop in the interest rate will shift the demand curves for stocks rightward.*

---

2    If you've studied *microeconomics,* you've learned another way to view the impact of interest rate changes on stock prices: Higher interest rates reduce the *present value* of any given stream of future profits.

Panels (a) and (b) of Figure 2 summarize the different forces that cause the demand curve for a stock to shift rightward or leftward.

## THE STOCK MARKET AND THE MACROECONOMY

As you can see in Figure 3, there is a *two-way* relationship between the stock market and the economy. That is, the performance of the stock market affects the performance of the economy, and vice versa. In the next two sections of this chapter, we'll look at this two-way relationship. Let's start with the impact of the stock market on the economy, as illustrated by the upper arrow in the figure.

### HOW THE STOCK MARKET AFFECTS THE ECONOMY

On October 19, 1987, there was a dramatic drop in the stock market. That day, the Dow Jones Industrial Average fell by 508 points—a drop of 23 percent—and about $500 billion in household wealth disappeared. That same evening, as President Reagan boarded his helicopter, a breathless Sam Donaldson of ABC News thrust a microphone in front of him and asked, "Mr. President, are you concerned about the 500-point drop in the Dow?" As Reagan entered his helicopter, he smiled calmly and replied, "Why, no, Sam. I don't own any stocks."

It was a curious exchange. Reagan was probably kidding—perhaps trying to calm a worried nation with his trademark humor. Or perhaps he was annoyed at a frantic reporter invading his personal space. Or he might have been caught off guard and said the first thing that popped into his head.

Whatever Reagan's intent, the statement was startling because, in fact, the stock market *does* matter to all Americans, whether they own stocks or not. As you are about to see, the ups and downs of stock prices—if they are big enough and sustained enough—can cause ups and downs in the overall economy.

**The Wealth Effect.** To understand how the market affects the economy, let's run through the following mental experiment: We'll suppose that, for *some* reason (we'll discuss specific reasons later), stock prices rise. As a result, those who own stock will feel wealthier. In fact, they *are* wealthier. After all, just as you measure the value of your house by the price at which you could sell it, the same is true of your financial assets, like stocks. When stock prices rise, so does household wealth.

**FIGURE 3**

**THE TWO-WAY RELATIONSHIP BETWEEN THE STOCK MARKET AND THE ECONOMY**

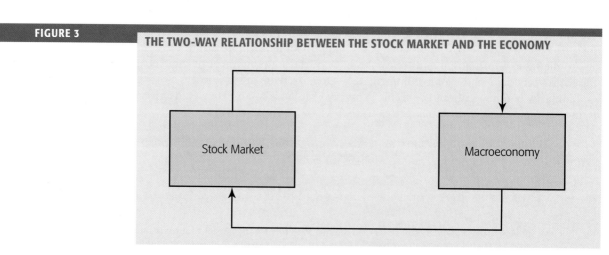

What do households do when their wealth increases? Typically, they increase their spending. In our short-run macro model, we would classify this is an increase in *autonomous consumption*—an increase in consumption spending at *any* level of disposable income.

The link between stock prices and consumer spending is an important one, so economists have given it a name: the *wealth effect*. And the wealth effect works in both directions: Just as an increase in stock prices increases autonomous consumption, so will a drop in stock prices—which decreases household wealth—cause autonomous consumption spending to fall.

More generally,

> *the wealth effect tells us that autonomous consumption spending tends to move in the same direction as stock prices. When stock prices rise, autonomous consumption spending rises; when stock prices fall, autonomous consumption spending falls with it.*

**The Wealth Effect and Equilibrium GDP.** As you learned when you studied the short-run macroeconomic model, autonomous consumption is a component of total spending. And an increase in total spending tends to increase equilibrium real GDP, as shown in panel (a) of Figure 4. There, when stock prices rise, the increase in real wealth causes the aggregate expenditure line to shift upward, and increases the economy's equilibrium GDP from $Y_1$ to $Y_2$.

Panel (b) of Figure 4 shows a more complete way to view the impact of rising stock prices. In this panel, the increase in equilibrium GDP at any given price level is shown as a rightward shift in the economy's $AD$ curve. And—in the absence of

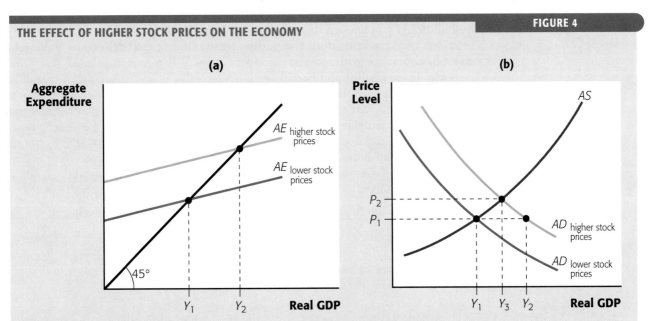

**THE EFFECT OF HIGHER STOCK PRICES ON THE ECONOMY**

**FIGURE 4**

**(a)**

**(b)**

Higher stock prices have a wealth effect on spending, increasing consumption spending at any level of real GDP. In panel (a), the wealth effect of higher stock prices shifts the aggregate expenditure line upward, raising equilibrium GDP from $Y_1$ to $Y_2$. Panel (b) shows a more complete way of illustrating the wealth effect: Higher stock prices shift the aggregate demand curve rightward, increasing both equilibrium real GDP and the price level.

any change in government policy—this shift of the *AD* curve will increase both equilibrium GDP (to $Y_3$) and the price level (to $P_2$). (Why does equilibrium GDP increase by less in panel (b) than in panel (a)?)

We can summarize the logic of the wealth effect as follows:

In words:

> *Changes in stock prices—through the wealth effect—cause both equilibrium GDP and the price level to move in the same direction. That is, an increase in stock prices will raise equilibrium GDP and the price level, while a decrease in stock prices will decrease both equilibrium GDP and the price level.*

How important is the wealth effect? Economic research shows that the *marginal propensity to consume out of wealth*—the change in consumption spending for each one-dollar rise in wealth—is between 0.03 and 0.05. In other words, when household wealth rises by a dollar, all else remaining the same, consumption spending tends to rise by between 3 and 5 cents. Moreover, recent research suggests that virtually *all* of the increase in consumption comes rather quickly—within one quarter (3 months) after the quarter in which stock prices rise.[3] Let's translate this into some practical numbers.

First, as a rule of thumb, a 100-point rise in the DJIA—which generally means a rise in stock prices in general—causes household wealth to rise by about $100 billion. This rise in household wealth, we've now learned, will increase autonomous consumption spending by between $3 billion and $5 billion—we'll say $4 billion. As you learned several chapters ago, the multiplier in the real world—after we take account of all the automatic stabilizers that reduce its value—is equal to about 1.5, with most of its impact in the first nine months to a year after a shock. Thus, a 100-point rise in the DJIA, which causes consumption spending to rise by about $4 billion, will cause real GDP to increase by about $4 billion × 1.5 = $6 billion. Extrapolating from these results, a 6,000- or so point rise in the Dow—such as we saw in the second half of the 1990s—would generate about $240 billion in additional consumption spending, and drive up real GDP by about $360 billion—an increase of about 4 percent. This is in addition to the normal rise in real GDP that would be occurring anyway, as income grows and spending grows with it. Thus,

> *rapid increases in stock prices—such as those that have occurred over the past five years—can cause significant positive demand shocks to the economy, shocks that policy makers cannot ignore. Similarly, rapid decreases in stock prices can cause significant negative demand shocks to the economy, which would be a major concern for policy makers.*

---

[3]    Sydney Ludvigson and Charles Steindel, "How Important Is the Stock Market Effect on Consumption?" New York Federal Reserve Bank *Policy Review*, July 1999. (Also available at *http://www.ny.frb. org/rmaghome/econ_pol/799lud.htm.*)

## HOW THE ECONOMY AFFECTS THE STOCK MARKET

Now that we've explored how the stock market affects the economy, let's look at the other side of the two-way relationship: how the economy affects stock prices.

Actually, many different types of changes in the overall economy can affect the stock market. Some—like the revolution in telecommunications that took place in the 1990s—are rare, happening once or twice a century. Others—like the impact of macroeconomic fluctuations—happen much more frequently. In this section, we'll focus on the more frequent scenario: how the stock market responds as the economy goes through expansions and recessions in the short run.

Let's start by looking at the typical expansion, in which real GDP rises rapidly over several years. In the typical expansion, profits will rise along with GDP. Higher profits are themselves enough to make stocks look more attractive. But the process is further helped by another factor: an improvement in investor psychology. In an expansion, not only are corporate profits rising, but also the unemployment rate falls, and household incomes rise. Memories of the last recession are dim, and it looks as if the economy will continue to grow and grow, perhaps forever. This optimistic outlook raises estimates of future profits—sometimes dramatically. The demand curves for stocks will shift rightward, and stock prices will rise.

We can summarize the impact of an expansion on the market as follows:

**In an Expansion:**

Of course, the process also works in reverse. When a recession strikes, corporate profits drop, unemployment rises, and the economy begins to look bleak. Stockholders turn pessimistic, and expect lower profits in the future. The demand curves for stocks shift leftward, driving stock prices down:

**In a Recession:**

In sum,

> *in the typical expansion, higher profits and stockholder optimism cause stock prices to rise. In the typical recession, lower profits and stockholder pessimism cause stock prices to fall.*

## WHAT HAPPENS WHEN THINGS CHANGE?

Now that you understand how stock prices affect the overall economy, and how the economy can affect stock prices—it's time to apply Key Step #4 one more time. But this time, we'll apply it very broadly: We'll observe how *both* the stock market and the macroeconomy are affected when *something* changes.

But . . . *what* changes?

**FIGURE 5**

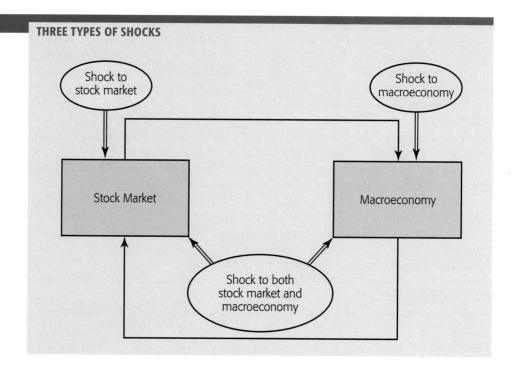

**THREE TYPES OF SHOCKS**

Figure 5 illustrates three different types of changes we might explore. A change might have most of its initial impact on the overall economy, rather than the stock market. For example, a change in government spending or taxes—with an unchanged interest rate target by the Fed—would initially affect real GDP, rather than the stock market. Ultimately, stock prices would be affected, but primarily *through* the change in real GDP

Alternatively, there might be a shock that initially affects the stock market. An example would be a change in the duration of patent protection for intellectual property, which would change the expected profits of firms and shift the demand curves for stocks.

Finally, a shock could have powerful, initial impacts on *both* the stock market *and* the overall economy. An example is the technological revolution of the late 1990s and early 2000s, which has rocked both the economy and the stock market.

In the next section, we'll explore the consequences of an initial shock to the *economy*. Then, we'll turn our attention to a shock that simultaneously hits the market and the economy, as occurred during the 1990s. Finally, in the end-of-chapter questions, you'll be asked to address the remaining case: a shock that initially hits just the stock market.

## A SHOCK TO THE ECONOMY

Imagine that new legislation greatly increases government purchases—say, to equip public schools with more sophisticated telecommunications equipment, or to increase the strength of our armed forces. This spending shock—and increase in government purchases—will have its primary initial impact on the overall economy, rather than the stock market. Let's suppose, too, that the Fed maintains its interest rate target, so there is no direct impact on the stock market from changes in the interest rate. What will happen?

As you've learned in your study of macroeconomics, the rise in government purchases will first increase real GDP through the expenditure multiplier:

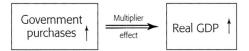

In previous chapters, the multiplier process was a simple one: Increases in output and income cause increases in consumption, which cause further increases in output and income and then further increases in consumption, and so on. But now, there is a *new* contributor to the multiplier process: the stock market.

First, remember that increases in real GDP cause increases in corporate profits. This, in turn, leads to investor optimism about *future* profits, shifting the demand curves for stocks rightward, and increasing the average price of stocks.

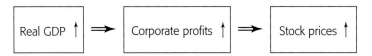

But the story doesn't end there. The increase in stock prices will—through the wealth effect—cause an increase in autonomous consumption spending. Note that this is *in addition* to the increase in consumption spending caused by the normal multiplier process. Indeed, the increase in autonomous consumption spending caused by the wealth effect sets off its *own* multiplier process, further increasing real GDP:

Now, look back at the three cause-and-effect chains just presented. You can see that an increase in government purchases will cause a *larger* rise in real GDP when we include the effects of the stock market. Another way of saying this is that,

> *when we include the effects of the stock market, the expenditure multiplier is larger. An increase in spending that increases real GDP will also cause stock prices to rise, causing still greater increases in real GDP. Similarly, a decrease in spending that causes real GDP to fall will also cause stock prices to fall, causing still greater decreases in real GDP.*

When you first learned about the multiplier, you learned about automatic stabilizers—features of the economy, such as the income tax or unemployment insurance payments, that make the expenditure multiplier smaller, and thus help to stabilize real GDP. Now you can see that the normal behavior of the stock market—which makes the expenditure multiplier larger—works as an *automatic destabilizer*. This is one reason why stock prices are so carefully watched by policy makers, and matter for everyone—whether they own stocks themselves or not.

## A SHOCK TO THE ECONOMY *AND* THE STOCK MARKET: THE 1990s

The 1990s—especially the second half of the 1990s—saw a dramatic rise in stock prices. Both the Dow Jones Industrial Average and the Standard & Poor's 500 more than quadrupled over the period, and the NASDAQ increased almost ninefold.

The 1990s were also a period of rapid expansion, especially the period from 1995 to 1999, in which economic growth averaged 4.2 percent per year—much faster than in previous decades.

In part, the economic expansion and the rise in stock prices were reinforcing: each contributed to the other, as we've seen in this chapter. But the expansion and the climb in stocks were *initiated* by a common shock: a technological revolution, led by the Internet.

The Internet had a direct impact on the stock market through its effect on expected future profits of U.S. firms. In particular, stockholders (and potential stockholders) believed that the new technology would enable firms to produce goods and services at much lower costs than before, and that this reduction in costs would translate into an increase in profit. The increase in expected future profits translated into a rightward shift of the demand curve for stocks at virtually any firm that had the potential to exploit the new technology, or help other firms exploit it.

For example, during this period, AT&T positioned itself to be a major supplier of information and voice communication using the Internet and other new technologies. As a result, the demand curve for AT&T stock shifted rightward—enough to drive the price of AT&T stock from $28 per share in early 1997 to $58 by the end of 1999.

At the same time, the technological revolution was having a huge impact on the overall economy. Investment spending rose, as business firms—in order to take advantage of the new technology—invested in new plant and equipment. Autonomous consumption spending also rose: consumers wanted new gadgets that would enable them to enjoy new types of services—new cellular phones, new computers, palm pilots, high-speed Internet connections, and more.

Faced with these demand shocks, the Federal Reserve would ordinarily have raised its interest rate target to prevent real GDP from exceeding potential output. But the technological revolution of the 1990s was having *another* effect on the economy: It *increased* potential output more rapidly than before. New computers, new software, and other forms of new capital equipment—along with the increased skills and training of the workforce—raised the typical worker's hourly output by about 22 percent over the decade.

The technological changes of the 1990s were an example of a shock to both the stock market *and* the economy. But remember that each of these also influences the other. As the expansion gained steam and real GDP was growing steadily and rapidly, profits and expected profits soared, pushing stock prices up further. And as stock prices rose, the wealth effect worked to propel consumer spending still higher. The result was a market and an economy that were feeding on each other, sending both to new performance heights. Was this a good thing?

Yes, and no. Higher stock prices certainly make stockholders happy. And a rapid expansion is good for workers, since it makes it easy to find jobs and forces firms to compete for workers by offering higher wages and better fringe benefits. Indeed, from a high of almost 8 percent in 1991, the unemployment rate dropped steadily during the 1990s, reaching 4 percent at the end of the decade.

But in spite of all this good news, there were dark clouds on the horizon . . . at least from the Fed's point of view.

## THE FED'S DILEMMA IN THE LATE 1990s AND EARLY 2000

As stocks soared during the late 1990s, many people began to wonder: Did the realities of the late-1990s economy justify the heights to which stock prices had risen? Clearly, many people in the market thought so, or they wouldn't have been willing to hold stocks at those high prices. But around 1995 and 1996, others—including some officials at the U.S. Federal Reserve—began to worry that share prices were rising out of proportion to the future profits they would be able to deliver to their owners. The Fed was worried that the market was experiencing a speculative *bubble*—a frenzy of buying that encouraged people to buy stocks and drive up their price because . . . well, just because their prices were rising.

In this view, the market in the late 1990s resembled the stock market in the 1920s, which is also often considered a bubble. While there were indeed reasons for optimism in the 1920s, there also seemed to be a speculative frenzy: Many investors borrowed money to buy stocks in companies they knew nothing about, just because of an anonymous tip or because they were watching the price of the stock go up. Indeed, the Dow Jones Industrial Average almost quadrupled from early 1920 to September 1929—just as it did during the 1990s. But when the bubble burst, it burst hard. From September 3, 1929 to July 8, 1932, the DJIA fell from 381 to 41—about a 90 percent decline.[4] Many stocks of the most reliable and successful corporations (the so-called "blue chip" corporations) fell to only tiny fractions of their highs. General Electric stock, for example, fell from a high of 396¼ in 1929 to 8½ in 1932; Bethlehem Steel from 140⅜ to 7¼; and RCA from 101 to 2½. Millions of people were financially wiped out—in itself, a human tragedy.

In 1996, when Alan Greenspan first made his "irrational exuberance" speech, he seemed to side with those who believed that the stock market was in the midst of a speculative bubble. His fear was that when the bubble burst—when people realized that there weren't sufficient buyers to keep propping up stock prices out of proportion to their future profits—then stock prices would come plummeting down to earth. And a burst bubble would be painful—millions of people would lose substantial amounts of wealth. Moreover, the Fed would be forced to intervene to prevent the wealth effect—this time in a negative direction—from creating a recession.

Could the Fed do so? Probably. We understand how the economy works much better today than we did in 1929, when—in retrospect—the Fed made several mistakes after the stock market crashed. But the Fed's knowledge isn't perfect and—as you've learned—Fed intervention is still fraught with uncertainty. There is always a chance the Fed will react too strongly, or not enough. From the Fed's point of view in the mid-1990s, the best economy would be one that hummed along without needing any policy intervention. That is, an economy with stock prices rising steadily and *slowly*, rather than a bubble that might burst and require a big policy shift.

In the mid-1990s, Greenspan seemed to be trying to "talk the market down" by letting stockholders know that he thought share prices were too high. The implied threat: If stocks rose any higher, the Fed would raise interest rates and bring them down. Indeed, according to many observers, merely hinting that the Fed *might* raise interest rates was designed to keep stock prices from rising too rapidly, and perhaps bring them down gently.

Only it didn't work. While Greenspan's irrational exuberance speech did bring the market down for a day or so, the relentless rise in stock prices continued. In October 1996, just before Greenpan's speech, the DJIA stood at about 6,500. By March 1999—less than three years later—it had reached 10,000.

Not only were Greenspan's efforts to "talk the market down" unsuccessful, they were also widely criticized. In the view of his critics, the value of stocks should be based on the decisions of those who buy and sell them. If people believe that a

---

[4] The Dow Jones Industrial Average measures *nominal* stock prices. Since the price level decreased over this period, the decline in *real* stock prices was less than 90 percent, but still a substantial loss.

company is onto something good and that its future profits justify a doubling or tripling of its stock price within a short time, what business is it of the Fed to say they are wrong? After all, stock buying—and the funds it has made available to American corporations—is partly responsible for the remarkable rise in U.S. living standards over the past century. Moreover, the stock market has been especially effective in funneling funds to good ideas and away from bad ones because it relies on *decentralized* decision making. Those who put their money at risk decide for themselves what is and is not a good idea.

Greenspan himself seemed to change his tune as the 1990s continued. By 1998, he had stopped referring to exuberance—rational or irrational. Instead, he began to stress the remarkable changes in the economy, the rapid rise in productivity and potential output, and the fact that the American people—who buy and sell stocks—have a certain wisdom that should not be second-guessed by government officials. It was almost a complete reversal.

But as the 1990s came to a close, and the stock market continued to soar, the Fed faced a new problem: *the wealth effect*. Justified or not, share prices had continued to rise—and they rose a lot. In the two and a half years after Greenspan's famous irrational exuberance remarks in 1996, about $3 trillion in new wealth was created. Consumer spending was rising dramatically, and the Fed began to worry that the economy might be exceeding—or would soon exceed—its potential output.

Figure 6 shows one way we can view the Fed's problem: with aggregate demand and supply curves. In panel (a), the wealth effect of rising stock prices shifts the aggregate demand curve from $AD_1$ to $AD_2$, causing an increase in real GDP from $Y_1$ to $Y_2$ along with a rise in the price level. The question is: What happens next? That depends on where our potential output is relative to $Y_2$. If $Y_2$ is greater than potential output, the self-correcting mechanism will begin to work: The price level will rise further, bringing the economy back to potential output (assumed to be $Y_1$ in the figure). This is something the Fed has worked hard to avoid. As you've learned, inflation—once it begins—tends to be self-perpetuating. People begin to expect it. And once the

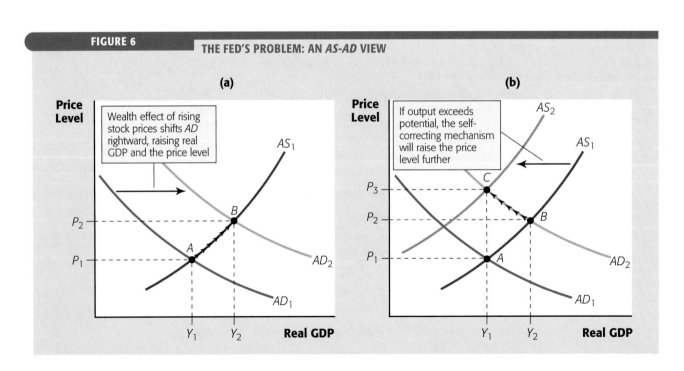

**FIGURE 6**     **THE FED'S PROBLEM: AN *AS-AD* VIEW**

(a)

Price Level

Wealth effect of rising stock prices shifts *AD* rightward, raising real GDP and the price level

$AS_1$

$B$

$A$

$P_2$

$P_1$

$AD_2$

$AD_1$

$Y_1$   $Y_2$   **Real GDP**

(b)

Price Level

If output exceeds potential, the self-correcting mechanism will raise the price level further

$AS_2$

$AS_1$

$C$

$B$

$A$

$P_3$

$P_2$

$P_1$

$AD_2$

$AD_1$

$Y_1$   $Y_2$   **Real GDP**

inflation is embedded in the economy, eradicating it is painful: The Fed would have to raise interest rates and slow the economy by more than would have been necessary to prevent the inflation in the first place. Moreover, in the past, efforts to bring the inflation rate down have triggered deep recessions. From the Fed's point of view, preventing inflation in the first place is always the preferred alternative.

Figure 6 is useful, but it has a serious limitation: It doesn't take account of the rise in potential output. Each year, potential output increases because the population is growing, and because productivity—output per worker—is growing. In the 1990s and through early 2000, potential output was growing even more rapidly than in previous decades. We could illustrate this on an *AS-AD* diagram by shifting the *AS* curve rightward and downward over time. That is, due to changes in population and productivity, we could produce more output at any given price level, or have a lower price level at any given level of output. With a shifting *AS* curve, the Fed's goal is to shift the *AD* curve rightward each year by just enough to prevent inflation.

But the Phillips curve can illustrate the Fed's goal more easily. Look first at panel (a) of Figure 7, where the position of the economy in late 1999 and early 2000 is represented by point *A* on the Phillips curve $PC_1$: 4 percent unemployment and a 2.5 percent annual inflation rate. As you learned a few chapters ago (Inflation and Monetary Policy), the Fed can *keep* the economy at point *A* only if the actual unemployment rate, 4 percent, is also the *natural* rate of unemployment. In that case, the Fed—by keeping the economy at point *A*—would be allowing actual output to rise each year by just enough to keep it equal to potential output.

But what if the natural rate of unemployment is *greater* than 4 percent—say, 5 percent? Then—as you can see in panel (b)—the economy would need to operate at point *B* to be at the natural rate. Point *A* now represents an overheated economy, with output greater than potential output. If we remain at point *A*, then over time

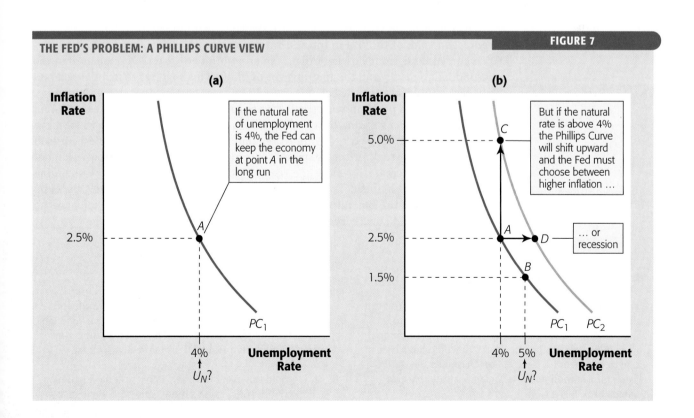

**THE FED'S PROBLEM: A PHILLIPS CURVE VIEW**   **FIGURE 7**

the entire Phillips curve would shift upward, to the curve labeled $PC_2$, and point $A$ would no longer be an option. If the Fed tried to maintain a 4 percent unemployment rate, the economy would then be at point $C$, with a rise in the inflation rate to 5 percent. To prevent any rise in inflation, the Fed would have to engineer a recession, bringing the economy to point $D$ with unemployment above the natural rate.

To keep inflation low and stable without needing corrective recessions, the Fed strives to maintain unemployment at its natural rate. But no one—including the Fed—knows what the natural rate of unemployment *is* during any given year. We know that it is lower today than in the early 1990s—when it was believed to be about 5.5 or 6 percent. But no one knows how far it has fallen since then.

You might think that the Fed can estimate the natural rate by a process of trial and error—bringing the unemployment rate to a certain level (such as 4 percent) and seeing what happens to inflation. Then, if the inflation rate rises, the Fed would know that it had underestimated the natural rate. It could then slow the economy and bring unemployment back up to the natural rate.

Unfortunately, things are not so simple. In the real world, when the economy overheats, the inflation rate begins to rise only after a lag of several quarters or longer. By the time the Fed notices a rise in the inflation rate, the economy may have been overheated for months, and the Fed may have to take even more drastic action to bring us back to potential output. For this reason, the Fed looks ahead, and determines whether *current* economic conditions are likely to raise the inflation rate in the *future*.

And that is just what the Fed did beginning in mid-1999. With the unemployment rate near 4 percent, the economy growing at a rapid 3.8 percent clip for a year, and the stock market continuing to rise to record levels, Fed officials believed that the wealth effect would overheat the economy if nothing were done. So the Fed took action, even though inflation was still low and stable. From June 1999 through May 2000, the Fed raised its target for the federal funds rate six times: from 4.75 percent to 6.5 percent.

As this is being written (May 2000), the Fed's caution seems to have been warranted. In spite of the rise in interest rates, the unemployment rate remained at 4 percent. And far from slowing down, the growth rate of real GDP increased in the second half of 1999 and the first quarter of 2000. This suggests that if the Fed had *not* raised interest rates, the economy would, indeed, have overheated.

But there is a problem with the Fed's approach. Raising interest rates to rein in the economy can *also* bring down stock prices. Thus the Fed, in trying to steer the economy, can be accused of trying to regulate stock prices. Indeed, the Fed itself seems to regard stock prices as one of its tools for steering the economy: Higher interest rates decrease (or slow the rise in) stock prices, and thus slow spending through the wealth effect. Thus, we are back to the debate of the mid-1990s: Who should be setting the general level of share prices—the millions of stockholders who buy and sell shares, or the Federal Reserve?

## PROBLEMS AND EXERCISES

1. The chapter contains the following statement: "You can also see that the 1990s were a good decade for stocks. Someone who invested $10,000 in a typical group of S&P 500 stocks on January 1, 1990 would have been able to sell them for $41,523 on December 31, 1999." Using information in Table 1, demonstrate that this statement is correct.

2. Suppose the corporate profits tax rate is reduced, and other taxes in the economy are increased by just enough to leave total tax revenue unchanged. Thus, the economy's equilibrium real GDP is unaffected, at least initially.
   a. Would this event have any impact on the stock market? Illustrate, using supply and demand curves for

the typical stock. What will happen to the price of the typical stock?

b.   Using cause-and-effect diagrams like the ones in this chapter, show how this change in tax policy would first affect the stock market, then affect the economy, and then create feedback effects in the stock market.

c.   When we include feedback effects from the macro-economy, is the ultimate effect on stock prices greater or smaller than the initial impact in (a) above? Explain.

3.   Sometimes corporations will use their profits to buy back their own shares.

a.   Explain why this action—using funds that could have been given to shareholders as dividends—might actually benefit shareholders. (*Hint:* Draw a supply and demand diagram for the corporation's shares. Which curve is affected by a stock buy-back?)

b.   In the United States, the tax rate on long-term capital gains (capital gains on assets held longer than one year) is lower than the tax rate on ordinary income, including income from dividends. Does this help explain why corporations sometimes buy back their own shares? Explain.

4.   Suppose that, over time, people become more sophisticated about changes in stock prices. Specifically, they realize that while stock prices go down in a recession, they tend to rise when the recession ends. Would this change the way the economy affects stock prices? Would it change our view of the stock market as an automatic destabilizer over the business cycle? Explain.

5.   Classify each of the following events as a shock that initially affects (a) primarily the economy; (b) primarily the stock market; (c) both the stock market and the economy. Justify your answer in each case.

a.   Government spending increases, while the Fed leaves its interest rate target unchanged.

b.   The Fed—beginning to worry about inflation—increases its interest rate target.

6.   In the section *"A Shock to the Economy,"* we explored the impact of an increase in government purchases with an unchanged interest rate target by the Fed.

a.   In order to maintain an unchanged interest rate target, will the Fed have to increase or decrease the money supply? Illustrate with a diagram of the money market.

b.   Suppose the Fed instead decides to pursue a completely passive monetary policy—leaving the *money supply* unchanged. What will happen to the interest rate? (Illustrate with another diagram of the money market.)

c.   Under a passive monetary policy, does the change in government spending have more or less of an initial impact on the stock market (compared to the policy of maintaining an unchanged interest rate target)?

7.   When population and productivity are increasing, potential output increases each year. One way to illustrate this is to shift the economy's *AS* curve rightward (and downward) each year. Assume that there is no expected inflation embedded in the economy, so that the ongoing inflation rate is zero. Using *AS-AD* diagrams, illustrate each of the following scenarios.

a.   Potential output is increasing, and the Fed allows actual output to rise just enough to keep up with potential.

b.   Potential output is increasing, and the Fed allows actual output to rise above potential.

c.   Potential output is increasing, and the Fed allows so little growth that output falls below potential.

8.   Using a diagram similar to panel (b) of Figure 7, show what happens over time if the Fed maintains an unemployment rate of 4 percent when the *natural* rate of unemployment is actually 3.5 percent.

## C H A L L E N G E   Q U E S T I O N

1.   In addition to its short-run effects on the economy via the wealth effect, the stock market affects the economy in another way: It is part of the loanable funds market in which households make their saving available to firms. Thus, the *existence* of a stock market should affect the economy in the long run.

a.   Do stocks have any advantages for households over other forms of saving? If so, what are they? (Think of yourself or your family. Why might you want to hold some of your wealth in the form of stocks, rather than hold all of it in other forms such as bonds or cash?)

b.   Using a loanable funds diagram, and your answer in part (a), show what happens—in an economy that is initially without a stock market—when a viable stock market is introduced. In particular, which curve will shift?

c.   Using your graph from part (b), how does introducing a stock market into the economy affect the level of investment spending and the standard of living over the long run?

d.   Do stocks have any advantages for business firms over other ways of obtaining funds for investment projects? If so, what are they?

e.   On your loanable funds diagram, and using your answer from part (d), illustrate the impact of the stock market on the investment demand curve. Does this contribute to, or work against, the impact of the stock market on the economy that you found in part (c)?

# PHOTO CREDITS

# GLOSSARY

## A

**Absolute advantage** The ability to produce a good or service, using fewer resources than other producers use.

**Active monetary policy** When the Fed changes the money supply to achieve some objective.

**Alternate goods** Other goods that a firm could produce, using some of the same types of inputs as the good in question.

**Aggregate demand (*AD*) curve** A curve indicating equilibrium GDP at each price level.

**Aggregate expenditure (*AE*)** The sum of spending by households, business firms, the government, and foreigners on final goods and services produced in the United States.

**Aggregate production function** The relationship showing how much total output can be produced with different quantities of labor, with land, capital, and technology held constant.

**Aggregate supply (*AS*) curve** A curve indicating the price level consistent with firms' unit costs and markups for any level of output over the short run.

**Aggregation** The process of combining different things into a single category.

**Appreciation** An increase in the price of a currency in a loating-rate system.

**Arbitrage** Simultaneous buying and selling of a foreign currency in order to profit from a difference in exchange rates.

**Automatic stabilizers** Forces that reduce the size of the expenditure multiplier and diminish the impact of spending shocks.

**Autonomous consumption spending** The part of consumption spending that is independent of income; also, the vertical intercept of the consumption function.

**Average standard of living** Total output (real GDP) per person.

**Average tax rate** The fraction of a given income paid in taxes.

## B

**Balance sheet** A financial statement showing assets, liabilities, and net worth at a point in time.

**Banking panic** A situation in which depositors attempt to withdraw funds from many banks simultaneously.

**Bilateral arbitrage** Arbitrage involving one pair of currencies.

**Bond** An IOU issued by a corporation or government agency when it borrows funds.

**Boom** A period of time during which real GDP is above potential GDP.

**Budget deficit** The excess of government purchases over net taxes.

**Budget of surplus** The excess of net taxes over government purchases.

**Business cycles** Fluctuations in real GDP around its long-term growth trend.

## C

**Capital** Long-lasting tools used in producing goods and services.

**Capital gains tax** A tax on profits earned when a financial asset is sold at more than its acquisition price.

**Capital per worker** The total capital stock divided by total employment.

**Capital stock** The total value of all goods that will provide useful services in future years.

**Capitalism** A type of economic system in which most resources are owned privately.

**Cash in the hands of the public** Currency and coins held outside of banks.

**Central bank** A nation's principal monetary authority.

**Critical assumption** Any assumption that affects the conclusions of a model in an important way.

**Comparative advantage** The ability to produce a good or service at a lower opportunity cost than other producers.

**Command or centrally planned economy** An economic system in which resources are allocated according to explicit instructions from a central authority.

**Communism** A type of economic system in which most resources are owned in common.

**Change in demand** A shift of a demand curve in response to a change in some variable other than price.

**Change in quantity demanded** A movement along a demand curve in response to a change in price.

**Change in quantity supplied** A movement along a supply curve in response to a change in price.

**Change in supply** A shift of a supply curve in response to some variable other than price.

**Circular flow** A diagram that shows how goods, resources, and dollar payments flow between households and firms.

**Classical model** A macroeconomic model that explains the long-run behavior of the economy, assuming that all markets clear.

**Complement** A good that is used *together with* some other good.

**Complete crowding out** A dollar-for-dollar decline in one sector's spending caused by an increase in some other sector's spending.

**Consumer Price Index** An index of the cost, through time, of a fixed market basket of goods purchased by a typical household in some base period.

**Consumption (C)** The part of GDP purchased by households as final users.

**Corporate profits tax** A tax on the profits earned by corporations.

**Consumption tax** A tax on the part of their income that households spend.

**Consumption function** A positively sloped relationship between real consumption spending and real disposable income.

**Consumption-income line** A line showing aggregate consumption spending at each level of income or GDP.

**Countercyclical fiscal policy** Changes in taxes or government spending designed to counteract economic fluctuations.

**Crowding out** A decline in one sector's spending caused by an increase in some other sector's spending.

**Cyclical deficit** The part of the federal budget deficit that varies with the business cycle.

**Cyclical unemployment** Joblessness arising from changes in production over the business cycle.

## D

**Deflation** A *decrease* in the price level from one period to the next.

**Demand curve for foreign currency** A curve indicating the quantity of a specific foreign currency that Americans will want to buy, during a given period, at each different exchange rate.

**Demand deposits** Checking accounts that do not pay interest.

**Demand deposit multiplier** The number by which a change in reserves is multiplied to determine the resulting change in demand deposits.

**Demand schedule** A list showing the quantities of a good that consumers would choose to purchase at different prices, with all other variables held constant.

**Demand shock** Any event that causes the *AD* curve to shift.

**Depreciation** A decrease in the price of a currency in a floating-rate system.

**Depression** An unusually severe recession.

**Devaluation** A change in the exchange rate from a higher fixed rate to a lower fixed rate.

**Discount rate** The interest rate the Fed charges on loans to banks.

**Discouraged workers** Individuals who would like a job, but have given up searching for one.

**Disequilibrium** A situation in which a market does not clear—quantity supplied is not equal to quantity demanded.

**Disposable income** The part of household income that remains after paying taxes.

## E

**Economic system** A system of resource allocation and resource ownership.

**Economics** The study of choice under conditions of scarcity.

**Excess demand** At a given price, the excess of quantity demanded over quantity supplied.

**Excess demand for bonds** The amount of bonds demanded exceeds the amount supplied at a particular interest rate.

**Excess reserves** Reserves in excess of required reserves.

**Excess supply** At a given price, the excess of quantity supplied over quantity demanded.

**Excess supply of money** The amount of money supplied exceeds the amount demanded at a particular interest rate.

**Exchange** The act of trading with others to obtain what we desire.

**Exchange rate** The amount of one country's currency that is traded for one unit of another country's currency.

**Expansion** A period of increasing real GDP.

**Expenditure approach** Measuring GDP by adding the value of goods and services purchased by each type of final user.

**Equilibrium** A state of rest; a situation that, once achieved, will not change unless some external factor, previously held constant, changes.

**Equilibrium GDP** In the short run, the level of output at which output and aggregate expenditure are equal.

## F

**Firm's quantity supplied** The total amount of a good or service that an individual firm would choose to produce and sell at a given price.

**Final good** A good sold to its final user.

**Flow variable** A measure of a process that takes place over a period of time.

**Factor payments** Payments to the owners of resources that are used in production.

**Factor payments approach** Measuring GDP by summing the factor payments made by all firms in the economy.

**Frictional unemployment** Joblessness experienced by people who are between jobs or who are just entering or re-entering the labor market.

**Full employment** A situation in which there is no cyclical unemployment.

**Federal Reserve System** The central bank and national monetary authority of the United States.

**Fiat money** Anything that serves as a means of payment by government declaration.

**Fiscal policy** A change in government purchases or net taxes designed to change total spending and total output.

**Financial intermediary** A business firm that specializes in brokering between savers and borrowers.

**Federal Open Market Committee** A committee of Federal Reserve officials that establishes U.S. monetary policy.

**Federal funds rate** The interest rate charged for loans of reserves among banks.

**Foreign exchange market** The market in which one country's currency is traded for another country's.

**Floating exchange rate** An exchange rate that is freely determined by the forces of supply and demand.

**Fixed exchange rate** A government-declared exchange rate maintained by central bank intervention in the foreign exchange market.

**Foreign currency crisis** A loss of faith that a country can prevent a drop in its exchange rate, leading to a rapid depletion of its foreign currency (e.g., dollar) reserves.

## G

**GDP price index** An index of the price level for all final goods and services included in GDP.

**Government demand for funds curve** Indicates the amount of government borrowing at various interest rates.

**Government purchases (G)** Spending by federal, state, and local governments on goods and services.

**Gross Domestic Product (GDP)** The total value of all final goods and services produced for the marketplace during a given year, within the nation's borders.

## H

**(Household) saving** The portion of after-tax income that households do not spend on consumption goods.

**Human capital** The skills and training of the labor force.

**Human capital** Skills and knowledge possessed by workers.

## I

**Imperfectly competitive market** A market in which a single buyer or seller has the power to influence the price of the product.

**Income** The amount that a person or firm earns over a particular period.

**Individual's quantity demanded** The total amount of a good an individual would choose to purchase at a given price.

**Index** A series of numbers used to track a variable's rise or fall over time.

**Indexation** Adjusting the value of some nominal payment in proportion to a price index, in order to keep the real payment unchanged.

**Inferior good** A good that people demand less of as their income rises.

**Inflation rate** The percent change in the price level from one period to the next.

**Injections** Spending from sources other than households.

**Interest rate target** The interest rate the Federal Reserve aims to achieve by adjusting the money supply.

**Intermediate goods** Goods used up in producing final goods.

**Investment demand curve** Indicates the level of investment spending firms plan at various interest rates.

**Investment tax credit** A reduction in taxes for firms that invest in certain favored types of capital.

**Involuntary part-time workers** Individuals who would like a full-time job, but who are working only part time.

## L

**Labor** The time human beings spend producing goods and services.

**Labor demand curve** Indicates how many workers firms will want to hire at various wage rates.

**Labor force** Those people who have a job or who are looking for one.

**Labor productivity** Total output (real GDP) per worker.

**Labor supply curve** Indicates how many people will want to work at various wage rates.

**Land** The physical space on which production occurs, and the natural resources that come with it.

**Law of increasing opportunity cost** The more of something that is produced, the greater the opportunity cost of producing one more unit.

**Law of demand** As the price of a good increases, the quantity demanded decreases.

**Law of supply** As the price of a good increases, the quantity supplied increases.

**Leakages** Income earned, but not spent, by households during a given year.

**Liquidity** The property of being easily converted into cash.

**Loan** An IOU issued by a household or noncorporate business when it borrows funds.

**Loanable funds market** Arrangements through which households make their saving available to borrowers.

**Long-run aggregate supply curve** A vertical line indicating all possible output and price-level combinations at which the economy could end up in the long run.

**Long-run Phillips curve** A vertical line indicating that in the long run, unemployment must equal its natural rate, regardless of the rate of inflation.

## M

**M1** A standard measure of the money supply, including cash in the hands of the public, checking account deposits, and travelers checks.

**M2** M1 plus savings account balances, noninstitutional money market mutual fund balances, and small time deposits.

**Macroeconomics** The study of the economy as a whole.

**Managed float** A policy of frequent central bank intervention to move the exchange rate.

**Marginal propensity to consume** The amount by which consumption spending rises when disposable income rises by one dollar.

**Marginal tax rate** The fraction of an additional dollar of income paid in taxes.

**Market** A group of buyers and sellers with the potential to trade with each other.

**Market clearing** Adjustment of prices until quantities supplied and demanded are equal.

**Market demand curve** The graphical depiction of a demand schedule; a curve showing the quantity of a good or service demanded at various prices, with all other variables held constant.

**Market economy** An economic system in which resources are allocated through individual decision making.

**Market quantity demanded** The total amount of a good that all buyers in the market would choose to purchase at a given price.

**Market quantity supplied** The total amount of a good or service that all producers in a market would choose to produce and sell at a given price.

**Means of payment** Anything acceptable as payment for goods and services.

**Microeconomics** The study of the behavior of individual households, firms, and governments; the choices they make; and their interaction in specific markets.

**Model** An abstract representation of reality.

**Money demand curve** A curve indicating how much money will be willingly held at each interest rate.

**Money supply curve** A line showing the total quantity of money in the economy at each interest rate.

## N

**National debt** The total amount of government debt outstanding.

**Natural rate of unemployment** The unemployment rate when there is no cyclical unemployment.

**Net capital inflow** An inflow of funds equal to a nation's trade deficit.

**Net exports (NX)** Total exports minus total imports.

**Net investment** Total investment minus depreciation.

**Net taxes** Government tax revenues minus transfer payments.

**Net worth** The difference between assets and liabilities.

**Nominal variable** A variable measured without adjustment for the dollar's changing value.

**Nominal variable** A variable measured in current dollars.

**Nominal interest rate** The annual percent increase in a lender's *dollars* from making a loan.

**Nonmarket production** Goods and services that are produced, but not sold in a market.

**Normal good** A good that people demand more of as their income rises.

**Normative economics** The study of what *should be;* it is used to make value judgments, identify problems, and prescribe solutions.

## O

**Open market operations** Purchases or sales of bonds by the Federal Reserve System.

**Opportunity cost** The value of the best alternative sacrificed when taking an action.

**Optimum currency area** A region whose economies perform better with a single currency than with separate national currencies.

## P

**Passive monetary policy** When the Fed keeps the money supply constant regardless of shocks to the economy.

**Patent protection** A government grant of exclusive rights to use or sell a new technology.

**Peak** The point at which real GDP reaches its highest level during an expansion.

**Perfectly competitive market** A market in which no buyer or seller has the power to influence the price.

**Phillips curve** A curve indicating the Fed's choice between inflation and unemployment in the short run.

**Planned investment spending** Business purchases of plant and equipment.

**Positive economics** The study of what *is,* of how the economy works.

**Potential output** The level of output the economy could produce if operating at full employment.

**Production possibilities frontier (PPF)** A curve showing all combinations of two goods that can be produced with the resources and technology currently available.

**Productive inefficiency** A situation in which more of at least one good can be produced without sacrificing the production of any other good.

**Progressive tax** A tax whose rate increases as income increases.

**Price** The amount of money that must be paid to a seller to obtain a good or service.

**Price level** The average level of dollar prices in the economy.

**Private investment (I)** The sum of business plant and equipment purchases, new home construction, and inventory changes.

**Purchasing power parity (PPP) theory** The idea that the exchange rate will adjust in the long run so that the average price of goods in two countries will be roughly the same.

## R

**Real interest rate** The annual percent increase in a lender's *purchasing power* from making a loan.

**Real variable** A variable adjusted for changes in the dollar's value.

**Real variable** A variable measured in terms of purchasing power.

**Recession** A period of declining or abnormally low real GDP.

**Required reserve ratio** The minimum fraction of checking account balances that banks must hold as reserves.

**Required reserves** The minimum amount of reserves a bank must hold, depending on the amount of its deposit liabilities.

**Reserves** Vault cash plus balances held at the Fed.

**Resources** The land, labor, and capital that are used to produce goods and services.

**Resource allocation** A method of determining which goods and services will be produced, how they will be produced, and who will get them.

**Run on the bank** An attempt by many of a bank's depositors to withdraw their funds.

## S

**Say's law** The idea that total spending will be sufficient to purchase the total output produced.

**Scarcity** A situation in which the amount of something available is insufficient to satisfy the desire for it.

**Seasonal unemployment** Joblessness related to changes in weather, tourist patterns, or other seasonal factors.

**Self-correcting mechanism** The adjustment process through which price and wage changes return the economy to full-employment output in the long run.

**Short-run macro model** A macroeconomic model that explains how changes in spending can affect real GDP in the short run.

**Short-run macroeconomic equilibrium** A combination of price level and GDP consistent with both the *AD* and *AS* curves.

**Simplifying assumption** Any assumption that makes a model simpler without affecting any of its important conclusions.

**Socialism** A type of economic system in which most resources are owned by the state.

**Specialization** A method of production in which each person concentrates on a limited number of activities.

**Spending shock** A change in spending that ultimately affects the entire economy.

**Stagflation** The combination of falling output and rising prices.

**Stock Variable** A measure of an amount that exists at a moment in time.

**Structural deficit** The part of the federal budget deficit that is independent of the business cycle.

**Structural unemployment** Joblessness arising from mismatches between workers' skills and employers' requirements or between workers' locations and employers' locations.

**Substitute** A good that can be used in place of some other good and that fulfills more or less the same purpose.

**Supply curve** A graphical depiction of a supply schedule; a curve showing the quantity of a good or service supplied at various prices, with all other variables held constant.

**Supply curve for foreign currency** A curve indicating the quantity of a specific foreign currency that will be supplied, during a given period, at each different exchange rate.

**Supply of funds curve** Indicates the level of household saving at various interest rates.

**Supply schedule** A list showing the quantities of a good or service that firms would choose to produce and sell at different prices, with all other variables held constant.

**Supply shock** Any event that causes the *AS* curve to shift.

## T

**Technological change** The invention or discovery of new inputs, new outputs, or new production methods.

**Technology** The set of methods a firm can use to turn inputs into outputs

**Total demand for funds curve** Indicates the total amount of borrowing at various interest rates.

**Traditional economy** An economy in which resources are allocated according to long-lived practices from the past.

**Transfer payment** Any payment that is not compensation for supplying goods or services.

**Triangular arbitrage** Arbitrage involving trades among three (or more) currencies.

**Trough** The point at which real GPD reaches its lowest level during a recession.

## U

**Unemployment rate** The fraction of the labor force that is without a job.

**Unit of value** A common unit for measuring how much something is worth.

## V

**Value added** The revenue a firm receives minus the cost of the intermediate goods it buys.

**Value-added approach** Measuring GDP by summing the value added by all firms in the economy.

## W

**Wealth** The total value of everything a person or firm owns, at a point in time, minus the total value of everything owed.

**Wealth constraint** At any point in time, wealth is fixed.

# INDEX